THE A TO Z OF ARTS MANAGEMENT

The A to Z of Arts Management, Second Edition covers 97 topics about the management of arts and cultural organisations.

Each section offers a theoretical and conceptual introduction to the topic, as well as storytelling and reflections about the meaning and application of such theories in the real world. Drawing on the author's past as a manager running media and performing arts companies and her present as a consultant helping Boards and managers, this book covers a wide range of topics, from leadership, motivation and cultural policy to passion, coffee and laughter. This second edition includes even more coverage and stories about the challenges of arts management, and new topics such as harassment, philanthropy and venues.

Written for arts managers, students and Board members anywhere in the world, *The A to Z of Arts Management* provides information about research and academic best practice in arts management alongside stories about the reality of working in the arts and cultural industries.

Ann Tonks is a management practitioner, consultant and academic specialising in arts and cultural management. She has been an Honorary Fellow at the University of Melbourne and was the Managing Director of Melbourne Theatre Company. She has been on the Boards of dance, theatre, opera, employer and advisory organisations and provides advice and guidance to a wide range of companies.

THE A TO Z OF ARTS MANAGEMENT

REFLECTIONS ON THEORY AND REALITY

SECOND EDITION

ANN TONKS

Routledge
Taylor & Francis Group

NEW YORK AND LONDON

Second edition published 2020
by Routledge
52 Vanderbilt Avenue, New York, NY 10017

and by Routledge
2 Park Square, Milton Park, Abingdon, Oxon, OX14 4RN

Routledge is an imprint of the Taylor & Francis Group, an informa business

First edition published by Tilde Publishing 2016

Library of Congress Cataloging-in-Publication Data
A catalog record has been requested for this book

ISBN: 978-0-367-35135-9 (hbk)
ISBN: 978-0-367-35139-7 (pbk)
ISBN: 978-0-429-33000-1 (ebk)

Typeset in AkzidenzGroteskBE Light
by Newgen Publishing UK

To Susan and Sebastian for providing real and emotional nourishment.

CONTENTS

Contents

PREFACE

Some of the best qualities of a manager:

> … the king-becoming graces,
> As justice, verity, temperance, stableness,
> Bounty, perseverance, mercy, lowliness,
> Devotion, patience, courage, fortitude.
> *Macbeth*, Act IV, 91–94

INTRODUCTION

Management is an art, not a science. You can't learn to do it all from a textbook or even a brilliant lecturer. But if you want to be a good manager, you can build on the work of others – their research, their experience, their knowledge – find out as much as you can about a manager's work and determine the most humanistic, thoughtful and effective way to complete those tasks.

I decided to write this book because I love the arts and if any small part of my experience can help arts managers use their companies' limited resources in a better way to create great art, then I can justify the fact that I've earned my living being an arts manager for the last 30 years. I've managed a community radio station and worked as a senior manager in the Australian Broadcasting Corporation. I spent 18 years running one of Australia's most prestigious theatre companies. I've been on the Board of theatre, opera and dance companies as well as networking, lobbying and employer associations. Since creating the first edition of this book, I've been a consultant and mentor in the non-profit industries. I've reviewed organisations, programs and Boards. I've even returned to the small to medium arts environment as a CEO. On and off for the same period of time, I've taught arts management and leadership and for the last few years have researched and written about leadership as well.

What you get in this book is a reflection of all the topics that have been important to me in these roles. Some topics will be much longer than others because I have more experience or more to say on one than the other, not necessarily because one is more important than the other. Some topics will be unlikely entries in a book on management (coffee, humour) but it's for the same reason that they have been important in my life as an arts manager. But I did check with a wide range of my arts colleagues in Australia to ask them what they wished they'd known more about when they started their roles just to make sure I wasn't missing out on something vital – and I think I've covered most of the things we do or worry about as arts managers.

There are a range of good arts management books around (see Appendix), but while you find the voices of academics, theoreticians and consultants in such books, you don't hear the voices of managers very often. The role of management education should be to stimulate the student to new ways of thinking that will help them better fulfil the management role they've decided to take on. Unlike the management of a set of accounts, there isn't a neat set of rules when it comes to managing people. And people management is the main part of our work. So, this book is not about rules or techniques: it's about storytelling and reflection. Research and theories come into it because I've learnt from other people's wisdom. But if you want a management book that lists, for example, all the theories on motivation or how to fundraise, there are better books to read.

Management knowledge isn't an abstract and established body of concepts and theories (Grey & Antonacopoulou 2004) but rather a contested social practice. I'm putting my views on the line so that you can challenge and disagree with me and in that process, you'll start that most important process for any manager – reflecting on how to do your job better. My advice and opinions are not prescriptive. They are simply personal reflections that will hopefully spark a response – of either agreement or disagreement, hysteria or outright disbelief, enthusiasm or gratitude. They hopefully will be part of a learning process that will contribute to better arts leadership and management. And at this point I should thank the University of Melbourne for providing me with funded time to write some of this book and to many arts colleagues, particularly at Melbourne Theatre Company, who have been part of some of the stories you'll read in this book.

The structure of this book is perfectly obvious. In each section I've provided some theory and concepts developed by other writers as a context for my considerations. As one of my favourite writers on organisations says, "theory is about mobilizing ideas, arguments and explanations to try to make sense of practice but also to influence practice" (Grey 2005, 14). There are endless articles, texts and advice books about management and I've cheated by choosing to share the theories that are most interesting or feel most connected to my years of practice. But this book is not a recipe book on "how to do it" because I'm not any sort of "heroic" leader who has got it right all the time. In a review of arts management textbooks, Fitzgibbon (2012, 96) notes that knowledge can "be acquired through the thoughtful examination of best practices with the exploration of scenarios". Although I can't say that what I've been doing for years is "best practice", I've been part of lots of "scenarios". So what you will hear is my voice based on that experience talking directly to you as we ponder together some of the challenges of managing arts and cultural organisations.

What I hope I've avoided is "inanities masquerading as profound insights", a warning that Stewart (2009, 147) gives about management gurus in his insightful book *The Management Myth*. For those who want to have access to better minds than mine, I've included references for every section as well as some recommended reading in the Appendix. For those who are curious about the stories I tell, some of them are mine and some of them belong to others. Some of the stories have been changed to protect both the innocent and the guilty. But all of the opinions are mine.

In some ways my experience is limited: being a CEO/senior manager in five cultural organisations, overseeing arts management on half a dozen Boards, and teaching it at some universities. I'm not a charismatic leader, more of a servant leader. I've only worked in the non-profit world. I've worked in the performing arts and media but not in the visual arts or museum sectors. And although I've taught in some other countries, I've only worked in Australia. It's best to keep in mind when reading this book that someone else could have been a much better manager of Melbourne Theatre Company (MTC) than me. They might have reached all the goals I boast about in a shorter period of time; in a more effective manner; in an organisation where people were better paid and valued. Obviously, there are many aspects of organisational and cultural life in Australia that are different to other Western countries, let alone countries in Asia and Africa, but there's also a lot of similarity in what's required of arts managers around the world – finding money, looking after people, serving artists and audiences. If reading some of these stories and insights causes you to reflect on your own practices and be inspired to try new things or sort stuff out or go back to study or find a mentor to help you improve, then that's all I can hope for.

When I first wrote this introduction, I realised that I was doing a traditionally female thing. Apologising and justifying and excusing the fact that I've been bold enough to put pen to paper on the complex subject of arts management. So

I should just stop there and get on with it but I do have a couple of more comments to make. This is a "textbook" in as much as I hope that arts management students will read it. But I also hope that practicing arts managers and even arts Board members will also take the occasional minute out of busy and complex lives to dip and in out of topics of interest. One of the most wonderful moments I had in response to the first edition of this book was from a manager in a small to medium-sized company in Australia. They said that it sat on the bookshelf at work and they read it whenever they had a problem or needed some inspiration. I couldn't have asked for more.

Let me share Grey's words of warning from his wonderful book called *A Very Short, Fairly Interesting and Reasonably Cheap Book About Studying Organisations*. In it, he reminds us that management is a continually failing enterprise: that no matter what a manager does, they can't control (and shouldn't control) every aspect of people's lives. And even important to remember, work isn't everything. When you work in the arts and cultural industries, that last point is a hard one to grasp as we see artists and arts workers work for a pittance, work long into the night, work to the detriment of their own health and their relationships with family and friends. The best we can do is to be the best we can – balancing passion with humility, skill with ethics, and caring for the people we work with. And I have worked with some wonderful people. From the volunteer radio announcers who first encouraged me to be an arts manager to the management team I had at MTC, from inspiring Board Chairs to enthusiastic casual ticket sellers, from the brilliant leaders of small companies to hard-working arts bureaucrats, from my peers in other companies to the skilled artisans who'd plied their craft for decades, from thoughtful teachers to great academic colleagues, and of course all the artists I've worked with who are the reason we do what we do. I hope that reading this book will help you to serve them with grace and dexterity.

The world of arts management is a world of complexity and uncertainty, of creativity and poverty, of joy and frustration. Each day you'll spend time dealing with people and thinking about money. You will lose sleep and get depressed, but you'll also be rewarded by the sheer exhilaration of being surrounded by artists making great works for diverse audiences.

Ann Tonks
Melbourne
January 2020

A Note About Language

I've called this book *Arts Management* but I might have just as easily called it *Arts Leadership* or *Cultural Leadership* or even the name of the first course in this area that I studied, *Arts Administration*. I chose "management" because "manager" has been in my title for most of my career and I'm yet to meet anyone whose formal title includes the word "leader" or who runs an organisation with the title "administrator".

Language becomes messy in studying management. Should you have a vision or mission? Is charismatic leadership the same as transformational leadership? Can you be a manager and a leader or is one part of the other? Do you devalue the making of art if you talk about the arts "industry"?

My advice is simple – don't get too hung up on definitions and language shifts as long as you understand where it's come from. For example, the shift from "administrator" to "manager" was to do with the professionalisation of the work. The use of the word "industry" started to happen when valuing the economic impact of the arts became an important part of arts policy. "Cultural leadership" started to appear in the late 20th century when various public crises in arts companies in Great Britain lead to a debate about a failure of leadership. In other words, follow the policy and theoretical changes in arts and culture and you'll make sense of the language shifts. But the underlying nature of your job won't have changed.

And one final point about language. In *Manufacturing the Employee*, Roy Jacques (1996) opts to leave his/him in place for references prior to 1970 and "sic" if the writer continues to use such language after that date. I love this idea of drawing attention to sexist language but I'm not willing to say that I was conscious of it as an issue in 1970 when I was still at my very safe single sex convent school. Instead, I've chosen the date when I walked out of a presentation at an industrial relations conference which I'd helped organise – it was yet one more presentation where "she" failed to get a mention. So my date of choice is 1978.

References

Fitzgibbon, C. 2012 "Review of 'The Arts Management Handbook: New Directions for Students and Practitioner,' edited by Meg Brindle and Constance DeVereaux", *The Journal of Arts Management, Law, and Society*, 42(2), 96–98.

Grey, C. 2005 *A Very Short, Fairly Interesting and Reasonably Cheap Book about Studying Organisations*, London: Sage Publications.

Grey, C. & Antonacopoulou, E. (eds) 2004 *Essential Readings in Management Learning*, London: Sage Publications.

Jacques, R. 1996 *Manufacturing the Employee*, London: Sage Publications.

Steward, M. 2009 *The Management Myth*, New York: W.W. Norton & Co.

A

Artists

It is appropriate that the first topic on arts management should be about artists because we don't have a job without them. The first question that people always ask when they discover that you're an arts manager is "What are artists like?" They're waiting for the story about the mad genius or the charismatic beauty. Some writers are quite clear on their position. Wesley Enoch (2014, 12), playwright, theatre and festival director, describes them as "rogues and philosophers – instinctual, naughty, vibrant, edgy, fringe-dwellers who use their wits to survive in a world that pressures its citizens into many shades of conformity". After examining the operations of arts organisations, Hewison and Holden (2011, 91) conclude:

> There is no doubt that creative people are special people.

However, "special" doesn't mean they are all the same and "special" doesn't mean "mad genius". "Special" does mean having to work harder and longer and with less pay and security than the general population because of the desire to create (Beirne 2012). In an article about the lives of Irish artists, McCall captures all the challenges of such work:

> Those engaged in [cultural] work often experience uncomfortable working conditions, peripatetic payment, and the precarity of self-employment. Unpaid work is common, as are long hours, and standard work benefits (for example, sick leave or holiday pay) are often absent. Lack of employment security, along with unclear career progression or pathways, also are prominent. Hidden costs are also apparent, and many cultural workers experience physical and mental stress and have limited choice about where and how to live, an inability to plan for the future, and difficulty sustaining a reasonable livelihood.
>
> (McCall 2019, 168–169)

The image that stayed with me reading her stories of cultural workers in Ireland was the cold – not being able to afford the basic necessity of warming one's home.

The gratification of producing art is seen as partial compensation for their labour and one could say that the largest subsidy to the arts has always come from arts workers themselves (Ross 2003). A 2015 report on the arts by the Australia Council paints a picture of a thriving arts scene but where living as an artist means less pay than average, with only 17% of people working full time in their chosen artistic career earning more than the poverty line.

The starting point for a manager's relationship with an artist is to acknowledge that without them, we don't have a rationale let alone a job. The next is to understand them and the challenges they face. For artists, work and art are usually indistinguishable and this means their identity is also tied to work. There's no clear differentiation between you as the musician at work and you as the person at home as there might be for the accountant or the set builder. "Their output is often seen as an extension of the inner worlds of its creator(s) and a symbol of their identities, both by the creators themselves and by audience or consumers" (Hoedemaekers & Ybema 2015, 172).

Thomas (2008), an experienced American arts manager, summarises what she claims is the shared view of "highly qualified leaders who have many years of working with artists of all sorts" as:

- Artists tend to be either up or down and their moods shift with incredible speed
- Problems are catastrophes
- Their needs are immediate
- Attention and praise are necessities of life; the need for applause is real
- Basic insecurity is nearly always present
- Real desire to be #1 (2–3).

However, this feels like a rather stereotypical approach to artists, painting them as child-like. Hein (2011) gives a more nuanced set of artist-archetypes, each with their own motivational profile including the prima donna whose work is their calling; the performance addict, both introvert and extrovert, who want to be the best in their field; the pragmatist who gives priority to work-life balance; and the pay check worker for whom work is a means to resources that provide satisfaction outside of work. This sounds more like a range of approaches to life that could also match those of us who aren't artists. It's not so much the archetype that's the issue but rather the nature of creative work and what that means when it comes to working with artists.

The best advice that I've read comes from the choreographer Mark Morris. When asked how to work with artists, he said handle them with "unconventional sensitivity steeled with radical honesty" (Morris 2001, 63).

After senior politicians and murderers, artists face more scrutiny than any other person in our community. Critics, good and bad, have opinions about every aspect of their work; bloggers and tweeters have opinions about every aspect of their life. To be an artist you have to be able to cope with such exposure but in order to do that, you want to feel protected and supported by those you work with. Ginther (2010, 2) claims that "in large hierarchical organisations, artists are on the fringes, at the mercy of a patriarchal Board in change of their art and their livelihood". But is this true? In the organisations she's talking about – symphony orchestras, ballet and opera companies – and one can add theatre companies – artists are either leaders or co-leaders of the organisation. The largest single group of people employed by these companies are artists. In some of these companies, artists are permanent members of the company just the same as the accountant or the receptionist. In areas such as marketing and communication, artists are consulted about how their images and their stories are to be told. And in some cases, artists are on the Board.

In companies without ensembles such as Melbourne Theatre Company, there was rarely a moment when our HQ wasn't full of actors or designers working and rehearsing. However, it's important to note that a freelance or contract worker doesn't feel as connected to a company as a permanent staff member. Our role was to make them feel as if the company was theirs just as much as ours. We provided welcome morning teas and induction processes; we made sure that all members of the management team from marketing to finance went to see the show and talked to the cast afterwards; we provided champagne and audience feedback; and we had staff whose main job was to make the artists feel looked after.

It's harder is for writers and composers and lyricists who work outside of a company environment. And it's even more challenging to be connected to the artists that want to work with you but can't see how they can because of what looks like a large, impenetrable organisation.

Just as you need to invest in developing new audiences, you need to invest in developing artists through commissions, associate positions and access to resources and advice.

The hardest thing as an arts manager is to say "no" to an artist. Hearing the person that is supposed to be supporting you and doing everything in their power to enable you to produce great art say "no" can be difficult. But if you're saying "no" for good reasons, for the benefit of the art, for the future of the company, and you can clearly articulate that point of view, then usually you'll be heard and usually the relationship will be stronger for it.

I can still remember my first major argument with Roger Hodgman, Artistic Director of MTC (1987–1999). It's a particularly clear memory because we were caught arguing by the Chairman of the Board in my office. It was the day of the first preview of Roger's production of *A Little Night Music* with Ruth Cracknell, Helen Morse and Pamela Rabe, amongst others, and Roger wanted to cancel the preview because, in his view, the production wasn't ready to be seen.

My view (having seen a dress rehearsal) was that it had a way to go but that's what previews are all about – getting the show in front of an audience and running it until it settles. I'd seen shows that were in disarray at preview time but this wasn't one of them. It just needed refinement. That was my perspective as an audience member. As a General Manager my view was that it was:

- 2pm in the afternoon and it was going to be hard to inform the audience in advance about the cancellation (pre-text and universal mobile phones)
- There was nearly full house, i.e. 800 people who'd travelled from all over Melbourne were going to be very annoyed
- That given a short season, there would be no guarantee that we'd get most of those people back into see the show and so income would be lost
- And this was all at a time when the company was in debt and trying to rebuild subscribers.

I won the argument, the preview went on, the musical went on to be one of the best-selling and most awarded shows in the company's history with an extension season in the Princess Theatre and a season in Sydney. So I called it as I saw it – and was right. But there is no guarantee. You just have to make the decision with the best information available and the best intentions in the world.

I had members of my senior management team who didn't think I said "no" often enough, particularly when it came to keeping on budget. Hearing "no, you can't spend money" for an artist is tougher than for a marketing manager. The latter won't be able to do all the elements of their marketing plan, which will be disappointing, but the artist may not be able to make the integrated creation that they had in their mind. So I'm more likely to take a risk on an artistic overspend than when the IT manager wants to buy new computer screens for everyone.

The most challenging aspect of working with artists is working with "divas". Artists are sometimes described as having huge egos and being overly demanding but sometimes there is good reason for behaviour that could be seen as excessive or irrational. The position of one Australian impresario, for example, is that artists are brave souls, exposing themselves in a way that most of us never have to do. Therefore, he will put up with any behaviour that is related to someone taking that deep breath and getting on stage to perform.

In an interview when he was CEO of the Royal Opera House, Covent Garden, Jeremy Isaacs described his role as "broadly approve the repertory in ballet and opera that is put in front of me and I watch other people get on with it – and I cheer them up!" The interviewer said "That's important?" and he replied:

> Yes, very. Because if you don't hold their hand, you're denying them something that they need to rely on. They need somebody they can fall back on and they need to be encouraged in this work because aspects of it are terribly lonely. When a singer goes out on the stage, it doesn't matter how good he

or she is, they are entirely on their own and they risk their lives in a way, each time any of them givers a fully committed performance. Now, they may be a pain in the neck but they deserve support. Because without encouragement, commendation, praise, they wouldn't be able to do that.

(Fitzgibbon & Isaacs 1997, 42)

Arts managers need to have "some compassion, to recognise the insecurity, vulnerability and self-doubt that can plague some creative people, and to seek to support and protect them, where possible, rather than attack them because they make inconvenient demands on us now and then" (Saintilan & Schreiber 2018, 244).

In an article about a Norwegian theatre company, Røyseng (2008, 46) quotes a sales marketing manager who had the experience of an artist upset that his name had been spelt wrongly. The result was additional cost to reprint the marketing material. "I understand him, because it's his identity, his artistic integrity that's at stake." I had similar experiences with distraught people when an actor's name was left out of a programme or where a photo was used of two people out of a cast of three. I'm not normally comfortable with high-pitched emotion but I understood their hurt. Given the public nature of the business of being an artist and the mainly modest financial outcomes, being acknowledged publicly is an important reward for them.

In addition, Røyseng (2008, 46) describes artists who are "groundless aggressive towards their colleagues" and goes on to say that the non-artists emphasise that

> this type of irrationality of the actors is part of their inner life of the theater which you have to accept if you want to hold a non-artistic position here … actors and artists are seen to be exempted from the normal rules of other working environments.

I discussed this perspective with my arts management students and their response to this point was interesting – because what's described could be defined as bullying. The

Executive Director of the theatre company is quoted as saying that she advises new staff that they will have to put up with it and if they are not comfortable with it then they should find another job. The students concluded that a critical point could be reached where other people would be damaged by such "groundless aggression" and that's what an arts manager had to look out for. I can think of stage managers who demonstrated an extraordinary resilience of spirit when it came to demanding Directors and actors but I can also remember employing someone who had been so damaged in the work environment by an artist that they could no longer do their job properly. There is a point where performance preparation turns into bullying and we have to draw the line.

In summary, artists on one level are simply people with ideas and ambitions, families and loved ones, needs and fears, like all the other people in your organisation. But on the other hand, they do have a special set of skills that need nurturing for their creativity to flower and for your arts organisation to be a success. Sometimes, they will step out of line for reasons that are forgivable and sometimes you'll need to exert control for the safety and benefit of those around them. Most of the time, it's an honour to work with creative people. As Enoch (2014, 12) says: "Artists are at the heart of this relationship between the 'who we are' and 'who we might become'. Artists synthesize the ephemeral into something tangible for a society and as such are often at the edge of societal change." And this is why we value them and want to work for and with them.

See also: Arts, Arts Managers, Arts Leaders, Bullying, People

References

Australia Council 2015 *Arts Nation: An Overview of Australian Arts*, Sydney: Australia Council.

Beirne, M. 2012 "Creative Tension? Negotiating the Space between the Arts and Management", *Journal of Arts & Communities*, 4(3), 149–160.

Enoch, W. 2014 *Take Me to Your Leader: The Dilemma of Cultural Leadership*, Platform Paper No. 40, Sydney: Currency House.

Fitzgibbon, M. & Isaacs, J. 1997 "Speaking for Themselves Part 1", in Fitzgibbon, M. & Kelly, A. (eds) *From Maestro to Manager*, Dublin: Oak Tree Press, 41–51.

Ginther, R. 2010 *Making the Case for Change: Challenging Hierarchy in Arts and Cultural Organizations*, Canada: Athabasca University.

Hein, H. H. 2011 "Stepping into Character", Antwerp: 11th AIMAC International Conference.

Hewison, R. & Holden, J. 2011 *The Cultural Leadership Handbook*, Farnham: F Gower.

Hoedemaekers, C. & Ybema, S. 2015 "All of Me: Art, Industry and Identity Struggles", in Beech, N. & Gilmore, C. (eds) *Organising Music: Theory, Practice, Performance*, Cambridge: Cambridge University Press, 172–180.

McCall, K. 2019 "The Reality of Cultural Work", in DeVereaux, C. (ed.) *Arts and Cultural Management: Sense and Sensibility in the State of the Field*, New York: Routledge, 167–184.

Morris, M. 2001 "Genius at Work: A Conversation with Mark Morris", *Harvard Business Review*, 79(9), 63–68.

Ross, A. 2003 *No Collar: The Human Workplace and Its Hidden Costs*, New York: Basic Books.

Røyseng, S. 2008 "Arts Management and the Autonomy of Art", *International Journal of Cultural Policy*, 14(1), 37–48.

Saintilan, P. & Schreiber, D. 2018 *Managing Organizations in the Creative Economy: Organizational Behaviour for the Cultural Sector*, Abingdon: Routledge.

Thomas, M. T. 2008, *Leadership in the Arts: An Inside View*, Bloomington, IN: AuthorHouse.

Arts

I'm going to take it as read that you know what books and film, theatre and dance, painting and sculpture, circus and cabaret, comedy and tragedy, opera and music are. And to extend the list one could add photography and computer games, television and radio, design and fashion. What's important for arts and cultural managers is to find the language that will convince stakeholders and potential audiences about the importance of the arts. There are endless writers and philosophers who can help so I'm going to provide you with some of my favourite quotes.

Tusa (2007a, 8) captures with grace and passion the contradictions and strengths, the paradoxes and weaknesses, of why the arts are important:

The arts matter because they are universal; because they are non-material; because they deal with daily experience in a transforming way; because they question the way we look at the world; because they offer different explanations of that world; because they link us to our past and open the door to the future; because they work beyond and outside routine categories; because they take us out of ourselves; because they make order out of disorder and stir up the stagnant; because they offer a shared experience rather than an isolated one; because they encourage the imagination, and attempt the pointless; because they offer beauty and confront us with the fact of ugliness; because they suggest explanations but no solutions; because they present a vision of integration rather than disintegration; because they force us to think about the difference between the good and the bad, the false and the true. The arts matter because they embrace, express and define the soul of a civilisation. A nation without arts would be a nation that had stopped talking to itself, stopped dreaming, and had lost interest in the past and lacked curiosity about the future.

I don't need to spend too much time convincing you, dear reader, of the value of the arts. But as we know, not everyone "gets it". There are the instrumental arguments about the arts – the economic impact, the stimulation of tourism, the redevelopment of urban spaces, the effect of creative practice in children on their capacity to learn in other areas, the contribution to the ideas economy, and so on. All of these are true but art is valuable for its own sake.

After giving a presentation about the arts leadership to a group of mainly middle-aged men who were not people who attended theatres and galleries as a normal part of their lives, I was asked why they should care about the arts. Most of them were married with kids and I asked them to imagine their child's life without the bedtime stories they told them, without the nursery rhymes, without the songs and craft making on *Playschool*,[1] without the dancing that children automatically do to music with rhythm, without the colourful drawings that were stuck on their fridges. In countries like Australia, every aspect of a young child's life is full of the arts. And then I asked them to imagine their child bought up under the Taliban – with no music, no dancing, no kite flying, no singing, no painting of the human figure, no historic sculptures left to look at and wonder about. Whose life is richer? Needless to say, this group suddenly started to connect to the value of the arts in their own lives.

De Botton (2009, 186) makes the beautiful point that

> many important truths will impress themselves upon our consciousness only if they have been moulded from sensory, emotive material. We may, for example, need a song to alert us in a visceral way to the importance of forgiving others … just as it may be only in front of a successful portrayal of an oak tree that we are in a position to feel, as opposed dutifully to accept, the significance of the natural world.

Years ago I queued for hours at the Young Vic in London to get a ticket to see Ian McKellan in Shakespeare's *Othello*. It was a long afternoon, my last in the city before returning to Australia, and as the hours ticked by and I ran out of things to read and water to drink, I wondered whether I might have used my time more productively. But, finally, my patience was rewarded and I got the very last ticket. I'd been a fan of McKellan since seeing him in the televised versions of *Edward II* and *Richard II* as a teenager but I'd never seen him perform live. The theatre was intimate and the production, with the US opera singer Willard White in the lead, was thrilling. But what remains in my mind is just one tiny moment. McKellan, as Iago, reaches over and delicately touches the back of Desdemona's neck. With a shiver, I suddenly understood jealousy. Not Othello's murderous jealousy but the Iago's jealousy of Othello and his "ownership" of

a beautiful woman. Intellectually I'd understood the idea of this vice but I'd never felt it emotionally. And that's what I love about theatre. How you can suddenly not only see but feel the world from another's perspective.

After quoting one of my favourite philosopher/playwrights A. C. Grayling about art, Jo Caust (2018a, x) says that when she thinks about art, she thinks about the way it affects her: "it heightens my senses and makes me think about issues in a different way". She goes on to say:

> Art as defined by artists can be from somewhere unknown, is a mysterious phenomenon, a way an artist expresses their feelings, a means of communication with others or a process for observing and interpreting the world. Art is not one thing – it is both simple and complex, and it has multiple meanings for the artists as well as the observer.
>
> (Caust 2018, xi)

When I was co-writing a book (Brokensha & Tonks 1986) on cultural economics back in the 1980s, I was desperate to find language that wasn't just about market failures and externalities and I found Stover (1984), who argued that the arts contributed to the betterment of the common life as:

- A form and body of knowledge, valuable in its own right, and catalytic and informative in other fields
- A unique way of seeing, thinking, and knowing, useful in itself, especially for its focus on wholeness, qualities, and value, and helpful in overcoming the constraints of and in advancing other intellectual modes
- A discipline on science and technique
- A celebration of aesthetic values
- A storehouse and expression of culture and as well, a critique of cultures
- An entertainment, encouraging the mind to play, the spirit to recreate itself

- A demonstration of the reach of the mind and the human potentiality, an inspiration to both; and this,
- A perpetual promise of the possibility of something new and something grand (15).

This is still an inspiring collection of ideas.

It's not that the arts, or even discourse about the arts, are easy. The place that the arts can take us emotionally or intellectually can be a dark and violent place as well as an uplifting one (Caust 2018a). An arts manifesto written by Singaporean group ArtsEngage in 2013 (quoted in Chong 2015, 15) contains some wonderful elements:

- Art unifies and divides
- Art is about possibilities
- Art can be challenged but not censored
- Art is political
- Art draws us together and reveals universal truths. However, art can also unveil differences and contradictions.

Apparently even the making of that manifesto created differences and disagreements in the arts world of Singapore.

Steiner (quoted in Leceister 2007, 13) said:

The arts are more indispensable to men and women than even the best of science and technology (innumerable societies have long endured without these). ... We are an animal whose life-breath is that of spoken, painted, sculptured, sung dreams.

In the 2016 Stuart Challender Talk, conductor David Robertson posed the question "Why should you care about art?" and offered two answers:

1. Because you should be selfish
2. Because "art is the thing that allows all of us to join the highest achievements of the human imagination" (6).

While his first point may be somewhat of a shock, what he means is that each of us deserve to be able to experience the joy, the tears, the connection to others, the insights that the arts can give us.

Robertson concludes:

With so much evidence of how horrible man (sic) can behave, art is the counter balance which restores the soul, uplifts the spirit, inspires us to share what we love, and continues to remind us how lucky we are to be illuminated by that light.

(Robertson 2016, 6)

It's because we believe this that we work as arts managers.

See also: Cultural Policy, Economics, Evaluation

References

Brokensha, P. & Tonks, A. 1986 *Culture and Community: Economics and Expectations of the Arts in South Australia*, Sydney: Social Science Press.

Caust, J. 2018a *Arts Leadership in Contemporary Contexts*, London: Routledge.

Chong, T. 2015 "Deviance and Nation-building", in Caust, J. (ed.) *Arts and Cultural Leadership in Asia*, London: Routledge, 15–25.

De Botton, A. 2009 *The Pleasures and Sorrows of Work*, London: Hamish Hamilton.

Leicester, G. 2007 *Rising to the Occasion*, International Futures Forum, March.

Robertson, D. 2016 "Why Should You Care About Art?" Stuart Challender Talk, www.ampag.com.au/article/why-should-you-care-about-art [accessed 20 February 2019].

Stover, C. F. 1984 "A Public Interest in Art – Its Recognition and Stewardship", *Journal of Arts Management and Law*, 14(3), 5–12.

Tusa, J. 2007a *Engaged with the Arts*, London: I.B. Tauris & Co Ltd.

Arts Industry

As I'm originally an economist, I've never had any problem about being part of an "industry". While so much of what artists do is unique, many aspects of their work and their life contain elements found in other industries: employment, taxation, superannuation, occupational health and safety legislation, industrial awards and conditions, income and expenditure, marketing and public relations … and so the list goes on.

However, I should offer you an opposing view before I go any further. Julian Meyrick (2018, 32), theatre director, cultural academic (and friend), says that: "calling something 'an industry' or 'a profession' or 'a leisure pursuit' is a nominative act of great rhetorical force. It does more than describe something. It hails it into being." Protherough and Pick (2002) argued with passion for us to resist the language of "industry" and "product" and "consumer" but I'm in no position to object because I did co-write reports on the economics of the arts in South Australia back in the 1980s.

Radbourne and Fraser (1996) argue that the language of economics started to appear in Australia when the Industries Assistance Commission published a report on the performing arts in 1976. They say that the major impact of receiving recognition as an industry was professionalisation and point to shifts such as the need for trained managers, the need to work with business on a professional footing and the organisational impact of having to conform to employment legislation. However, I'm not convinced that the being named an "industry" caused such changes. For example, it is clear from archives and publications that companies such as MTC were managed in a highly professional way from the beginning – in its case, 1953. Professional arts organisations both for-profit and non-profit have existed for hundreds of years. For example, the Australian employer association for the live performance and entertainment industry Live Performance Australia (LPA) celebrated its 100th anniversary in 2017.

There are certainly more pieces of legislation that impact on arts organisations and more financial reporting requirements from funders that we have to deal with compared to arts CEOs 20 or 30 years ago. But the main change has been in the language of management rather than the tasks of management. My equivalent at MTC in the 1950s was called an Administrator rather than a General Manager or Managing Director but her concerns – about tickets sales and production costs, buildings and money, Boards and funding – were the same as mine.

Instead of having a section called *Arts Industry*, I could have opted for the "Creative" or "Cultural" industries because those phrases have been highly debated in recent years by academics and politicians. Part of the debate is about which forms of creativity can be grouped together. For example, those that require government support such as the performance and visual sector fit into "arts". "Culture" is then used to broaden that grouping to include other areas such as museums, literature, film, galleries and libraries. Finally, the "creative" industries include sectors where making of the product requires creativity (such as advertising or architecture or fashion) but where the products are sold for a commercial return.

This language shift has often been about politics. For example, China started using the concept of "cultural industry" in early 2000s in parallel with the move to a market economy (Qiao 2015, 30). The shift to the "creative" industries was generated by politicians in Western countries in the 1990s. When the UK Secretary of State for Culture (1997 to 2001) Chris Smith rebadged the "arts and cultural industries" as "creative industries", O'Connor (2014) describes this move as "a pragmatic shift from a subsidy-prone 'culture' to a sector at the cutting-edge of the information or knowledge economy, where the cognitive ability of workers to adapt information and manipulate symbols was central". By definition, the creative industry is bigger than the arts industry and this can enable people to argue the importance of the industry to a country's economy but that doesn't help the argument to support non-profit arts and cultural activities. I'm going to leave the academics to debate the importance of these differences between "art", "culture" and "creative" industries because I agree with cultural economist David Throsby on this topic. In a talk at a Social Theory, Politics and the Arts in Adelaide in 2015, I wrote down his description of the debates over "cultural" v "creative" industries as "trivial".

In my view, there's not much point in resisting the language of "industry" but there is perhaps more reason to resist some of the language of management. Reputable arts managers such as Tusa (2011) encourage arts organisations to use the language of art instead; language that includes concepts of risk and the long term and failure and uncertainty and shock and impulse. Taylor (2010) argues that arts organisations *are* businesses so whatever they do is *like* a business but they are also artistic endeavours so whatever they do is *like* an artist. Questions about whether one's value and importance as a cultural organisation is undermined by being called an "industry" or a "business" is much less important than questions such as is your organisation effective and does it have a compelling artistic vision?

See also: Arts Management, Cultural Policy, Economics, Risk, Uncertainty

References

Brokensha, P. & Tonks, A. 1986 *Culture and Community: Economics and Expectations of the Arts in South Australia*, Sydney: Social Science Press.

Meyrick, J., Phiddian, R. & Barnett, J. 2018 *What Matters? Talking Value in Australian Culture*, Melbourne: Monash University Publishing.

O'Connor, J. 2014 "What Got Lost Between 'Cultural' and 'Creative' Industries", 27 February, http://theconversation.com/what-got-lost-between-cultural-and-creative-industries-23658 [accessed 20 February 2019].

Qiao, L. 2015 "Re-negotiating the Arts in China", in Caust, J. (ed.) 2015a *Arts and Cultural Leadership in Asia*, London: Routledge, 26–38.

Radbourne, J. & Fraser, M. 1996 *Arts Management*, Sydney: Allen and Unwin.

Taylor, A. 2010 "Artists, Businesses, and Other Mythological Beasts", *The Artful Manager*, www.artsjournal.com/artfulmanager/main/artists_businesses_and_other_m.php [accessed 20 February 2019].

Tusa, J. 2011 "Finding a Necessary Language for the Arts", www.theguardian.com/culture-professionals-network/culture-professionals-blog/2011/nov/16/finding-necessary-language-arts [accessed 20 February 2019].

Arts Leaders

Most arts organisations such as museums and galleries, opera and dance companies, have artists as either leaders, co-leaders or in senior positions such as Music Directors in orchestras (MacNeill & Tonks 2013). Given the stereotypes about artists, one might be tempted to ask whether they are the appropriate people to run large, complex organisations. The description of a traditional theatre Artistic Director in Norway (and many other countries) is that he (sic) is a "charismatic artistic with little or no respect for or understanding of the economic and administrative rules and responsibilities that accompany the role of manager" (Røyseng 2008, 40).

While artist leaders may distain detailed, management tasks, they have to have qualities such as the ability to communicate a vision, a spirit of collaboration, capacity to think strategically as well as be creative (Caust 2018a, 92). In a study of the development of creativity in the rehearsal process at the Royal Danish Theatre, Hein (2011, 15) concluded:

> They must dare exposing themselves - their vision, their passion etc. Leaders must be courageous. They themselves must be willing to step outside their comfort zone. They must have the stamina to shield the creative workers from considerations (regarding budgetary decisions, strategic decisions etc.) that leaders often (mistakenly) share with their employees. They must inspire.

This is a good reminder of what all leaders should do. However, it's not always such a positive story.

Fitzgibbon (2001) argues that artistic leaders can be narcissistic and ego driven, veering towards an autocratic style. In Caust's (2013, 206) examination of artists running small arts organisations in South Australia, she reaches a different conclusion: that collaboration was "part of their process and essential to achieving successful outcomes. They do not reflect the stereotype of the difficult guru arts leaders who is driven by a pure (perhaps selfish) ego to achieve their vision."

Mintzberg (1998), a well-known management writer, spent a day with an orchestra conductor to see exactly what they did and concluded that the conductor didn't have control, wasn't directing per se, that the role wasn't about obedience and harmony but rather about dealing with nuances and constraint. In a survey of leaders of arts organisations in Great Britain, Sutherland and Gosling (2010, 9) concluded their language was imbued with concepts such as "agency, discretion, and effectiveness through facilitative enablement, 'encouraging', 'tweaking', and 'suggesting', rather than directing or dictating". In other words, there are probably times when the stereotypes are true but, more often, the requirements of creativity such as vision, imagination, collaboration, motivation and problem solving are the leadership qualities one sees in artists.

The type of leadership styles usually discussed in the context of arts organisations are charismatic, transformational, transactional, participatory or relationship (Cray, Inglis & Freeman 2007; Hewison & Holden 2011). In summary, the charismatic leader uses force of personality and individual abilities; the transactional leader has a focus on tasks; the transformational leader has a sense of purpose and mission that drives the organisation; the participatory leader includes followers in decision-making; the relationship leader helps a group move forward rather than a situation where the group follows a leader.

There are arguments that the best leader for an arts organisation is either a transformational leader (because the charismatic leader may end up being Fitzgibbon's narcissist) or a participatory leader (because a transactional leader's focus on operations may undermine artistic freedom). Hewison and Holden (2011, 31) argue for a relationship leader because their charisma will be felt but of "a quieter, gentler kind than a transformational leader". Cray, Inglis and Freeman (2007, 301) note successful leaders match their personal styles to the culture of the organisation and the demands of the

environment and that the artistic leadership style required for a stable, well-resourced, mainstream company may be very different to that exhibited by a founder-artist in a new company. As many arts organisations have a co-leadership model with an artist and a manager sharing the leadership role, one is likely to see different styles at work between the two, such as a charismatic leader working with a relationship-focus leader.

De Paoli (2011) tells a fascinating story of three successive Directors at Norway's National Museum of Art. In summary, the first director failed because even though he was a change-oriented leader he forgot to bring key staff along with him. The second director was an autocratic with little faith in the team of curators who'd been left out in the previous regime. And the final director seemed to be a success but didn't appear to have any of the qualities of charisma or transformation or even relationship building that we're told are the best leadership styles for arts organisations. In fact, he's described as keeping his door locked at all times, arriving at 9am and leaving at 4pm, making decisions without much consultation but not being authoritative. His key qualities seem to be that he had "the right education, the right cultural capital and the right connection" (De Paoli 2011, 11).

What are the lessons from this story? That you can have all the charisma and vision in the world but if you don't get people on side, you'll fail? Or did the first director really fail? After all, he changed the structure, introduced 125,000 people to contemporary art in three months and attracted lots of attention. Perhaps some of those changes stuck. Perhaps sometimes a visionary leader should only be around for a short time because that's their skill – introducing change and letting others manage it.

The lesson I take from the second director is that Boards don't really know how to make leadership appointments. After all the trauma in the previous couple of years, they should have looked for a leader with participative and healing skills. Instead they chose the opposite. And as for the third story, it's depressing to think that you can be born into the job but then so was Mikhail

Piotrovsky, Director of the State Hermitage Museum in St Petersburg, whose father had also been Director and there's great story of renewal and successful change bought about by the son (Cameron & Lapierre 2007, 2013).

Nisbett and Walmsley (2013) quote research that says charisma is not a thing that can be possessed by an individual but that it exists in the relationship between the leader and follower. In my experience, the qualities that make a leader charismatic exist prior to any such relationship, so I'm not convinced on that point. I think it is both a gift and a relationship. I remember attending a presentation by Peter Sellars before his artistic directorship of the Adelaide Festival failed and being told afterwards in awed terms how charismatic he was. I failed as a follower because all I heard on that day was an ill-informed, self-focused person.

It's interesting to reflect on my time at MTC with Simon Phillips as CEO/Artistic Director. He is described as charismatic by almost all who have met him. Nisbett and Walmsley's (2013) research on charismatic arts leaders partly came about as a result of research they did with MTC audiences who talked in glowing terms about Simon.

> Figures such as Simon Phillips from Melbourne Theatre Company were eulogised with an abundance of positive epithets such as "clever", "charming" and "charismatic". Interviewees appeared to be personally excited by chance encounters with such individuals, emphasising any sort of exchange or interaction with the artistic Directors – from meeting in the foyer after a production to observing what colour socks a particular director wore.
>
> (Nisbettt & Walmsley 2013, 1151)

The authors go on to discuss the dark side of charisma, including issues such as vanity and egotism, narcissism and manipulation, but don't seem to have evidence from their two case studies. My reading of the MTC aspects of the research is that there really was an artistic leader with positive charisma that reached out to people. Although the audience members may not actually know "Simon Phillips", the qualities they responded to such as warmth, playfulness and charm were real.

With the artists and staff, there was a sense that people did whatever Simon wanted because it was Simon – whether it was working later or longer or harder. He bought change to the organisation such as the visual marketing image and the number of "stars" performing with the company but the core artistic product remained exactly the same. Simon didn't want to change the nature of the organisation. He'd had his first professional job with the company and loved it. He just wanted the product to be even better. The main change that came during this time was physical – a new theatre and new headquarters – and that change was mainly driven by the uncharismatic member of the leadership team.

So, was he a charismatic or transformational or a relationship leader? I can't decide. But what I can say is that he was an effective arts leader. However, he suffered the same conflict that many artists do – how to combine their creative role with the requirements of running a company. Volz (2017, 71) quotes a USA Artistic Director decrying that fact that "For the artistic director, every moment spent on business issues takes away from time spent envisioning the future, researching and reading plays, casting and hiring, designing, playwriting, directing, acting and teaching."

That story can be heard in voices of some Australian Artistic Directors:

> How much should I actually do myself? How much when balancing that with the administration and planning? That is a juggling act I'm yet to conquer. Last year I did three major works, that was too much. This year I'm doing two, maybe that's too little. I can't say I'm in control of it.
>
> I would say I am feeling exhausted by it already, yes. Institutionalised, I suppose. I would like to go back to just doing what I do, but I know I'm lucky to be here.

I'm looking forward to enjoying what I do more rather than be worried about deadlines or outcomes or responsibility.

(Quoted in Hands 2011, 6)

This tension between art making and management/leadership can be one of the reasons why it's sometimes hard to get great artists to step up to be CEOs of arts companies. As Caust (2018a, 99) says: "While they may see themselves as a 'leader' in their artistic field, they don't want to have the additional responsibility of being an organisational leader." This can be a challenge for a Board in the search for a new artistic leader.

As an arts manager working with an Artistic Director, you have to continually be aware of the contradictions they face. Sometimes, it plays out literally. For example, one Artistic Director would participate in discussions about budgets and put strict limits on even his own productions. But once the annual budget was signed off and the company was committed to shows, concern for working within the budget tended to disappear. There were two very distinct characters in the one person – the CEO and the theatre director. The desire for the artist to concentrate on art making and ignore the management detail may be part of the reason for the increased power of arts managers and the increased number of co-leadership partnerships that one sees, particularly in the performing arts.

Another challenge for artistic leaders is knowing when to leave. When you've founded a company, it's particularly hard to let go but it's even more ugly to be forced out by a Board. One of the rare successful transitions in Australia is when John Bell, founder of Bell Shakespeare, handed over the artistic reins to Peter Evans. Peter was invited into the company to work for a period as co-Artistic Director before all parties agreed to the final change. Other stories are not nearly so positive with founders not being willing to consider, let alone coach, a successor. They may also see the growth of organisational systems and structures as unnecessary bureaucracy and not be willing to share power with a management leader (Hudson 2009, 414).

Artists who have the capacity to not only make art but to provide leadership within an organisational structure are special. As an arts manager, you have to nurture those with potential as well as those in the job for your organisation to be successful.

See also: Artists, Arts Management, Boards, Co-leadership, Creativity, Cultural Leadership, Diversity, Gender, Leadership

References

Cameron, S. & Lapierre, L. 2007 "Mikhail Piotrovsky and the State Hermitage Museum", *International Journal of Arts Management*, 10(1), 65–77.

Cameron, S. & Lapierre, L. 2013 "Mikhail [double dot over his 'I'] Piotrovsky and the State Hermitage Museum", in Caust, J. (ed.) *Arts Leadership: Internal Case Studies*, Melbourne: Tilde University Press, 3–18.

Caust, J. 2013 "Thriving or Surviving: Artists as Leaders of Smaller Arts Organizations", in Caust, J. (ed.) *Arts Leadership: Internal Case Studies*, Melbourne: Tilde University Press, 194–209.

Caust, J. 2018a *Arts Leadership in Contemporary Contexts*, London: Routledge.

Cray, D., Inglis, L. & Freeman, S. 2007 "Managing the Arts: Leadership and Decision Making under Dual Rationalities", *The Journal of Arts Management, Law and Society*, 36(4), 295–313.

De Paoli, D. 2011 "The Role of Leadership in Changing Art Institutions – The Case of the National Museum of Art in Oslo, Norway", Antwerp: AIMAC.

Fitzgibbon, M. 2001 *Managing Innovation in the Arts*, Westport, CT: Quorum Books.

Hands, K. 2011 *The Impact of Artistic Directors on Australian Performing ArtsOrganisations*, Antwerp: AIMAC.

Helle Hedegaard Hein 2011 "Stepping into Character", Antwerp: AIMAC.

Hewison, R. & Holden, J. 2011 *The Cultural Leadership Handbook*, Farnham: F Gower.

Hudson, M. 2009 *Managing Without Profit: Leadership, Management and Governance of Third Sector Organisations in Australia*, Sydney: UNSW Press.

MacNeill, K. & Tonks, A. 2013 "Leadership in Australian Arts Companies: One Size Does Not Fit All", in Caust, J. (ed.) *Arts Leadership*, Melbourne: Tilde University Press.

Minzberg, H. 1998 "Covert Leadership", *Harvard Business Review*, November–December, https://hbr.org/1998/11/covert-leadership-notes-on-managing-professionals [accessed 16 March 2019].

Nisbett, M. & Walmsley, B. 2013 "The Romanticization of Charismatic Leadership in the Arts", Bogota: AIMAC, International Conference, 1145–1157.

Røyseng, S. 2008 "Arts Management and the Autonomy of Art", *International Journal of Cultural Policy*, 14(1), 37–48.

Sutherland, I. & Gosling, J. 2010 "Cultural Leadership: Mobilizing Culture from Affordances to Dwelling", *Journal of Arts Management, Law, and Society*, 40(1), 6–26.

Volz, J. 2017 *Introduction to Arts Management*, London: Bloomsbury Methuen Drama.

Arts Managers

Who are we?

In the early part of the 20th century we would have been impresarios rather than arts managers. Although I love the idea underlying the word "impresario" with its "hint of flair, even genius" (Cooke 1997, 33) I don't think I would have been a great success in such a role. Peterson (1986, 164) tells the story of one of the first people to train museum managers at a university.[2] The primary skill he taught his students was how to talk to wealthy prospective patrons. The impresario's style was based on flattering and cajoling the affluent elite "compared to the arts administrator who needs to be more even handed in his (sic) relationships". In 1981, DiMaggio hypothesised that arts organisations wanting government grants would have to become more managerial, create formal policies and plans and be more financially responsible and he was right as we have seen the shift from impresario to administrator to manager. For example, when I studied this subject in the mid-1980s, the course was called Arts Administration but now I teach arts management, although now the preferred term seems to be "cultural management" (DeVereaux 2019b). However, there is evidence that current managerial practices such as program planning and evaluation were happening long before the first tertiary educated "arts manager" was appointed to run a company.[3]

In an article about New Zealand arts managers, Major and Gould-Lardelli (2011) conclude that arts managers have diverse demographic characteristics, are highly educated and share a common passion for the arts. Many have previously pursued a career as a practicing artist or are what might be called "hobby artists" and most have a background in the arts rather than management. The people who responded to their survey were doing the job for "love" rather than money and had little interest in working as managers in other industries. Another insight from their research was that the arts managers often came to the role because a family member was a practising artist in need of management. In my case, it wasn't a family member but it was friends.

As the research subjects were young and old, male and female, local and immigrant, the authors concluded there was no such thing as a "typical" arts manager. However, the statistic of four women to one man in their research is reflective of what I have viewed over many years: the feminisation of arts management. In my post-graduate arts management class of 30–50 people, the number of men over the last five years has ranged from zero to eight.[4] A similar result was found in research on the sociology of French arts managers. In Dubois and Lepaux's (2019) survey, 80% of students enrolled in cultural management master's programs were women. Usually such gendered outcomes are a result of history, for example women as nurses, or exclusion, for example engineering as a male occupation. But the researchers say that cultural management positions are too recent to have a gendered identity. Perhaps one reason for this phenomenon is that more women than men participate and attend arts events. However, there's still a tension between creative and non-creative jobs with more men as artistic leaders of companies and the researchers also note that in their survey, more women than men give up artistic careers and might turn to management as a replacement.

The French results were also similar to the New Zealand research in terms of the impact of family background with parents' involvement in the arts. More important than this specific connection, Dubois and Lepaux (2019) point out that an interest in this area of education requires knowledge and experience in the arts (either as audience or creator) and that tends to part of middle-class life.

Tusa (2007a) says that arts managers can be introvert or extrovert, specialist or generalist, but they need to be able to cope with a number of paradoxes: patience/impatience, risk/failure, short term/long term. The first and last set of paradoxes are linked. On the one hand, the curtain has to go up at exactly the right time. The exhibition has to be ready for the public when the website says it's going to open. But at the same time, many parts of your job as an arts manager are about projects that can take years, if not decades, to complete and sometimes you just won't be there to see them through. My predecessor at MTC worked hard to find a new theatre for the company but for reasons totally out of his control, the project never came off. If I'd had stayed for the traditional five to seven years as Managing Director,[5] I wouldn't have seen the project completed either. As an arts manager, you work for the future, for the next team, for the next generation as much as you work for yourself in the now.

Just as interesting as our backgrounds and our characteristics are the reasons for becoming arts managers. The words Major and Gould-Lardelli's (2011, 5) research subjects used to describe their arts management careers were without exception positive and included "intuitive, enriching, fun, successful, educational, personally satisfying, interesting, varied and challenging". The French students that Dubois and Lepaux (2019, 52) interviewed didn't aim to work in "a given occupation, function or structure". Cultural management was seen as a vocation and a desire to work in the cultural sector rather than to perform management tasks per se, whereas the New Zealand researchers concluded that the majority of their survey participants had both *chosen* to be a manager and chosen to be a manager *in the arts*.

The commitment to the arts is self-evident in the case of artistic leaders who have dedicated their lives to their art form but it's true for arts managers as well. The research that I did with Kate MacNeill and Sarah Reynolds on leadership in Australia's major performing arts companies showed that the majority of Managing Directors had an extensive background in the arts, and often as a performer. Of the 27 General Managers interviewed in our study, 17 originally trained as artists and had made the transition to management. As one Managing Director said, experience on the artistic side of the organisational fence enabled them "to understand [the artist's] needs, to be able to appreciate the art form from an insider's point of view, but to really understand the performance issues, or what it's like to be out there on stage". Of the 17 Managing Directors who had originally trained as an artist, nine had studied the particular art form practiced by the organisation. This is consistently quoted as a benefit: "I haven't played professionally in years but playing [particular instrument] … has been crucial for me in terms of understanding what musicians do and what their issues and challenges are." (MacNeill et al 2013, 1166)

Dubois and Lepaux (2019) ask the question of whether arts managers are failed artists and conclude that it's likely to be a more active choice than "failing" implies:

> Chronologically, [the desires that leads to one working as an arts manager] are expressed first under the romantic form of a yearning for art, lasting for the duration of the feeling of freedom and of open future dreams, experienced during high school or the first year of academic studies when familial, economic, and processional constraints are suspended. As personal experiences and parental or educational incentives reshape a space of possibilities, and as gradation nears, the same dispositions may be expressed in a related but outwardly less risky and seemingly more serious choice – that of cultural management. The choice is then not so much the result of renouncement as it is the translation of an artistic vocation under what may appear to be a more

reasonable form, that is, one adjusted to the constraints that were previously, and temporarily, put aside (50–51).

Michail Piotrovsky (2013), Director the Hermitage Museum in St Petersburg, is very clear on what makes a good museum director – being a specialist in the museum field. He says: "as a director, the fundamental principles guiding your actions have much more to do with the museum's mission – that is, the preservation and dissemination of your collection - than with notions of profitability" (Cameron & Lapierre 2013, 15).

I'm in Major and Gould-Lardelli's (2011) "hobby artist" category having produced and presented radio programmes as a volunteer before I became a station manager. I made the decision to do a post-graduate course in arts management after a drunken conversation on the last night of a university play I performed in called *Women Beware Women* that had been directed by the English actor Timothy West. [By "drunken" I mean I was. I don't want to speak on Mr West's behalf!] He challenged me to decide whether I wanted to remain an academic all my life or do something useful for the art form I loved. However, there are also arts managers who aren't artists, either amateur or professional, but who contribute knowledge built on the experience of being a dedicated audience member.

A head-hunter rang a few years ago to see if I was interested in managing an orchestra. I said "No, thank you – I fall asleep at concerts."[6] They said "That's ok. We're not looking for people who know anything about music. We just want a good manager." I said, "You're wrong" … and they were. What makes a good arts manager is someone who has a care for and a commitment to the art that's at the heart of their company's rationale for existence, as well as a bundle of management skills. The orchestra appointed someone from the commercial world who barely lasted a year in the job.

Jeremy Isaacs, when General Manager of the Royal Opera House, Covent Garden, said that an understanding of the arts and artists was essential to the role:

… you have to believe passionately enough in the product – ghastly word – in what is being created, to go through fire and water for it. If you don't do that, if you don't understand what people go through when they make things, you can't appreciate what they need to keep them going.

(Fitzgibbon & Isaacs 1997, 42–43)

Arts managers, whether artists or arts lovers, tend to view their work as a "vocation", not just a job that pays the bills or provides status. This vocation is based on a strong belief in and commitment to the intrinsic value of the arts and culture (Sutherland & Gosling 2010). However, having such a vocation is not always an easy path. There is research to suggest that whereas passion and a desire to answer one's calling is a strong motivator to pursue a career in arts management, it does not guarantee subjective and/or objective career success. Formal knowledge and maintaining positive professional networks are also necessary for facilitating professional development and recognition. Being tough and resilient enough to withstand the hard times when facing unexpected budget cuts or program failures was also identified as an essential skill (Rentschler, Jogulu & Richardson 2013).

What Is Our Role?

Radbourne and Fraser described it this way in 1996:

The arts manager's role is to facilitate the exchange of the artistic experience between the artists and the consumer through innovative cultural leadership.

(1996, 1)

Kevin Radbourne (1995) was more poetic in his description of the role:

role player extraordinaire, the arts manager performs as the casting director in requiring compatible players for the team; the orchestra conductor in ensuring that all members of the organisations play the same tune; the potter in shaping and moulding the organisation; the acrobat in administering upwards to the Board and downwards to the team while on the highwire balancing sponsors and subscriber needs with limited resources.

Although that language seems to paint the arts manager as an artist (and in some cases that's what they are), participants in Major and Gould-Lardelli's (2011, 6) research draw a clear distinction between the artist and the arts manager:

Artists were described as impulsive, creative, passionate and not wanting to think about real life responsibilities. Arts managers were described as less biased, more holistic, focused on fine tuning aspects such as how to manage the career, business, finance, marketing, be a promoter and take calculated risks based on reality not just passion. The arts manager role includes considering issues of sustainability and is focused on getting (mainly economic) results.

This differentiation is based on role rather than on skill set as an artist or creative specialist could and often are both artist and manager.

Kuester (2010) challenges the notion that arts managers are divorced from the actual process of producing and presenting art works with her survey of music managers of classical symphony orchestras, chamber orchestras, concert halls and music festivals in Germany. She concludes that they *were* involved in arts decision-making and that's my experience too. Of course, I was never part of the rehearsal process but I did express opinions on the choice of play, cast and creatives and occasionally my views ended up on stage.

Morrow (2018, 8) has reviewed the literature on whether an arts or artists manager's role is a creative one. Some people disagree with the conflation between creativity and management because it undermines the notion of creatively driven artistic work. Others point out that they are creative but in different ways. I find the argument somewhat pointless because one could argue that many jobs are creative and it just muddles the difference between artists and managers in way that adds nothing to the story. Some artists are also good managers. Some managers are particularly creative. Morrow (2018, 105–106) makes a further interesting point that

a one-dimensional understanding of the commerce versus creativity dichotomy will not serve artists or artist [or arts] managers in the future. Artists and artist managers have a duty of care to one another, and there is a need to respect each other's creativities and to not simply believe in a "creatives" versus "non-creatives" divide.

(2018, 105)

In cultural and creative organisations which have uncertain demand and high risk, the skills specifically required to manage such workplaces are:

- Communication and advocacy skills
- Ability to manage creative people
- Need to reconcile art and commerce
- Ability to manage diverse teams
- Ability to manage multiple projects simultaneously; and
- Ability to work in a fast-moving, competitive environment (Saintilan & Schreiber 2018, 9).

But even if we have all these skills, what do arts managers really contribute? Cooke (1997, 32) asks the question "Does the better management of the arts lead to more and better art, or simply to more, but not necessarily better artistic activity?" We'll never know the answer to that question but having played the role for so long, I have to be optimistic and hope that the answer is more and better art. I would like to think that the management commentator Charles Handy is right when he said of the arts managers he saw in 1994 at the London International Festival of Theatre:

watching them at work, I often felt that if only more businesses had their sort of infectious enthusiasm, blended with their talent for understated and almost invisible management, our economy would be different from what it is today.

(Quoted in Summerton & Hutchins 2005, 4)

Alice Nash, an arts manager based in Melbourne, beautifully describes the nature of what we do. She works for *Back to Back Theatre*, a company whose ensemble are actors with intellectual disabilities. Having been on the Board of the company for a number of years I appreciate how clear and honest the communication from the ensemble can be. "Sometimes," she says, "an actor will question what it is that I do and whether I am pulling my weight. This makes me laugh, but feels the right order of things." She goes on to say:

We inherit this fine culture and try to build on it, each in our own way, through attention and care, ingenuity and dexterity, doggedness, dedication, grit, solidarity and a simple desire to make *Back to Back* better.

(Quoted in Grehan & Eckersall 2013, 27)

Arts management is not necessarily work that will always be recognised. The public face of the company is most likely to be the arts leader. But if you've chosen your vocation because you love the arts, then the success of the artists will be your success too.

See also: Arts Leaders, Cultural Leadership, Leadership, Resilience, You

References

Cameron, S. & Lapierre, L. 2007 "Mikhail Piotrovsky and the State Hermitage Museum", *International Journal of Arts Management*, 10(1), 65–77.

Cameron, S. & Lapierre, L. 2013 "Mikhail Piotrovsky and the State Hermitage Museum", in Caust, J. (ed.) *Arts Leadership: Internal Case Studies*, Melbourne: Tilde University Press, 3–18.

Cooke, P. 1997 "The Culture of Management and the Management of Culture", in Fitzgibbon, M. & Kelly, A. (eds) *From Maestro to Manager*, Dublin: Oak Tree Press, 31–40.

DeVereaux, C. 2019b "Cultural Management as a Field", in DeVereaux, C. (ed.) *Arts and Cultural Management: Sense and Sensibility in the State of the Field*, New York: Routledge, 3–12.

DiMaggio, P. J. 1981 "The Impact of Public Funding on Organizations in the Arts", *Yale Program on Non-Profit Organizations Working Paper 31*, Yale University.

Fitzgibbon, M. & Isaacs, J. 1997 "Speaking for Themselves Part 1", Fitzgibbon, M. & Kelly, A. (eds) *From Maestro to Manager*, Dublin: Oak Tree Press, 41–51.

Grehan, H. & Eckersall, P. (eds) 2013 *We're People Who Do Shows' Back to Back Theatre*, Aberystwyth: Performance Research Books.

Kuester, I. 2010 "Arts Managers as Liaisons between Finance and Art: A Qualitative Study Inspired by the Theory of Functional Differentiation", *The Journal of Arts Management, Law, and Society*, 40(1), 43–57.

MacNeill, K., Reynolds. S. & Tonks, A. 2013 "A Double Act: Coleadership and the Performing Arts", Bogota: 12th AIMAC International Conference, 1158–1169.

Major, S. & Gould-Lardelli, R. 2011 "Becoming an Arts Manager: A Matter of Choice or Chance?", Antwerp: 11th AIMAC International Conference.

Morrow, G. 2018 *Artist Management: Agility and the Creative and Cultural Industries*, London: Routledge.

Peterson, R. A. 1986 "From Impresario to Arts Administrator", in DiMaggio, P. J. (ed.) *Nonprofit Enterprise in the Arts*, New York: Oxford University Press, 161–183.

Radbourne, J. & Fraser, M. 1996 *Arts Management*, Sydney: Allen and Unwin.

Radbourne, K. 1995 "What Is an Arts Manager", paper delivered to graduate arts administration students, Brisbane: QUT, 16 March.

Rentschler, R., Jogulu, U. & Richardson, J. 2013 "Occupational Calling as a Platform for Career Advancement in Arts Management: When Passion Isn't Enough", Bogota: 12th AIMAC International Conference, 46–54.

Saintilan, P. & Schreiber, D. 2018 *Managing Organizations in the Creative Economy: Organizational Behaviour for the Cultural Sector*, Abingdon: Routledge.

Summerton, J. & Hutchins, M. (eds) 2005 *Diverse Voices: Personal Journeys, All Ways Learning*, Brighton: All Ways Learning.

Sumner, J. 1993 *Recollections at Play*, Melbourne: Melbourne University Press.

Sutherland, I. & Gosling, J. 2010 "Cultural Leadership: Mobilizing Culture from Affordances to Dwelling", *Journal of Arts Management, Law, and Society*, 40(1), 6–26.

Tusa, J. 2007a *Engaged with the Arts*, London: I.B. Tauris & Co Ltd.

Arts Organisations

The key qualities of arts organisations are that they operate in a world of risk, they are filled with people who have actively chosen to work in a creative industry, they never have enough resources to achieve the dreams of all their artists and – for non-profit companies – they have a multitude of stakeholders to please.

Arts and cultural organisations come in all shapes and forms. Profit or non-profit. Producing or presenting companies. Collectives or hierarchies. Making art or exhibiting it. Enabling new work or preserving historical artifacts. Festivals or venues. Work made by groups or by individuals. Government or private funding bodies. There is no homogeneity about art or the organisations that facilitate its making and sharing (Caust 2005).

The environment in which much art is created is unstable and turbulent with a high degree of uncertainty (Fitzgibbon 2001). Funding is uncertain; the outcomes of an artistic project are uncertain; appeal to audiences is uncertain. While the same could be said for most for-profit companies, innovation and creativity is at the heart of our companies which increases the level of risk. As I used to say to managers from the for-profit world, imagine putting 12 brand-new products on sale every year without any market testing. Each play MTC produced was either an original work or a new production of an existing work. And each production ran the risk of losing $100–500,000 if the audiences decided not to come.

Most of the traditional art forms such as theatre, dance, opera and classical music are produced by non-profit companies, as are most of the organisations that exhibit art or nature or heritage. The challenge for such arts organisations is to put the needs of the artist or the creative worker at the forefront when there are many other stakeholders including other staff, audiences and funders. For-profit arts companies such as commercial theatre producers and music presenters face many of the same challenges because even though profit is the desired outcome, in my experience, people who work in this part of our world care about the art just as much. Can art be well served by an organisational structure that looks like any other business with hierarchies and policies, annual reports and business plans, financial goals and Boards? The answer is that we have to make it work because we're faced not only with historical models, but with current legal and governance requirements.

An equally challenging question is should an arts organisation's goal be to support the work of an individual artist or ensure the existence of the institution (McDaniel & Thorn 1993)? This is of particular concern to arts organisations as they transition from being small, founder-led groups to larger, more rule-bound structures. I've seen the heartbreak of a founder as they lost control of their company. At the point when an artistic founder leaves or can no longer produce great art, should the organisation live on? As a CEO or Managing Director of an arts or cultural organisation, you are basically holding it in trust for the artists who want to work with you and the audiences who want to experience art both now and in the future. But sometimes that trust means that you have to hand on the resources to another company. Sometimes organisations come to the end of their natural life – when audience tastes change or when a founder Artistic Director leaves or runs out of energy and ideas. The best thing to do is to make that choice before you have to. In this way you are being a positive trustee for the art form and audiences of the future.

See also: Audiences, Boards, Non-profit, Organisational Structure, Risk, Stakeholders, Succession, Uncertainty

References

Caust, J. 2005 "Does It Matter Who Is in Charge? The Influence of the Business Paradigm on

Arts Leadership and Management", *Asia Pacific Journal of Arts and Cultural Management*, 3(1), 153–165.

Fitzgibbon, M. 2001 *Managing Innovation in the Arts*, Westport, CT: Quorum Books.

McDaniel, N. & Thorn, G. 1993 *Towards A New Arts Order*, New York: Arts Action Research.

Audiences

Most arts and cultural companies produce or present a show, an exhibition, a book, a film, a YouTube clip – some form of art that requires an audience. Except art forms that are experienced alone, the audience is the finishing touch to the creation process because by immersing themselves in the experience and responding to it, they impact on its delivery (Ryan, Fenton & Sangioro 2010). Understanding why people buy tickets or go at a cultural event is essential for both organisational and artistic well-being.

Why Do People Choose Arts Experiences?

Walmsley (2012, 206) summarises a range of audience research about how audiences "value" cultural experiences:

> emotional impact, stimulation and flight; engagement and captivation; knowledge and risk; authenticity and collective engagement; learning and challenge; energy and tension; shared experience and atmosphere; personal resonance and inspiration; empowerment and renewal; aesthetic growth and self-actualization; improved social skills, better relationships and family cohesion.

Going to a concert is not the same as passively watching television. Tusa (2007, 90) describes it as "closer to an intellectual gymnasium, where minds are fed, intellects stretched and emotions challenged". The artistic experience is not the only benefit that the audience member receives (Boorsma & Chiaravallloti 2010). At the same time, they also receive recreational, social and learning experiences. As an audience member said:

It all depends on your rituals …You are there to see a show …you see it and you leave. On the other hand … if you are the "true consumer", you will want the dinner, the drinks, the shows, the coffee, the cake and so on.

(Quoted in Hume et al. 2006, 313)

As well as the regular quantitative and qualitative surveys and focus groups done at MTC, sometimes an interested researcher would come our way and provide insights into our audiences. Ben Walmsley, an English academic, was one such person. He did deep interviews with some our audience members and, along with comments from audiences at the West Yorkshire Playhouse, wrote a fascinating paper called *"A Big Part of My Life": A Qualitative Study of the Impact of Theatre* (2011). He concluded that "theatre-going is a complex pursuit that transcends the blurred boundaries of arts, entertainment and leisure" (2011, 1) and I suspect, for the all the attempts to divide art into high and popular boxes, that this is true of many cultural experiences.

The reasons his (my) audience gave as to why they went to the theatre included escapism and immersion, distraction and emotional release, feeding the imagination, relationship building, personal insight and having one's belief systems challenged. When asked what their life would be like without theatre responses varied "from a casual shrug to a devastated tear" (Walmsley 2011, 10).

MTC was doing its biennial audience research around the same time as Walmsely's interviews and the theatre experience was summed up the research company as offering a unique emotional and (often) intellectual experience which they refined to the idea that going to the theatre was to "exercise my emotions". And that, the researchers concluded, was why people kept coming back for more.

Phrases MTC audience members used about why they came to the theatre included:

- Immerse myself
- The surprise element
- Real and relevant issues – not superficial

- Passionate
- Expose my mind to different ideas
- Give myself over to storytelling
- As real as it gets
- Entertainment
- Watching the creative process
- Dramatic
- Intimate, moving
- Escapism
- Being taken on a journey
- Challenge myself
- Confronting, thought provoking.

These words are all common to research on European audiences (e.g. Cuadrado-García 2017; de Rooij & Bastiaansen 2017) and I suspect could be found through the voices of audiences in other parts of the world.

Each arts organisation should have its own understanding about why people turn into their audience members. Baxter (2010) makes some really good points about audience research. Her starting point is that in order to develop and grow audiences, we need to know and empathise with them. And this means not just finding out what they think about us, but to concentrate on finding out what they think about art and culture. Baxter (2010, 128) argues the case (and I agree with her) for the importance of qualitative research which helps us understand how our company is perceived, the motivational triggers that lead to participation and the degree to which various marketing and brand strategies appeal.

MTC had a good history of audience research but hadn't done much in the early 1990s because of financial pressures. Our initial venture back into the qualitative area was in the form of focus groups. One of the questions we used to determine how our brand was perceived was to ask what sort of animal the company was. To my absolute horror, the overwhelming answer was a wombat. For those who don't know this unique Australian animal, it could best be described as iconic, but also fat, brown, boring, slow (with occasional 90 second bursts of unexpected speed) burrowers. Not exactly how we viewed ourselves. A couple of years later, after

changes in programming, marketing and public relations, we asked the same question again and we had become labradors. Not the most glamorous of dogs but with a reputation for being friendly and hard-working and at least no long a boring brown. Needless to say, there were other animals in the mix but the result of asking the question was a fascinating conversion that unpacked a lot of unstated assumptions about the company. I have no idea where I picked up this idea of asking how the company was personified (or rather animalified), but 15 years later Baxter (2010, 133) was advising this sort of technique to help uncover unconscious insight from one's audience.

Who decides what the audience gets to experience?

Some art making engages audiences through story creation, through participation, through co-production. In these cases the audience is determining the nature of the final artistic output, but the majority of art making is still "curated" or "created" by someone else, the "artist". Tusa asks "does the audience know what it wants, and should the arts world to try to find out?" His answers, which I agree with, are "no" and "no" (Tusa 2007a, 90). Some writers would disagree. For example, Holden (2008) would see it as playing gatekeeper. Tusa and I would be judged as either "'malign experts' or professionals who use their knowledge to confound and patronise; the 'cultural snobs' who perpetuate processes of exclusion bound up in class and education; and the avant garde artists who've traditionally defined themselves in opposition to the masses" (27). The opposite position is put by Hackley (2015, 130) who says: "The very notion of giving consumers what they say they want … seems absurd in the context of creative industries. What consumers of art want … is to see something new and exciting that activates their sense of discernment." In other words, we should give audiences what they want through creative cultural leadership. What this means to me is that we should attend to the needs of the audience in a general sense rather than attend to their opinions.

Radbourne and Fraser (1996) would also probably disagree with Tusa and me. They say that "[p]roduct selection, whether the season's repertoire or calendar of events, is too often based on the desires of an artistic director who has little concern for or understanding of the needs of a presumed audience" (48). They see arts organisations as being product focused rather than audience focused. In my experience, that view is wrong. No Artistic Director wants to kill the organisation that allows them to live and work. No Artistic Director doesn't want to communicate with an audience. Individual artists at the beginning of their practice may be focused on art making rather than audience making but their passion will eventually make them lift up their head and find someone to share it with.

Programming is always based on more than the desires of the artistic leader. In an article about managing the orchestral performances of the City of Birmingham Symphony Orchestra, Simon Webb, who had been the Director of Orchestral Management, describes the elements that impacted on programming and all of it would be familiar to a dance company or a theatre company. They are a combination of:

- Taste/preference − of key artistic staff, musicians and visiting conductors
- Audience needs − balance between new work and familiar work − both for the musicians and audiences; audience appeal of works, conductors and musicians
- Time − availability of artists; audience preferences for summer/winter shows
- Money − cost implications of guest artists and cost-benefit analysis of guest artists
- Funders − impact of service level agreements with funders − government, corporate, private (Webb & Dowling 2015).

Of course, all of these "interests" are "mediated" by the Artistic Director (and Managing Director)

but consideration of the audience is a large part of the mix.

One needs to know about one's audience's interests but making programming decisions on what they want to see doesn't work. For example, our audience often said that they wanted to see the classics but when it came to buying tickets, they were much more interested in contemporary international work. On arriving at MTC, I looked at the company's most recent research and when asked what audiences most wanted to see, it was Shakespeare. However, that certainly wasn't the case in terms of what they bought, either as subscribers or single ticket buyers. Shortly after reading the research, MTC presented a brilliant production of *Hamlet* directed by Neil Armfield and staring people who are now household names − Richard Roxburgh, Geoffrey Rush, Cate Blanchett. And hardly anyone came. Occasionally a Shakespeare would break the 18,000-ticket barrier, but rarely. We got to the point where because of our audience lack of interest plus direct competition in the market from Bell Shakespeare and the Australian Shakespeare Company, we only did a Shakespeare play every couple of years. This was a tragedy in some ways because Simon Phillips, our Artistic Director at the time, was (and is) one of the best Directors of Shakespeare that I have seen in the English language world.

One year, Simon said "I've found the perfect actor and I really really really want to do *Richard III*." So I budgeted low for subscribers (correct), high for students (correct) and modestly for single tickets (wrong). It was a stunning, fast-moving, cleverly designed, brilliantly performed production. Ticket sales at preview time were low but within days the show sold out. A 12-year-old member of my family loved it so much that they came three times. The single ticket buyers weren't people who loved Shakespeare *per se*. They'd just heard that this show was fabulous and wanted to have the experience.

What you need to do is to watch how people respond to what you offer rather than ask them what they want. One of Simon Phillip's initiatives when he started as MTC's Artistic Director was the use of "stars" to attract subscribers back to the company and build new audiences. However, what we learnt over time was that although a famous name could be an attractor, it had to be combined with other performance aspects, such as whether they were well known for their theatrical craft and/or were rarely seen on stage and/or were in a well-known or well-loved play and/or by a well-known playwright. Putting a TV star into an unknown play didn't guarantee an audience. But putting a famous actor who didn't often appear on stage who was also an award-winning performer could help boost audience numbers.

In another example, if we'd been listening to the opinions of the main subscriber audience, MTC wouldn't have developed the *Neon* program of new independent work. But we were listening to their *needs*. They were an audience who wanted the stimulation of the "new" but who didn't necessarily know what the "new" looked like. In the first season (2013), the early committers were the traditional middle-aged subscribers. What they wanted was *emotional exercise* and we gave it to them. Norbury (2010, 52) says, "[c]ultural leaders can never afford to lose touch with their audience and stakeholders … creators can only exist if they have an audience". It's a question of how you listen to them that's important.

Where Do You Find an Audience?

Colbert (2009, 9) makes the insightful point that in many countries "the consumption of cultural products is a reality for 100% of the population". They listen to music on their iPhone, read books, take their children to museums, go to music festivals, watch movies, see shows. According to research by cultural economists and governments, most of them value the arts (e.g. Australia Council 2015). It's just that not all of them come to the organisations presenting opera or dance, theatre or art exhibitions.

We can agonise about why they don't come and the list of reasons is endless: double income families lacking time; families with children lacking money; decreasing amounts of students studying the arts at school or the humanities at university; digital consumption; increasing competition from almost everything. In an interesting paper exploring the impact of age, period and cohort on arts audiences, van den Broek (2013) concludes that even though increasing education attainment over the decades has increased the propensity to experience art, this has been counterbalanced if not outweighed by increasing competition. Bianchi (2008, 240) argues that as time is allocated to activities that enable simultaneous consumption (e.g. eating and playing on a computer), activities that are less dependent on goods and "more on a free use of time that relies on pauses and associations, on anticipation and memories" will lose out. One can get completely depressed. Colbert (2009, 2) claims that arts markets have reached saturation. However, because we believe so passionately in the value of the arts, we keep looking for audiences.

There are a multitude of books and articles about marketing the arts (and I'll add some opinions under M). Arts companies are always searching for new audiences, but most of time we don't find them – they find us because a loved one or a teacher brings them. Most of the blokes who worked in the set-making department of MTC were turned onto theatre because a girlfriend took them. Most young people in an Australian multi-state longitudinal study on theatre attendance went because their mother or grandmother took them to the theatre even before their teacher did (O'Toole et al. 2014). Of course, this doesn't mean that you sit back passively waiting for that to happen.

One approach to audience development is called MAO – motivation, ability, opportunity (Kempa & Pooleb 2015). These can be individually or collectively barriers to attendance. For example, if you don't think you're going to enjoy the experience or get anything out of it, what's the motivation to go? If you don't know anything about opera or contemporary art, then you may not have the ability to get meaning out of the experience. Lack of opportunity may be anything from problems of time or money or even knowing that an arts experience is on. Keeping all these barriers in mind can help you design marketing and access programs to stretch your reach to new audiences.

In 2018, the French Government started testing an arts app "like Tinder, but for the arts, and with benefits" (Henley 2018). On your 18th birthday the app came preloaded with 500 Euros of cultural credit. This helps with the Opportunity aspect of MAO but as some of the critics of the program said, access to culture is not just a financial issue. People need to feel confident that they can go to new art forms and enjoy them, not just to the ones they know. Apparently, a similar program in Italy saw culture passes being sold to the highest bidder on social media. Putting cynicism aside, I like the idea of an app that offers a diversity of culture and, for the right age group, free access.

Kaiser (2013, 79) said that his mantra used to be "good art, well marketed" but he now adds the ingredient of "family" – the people who routinely buy tickets for themselves, their friends and their children. But he doesn't just mean literal families. Part of the challenge in finding new audiences is how to make them feel part of the arts "family". Osborne and Rentschler (2010, 57) summarise the work of Donna Walker-Kuhne who presented a range of workshops in Australia on finding "new", particularly multicultural audiences. She said that "audiences will come if they feel that they will be welcome, if they feel they have a place, and if the programming is culturally relevant to them". In the late 1990s, MTC put on a play about the Latvian immigration experience in Australia. The marketing team worked efficiently to communicate with every Latvian association and communication outlet in Melbourne and the result was a number of new audience members who came to theatre. Somewhat cynically, the Chairman asked why we hadn't done a play about the Italian immigration experience because that community was 40 times the size of the Latvian community. This was in the days before MTC owned its own ticketing system so we couldn't keep track

to know whether those new audience members ever came back – something that is no longer a problem with sophisticated customer management systems.

Governments expect cultural activities to have instrumental benefits, including, for example, personal development at the individual level and community outcomes such as integration and socialisation. But the people who most need these outcomes are the least likely to be able to access cultural events and experiences. Bourder-Pailler and Urbain (2015) offer some thoughtful insights into why people who might be unemployed or otherwise in social or financial difficulty find it hard to access culture. Of course, the obvious answer is lack of money but just as important is the way that time is viewed. For those in work, culture takes place in "leisure" time but for those not in work, there is no such thing. One is always trying to ameliorate one's situation – looking for work, finding ways to save money, dealing the bureaucracies, being occupied with surviving – leaving no free time or energy to pursue cultural activities.

Sometimes, it's not about time or money or cultural relevance, but rather the accessibility of the form. In the 2000s MTC participated with other performing arts companies in an audience development program to attract more people from a non-English-speaking background. The most successful programs were run by classical music companies where language wasn't an issue. Hayes and Roodhouse (2010, 50) believe that this focus on building relationships with diverse audiences has been about meeting the policy objectives of governments and that there is little evidence to support the impact of such interventions. While this may be true for arts institutions in relation to new migrant communities, if art is successfully introduced and experienced in schools, then the second generation will be the new potential audience.

Kaiser (2013, 79) notes that the commercial world has to spend huge amounts on marketing art because few people either know or care who produces films or musicals or books. Audiences will be loyal to a writer or an actor or a painter or a musician but not to the organisation that publishes or produces or presents or records them. However, in the non-profit world, there are people who know the company and care about its health and its future. This means that every new project we do already has a potential group of supporters.

In my first year at MTC, we did some audience research and one of the topics was postcodes (zipcodes). I'd been in Melbourne for a couple of years and had finally saved up enough money to buy a house in a working-class northern suburb that was starting to be gentrified. I checked our subscriber list and not one of them lived in my new suburb. I found that particularly bizarre given that it was starting to fill with middle-class, educated people like me who were the key demographic for the company. At that time, we couldn't afford to buy suitable lists to mail subscription brochures to but what we could afford was me. So for a couple of weekends, I wandered around the neighbourhood looking for houses that showed signs of gentrification and popping an MTC brochure in their mail box. I don't know whether this technique worked or not but soon we had a couple of new subscribers. I don't necessarily recommend this as a cost-effective use of your time these days but the point is to analyse your data, find out who you're missing and find a way of talking to them.

To the cynical, subscribers are a group of old age, old-style, old-fashioned arts luvvies, taking good seats from the young, forcing conservative programming on companies and creating an audience of white and grey heads. To the theatre or ballet or symphony manager, they are the risk takers, the loyalists, the cash flow guarantors, the people who bring the next generation to us. Survey analysis from Scotland shows that

> those who participate most tend to be least concerned with traditionally conceived notions of art form and genre. Rather than restrict themselves to favourite forms, the most avid consumers of art and culture increasingly tend to engage with as wide a spectrum of experiences as possible,

cutting across old categories such as "high" and popular art.

> (Beech et al. 2015, 5)

They are also the audience members who are the most forgiving. If they see a show they don't like, they'll still come to the next one. In Obaudalahe et al.'s (2017) research on audience loyalty, their results showed that subscriber tolerance was manifested in two ways if they were disappointed with a show:

- Remembering the previous shows that had been good
- Balancing it out if the other aspects of the experience – social interaction, peripheral services – were highly satisfactory.

In the case of MTC, subscribers were (and presumably still are) the people who bought tickets to shows by authors they've never heard of, with actors who hadn't been cast, on subjects that were tough and demanding. Yes, there were 10,000 people in Melbourne willing to buy tickets to see a play about a man in love with a goat[7] long before the reviews came out. Yes, new Australian plays can start with an audience base of 16,000 or 17,000 people because of those subscribers who trust that an MTC production of Joanna Murray Smith's work[8] will be interesting even if they don't know who's going to be in it. Of course, there's risk for single ticket buyers too, but it's considerably reduced because unlike the subscribers who buy on reputation, the single ticket buyer has the advantage of reviews, interviews, social media and work of mouth (Meyrick et al. 2018).

How Should We Treat Them?

Contemporary arts audiences may be very different from those for whom many of our 19th- and 20th-century museums and theatres were built (Baxter 2010, 124). However, regardless of the proliferation of cultural choice and distribution, the new audience share something with the old audience: artistic appreciation of the cultural arts seems to increase with consumption. Therefore, one of our goals should be to get more people coming more often. As Boorsma and Chiaravalloti (2010, 305) note "[a]n established reputation with the audience and durable relations with customers form important intangible assets that can be created by a strategy focused on overall customer satisfaction". Those intangible assets can help an organisation survive a certain amount of breakdown in the artistic exchange: an exhibition that doesn't deliver, a play that doesn't appeal, a soloist who has a bad night. Obviously if this pattern continues for the long term you're in trouble, but having a good reputation does buy you time to take another risk. But while getting the art wrong sometimes is forgivable, getting the relationship wrong isn't. "I know of no arts organization that prides itself on rudeness, being closed to new ticket buyers, or an unwillingness to embrace new donors. And yet many are not successful in avoiding these disastrous traits," said Kaiser (2013, 84). We simply don't have the purchasing power of Hollywood or Sony to buy loyalty. In our world, we have to earn every ticket sale and every donation.

When I joined MTC in 1994, ticketing was in the form of hard tickets. At the launch of each subscription season, people would camp outside of the venue, just as they do for rock and roll concerts, to get the best tickets. I remember thinking as I wandered along the line of people in sleeping bags and on deck chairs, handing out coffees and an early edition of the local paper at 3am, "this is undignified" for the mainly middle-aged people who were there. The next year, we created a different model to enable the dedicated to get their tickets. We invited them to our workshops, gave them a presentation about the season, a glass of champagne and a seat to sit on while they filled in their booking form. By the time I left the company we'd moved from servicing a couple of hundred people this way to a launch in a venue seating 2,500 people. And we still had to give them that free champagne.

The point is, you need to look after your audiences. Whether it's the glass of champagne or driving the elderly ladies home who came with cash tucked into the top of their stockings, because in my view they were too tiddly to catch the tram, you need to ensure a real connection with the people who support you by buying tickets.

In an interesting examination of service elements in the performing arts, Hume et al. (2006, 311) claim that performing arts CEOs "appeared one-dimensional and focused on the show performance" and that "the service process commenced at the entrance into the venue and finished at the venue exit with little discussion of any factors that occurred before or after these activities". Issues included: seating, ushering, refreshment, comfort, ticketing, cloaking – and staff interaction at all these points. There is a growing body of literature on the role of the venue in enhancing the audience's experiences (Walmsley 2011, 6) and so it's hard to imagine why these managers weren't concerned about these issues. Hume et al. (2006, 311) go on to say that there was limited discussion on pre-arrival factors such as parking, accessibility, cafés, restaurants and "peripheral delivery factors" such as amenities, signposting, crowd traffic flow and venue accessibility, but these managers believed that consumers had a high zone of tolerance for service failures related to their factors.

They are wrong. Audiences are impacted not by just the show, but also by all those peripheral services as well as the social interaction not just between audience members but also with theatre personnel. Interestingly, there's evidence that men are more impacted by the services and women by the social interaction (Obaidalahe Sarlerno & Colbert 2017). Obviously, I wasn't part of Hume et al.'s research because I don't share the opinion of the managers they interviewed. In the first public document that I wrote to argue the case for a new MTC theatre in 1994, I talked about the ability to control factors such as service, ticketing and pre- and post-activities as well as the capacity to make money from parking, bars and cafés. I didn't win on all fronts because although the original plan for what became the

Southbank Theatre included parking, it didn't come to fruition. But we did win on the bar and café fronts.

A major reason for MTC to have its own theatre was the need to deliver the total service experience. No matter how good individual ticketing or front-of-house or even back of house staff were at the Arts Centre Melbourne (and there were some great people), they weren't our staff. We couldn't control the rosters for the lighting technicians. We couldn't ask for particular front-of-house staff to be on the doors for our shows. We couldn't get any action on undertrained bar staff because for most of the time I was at MTC they were the staff of a subcontractor. And we couldn't control the cost of the parking or the drinks or the food. But all these service experiences are important to the total experience of going to the theatre. As Hume et al. (2006) found, some of these elements may be less important to the dedicated theatre goer whose priority is the cultural experience, but for those more casual theatre goers, if you surround the risk of going to the theatre with poor service, the odds aren't good that you'll get them back.

As for the notion of having a "high zone of tolerance for service failures", I've always described audience responses to service needs in the same language as Herzberg's motivation factors. He divides these factors into two groups – Hygiene factors and Motivators. His theory is that hygiene factors don't provide positive motivation; they don't make people happy; they just stop people from being unhappy. In the case of the performing arts, no-one is going to be positively excited that they found a parking spot easily, that the interval drinks were reasonably priced, that the queue for the ladies' toilets didn't go on forever, whereas they will be positively excited if the show was amazing. But if they walk into the theatre grumpy to start with because they couldn't find a carpark, because the toilets didn't have paper and that they had to wait for 10 minutes to pick up their ticket, it's going to take them longer to relax into the world of the show and that might just be enough to stop them

have a great night out. Interestingly, Hume et al. (2006, 317) use very similar language in their research but with a slight twist: highly involved customers focused primarily on satisfiers while general entertainment consumers emphasised avoiding dissatisfiers such as queuing, the price of parking, venue signposting, the quality of refreshments, position and comfort of seats.

Theatre seating is always a trade-off. You can make it easy for people to get past other audience members but that adds metres onto the distance between the last row and the stage. You can have truly glamorous seats but they aren't always comfortable. Some will say that the trade-off we did in the Southbank Theatre isn't perfect – it's a tight squeeze to get past someone to your seat but the theatre is very intimate and the seats are comfortable. But I'd rather be comfortable for three hours with great sight lines and be slightly awkward for a minute or two getting to my seat. There are some very stylish foyer seats in the theatre – like black thrones. But as soon as I sat in one, I knew that I'd been wrong to let Simon Phillips choose them by himself. They were perfect for slender-hipped people like him but not for plumped-bottom people like me. That's how I chose the seats for the Fairfax Theatre when it was refurbished in the 1990s. My logic was that I was the perfect subscriber profile on a socio-demographic basis but probably fatter than most, so if the seat was a comfortable fit for me then odds were it was going to be comfortable for an ever-increasingly sized future audience member as well. Twenty years on, they are still great seats.

Hume et al.'s (2006) satisfiers for the highly involved audience members were (in order):

1. Complimentary extras, e.g. refreshments/ programs
2. Show experience
3. Preferential or upgraded seating and ticketing
4. Exceptional personal treatment (317).

The critical factors that, positive or negative, have to be part of the service offering were (in order):

1. Value-for-money
2. Timeliness: long queue times, parking accessibility
3. Responsiveness: courteous, friendly staff behaviour
4. Accessibility: venue mapping and signposting
5. Empathy: service recovering and attention by staff in service failure situation
6. Assurance and reliability: show publicity and critic reflect the production
7. Safety: overcrowding and crowd behaviour
8. Emotional exhilaration/show quality.

Although all of those factors have been on my service list, I confess to being completely surprised that the show quality is last on the list. The only reason I can think of for such a result is that because every show is unique, there can be no guarantee that the show quality of one production will have any impact on the show quality of the next. And I'm not entirely convinced that a survey of MTC subscribers would result in a list in the same order.

Hume et al. (2006) also claimed that there were neutral factors which have little influence on consumer judgement and they were the physical surrounding and venue décor (excluding accessibility and amenities) and programme and promotional collateral (excluding critic reviews and show description and schedules). The first point will of course shatter every theatre architect, but all my years of theatre-going would probably lead me to agree because I've had wonderful experiences in dingy, grimy, cold, uncomfortable spaces. But on the other hand, the décor does sometimes have an impact on whether people feel comfortable and welcomed into a space. The luscious over-decorative Melbourne theatres of the early 20th century do provide a wonderful atmosphere of specialness for those expensive musical nights out. But a venue with red velvet and gold sends a very different message to a venue that's white and wood.

So for me, every aspect of the experience from the first contact with the website or the ticketing service through to the chance for a post-show debrief is important. It's one of the reasons why I became completely obsessed about getting the toilets right in the Southbank Theatre. Of course, one can never have enough women's toilets to avoid a queue. You'd end up with no foyer space at all. But you can make sure that you have more than the standard building requirements and that they provide a number of extra services such as extra rolls for loo paper, having somewhere to put your programme or your clutch, making sure that each cubicle is wide enough that you don't have to half sit on the disposal bin – and most importantly, that there's a reason to smile when you go in. I spent a couple of years with a disposable camera and a tape measure in my handbag measuring toilet dimensions in venues all over the world trying to get those features right. I still experience moments of pride when I'm in the first-floor women's toilets in the Southbank Theatre and I hear women say "look at the walls, aren't they great" or when I'm in the ground-floor ones and someone says "thank god for soft light" as they repair their makeup. Ashton Raggatt McDougall came up with some brilliant shiny colours for the ground-floor toilets but Simon Phillips came up with the idea to create an amazing theatrical effect upstairs. Small sepia photos of old set backdrops were given to a group of talented scenic artists. They imagined the colours their historic peers would have used, painted them in watercolours or acrylics, and then we turned their original artwork into wallpaper.

The point of this story is that if you care about the art, you want to make sure every aspect of the audience's experience will deliver them to the door in the mood to engage emotionally. And that when they leave, the stories they tell their friends will be about the magnificence of the performance or the set or the direction and not the endless loo queues or the grumpy usher or the overpriced stale sandwich.

Another battle I had with the Arts Centre Melbourne was queueing for tickets. It was completely illogical to me why I should wait in a queue to simply pick up a ticket because someone in front of me was buying one. It took me months before I finally convinced them to try using two lines in the period before a show. The result was there was very little waiting time for the people who'd already bought their tickets and with little waiting time, little time to get irritated.

Ultimately, it's all about the relationship you have with your audience. Avery, Fournier and Wittenbrake (2014, 79) give an example of Siminn, an Icelandic telecommunications company that implemented an 18-month training program "to help every employee, from receptionist to ditch digger to software engineer, become immersed in the company's relationship-oriented strategy and learn how to translate it to their jobs". And this of course comes back to staff. MTC is lucky that most of its staff have enthusiastically joined the company because they love theatre. But what you need is for that "love" to be translated into service. One of the best ushers at the Arts Centre Melbourne had been an usher for MTC. When the company closed Russell St Theatre in 1994, we helped all who were interested to make the transition to the Arts Centre where we were going to be presenting our plays in the future. He was a great ambassador for MTC because he loved his job – he loved the theatre and the audience. Every time I watched him at work he was open, smiling, welcoming and in some circumstances, even knew the old subscribers by name. What I didn't discover until his funeral was that he mentored all the young ushers and helped them learn his qualities. He was a casual staff member, not paid particularly well, with very little status, but he has fabulously good at his job and proud to do it well.

On the other side of the fence was a young usher who generated a number of complaints about his attitude and rudeness to customers. After the first complaint, he received feedback and extra training but then came the second and third complaint. At each feedback session he denied the problem, and found a way to blame the audience member (too old, too slow, too rude). My response to such people is simple: "you're in the wrong job". Being nice to old, slow, rude strangers isn't everyone's cup of tea, but sometimes it's what you have to do.

What Is Happening to Our Audience?

Whether it's because we've become "hypermodern" individuals "detached from the past and future, no longer able to distinguish what's essential to build meaning" due to the impact of technology (Fortier & Castenllanos Juarez 2017, 209) or because we don't have time or money for more pragmatic reasons such as our hours of work and the economic climate, there's a sense that our audience numbers are decreasing. Webb (2017) proposes a variety of reasons for this including:

- Demand for more stimulation: we're increasingly used to multisensory engagement – watching, hearing, reading simultaneously – so we have higher satisfaction expectations than participation in one art form might allow
- Demand for convenience: we don't have much tolerance for bad sightlines or lack of pre- or post-show facilities
- Risk versus reward: "because of the cost (time and money) of participating, audiences are generally less willing to take risks and more willing to pay large sums for a guaranteed 'home run' experience" but less often – the blockbuster effect
- Decline of traditional media and the challenge of cut through in a busy media world.

To this list, I'd also add issues such as decreasing arts education, increasing ticket prices because of the decrease in government funding, shrinking of the middle class, lack of appeal of traditional art forms to members of increasingly multicultural societies, and because we can access so much more via digital means rather than having to go to the theatre or the gallery.

Each country will be going through a different set of experiences as audience taste changes. The performing arts audience patterns in the USA, for example, is a flat participation rate with declining adult attendance for traditional forms such as jazz, classical music, opera, musicals, plays and ballet, with increased consumption through electronic media (Webb 2017, 46). In Australia, the attendance pattern is much more mixed with opera down but theatre up; children's and family performances down but circus and physical theatre up; classical music and ballet steady but contemporary music increasing (Live Performance Australia 2017). In developing countries such as China there may be increases in audiences for traditional and contemporary Western art forms and decreases in audiences for their own traditional forms.

Some of these problems we can address through audience development and marketing strategies; some of these problems we can only address collectively through changes to government policy. And then there's the role of the individual consumer. A manifesto on cultural rights from Taiwan proposed an idea that I hadn't considered before. As well as acknowledging that cultural rights were as important as human, political and economic rights and that governments have a "responsibility to provide enough cultural resources to satisfy their citizen's needs" (Hsin-tien 2015, 52), this manifesto also said: "Citizens have the responsibility to undertake, participate, support, maintain, and promote the development of arts resources." In other words, that it's not just up to the artists and government to create a vibrant cultural environment but us, the (potential) audience, too.

Conclusion

We need to provide our artistic and creative staff with audience members ready and open to a new emotional experience, be it at a commercial musical or an exhibition of cutting-edge art. To do this we need to understand our audience and communicate effectively with them. Of course, if the art doesn't work, it doesn't work, but if we've made the audience feel valued they may take a risk and visit us again.

See also: Buildings, Communication, Marketing, Media, Money, People

References

Australia Council 2015 *Arts Nation: An Overview of Australian Arts*, Sydney: Australia Council.

Avery, J., Fournier, S. & Wittenbrake, J. 2014 "Unlock the Mysteries of Your Customer Relationships", *Harvard Business Review*, 92(7/8), 72–81.

Baxter, L. 2010 "From Luxury to Necessity: The Changing Role of Qualitative Research in the Arts", in O'Reilly, D. & Kerrigan, F. (eds) *Marketing the Arts: A Fresh Approach*, London: Routledge, 121–140.

Beech, N., Broad, S., Cunliffe, A., Duffy, C. & Gilmore, C. 2015 "Developments in Organisation Theory and Organising Music", in Beech, N. & Gilmore, C. (eds) *Organising Music: Theory, Practice, Performance*, Cambridge: Cambridge University Press, 1–24.

Bianchi, M. 2008 "Time and Preferences in Cultural Consumption", in Hutter, M. & Throsby, D. (eds) *Beyond Price*, Cambridge: Cambridge University Press, 236–257.

Boorsma, M. & Chiaravalloti, F. 2010 "Arts Marketing Performance: An Artistic-Mission-Led Approach to Evaluation", *The Journal of Arts Management, Law, and Society*, 40(4), 297–317.

Boudier-Pailler, D. & Urbain, C. 2015 "How Do the Underprivileged Access Culture?", *International Journal of Arts Manager*, 18(1), 65–77.

Colbert, F. 2009 *Beyond Branding: Contemporary Marketing Challenges for Arts Organizations*, Geelong: Kenneth Myer Lecture, Deakin University.

Cuadrado-García, M. 2017 "Teatro Olympia: A Family-Run Venue Entering a New Century", *International Journal of Arts Management*, 19(3), 71–78.

De Rooij, P. & Bastiaansen, M. 2017 "Understanding and Measuring Consumption Motives in the Performing Arts", *Journal of Arts Management, Law and Society*, 47(2), 118–135.

Fortier, I. & Castellanos Juarez, M. 2017 "How Hypermodern and Accelerated Society is Challenging the Cultural Sector", *The Journal of Arts Management, Law, and Society*, 47(4), 209–217.

Hackley, C. 2015 "Branding and the Music Market", in Beech, N. & Gilmore, C. (eds) *Organising Music: Theory, Practice, Performance*, Cambridge: Cambridge University Press, 127–134.

Hayes, D. & Roodhouse, S. 2010 "From Missionary to Market Maker", in O'Reilly, D. & Kerrigan, F. (eds) *Marketing the Arts: A Fresh Approach*, London: Routledge, 40–53.

Henley, J. 2018 "French Teenagers Swipe Up for Arts on Macron's App", *The Guardian*, 18 August, www.theguardian.com/world/2018/aug/18/french-teenagers-swipe-up-for-arts-electronic-culture-pass-emmanuel-macron [accessed 20 February 2019].

Holden, J. 2008. *Democratic Culture: Opening up the Arts to Everyone*, London: Demos.

Hsin-tien, L. 2015 "Interlocution and engagement", in Caust, J. (ed.) *Arts and Cultural Leadership in Asia*, London: Routledge, 48–58.

Hume, M., Mort, G. S., Liesch, P. W. & Winzar, H. 2006 "Understanding Service Experience in Non-profit Performing Arts: Implications for Operations and Service Management", *Journal of Operations Management*, 24, 304–324.

Kaiser, M. M. 2013 *The Circle*, Waltham, MA: Brandeis University Press.

Kempa, E. & Pooleb, S. M. 2016 "Arts Audiences: Establishing a Gateway to Audience Development and Engagement", *Journal of Arts Management, Law and Society*, 64(2), 53–62.

Live Performance Australia 2017 *LPA Ticket Attendance and Revenue Report 2017*, Melbourne: LPA.

Meyrick, J., Phiddian, R. & Barnett, J. 2018 *What Matters? Talking Value in Australian Culture*, Melbourne: Monash University Publishing.

Norbury, C. 2010 "Relationships Are at the Heart of Good Cultural Leadership", in Kay. S. & Venner, K. (eds) *A Cultural Leaders' Handbook*, London: Creative Choices, 50–57.

Obaidalahe, Z., Sarlerno, F. & Colbert, F. 2017 "Subscribers' Overall Evaluation of a Multi-experience Cultural Service, Tolerance for Disappointment, and Sustainable Loyalty", *International Journal of Arts Management*, 20(1), 21–30.

Osborne, A. & Rentschler, R. "Conversation, Collaboration and Cooperation", in O'Reilly, D. & Kerrigan, F. (eds) *Marketing the Arts: A Fresh Approach*, London: Routledge, 54–71.

O'Toole, J., Anderson, M., Adam, R., Burton, B. & Ewing, R. (eds) 2014 *Young Audiences, Theatre and the Cultural Conversation*, Netherlands: Springer, Netherlands.

Radbourne, J. & Fraser, M. 1996 *Arts Management*, Sydney: Allen and Unwin.

Ryan, A., Fenton, M. & Sangiori, D. 2010 "A Night at the Theatre", in O'Reilly, D. & Kerrigan, F. (eds) *Marketing the Arts: A Fresh Approach*, London: Routledge, 214–230.

Tusa, J. 2007 *Engaged with the Arts*, London: I.B. Tauris & Co.

Van Den Broek, A. 2013 "Arts Participation and the Three Faces of Time: A Reflection on Disentangling the Impact of Life Stage, Period and Socialization on Arts Participation, Exemplified by an Analysis of the US Arts Audience", *Cultural Trends*, 22(1), 46–53.

Walmsley, B. 2011 "'A Big Part of My Life': A Qualitative Study of the Impact of Theatre", Antwerp: AIMAC 11th International Conference.

Walmsley, B. 2012 "Whose Value Is It Anyway? A Neo-institutionalist Approach to Articulating and Evaluating Artistic Value", *Journal of Arts and Communities*, 4(3), 199–215.

Webb, D. 2017 "Trends in the Development and Operation of Performing Arts Centers", in Lambert, P. D. & Williams, R. (eds) *Performing Arts Center Management*, New York: Routledge, 45–62.

Webb, S. & Dowling, M. 2015 "The Organising and Artistic Demands of Orchestral Performances", in Beech, N. and Gilmore. (eds) *Organising Music: Theory, Practice, Performance*, Cambridge: Cambridge University Press, 251–257.

Authenticity

One of the most popular topics in leadership research in recent times has been "authenticity". Being authentic is seen to be an important attribute of a good leader. For example, a high-profile bank executive said:

> I am a big believer in being authentic and sharing my vulnerabilities with my team. It empowers them to do the same and also step up and into issues that I require their support to move forward.
>
> (Louise Bourguignon, quoted in Swanson 2014, 40)

Academics have taken the notion of authenticity in leadership further than the standard dictionary definition of being reliable, trustworthy and genuine. An authentic leader is defined as someone who has four qualities: self-awareness, balanced processing of information, relational transparency and internalised moral perspective (Walumbwa et al. 2008). Kate MacNeill, Sarah Reynolds and I (2012[9]) decided to test whether "authenticity" was a quality to be found amongst arts leaders who operated in a co-leadership model in Australian performing arts companies. We took the position that leadership in the performing arts has likely to be more authentic than in many other organisations/industries because of:

1. The value centred nature of the arts
2. The cooperative nature of the performing arts
3. The requirements of effective co-leadership which include shared vision, trust and effective communication.

Our hypothesis was that individuals in co-leadership arrangements would display the characteristics of authentic leadership. This doesn't mean that we expected all such arts leaders to be authentic but that the better ones would be. And we did find evidence of authentic qualities in the teams of co-leaders that we interviewed.

Goldman and Kernis (2002, 18) have described self-awareness as having an "awareness of, and trust in, one's motives, feelings, desires and self-relevant cognitions". They go on to describe being able to identify one's strengths and weaknesses, being aware of one's emotions and trait characteristics and having knowledge about one's behaviour in particular circumstances, as being indicative of self-awareness. From an examination of the interviews we did, evidence of self-awareness was found in the way in which interviewees were clear about their own strengths and/or weaknesses.

> I manage like an artist, not like a manager. And sometimes that can be less effective ... I try not to be but I think some decision-making can be very emotional. And I think that's something that I've really tried to change in myself because the organization is like a big family and I think sometimes that can be dysfunctional. [AD5][10]

> I guess I'm reasonably intuitive and reasonably quick. ... I am able to juggle; I'm a good juggler I think as most general managers are, can keep multiple balls going at once and prioritize instinctively to keep them going. [GM4]

Self-awareness was also evident in the way some interviewees spoke about their own personality type – often in relation to the other:

> On the whole I think personality wise on many levels we're actually quite similar, we're quite pushy. It's funny that whole nurturing mum, dad notion of relationship or whatever doesn't really – it doesn't feel like that particularly, I don't think one or the other nurtures more than the other. We will take turns in it, we'll sometimes do a little bit of good cop, bad cop thing with staff sometimes, or with management issues. On the whole I would say actually we've reasonably similar style of management with slightly different focuses. [GM4]

While indicating self-awareness, this quote also notes the similarities between the two leaders in their personality type. More often the interviewees highlighted the skill set of their co-leader and noted differing strengths. A recurrent theme in these interviews was an awareness of the complementary nature of their respective skills. The self-awareness observed in the interviewees' statements may have arisen, or been developed, as a result of being in a co-leadership arrangement where each must be aware of the complementary roles that they play and the skills that they bring to the partnership.

Balanced processing consists of listening, consulting and understanding beyond oneself. According to Kernis (2003), balanced processing relates to "not denying, distorting, exaggerating or ignoring private knowledge, internal experiences, and externally based evaluative information" (2003, 14). Self-awareness must contribute substantially to one's capacity to practice balanced processing in that knowledge of oneself would enhance a reflective approach to decision-making. However, as Kernis's definition suggests, balanced processing also requires taking into account knowledge obtained from a variety of sources. Within a co-leadership arrangement these sources are structurally augmented by the presence of a colleague with whom many major decisions must be made and consultative decision-making is evident in the accounts provided by the interviewees. Nonetheless, the degree to which consultative decision-making is utilised as a formal mechanism varies.

> We do discuss everything. [GM2]

> When you say shared decision-making, not all decisions are made jointly and so there's almost a kind of scale. [GM4]

> [The General Manager] is as much an integral part of the artistic decision-making process of this company as anybody else in it, including artistic associates and resident director and so on. [AD3]

Despite this range, what was clearly outlined by the majority of interviewees is that consultation and discussion is necessary in relation to large decisions.

> We catch up a lot and most of the big decisions we do together. [AD6]

More than merely discussing key decisions with their co-leader, many interviewees acknowledged the positive impact that such discussions have on the decision-making process. This suggests an awareness of the importance of balanced decision-making and being receptive to the views of their co-leader. In a number of cases, interviewees noted that consultation and listening to other people's views is not limited to the co-leader but extends to the wider organisation. Consultation and inclusion can indeed be a characteristic of the creative process in the performing arts and hence is intrinsic to the work practices of some Artistic Directors:

> I like to be collaborative. I like to work as a team. I like working with the executive. I like picking everyone's brains and their specific expertise to come up with a decision … And also I like people to challenge me. [AD5]

In our study it was often the case that the manager director had a developed understanding of the art form. They consistently stated that their role was to facilitate the Artistic Director's vision for the company, yet to so do within very clear constraints. This would encourage balanced processing as the Managing Director must explain why something is not possible and the Artistic Director must make decisions in the knowledge that there are implicit limits.

A key component of relational transparency has been described as striving for "open and truthful relationships" (Spitzmuller & Ilies 2010, 311). In order to have open and truthful relationships, communication is paramount. The majority of interviewees commented not only on the importance of communication with their co-leader, but also on its frequency and the manner in which it occurred. The communication that took place in the majority of these relationships was intense, frequent and predominantly informal. This pattern of communication often extended beyond the co-leaders and was part of the organisational culture.

> We spoke every day even if we were out of town. [AD5]

> In terms of communication we talk daily: by text message, telephone, e-mail, coffee – just to keep in touch. [GM6]

Ilies, Morgeson and Nahrgang (2005) argue that open and truthful relationships result in a high degree of trust. According to our interviewees, this appeared to be essential for co-leadership arrangements; indeed, all interviewees emphasise the necessity for mutual trust. For some, this was posed as a necessity of such a relationship; for others it has emerged from the experience of working together; and for others it is a prerequisite to taking on such a role.

> Ultimately it's about trust. I have to trust [the Artistic Director] to make the best art for the company and he has to trust me to do all the other bits and bobs that are needed to ensure that [the Artistic Director] has got the space to make the best art. So, trust in a way … it's almost unspoken and with that trust comes respect because you can't trust

... in someone you don't respect and vice versa. [GM1]

It may be that to be effective the co-leadership structure requires a focus on communication, particularly with your co-leader, otherwise the relationship will deteriorate. The trust between the co-leaders appeared to develop out of the iterative nature of the decision-making, a process that gave rise to a confidence on the part of each party that each would speak the truth.

A key component of internalised moral perspective is authentic behaviour, which relates to the tendency "to act based on values, personal preferences, and needs" (Spitzmuller & Ilies 2010, 310). The importance of values, in particular shared values, was most evident in the relationship that the interviewees had to the artistic rationale of the company. A common attitude was that the art itself is central to the company and therefore the role of the manager was to support the Artistic Director in implementing their vision for the company.

> The organization only exists because it's an arts organization; it only exists because of the artistic vision of that leader. [GM1]
>
> I feel like [the General Manager] is totally supporting me in my artistic vision. [AD4]

This focus on the primacy of the art and a belief that the art form is central to the identity of the company means that both the managing and Artistic Directors are not only acting with a strong value base, but that it is a shared value base.

Our research didn't demonstrate that all performing arts co-leaders are "authentic" leaders because we were talking to people who had effective working relationships, often for a long time. But what we did conclude was that successful co-leadership relationships seem to demand and/or build authentic leaders. Ideas such as open and regular communication, shared vision and values and self-knowledge seem to contribute to effective leadership. When talking

about how he'd kept a team of talented people around him, choreographer Bill T. Jones said "showing vulnerability. You've got to know how to say 'I made a mistake'. People also forgive a lot when they know what you love. They might say, 'this guy I work with is crazy. But there's something about him. He's so real ....' People recognize there's something authentic here" (Lissing & Beard 2015).

Rosh and Offerman (2013) note that authenticity begins with knowing who you are – your values, emotions and competencies. However, those values may not always be positive ones. Sendjaya et al. (2016) offer some interesting insights into the leader who may have Machiavellian traits. Such a leader might have great self-awareness and a clear, internalised moral perspective, but that perspective may be, for example, that the end justifies the means, resulting in less than positive outcomes for the people they lead.

Equally important to consider is knowing how you are perceived by others. Authentic leadership is not an obsession about the self. Sinclair (2007) provides a series of warnings that are worth noting. For one, "authentic" behaviours are not gender neutral. An assertive female leader will be read differently to an assertive male leader. Nor are the perceptions of leadership behaviours free from the stereotypes and the social and cultural norms that people bring into the workplace. In other words, leadership is two way – you may be being authentic but it may not be read that way by the receiver.

Another warning that she offers is that to be yourself, if "yourself" is different from standard perceptions of leaders, may be risky in the professional context (Sinclair 2007). That difference may be as minor as the clothes you wear or as major as the fact that you're a loud, opinionated female. She recommends selective self-disclosure attuned to cultural and contextual cues. This is not to split the "real you" from the "work you", but simply an acknowledgement that we have multiple selves (Sinclair 2005).

As long as self-awareness includes contextual awareness, that there is consistency and openness in how you behave in the work place, and the moral and ethical aspects of your leadership remain true to self and with a focus on the well-being of others, then authenticity is an important aspect of your role as a leader.

Also see: Co-leadership, Ethics, Gender, Leadership, Trust

References

Goldman, B. M. & Kernis, M. H. 2002 "The Role of Authenticity in Healthy Psychological Functioning and Subjective Well-being", *Annals of the American Psychotherapy Association*, 5(6), 18–20.

Ilies, R., Morgeson, F. P. & Nahrgang, J. D. 2005 "Authentic Leadership and Eudaemonic Well-being: Understanding Leader-follower Outcomes", *The Leadership Quarterly*, 16(3), 373–394.

Kernis, M. H. 2003 "Toward a Conceptualization of Optimal Self-esteem", *Psychological Inquiry*, 14(1), 1–26.

Lissy, D. & Beard, A. 2015 "Life's Work: An Interview with Bill T. Jones", *Harvard Business Review*, November, 156.

MacNeil, K., Tonks, A. & Reynolds, S. 2012 "Authenticity and the Other", *Journal of Leadership Studies*, 6(3), 6–16.

Rosh, L. & Offermann, L. 2013 "Be Yourself, But Carefully", *Harvard Business Review*, 91(10), 135–139.

Sendjaya, S., Pekertie, A., Hartel, C., Hirst, G. & Butarbutar, I. 2016 "Are Authentic Leaders Always Moral? The Role of Machiavellianism in the Relationship Between Authentic Leadership and Morality", *Journal of Business Ethics*, 133(1), 125–139.

Sinclair, A. 2005 *Doing Leadership Differently*, Melbourne: Melbourne University Press.

Sinclair, A. 2007 *Leadership for the Disillusioned*, Sydney: Allen & Unwin.

Spitzmuller, M. & Ilies, R. 2010 "Do They [All] See My True Self? Leader's Relational Authenticity and Followers' Assessment of Transformational Leadership", *European Journal of Work and Organizational Psychology*, 19(3), 304–332.

Swanson, C. 2014 "A Balancing Act", *Superfunds*, October, 39–40.

Walumbwa, F. O., Avolio, B. J., Gardner, W. L., Wernsing, T. S. & Peterson, S. J. 2008 "Authentic Leadership: Development and Validation of a Theory-based Measure", *Journal of Management*, 34(1), 89–126.

Notes

1 A long-running Australian television program for children.
2 Paul Sachs who taught several generations of students at Harvard University after World War 1.
3 See for example John Sumner's autobiography, *Recollections at Play*.
4 Although the number of women studying arts management and entering into the industry is high, there is still a sense that don't always achieve the top jobs – see Gender.
5 The titles of the senior management leader in arts organisations can include General Manager, Managing Director, Executive Producer, Director, so for consistency, I shall use Managing Director for this role.
6 Much as I love classical music, there isn't enough action on stage for me.
7 Edward Albee's *The Goat or Who is Sylvia?*
8 https://australianplays.org/playwright/CP-murfit
9 The following comments are extracts from this paper.
10 Participants were kept anonymous and labelled by role (Artistic Director – AD; General Manager/Executive Director/Managing Director – GM) and a randomly allocated number.

B

Boards

Why Do We Have Boards?

When asked what a Board is, most of my students will say something along the lines of "the group of people that watch over the company". And that in a nutshell is it. But as a huge amount of any CEO's energy goes into managing the Board, it's worth spending time on the key issues of membership, role and relationships.

Most non-profit arts organisations in Commonwealth countries[1] and the USA have a Board, a group of people that are either elected or selected to oversee the organisation. This model is appearing in more European countries as government funding decreases and new structures to enable other fundraising is put into place (e.g. see Dubini & Monti's 2018 article about Italy). They usually have a constitution that is based on some legal format and have become necessary even for small arts organisations because funders, both public and private, believe that they are required for the efficient operation of the company.

In David Fishel's informative book on Boards, the heading of Chapter 2 (2003, 10) is "Why do we have a Board?" And the answer from most arts managers would be "indeed" (with an ironic inflection). Organisations have Boards because governments require them. Whether the organisation is a statutory authority, a for-profit company listed on the stock exchange, a company limited by guarantee, an incorporated association or another form of legal structure, there will be a Board. Even when it isn't technically required there may still be a "Board". For example, MTC is a semi-autonomous department of the University of Melbourne and as such doesn't have to have a Board. But the University Regulations which determine its structure and reporting relations include a Board of management.

Adirondack (2005, 12) also asks the question of why non-profit organisations have Boards and her conclusion is:

- To ensure the organisation meets the needs of its members, its users or clients and/or the community it serves
- To draw on people's experience or expertise in making decisions about the organisation
- To ensure the organisation is accountable to its members, users or clients, the community it services and/or its funders
- Because donors or funders want to know financial and other decisions are being made properly, and not just by one or two people
- Because the structure of the organisation requires it to have a governing body.

Whether the Board format is the best one for an arts organisation hasn't been conclusively determined, but both law and policy require it in many circumstances.

Given a choice, most CEOs would love a good mentor and a donor committee and would quite happily live without a Board. Adirondack (2005, 12) notes: "Managers and staff … sometimes feel a management committee is more trouble that it is worth and say committee members constantly interfere with their work or, at the other extreme, never show any interest in the organisation." In talking to one art CEO, they said that their Board didn't understand the business, didn't know how hard the management team worked, were always trying to show off, were continually telling management what to do and questioning their decisions.

In *Daring to Lead 2006: A National Study of Nonprofit Executive Leadership* (Bell, Moyers & Wolfred 2006) the searchers discovered that only one in three executives agreed strongly that their Boards challenged them in ways that make them more effective and only one in three executives agreed strongly that their staff view the Board as an engaged leadership body.

Some of the quotes from managers include:

I find that boards want to do all the wrong things. I don't want them to set policy; they're business people.

Why is there so much rhetoric that touts the significance and centrality of non-profit boards, but so much empirical and anecdotal evidence that boards of trustees are only marginally relevant or intermittently consequential?

To me the whole role of the Board and the interaction between the ED and Board and the governance structure are what I find the most challenging. I can't say that I hate it, but I honestly think that it's seriously flawed.
(Bell, Moyers & Wolfred 2006, 10)

In a follow-up survey in 2011, nearly a third of non-profit executives reported that they were very unsatisfied or only a little satisfied with their Boards and 48% were only somewhat satisfied (Moyers 2011, 2). Summerton and Hutchins (2005, 52) reflect on the belief that organisational structures such as companies limited by guarantee (a model found in Australia and the UK) "are restrictive and the time and energy absorbed in making them work are not justified". They note the anxiety expressed by arts managers that

these boards, while having the ultimate responsibility for the company, and often the goodwill to act conscientiously, are not best placed for the role. There is the danger that they can do little more than serve a ritualistic function, providing a reason for management teams to produce reports and review their progress.

In a 2015 survey about non-profit US Boards of Directors (Larcker et al.), a surprising number of Directors lacked a deep understanding of their organisation and weren't satisfied with the Board's ability to evaluate its performance. An equally surprising number didn't have audit or finance committees and didn't have performance targets for their CEO. However, almost all of them were satisfied with the performance of their CEO, their Board and their organisation. It's hard to put those two sets of results logically together.

Of course, it's not just arts managers and academics that feel uneasy about Boards. In an article on Boards in the *Harvard Business Review*, Parsons and Feigen (2014, 101) quote a former CEO of a Fortune 50 company: "Directors who don't know my business are often off base. We have to humor them and manage them, but in truth they don't add much."

However, unless you work in organisations directly funded by government, you are probably going to have to work with Boards. "From the point of view of general management … boards of management are perceived a little in the same way as democracy: that is to say, the least bad of all the different forms of government" (Ouellet & Lapierre 1997, 371). Another approach is to take the position that Australian creative producer Scott Rankin did and try to minimise the work you have to do with your Board. Rankin (2014) tells a story of Mr Crips, the elderly semi-retired local lawyer who offered to do pro bono work to set up Big hART,[2] Rankin's company. He offered to do it for Rankin but on three conditions:

1. The Board should be as small as possible
2. It should meet as infrequently as was legal
3. Its constitution was to be minimal "and we had to promise never to read it" (10).

Given that you have to have a Board, the role of management is to work as effectively as possible with the Chair and Board members to ensure that this somewhat unloved form of governance works for the betterment of the company.

Who Are They?

The people on arts Boards are "the men and women who operate in an emotionally laden space, requiring them to raise funds, advocate for the organisation, liaise at the highest levels of government, and remain loyal beyond reason, all predominantly pro bono" (Rentscheler 2015, 9).

While Artistic Director Ralph Myers (2014, 3) believes that theatre Boards in Australia mainly consist of "suits", that is, wealthy white men (and the occasional woman), Rentschler's (2015) research on a broader range of arts organisations in Australia concludes that gender diversity is pushing 50% with ethnic diversity up to 25%. She notes that this is very different from the corporate world where Boards are "often monocultural and monochrome". The irony of this result is that she didn't uncover any hard evidence that "diversity of and by itself leads to better Board performance" (100). Some other qualities which she found presumably do have a more direct linkage to effective performance such as expertise in the areas of law, finance, marketing, management, research and fundraising (101).

Having noted that passion or interest in the arts isn't generally one of the selection criterion for Boards, Rentschler says that "passion is a driving force in people's appointment to an arts boards", noting at the same time that this passion can occasionally be a destructive for arts organisations (Rentschler 2015, 119). "Without passion," she says "there would be little to attract capable people to the hard grind of serving on an arts Board" (120). I don't necessarily agree with this point. I've joined Boards because I was asked to help rather than because I particularly cared or knew much about the art form. I've seen people join arts Boards because of a desire for status and power, a commitment to volunteerism or community, a desire to fill in retirement hours, peer pressure, a call from help from a friend, career development as well as because they care about the art form. A commitment to shared values about the general importance of the arts and to effective governance may be all that's required in addition to pragmatic skills such as those listed above.

The expertise of Board Members is particularly important for small to medium-sized arts organisations that may not have such skill in-house or even be able to afford to buy it, such as legal or financial advice. The challenge in these situations is to get the balance between governance and management right when Board members end up doing what is actually the work of staff. While hands on work by Board members may be necessary in the most under-resourced arts company, it is often a difficulty for Board members with specific expertise when organisations have professional staff. I have seen the frustration of both Board and staff members when the Board person who has been appointed (amongst other things) for their marketing kudos expresses opinions that don't fit within the strategic plan of the marketing director. When the Board member's expertise is a specialisation that the company doesn't have, such as the law, the application of the Board member's skill is much easier.

Fishel (2003, 15) makes a good point when he says:

[t]he paradox is that the Board needs to get a close-up understanding of the operation

in order to be able to stand back and play a productive role at a higher level … But the closer the Board gets to the operations, the more anxious the senior staff become about unwelcome interference.

He describes the process of getting involved in the detail as "seductive". However, I think there is a more prosaic reason behind this problematic outcome. Most arts Board members are managers and professionals in their own right. In fact, funding organisations in Australia, for example, have pushed for this set of skills on Boards. Board members are likely to know more about managing companies than creating art so they fall back on commenting on the things they know best.

Most Boards will do an audit on a regular basis to check that they have the required range of skills and diversity. The skill set usually includes accounting and finance, law, marketing, fundraising and other specialities at particular times. For example, an organisation planning to renovate a building looked for an architect to join their Board. As well as ensuring that you have a range of skills on your Board, Rentschler (2015, 141) suggests that you have a range of strategic types including the mission-driven, the commanding (political and connected), the shape shifting (catalyst for change) and community minded. Other elements in a Board matrix might cover a range of ages, gender and race/ethnicity. While it's easy to do a matrix and get your collection of skills and diversity right, it's not quite so easy to determine what personality types you'll end up with.

Another challenge for Boards is how much arts expertise there needs to be amongst their members. At the beginning of the life of many arts companies, the Board will consist of friends and peers. The pattern usually goes like this: an artist works on a volunteer basis and then receives a modest project grant or donation. This may mean that another organisation has to auspice the grant and if the artist wants more in the future, they need to establish a legal entity of some form which will require a Board. The initial

Board members will often be friends, family or fellow artists who all share a passion for the work. Over time, there will be a need to bring some specialist knowledge to the Board such as finance or marketing or legal skills. The new Board members will have in interest in the art form but not usually the same passion as the original members. Their interest will be more about organisational effectiveness and governance than necessarily the art. The new Board will want more policies and reports than the old Board. And finally, there will be the moment when the Chair challenges the Artistic Director on why a certain project is being undertaken, the Artistic Director looks around and realises that it's turned from a room full of friends to a room full of strangers.

At this point, there are three choices:

1. Bring some artists onto the Board
2. Spend more time educating the Board about the art
3. The Artistic Director and the Chair spend some reflection time together to develop a new relationship.

It might be also be indicative that the founder Artistic Director may need to contemplate their own future and whether they have achieved all they need to with this particular organisation.

There isn't agreement about whether artists should be on Boards of arts organisations. An artist/CEO, Richard Mills (2003, 15) said "artists can be a damn nuisance on boards". MTC didn't have an artist on the Board for years because Artistic Directors have said that they don't want to spend their lives being second-guessed by people who wanted to work for the company. I've heard of examples where this has indeed been the result, with conflict between Artistic Director and artist Board members over the direction of the company and choice of repertoire. My sense is that the Artistic CEO has been appointed to provide the vision for the company and that's the vision that should be heard most clearly.

However, I should also offer a contrary view. Artistic Director Ralph Myers wants more artists, maybe even a majority of artists, on Boards. He's particularly concerned because of the lack of the artists' voice when it comes to choosing the artistic leader (see below for more discussion). Summerton and Hutchins (2005) point out that when the company is artist-led and a vehicle for the artist's talents, a Board without artistic expertise may not feel able to challenge artistic matters. Whether having more artists on Boards would actually change that situation or just make it more complex is moot.

In summary, the qualities that arts organisations look for in Board members include:

- Business experience of some sort e.g. specialisation in marketing or law
- Ability to judge whether the organisation is achieving its mission
- Capacity to read financial statements
- Time to be able to attend not only Board meetings but sub-committees and opening nights and fundraisers
- Money – moving towards an US model where Board members are expected to donate (or open doors).

As an arts manager, what I want from a Board is:

- A Chair who listens, can run a meeting, is available when I need them
- Board members who give of their expertise when asked but don't try to tell my staff how to do their job
- A Board that's prepared to take the hard decision when an Executive has to be fired
- People who will donate when we need it and if they can't afford to, solicit people who can
- People who can, through mentorship and leadership, teach me how to be a better manager
- Being able to have discussions in confidence with the Chair (about future ideas, other management staff, performance of the Board, personal directions)
- Board members who can give time and ideas when needed

- People who will resign when they realise that they can't contribute enough.

What Do Boards Do?

Boards are essential to the way an organisation is governed and "governance" is often used as a synonym for a discussion of Boards. Both Turbide (2011) and Rentschler (2015) offer a definition of non-profit governance based on the work of Renz (2004), with Rentschler adding some extra words in italics:

> Governance is the process of providing strategic leadership to a nonprofit organisation. It entails the functions of setting direction, making policy and strategy decisions, overseeing and monitoring organisational performance, and ensuring overall accountability. Nonprofit governance is a political and organisational process *that mediates between external stakeholders and internal challenges, balancing the aesthetic and business needs of the organisation* (19).

Another way of thinking about governance is that it's the connection point between an organisation's internal rules, the external rules that it's supposed to comply with and the organisation's culture.

There are an endless numbers of theories on Board governance which have the Board playing roles such as managing the conflict between owners and managers (Agency), working with management to improve performance (Stewardship), representing members (Democratic), because they provide resources (Resource Dependency), making strategic decisions (Strategy), providing a mix of skills to help the organisation (Social Capital) and rubber-stamping management's decisions (Managerial Hegemony), amongst others (Turbide 2011; Rentschler 2015). Both Turbide and Rentschler conclude (and I agree) that using a multi-focus approach to governance is the one that provides the most richness in our understanding of Boards.

In other words, whether it's sociology or management theory, economics and law or psychology, a range of theories can help us understand how Boards operate.

Board members need to understand the organisation they are governing and the environment in which it operates. Rentschler (2015) describes this in terms of oversight (taking into account the culture and values of the company), insight (into the company's financial position and their own roles and responsibilities) and foresight (in having effective relations with key internal and external stakeholders).

However, governance is not just about the role of the Board. It is also about the management team. Both have a responsibility to ensure the artistic and financial well-being and future of the company.

So what is the role of a Board? An Australian expert on Boards summarises the role of Board members neatly: support and accountability (Fishel 2003). But while that's neat, it needs to be unpacked to help us see what a Board does. One of the best writers on arts Boards from an US perspective is Michael Kaiser (2013). His list of the roles of a Board is:

1. Developing, approving, and monitoring the implementation of strategic plans
2. Understanding and approving the annual budget
3. Hiring, firing, compensating, and motivating staff members who report directly to the Board
4. Participating in resource generation
5. Serving as ambassadors for the organization (91–92).

To this list one could add providing advice and challenging management, holding management to account and guarding the organisation's assets and its long-term future (Hudson 2009).

The Australia Council (Golding 2011) has produced a useful document on the governance of arts organisations and their advice to Boards is to:

1. Lay solid foundations for management and oversight
2. Structure the Board to add value
3. Promote ethical and responsible decision-making
4. Promote diversity
5. Safeguard integrity in financial reporting
6. Recognise the legitimate interests of stakeholders
7. Recognise and manage risk
8. Remunerate fairly and responsibly.

The two most controversial roles an arts Board plays are around the art itself – the mission of the organisation and the appointment of its artistic leader.

Mission/Strategy

Rentschler (2015, 17) claims that "[a]rts Board members make creative choices, incorporating new ideas on art". I suspect that most arts leaders would be surprised by that claim. If what she means is that Boards are involved in setting the mission and vision of the organisation and oversee the money which has the potential to have a profound impact on the strategic choices about repertoire, art making and staffing, then there probably wouldn't be any disagreement. The tension lies in Rentschler's use of the word "determining" when talking about the creation of the aesthetic mission. In my experience, Boards approve a mission but don't determine it and even the Board Chairs and members interviewed by Rentschler (2015) indicated that it was usually the CEO who initiated discussions on strategy and that there was a range in how much Board members actually engaged with strategy making.

Because most non-profit arts organisations don't have "owners" per se "the moral assumption is that the Board conducts the organization's affairs as a steward of the public interest, in a manner consistent with the wishes and needs of the larger community" (Herman 2010, 159). And so they do have ultimate responsibility for the mission of the organisation, regardless of whether they "determine" it or not.

That sense of ownership is a complex idea to unpack. If you ask a staff member who owns the arts company they work for, they will usually just look puzzled and would rarely say "the Board". The Board is that collection of well-dressed people who come to visit once a month. Their connection with the company is seen to be considerably less than the staff's – and in terms of time, energy and commitment, that's probably true. The Board "own" the company because the law says they do. In reality they have to share that sense of ownership with many other stakeholders including staff, artists, the audience, members, donors and even government when grants are involved.

Hudson (2009) uses the same word as Rentschler, saying that the Board should determine the mission of an organisation, and Kaiser (2103) says that Board members should help create the mission statement, but in my view the balance is more in favour of the artistic leader (and their management partner) when it comes to "determining" and "creating" the mission. While a Board may make the big decisions, these are usually more in the form of approval in response to what the leadership of the organisation wants. For example, a Board will usually choose an Artistic Director or CEO *because* of their vision for the company. While what makes sense in an interview room then has to be given a reality check, the Board will be more likely to stretch and support that new leader rather than provide them with an artistic mission. Where the Board's role comes in is to ensure that mission is effectively reflected in the strategic plan.

Boards will play a variety of roles in contributing to a strategic plan from participating in planning days to simply signing off on the plan. Their main role when it comes to planning should be to review the implementation of the strategic plan and this role is important because the leadership of an organisation can get distracted by the day-to-day or be focused on their favourite task and fail to take a longer, harder look at where the organisation is heading.

Employing the CEO

While the mission should be created by the artistic leader, that person is appointed by the Board in one their most important decisions for the future of the company.

Scene: Chairman (in tuxedo, smoking a cigar) talking to Festival General Manager (drinking a beer)
Chair: Can I say something, personally, off the record?
GM: Sure
Chair: This Festival needs an Artistic Director with a strong business background. More business savvy than theatre savvy.
GM: True
Chair: Why have a crazy artist to hire other crazy fucking artists?
GM: You're right
Chair: I'm right.
GM: Yep
[Pause]
Chair: So how would you like the job?

This extract is from one of my favourite TV series, *Slings and Arrows*. Made in Canada, it's supposedly based on the Stratford Festival, the biggest theatre company in North America. It's both very funny and full of lessons for anyone in a leadership or Board role in an arts company.

I don't know whether Ralph Myers, the Artistic Director of Belvoir Theatre, Sydney, at the time had seen that particular excerpt before he gave his Philip Parsons Memorial Lecture in 2014. He saw a grave threat to the artistic life of Australia through the creeping replacements of artistic leaders who are actually practicing artists with managers and producers. Part of the reason for this shift, he said, was because Boards appoint Artistic Directors and those Boards are overwhelming dominated by business people.

And therefore, because we're comfortable with people similar to ourselves, Boards "are appointing people who they instinctively trust and understand. People like them" (Myer 2014, 3).

I'm not convinced this is the problem. For example, the MTC Board that chose exciting but occasionally profligate theatre director Simon Phillips had the same structure and some of the same people that appointed non-practicing artist Brett Sheehy. The problem is not that they appoint people like themselves, but they don't know how to judge an artistic leader. While they are usually well-positioned to review HR and risk policies, financial accounts and marketing strategies, and appoint Managing Directors, they are usually badly placed to choose Artist Directors and review artistic programs.

Myers' (2014, 5) suggestions to solve the problem are more artists on Boards and an expert panel (not head-hunters) to make the choice who, because they "are actually involved in the process of making or commentating on theatre or dance … [will] have a deep understanding of who will be right for the position". Another way of making better employment decisions is to appoint external artists to the selection panel. However, the community of artists may be so small that the most suitable candidates for the committee will also be the most suitable candidates for the position. An alternative approach is for the Managing Director, regardless of whether they are the CEO, joint CEO or reporting to the Artistic Director, to be an integral part of the process because of their knowledge of the industry, the community of artists and the company.

A classic example of where a Board doesn't know what the organisation needs is in the story of the National Museum of Art, Architecture and Design in Norway. When an international director left after successfully introducing new audiences to new art but failing to bring his curators and the art establishment with him, the Board made an appointment that should have seemed obviously wrong at the time. They appointed another overseas candidate who was described as "a debated and criticized leader" even before she'd started (Di Paoli 2011, 8). From reading the case study it's clear that the organisation needed a local, someone who understood the political and cultural world of Norway, someone capable of

healing and bringing the curators on the forward journey, a relationship-focused leader who could take the new initiatives of the first director, refine them and bed them down. I don't know whether the Board consulted with staff or the museum and arts community but it's hard to image that they would have made the same poor decision if they had.

Money

The day-to-day work (or rather the month-to-month work) of a Board is in the area that Fishel (2003, 12) describes as the "hygiene"[3] or "caretaker" factors: "managed cash-flow, legal compliance, a safe working environment for staff and volunteers. Without these basics, the organisation operates in peril." Given the skill set of contemporary Board members usually with strong business backgrounds, overseeing the financial operations of a company should be the easiest part of their role. However, I'm very conscious that this is not necessarily the case. When I told an arts industry friend that I was applying for the role of General Manager (as it was then called) of MTC, they said "You're mad. They're a million dollars in debt." Always one for a challenge (and not believing for a minute that I'd get the job), I asked the interview panel about the financial situation. "We're about $2 million dollars in the red," they said. When I got into the company and reviewed the situation, the answer was closer to $4 million dollars in debt. It was hard to tell whether the Board's lack of knowledge was caused by their failure to ask hard questions, management that was trying to shield them from the awful truth, a finance system that wasn't capable of generating useful figures or a Finance Director who didn't understand forecasting.

Turbide (2011) tells the story of a number of cases of financial crises in Canadian arts companies. In each of them she describes the CEOs as having the full confidence of their Board members and Chairs; however, in all but two cases, the Board members were passive. In the remaining cases, Board members were a little more active but the situation was still controlled by the CEO, "by means of his expertise and his reputation" (2011, 6).

Boards are often in a situation of approving budgets without understanding the underlying operational assumptions of the company (Kaiser 2010). We shouldn't be surprised that our Boards don't have a clear understanding of what we do. In 2013, only 22% of for-profit Directors surveyed thought their Boards were completely aware of how their firms created value and just 16% claimed their Board had a strong understanding of the dynamics of their firm's industries (Barton & Wiseman 2015). Some organisations will resolve this problem by having a highly skilled Finance Subcommittee to monitor both the creation of the budget and regular forecast updates. However, sometimes this can turn into a Board fetish about money and doing better than budget rather keeping in mind the achievement of the mission. The management team has the responsibility to educate the Board about the financial structure of the company, provide meaningful reports and budgets and put them in a context that enables Boards to make appropriate financial decisions.

For non-profits art organisations, there's always an income gap between what can be earned and what's required to spend to cover operational costs and build reserves. Unlike the system in the USA where Board members are expected to both give and get, this focus on raising money isn't as strong in other countries. In more recent years, with economic crises, governments in Commonwealth countries and even European and Asian countries where state funding has been more generous have been pushing arts organisations to increase their fundraising efforts. One aspect of this is for Board members to set an example by donating to their company. People who are mostly likely to able to give are those in senior management in the public or private sector. Those who are least likely to be able to give are artists and community members in lower paid jobs or students or pensioners. These people may be able to make important but different contributions to a

Board but the financial pressures may be such that they become less likely to be an "attractive" Board member. On the other hand, I have seen people appointed onto the Board, because of their personal wealth, who fail to give generously or because of their wealthy networks who fail to use them. The only way to solve this is for the Board to have a clear policy about what their financial expectations are, both (to use the American terminology) in terms of "giving" and "getting".

On the surface, being a positive and public supporter of the organisation should be one of the least controversial roles of a Board member. After all, they are there to ensure the ongoing welfare of the company and one way of doing that is to talk it up. In order to this effectively, they have to have a good understanding of the range of work the organisation does and feel confident in telling its story. Even though Board members may be passionate about the art form, they may be embarrassed by the organisation, whether because of the financial results, a particular show or even aspects of the company's operations (Kaiser 2010). They also may be uncomfortable about asking for money or help. The role of management is to solve all these problems and provide appropriate support and briefings so that the Board member can feel comfortable and informed when it comes to "selling" the company to potential funders and the broader community.

One of the most powerful lobbying groups in the non-profit arts world in Australia came out of some breakfasts in the MTC café. We invited the Chairs of other performing arts companies in Melbourne to come together to discuss government policy and out of that came the Australian Major Performing Arts Group. It consists of Chairs of these companies and, as experience has shown, any one of those influential people is much more likely to get access to the Prime Minister or the Minister of the Arts than an Artistic Director or a Managing Director, and, through such connections, impact positively on the financial health of the company.

Relationships and Processes

As an arts manager it's going to be up to you ensure that your Board isn't one of those that Kaiser (2013) gives a score of 1 out of 5 to: a Board does not know how to plan, has no budget, has no relationship with the senior staff, gives and gets nothing, and actively bad-mouths the organisation in public. What we're all looking for is a 5 out of 5 Board: the plan is strong and monitored well, the budget is believable, the senior staff well-hired and supported and the Board members are generous, actively participate in the development efforts and are excellent emissaries in the community.

The starting point is to have a Charter which gives Board members as much guidance as possible about their role and that helps to provide a framework for good governance. If your organisation doesn't have a Board Charter then you should work with the Chair to create one containing information such as Board structure (composition and tenure, code of conduct, decision-making requirements, role of the Chair, management delegates, conflict resolution, Board policies and assessment processes). It's a useful document not only for new Board members but a good one to revisit every year to make sure that the Board is on track. You don't have to be a large organisation for this to be a helpful document. One of the most detailed and carefully considered Board Charters I've seen had been created by a medium-sized arts organisation that had a series of effective Chairs and CEOs who were determined to keep both Board and management moving forward together.

Any new Board member should be treated the same as any new staff member: by being given an induction. I have been to my first Board meeting as a new member without any information about the state of the company apart from what I could scrounge from annual reports, gossip and the internet. A Board member needs to feel confident about you and the organisation at the beginning. Fishel (2003, 35) tells the story about a theatre company having a Board retreat, the first one for many years. "On the first evening of the retreat a Board member confided that she had been one the Board for six years but this was the first time she had understood her role, and the first time she felt able to make a practical contribution." I find this a depressing tale about both the organisation and the Board member.

One would think that the Chair would do the induction but don't make that assumption. It may seem slightly odd to the have the CEO induct their "employer" but the Charter can help provide a discussion framework for the responsibilities of a Board member. An important point that you need to get across to new Board members, particularly from the corporate world, is that an understanding of the for-profit world doesn't necessarily translate to the non-profit world. The main concern in the business sector is increasing shareholder value but for a non-profit, financial considerations are only part of the mission (McFarlan 1999). What's required from arts Board members is empathy about the artistic mission and an awareness of a different set of measurements and judgements about whether the organisation is operating effectively.

It's not always new Board members who are unsure about their roles. I've run training sessions with experienced Board members and when asked what they really wanted to know about being a good member, they will offer comments such as "to be aware of when to ask further questions about particular issues" and "what specific role should I play in advocacy". When asked what makes them uncertain about their role on the Board, answers included: "to understand how far the Board should continue to ask questions or when it's a management issue" and "when to receive information, when to question information, when to *do* something and when to shut up because it's none of my business" and "to what extent must I understand topics outside my areas of knowledge" Your role is help them overcome such uncertainties in order to contribute effectively to the company.

While good governance practice these days includes the use of Board orientation, strategic planning sessions and Board appraisals, according to Tshirhart's (1996) research, this made no significant difference to whether CEOs reported problems with their Board members. This is a depressing outcome which hopefully may have changed over the last 20 years with more emphases on Board training and effectiveness. But it's not a result which would stop me as a manager having meetings with potential Board members, providing a proper induction process and encouraging my Chair to have an appraisal process to enable a private conversation with ineffective Board members.

The main format in which Boards do their work is a meeting. Although ultimately how such meetings are run is in the hands of the Chair, there are some principles which you may be able to put in place to help them work. As Kaiser (2013, 96) says, an important element in engaging a Board "is to ensure that Board meetings and committee meetings are interesting, enjoyable, productive … and short".

When I started at MTC, Board meetings were held at lunchtime in a wood-panelled room with walls covered by paintings of serious, middle-aged men.[4] The communication process was very formal with every question being directed through the Chairman. Sandwiches were served but rarely eaten as everyone was determined to be formal and dignified. With a change of Chair, the dynamic – and in my view, the effectiveness – of the meetings changed dramatically. One of the changes wasn't originally to my taste. 8am starts. For a theatre company, that's a shocking idea particularly if there's been an opening night finishing up just hours beforehand. But I learned to love that start time. Board members were fresh at the beginning of the day. They had a desire to work quickly in order to get to their offices at a reasonable hour. And I found a way to help ensure the brevity of the meeting. Unlike night-time meetings where substantial food (and occasionally wine) is required, I simply served water and bad coffee. The latter was a deliberate strategy. MTC had its own café at which you could get not only good espresso but also a great chocolate muffin. Knowing that this was waiting for them, Board meetings were usually over in an hour and a half. This also meant that they were inclined to give whole days when we needed them for strategy and planning sessions.

There's an interesting new practice taken by corporate Boards partly as a result of a fallout of the Global Financial Crisis. Boards are regularly meeting without the CEO in the room for at least part of the meeting (Parsons 2014, 99). Some arts Boards rarely have sessions without the CEO and/or senior staff and some arts Boards always have sessions without them. My initial reaction to the latter was that it leads to paranoia and lack of trust on the part of both parties except for obvious and agreed topics of conversation such as CEO pay and performance. If the conversation is on other topics, the Board members never learn to clearly express their concerns to the CEO and the CEO assumes that the Board members are having ill-informed conversations usually about management issues rather than strategic issues. However, I am now on a Board when there is a programmed session without the CEO and staff. To date, little is discussed but by making it a regular part of the Board meeting, the paranoia can be reduced.

And perhaps a little paranoia is a good thing. Turbide (2011, 13) reached an interesting conclusion after her stories of company failures:

> To improve governance, we believe that a combination of trust and *distrust* [my emphasis] might be key to balancing relations between Board and staff. It seems that the Executive Director will always be the person (along with his (sic) team) with the knowledge and the expertise to inform Board members about activities, risks and possible consequences. However, boards need to be able to challenge the artistic vision and to ask "why" the decision should be taken instead of just asking "how" it will be done.

Where you can have a direct effect on the function of the Board is how and when you give them the information they need to make the right decision. I heard a recent conversation between two people about the CEO and the Board of an Arts organisation. The organisation needs to move. The CEO had found a great new location and was going to inform the Board of his decision. The response of the two people I was overhearing was that this demonstrated the naivety of the CEO in failing to realise that, at the very least, they had to present a business case to the Board and let the Board make the final decision. It's another one of the stories about the subtlety of governance and the interlinked roles of the Board and the CEO. On the one hand the Board is not in a position to research all the relocation options but because it's a major decision, they do want to have the final say. The CEO is best placed to make the most meaningful choice for the organisation but they do need to let that choice be examined and challenged by the Board. Technically the Board is responsible for long-term strategy and policy, but usually is in no position due to lack of expertise and time to develop it. The best approach for a CEO is to ensure that the Board is as well informed as it can be about the state and the future of the company so that when it comes to crucial decisions, they can bring that "informedness" as well as a trust in the CEO to play when making the final call.

A neat way of describing this role is what David Herman (2010, 166) describes as "laying a bread crumb trail". In offering advice on dealing with Boards, he suggests providing them with information formally and informally about possible issues and changes so that when a decision is finally required it is (in his words) a foregone conclusion – or perhaps more accurately, not as fraught or drawn-out a decision-making process as it might have been. And that last point captures what many CEOs believe about Boards: that it's management that is mainly responsible for ensuring that Board members can effectively undertake their roles. Without the detailed work and support of the management team, it's rare that a Board can notice anything but major problems. The most important document that helps the Board in fulfilling their role is your report. Fishel (2003, 12–13) suggests that

factors such as finance reports and legal compliance (his "hygiene" factors) should be

> "dealt with speedily through clear, reliable reports which have been circulated and read in advance of Board meetings. This leaves the Board free to devote the majority of their time to higher level issues which make a real difference to the organisation's work.

Getting the Board reporting balance right is often a challenge. Morgan and Rentscheler (2011) quote the work of Harris (1989) who says that executives may not always share information and problems with their Board for a variety of reasons, such as to retain power by limiting access by the Board to information; to save Board members time; assuming that the Board may not be interested; or having a perception that these things are not relevant to the work of a Board. The result is that Boards will lose trust, not understand what is actually happening in the company nor have enough information to make good decisions. Some arts managers prefer giving verbal reports rather than lengthy written reports to both save the manager's time and to keep the Board focused on the issues that the manager thinks are important. Other arts managers spend days writing extraordinarily detailed reports and then insist on talking through the detail at the Board meeting. Needless to say, I sit somewhere in-between based on what I want when I'm a Board member:

- I want to know what's going on but I don't want to spend my life second guessing the manager
- I can read and if I have read the report then I don't need it explained to me; if I have questions, I'll ask them
- I want to feel confident that the company is in a good state, both financially and legally, and that the management team is working well together
- I don't want any surprises such as the "you're on notice" letter from the funding body

- Like every Board member I've ever known, I don't remember what we decided on that particular issue or policy three or six or 12 months ago so don't wait for me to ask for an update.

Parsons and Feigen (2014, 102) say that when meeting with the Board, "even well-intentioned managers may succumb to a normal human tendency to overstate opportunity, understate risk, or sugar-coat problems". I tended to do the opposite. The best that can be done for Board members is to give them relevant written information in a timely manner, assume that they have done their homework but may have operational questions, focus their attention on the most important issues to hand for the organisation and capture the actions required in the minutes, not the conversation around decisions.

Hudson (2009, 89) provides the following guide lines for effective Board communication:

- Minutes are succinct high-level summary of decisions and actions – circulated within a week of the meeting
- Make agendas, minutes, non-confidential papers available to staff [he doesn't exactly say that but I think that's what he means]
- Circulate a summary of Board decisions
- Have a regular item about Board matters in internal newsletters
- Invite managers or staff to attend parts of meetings
- Invite staff and managers to meet informally with the Board
- Invite the Board to social gatherings of staff.

Of Hudson's list, I was much bolder with some aspects and less so with others. For example, I resisted letting Board members come to the staff Christmas party until the year I left. The vision of men and women in suits just didn't fit the atmosphere of carefree fun that people wanted to have and I didn't want to put any potential dampener on the festivities. Having said that,

for that last party, the Board members who were more comfortable with fun came but had enough sense to leave early so that people could really relax. It was a very amusing Board meeting on the morning of the party because the theme of the party was "A" – because I was leaving as was another senior staff member whose name began with A. So we had a number of angels at the Board meeting plus an Amelia Earhart but the funniest moment was when I realised that the Chairman had come as me – with brightly coloured glasses, a silk scarf and a large diamante brooch.

When you're writing a Board report, use your strategic plan as the framework for it. The Board doesn't need to know every detail of your activities but they do need to know what you're doing to ensure that the company is on track. Encourage the Board to want to have your senior management team at meetings and present their reports directly. I got my team to attend not just the part of the meeting that covered their topic, but all of the meeting. I wanted the Board to know them and for the managers to know the Board's views and the challenges they gave me. The only confidential meetings the Board ever had were on salaries, CEO appointments and the occasional tricky stakeholder situation. Never assume that Board members read anything more than Board papers and mainstream media. And I can say this after watching Board members in action and being a Board member. It's useful if they are aware of the changes and developments that happen in industry context in which the company sits, but they only way they are going to find out is if you tell them.

Hudson's right to say that one needs to be more proactive about ensuring that staff understand the role of the Board, the issues that they discuss and the decisions they make. For years, I left a copy of the Board papers outside my office for anyone to read. But I have to confess that only one person regularly did.

A curious phrase that has been used about Board/Executive relationships is "strange loops and tangled hierarchies" (Middleton 1987, 149). I'd tend to turn it around and say "strange hierarchies and tangled loops". "Strange hierarchies" because even though the Board technically hires and fires the CEO and is their "boss", the Board knows almost nothing about the organisation without the CEO's work. They are at the whim of the CEO which is why, so often, Boards don't know about a crisis until there's a whistle-blower or an article in the paper. "Tangled loops" because different Board members will have different relationships with the CEO and that will mean different relationships between Board members. For example, in a small organisation where the Board Treasurer works with the CEO on budgets and accounts, they are much more informed than anyone else. Similarly, if there is a Board subcommittee that is focused on risk, their understanding of the operations of the organisation will be much clearer than those of other Board members.

Herman (2010, 162–163) recommends the following actions in what he calls Board-centred leadership by executives:

1. Facilitate interaction in Board relationships (listening and hearing the concerns of members)
2. Show consideration and respect toward Board members
3. Envision change and innovation for the organization with the Board
4. Provide useful and helpful information to the Board
5. Initiate and maintain structure for the Board
6. Promote Board accomplishments and productivity.

You should try to see Board members as people who can help you rather than view them as people who unnecessarily absorb your time. Fishel (2003, 12) also advises CEOs to invest time in Board members outside of Board meetings, to get to know them individually and (one of my favourite phrases), to say "thank you".

The most important set of communication requirements is between the Chair and the CEO. There are all sorts of Chairs:

- The Chair who wants your job
- The Chair that can't run a meeting
- The Chair that insists on meeting with your staff without you
- The Chair that doesn't donate time, money or skill
- The Chair that can't remember what was agreed last week.

And of course, there are good ones who know what their job is: to hire and fire the CEO and to make sure that organisation is fulfilling its mission and is on track to meet its strategic goals.

But what if you have one of the bad ones? Your options are to work around them, to put up with them or to have a very open one-on-one conversation with them, knowing that one of the results might be that you have to leave. Why is it so hard to manage your Chair? They are usually senior executives in their own world where no-one would tell them how to behave. There are plenty of examples of bad management in the corporate world and it's certainly a less collegiate world than you'll find in the arts.

I've been extremely lucky with the Chairs of organisations that I've managed. They have been intelligent and generous men and women who have given of their time (and often their money) for the good of the organisation. Their most important virtue was that they all understood the role of both a Chair and a Board. I've also been on Boards of organisation where, again, the Chairs, in this case mainly women, were well informed about the best way a Board can contribute to an arts organisation.

I have heard horror stories of Board Chairs involving attempts to micromanage the CEO, holding secret meetings without the CEO, attempting to impose organisational change on companies. One story is documented in Kirby and Myer's (2009) biography of Richard Pratt. In it they describe, without ever questioning his behaviour, an attempt by Pratt as Chairman to run the Victorian Arts Centre (VAC).[5] It included bringing in "his own man to be his eyes and ears in the VAC "(114) and what Sue Nattrass, CEO at the time, politely described as "legendary arguments" (115).

The negative impact on both the CEO and the organisation of this attempt by the Chair to manage the arts centre led a number of the major hirers to go to the Premier of Victoria and ask (unsuccessfully) for the Chairman to be removed. The biographers say that Pratt was trying to turn the arts centre into a "people's palace" and put it on a more commercial footing but

> [o]bservers said that some of the discord at the VAC was deliberately created by Pratt in the way it was in his business. He felt it useful to provoke people to see what they really thought and felt about issues to allow him maximum information of decision-making. The difference was, however, that at the VAC he was not making decisions alone.
> (Kirby & Myer 2009, 116)

This last point is telling because it captures one of the major problems – a Chairman who was used to running his own company and clearly didn't understand the role of a non-executive Board in an arts organisation with its multitude of stakeholders and its complex mission.

As for using discord to provoke people, I remember being in a meeting with Pratt as he described some of his more outlandish plans for the arts centre including serving yum cha in the Concert Hall when it wasn't being used or turning the balconies of the State Theatre into closed corporate boxes such as found at sports venues. There was no sense in that meeting that he was interested in our ideas or even our views on his ideas. His biographers describe the managers of the major hirers as an "arts elite" who were opposed to both his style and his desire to bring a more commercial approach to the organisation (Kirby & Myer 2009, 77). Rather than the dismissive use of "elites" I think it's more accurate to describe us as good managers with effective Chairs who therefore knew how a Board should operate.

The relationship between Board and CEO is more subtle in arts organisations than in corporate Boards because a volunteer committee is overseeing the work of a professional CEO

(Fishel 2003). If the relationship in a co-leadership model between Artistic and Managing Director is like a marriage, then so too is the relationship between the Board Chair and the CEOs. But there are a couple of interesting dimensions to this "marriage". From one perspective there is an imbalance of power because the Chair can choose the CEO but not vice versa. However, from another perspective, the CEO has more power because without their reports, the Chair can be completely in the dark about what is actually going on in the company.

In a conversation with a peer, we were discussing the Chair of a particular organisation that was searching for a new CEO. I asked if my compatriot was going to apply for the job and the answer was "no". Not because they weren't interested in the job and the organisation but because they knew the Chair and didn't think their working styles would be compatible. Being able to find that out in advance can be a problem. The Chair should be on the interview committee so you'll have a chance to see them in action and can ask them some questions. However, they are not going to confess that they are micromanagers or never available to make a decision or bad in a crisis. It's one of the risks you have to take when working as a CEO or co-leader. Before you take on a job, you should insist on having a one-on-one meeting with the Chair to try and tease out their way of operating and being upfront about what you expect from them. This is an example where truth telling will pay off. Ultimately, the existing partner will have to adjust their approach to the new person (Hudson 2005).

Obviously, if neither party is good at their job, the relationship and therefore the organisation will suffer. Support and respect are interlinked. A CEO needs to feel that the Chair will back their decisions but, equally, the Chair needs to feel that the CEO is giving them enough information to do *their* job. A Managing Director told me that their Chair would talk over them, not listen to them, have meetings with other Board members and staff without them and – not surprisingly – the MD felt completely undermined by the Chair. We don't respect our staff who aren't good at their job. The same applies if it's the Chair.

Boards only gather for conversation on a limited number of occasions. They may wave across the room at an opening but Board meetings usually happen between six and 12 times a year. A lot can happen in a month, let alone two, so it's important to keep your Chair in the loop about issues with the potential to create trouble. "The CEO wants support and advice. The Chair wants no surprises. The CEO wants the space to get on with the job. The Chair wants to be associated with a successful organisation" (Fishel 2003, 164).

I've only had a Chair give me a good telling off twice. I've already referred to one case already – when the group of Melbourne arts managers talked to the Premier about not renewing Richard Pratt's chairmanship of the Victorian Arts Centre (as it was then called). By the next morning, Pratt had rung all the Chairs to express his extreme displeasure and mine rang me to find out what the hell I'd been up to. In the end, he didn't disagree with the position that I'd taken but he would have liked to discuss it with me first. He was right.

The second case concerned a case of staff theft. I had proved the case, the person had confessed, they had repaid the amount (not a large sum, but not a small one either) and I had let them resign because there were a range of issues that, if not acceptable, were understandable that had led to the theft. The Chair was furious that I'd just let the person go without calling the police and firing them. In this case, I'm not so sure that he was right. Maybe it's the ex-Catholic in me where one can confess one's sins and be forgiven.

The communication between Chair and CEO varies. Some talk every week. Fishel (2003, 164) claims some talk every day. In my experience it depends on two key factors – the experience of either of the parties and the immediacy of the challenges faced by the organisation. A new Chair and a new CEO are going to want to learn, to be nurtured, to be informed, to be supported, and all of this requires communication. After the

first couple of months of working with a particular Chair, I was beginning to despair about whether we were ever going to get along. I respected his intelligence, his incisiveness, his care for the organisation and his networks, but he was tough. Always pushing, always questioning. And then during one Board meeting, he was quiet. He was still focused on the task at hand and on the effective operations of both the Board and the company but the nitpicking and aggression disappeared. It took me months to finally realise what had happened. When he took over the Chair's role, the company wasn't in great shape and I was comparatively new. It was simple. Was I capable of doing the job required to re-orient the company? That's what all his questions and challenges were about. Once he'd decided that I was competent and could be trusted, he could relax. However, I've heard of Managing Directors who've been completely demoralised as the Board Chair and members continually question their intentions, their actions and their decisions.

By the time I left MTC, I had worked with the then Chair either in that role or as Board member for 18 years. The company was in a good place with a new theatre, new headquarters, a new Artistic Director, a new strategic plan and money in the bank. We hardly needed to talk between Board meetings at all.

One of the best bonding processes that I have ever seen play out between Board Chair and CEO was an unintended consequence of an investment by the Australia Council in philanthropy. They created a learning program in New York for Chairs and Managing Directors of Australia's major performing arts companies. The program was well structured and we traipsed all over Manhattan and Brooklyn visiting arts companies and learning about their fundraising strategies. But the best outcome that I observed was Chairs and MDs learning about each other over breakfast and in the hotel bar at the end of the night and as they negotiated the subway and compared notes on their response to the visits. Suddenly, we were on a level learning field and the relationships were strengthened.

In an interesting article about Board/CEO relations, four European non-profit organisations that faced generally externally generated conflict between the Board Chair and the CEO were examined (Jager & Rehli 2012). In all cases, the Chair and the CEO were replaced and the replacements were seen to be much more equivalent in terms of capabilities to work effectively and efficiently with each other. Both roles required strategic thinking and leadership strengths but each team was seen to have complementary preferences in the governance and management of the organisation. The keys to the relationship between the Chair and the CEO are respect, support and competence (Fishel 2003, 177), to which I would add trust. One has to be able to have conversations in confidence about everything from the performance of the Board, the management team, your co-leader, ideas for the future and your future.

For arts organisations with a co-leadership model, the Board has an important additional role as mediator and conflict manager between Artistic and Managing Director. Often the conflict is about the type of work, and more specifically the cost of the work, that a company wants to create. Usually, if such conflict continues, one of the co-leaders will leave, sometimes voluntarily and sometimes not. If the Board hasn't been able to resolve the conflict then they will have to make a decision over which member of the partnership is asked to leave.

In one such example, the Board decided to support the Managing Director rather than the Artistic Director and so terminated the latter. However, there were lots of artists and community members who supported the Artistic Director and a committee got together to try and have the Artistic Director reinstated. When the Board refused to do so, the committee's next action was to try and take over the Board. This was possible because Board membership was done by vote of the company membership. The reinstatement committee decided to call for the Board to stand down and to be followed by new elections. This required the calling of a Special General Meeting, but more importantly, getting friends and supporters to become members so that they could vote. At the Special General Meeting, the Artist Director's supporters lost the vote but this spurred them on to an even bigger recruitment drive. Not surprisingly, supporters of the Board were doing the same thing.

Finally, the Annual General Meeting came around and instead of the usual 15–20 members turning up, the room was filled with hundreds of people. Independent auditors had been called in to count the vote. On the motion for the Board to step down, a vote by voice was called – but the auditors couldn't decide. A vote by hands was called but again, it was too close to call. Finally, the auditors asked people to go to either side of the room to be counted. I remember that my father (a supporter of the Board) looked at me sadly before we walked to opposite sides of the room.

The reinstatement committee won the vote, the Board stood down, all positions were declared vacant and the resulting Board saw the Artistic Director's supporters in the Chair's role and four positions,[6] and the old Board members retained four positions. The battle wasn't quite finished because the Managing Director tried to work with the new Board and the reinstated Artistic Director, but couldn't. Although this process was traumatic for many individuals, it did give a whole new energy to the company with a new Chair and a new Managing Director.

Because there is a paradox about exactly how much control Boards have, it's hard to actually review their performance. It's easier to review the individual Board member: did they appear to prepare for meetings, attend meetings, contribute thoughtfully to discussions, publicly support the organisation, provide a financial contribution if that's required, put the interests of the company before their own? Morgan and Rentscheler (2011, 7) quote a 1996 survey which asked the following question: Does the Board of Directors determine whether the organisation is or is not accomplishing its mission? And the answer was: "The vast majority of respondents did not know whether their actions or Board contributions contributed to the organisation's mission" (8).

One way of finding out whether a Board is working effectively is to bring in an outsider to do a review. Usually this will involve asking a range of questions about individual and collective performance. I've completed such reviews as a Board member and undertaken them as a consultant and my preference, informed by these experiences, is that a face-to-face interview is more useful than completing an online survey. If people know that their comments are confidential, they'll share more with a person than a computer and, with the right questions, will also offer unexpected ideas to help improve Board performance.

Technically, the whole Board is responsible if they make the wrong choice of CEO, if they let the financial situation get away from them, if they approve projects that over-stretch the organisation. But in all but the first scenario, they don't actively create the environment in which organisations fail. If they can't anticipate and control failure, they also rarely get congratulated when a company is successful (Turbide 2011). In my experience, a good Board does contribute to the success of a company's mission through good governance, wisdom, financial and moral support.

Being on Boards

At some point in time, an experienced arts manager will be asked to join a Board. The most pragmatic and sensible book of advice for such a role is one I've quoted from already: David Fishel's *The Book of the Board* (2003).

Fishel (2003, 219) lists the key elements to good governance and there are ones that you should keep in mind in your new role:

1. Commitment to organisational performance as well as to compliance
2. Structure and rational approaches to decision-making
3. Careful selection of the CEO
4. Strategic thinking and openness to the demands of a changing environment

5. Prediction and mitigation of risk in your operations
6. Proper attention to the Board's own health – through its recruitment, induction, meeting procedures and leadership.

The most important thing you can know is when to ask questions. It all comes back to your role in managing risk and performance. Assuming that you are receiving regular and reasonable written reports on the activities of the company, ask about:

- Anything you don't understand
- Anything that holds a risk for the company
- Anything which you think implies performance problems
- Anything in your area of expertise where you think things could be done better.

Some of the language around Boards' responsibilities seems overly dense but unpacked, it is full of ideas that apply to management generally. For example, leaving the exact legal meaning of the phrase "duty to exercise care and diligence" to one side, the vision of doing your job as a Board member or a manager with care and effort seems highly appropriate to a mission-driven organisation. Similarly, "duty to act in good faith and for a proper purpose" is about values such as honesty and appropriate use of power. A "duty to disclose interests" and to avoid conflicts of interest and a "duty not to improperly use position of information" are examples of behaving ethically.[7]

In Australia in 2019 as a result of a Royal Commission into Misconduct in the Banking, Superannuation and Finance Services Industry[8] there has been considerable discussion about the responsibility of Boards. Those industries may seem very distant from our industries but some of the insights drawn from the Commission are important to note for Board members. The traditional view of their role in hiring and firing the CEO and making sure the organisation is solvent is no longer enough. Boards also have to be responsible for the culture and ethics of our companies.

Conclusion

In a presentation to a small arts organisation, a legal firm provided the following useful takeaways for Board members:

- Remember to speak up if you don't agree with Board's strategy
- Read the Board Papers
- Make sure you understand the fundamentals of the company's business
- Find out how significant proposals will impact the company
- Ensure the Board minutes are accurate
- Consider training for specific financial and accounting issues
- You are entitled to information you need in an understandable form and in time to properly consider it
- Apply an independent and inquiring mind to the information with which you are presented
- Recognise situations where it would be difficult to rely on the advice and conduct of others and complete own investigation or seek independent expert advice.

I re-offer these points because, regardless of whether you are on a Board yet, you probably will be in the future and this is what your Board has in mind when they challenge your bright new idea or ask for more detail on the finance report – they are just doing their job.

There is a paradox at the heart of the Board-Executive relationship. The Board hires and can fire the CEO but completely relies on them to provide the information which enables proper governance. It's a paradox we have to live with.

See also: Artistic Leaders, Conflict, Ethics, Fundraising, Meetings, Money, Strategic Plan, Trust

References

Adirondack, S. 2005 *Just About Managing?* (4th ed), London: London Voluntary Service Council.

Barton, D. & Wiseman, M. 2015 "Where Boards Fall Short", *Harvard Business Review*, 93(1/2), 98–104.

Bell, J., Moyers, R. & Wolfred, T. 2006 *Daring to Lead 2006: A National Study of Nonprofit Executive Leadership*, www.compasspoint.org/sites/default/files/documents/194_daringtolead06final.pdf [accessed 22 February 2019].

De Paoli, D. 2011 "The Role of Leadership in Changing Art Institutions – The Case of the National Museum of Art in Oslo, Norway", Antwerp: 11th AIMAC International Conference.

Dubini, P. & Monti, A. 2018 "Board Composition and Organizational Performance in the Cultural Sector: The Case of Italian Opera Houses", *International Journal of Arts Management*, 20(2), 56–71.

Fishel, D. 2003 *The Book of The Board*, Sydney: Federation Press.

Ginther, R. 2010 *Making the Case for Change: Challenging Hierarchy in Arts and Cultural Organizations*, Canada: Athabasca University.

Golding, K. 2011 *Essential Governance Practices for Arts Organisations*, Sydney: Australia Council.

Harris, M. 1989 "The Governing Body Role: Problems and Perceptions in Implementation", *Non-profit and Voluntary Sector Quarterly*, 18 (3), 317–232.

Herman, R. D. 2010 "Executive Leadership", in Renz, D. O. (ed.) *The Jossey-Bass Handbook of Nonprofit Leadership and Management* (3rd ed), San Francisco, CA: John Wiley & Sons, 157–177.

Hubbard, D. 1992 "The Effective Board", in Drucker, P. (ed.) *Managing the Non-profit Organisation*, London: Buttersworth Heinemann.

Hudson, M. 2005 *Managing at the Leading Edge*, San Francisco, CA: John Wiley.

Hudson, M. 2009 *Managing Without Profit: Leadership, Management and Governance of Third Sector Organisations in Australia*, Sydney: UNSW Press.

Jager, U. P. & Rehli, F. 2012 "Cooperative Power Relations between Nonprofit Board Chairs and Executive Directors", *Nonprofit Management & Leadership*, 23(2), 219–236.

Kaiser, M. M. 2010 *Leading Roles*, Waltham, MA: Brandeis University Press.

Kaiser, M. M. 2013 *The Circle*, Waltham, MA: Brandeis University Press.

Kirby, J. & Myer, R. 2009, *Richard Pratt: One Out of the Box*, Milton, QLD: John Wiley & Sons.

Larcker, D. F., Meehan, W. F., Donatiello, N. & Tayan, B. 2015 *Survey on Board of Directors of Nonprofit Organisations*, Stanford, CA: Stanford Graduate School of Business & Rock Center for Corporate Governance.

McFarlan, F. W. 1999 "Working on Nonprofit Boards – Don't Assume the Shoe Fits", *Harvard Business Review*, 77(6), 64–80.

Middleton, M. 1987 "Nonprofit Boards of Directors: beyond the Governance Function", in Powell, W. W. (ed.) *The Nonprofit Sector: A Research Handbook*, New Haven, CT: Yale University Press.

Mills, R. 2003 *The Australian*, 4 July, 15.

Morgan, M. & Rentschler, R. 2011 "Mission Fulfilment: The Role of Board Performance", Antwerp: AIMAC 11th International Conference.

Moyers, R. 2011 *Daring to Lead 2011 – The Board Paradox*, Meyer Foundation http://daringtolead. org/wp-content/uploads/Daring-Brief-3-080511.pdf [accessed 22 February 2019].

Myers, R. 2014 "The Artistic Director: On the Way to Extinction", 2014 Philip Parsons Memorial Lecture, http://belvoir.com.au/wp-content/uploads/2014/12/2014-Philip-Parsons-Memorial-Lecture-by-Ralph-Myers.pdf [accessed 9 January 2015].

Ouellett, P. & Lapierre, L. 1997 "Management Boards of Arts Organisations", in Fitzgibbon, M. & Kelly, A. (eds) *From Maestro to Manager*, Dublin: Oak Tree Press, 367–377.

Parsons, R. D. & Feigen, M. A. 2014 "The Boardroom's Quiet Revolution", *Harvard Business Review*, 92(3), 99–104.

Rankin, S. 2014 "Soggy Biscuit", in Schultz, J. (ed.) *Griffith Review 44*, Brisbane: Griffith University, 12–32.

Rentschler, R. 2015 *Arts Governance: People, Passion Performance*, Abingdon, Oxon: Routledge.

Renz, D. O. 2004 "An Overview of Nonprofit Governance", *Philanthropy in America*, www.energycollection.us/Board-Of-Directors/Governance/Overview-Nonprofit-governance.pdf [accessed 15 March 2015].

Summerton, J. & Hutchins, M. (eds) 2005 *Diverse Voices: Personal Journeys, All Ways Learning*, Brighton: All Ways Learning.

Tshirhart, M. 1996 *Artful Leadership*, Bloomington, IN: Indiana University Press.

Turbide, J. 2011 "Poor Governance Sickens the Arts – We Have the Cure", *Kenneth Myer Lecture*, Geelong: Deakin University.

Buildings

While there's probably a lot of theory about managing building projects, there isn't much on managing theatre building projects so what follows is a very practical story. Cray and Inglis (2011) interviewed 14 Canadian arts organisations of different sizes and types to see what the most important strategic decisions had been in the previous five years and the overwhelming answer (80%) was buildings (new, renovated, expanded). I have been involved in building a new radio station, moving people from six different buildings into one new media headquarters, refurbishing an office and work spaces for a theatre company, building a new theatre and, as I type, working with architects and bureaucrats to find a new home for a dance company. I'm going to tell the story of the Southbank Theatre[9] because that is the most complex of those projects and in the process, I'll offer some practical advice for those who want to create venues as well as art and because it's the project of which I'm still inordinately proud.

That hubris may be a reflection of what is commonly called the "edifice complex" where governments and organisations invest a lot of money (and energy) into the "hardware" of bricks and mortar of cultural venues at the expense of "software", the artists and shows. For example, in an article by Australian cultural policy blogger Ben Eltham (2012), he talked about the challenge between investing in buildings and investing in art and gave the example of the Albany Entertainment Centre which opened in December 2010 with a 620-seat theatre and a 200-seat studio. Both were "state of the art" but mainly empty in the first part of 2011 with eight days used in March and only four in April and May.[10] The City of Albany, population 36,000, couldn't afford to run the venue at the time, let alone have an Artistic Director or a programming budget.

Examples of the edifice complex can also be seen in other countries. Caust (2015, 6) describes the export of cultural edifices from Europe initially through the process of colonisation and then with their creation as signs of a shift from a Third World country status such as the building program of arts centres in China over the last decade. It's much more comfortable for governments, democratic or not, to spend arts dollars on buildings which can be controlled in both a practical and a symbolic sense than on artists which can't. Qiao (2015) notes that that many of China's new venues are designed by foreigners without consideration for Chinese style or characteristics and that they are large and expensive to run, making them inaccessible or inappropriate for mid-sized companies to use. And ironically, existing old theatres and opera houses have to close or repurpose in the face of shiny new competition. One of the set of demands made to the Taiwanese Government in 2011 by a group of artists, Directors and writers was: "The government should stop wasting expenditure on cultural facilities and end the distortion of cultural development" (Hsin-tien 2015, 49).

MTC's situation was almost the opposite of the edifice complex. The company had been investing in art making for decades and now wanted some infrastructure to enhance its activities. And for a long time, the State Government in Victoria didn't want to invest money in a building for us.

Does a theatre company always need a theatre? The answer is not always "yes". If a company produces a couple of shows a year then the answer is probably "no". If a company tours a lot then the answer is probably "no". If a company has been given access to a building for a peppercorn[11] rent then the answer is probably "no". If a company has to take on the depreciation and the potential replacement of a building then the answer is probably "no".

MTC was founded as the Union Repertory Theatre Company in 1953 and from the beginning had a structure unique amongst Australian performing arts companies – it's a department of the University of Melbourne. The company started its life having free access to a theatre for six months a year – the Union Theatre on the campus of the University. As the company expanded its audience and repertoire, the University bought it the 420-seat Russell St Theatre in the Melbourne CBD in 1966. The theatre wasn't new, wasn't posh and had basic flying and technical facilities, but in the 1960s it was a really good deal.

In 1960, the State Government of Victoria decided to build an arts centre[12] – with a concert hall, a lyric theatre, a playhouse and a black box space. The assumption was that the playhouse would become MTC's home with the black box space being an accessible and flexible room for smaller and more experimental companies. However, the arts centre took over 20 years to be built and, in the process, the entertainment and leisure market became denser and the audience for live, text-based theatre started to drop. So, by the time the Playhouse came online in 1984 with 850 seats, it was too big for even MTC, Victoria's largest theatre company, to fill on a regular basis. So MTC continued to use the Russell St Theatre in the city and only presented work in the Playhouse a couple of times a year.

However, Russell St was falling apart. Although the University had bought the building for the company, they didn't provide any money to maintain it let alone improve it and the company invested the resources it had in what it put *on* stage rather than the stage itself. As the building disintegrated, audience expectations were increasing. People wanted comfortable seats, good sightlines, a cosy bar, roomy foyers, entertainment spaces for sponsors and special events – and Russell St had none of this. Even actors were beginning to find the challenge of dark and tiny dressing rooms unacceptable.

So in the late 1980s, MTC started to look for a replacement theatre and knowing that Russell St was likely to fall apart before they succeeded, the company started to talk to the arts centre about using the black box space (Fairfax Studio) and reducing the cost of renting the Playhouse in order to make it more financially viable, even for small houses. At that point in time there were two viable options: replace Russell St or become the full-time tenant of a state-built and subsidised arts centre. MTC chose the latter for the short term but kept the former goal as the dream.

Why wasn't being a tenant in the Arts Centre enough? When a person decides to go to the Arts Centre to see an MTC show, they are sold a ticket by an Arts Centre staff member, park in a car park which benefits the Arts Centre, are shown to their seat by an usher trained by the Arts Centre, buy a drink at a bar where MTC doesn't get to choose the wine or share in the profit and see a show where the technical staff aren't MTC staff and may change week to week. In other words, MTC has no control whatsoever about the experience that the audience has when they go to the theatre and the company doesn't have access to any of the additional income from the money they spend during their time in the venue. And because the Arts Centre contracted out ticketing services at the time, we couldn't even get the contact information for the single ticket buyers in order to talk to them about their experience or offer them a chance to see another MTC show.

Although MTC brought more people to the Arts Centre during the 1990s and 2000s than any other organisation, we had little bargaining power as a hirer because we had nowhere else to go. There are no other suitably sized theatres in Melbourne. So we had no opportunity to negotiate better rental rates, we had to pay higher staffing costs for the Centre's staff than we did for our own staff, we had to accept the charges of their ticketing agency, we had to accept the dates they offered even though they didn't always suit us, we had to sign contracts we didn't agree with or otherwise they wouldn't put our single tickets on sale and we had to accept their marketing policies about our material.[13] Not surprisingly, even though the Arts Centre in Melbourne has two beautiful theatres that we wanted to keep using, we also wanted to have our own space.

So what did we claim were to be the benefits of a new theatre? For MTC, the new theatre would:

- Reduce the amount of rent for subscription and education productions
- Increase income through bar and restaurant takings, conference and other rental
- Decrease the cost of servicing sponsors and patrons
- Enable extended seasons of successful productions
- Provide a more appropriate theatre size for the majority of plays, leading to a better experience for actors and audience as well as reducing the cost per seat
- Create a physical environment more appropriate to the style of the company
- Provide the opportunity to present a range of new theatrical experiences such as cabaret, late-night comedy, play readings, children's shows
- Enhance our identity as a Melbourne institution through having our own home *again*.

Arguing the case for a new theatre building has to be more than just a selfish exercise of what your company is going to get out of it so we also argued that Melbourne would benefit in a variety of ways.

For the Arts Community:

- A financially healthy MTC with a guaranteed future
- Ongoing employment for actors, Directors, designers, choreographers, composers and writers
- Access to a new, intimate and modern performance space of a size that doesn't exist in central Melbourne
- Increased access for other companies to the Arts Centre theatres (as we vacated 50% our previous bookings).

For the audience:

- A comfortable, attractive venue in which to enjoy a stimulating evening centred on a play but including bars, a restaurant and other forms of entertainment
- An intimate venue in which to view theatrical performances of international standard
- A lively environment with day-long activity in addition to evening performances
- New theatrical activity due to the improved financial state of MTC.

For the stakeholders – the State Government and the University of Melbourne

- An iconic building for locals and tourists to enjoy
- A stronger major arts organisation
- Increased arts activity.

Of course, this was all very well but when you have no money, how do you build a theatre? The answer was "partners". We looked everywhere: commercial companies that might have included a theatre at the bottom of an office block or an apartment high rise building; a developer that wanted access to government-owned land and might have been willing to build a theatre as part of their "community service"; a government that wanted to invest in cultural infrastructure or renovate an existing theatre. We tried all these approaches and eventually ended up with a partnership between the State Government of Victoria and the University of Melbourne. The University owned land close to other cultural infrastructure in Southbank and the Victorian Government had been lobbied by music lovers to build a 1,000-seat recital hall. The land was big enough to fit a 500-seat theatre as well as a recital hall. So the initial logic was that the University gave the land to the state and in exchange the state built a theatre for MTC. Needless to say, the finances didn't work quite as neatly as that and the University ended up investing millions of dollars in cash as well.

Although this deal meant that we got "in-principle" agreement to the building of a theatre, it also created a series of tough challenges at every step in the journey. Why? Because the Government department which funded the arts, Arts Victoria, was technically the client and another Government department, Major Projects Victoria, was the project manager. And MTC wasn't part of the picture – we didn't have any voice – until we fought and clawed our way into the process.

Did we get the building we wanted? For the most part "yes". There were compromises along the way (more of that later) but the building (along with its neighbour, the Melbourne Recital Centre) has won a number of architectural awards[14] and most days, tourists can be seen outside taking photographs of it. Architecturally it's a great success. More importantly, the feedback from the artists, actors and directors and designers who work in the building has been extremely positive. And the audience for the most part (and more of that later as well) love the experience of coming to the building.

So what did we do right? We had workshops with actors and directors and technical staff to collect their ideas and their needs. Consultation is essential at this point and people who are going to live in a space deserve to be asked their opinion. As a result of such consultation, for example, the dressing rooms in the Southbank Theatre have natural light whenever possible plus convertible sofa beds – because that's what the actors wanted.

We checked research on what audiences wanted out of their theatre-going experience. I travelled around Australia and Great Britain and checked the strengths and weaknesses of every theatre that had been built in the previous ten years. We reviewed every architectural and theatre and lighting design magazine for inspiration. And in the end, we created an extremely specific briefing document with every room and every space, the relationship between the audience and the actor, and the technical requirements, spelt out in great detail.

The shape of a theatre is usually going to be a compromise between the land footprint and the desire of the theatre consultant and directors and designers. Richard Pilbrow (2017) argues the case that new theatres should be like the English theatres of Shakespeare's time – wrapped around the stage and intimate. He likes layered theatres with audiences down the side as well as facing the stage: "Enwrapping balconies and boxes bought all the audience around the room into a tight embrace of the actor, and all shared together the immediacy of each moment" (92). I have to confess that we fought this idea when building the Southbank Theatre. Different layers of seats has always felt very hierarchical, almost anti-democratic, to me and there's an energy that comes from people being in the same room. And for Australian performing arts companies that don't get the same sort of subsidy as British or European ones, the idea that a portion of your audience wouldn't experience good sight lines or comfortable seats for the same ticket price (or you have to lose income by reducing your price) wasn't a good option. Having said that, I agree with Pilbrow that "[s]maller will always be better, lively will always be more appealing, and warmth will always attract" (Pilbrow 2017, 100).

When it came to the outside of the building, we knew that we couldn't "control" it – that part of the design had to be in the hands of the architect. But we used words and images to excite their imagination and all of those words – bold, intimate, colourful, entertaining, adventurous, beautiful, provocative, warm, layers of history, stylish, inspirational, light, natural, inviting, relaxed – can be found in some aspect of the Southbank Theatre.

In Cray and Inglis' (2011, 91) research on strategic decisions by Canadian cultural organisations, they did find one where the choice of architect was viewed as even more important that the building itself.

> In part, the salience of this decision was linked to the prestige of the architect and its projected effect on raising the necessary funds, but it was also a result of the specific aesthetic statement the organization wished to make about its identify and the path it intended to follow in the future.

We were equally passionate about the choice of architect. Because the building project was a Government tender, we initially didn't have any say in choosing the architect. In my view this wasn't acceptable because although we weren't technically the client, we were the people who were going to have to live with the results for the rest of our lives (and longer!) We fought hard to be part of the committee that chose the architects. I would have to say that the final choice, Ashton Raggatt McDougall[15] (ARM), wasn't our first choice but as the project developed, we gained an ever-increasing

respect for their achievement and their willingness to engage with us. We learnt to understand their language and their output as we worked on building a relationship with them. We explored the buildings they had already designed sometimes with them and sometimes through talking to the users of their buildings. And we spent lots of time sitting around talking to them about art and design.

I suspect that didn't happen between the architects and the arts teams that work in the building I spent time in during 2018. It's an arts building that has won awards and accolades and is viewed as an architectural icon in Melbourne. From the outside, it may have many outstanding architectural properties. From the inside, it's a disaster. I sat in an office with endless noise from the next-door plant room. It was one of many rooms in the building with no light. The angularity of the building meant that studio spaces were compromised in their shape. There were wasted spaces in some areas and not enough space in others. Every aspect of work felt compromised because of the design. If you ever have a chance to influence the creation of a new arts building, fight hard to be heard because while the architect can put their award on a shelf and move on, you'll be living in unhappy circumstances for years to come.

We were nervous because ARM had never designed a theatre before – but they had designed a number of cultural buildings.[16] And we were nervous because some of their designs had created major divisions with the public loving or loathing them, such as Storey Hall for RMIT University in Melbourne. At one stage ARM's first image on their website was the outside of our theatre with the words "not for everyone" in bright pink. However, the very first design presentation by the architects for our theatre captured all the elements we wanted and was a thrill to see. ARM responded to the "magic" of theatre and the fact that we create houses out of cardboard and worlds out of light. They took the idea of contemporary *trompe-l'oeil*[17] and, based on the work of USA artist Al Held, created an external pipe framework which is both two-dimensional and three-dimensional. They also took on board our desire to have a building that is at its strongest when most people experience theatre. Through reflective paint and light, the Southbank Theatre glows with energy – at night, in the dark.

If we were nervous because ARM hadn't designed a theatre, our angst increased when we discovered that the builders Bovis Lend Lease had never built a theatre. The building project included theatre designers and acousticians but we knew what we wanted and had to fight hard sometimes to get it. Without that detailed brief, we wouldn't have reached our goal. Of course, there were compromises. There's never enough money to build the perfect building so we lost the battle to make the building stand alone,[18] we lost the battle to make the building green, we lost public rooms and storage space, we lost some backstage space but, generally, we got what we wanted.

Some of the battles we fought might seem trivial but they were worth the agony. My next story is really for the women reading this book. You know those endless interval queues? You know those tiny cubicles where there's nowhere to put your theatre programme let along your clutch purse and the toilet paper has always run out? You know those spaces where the light is too bright or too dim or the environment is simply seedy? For months, every time I went to a theatre in another building or another city or another country, I took a tape measure and a camera. I measured toilets, took pictures of toilets, reviewed endless design magazines about toilets, discovered obscure research about toilets – all in order to achieve a reasonable number of toilets of a reasonable size in a pleasant space. And we did. Yes, there are queues at interval but they're short and people don't mind waiting in the architectural follies we created based on scenic backdrops from the early 20th century (Philips & Tonks 2012).

Ultimately, you can't control everything. I had to trade off the space between rows in order to get great sight lines and comfortable seats. There's a fabulous foyer upstairs but

most people don't want to make the effort of going up one floor and so remain jammed in downstairs (although this adds to the excitement and anticipation). I didn't get parking which was going to provide income as well as convenience. But I fought to keep space for the studio/rehearsal space and the café/bar even though the fit-out expenditure was cut from the budget.

The University of Chicago's Cultural Studies Center did a major study of cultural building projects in the United States – looking at the building boom between 1994 and 2008 that included museums, performing arts centres (PACs) and theatres (Woronkowicz et al. 2012). They found that there was overinvestment during this time, "especially when coupled with the number of organizations we studied that experienced financial difficulties post-building. Eighty percent of the projects we studied ran over budget, some by as much as 200 percent." They identified four characteristics that led to more or less successful projects:

1. The project's motivation, driven by both the organization's artistic mission and by organizational need, was the primary purpose for building
2. Project leadership that was clear and consistent throughout the planning and building process improved the chance of positive outcomes
3. Efficient project timelines and the effectiveness of the project leadership helped determine a project's success in implementation
4. Project outcomes were influenced by how flexible the organization was in generating revenue post-project completion, and how effective the project leaders were at controlling expenses.

The Southbank Theatre was a very particular project but it did come in on time and on budget. In addition to Woronkowicz et al.'s (2012) recommendations there are additional lessons to be learnt in how we got what we wanted:

1. Prepare a detailed brief based on feedback from artists, best practice and the knowledge of your technical staff
2. Ensure that you are part of the process to choose the architect
3. Employ someone to be your eyes and ears on the project
4. Develop a meaningful relationship with the architects, builders and consultants
5. Fight to keep the elements of the project that are most important to you but be willing to compromise to get the project across the line.

We invested lots of time in building rapport with ARM. Our Artistic Director was a designed focus artist who could share a language with the architects (and an interest in red wine). No matter how strong our disagreements about issues, we could always talk to them online and offline and find a way through to a solution that was a new answer rather than a begrudgingly accepted compromise.

We appointed a Project Manager with a technical theatre background, experience in working on the creation of other cultural buildings and a great eye for detail. I have no capacity to think in three-dimensions. My knowledge of flying systems was non-existent. I had to run a theatre company and (as it turns out) solve another building problem as our headquarters sank further into the Yarra River each day. Without someone to check the details, read every plan, ensure that the implementation of every plan worked, we wouldn't have got the result we did. This didn't make my Project Manager the most popular person on the block but it was worth every argument. And when the building project managers tried to ignore us or bypass us or undermine us, we just kept plugging away: keeping minutes, documenting responses, following up on issues, developing direct relationships with the builders and subcontractors, poking our nose into every issue.

At one stage in the "value management" process (which translates in Australia to mean what can you cut out to decrease the cost?), it looked as if we were going to lose our rehearsal/studio space. Simon Phillips, the Artistic Director, and I played a bold hand. The cost of the exterior design elements (which we loved) were about the same price as the studio space. We said we'd rather have a black box with no decoration and a useful performance space. Needless to say, the architects were horrified and joined with us to argue for additional funding to keep their design in tract and deliver our studio.

By immersing ourselves in the project, we achieved some beautiful results. For example, the acousticians wanted wooden panels in the Sumner auditorium to facilitate the best sound. The architects came up with the idea of putting lights behind those wooden panels. We then collectively said if there can be lights and holes there can be words. And then we came up with 70 theatrical quotes to fill the walls.[19] The result is a unique contemporary version of the 19th- and early 20th-century decorative theatre auditoriums.

At the same time all this was going on, the company continued to produce its usual output of a dozen main stage plays for 250,000 people each year plus education, touring and play development activity plus the redevelopment of a car showroom and warehouse into a new headquarters for the company. And while we continued business as usual during the design and build period of the new theatre (2004–2008), we had to create a new business model and organisational structure for the theatre, including a new ticketing system, website, brand, capital campaign plus the implementation plan to open and run the building including a tender for the café operator.

I would have to say that we got some of this right and some of this wrong. Having a new building means that by definition you have a new image of yourself and you can lever a new energy, a new communications structure, a new relationship, a new brand off that new look. We invested money in audience research to make sure that we really understood our audience as we moved into the new space and worked with an advertising agency to refine our brand and develop a new logo.

We used the existence of the new theatre as a reason to buy and implement a new ticketing system (Tessitura) and test it with our subscribers a year before the building came online. This meant the company had a great Customer Relationship Management capacity going into the building and that the transition to selling single tickets in the new theatre was an easy one. It even made moments like our first cancelled show in the new theatre bearable because we could text people on their mobile phones and give them the bad news before they'd left work or home.

We initiated the company's first capital campaign (mtc@home) to raise money to underpin the cost of both the new theatre and the refurbishment of our new headquarters. While we needed more money for the HQ than for theatre, a new public space is more appealing than offices and workshops and we successfully used the sparkle of the new theatre to fund both – until the Global Financial Crisis hit and slowed our fundraising down to next to nothing. We were willing to "sell" naming rights to some rooms[20] in the building plus every seat and every auditorium wall quote.

It's worth noting that we achieved these major initiatives with only two new ongoing full-time staff positions prior to staffing the new theatre: one created when we split the job of Marketing and Development Director in two and one to manage our new ticketing service.

We had developed a detailed financial business plan with high-level sensitivity analysis for the new theatre. We'd benchmarked costs and staffing levels against other similar theatres and we kept (we thought) our income projections at a modest level. However, we got it wrong in a number of unexpected areas: more expensive electricity bills, higher staffing costs and the Global Financial Crisis (GFC) impacted on our capacity to find new sponsors. In other words, less income and more cost than we expected. Mind you, we weren't alone in this. Apparently, in the USA between 1994 and 2008, 54% of cultural building projects had lower revenues than projected and 59% had higher expenses

than projected (Woronkowicz 2017, 113). Woronkowicz also quotes research to say that 91% of newly constructed performing arts centres (PACs) went over budget, 73% when over by at least 50% and 40% of these projects took longer than originally planned (116).

We didn't do enough preparation work on the administrative processes for the building. For example, we didn't have risk documents such as evacuation and emergency procedures ready when we moved in. We didn't have hiring agreements ready when we moved in. But we had an excuse. The building finished three months *early* and although there was a warning that this might happen, the project managers wouldn't commit to a completion date. However, we should have been just as focused on processes as we were on bricks and mortar.

We found a new group of energetic and enthusiastic staff for the building – front-of-house and back-of-house – and trained and inducted them. However, there were challenges in this area that took a long time to solve. MTC has been around since 1953. Some of our staff had been with the company for over 30 years. The great strength of the company is that most of the staff spend most of their time together: set and props workshops, costume making, rehearsal rooms, lighting and sound staff, marketing and development, casting and creative, finance and IT – all under one roof. But suddenly there were two roofs. There was a new team of permanent and casual staff as well as the catering contractor's staff 10 minutes' walk away. And no matter how hard you try, you can't be in two places at once.

The new theatre people had a completely different relationship to the company to those at HQ (or the "mother ship" as the new staff call it). How do you connect the two? When you have back of house staff who share skills with people at HQ, do you integrate them into one production department or have them reporting directly to the theatre manager? How do you ensure that the new staff meet the old staff? How do you ensure that the old staff value the new staff? How do you explain why the new staff seem to be getting new everything – desks, chairs, computers, technology – when for years you've asked the old staff to be frugal?

Even by the time I'd left the company, I don't think I'd been successful in managing the integration of the two sets of staff. We tried lots of strategies, including joint events for staff, inductions that covered both buildings, photos of the new staff in the old building, presentations from old staff as part of the training of new staff, encouraging new staff to see shows and start to get the feel of the company's work than just standing on the outside of the auditorium. And then there were the staff employed by the café operator. If it's a challenge to integrate one's own new staff, it's even harder to ensure that someone else's employees fit your service standards.

Back at HQ almost everyone had to face an increase in their workload because of the new theatre. There were more people on staff for the payroll clerk to process. There was more marketing required because of the building itself. We were making more shows so the production staff were stretched. We needed to raise more money and so the fundraising staff had to be nice to more people. While we built new staffing structures for ticketing and website management and theatre operations into our business model, we didn't build many new positions into the general overhead operation of the company. And we should have.

Another group of people that need to be looked after are the stakeholders – from politicians and the media, to donors and audience members. Once the decision to create a new building is made, there's an endless array of opportunities to build relationships and increase the institutional profile of the company. Kaiser (2013, 72–73) lists a number of announcements that can surround a building project:

- Decision to build a new building
- Selection of the architect
- Announcement of a capital campaign
- Renderings of a building
- Programming to be housed
- Success with the capital campaign

- Plans for reopening
- Opening ceremonies.

With the Southbank Theatre, MTC did all the things on Kaiser's list and added a series of events including:

- Sod turning
- Theatre naming
- Patron tours of the half-built construction
- Open house for the general public
- Being part of other civic events which invited people to visit this building amongst others.

We didn't want to risk the opening of the theatre being tied up with the audience response to a brand-new play. We'd seen that happen when the Sydney Theatre[21] opened a few years earlier and both the theatre and the new plays suffered because of it. Instead, we decided to show off the building itself. We presented two theatrical concerts in order to be able to fit in MTC staff and the staff of the architects, builders and subcontractors as well as the VIPs. And we did show off what the Sumner Theatre could do: the Chancellor of the University arrived to make his speech on a cherry picker; the Victorian Minister for the Arts came up through a trap in the stage floor on an elevated work platform; the Chairman of the MTC Board became part of a slapstick comedy routine after his speech. And everyone had a jolly good time. Once we'd got that out of the way, we could spend the next two months commissioning the technical equipment, training staff and fine-tuning the building for the first production, *Poor Boy*, which opened in the Sumner Theatre on 27 January 2009. The first meal in Script Bar and Bistro, the Theatre café, was consumed on 8 July 2009. The first public play reading in the Lawler Studio was on 14 July 2009. And the first major catastrophe happened with massive damage due to an hail storm in March 2010. Thank goodness for insurance.

Unlike the 1960s, when theatre patrons were quite happy to race across from Russell St Theatre to the nearby pub to get an interval drink and eat their ice-cream on the street because there wasn't enough room in the foyer, audiences these days want to combine a cultural experience with an entertainment one, preferably one including a bar and/or a café. In research about the role of cafés in museums, McIntyre (2008, 182) describes the cultural experience as "warm" complemented by a "cool" space to allow reflection, consideration, relaxation and a bar, bistro or restaurant plays the cool function. As well as detailing the theatre, we also put a lot of energy into the service areas such as the bars and restaurant.

Relationships between café operators and the theatres in which they operate are notoriously fraught. We hoped that we'd be able to do it better than most by a thorough tender process that included a specialist in catering and café operations. Every tenderer wanted to operate the bars as well as the café but theatre bars are difficult to get right. In 10 minutes, you have to serve the audience with wine and beer, coffee and ice-creams, lollies and cakes so they have at least ten minutes to enjoy them before going back into the theatre. If an outside caterer is running the bar, because they have to pay casual staff by the hour, the temptation is to understaff it. I remember being horrified on one opening night at the Arts Centre Melbourne to discover that there was only one person on the downstairs bar which was supposed to service the 500 people in the stalls. My response was to race behind the bar to serve people.

Years of experience drinking (modest amounts) in bars across the world led me to believe that MTC could do it more effectively and efficiently by adding bar service onto the job descriptions of the ushers but intuition isn't proof. We agreed to let the winning company take on the bars as well as the restaurant and catering but with a two-year limit to the former and a chance to review after a year. And sure enough, I was right. We took back operations of the bar[22] and MTC staff now serve you.

On a more positive note, the café continues to be full before every show. It can also be a safe space to be alone. I've spent years going to the theatre by myself and the idea that one can sit before or after in a "safe" space that understands single dinners add to one's entertainment experience. Script, the restaurant in the Southbank Theatre, understands this and was voted number one in the country for solo diners in 2014 by Australia's largest online reservations service, Dimmi.[23]

Bowman (2011, 84) suggests considering the following ideas if a non-profit organisation is thinking about whether to own a building:

1. Are the annual costs of maintaining and operating property likely to be less than rental payment?
2. Rental property tends to be standardised and office space so if you need more specialised space you may have to buy – but maybe only if the leasehold improvements cost more than the build-to-own costs
3. You may not be able to all fit into one building and face-to-face communication is important
4. Renters are vulnerable to losing their lease or facing rent hikes.

The trouble with renting is that you ultimately have no control over the future. After 42 years of leasing an old stable, La Mama theatre in Melbourne was given a short window in 2008 to buy the building. They managed to raise the A$1.7 million required but not many companies would have that capacity. In 2018, Gertrude Contemporary art gallery was given notice after 32 years and had to head kilometres further north in Melbourne to find an affordable space, given the gentrification of area around their original home – a gentrification they had contributed to by their very existence in Fitzroy.

On the other hand, there can be real difficulties in owning a building. As a producing company, MTC is always going to want to spend more money on the art than on buildings. That's why the company didn't invest in its earlier theatre in Russell St and it fell apart. That's why the company didn't fix up its Ferrars St HQ as it sank into the river. The very reason that you want a theatre – to ensure that people come and have a fabulous time seeing your shows – is the very reason that can undermine either the financial stability or the artistic output of the company.

If you don't have the money to maintain the building, the experience will be less and less pleasurable for the audience. If you have to spend too much money on the building, you potentially lose your artistic competitive advantage. In the long run, no non-profit theatre company can afford the major structural upkeep of a theatre. Our building ended up costing $55 million. Depreciation of 3% a year would mean $1.65 million per annum. That was more than our total annual state and Federal Government grant combined. Building issues that need to be sorted out in advance include:

- Depreciation – if the depreciation for a multimillion-dollar building ends up on your annual accounts, the odds are that you have going to have continual deficits. Although they are only paper deficits, what does this mean to the outside world? Journalists aren't very good at reading accounts. We solved the problem by arguing that the building should be on the University's balance sheet, not ours.
- Defects – there was a 12-month defect process which ensured that such mistakes were fixed at the cost of the builder but there will always be elements of such a project that seem to be defects but won't be accepted by the Building Supervisor as such. In MTC's case, for example, there wasn't an airlock on the front door and this has an impact on the internal temperature and therefore on heating and cooling costs. A defect or not?
- Fixing things – who is going to fix things in the long term? Again, it depends on the owner. Most governments don't plan to upgrade and replace buildings. It becomes part of a cycle of planning and budgeting

and eventually you'll get your money. MTC budgeted for operational maintenance for the building but replacing large cost items such as the theatre seats or upgrading the flying system or fixing the shared chiller plant are going to be the subject of endless debate in the future.

- Fixing things up in the short term – a theatre is a public space and if the front door won't open or the lift won't work or the toilets won't flush, you can't afford to wait for a week or even a day to fix things up. For example, MTC is owned by the University of Melbourne. For six weeks, the heating system in the Vice Chancellor's building didn't work. He might have been willing to put up with that but six weeks x eight performances x 500 people wouldn't be prepared to put up with it at the theatre.

As Hewison and Holden (2011, 162) note and MTC experienced:

> [b]uildings have a tendency to produce nasty shocks, such as getting an electricity bill that has increased way beyond the rate of inflation, when on the income side your grant is limited to inflation itself (if you're lucky). Lots of shiny glass means lots of grumpy window cleaners.

They propose three good guiding principles:

1. Build up financial contingency in the form of a maintenance fund – "it is not rocket science to work out the life of the carpeting or seating in your auditorium".
2. Insure against the completely unforeseen
3. Build a team of staff who you can trust to manage the building efficiently and effectively.

Another challenge for MTC was becoming a landlord. Suddenly, after years of whinging about the service standards and cost and staffing and contracts and policies and rules and regulations of other theatres, MTC turned into a landlord for other arts companies. What Donnelly (2011, 14) said about performing arts centres now applied to MTC: "By necessity, the centre manages its venues from a point of view that is distinct from that of its clients." What suits the company and its operations isn't necessarily what an outside commercial or non-profit hirer is going to desire or expect. For example, MTC has a sophisticated risk management process when it comes to theatre design. What happens when a small theatre company with no such process wants to hire the Lawler Studio? And climb up ladders without supervision? And work without 10 hour breaks? And use sand in the set that hasn't been risk assessed? Do we let them? The company needs to make as much money as it can from venue hire to cover maintenance and operating costs. What are appropriate rates to charge hirers, particularly non-profit companies with modest budgets? How much of our website and ticketing services do we divert to supporting hirers when our first priority is always to get people to see our shows? And of course, there is now no-one to blame when things go wrong. If staff are rude to customers, it's MTC's problem to manage. If back-of-house staff won't help out changing light globes at the front of house, it's the company's approach to multi-skilling that needs fixing. If the marketing material isn't always up to date, there's no-one else to blame.

So was it worth it? All that time and money and angst? Of course, my answer's "yes". But people will only keep going to the Southbank Theatre as long as MTC creates great theatre. They will still go to Script café if it's well run but that experience need only cost the price of cappuccino. One needs to take a much bigger risk and pay considerably more to go to the theatre. We only wanted a theatre in order to create the best possible art in the best possible environment for artists and audiences. While it's great to 'own' an icon, it's only as good as the theatre we make and present inside it.

See also: Audiences, Money, Offices, Risk, Stakeholders, Strategic Planning

References

Bowman, W. 2011 Finance Fundamentals for Non-profits, Hoboken, NJ: John Wiley & Sons.

Caust, J. (ed.) 2015 *Arts and Cultural Leadership in Asia*, London: Routledge.

Cray, D. & Inglis, I. 2011 "Strategic Decision Making in Arts Organizations", *Journal of Arts Management, Law and Society*, 41(2), 84–102.

Donnelly, P. 2011 "Facilities Management", in Brindle, M. & DeVereaux, C. (eds) *The Arts Management Handbook*, Armon, NY: M.E. Sharpe, 13–37.

Eltham, B. 2012 "The State of Australia's Performing Arts Centres, and What it Tells Us About the State of the Australian Arts", *Meanjin*, 71(3), 92–101.

Hewison, R. & Holden, J. 2011 *The Cultural Leadership Handbook*, Farnham: F Gower.

Hsin-tien, L. 2015 "Interlocution and Engagement", in Caust, J. (ed.) *Arts and Cultural Leadership in Asia*, London: Routledge, 48–58.

Kaiser, M. M. 2013 *The Circle*, Waltham, MA: Brandeis University Press.

McIntyre, C. 2008 "Museum Food Service Offers – Experience Design Dimensions", *Journal of Foodservice*, 19(3), 177–188.

Phillips, S. & Tonks, A. 2012 *Play On: Melbourne Theatre Company 2000–2011*, Melbourne: MTC.

Pilbrow, R. 2017 "Magic of Place: An Unrecognized Revolution in Theater Architecture", in Lambert, P. D. & Williams, R. (eds) *Performing Arts Center Management*, New York: Routledge, 84–102.

Qiao, L. 2015 "Re-negotiating the Arts in China", in Caust, J. (ed.) *Arts and Cultural Leadership in Asia*, London: Routledge, 26–38.

Tonks, A. 2009 "Building a Theatre in the 21st Century", in *Innovation and Transformation*, Kaohsiung, Taiwan: 2009 International Symposium on Theater Arts and Cultural Administration.

Woronkowicz, J. 2017 "Building Performing Arts Centers", in Lambert, P. D. & Williams, R. (eds) *Performing Arts Center Management*, New York: Routledge, 102–109.

Woronkowicz, J., Joynes, D. C., Frumkin, D., Kolendo, A., Seaman, B., Gertner, R. & Bradburn, N. 2012 *Set in Stone: Building America's New Generation of Arts Facilities, 1994–2008*, Cultural Policy Center, University of Chicago. http://culturalpolicy.uchicago.edu/setinstone/ [accessed 20 February 2019].

Bullying

Bullying in the workplace is illegal in countries like Australia, but what is it? Examples may include persecuting or ganging up on an individual, making unreasonable demands or setting impossible work targets, making restrictive and petty work rules, constant intrusive surveillance, shouting, abusive language, physical assault, and open or implied threats of dismissal or demotion.

(Stone 2013, 549).

In other words, bullying can be done by co-workers and Board members as well as managers. Galanaki and Papalexandris (2013) describe it as behaviour that is repeated and aggressive and intended to be hostile or seen as hostile by the victim. Some of the effects on individuals include anxiety, irritability, feelings of depression, paranoia, mood swings, feelings of helplessness, lowered self-esteem, physical symptoms, social isolation and maladjustment, psychosomatic illnesses, depressions, helplessness, anger, anxiety, despair, burnout and lowered job satisfaction and well-being. To this depressing list of symptoms, one can add the impact of the behaviour of the bully and the response of the bullied on other staff and the culture of the organisation. Organisational impacts include increased absenteeism, stress and turnover and decreased productivity and motivation (Quigg 2011).

The Australian Fairwork Ombudsman's website defines bullying this way:

> A worker is bullied at work if:
> - a person or group of people repeatedly act unreasonably towards them or a group of workers
> - the behaviour creates a risk to health and safety.
>
> Unreasonable behaviour includes victimising, humiliating, intimidating or threatening. Whether a behaviour is unreasonable can depend on whether a reasonable person might see the behaviour as unreasonable in the circumstances. Examples of bullying include:
> - behaving aggressively

> - teasing or practical jokes
> - pressuring someone to behave inappropriately
> - excluding someone from work-related events or
> - unreasonable work demands.

What isn't bullying is reasonable management actions carried out in a reasonable way such as performance appraisal, directing people how to work and maintaining rational workplace goals and standards. One of the key points to note in the Ombudsman's definition is "repeatedly" and another is the notion of the "reasonable person". In countries where there is legislation that covers bullying it's important to read the resources legislators provide, have a company policy about bullying and know when to ask for legal advice.

That's the pragmatic approach to the question of bullying. But the arts face a particular additional challenge. Quigg (2011), who has written an entire book about bullying in the arts, quotes research from Great Britain to the effect that more bullying occurs in the arts than in any other employment sector. This may be because there's a sense amongst managers and employees that the arts are different to other industries and that the same rules don't apply. She disagrees and so do I. The bullying that goes on in the arts is the same as in other organisations with one particular difference – our opinions are coloured by the notion of creative genius and artistic temperament. Artistic leaders of companies, particular people who are directors and choreographers and conductors have enormous individual power. This is used to pursue their artistic vision but can also be used to treat the people they work with with disrespect and even emotional and physical violence (Cray, Inglis & Freeman 2007). One does experience and hear stories of where abusive behaviour is allowed in order to get the show on and this may be the reason why there is a high incidence of bullying behaviour, particularly in the team-based world of the performing arts. But this is not the only sector where one can find bad behaviour. Ian McEwan's Booker Prize winning book *Amsterdam*, a book I confess that I don't like, has a composer as a main character. He turns out to be someone who will sacrifice the well-being of a young woman for his music but before that the event, he's pondering whether to back out of various engagements "by assuming the licence of the free artistic spirit, but he loathed such arrogance". Clive, the composer, goes on to say: "These types … managed to convince friends and families that not only their working hours, but every nap and stroll, every fit of silence, depression or drunkenness bore the exculpatory ticket of high intent … He didn't doubt that the calling was high, but bad behaviour was not a part of it" (McEwan 1999, 61–62). In Quigg's (2011, 187) words, "creative genius may yield 'great art' but often at a terrible cost; and the latter is the result of artists behaving badly and is indefensible in the true professional".

Paul Saintilan and David Schreiber 2018 (99–100) describe the sacking of Jeremy Clarkson from *Top Gear* by the BBC after his abusive behaviour when he didn't get a hot meal, and the Managing Director of the Metropolitan Opera Company firing Kathleen Battle for insulting staff. Their implication was that while non-profit companies can take ethical standards, it wasn't necessarily the best decision to fire someone over such a small issue as a meal when £150 million of revenue was at stake. In my view, that's the type of thinking that enabled people such as Harvey Weinstein continuing to work.

I pose the following question to my students and the result is always robust debate:

> The artistic genius may be hell to work with, but the end result (the art) is exceptional so behaviour deemed unacceptable in normal circumstances must be tolerated. Agree or disagree?

The conclusion that my students usually reach is that it's not appropriate to expect people to put up with bad behaviour from colleagues just because they are "artists". To deal with artistic bullies you need a written policy, be seen to be available so that people will tell you what's going on, to deal with rather than ignore complaints, provide training for managers and staff, give feedback to the bully and not to re-employ artists who are bullies. Having said that, in my experience, artists get away with bad behaviour more than anyone else. For example, I'm aware of a group of actors who took the almost unprecedented step of complaining to management via their agents and union about a director's behaviour in the rehearsal room. They were told that the director and the production were too important to the company and that the director couldn't be removed. I'm also guilty of allowing a director who was known to be verbally abusive to stage managers to be re-employed. In the latter case, we provided feedback to the artist via their agent, employed an experienced stage manager who had worked with them before and could "control" them to a degree and provided that person with instant access to a support team if and when required. I would have preferred not to employ the director but the company wanted their specialist skills for a production. In the end, the resulting rehearsal and production process was uneventful but it was a risk that some may think that I shouldn't have taken.

The subtitle of Quigg's (2011) book is "vocation, exploitation and the abuse of power". Her definition also includes the notion of corporate bullying in which organisations employ unfair terms and conditions of work such as pay, hours and workplace policies. Although working conditions for arts organisations in countries like Australia are covered either by union agreements or legislation, there is still a tendency, particularly around working hours in arts organisations, for a bullying environment to be created. This may be because arts organisations under under-resourced and people have an intense commitment to the art, but it could also be because there is not strategic management of time and workloads. For example, in Australia there is usually a requirement in industrial awards for a ten-hour break to occur between work shifts with a financial penalty built in until that break can occur. One would think that this financial cost would be enough to prevent people from being forced to work unconscionable hours but this is not always the case.

Quigg (2011, 170) says that increased managerialism including the pressure to be more efficient and effective and have more control over what people do at work can create an environment where bullying may be more likely. Complaints about bullying sometimes are focused around performance appraisal. In some cases, someone's low resilience may mean that they think they've been bullied when they've received legitimate but critical feedback. On the other hand, it might be tempting to treat someone in a way that might be construed as bullying just because you want them to leave the organisation. Avoid the temptation and put in place a proper performance review and exit strategy.

The other challenge for managers, and again this is particularly true in the arts, is that people will put up with bullying behaviour because "he's always been like that but he's good at his job" or "she doesn't mean to yell, she just gets carried away" or "I don't want to complain because people will think I'm a wimp". One has to create an organisational culture where people feel free to complain about bad behaviour. Ultimately, one has to accept that most bullying is done by supervisors and managers (Quigg 2011) and that it's particularly difficult for people to complain about their boss or someone in power over them. You have to monitor your behaviour. You have to set a good example. If you're abusive or petty or persecute people you don't like or demand excessive work hours from staff, others will feel free to do the same.

Regardless of one's personal views on unions, they can be important in providing a voice for workers in an individual sense as well as a collective sense. Their role can help ensure that stories are told and real grievances are aired. On the other hand, because their role is to support their members regardless of the circumstances, they can sometimes end up on the side of the bully or turn a case of reasonable performance management into a putative bullying case.

Written policies are important but they have to cover the right topics and be implemented through training. Quigg (2011, 54) notes that in a UK survey of theatre companies and arts centres, many of the written policies covered violence and physical threats but not more subtle insulting behaviour that can result in psychological damage.

As well as taking responsibility for your staff, you may also have to take responsibility for yourself. Just because you're a manager doesn't mean that you can avoid being bullied. Quigg's (2011) first case study is of a Managing Director being bullied by a Board member. I have seen CEOs of organisations bullied by the Chair of their Board. Sometimes this has involved shouting and even threats of physical violence. Other times it has involved micromanagement including impossible demands and ongoing undermining of the person. In such cases, you have to make a decision about how much you're prepared to put up with before your health and your sanity suffer. Is the Chair vulnerable to being removed or coming to the end of their tenure? Is the Chair unique in their behaviour or does the rest of the Board behave similarly? In my experience most CEOs (like most arts workers) will put up with more than they should because they love the organisation. For me, life's too short to be shouted at or abused.

Quigg (2011, 216) concludes her book by noting the concept of "permissibility" which is when staff believe that bullying is condoned. This can happen when witnesses who are empowered to act fail to stop the actions of a bully, when an arts organisation is "in thrall to a creative genius" and unfair behaviour is excused in the name of artistic excellence, and when arts workers themselves tolerate poor terms and conditions, thus condoning a corporate culture that undermines health and safety.

In response to the #MeToo movement, industry associations and companies across the world have adopted polices to stop harassment, discrimination and bullying has usually been included in that list. For example, Live Performance Australia and the Screen Producers Association have produced draft policies for companies to adapt and run training programs to help with their implementation. Jo Caust (2018, 97) makes the interesting point that it's harder to get away with a bullying leadership style now because "[c]ommunication devices such as phones and tablet computers mean there is much greater transparency and the capacity for exhibiting uncivilized behavior without being caught out is quite low".

Our employees want to work in companies where respect and autonomy are at the heart our organisational culture, not fear and control. We all have to take responsibility to create a culture that is positive and free from bullying.

See also: Artists, Boards, Harassment, Hours, Industrial Relations, Law, Occupational Health and Safety, Organisational Culture, People, Performance Appraisal, Unions

References

Caust, J. 2018a *Arts Leadership in Contemporary Contexts*, London: Routledge.

Cray, D., Inglis, L. & Freeman, S. 2007 "Managing the Arts: Leadership and Decision Making under Dual Rationalities", *The Journal of Arts Management, Law and Society*, 36(4), 295–313.

Fairwork Ombudsman, www.fairwork.gov.au/employee-entitlements/bullying-and-harassment [accessed 20 February 2019].

Galanaki, E. & Papalexandris, M. 2013 "Measuring Workplace Bullying in Organisations", *The International Journal of Human Resource Management*, 24(3), 2107–2130.

Live Performance Australia n.d. *Australian Live Performance Industry Code of Practice: Discrimination, Harassment, Sexual Harassment and Bullying* http://members.liveperformance.com.au/uploads/files/Combined%20-%20LPA%20Discrimination.H.SH.B%20resources%20-%20Consultation%20Draft%2023.02.2018-1519365284.pdf [accessed 20 February 2019].

McEwan, I. 1999 *Amsterdam*, London: Vintage.

Quigg, A. M. 2011 *Bullying in the Arts*, Farnham: Gower.

Saintilan, P. & Schreiber, D. 2018 *Managing Organizations in the Creative Economy: Organizational Behaviour for the Cultural Sector*, Abingdon: Routledge.

Stone, R. J. 2013 *Managing Human Resources* (4th ed), Milton, QLD: John Wiley & Sons.

Notes

1 The British Commonwealth including countries such as England, Scotland, Wales, Northern Ireland, Eire, Canada, South Africa, Australia, Singapore, New Zealand.

2 http://bighart.org/

3 Based on Herzberg's theory of motivation.

4 University Vice-Chancellors.

5 Now called Arts Centre Melbourne.

6 One of which I held.

7 Examples taken from the Australian Corporations Act 2001.

8 https://financialservices.royalcommission.gov.au/Pages/default.aspx [accessed 22 February 2019].

9 I told this story at the 2009 International Symposium of Theater Arts and Cultural Administration in Taiwan and what follows is an edited and updated version of that paper.

10 The General Manager of the Perth Theatre Trust, owner of the Centre, in response to the article said that the main stage of the venue reached 62% capacity in 2011/12, the industry average.

11 Peppercorn = $1 per year, i.e. literally no rent.

12 Originally called the Victorian Arts Centre and now Arts Centre Melbourne.

13 For example, in 2008 we weren't allowed to display posters advertising our subscription season even though we had for every year prior to that.

14 Dulux Colour Award – MTC Theatre; Victorian Architecture Medal for Public Architecture – MTC Theatre and MRC; Public Buildings Award – MTC Theatre and MRC.

15 www.a-r-m.com.au/

16 E.g. Australian Museum (Canberra), Storey Hall (Melbourne), extension to the Shrine of Remembrance (Melbourne).

17 Meaning: trick of the eye.

18 We share chillers, a laneway, a service corridor, fire systems, an electrical substation, sewerage pipes with our neighbours the Melbourne Recital Centre.

19 You can see this auditorium on the book cover.

20 We refused to "sell" the two main performance spaces and named them after the founder director, John Sumner, and an early important Australian playwright who worked for the Company, Ray Lawler.

21 Now called the Roslyn Packer Theatre.

22 My going-away present from MTC when I left in 2012 was to name the bar after me – it's now called the Tonks Bar.

23 www.goodfood.com.au/good-food/eat-out/lone-diners-united-in-their-taste-for-melbourne-eateries-20140724-zucr2.html [accessed 13 November 2014].

C

Change

Introduction

Art is about change. Culture is about change. As Heinze said in an editorial in an Arts Management Newsletter (2013), arts organisations should have the capacity to change – in response to challenges from the environment and because of audience and stakeholder expectations. They should also be organisations where people are encouraged to challenge the ways things are done in order to more effectively use limited resources.

Most of the discussion around change in organisations is about how hard it is. But as it's inevitable, understanding the resistance to change is as important as creating a resilient organisation that can deal with change. Jim Phills (2005, 162) ran a number of arts leadership programs at Stanford University, and after discussions with the participants, concluded that "the notion of leadership as managing change in order to ensure the continued vibrancy and effectiveness of the organization was a recurring one". The equally telling point that he made was regardless of that belief, most of the arts leaders loved the idea of stability.

There's the change we seek, the unplanned change that is forced upon us, and the emergent change that just happens. Organisations change their current activities, they replace them with new ones and they undertake transformational changes, usually with new leadership or in times of crisis. We need to be ready for change. If you don't want to change anything then you're probably wrong. If you want to change everything, you're probably wrong. Even if you only want to make small changes, there will be resisters.

Resistance

In her PhD about the role of theatre practice in facilitating organisation innovation, Pässilä (2012) elegantly captures what she calls the "messy every day politics of organisational life" that get in the way of change and innovation:

> the complex feelings and emotions generated through interaction with practitioners and customers; established habits and attachments to routine ways of working that are resistant to change; individual and collective blame, apathy, and cynicism, and the silos created by them; the tensions within hierarchies; and the contradictory role assigned to managers and leaders, which asks them to be both the champions of change and the guardians of the status quo (36).

The list of why we resist change in the workplace when we're often inclined to embrace changes in our own lives such as new technology ranges from the pragmatic to the psychological. Change can lead to a loss of control, increased uncertainty, potential loss of status or even loss of a job, loss of colleagues and even the symbolism of losing touch with the past. Underlying this list is fear and as a result, some people become intransigent either actively or passively. As well as fear, there's scepticism ("will it really make a difference?") and cynicism ("the bosses don't know what they're doing").

Only an intrepid few desire the uncertainty of change over the security of the status quo.
(Welch McCarville 2003, 23)

One will find resistance to reasonable changes, right decisions and logical strategic choices and all of the reasons behind the resistance will be good from someone's perspective. In organisations, there is what Schien (1988) calls a psychological contract between management and employees. This contract contains elements such as money in exchange for time at work, social need satisfaction and security in exchange for hard work and loyalty, opportunities for challenging work in exchange for high-quality work and creative effort. Schien says that this contact is constantly being negotiated and this can make changes processes difficult when people don't agree with the change in the contract. For example, when I worked in the Australian Broadcasting Corporation, jobs were perceived as being for life but funding cuts meant that departments were closed and positions were lost.

People want to defend their jobs and their work practices and the view from an operational perspective is often different to the view from management. There's also a natural tendency to resist the unknown. Belief comes into it as well. People may simply not believe that a new strategy will solve a problem or that management has the capacity to implement effective change. And they may be right.

Reading Thomas (2015) reminded me that resistance to change isn't always bad even though it's often framed that way in management textbooks. She points out that we do generally admire people who "resist" but that's usually about politics – resist Wall Street, resist apartheid, resist bad Government arts policy. But in organisations, resisters are usually viewed as conservative or fearful or selfish. Pfeffer and Sutton (2006, 185) note that sometimes "resistance to change is well-founded, well-intentioned, and actually helpful in keeping companies from doing dumb things. Even presumably good changes carry substantial risks because of the disruption and uncertainty that occur while the transformation is taking place."

Resistance can show itself in outright conflict involving unions and industrial action, but more likely in arts organisations, it will show itself through delays and detachment where staff have no investment in the process or the outcome. Strategies can be practical (withholding information) and fanciful (escapism), verbal (satire, cynicism) or physical (damaging property or deleting files).

Advice on how to get over such resistance includes investing in training and development, finding people who are open to change, creating an environment where employees can voice their concerns, improving communication, confirming what won't change, including resisters in the planning process, helping people with counselling and the final strategy, using coercion to get things done including getting rid of the resisters (Walmsley 2013; Onsman 1991). Hagoort (2005) has a slightly more positive take on this last point, suggesting that there should be special farewell parties for those who can't face the new world and want to explore opportunities elsewhere.

While most of the challenges listed under the heading of "change" in management textbooks tend to be the response of individuals to change, Walmsley (2013, 227) points out that one of the biggest barriers for arts organisations is money. Because they tend to be underfunded and under-capitalised and with limited financial reserves, they lack what he calls the "requisite development capital to embark on any meaningful process of change and innovation".

Another approach to resistance is to "recast [it] as a resource and something to be encouraged – even celebrated – in order to arrive at a new and shared consensus of understanding. The change agent's role, rather than pre-empting, controlling and eradicating resistance, should be to invite it, encourage it and harness its value" (Thomas 2015, 64).

In other words, reaction to change could be seen as thoughtful, productive or facilitative rather than problematic.

Undertaking Change

The most famous writer on organisational change is John Kotter (1996). His direction for change, quoted in every management textbook I've read, consists of eight stages:

1. Establish an urgency for change
2. Form a powerful guiding coalition
3. Create a vision that people understand and aspire to
4. Communicate the vision
5. Empower others to act on the vision
6. Plan for an create short-term wins
7. Consolidate improvements that produce more change
8. Institutionalise new approaches.

A more sophisticated take on Kotter's advice can be found in Bolman and Deal (2013). They look at organisational change through what they call "frames" – structural, human resources, political and symbolic which add richness and density to Kotter's model. For example, in order to create a sense of urgency, one needs to involve people and get input (human resources), network with key players (political) and tell a compelling story (symbolic). In communicating the vision, they suggest it's done not just with words but with deeds such as visible leadership involvement and ceremonies (symbolic) while one builds alliances and defuses opposition (political) (391).

Another famous management writer, Henry Mintzberg (2009) challenges Kotter's change model and asks, for example, what happens when the driving leader leaves and whether transformational change couldn't come from the bottom up or the middle out? He's right to ask those questions but it doesn't mean that a number of the practical steps in Kotter's model aren't worth doing no matter where the idea of transformation starts.

Hudson (2009, 301) says that there are two components central to change management – the head elements (vision and analysis) and the heart elements (people and their emotions). Often organisations will create a plan for change based on good analysis and reflective of the mission but fail to take into account that change is about people even when it's about technology or structure or output. A strategic change in direction usually means a change in culture and management can overlook the impact of that change. If change by definition leads to uncertainty, it's important not just to change the organisation but also the way people think about themselves and their capacity to operate in the new world (Hewson & Holden 2011). Sometimes, getting people to re-envisage their organisation will help them come up with ideas for change. Bolman and Deal (2013, 262) talk about the power of the metaphor and give some wonderful examples as organisations imagine what they are and what they might become, such as a maze becoming a well-oiled wheel, a wet noodle turning into an oak tree, an aggregation of competing teams becoming a symphony orchestra.

Where it goes wrong in Bolman and Deal's (2013, 390) view is when management relies mainly on reason and structure while neglecting the human, political and symbolic elements. Hudson lists a number of common problems under the headings of process (for example, missing out a stage, talking too much and saying too little, writing a memo instead of lighting a fire, no quick wins) and people (disrespect of the past, staff voice isn't heard, too few innovators, unclear benefits).

As leadership is about taking an organisation forward, each different leadership style is connected to change outcomes. There is no doubt that autocratic and charismatic political leaders can deliver change, but often at great cost (think Stalin, Hitler, Pol Pot). Transformational, participatory and relationship leaders are better suited to change in arts organisations. To be an effective change leader you need to be very clear about key issues and flexible about detail, understand people's frustrations, expect to be criticised and allow time for reflection (Hudson 2009, 326).

Even if you have all these skills in your kitbag, there'll be challenges which may differ according to whether you're a newcomer or you're already leading the organisation. For example, if you're inside and get promoted, there may be resistance from your colleagues to accepting you as their new leader, your organisational peers may be jealous, you may have a one-sided view of the organisation and have limited experience in introducing change. If you've come from outside, you probably don't have a complete picture of the problems and face a steeper learning curve but you may have a more even-handed approach to the overall picture (Thomas 2008).

The story told by Hewison, Holden and Jones (2013) about the Royal Shakespeare Company is one where change is driven by both an incomer and someone who knew the company well. In reflecting on the outcome, the authors conclude that because organisational change occurs in already stretched organisations and where short-term pressures can distract from pursuing long-term goals, leaders need to be deeply involved in the change process. Through this, they demonstrate confidence and thus may help overcome peoples' fear and uncertainty.

Examples

There are differences in the capacity to embrace change between arts organisations because of size and sector as well as other qualities such as financial capacity and leadership. For example, established institutions such as art museums are difficult to change because of their history. As De Paoli (2011, 3) says "[a] high degree of institutionalizing leads to the conservation of values [and] traditions". A new organisation may be more fleet of foot even though their very newness may be the reason that they don't have to change much. A small organisation may also have the capacity to flex in terms of staff numbers and operations in a way that a larger, more unionised organisation may not.

Given the presumption that all arts organisations will change at some point but acknowledging that no two organisations are the same, it is still worth learning from the change experiences of others.

Tusa (2007a, 28) tells the story of becoming the manager of the BBC World Service and it reminded me of being Station Manager of ABC Radio National. The underlying view of the BBC staff was:

> Good broadcasting was good broadcasting; it took place in the studio not in the office. It could not be improved by being passed through an additional filter of so-called good management. Institutional sluggishness can be as hard to overcome as actual open resistance.

This was exactly the view of most of the Radio National staff when I was there. In main ways, I failed in my job as station manager. Although a range of changes that I was part of designing and implementing can still be heard on the station 30 years later, I wasn't successful in convincing the broadcasters that they needed a "manager". My direct manager, an intuitive and inspirational leader, solved the problem. He co-opted one of the objectors into the management team and because our collective management voice now had a respected broadcaster as part of it, we were heard more clearly and got more done.

Pfeffer and Sutton (2006, 178) claim that change happens when:

1. People are *dissatisfied* with the status quo
2. The *direction* they need to go is clear (at least most of the time) and they stay focused on that direction

3. There is confidence conveyed to others – more accurately *overconfidence* – that it will succeed (so long as it is punctuated by reflective self-doubt and updating as new information rolls in)
4. They accept that change is a *messy process* marked by episodes of confusion and anxiety that people must endure.

There's a certain amount of truth in that first statement. At the ABC, very few people in Radio National were dissatisfied with the on-air sound or thought that any change, apart from more resources, was required. This made change a hard slog. On the other hand, people at MTC knew that they hadn't had a pay increase for a couple of years because of the company's financial situation and were more open to change.

An example where I was more successful in managing change was the move of MTC from its headquarters in South Melbourne to a refurbished building in Southbank. Our old offices and workshops in Ferrars St were such that visitors (including new Board members worried about risk) gasped with horror – gaps in the walls, uneven floors, 30-year air conditioning, ancient furniture, plastic and gaffer tape holding asbestos at bay. One would think that people would be thrilled to move into a newly renovated building closer to our theatres but Ferrars St also had great strengths. The space was huge with three big rehearsal rooms, large workshops and storage spaces, great points of interconnection between departments, a café in the heart of the building and an undeniable sense of history. In the new Sturt St building, although there were some wonderful aspects, the spaces were sometimes smaller and there was a different physical relationship between peers with people on different floors. To follow Hudson's point, we had to make sure that both the head and the heart elements worked. The pragmatic issues were solved by employing someone 12 months out whose only task was to focus on managing the change and ensuring that all department heads were deeply involved in the refurbishment design. The heart part meant lots of communication,

asking for ideas about improvements even after the move, introducing people to the building at all stages as it moved from building site to final product, having points of light-hearted celebration, particularly through the move process such as Best Packing Award, and capturing the history of Ferrars St with photos and anecdotes in an e-book that everyone could treasure. And it worked. For a large, complex organisation it was a successful move with even the regular naysayers agreeing that the result was a good one.

Cultural change can be more challenging than physical change. I heard an interesting story from a colleague who took over a major cultural institution. Within days they discovered that:

• The previous manager was a bully
• Managers were encouraged to compete with each other rather than to support each other
• People didn't actually know who their senior managers were
• Information was kept secret
• Staff meetings were done electronically
• The manager had delegated work but not reward or praise
• People weren't used to telling the truth or trusting each other.

The new manager's response was to introduce open face-to-face staff meetings, wander the building introducing themselves to staff, encourage the management team to share information and respect, use words like "trust" and "like" and "thank you" and demonstrate qualities of manners and care. The change process involved lots of hard work on the part of the manager and the main challenge was to overcome distrust. The result (which took time) was positive and the part of the story that moved me the most were some quotes from the staff in response to the changes: "you have given me back my wife"[1] and "you've helped me find the truth again".

Some interesting stories on change in other arts organisations include Hewison, Holden and Jones (2013) on positive change within the Royal Shakespeare Company (RSC) and

Walmsley (2013) for not so successful change in the West Yorkshire Playhouse.

Hewison, Holden and Jones (2013) tell the story of a new leadership team in the RSC and their attempts to rebuild the morale of the organisation, its critical reputation, improve stakeholder relations, solve financial challenges and solve long-term structural problems. They conclude that:

- Crisis can provide an opportunity for change but ambition and energy are what make change happen
- Experimentation and constant small-scale innovations help change to happen
- Changing things depends on creating confidence and trust
- Change needs to be tested internally and externally.

Their case study is also an interesting example of the power of symbols as the leadership team took the idea of "ensemble" out of the rehearsal room and into the whole of the organisation to provide a framework to bring people together. Other conclusions reached by the researchers include that leaders need to embody the values they promote, to lead the change process, to acknowledge the emotional life of the organisation, to provide conceptual simplicity in response to organisational and contextual complexity and to be at the heart of the organisation not at the top of a pyramid.

The problems with the change process at the West Yorkshire Playhouse which was designed to increase the organisation's resilience in the face of artistic and financial challenges were because

- Half the staff participated in the process and this delivered a false sense of democratic decision-making when many of the actual decisions came from the top
- Ambitious programming didn't come to fruition because of funding cuts
- There was a lack of clarity about the role and power of participants

- Not all line managers were brought into the process (Walmsley 2013).

The question of how many people are involved in the decision-making part of a change processes is one that doesn't have a clear answer. Consensus building through using teams can be a slow but fruitful process; bringing the resisters into the process can eventually win them over but can create blockages and negativity to begin with. People can become disillusioned when their views aren't taken on board. Hagoort (2005) points out that in times of crisis, interactive processes can't necessarily be used and external guidance or an interim or new management team might be required. Although I did lots of consulting with MTC staff in order to develop new strategies, I confess that the decision-making wasn't a participatory process. Another colleague going into an organisation in crisis didn't even do the consultative process. They came into the organisation with a strong vision, quickly built a new management team and implemented very quick, very public change to the structure and the output of the organisation and then spent time with staff to see what else could be done.

Conclusion

Change is unavoidable and it's "messy, complex, unpredictable, situation-specific, multi-authored and multidimensional" (Thomas 2015, 67). People are rightly nervous about what change will deliver for them personally and for the organisation they value. We have to make sure that we're proposing change for the right reasons and ensuring that all elements of the change process including the emotional well-being of staff are considered. This latter point doesn't mean that everyone needs to be happy about the process. As De Pree (1997, 9) says, "[a]ll of us do many things we don't agree with". But that if we want "to live or work in a true community", then we need to accept even if we don't agree. I think that this is an interesting insight into the world of work. We may decide not to accept a change we disagree with if it's ethically wrong or if it creates an environment that no longer suits our skills or desires. But if we've had a chance to speak and been listened to and a decision is made that isn't ours, acceptance is a gracious way of being part of a community.

See also: Offices, Organisational Culture, People, Resilience, Strategic Planning

References

Bolman, L. G. & Deal, T. E. 2013 *Reframing Organizations*, (5th ed), San Francisco, CA: Jossey-Bass.

De Paoli, D. 2011 "The Role of Leadership in Changing Art Institutions – The Case of the National Museum of Art in Oslo, Norway", Antwerp: 11th AIMAC International Conference.

De Pree, M. 1997 *Leading Without Power*, Holland, MI: Shepherd Foundation.

Hagoort, G. 2005 *Art Management: Entrepreneurial Style*, (5th ed), Delft: Eburon.

Heinze, D. 2013 "Editorial", *Arts Management Newsletter*, October.

Hewison, R. & Holden, J. 2011 *The Cultural Leadership Handbook*, Farnham: F Gower.

Hewison, R., Holden, J. & Jones, S. 2013 "Leadership and Transformation at the Royal Shakespeare Company", in Caust, J. (ed.) *Arts Leadership*, Melbourne: Tilde University Press, 144–158.

Hudson, M. *Change Management*, http://compass partnership.co.uk/pdf/CM.pdf [accessed 20 February 2019].

Hudson, M. 2009 *Managing Without Profit: Leadership, Management and Governance of Third Sector Organisations in Australia*, Sydney: UNSW Press.

Kotter, J. P. 1996 *Leading Change*, Boston, MA: Harvard Business School Press.

Minzberg, H. 2009 "Rebuilding Companies as Communities", *Harvard Business Review*, https://hbr.org/2009/07/rebuilding-companies-as-communities [accessed 20 February 2019].

Onsman, H. 1991 *How to Manage Change in the Workplace*, Sydney: ABC.

Pässilä, A. 2012 *Reflexive Model of Research-Based Theatre*, Finland [document provided by author].

Pfeffer, J. & Sutton, R. I. 2006 *Hard Facts, Dangerous Half-Truths, and Total Nonsense*, Boston, MA: Harvard Business School Press.

Phills, J. A. 2005 *Integrating Mission and Strategy for Nonprofit Organizations*, New York: Oxford University Press.

Schien, E. H. 1988 *Organisational Psychology*, New York: Prentice Hall.

Thomas, M. T. 2008 *Leadership in the Arts: An Inside View*, Bloomington, IN: AuthorHouse.

Thomas, R. 2015 "Resisting Change and Changing Resistance", in Beech, N. & Gilmore, C. (eds) *Organising Music: Theory, Practice, Performance*, Cambridge: Cambridge University Press, 61–71.

Tusa, J. 2007a *Engaged with the Arts*, London: I.B. Tauris & Co. Ltd.

Walmsley, B. 2013 "Rethinking the Regional Theatre: Organizational Change at West Yorkshire Playhouse", Bogota: 12th AIMAC International Conference, 224–237.

Welch, R. & McCarville, R. E. 2003 "Discovering Conditions for Staff Acceptance of Organizational Change", *Journal of Park and Recreation Administration*, 21(2), 22–43.

Chief Executive Officer

Starting

You've got the job. The contract is signed. You've started. It may be with a company that is in fine form or a company in crisis. Tulsa (2007a, 25) offers a saying about whether to take over a successful or failing institution: "Take on the one in deep shtuck. You can only make it better." Regardless of a good or bad scenario, what do you need to be able to start off well? It helps if the outgoing or interim CEO can:

- Create a positive environment amongst the staff about the forthcoming change
- Ensure that the strategic plan is in place and people are implementing it
- Have a distributed leadership model that means middle managers feel empowered to get on with their job while you learn yours
- Document processes and practices
- Be honest about the organisation and key staff's strengths and weaknesses.

One past CEO gleefully told me that while he'd kept notes on all sorts of organisational skeletons, he'd destroyed them all before he left. I had to painfully come up against the shaking bones one by one.

In a book on how to manage leadership transition in non-profit companies, Dym, Egmon and

Watkins (2011) make the good point that a leadership change-over isn't the six month recruit, select and hire process, but rather an 18-month transition process. And I would agree. It can take at least a couple of years for a new CEO of a medium to large arts company to understand the complexities of its operations.

The CEO's job is less structured, more exposed, requiring a wider range of skills than you have to apply in middle management, and it's a lonely position. Hudson (2009, 333) summarises the work of CEO under three headings:

- Purpose: focus on the primary purpose, ensure the strategy is clear, pay attention to quality, ensure internal services and value, secure the economics of the organisation and encourage innovation
- Processes: work relentlessly to deliver effective processes, make sure managers manage, think carefully about the big decisions, judge who to involve, pace decisions, take care over timing and communicate massively
- People: build a strong management team, create a close working relationship with the Board, and work in partnership with the Chair.

The irony of becoming CEO is that unless you've already experienced this position of power, you suddenly become an amateur. You've been given the job because of your expertise in something else: being a Marketing or a Development or a Production or a Finance Manager, or managing a different type or size of organisation. In your new position, you're no longer the person with the most knowledge. As de Pree (1997, 76) says, "[y]ou have to shift from acting as an expert to becoming a quick learner". That's why I'm not one of those people that starts at an organisation with a plan to change everything. Often a new CEO will come in determined to put their stamp on an organisation but that can mean discarding what's best about old ideas and practices without knowing enough about them. Change for change's sake is a pointless start to

a job. First, you need to know what, if anything, needs to be changed.

I've always wanted to find out more about the organisation than one can possibly know from talking to the interview panel, reading annual reports, checking media coverage and websites and listening to gossip. The knowledge you need has to be narrative-based as well, reflecting the experience of staff and stakeholders, so that in Dym, Egmon and Watkin's (2011, 237) words, "the vision comes alive". The first couple of months at MTC included a couple of meetings every day with staff and by the end of the process, I'd spoken to every permanent member of staff to find out their views on the company's strengths and weaknesses and their own dreams for the future. I also poured over the company's financial reports because without that pragmatic information, it's hard to create a context for the future. Another part of learning about MTC was simply sitting quietly in rehearsals and the theatrical bump-in process, watching the business of the company being acted (pun intended) out.

Advice from another arts manager for new CEOs when having those one-on-one conversations to create relationships is to explain:

- Who am I?
- What do I stand for – my values?
- What do I expect from you?
- What can you expect from me?

In other words, you're building a contract with them. You're offering transparency in exchange for trust.

Staff, particularly those that have been in the company for years, will usually look at a new CEO with some cynicism. The early communication process will help unlock some of that negativity, but in some cases it can't be done and people may have to leave. I had the particularly difficult situation at MTC where one of the senior management team was sure they were going to get the Managing Director's job, that is, the job I got. They spent the next 18 months actively trying to undermine me and trying to recruit other staff to their "team". In such a situation people will eventually see that you are making a difference and creating a more positive environment and will come back to your team. Sometime after the person who wanted my job left, I had to deal with another person who desperately wanted the position. They were much more honest about their desire and instead of stabbing me in the back were very straightforward in their strategy. They would simply cut out job advertisements from the newspaper that they thought I should apply for and leave them on my desk every Monday morning.

Another requirement of a new CEO is to be seen and to see. You need to help staff understand what you are doing and you need to go out of your way to learn about them, their skills, their fears and their strengths. In a very public and forensic examination of the CEO of the Australian Broadcasting Corporation after she was fired in 2018, she was described this way:

> She was absent. She was hostile. She didn't understand public broadcasting. And she moved like a ghost through the foyer of the ABC on the odd occasion she was even there.
>
> (Price 2018)

This is not the way you'd want to be remembered.

Along with building relationships with staff and stakeholders comes the challenge of building a relationship with the Board and particularly the Board Chair. While this can be a passive process, played out through Board meetings, it's better if you work more actively including meeting with the Chair before Board meetings and having a planning meeting with the Board focused on the company's long-term future as soon as you feel confident that you have enough understanding of the organisation and the environment.

Corrigan (1999) spends half a chapter talking about the role of the Fool in *King Lear* and how every CEO could do with someone to play that truth-telling role because staff, concerned about their appraisal or their pay or their future and worried about the CEO's power,

may be tempted to tell you want you want to hear. The relationship with a boss can be uneasy because for the employee, the CEO is potentially both supporter and evaluator. Corrigan says that you need to look for a Fool because "he (sic) not only tells the king what he thinks, but he does so without being asked" (Corrigan 1999, 199).

How do you ensure that as CEO you can get to the truth? Part of it is using your power modestly. People need to know that they will not be punished for telling uncomfortable truths. Part of it is to have regular, open discussions with your management team about the state of the company. Some CEOs will have a mentor or a coach but they can't tell you what's going on inside the company. If you're lucky enough to work in an effective co-leadership model, then you'll find your support and your truth telling in your partner.

Someone suggested having a section about "a day in the life of a CEO" but my answer is that there's no single day that's like any other. Your work as CEO consists of all the topics and challenges and relationships covered in this book … and then some.

Leaving

So you did a fabulous job and you're thinking about leaving. How long should you stay as a CEO? And the answer is "it depends". If the fit is right, your relationship with the Board is good, your partnership with your Artistic Director and/or your management team is effective, then you will want to stay for more than a couple of years. If you are only going to stay for three or four years, you'll have time for some new, modest initiatives, maybe a new major funding source or two and to build a good team but you won't have time to do undertake and implement any major changes.

Perhaps I was just very ineffective but it took from 1994 to 2009 to do the three things I originally set out to do when I started at MTC. I had to solve the financial crisis, build a theatre and find new headquarters for the organisation and all of that took considerably longer than

I planned. In each circumstance I needed not just the support of stakeholders but major financial contributions. With the Southbank Theatre, the building process itself was an extremely effective 18 months because we had a great brief, good architects and a well-managed building company but trying to find the right site and the right funding mix took a decade. With the HQ project, again we had all the right elements to make it work but we had to raise $5 million and we were halfway there when the Global Financial Crisis hit and our fundraising ground to a holt. As did our building plan. This was a lucky outcome for the producers of the TV series *The Librarians* because it meant they could borrow the building in its pre-renovated state to film their show although I did watch the last episode of the first series with my heart in my mouth as the "library" burnt to the ground.

Once the theatre was open and we moved into our new HQ, I decided to stay for another year just to enjoy an office with light, windows that opened, a view of a telegraph pole and a gum tree, flat floors, straight walls and a door that could close if required – none of which I'd experienced for the previous 15 years. Just when I was ready to leave, the Artistic Director reached the same conclusion so I stayed to oversee the transition … which took somewhat longer than planned as the new AD couldn't start full time for 12 months. So two years later than planned I finally left MTC.

Sometimes, the leaving is even harder. You don't get on with your Chair; the staff aren't as open to change as you'd like; you can't find the financial resources to put your dream into action; no matter how hard you try, the funding bodies decide to defund you; your Board attempts to micromanage you. The two times I've left organisations because I was unhappy were because of incompetent or problematic bosses. No matter how much I loved the organisation, life was too short to be tormented on a daily basis. It's not that every day at work needs to be a happy one but if you are going to perform at your best, you need to be able to do so without the interference of another's poor management skills.

How can you best support the organisation in transition because much can be lost in this process? Transitions absorb time and energy from Boards and staff. They are costly.

Credibility may be sacrificed. Funders and partners wonder if the organization has lost its way, whether it will have the ability to carry our programs, and whether it is trustworthy. Program development tends to slow or stop, awaiting the approval and guidance of the new leader. Staff may grow indecisive or contentious without a leader to guide. Organizational memory can be lost.

(Dym, Egmon & Watkins 2011, 4)

During the transition the organisation has two tasks to manage – the process of finding the new CEO or co-leader and the day-to-day business of the organisation. This is why it's often good to have an interim CEO.[2] Usually organisations will look internally because that person comes with understanding of the company, its culture, its operations, its finances. This may also be a good development opportunity for that person. However, if that person is a candidate for the job, although it will provide the Board with a chance to see them at work in the desired position, it can be devastating if they aren't successful. In my experience, finding an outside expert who doesn't want the job is often a better approach. If there is someone in the organisation who has the potential to be the next CEO then their development opportunities should be ongoing – access to training, short-term acting roles, special projects – not just waiting until the CEO resigns.

See also: Board, Co-leadership, Leadership, People, You

References

Corrigan, P. 1999 *Shakespeare on Management*, London: Kogan Page.

De Pree, M. 1997 *Leading Without Power*, Holland, MI: Shepherd Foundation.

Dym, B., Egmont, S. & Watkins, L. 2011, *Managing Leadership Transition for Nonprofits*, Upper Saddle River, NJ: Pearson Educational.

Hudson, M. 2009 *Managing Without Profit: Leadership, Management and Governance of Third Sector Organisations in Australia*, Sydney: UNSW Press.

Price, J. 2018 "Guthrie's Morale Boost Fail Was Last Straw for Miserable ABC Staff", 25 September 2018, *Sydney Morning Herald*, www.smh.com. au/national/guthrie-s-morale-boost-fail-was-last-straw-for-miserable-abc-staff-20180924-p505p2.html [accessed 20 February 2019].

Tusa, T. 2007a *Engaged with the Arts*, London: I.B. Tauris & Co Ltd.

Coffee

I can say with some certainly that "coffee" (or your social beverage of choice) will not be in the index of any management textbooks. But it should be because our job is about relationships and there is research to show that when people hold a warm beverage, they tend to feel closer to the person with whom they are conversing (Moss, Callanan & Wilson 2012, 24).

In an article about how to design offices to get more communication and connection, Waber, Magolfi and Lindsay (2014) tell the story of a company which wanted to increase sales but didn't know which behaviours would help. The researchers used sociometric badges to map what 50 sales executives did throughout the day and the results showed that when a salesperson increased interactions with co-workers on other teams by 10%, their sales grew by 10%. The next question was how to design the office space to get sales people to run into colleagues. Answer: coffee. They had one coffee machine for every six people so they stripped them out and put in fewer but bigger ones and created a large cafeteria in place of a smaller one that few people used. Sales rose by 20%.

MTC had a café when I arrived and had done for a number of years. The story was that the Artistic Director (normally the calmest of men) couldn't operate without at least two macchiatos before 9am and as the building was stuck in an industrial wilderness without a coffee shop to be seen, the company decided to get an expresso machine. From that decision flowed a space in which fresh good food could also be obtained.

It was a space in which people from different departments caught up; where special events acknowledging cast arrivals and staff departures were held; where great savings were made on productivity because people were happy to come to MTC for a meeting knowing its reputation for muffins and handmade sausage rolls; where actors (usually poor) could get a cheap, healthy, fresh meal.

At two points during my time with the company, the question of whether we should have the café at all arose. Both times the question was driven by money. The first case was about operational costs – we subsidised the café. When the company was in debt and we were desperately looking for expenditure cuts (as well as new income sources), this was an obvious area to consider. So I did – and rejected the idea. The café was now so central to the culture of the organisation, that the damage would have far outweighed any short-term, modest financial gains.

The second time was when we were short of money to finish off the refurbishment of our new headquarters in Southbank. The University property people raised the question of the café in every design meeting but each time I pushed back, with the challenge to them to find other savings and the challenge to myself to raise enough money through our capital campaign to pay for it. And in the end, we got it. A small space admittedly, but light and airy with some greenery outside and the off-cuts of the beautiful jarrah floor from the Southbank Theatre foyer to provide "free" decoration.

And there is evidence to prove that a simple way of building higher performing, more cohesive teams is to encourage people to eat together. Whether it's free or subsidised food or bringing takeaway coffee to a meeting, there's more chance of people working together in a more timely and effective one if you do (HBR Editor 2015). The point is that investing in collective staff benefits is worthwhile if it helps bring people together, helps them work harder, rewards them, add to the positive culture, and if they are valued by the staff. It's research like that that justifies my sense of pride in winning those battles with the Board when I walk past MTC's HQ on the way to my current workplace and see the olive tree and herbs growing at the front of café.

In an article about how to get people who don't work for you to do things for you, Craumer (2013) includes an important coffee-related piece of advice. Pick up an extra coffee for the person who's helped you out … or take fruit to the project meeting or sweets to the presentation. As she says: "It's simple, but true: we like to be fed" (188). And it's not just the provision of coffee per se that's important, it's who provides the coffee. In an article about women in leadership, Ladkin (2010) describes a variety of positive and negative organisational cultures and how they can enable or frustrate women's participation. In one positive case, the clue to the success of the company in this area was in a simple gesture made by a male manager. He not only offered the researcher a coffee, but went off to get it – plus one for his secretary.

Of course, there are moments when it's a better use of your time if someone else gets the coffee while you get on with the meeting. I had a series of very smart assistants who had a schizophrenic job: half the time they were negotiating copyright licenses and the other half doing less than glamorous work such as filing – and getting the coffee. The important point was that it was made clear from the position description and the job interview that providing such services was part of the job so there were never any grumbles that such work was below them.

Having supported MTC's coffee culture for years, I finally gave up drinking it. This decision was a combination of being a coffee snob and (I'm sorry if this is going to insult my American readers) one too many trips to the USA and putting up with their bad coffee. When I got back to work and announced this change in behaviour I was expecting either pity ("you poor thing, was it hard?") or sarcasm ("how are you going to survive the next management meeting?") but I what didn't expect was hurt. The staff in the café, who'd all learnt how to make my coffee just the

way I liked it were upset and disconcerted that I'd given up. They thought that it was their fault. This was an unexpected reminder that people do care about doing their job well, even when it's just making a cup of coffee for the boss.

See also: CEO, Gender, Hiring, Motivation, Offices, People

References

Craumer, M. 2013 "When the Direct Approach Backfires, Try Indirect Influence", in Hill, L. A. & Lineback, K. (eds) "Managing your Boss", in *HBR Guide to Managing Up and Across*, Boston, MA: Harvard Business Review Press, 185–188.

HBR Editor 2015 "Collaboration: Team Building in the Cafeteria", *Harvard Business Review*, December, 24–25.

Ladkin, D. 2010 "Creating an Aesthetic of Inclusivity: A New Solution to the 'Problem' of Women Leaders", in Kay, S. & Venner, K. (eds) *A Cultural Leader's Handbook*, London: Creative Choices, 32–39.

Moss, S., Callanan, J. & Wilson, S. 2012 *The Moonlight Effect*, Melbourne: Tilde University Press.

Waber, B., Magnolfi, J. & Lindsay, G. 2014 "Workplaces That Move People", *Harvard Business Review*, November, 92(11), 69–77.

Co-Leadership

Introduction

When I started work as General Manager at Melbourne Theatre Company 15 years ago, I understood that I was 2IC[3] to the Artistic Director, Roger Hodgman. The Board had taken a punt in appointing me. Although I'd managed radio stations, I hadn't managed a theatre company and the company was in financial trouble. Within minutes I realised that I didn't actually have a boss but rather a partner in trying to solve the problems we faced. This was partly because like every Artistic Director I've ever met, Roger wanted to be in the rehearsal room more than the office. And partly because our skills were complimentary when it came to solving problems. He knew lots about theatre and I knew lots about managing people and resources. We had to work together to save the company. This type of relationship continued with two successive Artistic Directors.

In 2005, I asked an ivy-league management academic what he thought about co-leadership models and his response was: "don't be ridiculous – it never works". My response was: "Yes it does. MTC is the living proof." He continued: "No it doesn't – it's never an equal partnership, someone always has to be the boss." It clearly wasn't worth continuing the conversation but his response irritated me. A couple of years later, there was an article in the *Harvard Business Review* about what was called "complimentary" leadership (Miles & Watkins 2007) and I thought, finally, the academic and business worlds are starting to see the benefits of what the performing arts world has been practicing for years.[4]

In my spare time while managing MTC, I taught a unit in advanced arts management at the University of Melbourne where Kate MacNeill was the program coordinator. We were sitting around having coffee one day, chatting about life – and leadership in the arts. She said, "Is there any research about this subject?" And that was the beginning of our work together.[5] Much of what follows is based on the research we did, interviewing the leaders of Australia's major performing arts companies[6] plus some overseas leaders for comparison. Between us, we've written papers on gender and co-leadership, structure and co-leadership, authenticity and co-leadership and co-leadership *per se*.

The language of co-leadership includes words like "shared" and "joint" and "complementary" and "dual", "merged" and "invited" (see, for example, Järvinen, Ansio & Houni 2015), but as co-leadership is the phrase that people in the arts tend to use, that's the one we used to describe the working relationship between two (and sometimes three) senior executives.

In one the early academic papers on co-leadership O'Toole, Galbraith and Lawler (2002) listed 25 examples of such partnerships across 19 companies with financial services, entertainment and computer companies strongly

represented. In discussing why the idea of shared leadership hadn't taken off, the authors concluded: "this resistance to the notion of shared leadership stems from thousands of years of cultural conditioning. We are dealing with a near-universal myth: in the popular mind, leadership is always singular" (65). And that's clearly still true. In the top 827 companies that *Harvard Business Review* looked at to find their best-performing CEOs in 2014, only five had co-CEOs (Ignatius 2014) and there didn't appear to be any in their 2018 list.

Miles and Watkins (2007) provide examples of complementary leadership in the business world including those based on task (where the CEO looks after external matters and the COO[7] looks after internal matters), expertise (e.g. one with deep technical knowledge; one with general knowledge), cognitive difference (e.g. one creating compelling visions and strategies; the other implementing them) and role differences (e.g. the diplomat versus the warrior). The image that my students love the most is that of 17th-century pirate ships where the division was between the Captain (who led the battle) and the Quartermaster (who looked after the injured and the loot) (Rao 2010).

While in arts organisations such as museums, the leadership model tends to be the corporate standard, in many performing arts companies around the world, one sees a co-leadership model. Sometimes the Artistic Director will be the CEO, sometimes the Managing Director/General Manager and sometimes it's formally a joint CEO arrangement. But regardless of the technical organisational structure, the practice tends to be a shared role with the Board, the senior managers and the staff all viewing both people as leaders.

So when are two heads better than one? O'Toole, Galbraith and Lawler (2002, 68) say that it's "when the challenges a corporation faces are so complex that they require a set of skills too broad to be possessed by any one individual". Arts organisations, particularly those operating in the non-profit world with their ongoing tension between mission and money, are viewed as complex organisations. Whether companies such as those in the Australian Major Performing Arts Group were started by artists or entrepreneurs or collectives, the majority of them have moved to a co-leadership model with the exception of the orchestras where the Managing Director tends to be the CEO with a part-time, often overseas-based, Chief Conductor.

Roles, Skills and Traits

At its most simplistic, two things need to happen within arts organisations: art is either created or presented or displayed, and money is found to pay for it. Some people will take the view that as Artistic Directors exhibit traits that are creative, unpredictable, iconoclastic, spontaneous and socially critical, they are not necessarily well-positioned to look after the more rational, ordered parts of an organisation's needs (Beard 2012a). There's often an attempt to differentiate between the artist and the manager this way:

- Intuitive v rational
- Bohemian v Confirmist
- Low value if it can be planned v high value if it can be planned
- Things cannot be absolutely assessed v everything can be measured
- Money is not the only measure v money is the universal measure
- Unpredictable v predictable (quoted in Chew & Hallo 2015).

This reads more like a division between an anarchist and a neoliberal rather than the Artistic Directors and General Managers that I've known.

Another view is expressed in an interview with Jeremy Isaacs, then CEO of Covent Garden, where he takes the position that artists can be managers and that the best person to make decisions within arts organisations should be the person whose priorities are artistic. But at the same time "boundaries have to be set – will it ready on time; can we afford it; will the realisation of this piece prevent other people from realising their pieces?" (Fitzgibbon & Isaac

1997, 43). So while the artist *can* sort out the money, they may not want to or be best placed to do so. As can be seen in the *Artistic Leader* section, a number of our interviewees talked about the challenge of trying to balance their artistic expression with their role as organisational leader. As an arts manager working with an Artistic Director, you have to be continually aware of that tension.

All our interviewees, whether Artists Directors (AD) or General Manager/Managing Directors/Executive Director (GM), believed in the primacy of the art and this means the artist should (or at least appear) to be the organisational leader, but there was an acknowledgement that the artist often doesn't have the time or interest or skill set to lead the organisation alone. Some quotes help to illustrate this point:

> Really the fundamental job of the general manager is to enable the art to be made. [AD2][8]

> the company wouldn't run with just me as the CEO – it would be – fall apart into a chaotic shemozzle fairly quickly. [AD6]

> [The Artistic Director]'s just not interested in budgets and dealing with sponsors and strategy and policy development and all those sorts of areas. ... I get excited about trends and looking back at the information and churning figures through to see where we might be heading. [GM7]

The integrity and vision of the artistic leadership was regarded by our interviewees as crucial to the success of the company:

> you have to allow the artistic director to dream and come up with the craziest maddest ideas possible, but then be able to, and pull them back or coach them into seeing a different point of view if it's necessary. [GM]

There's a great quote from a stage director about the traditional perception of the difference between the Artistic Director and the Managing Director:

> One of them is supposed to "Yes" and "everything is possible" and such things and the other is supposed to say "No" and "No" and "No" and "No"!
>
> (Røyseng 2008, 41)

A more subtle view is expressed by Alice Nash, Executive Producer and co-CEO of Back to Back Theatre:

> I believe our collective job … is never to say "no" to the artistic team. In practice this involves listening as closely as possible to what the artists want to achieve, and then finding the means to make it happen.
>
> (Grehan & Eckersall 2013, 27)

In a co-leadership model, the role of CEO is divided with some parts shared and some parts managed separately. Usually, both leaders will participate in strategic planning and artistic planning but the public profile of the company must always be closely aligned to its artistic endeavours. In our research the charismatic presence of the artistic leaders was often referred to as a critical aspect of attracting audiences and fundraising while the GM may be engineering the encounters and closing the deals. Usually the GM will oversee the fundraising department but the AD is the person that all the donors want to engage with. Similarly, the GM will manage the Marketing department but the AD will want to be deeply involved in brand development. The two leaders will often share the management of people and stakeholders but most of the resource issues (money, buildings) will be managed by the GM. However, the two positions, although different, were seen by our interviewees as inescapably interdependent. The notion of a tension between the artistic goals of the company and its financial sustainability was seen as a productive tension rather than a potential conflict – almost an integral part of the conditions under which the artistic outcomes were achieved.

A number of interviewees talked about the importance of having complementary skills:

> The most important thing is that your co-CEO should have complementing abilities. So I wouldn't particularly want to work with someone who was very flighty and impulsive and not as methodical because I think that tends to be my sort of thing. I tend to be a bit impulsive. I like to be flexible. I like to make decisions probably on the go and at the last minute. And I like to work with someone who's very sensible, who plans ahead, who's flexible so that you can react but they can give you that support. And I tend to think of myself as being very right brain and the Executive Director tends to be very left brain. [AD1]

A common theme emerged that it was the responsibility of the GM to adjust and adapt their own work style to complement and suit their artistic partner. Numerous GMs made claims such as "you adapt to any different personality type" [GM12] and "he is, who he is and I just adapt to practices around to suit him … it's part of that flexibility of bringing up the rear and making sure that that person is there and then supporting him through their goals" [GM15].

The ability to "develop the bit that is missing" [GM3] seemed to stem from the acknowledgement that the art form and the work of the AD is central to the vibrancy of the organisation. One GM stated "there's no point in an institution thriving if the art doesn't. The art's got to come first in the minds of everyone" [GM14]. This focus on the art, and an understanding of the nature of the Artistic Director's role, possibly from a previous history and knowledge of the arts, seems to be a key requirement of the GM in dual leadership arrangements in the performing arts.

This leads us to a discussion of the GM as a servant leader, serving the art and the AD. Some writers such as Lapierre (2001) believe that only the artist can be the leader and that the GM in their service or support is "just" a manager. In a conversation with someone who teaches leadership in the corporate world, they were equally dismissive about the idea of equality in such co-leadership relationships. From their perspective, in an AD/GM combination the artist was likely to be the leader, providing vision and direction for the organisation, and the GM was "simply" a manager doing administrative tasks. Chew and Halo (2015, 131) also believe that co-leadership is a myth: "in reality, one person will usually dominate, so there is no equality of power". Of course, there are areas where one person will have a stronger opinion or a stronger right to an opinion, but this doesn't mean that overall the power is uneven.

While all the performing arts Managing Directors and General Managers that we have interviewed saw the AD as the mission driver of the organisation, there was no sense that they saw themselves as "just" administrators. While the shared vision for the company might be encapsulated in the artistic vision, both leaders appear well aware that the success of the company relies on their joint contributions. In other words, the AD in the best co-leadership arrangements acknowledges the essential leadership contribution made by the GM. Not that novelist Margaret Atwood would agree. In her book *Hag-seed* based on Shakespeare's *The Tempest*, the Prospero figure is the Artistic Director of a theatre company and the evil Duke of Milan role is played by company's General Manager:

> Finding the money had been Tony's thing. A lesser thing: the money was only a means to an end … Felix the cloud-riding enchanter, Tony the earth-based factotum and gold-grubber.
>
> (Atwood 2016, 12)

Needless to say, I refuse to identify with a bad character.

If we believe that both AD and GM are leaders, another perspective is that they are different types of leaders with the artistic leader representing a "transformational" style and the manager representing a "transactional" approach. The former is focused on relationship development and achieving change while the latter is task-oriented, outcome-driven and focused on achieving short-term goals (Caust 2010). However, a good GM is going to want to be transformational in their relations with staff in the same way that the artist manager wishes to be transformational with other artists and audiences. In research by Inglis, Cray and Freeman (2006), they concluded:

> Despite the fact that all four organizations were highly project driven, with deadlines to meet, key performance indicators to achieve for government and donor bodies, budgetary constraints, and high standards of performance, both administrative and artistic to meet, there was little evidence that the leaders were transactional with their staff (10).

However, interestingly, they also concluded that the focus of the GMs (who were the CEOs in their research) was "to ensure the financial security and long-term survival of the organization" and that the focus of the ADs was "more on short-term artistic recognition". They base this conclusion on the position that "it is essential that the artistic direction of the organization enhances [the Artistic Director's] reputation among peers" (3). While for a narcissistic leader this may be their purpose, for most arts leaders it's the passion for creating the art, not the passion for self-aggrandisement that's important. In my experience, they have a clear interest in the long-term survival of the company because without that framework, how can they make their art?

Benefits

Given the complexity of two people working so closely together, what are the benefits of the co-leadership model for the organisation? The starting point is that it frees the artist to concentrate on the art but still drive the mission. The most optimistic position is the hope that "the whole is greater than the parts" and that the resulting shared decision-making will benefit from the synergy of two minds at work. A more pragmatic position is that it solves the problem of not being able to find one person with all the skills to lead and manage a complex organisation.

Ralph Myer (2014), then Artistic Director of Belvoir Theatre, described the relationship this way:

> It's a winning combination, and one that allows the artistic director to keep wearing rags and doing the frankly extremely difficult job of programming and inspiring a season, while the general manager can power dress and focus on the pragmatic task of implementing whatever harebrained and nutty ideas the artistic director has had. It's ying and yang and good cop, bad cop all at the same time.
>
> The key glue in this relationship is trust. I don't try and do Brenna's [Hobson, the company's General Manager at the time] job, except when she's wrong, and on the whole she doesn't try and do mine. The truth is, I'd be a terrible general manager, but it's surprising how many artistic directors get involved in stuff they really should stay out of (9).

His comments capture the nature of the relationship so well that here are some more of his insights:

> Good general managers have well-honed artistic instincts. And good artistic directors love pulling a crowd and making a buck. But broadly speaking this structure allows each of us to work to our strengths, rather than having to be someone who we are not.
>
> Brenna and I share an office now, so we can fight all the time, but until I moved in last year, I would spend an hour or so sitting in the armchair opposite her desk each morning rolling through – and fighting out – the issues of the day, finding practical, affordable, sustainable solutions to the difficult task of producing unaffordable, impractical and unsustainable theatre.
>
> The critical thing is that we can battle this stuff out because we're separate people. It'd be very hard to do this if both our jobs were rolled into one position.

Another description of a co-leadership relationship, this time from a researcher (Reid 2013), also tells the story well: "they each understand and have lived the other's reality". Her AD and GM share a similar approach to work, they hold back rather than confront, they have different personalities (102) and although they relate closely in their professional life, they only socialise outside the theatre once a year (103). The qualities that I particularly like, confirmed by staff, is "Everything is undertaken naturally with good humor and good understanding" (103).

Another perspective is offered by Simon Webb, who was the Director of Orchestral Management at the City of Birmingham Symphony Orchestra, when reflecting on the link between the organisation and creativity:

> I think ... that the two are inseparable: there is no single part of the operation that you could consider either as artistic or operational ... If any time we are tempted to look at one part of the operation without considering the others we force ourselves to bring other aspects in to the discussion. The danger of having one part of the organisation thinking artistically, one part thinking financially and one part operationally is that things just start to unravel; what we have done over a number of years here is to make sure that that conversation is right at the heart of everything. Whenever somebody is making a very strong economic point we would always bring in the artistic balances and vice versa, and that is how you make the strong decisions.
>
> (Webb & Dowling 2015, 256)

Given these benefits, even if your organisation doesn't have a formal co-leadership structure, you may want to develop a shared leadership regime anyway. If it's a small organisation where the Board Chair is an important volunteer contributor, then that's the relationship it's important to develop. If you have a deputy, then sharing leadership and management roles rather than simply delegating work may be effective.

What Makes It Work?

Miles and Watkins (2007) suggest four qualities of effective complimentary leadership and three of the four were topics that dominated our research:

1. Common Vision
2. Common Incentives
3. Communications
4. Trust.

In our research (MacNeill, Reynolds & Tonks 2013), 38 of the 46 leaders mentioned the need for a shared vision and values for an organisation in a co-leadership arrangement.

> I think we've got the basic philosophy right, the intention and the sort of shared aims, everything else will look after itself, then you wipe ego out of the equation, there is nothing to worry about except communication. [AD9]

> I think as long as the two people that are doing it are on the same page there's not an issue. If you've got someone who's diametrically opposed to what you're doing, then yeah, it won't work. [AD6].

The artist creates the vision, but the manager has to "interpret the vision and sell it to the world at large" (Caust 2010, 577).

Communication was a recurring theme with 44 leaders commenting on it. Although it was less intense in organisations such as orchestras where the Chief Conductor was often part time and overseas, where a true co-partnership did exist, the communication was intensely regular.

Most of that communication just takes place about making meetings he might say what you doing for lunch, let's have a coffee and we'll talk about a few things. [AD3]

> We have a lot of coffees – which sounds big wanky but it's actually good to get out of an office environment and discuss particular issues. [GM8]

> He rings me every lunchtime. … and then maybe once a week we'll see each other in evening. Or half a day on the weekend. … Because we discuss everything. [GM5]

Trust between the Artistic and Managing Director was mentioned by 70% of those interviewed. Those who commented on trust mentioned its high importance, making claims such as "trust I think is the most important" [AD6] and "that's probably the biggest thing, is trusting each other" [GM20]. This development of a sense of trust appears to aid the decision-making process with many respondents commenting along the lines of "there's enough trust between the two of us to have the difficult conversations when we need to" [GM16]. Trust develops over time, "[it was] kind of a process, and me learning to trust him" [GM5] and "[trust is] normally borne of experience of each other … I think a year is about enough. You'll know whether you've got a marriage or not at the end of that, and whether you should get into bed together or stay in bed together" [AD19].

As you can imagine, the question of common incentives didn't come up in conversation with our arts leaders at all.

Another required quality for the relationships to work that regularly appears in academic literature is conflict management skills (Reid & Karambayya 2009), to which I would add experience in/passion about the art form and the capacity and willingness to make joint decisions. In our research, decisions that affected the organisation as a whole and impacted the managers' respective responsibilities were often discussed together: "Most of the big decisions we do together, we definitely do together" [AD10] and "we try and consult on things that are very obviously public in terms of the organisation, its message, its branding, its core values and so on" [GM7]. The interviews revealed that some decisions were made separately; however, this depended on the scale and potential impacts, "of course, some things I can [say] … fall completely within the administrative envelope and so on … (But) let's say you wanted to change a marketing approach. Can that be done without talking to the Artistic Director? I don't think so" [GM18].

Love and Gender

We found shared vision in our discussions. We also found endless communication with relationships negotiated on an informal and often daily basis. And as well as trust we also found "love" and "passion":

> You're working for love basically, so you actually have to enjoy what you're doing. [GM7]

> I think the motivating force is a general love of [name of organisation]. [GM6]

> I can't work with anyone I don't love in this business. If I'm not in love with my Artistic Director I can't do it. And so there is automatically a relationship that is deeply personal and deeply respectful. [GM5]

So we have two people who talk and trust and love and share. One of them is supposedly the single focused, heroic leader. And the other is the facilitative servant/leader. Are you starting to get the picture? Is this that old fashion relationship − marriage?

> you end up being Mum and Dad in an organisation and I'm possibly the more nurturing, encouraging, more access to … and AD's much less effusive with his praise but when it comes, it's more important and meaningful. [GM7]

Maybe … because some of these partnerships were male ADs and female GMs. But then some of them weren't. If what we saw at play in the leadership partnership in the performing arts is marriage, it's a thoroughly reconstructed model of marriage:

> I don't think that gender really plays a part in it − it might provide a convenient psychological paradigm for the rest of the company who might like to refer to "mum and dad", but in the theatre of course one could have same-sex parents and it wouldn't be that surprising. [GM2]

Although the metaphors of family, mother and father were pervasive within the language of the people we spoke to, it was in a very self-aware way and one that was disconnected from any sex-based stereotypes.

> I don't think that AD is a really blokey bloke or that I'm a really girly girl. [GM7]

> I guess you'd say that they're fairly ideologically sound men or politically reconstructed men or feminist men or what have you. [GM6]

If one takes the standard definition of male leadership (self-assertion, separation, independence, control, competition, focused perception, rationality, analysis) and female leadership (interdependence, cooperation, receptivity, wholes and contexts, emotional tone, personalistic perception, connective leadership caring) (Billing & Alvesson 2000) then they can be seen as shared across both roles. Some of the "masculine" qualities could be considered values of a theatre director or a choreographer or a music director (self-assertion, focused perception) but others are the necessary requirements of the GM within an arts organisation (rationality, analysis). But equally an artistic leader needs a number of the "feminine" qualities (emotional tone, connective leadership, wholes and contexts) and the GM working with artists in underfunded organisations needs some of those qualities too (cooperation, caring).

The Managing Directors and General Managers we interviewed required a sophisticated set of management skills and qualities that were both "masculine" and "feminine" in order to have a successful co-partnership with an artist and manage a complex organisation. Metaphors of passion and love and family infuse their conversation but the relationships described aren't stereotypical or traditional ones. Although images of "mum" and "dad" make sense given that the best co-partnership intuitively reflects the respect and love found in a good marriage, it's a complex modern marriage where gender is irrelevant to the roles. In order to work with an artist to produce great music or dance or circus or theatre, our artistic and management co-leaders combined rationality and passion, analysis and feeling, single mindedness and caring – regardless of gender.

Problems

All of the people we interviewed were engaged in positive co-leadership relationships but they also offered insights into previous relationships where co-leadership didn't work. Stories included lack of trust, extensive differences in experience, lack of agreement about strategy, ambiguity about role responsibility, lack of clear communication and lack of shared values:

> I don't think we had shared values. I don't think we shared the same goals … So every idea I put forward or vision I had for the company was something to be suspicious of. [AD13]

There can be a conflict at the heart of non-profit arts organisations:

> an artistic director may argue for quality, artistic development and the risk of innovation while the executive director prioritizes efficiency and conservative, predictable, widely-accepted programming. These differences, taken to the extreme, would mean that if the artistic mission is unchecked it may threaten the organization's stability. Conversely if financial limitations are too rigid, the organization cannot realize its mission.
>
> (Beard 2012a, 21)

The best way of seeing a number of these challenges play out is the engaging Canadian TV series *Slings and Arrows*. Set in a theatre company, each episode shows an interaction between Artistic Director and General Manager. It's both entertaining and informative about the challenges of running an arts organisation in conjunction with another person.

Just because our interviewees were in successful relationships didn't mean to say that conflict didn't occur: 11% of our GMs and 10% of our ADs mentioned varying degrees of conflict. Conflict, however, was not always depicted in a negative light, with many mentioning that this conflict "was actually a positive resource" [GM21]. "You've got to create a really powerful partnership. And that doesn't mean you're going to agree with everything. I think half the fun is that you won't … I will always come from this perspective, and you will always come from that perspective, and we find a middle ground and have that good debate" [GM19]. As not everyone comes to a relationship with equal skills in managing conflict, Reid and Karambayya (2009) recommend that developing such skills is an important contributor to having an effective relationship.

Other problems that can arise out of co-leadership relationships include the lack of clear leadership from the perspective of staff (and the capacity for leaders to be played off against each other), a sense that too much compromise has to happen for decisions to be reached, and that de facto power actually lying in one person's hands. O'Toole, Galbraith and Lawler's (2002) focus is the business world but some of their comments could be relevant to the arts world such as the requirement to manage egos and let one person take the credit, and political issues around power that come out of role ambiguities. Solving such problems can only be done in two ways: if the individuals can't work it out between them the Board successfully mediates or one person leaves.

As I've noted earlier, communication is key to effective co-leadership and if that process breaks down, then the relationship may be damaged irreparably. In one case I'm aware of, one partner started working from home so that they didn't have to see, let alone talk to, the other. It may take a while for the Board to notice such a breakdown but it's an important signal that all may not be well. Proposals about how to improve communications between leaders include "sharing office space and holding regular, informal meetings between the two leaders and between the leadership duo and the other staff" (Järvinen, Ansio & Houni 2015, 25).

Beirne and Knight (2002) provide an example where a Managing Director was added into a company to free the Artistic Director up to pursue the art and where the results was catastrophic. However, this isn't the fault co-leadership *per se* which clearly works in many organisations. The problem (which staff called "the crazy time" (84)) could have been caused by any number of issues – personalities, lack of trust and communication, blurred reporting lines, poor implementation of the new model – rather than assuming that drawing a line (albeit a permeable one) between creative activities and organisational tasks is impossible.

Hiring

One way of anticipating problems is to use the hiring process to set up the best structure and get the best possible partnership. The question about structure is who should be the CEO? The artistic leader? The management leader? Both? The majority of performing arts companies we explored where co-leadership was practiced maintained a formal structure with the Executive Director or General Manager as CEO. However, taking out orchestras, there were more companies with formal shared leadership than where either the AD or GM were sole CEOs (Reynolds, Tonks & MacNeill 2017). Even in the situations where the model was a solo CEO (as my case at MTC), the reality was that most of the partners behaved as if they were equal partners in leadership.

A number of Managing Directors and General Managers were emphatic in their support for the Artistic Director to be the Chief Executive Officer of the company. This was in order to signal the pre-eminent position of art in the organisation's mission. In this capacity they would also have the ultimate decision as to the appointment to the GM role. The reason for this was practical: if the Artistic Director is constrained by an uncomfortable relationship with the General Manager or Managing Director then the company as a whole is hampered. However, if the Board is confident that the partnership is a strong one and that the Board has the skills to manage any disagreements, I'd recommend a co-CEO arrangement.

Regardless of the structure, the organisation's well-being demands an effective partnership. When it comes to hiring new leaders, there are number of different views on how to do this. There is some evidence that it's good practice to involve the current leader in the selection of his or her new partner (O'Toole, Galbraith & Lawler 2002). In a Canadian theatre case study, Reid (2013) reports that the Managing Director was on the selection committee for the Artistic Director. Our interviewees tended to look at the situation from the opposite point of view:

> It's absolutely crucial that the Board ensures that each new artistic director has their own general manager. … I would recommend to any Board of any organization that the most important thing that a theatre company does is to employ an artistic director. So it's absolutely crucial that they have in mind that the artistic director will pair themselves with a person that they want to work with. [AD2]

My view is that as we're talking about arts organisations and even though the partnership should be an equal one on the ground, the artist is the most important person for the health of the mission and vision of the company. Therefore, they should be able to choose their management partner. When Roger Hodgman, the first AD I worked with, resigned, I submitted my "in-principle" resignation immediately because it had become clear to me that a partnership was required to run a company like ours and if the new AD wanted to work with someone else, then so be it. As it turned out, the Board decided that they didn't want two people leaving at the same time and so told the next AD that he had to work with me for the next two years. He did, we forged a relationship, and he forgot that he had the option to find a new partner. So our co-leadership lasted for 11 years.

In 2018, I helped an arts organisation implement a bold hiring process when both AD and GM were leaving with a six-month timeframe. Instead of advertising for the artistic leader who would then be involved in picking their management team mate, the Board put out an expression of interest for the artistic leadership of the company. They were open to any combination — solo AD, team of artists, AD/GM team, even another small company that may have wanted to amalgamate. The short list included three solo ADs and three teams and the final choice was a team made up of Artistic Director, Executive Director and Program Producer. The AD and ED had danced together before one turned to choreography and the other to producing work, but they haven't worked together in these roles. It will be interesting to see how this team performs in the future.

If an organisation is adopting a co-leadership model for the first time, Järvinen, Ansio and Houni (2015) recommend that you need to do some preparation beforehand. What you need are structures that are going to make it more likely than not that the requirements of such a relationship — trust, communication, shared vision and so on — can actually happen. For example, being clear — particularly to company members — about who's doing what and putting in place conflict resolution processes.

Conclusion

After interviewing Artistic Directors and Managing Directors/General Managers/Executive Directors of performing arts companies in Australia, the USA and UK we concluded:

- The roles of AD and GM are distinctly different but absolutely interdependent
- Regardless of whether the AD or the GM was the CEO, the majority of people thought that the AD needed to be the symbolic and public leader
- The primacy of the art is reinforced by the acknowledgement that the AD should have their choice of GM
- The GM is seen to be leading from behind, a facilitative role that enables the company and the artists to get on with their primary role of creating the art
- But there was a clear understanding about the dependence of the AD on the GM.

The most compelling feature of collaborative leadership was the inherent interdependency between the two leaders. The success of the company relied upon both entities meeting their own imperatives — artistic excellence and financial sustainability — and that one could not be met at the expense of the other. Achieving the win-win outcome for the organization overall required give and take, which when repeated over iterative decision making built trust and respect in the relationship.

(Reynolds, MacNeill &Tonks 2017, 102)

In my experience, co-leadership is hard work because you have to continually think about someone else's world view. Common vision, communication and trust are essential for success. But when it works, the result is great for the organisation and the staff. My Artistic Directors couldn't have run the organisation without a managing partner, but regardless of my love for and understanding of theatre, I was never going to be a great visionary leader for the organisation.

In the relationships we've been discussing, the two leaders are completely reliant on each other: "the Artistic Director on the executive for the resources to satisfy his or her ambitions and taste; the Executive Director on the artistic for programming that satisfies audiences, artists, donors and other external constituents" (Beard 2012a, 22). Not only do they have to manage the specific requirements of their role, they also have to manage the relationship itself.

See also: Arts Leaders, Arts Managers, Communication, Gender, Leadership, Organisational Structure

References

Atwood, M. 2016 *Hag-seed*, London: Hogarth.

Beard, A. 2012a "Dual Leadership and Budgeting in the Performing Arts: A Tale of Two Organizations", in Beard, A. (ed.) *No Money, No Mission – Financial Performance, Leadership Structure and Budgeting in Nonprofit Performing Arts Organisations*, PhD, New York, 9–54.

Beirne, M. & Knight, S. 2002 "Principles and Consistent Management in the Arts: Lessons from British Theatre", *International Journal of Cultural Policy*, 8(1), 75–89.

Billing, Y. D. & Alversson M. 2000 "Questioning the Notion of Feminine Leadership: A Critical Perspective on the Gender Labelling of Leadership", *Gender, Work & Organization*, 7(3), 144–157.

Caust, J. 2010 "Does the Art End When the Management Begins?" *Asia Pacific Journal of Arts and Cultural Management*, 7(2), 570–584.

Chew, S. & Hallo, L. 2015 "On Your Toes: Perception of Leadership Influences in Dance Companies in Singapore", in Caust, J. (ed.) *Arts and Cultural Leadership in Asia*, London: Routledge, 129–147.

Fitzgibbon, M. & Isaacs, J. 1997 "Speaking for Themselves Part 1", in Fitzgibbon, M. & Kelly, A. (eds) *From Maestro to Manager*, Dublin: Oak Tree Press, 41–51.

Grehan, H. & Eckersall, P. (eds) 2013 *"We're People Who Do Shows": Back to Back Theatre*, Aberystwyth: Performance Research Books.

Ignatius, A. 2014 "Leaders for the Long Term", *Harvard Business Review*, 92(11), 48–56.

Inglis, I., Cray, D. & Freeman, S. 2006 *Leading Arts Organizations: Traditional Styles or Different Realities?*, Department of Management Working Paper, Melbourne: Monash University.

Järvinen, M., Ansio, H. & Houni, P. 2015 "New Variations of Dual Leadership: Insights from Finnish Theatre", *International Journal of Arts Management*, 17(3), 16–27.

Lapierre, L. 2001 "Leadership and Arts Management", *International Journal of Arts Management*, 3(3), 4–12.

MacNeill, K. & Tonks, A. 2009 "Co-leadership and Gender in the Performing Arts", *Asia Pacific Journal of Arts and Cultural Management*, 6(1), 291–404.

MacNeill, K. & Tonks, A. 2013 "Leadership in Australian Arts Companies: One Size Does Not Fit All", in Caust, J. (ed.) *Arts Leadership*, Melbourne: Tilde University Press.

MacNeill, K., Tonks, A. & Reynolds, S. 2012 "Authenticity and the Other", *Journal of Leadership Studies*, 6(3), 6–16.

MacNeill, K., Reynolds, S. & Tonks, A. 2013 "A Double Act: Coleadership and the Performing Arts", Bogota: 12th AIMAC International Conference, 1158–1169.

Miles, S. A. & Watkins, M. D. 2007 "The Leadership Team: Complementary Strengths Or Conflicting Agendas", *Harvard Business Review*, 85(4), 90–98.

Myers, R. 2014 "The Artistic Director: On the Way to Extinction", 2014 Philip Parsons Memorial Lecture, http://belvoir.com.au/wp-content/uploads/2014/12/2014-Philip-Parsons-Memorial-Lecture-by-Ralph-Myers.pdf [accessed 20 February 2019].

O'Toole, J., Galbraith, J. & Lawler, E. E. 2002 "When Two (or More) Heads are Better than One", *California Management Review*, 44(4), 65–83.

Rao, H. 2010 "What 17th-Century Pirates Can Teach About Job Design", *Harvard Business Review*, 88(10), 44.

Reid, W. 2013 "Dual Executive Leadership in the Arts", in Caust, J. (ed.) *Arts Leadership: Internal Case Studies*, Melbourne: Tilde University Press, 98–111.

Reid, W. & Karambayya, R. 2009 "Impact of Dual Executive Leadership Dynamics in Creative Organizations", *Human Relations*, 62(7), 1073–1112.

Reynolds, S., Tonks A. & MacNeill, K. 2017 "Collaborative Leadership in the Arts as a Unique Form of Dual Leadership", *The Journal of Arts Management, Law, and Society*, 47(2), 89–104.

Røyseng, S. 2008 "Arts Management and the Autonomy of Art", *International Journal of Cultural Policy*, 14(1), 37–48.

Webb, S. & Dowling, M. 2015 "The Organising and Artistic Demands of Orchestral Performances", in Beech, N. & Gilmore, C. (eds) *Organising Music: Theory, Practice, Performance*, Cambridge: Cambridge University Press, 251–257.

Communication

To be an influential manager, you will need to be able to interview, counsel, coach and motivate people, make written and verbal presentations, argue a position and make a case, chair meetings, convince stakeholders – and so the list goes on. As Adams (2007, 190) says, "management is, principally, refined communication". Other writers describe organisations as ongoing communication (e.g. Stahl & Tröndle 2019). After listing listening as his first leadership competence, Drucker's (1990, 20) second competence is "the willingness to communicate, to make yourself understood". This, he goes on to say, "requires infinite patience".

It's also a series of skills that can be learned. I'm a shy person. I'm the sort of person that had to be forced to go to school dances by the nuns who were worried about my social skills. I used to take books of poetry to parties so that I could pretend to be busy and not have to talk to anyone. Now, no-one believes those stories because I can give a witty speech at a sponsor event, present an informative and engaging paper at a conference, handle a media interview with aplomb and generally seem to be an effective communicator. It's all about learning the craft of communication. I learnt that from my father who came back from World War 2 with a nervous stutter. To help overcome it, he joined a drama club and a public speaking organisation. He wasn't ever comfortable in those roles but he overcame his handicap. If you're nervous about speaking in public or writing Board papers or giving feedback to staff, find an education program that

will help you learn those skills. At one university where I teach, the MBA program has been restructured to make effective business communication one of the compulsory units, one of the so-called "soft" skills that employers expect from graduates.

Just because communication is learnable, doesn't mean that it's simple. Human communications is complex because of all the different elements that make up the moment – the context in which it happens, the language understanding of the manager and the employee, the ability to create a precise message, the ability to send and hear it, the non-verbal cues that surround the message as well as the form in which it's sent (Dickie & Dickie 2011). Because of this complexity, there are barriers that prevent effective communication. One of the main ones is the assumption that because you're the manager it must be perfectly obvious what you want – you announce it and everyone understands. No-one does as a rule, without considerable effort to make yourself understood (Drucker 1990). I was guilty of assuming people also knew what was required – I tended to brief people and send them on their way when I should have been providing more detail and context; explaining what I expected from them; what their focus should be; where they should be spending their time and effort; and making sure they understood.

Other barriers include (but are certainly not limited to) differences in perception and values, inconsistency between spoken and non-verbal messages, differences in cultural conventions, boredom or lack of interest, being egotistical or off message, dislike of the communicator, using the form for the message. Any good textbook[9] on communication will expand this list and provide strategies to overcome the barriers but some simple advice is listen carefully, speak clearly and directly, limit the use of jargon, ask questions, give feedback, be ethical and focus on the audience who is going to receive the message. Another approach is to think about all the terrible presentations you've attended (the boring post-show sponsor thank you or the endless PowerPoint slides) or the unreadable memos or Board reports you've received or the briefing when the meaning was completely opaque, and work out what would have made them better.

In my first management position, I had a portable computer the size of a sewing machine with a green and black screen that helped me write letters – a great improvement on the typewriter. During that period in the 1980s and 1990s, the change in communication was about the speed with which information could be created and delivered with a matching expectation of an increasingly prompt response. According to Mankins, Brahm and Caimi (2014) the approximate number of communications per executive per year has increased from 1,000 in 1970 to 4,000 in the 1980s (the rise of voicemail), 9,000 in the 1990s (email), 25,000 in the 2000s to 30,000 in the 2010. In the year that I'm writing this, people text more than ring, email more than write a letter, update their Facebook page rather than talk to a friend, Twitter rather than engage in a debate with a person. But each of those communication forms has their strengths and weaknesses and as managers we need to be sophisticated in their use.

For example, in an article about emails, Brown, Killick and Renaud (2013) point to the negative impact that they can have on an organisation's efficiency. They proposed training executives to be more judicious in their use of email and to be more strategic about which communication form to use. The article also reminds us that:

> In a phone call, for example, vocal tone provides real-time feedback on whether the message is being understood – something that's missing in the low-bandwidth email channel. Facial expressions and body language make in-person meetings an even richer method of communication (26).

Rosner and Halcrow (2010) also recommend not hiding behind email for the same reason and I couldn't resist sharing their cultural metaphor:

> the more dependent you are on email, the more mysterious you become. Even the Wizard of Oz learned that being the man behind the curtain only gets you so far. Go down the hall, hang out in the lunchroom, or pick up the phone at least some of the time (288).

In an article about work-life balance, nearly all the interviewees talked about the need to corral their electronic communication whether it was emails or text messages. Reasons for applying some discipline included the need to give some things undivided attention, trying to avoid "frenetic responsiveness", wanting to exchange and analyse ideas rather than simply broadcasting them and using face-to-face communication, particularly when listening was important (Groysberg & Abrahams 2014). The authors conclude: "[m]ake yourself available but not *too* available to your team; be honest with yourself about how much you can multitask; build relationships and trust through face time; and keep your in-box under control" (63).

Face-to-face communication, while sometimes challenging, is usually more effective than phone calls or emails, let alone texts. Facebook is an interesting phenomenon in this regard. People often assume that everyone knows what's happening because they've posted information about a gig or a new love or a change of job on Facebook. They don't actively communicate with friends to make sure that they have the information. Just because you've sent an email doesn't mean that someone's read it. If you have a project for someone to do, then of course it's a good idea to summarise the requirements and goals of the projects in writing, but talk to them first. First, find out if they are up to it; what support they need; what changes they may like to make; what resources are required. And if you're dealing with difficult news – what Volz (2017, 129) calls "sad, bad, or troubling" news – then you are always best to do it in person. You need to respect the person receiving such news by being there to engage with the emotional impact of the communication.

We've all experienced emotion on receiving the irritating email that was sent too broadly, the confusing email that doesn't make sense, and the angry email full of capital letters. Having a policy about email etiquette for the whole company can help both reduce the number of emails and reduce the miscommunication that they can sometimes cause. Face-to-face communication can be misinterpreted too but at least you have the chance to unpack the meaning of the message at the time.

In describing how he changed organisational culture at the Barbican Arts Centre in London, John Tusa's first point was about opening up communication with staff. "Information, freely offered as a right belonging to colleagues, is at the heart of any institution, certainly one that is on a steady trajectory of change" (Tusa 2007a, 30). He talks about having an Annual General Meeting for staff in which the business plan and the annual report are shared. Over the years at MTC, I tried a variety of information sharing processes, the most regular of which were fortnightly newsletters and staff meetings. Each waxed and waned in effectiveness as processes of getting staff interested and enthusiastic and encouraging them to tell their stories. Some departments loved providing information and others didn't. Some wanted just to get on with the job and some enjoyed the cross-departmental interaction. When there was important news to share, we did it well, but when life was going on as usual, I would have to say we didn't do so well. Both the CEO and the staff preferred a staff barbeque to a staff meeting. The key point about communicating with staff is to share information. As Lambert et al. (2017, 246) concluded, "[t]hose who work in a silo and keep all of the information too close will not succeed as a leader". They also say that it's almost impossible, as a manager, to communicate too much.

Whatever form of communication you use, it's better that people are finding out from you rather than via Twitter or at the local bar. As it's no longer the case that information about the company stays in the company given the ubiquity of social media, it's worth having a policy on how and when people can comment about the company in that form. However, a policy won't be as effective at stopping online complaints and gossip as a good organisational culture and meaningful two-way communication within the organisation.

You have to find a way to ensure that your staff have a voice, to be able to "raise concerns, express and advance their interests, opinions and ideas, solve problems, and contribute to and participate in workplace decision-making with management" (Pyman et al. 2013, 119). Often this "voice" will be facilitated through unions but many organisations these days don't have a strong union presence. Research in those organisations in Australian showed that 83% of staff in 2010 reported the presence of an "open door" policy to express problems with their managers and regular staff meetings had increased from 65% in 2004 to 70% in 2010. However, employee involvement programmes where actual decision-making took place had reduced from 40% in 2004 to 33% in 2010 (Pyman et al. 2013). I had an open door policy for many years simply because the building we were in was so decrepit that my door couldn't be closed. And there is an irony in having an open door policy because the moment you close it, people assume there's a problem.

Having said that, I've always had an open door policy – are there really people who don't?[10] But was it really always open? Sometimes, we are so busy that we don't want someone to come in and interrupt us and sometimes, even in an organisation with a positive work culture, you're still the boss. You might not think that you're scary but you'd be surprised how a title creates a barrier. Detert and Burris (2016) explored reasons why an open door wasn't enough of a communication policy and offer some advice on how to improve feedback mechanisms in companies. They also offer evidence about the positive impact on organisations when employees can voice their concerns freely, such as increased retention, stronger performance, better financial results and improvements that save money (82).

Sometimes, a way to get over the reticence of staff to share their views or offer opinions is to have anonymous surveys but Detert and Burris (2016) aren't convinced this is the right approach. Apart from anything else it sends a message that it's not safe to speak up and if the issue is about discrimination or harassment, then you can't seriously address the problem without more details.

The depressing point about Detert and Burris' (2016) research is that the reasons why most people withhold ideas and concerns isn't fear but "the belief that managers wouldn't do anything about them anyway" (84). For example, if when you start a new job, you have open conversations with everyone about their work and the company (as I did at both Melbourne Theatre Company and more recently at Chunky Move and the Australian Dance Theatre), these meetings can backfire if you don't actually address people's concerns.

Deter and Burris' (2016) recommendations for creating a more vocal culture include:

- Making feedback a regular, casual exchange
- Be transparent about feedback processes including telling people what you've done in response
- Ask people – reach out – be proactive rather than passive
- Soften the power cues so you're not the scary boss
- And if you're not the CEO, set a good example to your staff by taking their concerns up to the top.

"Management by walking around" can help elicit feedback because suddenly you're on your staff's territory, not in your office.

Even when you're following up all these strategies, there's no guarantee that the communication processes will be equally two way. Whereas clear and honest communication is necessary, particularly

if you want to encourage employee empowerment, it requires training in interpersonal skills, particularly for non-managerial staff. When I started at MTC, everyone there knew more than I did about making theatre. Although I was the boss, I was the newest kid on the block. One way of learning was not just talking to people but listening to people. For a while I felt that this gave people, particularly the long-term arts workers, considerable power in our relationship. But knowledge and experience aren't always enough. I learnt through the first enterprise bargaining process that the staff representatives felt that they lacked the capacity to communicate their concerns and their demands effectively. In order to enable a better power balance in our discussions, I paid for them all to attend a union-run training program on negotiation.

One of the key communication processes in use inside and outside arts organisations is public speaking and whether it's a presentation to the staff, the Board, at a sponsor event, to the media, that's usually the time when most managers are most nervous. Again, this is a challenge that can be solved by the right technique. It's just a matter of finding what works for you. I was at a recent meeting when someone said "Why do people in the visual arts always read their speeches?" The underlying meaning of the comment was that they weren't good communicators. I think that it's perfectly reasonable to read a speech as long as sentences are constructed to be read out loud rather than on the page and if you do it with some verve and enthusiasm. The people who can riff on a topic effectively without notes are rare. One of my Artistic Directors could do it – but he needed a couple of glasses of wine beforehand. I looked as if I could do it but always needed to write and semi-learn it first and saved the glass of wine until afterwards. The lesson is, you can learn how to speak in public. You might need a coach. You might need to join a group. You might need lots of practice. Or you might just need technology. At a public event I attended, an actor gave a particularly impressive presentation without notes. Afterwards, I went up to congratulate her on speaking so well and it was only then that I spotted the translucent electronic displays which had contained all her words.

One also needs to be able to speak fluently and passionately when unprepared and in the most unlikely of places. Because of my public role at MTC people knew me and because the MTC audience saw themselves as a family, they assumed I knew them. I've had a number of conversations with people at times when I'd rather not – in one's daggy clothes at the supermarket on a weekend; at the beginning of a holiday on a gulet in Turkey; spectacle-less in one's bathers at an aqua aerobics class. And each time, you have to be the company's ambassador.

Covey (1992) offers some advice on attitudes that I agree help develop good communication lines: assume good faith, care about relationships and be open to change. In his book on principle-centred leadership he says:

> When there is high trust and good feeling, we don't have to "watch our words" at all. We can smile or not and still communicate meaning and achieve understanding (112).

That feels like an organisation I want to work in.

See also: Empowerment, Listening, Marketing, People, Trust

References

Adams, J. 2007 *Managing People in Organizations: Contemporary Theory and Practice*, Basingstoke: Palgrave Macmillan.

Archee, R., Gurney, M. & Mohan, T. 2013 *Communicating as Professionals* (3rd ed), Melbourne: Cengage.

Brown, C., Killick, A. & Renaud, K. 2013 "To Reduce E-mail, Start at the Top", *Harvard Business Review*, 91(9), 26.

Covey, S. R. 1992 *Principle-Centred Leadership*, London: Pocket Books.

Detert, J. R. & Burris, E. R. 2016 "Can Your Employees Really Speak Freely?", *Harvard Business Review*, January–February, 81–87.

Dickie, L. & Dickie, C. 2011 *Cornerstones of Management* (2nd ed), Melbourne: Tilde University Press.

Drucker, P. F. 1990 *Managing the Nonprofit Organization*, New York: HarperCollins.

Dwyer, J. 2009 *Communication in Business* (4th ed), Sydney: Pearson.

Groysberg, B. & Abrahams, R. 2014 "Manager Your Work, Manager Your Life", *Harvard Business Review*, 92(3), 58–66.

Lambert, P. D. & Williams, R. (eds) 2017a Performing Arts Center Management, New York: Routledge.

Mankins, M., Brahm, C. & and Caimi, G. 2014 "Your Scarcest Resource", *Harvard Business Review*, 92(5), 74–80.

Pyman, A., Holland, P., Teicher, J. & Cooper, B. 2013 "The Dynamics of Employee Voice in Australia", in Teicher, J., Holland, P. & Gough, R. (eds) *Australian Workplace Relations*, Cambridge: Cambridge University Press, 118–136.

Rosner, B. & Halcrow, A. 2010 *The Boss's Survival Guide* (2nd ed), New York: McGraw Hill.

Stahl, J. & Tröndle, M. 2019 "Toward a Practical Theory of Managing the Arts", in DeVereaux, C. (ed.) *Arts and Cultural Management: Sense and Sensibility in the State of the Field*, New York: Routledge, 245–266.

Tusa, J. 2007a, *Engaged with the Arts*, London: I.B. Tauris & Co Ltd.

Volz, J. 2017 *Introduction to Arts Management*, London: Bloomsbury Methuen Drama.

Williams, R., Harris, K. & Lambert, P. D. 2017 "Executive Leadership for Performing Arts Centers", in Lambert, P. D. & Williams, R. (eds) *Performing Arts Center Management*, New York: Routledge, 238–259.

Conflict

Reid (2013) summarises three different types of conflict:

1. Task conflict which involves a focus on what is to be done. She describes this type of conflict as having a dynamic that is positive and enables creative solutions
2. Process conflict which concerns who does what and how. "It can remain positive and similar to task conflict, or it can evolve into negative and emotional conflict, especially if opposition concerns territory and personal power."
3. Emotional or value-based conflict which is "least likely to have rational resolution, erodes trust in any relationship,

and can be dispersed into the rest of the organization" (106).

Reid (2013) says that the latter form is what most people think of as conflict and forget that some conflict can be productive and useful. Autry (2001, 171) also makes the distinction between disagreements over processes and personality. He says that most conflict in the organisations is about personality and style but not most disagreements. In his view, although disagreement can change into conflict, "constructive disagreement is often the fertile medium in which better ideas grow".

Disagreements happen because there are differences of opinion or perceptions about everything from the power of management to the strategies of the organisation. They can occur when there are limited resources to go around and if people's tasks are interdependent. If people feel undervalued or under pressure, disagreements can surface. Personality or cultural differences can lead to disagreements, as can communication problems. Some disagreements can be driven by outside forces such as unions or funding agencies.

Adirondack (2005, 126) gives examples of conflict that are personal, historical or about hidden issues and these are some of the most difficult disagreements to deal with:

- "Ownership", which can lead to emotional investment where there is not room for other people's views
- Allegations of racism, sexism and so on which may get all the attention but the underlying problems are something else
- Group history with past grievances that haven't been resolved
- Mistrust getting in the way of work.

Value-driven disagreements can be particularly problematic for non-profit arts organisations as the mission is the key driver of company activity. For example, what if you joined the company when it had a specific emphasis on creating work for secondary school students but that focus changed towards post-teen young adults?

As a volunteer at a community radio station, I was part of a very laid-back, cool group of people who presented a Sunday morning music program. The idea of the program was that our listeners, that is, people like us, were probably going to be hung over at 8am in the morning when the show started so the music in the first part was quiet, gentle, reflective – jazz or classical or blues. Then as the hours passed, the energy level of the program would build and other forms of music would be introduced and by midday when our listeners were up and about, there was rock and reggae as well.

A few years later, I became the General Manager of the station and my values had shifted from being laid back to being concerned about the presentation qualities of the program. When people were late or swore on air or left radio silence while they nicked out for a cigarette, I was no longer so forgiving. After warning one member of the presentation team a couple of times, I finally banned him from the station for a period of time – and all hell broke loose. It wasn't so much that the station manager had made that particular decision, but rather it was because I, a past member of the group, had made the decision. Eventually, calm was restored, behaviour improved, and the program continued to run for many years. But it's a classic example of the conflict that can happen when a team member becomes a manager and suddenly has a different set of priorities and values.

When disagreements are not about opinions or values or personalities but rather about the work contract – pay, hours, promotion – unions or third parties such as government employment agencies will become involved. Having proper employment contracts, understanding the legal employment environment and having access to advice through, for example, an employer's association are techniques to help mitigate this form of conflict.

Some writers claim that conflict benefits organisations. For example, Heffron (1989, 130) says:

Conflict challenges the status quo, stimulates interest and curiosity. It is the root of personal and social change, creativity and innovation. Conflict encourages new ideas and approaches to problems, stimulating innovation.

But this feels like competitive for-profit hyperbole to me. A creative organisation can contain productive disagreement without having conflict at the heart of its organisational culture.

Just as there are many sources of disagreement and conflict in the workplace, there are many ways of resolving it. The standard approach can be found in a matrix of assertiveness and cooperation that is found in most textbooks where the processes can include competing (using power to impose a decision), collaborating (getting everyone committed to the decision), avoiding (hoping the conflict will go away or diplomatically sidestepping it until another day), accommodating (which could be selflessly generous or resentfully submitting) and compromise (where you spit the difference) (Dickie & Dickie 2011). Collaboration is usually proposed as the win-win situation but even from the brief descriptions, you can see that other approaches might be suitable at different times. Compromise, for example, can result in both sides coming away with something to their liking but only if ethics and values aren't sacrificed in the process.

Teicher, Holland and Gough (2006) offer a fairly comprehensive list of conflict resolution techniques, starting from the one-on-one session and ending in a formal industrial relations process when conflict is collective:

- Open door policy – ad hoc facilitation or resolution by the manager
- Hotline – anonymous access to adviser or other senior manager (e.g. harassment counsellors)
- Mediation – third party who helps the parties resolve differences but doesn't impose a decision
- Fact-finding – when the disputants are so emotionally involved that the facts of the case are hard to determine

- Conciliation and/or arbitration by third parties
- Mini-trials – with a private "judges" providing a "verdict"
- Peer review – where employee representatives have a majority over management representatives to balance the power inequality
- Internal ombudsperson – in large organisations
- Collective bargaining or negotiation.

With the exception of mini-trials, peer review and the internal ombudsmen, I've used all of these approaches. One can also add crisis intervention to the list where one literally throws oneself in-between people to give them a change to calm down. And the final scenario might be (unfortunately) settlement through a legal process or litigation. Managing disagreements before they turn into conflict is best but can't always be done and, sometimes, conflict becomes so intractable that you need outside help.

The starting point is usually when someone complains or a manager notices an interpersonal conflict. People often feel uncomfortable talking to their manager about their problems, but if they believe the open door policy is real and that you can be trusted, the problem will be reported. Autry (2001, 189) claims that the most important thing you can do as manager is to bring the disagreeing parties together to discuss their differences before they reach a point of conflict or hostility or formal complaint. If the disagreement is about resources or processes, Drucker (1990, 127) suggests getting people who do disagree to work together and see if they can reach a common decision and perhaps help them to get started by working out what they do agree on. He also proposes calling for dissent and disagreement in order to resolve conflict. This way, the objectors get heard and in some cases their position can be accommodated. Although I haven't tried it, I like the idea of one boss's conflict resolution strategy. "He has a standing offer to any two employees engaged in a conflict: he'll buy them lunch to work out their problems. The catch? They have to come back and tell him how they've resolved their differences. He calls it 'the cheapest problem-solving tool ever'" (Rosner & Halcrow 2010, 180).

For joint solutions to be reached through consensus or compromise, the parties have to be willing to engage. In a section called DIY conflict resolution, Adirondack (2005, 128) says they have to:

- Want to find a solution
- Be willing to talk rationally to each other
- Be willing to listen to each other
- Be willing to explore a range of solutions, not just their own
- Be willing to accept a solution even if it does not meet all their needs and wants.

Sometimes when people can't work out their differences, a solution may have to be imposed, but while it might solve the problem in the short term, it rarely works in the long term. In one department, disagreements which had been simmering for years finally surfaced as a perceived conflict between a department head and their deputy with people taking sides. The conflict initially appeared to be about tasks and a series of one-on-one and then joint meetings were held to work out new ways of working together. Although the two people appeared to agree, at heart they didn't and so what looked like an agreement was in reality simply what I thought was the best answer to the problem. In fact, I'd failed to realise that the conflict was as much about values and respect as it was about tasks. While my "imposed" solution worked for a while, the unresolved conflict resurfaced at an even higher emotional pitch. This time, I turned to expert mediators but even they couldn't facilitate a solution and eventually one of the parties left – which is often the way that emotional conflict is resolved.

In their research on a number of Artistic Director/Managing Director partnerships in Canada, Reid and Karambayya (2009) talk about what they call a previously unreported form of conflict behaviour: conflict dissemination. If the conflict between the co-leaders was about tasks (i.e. on substantive choices involved in making a decision), it was solved either within the team or through seeking advice. If the issue was process conflict (e.g. who does what) then again, it was either retained in the team or disseminated through alliance or advice seeking. If it was emotional conflict (e.g. about values) and thus more likely to generate responses like anger of hostility, it was more likely to be disseminated either in the form of mediation, alliance-seeking or abdication. However, this last case was likely to lead to weaker leadership and lower morale amongst staff. On the other hand, where conflict was retained between the co-leadership duo, the effect tended to be positive for the organisation because the two leaders were seen to be working well together.

The desired outcome of any conflict scenario is agreement on how the problem should be dealt with, a specific set of steps to end the conflict and some form of reconciliation to ensure that people can continue to work effectively and respectively together (Adirondack 2005). I'm not a natural conflict resolver because I'm more comfortable avoiding conflict and so most of my experience is based on preventing disagreements turning into conflict. However, I do know that as a manager, some conflict will be unavoidable. Helping people to resolve their differences is the best outcome but sometimes the organisation and its mission has to be protected from conflict that undermines the work we're so committed to do. While task and processes conflict can often be resolved and in some cases provide positive new approaches to work, personality and emotional clashes are more challenging. In those cases, before you end up in the courts because someone claims to have been harassed or bullied, the best result may be for one of the parties to leave.

See also: Co-leadership, Communication, Ethics, Firing, Harassment, Industrial Relations, Organisational Culture, People, Unions, Work

References

Adirondack, S. 2005 *Just About Managing?* (4th ed), London: London Voluntary Service Council.

Autry, J. A. 2001 *The Servant Leader*, New York: Three Rivers Press.

Dickie, L. & Dickie, C. 2011, *Cornerstones of Management* (2nd ed), Melbourne: Tilde University Press.

Drucker, P. F. 1990 *Managing the Nonprofit Organization*, New York: HarperCollins.

Heffron, F. 1989, *Organisation Theory and Public Organisations: The Political Connection*, Englewood Cliffs, NJ: Prentice Hall.

Reid, W. 2013 "Dual Executive Leadership in the Arts", in Caust, J. (ed.) *Arts Leadership: Internal Case Studies*, Melbourne: Tilde University Press, 98–111.

Reid, W. & Karambayya, R. 2009 "Impact of Dual Executive Leadership Dynamics in Creative Organizations", *Human Relations*, 62(7), 1073–1112.

Rosner, B. & Halcrow, A. 2010 *The Boss's Survival Guide* (2nd ed), New York: McGraw Hill.

Teicher, J., Holland, P. & Gough, R. 2006 *Employee Relations Management* (2nd ed), Sydney: Pearson Education Australia.

Control

In his very short but very interesting book about organisations, Grey (2005, 107) says that "the conceit of management knowledge to offer a way of exercising systematic, predictable control over organizations is just that, a conceit: flawed, incoherent in theory, unrealizable in practice".

But there's control and there's control. What Grey means is that we live in a world of complexity and uncertainty and that we can't expect to "control" people (except in limited and agreed upon terms) or the environment. However, within organisations there are "controls" which can contribute to success.

Control is a word that a lot of arts workers feel uncomfortable about. Ironically, it is an underlying feature of most arts practice but when combined with the word *management*, it feels wrong – undemocratic. In an article about management control in the arts and cultural sector, the authors provided these quotes from arts managers:

- Management control is not important for small organisations
- Controls contribute to the creation of a climate of suspicion at odds with artistic and cultural philosophy
- An organisation that has confidence in its employees has no need for an elaborate management control system
- Since an annual external audit is sufficient means of detecting fraud and errors, no additional controls are required
- In my view, internal control is an essential element of sound management (Lafortune, Rousseau & Begin 1999, 73).

Admittedly the research was from the 1990s but, with the exception of the last quote, it does demonstrate a combination of naivety and (dare one say it?) stupidity. "Management control is not important for small organisations"? Really? In some ways, small organisations are the most vulnerable to things going wrong so control as I'm about to describe it is very important. Arts organisations suffer from what Fitzgibbon (2001, 161) describes as a control/creativity paradox. On the one hand, they usually look very informal – in demeanour, attire and ways of interrelating – but low formality co-exists with what she calls the "firm trellis of discipline and control" necessary for high creative output. If there are layers of control in the making of art, there also need to be layers of control in the management of art.

Arts and cultural organisations develop control processes for a variety of reasons such as:

1. You have to, e.g. because funders want to see measurements and how objectives are being met
2. You think you should, e.g. we're a business so we need to behave like a business
3. You think it's right to do so, e.g. planning and evaluation are seen as important *per se* (Tucker & Parker 2013).

One way to think about what sort of controls you should have is to follow the list created by Lafortune, Rousseau and Begin (1999):

1. Structural components such as organizational charts and job descriptions

2. Management systems such as strategic plans, monthly budget forecasts, variance analysis, industry comparisons, trend analysis

3. Internal financial controls to protect from errors and prevent fraud

4. Performance evaluation.

To this list I'd also add policies that reflect your organisational values about how people should behave both to encourage positive relationships (such as respect) and protect people from negative outcomes (such as bullying and harassment).

Another way of looking at control systems is that some are diagnostic and some are inter-active. Diagnostic controls are the ones where you're monitoring results, reviewing key measures, tracking progress towards goals and comparing outcomes to expectations. Interactive control systems are ones in which people come together to use the diagnostic information to make sure the organisation is on track, such as having discussion and debates in management and strategic planning meetings (Tucker & Parker 2013).

Most arts organisations aren't going to set out to be overly controlling of people with rigid bureaucracies and expectations of highly controlled behaviour. But frameworks around performance, expected outcomes and actions can provide people with useful guidance about how to do their jobs well. Organisational charts and job descriptions help clarify reporting relationships and roles. Controls that protect individuals from bad behaviour and organisations from financial catastrophe are positive contributions to an effective organisation.

See also: Harassment, Money, People, Performance Management, Policies

References

Fitzgibbon, M. 2001, Managing Innovation in the Arts, Westport, CT: Quorum Books.

Grey, C. 2005 *A Very Short, Fairly Interesting and Reasonably Cheap Book About Studying Organisations*, London: Sage Publications.

La Fortune, A., Rousseau, J. G. & Begin, L. 1999 "An Exploration of Management Control in the Arts and Cultural Sector", *International Journal of Arts Management*, 2(1), 64–76.

Tucker, P. B. & Parker, L. D. 2013 "Managerial Control and Strategy in Nonprofit Organizations", *Nonprofit Management and Leadership*, 24(1), 87–107.

Creativity

Creativity operates at a number of levels in arts and cultural organisations. To begin with, it's an implicit requirement of art making and, thus, at the core of most our mission statements. Second, as it's a requisite part of making ("creating") art, it's a skill of many of the people employed by our organisations. And as we're usually operating in organisations with limited resources, we want all the people in our organisation to be creative in the way they do their jobs. This puts creativity at the heart of our organisations.

There's an assumption that only "artistic" people are creative but there is evidence that almost anyone is capable of doing some sort of creative work (Quigg 2011). The Concise Oxford English Dictionary definition of being "creative" is to be inventive, showing imagination as well as routine skill. So the myth that creativity belongs to a small number of geniuses is not true. On that basis, creativity can exist at all levels in an organisation.[11] According to one of the important theorists about creativity in business, to be creative one needs expertise, to be able to put ideas together in new combinations, and to have intrinsic motivation (Amabile 1996). Hein (2013) adds to this list and says that as well as individual factors such as knowledge, skills and a personality that lends itself towards coping with creative work, one also needs to be in a context where leadership fosters creativity.

Given that "creativity" has expanded beyond the arts to be a generalised ability to solve problems, generate new ideas and have the capacity to be innovative and flexible, Bilton and Leary (2010, 49) make the neat ironic point that these days no-one is going to admit to being "uncreative". Having said that, I've never viewed myself as "creative" in the traditional sense. I've failed at every type of creative process I've tried from weaving and enamelling to drawing and painting. However, almost every day at work, I'd have a small, modest idea about something new. It may have been in response to something that already existed, for example a small improvement to the website; or it may have been about how best to help a staff member do their job more effectively. The point is, a manager needs to keep thinking of new and better ways to do things. This may be more about innovation than creativity but in much management writing, creativity and innovation are intertwined and usually refer to the capacity to do things differently by adding value to a service or product or method or creating something completely new. Varbanova (2013, 9) provides a neat definition of these terms: "[c]reativity is thinking up new things. Innovation is doing new things". She goes on to say:

> To be successful and sustainable, an arts organisation needs to develop new ideas on an ongoing basis and at all management levels, as well as to elaborate mechanisms to implement these ideas and transform them into opportunities (13).

Hein (2013) summarises the work of a number of researchers about the preconditions for creativity and her list includes undisturbed concentration for a considerable period of time, moderate time pressure, the feeling of being on a mission, the realisation that creativity is enabled through hard work rather than divine inspiration, a willingness to step outside one's comfort zone and having ways of coping with the cognitive and psychological barriers of doing creative work (e.g. coping with failure, procrastination).

Another myth about creativity (Coffee 2013) is that to be creative you need to be free from boundaries but there is evidence that boundaries of space, time, interpretation and expression help creativity (Hein 2013). Twyla Tharp (2003, 78–79), US choreographer, says

"[b]efore you can think out of the box, you have to start with a box". Bilton and Leary (2010) believe that managing creativity is not about managing the individual, but rather the process, so the question is: What is going to get the process going? For example, corporate employees (or those in positions that aren't "artistic") may need to be stimulated by thinking outside the box but they agree with Tharp that artists may respond better to approaches that emphasise discipline, organisation, repetition and logic. They seem to be supporting one element of John Kao's *Creativity Bill of Rights* (quoted in McCann 2008, 14) which is "[c]reative work is not an excuse for chaos, disarray or sloppiness in execution". Bilton and Leary (2010, 56) conclude: "For most artists and arts organisations the challenge is not 'thinking out of the box', the challenge Is rather to 'redefine the box', establish rules and boundaries within which creative ideas can be shaped and developed."

There is clearly a tension between this idea of creating a framework of discipline for creative work and also enabling the qualities of an innovative organisation. Having an organic structure with "intense communications and interactions, mutual adjustment, flexibility, informality, and integration" (Fitzgibbon 2001, 36) is regularly seen as a requirement for innovation. After studying three theatre companies in Ireland, Fitzgibbon concluded that was no single formula for successful innovation management in arts companies except for shared qualities of being focused, driven, lacking in complacency, with a single-minded commitment and that it wasn't a scenario for the fainthearted. "The production of high-quality innovative work involves real labour and often considerable sacrifice" (Fitzgibbon 2001, 176).

The challenge in creating innovative art for larger organisations is to replicate the organic characteristics of small or new groups such as "lack of formality, a familial atmosphere, a spirit of enterprise" (Fitzgibbon 2001, 26). This is not always a quick or easy process and innovation is as much about small, modest changes as major advances (Cloake 1997). An example from MTC serves to illustrate the point. There are two theatre spaces in the Southbank Theatre, the 550 seat Sumner Theatre[12] and the 120 seat Lawler Studio.[13] We almost lost the studio space in the process of "value management" (i.e. reducing the costs of a building project) but I just kept saying that you couldn't build a theatre without a rehearsal space, knowing full well that what we really wanted was a space for new and/or experimental work. Repetition (and one could say endless white lies) worked and we kept the space, although not the funding to fit it out which we had to raise ourselves. Finally, by the middle of 2009, we had a flexible performance space.

It's difficult for a large theatre "machine" like MTC to produce experimental work. First, there are a group of cost issues: our salaries are higher than those in small to medium-sized companies; we pay all the artists involved in a production; we have overheads that are higher than smaller companies. Second, while a section of the company's subscriber base are theatre diehards who'll go to anything, the company's brand doesn't say "experimental". Third, directors and designers who'd worked with us on main stage shows were used to large budgets and were shocked, even disbelieving, about the modest amounts of money we provided for experimental studio work in the Lawler Studio.

We tried a variety of models over the first couple of years – a new European work as an add-on to the subscriber season; providing free rent to independent producers to put on their work; putting on a short season of new Australian plays. Although some of them did well in terms of attracting audiences, the feeling was that we still weren't getting it right. Our strengths were effective production and marketing teams. Our weaknesses were brand and cost structure. Finally, we worked out a model that solved the problems by inviting a group of small, innovative companies to put on their plays in our venue, under a new marketing umbrella (Neon Festival of Independent Theatre). We provided the theatre space, the marketing, the production advice, ticketing, venue staff and a cash grant and the companies used their own financial resources

to produce the work and brought their already committed audiences into our world. It took five years of experimentation until MTC finally found a model that worked. During the process, we had to learn to tweak and adapt many of our activities to match the needs of these new relationships.

A number of writers on creativity present the following "6 Golden Rules" for organisations that want to encourage creativity at every level:

1. Allow everyone to contribute to the big picture
2. Accept that life is full of contradictions
3. Correct processes will allow adaptable organisations to respond
4. Value diversity, fun, enjoyment, commitment and spirit
5. Accept change – be open to surprises
6. Continually question your own behaviour and ideas, find new directions, challenge boundaries and reshape goals.

The resulting environment should be one in which staff are encouraged to explore new fields of knowledge, where they're comfortable to try new approaches to solve problems and new ways to do tasks, and that they know that new ideas are valued (Lang & Lee 2010). The key to this approach is support for risk taking and a tolerance for mistakes. This is a scary position to take sometimes when resources and time are tight, but the very fact of trying something new without being absolutely certain that it's going to work means that failure is an option.

In a fascinating PhD dissertation, Pässilä (2012) used theatre practices as a way of enabling innovation within organisations such as factories and health services. The process of Research-Based Theatre worked because it enabled people at different levels and in different occupations within an organisation to move from "what we're always done" to imagining "what if" scenarios. In her words:

This approach encourages reflection on the difference between knowledge that is experienced from within a role (as a worker, manager, leader) and knowledge that is generated from collective, critical reflection on roles (174).

Through the creation of space for people to think reflectively about their work, the dynamics of what promoted and prevented innovation was uncovered. I don't think that I could have used such a process within a professional theatre company because there would too much ownership of performance as art but it was a great reminder that problem solving and innovation come through trust and communication, stories and metaphors.

Canadian cultural entrepreneur, Roger Parent, has been credited with some clever metaphors about how to run a creative organisation (Cyr 2014). One that I like is the vision of being an "amoeba", as opposed to being a little square in an organisational chart. You're given lots of freedom and the workflow is designed so that you can grow and develop within an area that interests you. Although I didn't have this image in mind, it relates to some of the best inter-organisational shifts that some of my staff made as they explored their interests and increased their contribution to the organisation by being able to move outside the restraints of their position description. Another metaphor that appeals is the "spaceship". The idea is that everyone has to agree to determine objectives together and to go in the same direction but once the course is set, you can be independent. But to be independent you have to keep your word, and in Parent's words (Cyr 2014, 62) this means "[y]ou can have as much fun as you want, but you start on such and such a date and you spend only so much". It's another example of freedom and discipline enabling a framework for creative work.

Jaskyte et al. (2010) did research in a faith-based non-profit organisation, and unpacking the elements of the workplace were conducive to creativity. Based on insights from staff, the results were clustered into five areas: workplace setting and resources, co-workers, time, organisational culture and the influence of authority.

Some of the outcomes were fascinating such as the importance of décor that included colourful walls, rugs, artwork and good lighting in order to create a pleasant work environment. Working in small groups with other creative people was important but so were productive meetings. People wanted sufficient time to follow through with ideas but also wanted quiet time, time for brainstorming and simply time to break the routine. They wanted a safe environment to make mistakes with a non-judgemental attitude towards new ideas with a culture that reflected open communication and an openness to change. Finally, staff wanted authority figures that in the process of clearly communicating vision, purpose and goals also encouraged creativity and gave people control of their tasks. All of these qualities and practices should fit comfortably in an arts organisation.

In a review on an arts management textbook, Fitzgibbon (2012, 96) comments on Brindle and DeVereaux's (2011) claim that arts managers are creators executing vision equal to the creative process. She says (and I tend to agree with her) that while many artists would take issue with that claim, "there is truth in the fact that sound management and exemplary leadership requires critical thinking and creative problem solving to assist organizations to thrive in this dynamic environment".

If creativity is at the heart of what we manage, then we have to be creative and innovative too.

See also: Artists, Offices, Organisational Structure, People

References

Amabile, T. M. 1996 *Creativity in Context*, Boulder, CO: Westview Press.

Bilton, C. & Leary, R. 2010 "What Can Managers Do for Creativity? Brokering Creativity in the Creative Industries", *International Journal of Cultural Policy*, 8(1) 49–64.

Brindle, M. & DeVereaux, C. (eds) 2011 *The Arts Management Handbook: New Directions for Students and Practitioner*, Armon, NY: M.E. Sharpe.

Cloake, M. 1997 "Management, The Arts and Innovation", in Fitzgibbon, M. & Kelly, A. (eds)

From Maestro to Manager, Dublin: Oak Tree Press, 271–295.

Coffee, S. 2013 "Top Ten Myths about Creativity", *Arts Hub*, 18 August, www.artshub.com.au/news-article/features/trends-and-analysis/top-ten-myths-about-creativity-196291 [accessed 20 February 2019].

Cyr, C. 2014 "Roger Parent and Realizations Inc. Montreal: A Flair for Creativity", *International Journal of Arts Management*, 16(3), 60–70.

Fitzgibbon, C. 2012 "Review of 'The Arts Management Handbook: New Directions for Students and Practitioner', edited by Meg Brindle and Constance DeVereaux", *The Journal of Arts Management, Law, and Society*, 42(2), 96–98.

Fitzgibbon, M. 2001 *Managing Innovation in the Arts*, Westport, CT: Quorum Books.

Hein, H. H. 2011 "Stepping into Character", Antwerp: AIMAC International Conference.

Jaskyte, K., Byerly, C. Bryant, A. & Koksarova, J. 2010 "Transforming a Nonprofit Work Environment for Creativity", *Nonprofit Management & Leadership*, 21(1), 77–92.

Lang, C. & Lee, C. H. 2010 "Workplace Humor and Organizational Creativity", *The International Journal of Human Resource Management*, 21(1), 46–60.

McCann, J. M. 2008 "Development: Leadership as Creativity", *Arts Management Newsletter*, No. 82.

Pässilä, A. 2012 *Reflexive Model of Research-Based Theatre*, Finland [document provided by author].

Quigg, A. M. 2011 *Bullying in the Arts*, Farnham: Gower.

Tharp, T. 2003 *The Creative Habit. Learnt It and Use It for Life*, New York: Simon & Schuster.

Varbanova, L. 2013 *Strategic Management in the Arts*, New York: Routledge.

Crisis

Arts companies can get into trouble for an endless array of internal reasons such as an unclear mission, poor programming, ineffective marketing, weak Boards, poor expenditure control, lack of diversity in income or just lack of income (Kaiser 2013), plus external reasons such as increased competition, change in government policy or an economic downturn. In some cases, you can see the crash coming as funders announce reviews or trends show that audience numbers are going down, but in other cases, the crash just happens. The GFC hits or your Artistic Director dies. Drucker (1990) said that leaders need to anticipate crises by building an organisation's capacity through innovation and constant renewal. "You cannot prevent a major catastrophe, but you can build an organisation that is battle-ready, that has high morale, and also has been through a crisis, knows how to behave, trusts itself, and where people trust one another" (9). In other words, if both you and your organisation are resilient, you may survive the crisis.

An example of this resilience is when a fire swept through La Mama's theatre in Melbourne in 2018. La Mama is an iconic theatre established in 1967 and the place where most local playwrights receive their first production. The theatre is in an old stables building and in 2008 the owners decided to sell it. La Mama launched a fundraising campaign and attracted enough donations enough to buy it. The company has an extended support network – 60 years' worth of actors and playwrights and creatives and audiences – and the campaign enabled to them to update their connections with these stakeholders. When the fire happened, the response was immediate. The company has a dedicated team of workers and artists (many of whom I know) and within days, La Mama announced that it was able to move its productions to other venues and keep making great theatre as well as start another fundraising effort to rebuild. La Mama proved once again that a company with modest resources but great heart can survive such disasters.

One of the most informative stories of arts leadership in crisis is the case study (Cameron & Lapierre 2007, 2013) about the role of Mikhail Piotrovsky, Director of Leningrad's State Hermitage Museum, in the aftermath of the end of *perestroika* in the early 1990s. Students find it a fascinating read because it tells the story of a leader who looked outward to find support for his organisation but also looked inward to ensure that even in the most challenging of times, his staff were encouraged to come up with new ideas and work collectively. No staff were laid off, even during periods of intense financial stress, and they were clearly considered key partners in the change process. His management approach was guided by four principles:

- The central mission
- A strong work ethic
- Openness to opportunities; and
- Upholding of traditions (Cameron & Lapierre 2013, 8).

In a number of the organisations in which I've been a CEO/senior manager, there has been a crisis. At 6UVS-FM,[14] one of the major funders threatened to withdraw its financial support which would have led to the closure of the station. I was extremely lucky because I got wind of the proposal to cut funding before the decision had been approved. As I thought the decision was unfair and ill-informed and because the amount of the grant was going to be impossible to replace, I decided to communicate with and get as many people on our side as possible. With the help of the station's volunteers, we told our story on TV, on radio, in meetings, in print (and because this was before the days of the internet) via postcards and petitions. The community response was extremely positive and the proposal to cut our funding failed. That didn't stop the major funder, a university, making the same decision years later, but the station was then well-positioned to reinvent itself.

At the Australian Broadcasting Corporation, the crisis was also one of funding. As the majority of the Radio Division's costs were in people, government funding cuts meant job losses and the results were strikes and picket lines, demonstrations and angry staff meetings, and the heartache of making people redundant.

When the University of Melbourne indicated that it was so unhappy with MTC that it was seriously considering closing the company, our strategy was to downscale in order to reduce losses and gain the energy to improve the quality of our work. We had to convince the University that we had a workable strategic plan and ask for enough time to demonstrate its effect.

The reason that I worked as a locum CEO at Chunky Move dance company was because of the Board's response to the crisis when both the Artistic Director and the Executive Director left within six months of each other. By having someone come into the company to provide a steady hand, support the good remaining staff and help with the recruitment process, the company stayed in good shape during the leadership transition.

A financial crisis is often created by an external party such as the withdrawal or reduction of a major grant giver, sponsor or donor. Since the GFC, many arts organisations have suffered financial cutbacks. In countries such as the UK and the European Union where governments have been generous to arts organisations in the past, that generosity has faded with more and more pressure on companies to find alternative funding sources. Watts (2013) came up with a range of strategies based on feedback from arts managers about what to do when you lose (or fail to get) government funding:

1. Don't panic – consider your business case again and communicate your story in the hope of finding other funding
2. Get feedback on your application
3. Strategise, get community support and seek funding from other sources such as crowdfunding
4. Downscale and diversify
5. Take drastic action and reshape yourself
6. Go it alone.

Usually crises that are generated externally come out of the blue but internal crises tend to have been a long time coming. When an organisation is in debt, when the news hasn't been good for a while, when people don't feel confident about the future, then there's usually a sense of exhaustion which makes it hard to re-energise people to make the necessary changes to keep going. The management team may be equally exhausted, having been avoiding the issue for a long time or, in fact, be the problem. Some of the leadership symptoms of an organisation out of control are misplaced confidence or blame deflection (Dickie & Dickie 2011, 102). Another symptom is being frozen into inaction.

Turbide (2011) examined a number of Canadian arts organisations in financial crisis and noted that before the storm, the Board tended to be highly trusting of the executive, rubber-stamping their decisions. The crisis trigger seemed to come from outside the organisations such as legal action, limits placed on credit and governments refusing to provide short-term funding. Then, the Board took over. The next stage tended to involve new players with changes in either the Chair or the Executive, leading to what Turbide (2011, 8) calls "a more mature and collaborative relationship".

As changing leadership heads can take time, the temptation at a time of crisis is to call in the experts. Often that fails because they are either called in too late or the staff respond negatively to outsiders and don't provide them with the information they need to make their recommendations as good as they should be.

Sometimes when audiences lose interest, when funders decrease their support, when economic times are dismal or when stakeholders no longer value what you do, the right decision may be to close – a hard, but a good decision to make. But usually, you want the organisation to survive or because it's such an iconic part of a community, you have no choice but to see it through the bad times. Your starting point always must be the vision. Is it still relevant? Are you still delivering on the artistic or cultural promise implicit in the vision? If not, then you either change the vision or change the artistic leadership to better reflect the vision. Poisson-de Haro and Montpetit (2012) argue that the key resources of an arts organisation are both tangible (people, technology, buildings) and intangible (reputation and knowledge). When an organisation is in trouble, they probably all need to be reconfigured but that artistry, the basis of reputation, is the most important part of the organisation's resources to be preserved in times of turmoil. Reputational resources are the ones that need to be kept in good standing so that stakeholders continue to support you.

In Turbide's (2011) study she concluded that there were two major causes for the crises: first, an expanded program of activities due to a positive artistic reputation of the CEO or the company, or, second, an expanded building due to the quality of the collection (museum settings) or due to a willingness to develop new markets or activities (performing arts settings). Why did what look on the surface to be positive scenarios – great art and expansion – cause financial problems? Mainly, because revenues did not expand at the same rate as the expenses incurred by the new events or bigger facilities.

If you want to read some fascinating stories about arts companies in crisis, check out Michael Kaiser's book *The Art of the Turnaround* (2008). Kaiser has been the CEO of four companies in crisis – Kansas City Ballet, Alvin Ailey Dance Theater, the American Ballet Theatre and the Royal Opera House. His first piece of advice (which is easy to say but not easy to do) is "don't panic". His second piece of advice, particularly if the crisis is financial, is not to cut expenditure but to find additional revenue quickly (Kaiser 2010, 102). Kaiser (2008) provides ten rules on how to get an organisation out of crisis. Although I'm not that fond of rules in textbooks, I'm always interested in hearing the advice of arts managers who have the lived experience on which they are commenting. While one may not agree with every piece of advice, hearing the story of how the rules were put into in practice provides a useful context when it comes to deciding whether they are right for you in your circumstances. His rules are:

1. Someone must lead – for example, the Royal Opera Board was meeting every week during part of their crisis but managing a problem by part-time committee is not the ideal process. Kaiser describes the effective crisis leader as having a unified vision, courage to make difficult decisions, strong negotiating skills, the respect of all parts concerned, the capacity to work incredibly hard and have an obsessive focus on solving the problem. With the challenge at 6UVS-FM, it was easy to be the public figurehead and lead the team because the problem was

simple – live or die on one decision. At MTC it was more complex and less public than some of Kaiser's cases so my role as leader was behind the scenes, working with the Board and developing and implementing plans with staff.

2. The leader must have a plan – Kaiser's planning process is the standard way of developing a strategic plan that you'll find in most textbooks. It starts with the mission, follows with an environmental review, an honest evaluation of the organisation's strengths and weaknesses, a set of strategies that will help the organisation achieve its mission and detailed implementation and financial plans. Without a plan, responses to each stage of a crisis will be ill-considered and reactive.

3. You can't save your way to health – his description of the financial framework for a performing arts company is quite simple. One has limited capacity to improve productivity (yes, you can do *Hamlet* with 12 people and not 24 people, but you can't do *Art* without the three characters created by Yasmina Reza); limited ability to expand ticket sales for live performance; increasing ticket prices can be counterproductive. Which leaves you with finding more funding sources or earning more income through non-performance sources. One can see the temptation to cut costs. However, when one cuts artistic initiatives and marketing, "one cuts the very reason people supply revenue to the arts organization" (xi). His point is to be careful about where you cut costs.

4. Focus on today and tomorrow, not yesterday – what he's really saying is that although in a crisis there will be short-term problems that need solving, one needs to find the time to think about ideas and strategies that will make future years easier.

5. Extend your programming planning calendar – this, again, is Kaiser's way of

reminding us that the art is at the heart of any turnaround. Unless you are already or extremely likely to be insolvent no matter what you do, planning an artistically vibrant future will not only attract the artists you want to work with, but the donors, foundations and audiences that want to support you.

6. Marketing is more than brochures and advertisements – Kaiser's approach is focused on institutional marketing in addition to programming marketing. This can be harder in some environments than others and he was particularly stunned by the ferocity of the UK press when he joined the Royal Opera House.

7. There must be only one spokesman (sic) and the message must be positive – while the idea that the organisation controls who speaks to the press and with what message is sensible, in this world of social media, it's much more difficult than it used to be to control the message. However, demonstrating optimism and belief in the future can be catching.

8. Fundraising must focus on the larger donor, but don't aim too high – this is a particularly American "rule" where donations make up a higher percentage of turnover than in countries like the UK, Australia or Europe. However, the idea of finding the right pitch and the right time to talk to donors is sensible.

9. The Board must allow itself to be restructured – Kaiser's approach is concerned with the Board's role in fundraising but the "rule" can apply in other cases such as if there has been Board conflict, if the Board hasn't been able to operate efficiently during the crisis, if the Board was part of the cause of the crisis or if members of the Board have contributed negatively to the company.

His Rule #10 is a summary – have the discipline to follow the rules (Kaiser 2008, 14).

In telling the story of the Royal Opera House, Kaiser (2008, 111) notes that "In the most troubled organizations, the staff will support your work once it is clear that you offer hope and excitement." This was true at 6UVS-FM but not true in the early days of MTC. In the former case it was easier to offer the hope that if we all worked amazingly hard for 10 days, there was a chance that we'd survive and there was plenty of excitement in the remorseless publicity campaign that we put in place. At MTC, the future wasn't nearly as clear and the excitement was a long time coming. One series of actions that Kaiser took which I'd also recommend is that he made an effort to talk to every employee (including travelling to catch up with a group on tour) as soon as he could. Similarly, at the beginning of my time at MTC, I had an hour-long meeting with every staff member, including part-timers, to find out their concerns and their dreams for a better future.

Art soothes and comforts, stimulates and entertains, but it also challenges. And every so often someone won't like the content of what you do. Sometimes their response will be to take an injunction to try and stop you. Sometimes the reaction will be louder or more violent. This is not a new phenomenon. A fascinating exhibition at Tate Britain in 2012 showed historic art that had been defaced for religious reasons, by feminists and by political activists. And in these days of social media, a play in Australia can garner worldwide antipathy within minutes.

Back to Back Theatre is a company of intellectually disabled actors who do innovative work devised by the actors working with non-disabled creatives.[15] In 2011, they were about to present a new work called *Ganesh and Third Reich* when an international furore started. The play's plot is a journey by Lord Ganesh, a Hindu god, travelling through Nazi Germany to reclaim the swastika. Before the internet, no-one outside of Australia would have seen the original marketing material which featured Ganesh but the world has changed. Two weeks before the play opening, having neither read the script nor seen the show, Nevada's self-proclaimed "Hindu

statesman", Rajan Zed, saw publicity about the show and issued a statement declaring that the "Lord Ganesh was meant to be worshipped in temples and home shrines and not to be made a laughing stock on theatre stages" (quoted in Coslovich 2011), and the ruckus started. In a world where perceived blasphemy can lead to murder,[16] the very public international response led to abusive emails, threats and demands the play be cancelled, creating a crisis for the company. Their initial response was to leave the script intact, modify the marketing material, clarify the nature of the play on their website and talk to the media about the nature of the company and the production. They also invited concerned members of the public and the Hindu community in particular to see the play. A meeting was arranged between members of the local Hindu community and the company at the Office of Multicultural Affairs and the discussion, though apparently moderate, did include calls for the script to be vetted. Back to Back refused and the play went ahead although there were still security guards at the theatre on the night I saw it. The production went on to have successful, award-winning and uneventful international seasons.[17] Although differences in response to the play continued after its opening, tension did dissipate when those who took up the invitation to see it did see the positive rationale behind the story, realising that in fact "[t]he play goes some distance towards redeeming the swastika and restoring it to its proper godly position".[18]

Luckily, in Australia artists haven't suffered the physical violence their peers have in countries like Palestine[19] and France, but I have received a death threat for putting on a play about the 1992–1995 war in Bosnia-Herzegovina. The play *Miss Bosnia*[20] was a political comedy and some members of the Bosnian community took exception to the production. The response included a call for the play to be cancelled and demonstrations outside the theatre, all of which were fine, but it wasn't so fine when a bomb threat came and I had to consider the welfare of my actors, production staff and audience. It became more personal when I invited some of the demonstrators to a meeting to talk about the play and was issued a death threat. In the end, there was no violence and the play continued in the face of legal challenge via the Victorian Human Rights and Equal Opportunity Commission (HREOC) to close it and prevent future productions. The legal process can be a slow one so it took a couple of years before HREOC decided that MTC was not guilty of racial vilification by staging the play.

A slightly less dangerous crisis happened to MTC a couple of years later. I'll let the author of the play tell the story. On 11 March 1999, David Hare was performing in previews of his play *Via Dolorosa* in New York when he received some news from Australia.

> A member of the Melbourne audience has complained about my play *The Judas Kiss* to the police. The vice squad have been twice to see the shows, which is about Oscar Wilde, and have now threated to close it down. There have been huge amounts of attendant publicity, and jeering articles asking why the Melbourne vice squad has to see something twice to know whether it's obscene or not. Needleless to say, the few remaining seats have now been sold.

You can never prepare for these moments. Sometimes you'll need the help of lawyers, sometimes of the police, sometimes of the security forces. And the challenge will be to balance your commitment to the art and the protection of the people involved in the project.[21] Should you withdraw a piece of art if it's too controversial? Should you cancel a production because it might upset a section of the community? What is the balance between freedom of expression and community sensitivities? If there was a simple answer, I'd give it, but there isn't.

And everyone's going to have an opinion about your crisis anyway in this world of social media. In most crises, you'll need to be communicating inside and outside. If you can't afford expert help, steps such as having a crisis communication plan, including who's going to speak to the media and how the senior group can get together quickly, helps. The best approach for a small to medium non-profit organisation is offered by Our Community Group: don't run, don't hide. More specifically:

- Acknowledge there's a crisis
- Decide who will be the spokesperson
- Speak to the media with your real audience in mind
- Act quickly and make first impressions count
- Say only what you know to be true and avoid speculation
- Challenge information you know to be wrong
- Show concern and don't shoot the messenger.

Some of the seven essential lessons that Mitroff (2005) proposes for companies in crisis have a particular resonance for the scenarios we can find ourselves in. I particularly respond to the ideas of Right Heart (emotional resilience), Right Thinking (on the spot creative thinking) and the more pragmatic Right Social and Political Skills. Autry (2001, 236–237) uses King Henry's St Crispin Day speech from Shakespeare's *Henry V*[22] to illustrate what one needs to survive a crisis and even though the example is a potential military disaster, the core of it should ring true for an arts organisation. Shakespeare gives King Henry the words that present a compelling vision, connect that vision with each soldier's vision of how life will be if they live through the battle, and the words to build a community in the sense that they are all in it together.

The crisis may have come from inside or out, but while leadership will be required to guide the organisation, it's the people in it who provide the energy and the skills to turn the company around.

See also: Boards, Change, Cultural Policy, Marketing, Media, Money, Strategic Plan, Resilience

References

Autry, J. A. 2001 *The Servant Leader*, New York: Three Rivers Press.

Cameron, S. & Lapierre, L. 2007 "Mikhail Piotrovsky and the State Hermitage Museum", *International Journal of Arts Management*, 10(1), 65–77.

Cameron, S. & Lapierre, L. 2013 "Mikhail Piotrovsky and the State Hermitage Museum", in Caust, J. (ed.) *Arts Leadership: Internal Case Studies*, Melbourne: Tilde University Press, 3–18.

Coslovich, G. 2011 "If Religious Zeal Inhibits Art We Are All Poorer", *The Age*, 3 October, www.theage.com.au/it-pro/if-religious-zeal-inhibits-art-we-are-all-poorer-20111002-1l3q3.html [accessed 20 February 2019].

Dickie, L. & Dickie, C. 2011 *Cornerstones of Management* (2nd ed), Melbourne: Tilde University Press.

Drucker, P. F. 1990 *Managing the Nonprofit Organization*, New York: HarperCollins.

Hare, D. 2004 *Acting Up* (2nd ed), London: Faber and Faber.

Kaiser, M. M. 2008 *The Art of the Turnaround: Creating and Maintaining Healthy Arts Organizations*, Waltham, MA: Brandeis University Press.

Kaiser, M. M. 2010 *Leading Roles*, Waltham, MA: Brandeis University Press.

Kaiser, M. M. 2013 *The Circle*, Waltham, MA: Brandeis University Press.

Mitroff, I. 2005, *Why Some Companies Emerge Stronger and Better from a Crisis: 7 Essential Lessons for Surviving Disaster*, Saranac Lake, NY: AMACOM Books.

Our Community Group, "Managing a Media Crisis", www.ourcommunity.com.au/marketing/marketing_article.jsp?articleId=1520 [accessed 2 September 2019].

Poisson-de Haro, S. & Montpetit, D. 2012 "Surviving in Times of Turmoil: Adaptation of the Theatre Les Deux Mondes Business Model", *International Journal of Arts Management*, 14(1), 16–31.

Turbide, J. 2011 "Poor Governance Sickens the Arts – We Have the Cure", *Kenneth Myer Lecture*, Geelong: Deakin University.

Watts, R. 2013 "What To Do When You're Defunded?" *Arts Hub*, 7 November, www.artshub.com.au/news-article/news-article/feature/all-arts/what-to-do-when-youre-defunded-197230 [accessed 20 February 2019].

Cultural Leadership

Having had a section on *Arts Management* and *Artistic Leadership*, why is there a separate section on cultural leadership? It's to emphasise the point that there's a responsibility for those of us with a voice that can be heard to speak out about the importance of arts and culture in our community. Cultural leadership is "advocacy for, and facilitation of, cultural activity" (Sutherland & Gosling 2010, 6). The voice of the artist can be lost in media that's more interested in entertainment or sport; in politics where the arguments can be about the instrumental rather than the intrinsic value of the arts; in the broader community where arts practice can be seen as an indulgence and arts attendance as a middle class or elite pursuit.

"Leading" in the arts is not only providing direction and inspiration for people in your organisation, but actually being out in the public purview expressing a belief in the value and benefits of culture. From the time of my first management job in the cultural industries, I have immersed myself in lobbying, industry development and providing political advice. I helped start a state-based public broadcasting organisation, worked to present the first state-wide radio festival and conference and joined a government advisory body on media. When I shifted into the performing arts, I joined industry and arts management advisory groups, participated in lobbying activities, gave public speeches about the importance of not just my company, but the arts in general, and participated in forums about the arts and culture. The point is to push the cultural agenda in order to make sure that the message is heard by decision makers and funders at all levels of government and civic society (Sutherland & Gosling 2010). Tusa (2007a, 16) makes the lovely point that being a leader in the arts and cultural world is all about caring without moderation or qualification. Whether its public speeches or fighting for resources, each action is a demonstration of that care.

The voice of artists will be heard more loudly than that of managers which is as it should be. Ralph Myers, when he was Artistic Director of Belvoir St Theatre (2014, 2) described the role of Artistic Directors to "inspire, encourage and defend the work their company makes, and our culture more broadly". In a 2014 Currency Press Platform Paper, Wesley Enoch, then Artistic Director of Queensland Theatre Company, called for arts leaders to both "make art that excites and challenges the country to be better, be more humane, more ambitious" and to "be public, more engaged, more passionate" (2014, 10). He argues that cultural leadership is about "creating space for the opposing voices, about imagining a future, exploring the repercussions of our values and promulgating public debate through the work we make and the relationships we create". But arts managers have a role as cultural leaders as well. In Australia in 2016/17 when the Federal Government made a change to cultural policy that had a potentially devastating effect on funding, it was the managers of the small to medium-sized companies who stood up, argued their case in Parliament, and won the day.

But regardless of who's presenting the pitch, sometimes it can be hard to be a cultural leader particularly if you're facing a government with cultural or other policies with which you don't agree. Cate Blanchett, for example, when she was co-CEO of Sydney Theatre Company, actively participated in the greening the arts debate and implemented a range of green policies including water capture and solar panels at the company. But when she spoke out publicly about global warming and a carbon tax she was publicly rebuked by politicians and commentators for misusing her "star" capacity (Coorey 2011). It can feel safer in such circumstances to back down and protect the organisation but sometimes that's not the right call. The threat can be a bluff, particularly when you're running an important iconic company and it's unlikely, given democratic processes, that you'll be targeted and defunded so sometimes it's right simply to take a deep breath and stand up for what you believe in. Sometimes it's easier to do that in concert with others through advocacy organisations such as Americans for the Arts in the USA or What Next? in the UK or through specialist interest groups such as Theatre Network Australia or the National Association for the Visual Arts.

In a speech by Lyn Wallis (2011), when Director of the Theatre Board of the Australia Council, she described what cultural leaders looked like from the Council's perspective – people with cool ideas and the strategies to make those ideas play out. They were the people who "have incredible vision, they motivate others and demonstrate fortitude in the face of adversity. More importantly, they possess that intangible gift: the ability to inspire change."

Enoch (2014, 67) concludes his "letter" to Australian theatre artists with some challenges: "If you can't articulate your work as a vision for a better, more humane society, then give it up. If all you have to offer is beauty and distraction, work harder." Equally, one could say that if all you have to offer is good financial analysis and strategic planning skills, then you have to work harder. Not everyone is convinced about the value of arts and culture and as a manager privileged to be working in the sector, an important part of your job is to be a cultural leader.

See also: Arts Leaders, Arts Managers, Cultural Policy

References

Coorey, P. 2011 "I Want to Be Able to Look My Children in the Face", *Sydney Morning Herald*, www.smh.com.au/environment/climate-change/i-want-to-be-able-to-look-my-children-in-the-face-20110530-1fd01.html [accessed on 20 February 2019].

Enoch, W. 2014 *Take Me to Your Leader: The Dilemma of Cultural Leadership*, Platform Paper No. 40, Sydney: Currency Press.

Myers, R. 2014 "The Artistic Director: On the Way to Extinction", Philip Parsons Memorial Lecture, http://belvoir.com.au/wp-content/uploads/2014/12/2014-Philip-Parsons-Memorial-Lecture-by-Ralph-Myers.pdf [accessed 20 February 2019].

Sutherland, I. & Gosling, J. 2010 "Cultural Leadership: Mobilizing Culture from Affordances to Dwelling", *Journal of Arts Management, Law, and Society*, 40(1), 6–26.

Tusa, J. 2007a, *Engaged with the Arts*, London: I.B. Tauris & Co Ltd.

Wallis, L. 2011 "Opinion: Cultural Leadership in the Arts", Australia Council, Sydney,

Cultural Policy

"Culture" is one of those words that has an almost overwhelming richness of meanings. As Schultz (2014, 8) says:

> Culture is complex, it is everything – language, heritage, art, social relations, education, identity – and at the same time, it is annoyingly intangible. It is the essential glue that binds us, it enriches and informs our lives every day, it is something we make and something we participate in as a human right, and while its public value can be assessed it resists conventional measurement.

In 1994, an Australian Government advisory committee recommended a Charter of "Cultural Rights" that would guarantee all Australians:

- The right to an education that develops individual creativity and appreciation of the creativity of others
- The right of access to our intellectual and cultural heritage
- The right to new intellectual and artistic works; and
- The right to community participation in cultural and intellectual life (Enoch 2014, 36).

Needless to say, we don't have such a Charter yet in Australia but these rights do underlie much cultural policy. Most political parties have policies on arts and culture, even Australia's Motoring Enthusiasts Party has a policy on motoring "culture"! Such policies vary from country to country, government level to government level, political party to political party, and change over time. For example, in Australia in the 1970s, the emphasis was on high arts and notions of excellence; in the 1980s the focus changed to promoting access and equity; and by the 1990s the interests of audiences were seen as more important than artists and the focus was on exports and cost-efficiencies (Caust 2003). But in each of these decades there were both conservative and left-wing parties in power so one can't necessarily match a policy to a party. For example, large performing arts companies did well in the 2000s under a conservative party, the same party that decades earlier introduced and supported community radio stations: high arts and community arts encouraged by the same party. Even within political parties, support for the arts varies over time. Australia's Labor (left-wing) party has had leaders who were passionate supporters of the arts and ones that exhibited almost no interest in the arts. Back in the 1980s, Peter Brokensha and I (1986, 21) said that "having the leader of a government who is philosophically committed to the arts can have a major influence on funding" and even that's not the answer. From 2015-18, Australia has had a conservative Prime Minister who regularly attended the performing and visual arts but the cultural policy environment under his leadership was a negative one. The previous left-wing Prime Minister had no interest in the arts (only attending one musical in her time as PM) but her government produced a reasonable cultural policy.

The language of policy can shift over time, sometimes disguising the real intent of governments. For example, "creative industries", a term including lots of private as well as public activity (adding industries such as advertising, architecture, design, fashion, video games into the list of more traditional arts activities) became popular from the late 1990s. Some see it as part of a neoliberal cultural policy agenda leading to reductions in grants (Haves & Roodhouse 2010), but in 2014, it was a newly elected Labour government in Victoria that adopted the words, with the Shadow Minister for the Arts becoming the Minister for Creative Industries.

Most governments support the arts. It's not just a Western tradition. Poor communist countries such as Vietnam and Cuba invest in the arts. Governments in some Middle East countries are following the example of countries like Singapore and creating arts infrastructure to attract tourists and expats to live and work there as well as to celebrate their own culture. The reasons governments give for investing[23] in the arts in the 21st century are mainly what are described as instrumental values – what the arts can do for communities and individuals. For example, their contribution to urban renewal or regional development, creation of employment, tourism or general community creativity, their contribution to people's health and well-being, to better exam results for children, to better rehabilitation outcomes for prisoners and so on. However, while most governments provide financial support to the arts, it is usually given a low priority. Ironically, this is because of the very small budgets involved (van den Born, van Klink & Witteloostuijn 2011) and because governments have an ambivalent relationship with the arts which is sometimes seen as "oppositional and troublesome" (Hewison & Holden 2011, 73). The state is much more comfortable with traditional art forms such as symphonies or ballets because they don't challenge the status quo. The state

> is less comfortable with contemporary arts practice as it presents a different world view to its own. Some art practice then represents a power that the state finds hard to control and so it resists it in whatever way it can.
>
> (Caust 2018a, 7)

While there's lots of evidence to demonstrate the positive impact of arts and culture via these instrumental outcomes and most arts workers would agree that such outcomes are important, they are not the only reasons why artists make work and arts organisations exist. The intrinsic value of the arts is why most of us have committed to work in the industry. These are the "difficult to describe, let alone measure" qualities of the arts. They are the qualities that affect our emotion, our mind and even our spirit (Hewison & Holden 2011). Walmsley (2012, 200) argues that for the last three decades, "successive UK governments from both right and left have conspired to industrialize and monetize

the arts and culture to a point where their real (social and intrinsic) value has become secondary". Writers and arts managers in Australia and, I suspect, many other countries would agree that this has happened in their political environments as well. As Morganti and Nuccio (2011, 2) remind us:

"That art is useful is rhetoric. The debate about its value is everlasting."

It's not surprising that government policy makers (whether politicians or bureaucrats) are more comfortable in the realm of the instrumental benefits of the arts because intrinsic benefits are very individual and specific to the person having the arts experience even though there may be flow-on societal benefits. Governments are interested in providing measurable economic benefits rather than investing in the messy and hard to conceptualise, let alone measure world of emotions.

Mullen (2012) has written a research paper about how a company specialising in applied theatre (participatory theatre practices underpinned by social intentions) negotiated its relationships with government-funding bodies. You'd think that such a company, offering instrumental benefits to the community, would be in a good funding position, but the story offers interesting insights into the impact of a shift towards the achievement of measurable outcomes. Initially, the relation between the company and the funder was seen as a value-centre contract where the communities involved were equal stakeholders but then it shifted to an outputs-based contract where the communities became recipients of a service and the theatre company was working for the funders rather than working with the communities. The problem seems to be that a reliance on quantitative information led to a lack of understanding about more intrinsic values. The company's response to new policies that prioritised value for money and evidence-based research was to engage in strategies to ensure the survival of the company through advocacy from longstanding supporters, presenting evidence-based research and evaluation and engaging the support of powerful allies. In other words, they found a way to adapt to the new cultural policy but in the process the artists felt that any sense of the real value and meaning of their work was lost.

In amongst the cultural policies that require instrumental and measureable outcomes, there is still usually an acceptance that art practice and arts organisations are "good" *per se* for a community. For example, MTC employed people, added to Melbourne's vibrant city life, had an education program, promoted Australia's national identity through international touring, attracted tourists and so on. But one suspects that the real reason it was funded by State and Federal Governments was because if Melbourne wants to continue to be one of the world's most liveable cities, it has to have an excellent internationally renowned theatre company. This is not just about tourism or attracting people to live in the city but that people value, whether they go to it or not, a high-quality organisation that makes and presents plays.

Frey (2008) picks up an interesting irony in the fact that "arts people" focus on economic impact studies (and I'm guilty of that – see *Economics*) whereas "arts economists" concentrate on people's willingness to pay for arts and culture, even if they don't participate themselves. Why? Because, Frey argues, the arts people take the artistic value as given and see no need to establish that it contributes to human welfare but given the current policy climate, feel that decision makers can best be convinced to support the arts when economic (i.e. instrumental) benefits are demonstrated. Arts economists think that they need to establish the need for government support of art first. The only rationale for such support according to classical economics is that art produces external effects not captured by the market. If this can be proved, there is a justification for funding. And willingness-to-pay surveys are one way of capturing these external effects.

The use of economic value arguments about the arts may be required to help legitimise government funding in the eyes of "hard-headed economic policy makers" and Throsby (2010, 7) says that it may have an additional benefit

of acting like a Trojan horse and at least getting arts and culture onto the policy agenda. In powerful government agencies such as Treasury or Finance, bureaucrats are still highly sceptical of the arts seeing them as "warm and fuzzy window-dressing compared to the serious stuff of roads, schools and hospitals" (Eltham 2013). Once you're in the door to these agencies then, Throsby says, you can start to argue the case for cultural values, such as producing and consuming the arts, cultural identity and symbolism, cultural diversity and cultural preservation and continuity. Regardless of our personal views about the importance of the arts, governments have to make choices. As Bakhs, Freeman and Hitchens (2009, 17) pragmatically note, governments can't spend the same money twice – on a hospital and an art gallery. Evidence-based policy would say invest the money in the hospital because it saves more lives in the short term but what's the long-term impact on people's well-being through participation in and experience of the arts?

So what do the politicians spend money on? The debate is usually phrased in economic terms – should the "investment" be on the supply side or the demand side? The general view is that there is an excess of supply of both arts labour and arts output (Throsby 1992, 1994). However, in most countries, government policy is focused on giving grants to arts and companies to make more "products". Other policy options are to let the market do its work (i.e. no investment), restrict arts supply (e.g. reduce arts training courses) or stimulate arts demand (Hewison & Holden 2011, 7). One could stimulate demand by giving vouchers to people to "buy" art or to arts organisations to reduce prices or improve their marketing. Other ideas include prizes or tax credits instead of grants (Potts 2013).

It's not just direct investment in the arts through an Arts or Culture department that impact on an arts company. DeVereaux (2011, 228) provides a list of all the potential policy areas that impact on the arts including, education, censorship, community cultural development, tourism, heritage, human rights, trade, intellectual property, public art, artists' rights, tax deductibility, health, immigration and so the list goes on. Sometimes those policies have specific and direct impacts on the arts such what gets taught in schools. Sometimes the polices have an accidental impact such as the Victorian State tax rule that universities pay payroll tax but non-profit arts organisations don't. We fitted into both categories because the University of Melbourne owned us. As the State Revenue Office didn't want to create a precedent, it wouldn't give MTC an exemption and so in my final year at the company, our gross state grant was around A$400,000 but our net state grant was about A$10,000 because we paid tax. Sometimes, policies or decisions on the same subject result in contradictory and often unfortunate outcomes. For example, in 2014 the Federal Arts Minister gave Disney a grant of A$21.6 million to make a film in Australia (plus access to millions of dollars of tax offsets) at the same time that the country's premier film funder Screen Australia was told that its funding was to be cut by A$38 million over four years (Connolly 2015).

Arts organisations respond to changes in cultural policy in a number of ways. For example, we sometimes attempt to link our activities to government policies on topics such as education or regional development to attract funds. This may be pragmatic but may divert companies from their mission. Evidence-based funding has changed the emphasis from inputs to outputs which in turn leads to a more demand-oriented management of cultural organisations. An organisation's success might be measured on the numbers of shows they put on rather than the artists they employ; on the number of plays that are written rather than the commissions that are offered. And again, this may not be the best way of measuring the effectiveness of an arts organisation (Lindqvist 2012). And the other response is to try and change policy.

While policy making is largely driven by public servants, agenda setting on cultural issues can be done in a variety of different ways such as within political parties (particularly in the lead up to an election), through lobbying and advocacy by special interest groups, in response to environmental changes (both literal and eco-nomical) and in response to media attention on issues (DeVereaux 2011). From my first management role, I was actively involved in talking to government. If you don't participate in lobbying organisations or consultation processes, meetings with politicians or briefing of political advisers, joining advisory bodies or speaking out on matters of importance, then you miss out on the chance to have your say on policies that will impact on your organisation. Some art forms are better at this than others. The community broadcasting sector held annual Board meetings in Canberra to ensure that its Board could have conversations with Federal politicians but it took AMPAG,[24] representing the major performing arts group of companies, years after its formation to finally hold a gathering in Australia's political capital.

Most of the time, the arts community will come together at a time of crisis to battle government policy. Government cutbacks were so dire in Australia in 2016 that artists and cultural workers founded the Arts Party[25] entirely on crowdfunding and put forward 20 candidates in the next Federal election. They didn't win any seats but the arts voice was heard (White 2017). This isn't always the case. In some circumstances, organisations and their Boards don't respond critically to cultural policy decisions because of an unwillingness to upset the current government in a world of competitive grants.

Sometimes cultural policy can set companies and sectors against each other. In 2018, the Cultural Ministers Council in Australia launched a review into the funding model for the major performing arts companies. They held a series of meetings around Australia and I attended one in Melbourne. The atmosphere was bitter with many people attacking the major companies for their very existence as bastions of Western white culture. But the underlying bitterness was about money. Why should some large companies receive ongoing funding and not face competition when the small to medium sector is starved of funds? This is not just an

Australian story. There's a quote in an article about the Hong Kong Arts Development Council which could be word for word what the Australian small to medium companies think about the majors: that they don't "foster high artistic standards or sustained indigenous creativity [whereas] the ideas generated by smaller troupes are innovative but short-lived" (Chin & Yun 2013, 44). Cultural policy can divide us as well as unite us.

By staying on top of government decisions and policies, arts managers can ensure that their organisation is complying with laws and government regulations, can adapt to changing policy conditions, is prepared financially for policy decisions that may have a fiscal impact and can rally friends and supporters to pre-emptively oppose policy decisions that affect the core mission or programs (DeVereaux 2011).

The biggest issue that arts organisations face in Western democracies[26] is the pattern of reducing government support for the art and the pressure on companies to find replacement funding from corporate sponsors and private patronage. Regardless of whether that push has been effective or not, there are issues for organisations in increasing their reliance on such funding sources and there are also questions about whether letting wealthy individuals "determine" government expenditure in the form of tax deduction is appropriate (Throsby 2010).

Throsby (2010, 235), one of the most reputable and thoughtful cultural economists, concludes one of his books with the advice that governments interested in protecting and advancing the public interest

> will require constant vigilance to ensure that the right balance is struck between fostering the economic potential of the cultural industries in all their various guises, promoting beneficial social change, and ensuring the long-term health and vitality of the art and culture that is the cornerstone of civilisation.

As the weight is more on the side of the economic potential at the moment, we in the arts and cultural industries have to be equally vigilant in making sure the arguments about the intrinsic value of the arts are heard and that artists and companies that advance those values are supported. Outputs such as excellence, innovation and risk taking are just as important as employment, exam results and tourist numbers.

See also: Cultural Leadership, Economics, Evaluation, Fundraising, Philanthropy, Sponsorship, Stakeholders

References

Bakhshi, H., Freeman, A. & Hitchen, G. 2009 *Measuring Intrinsic Value: How to Stop Worrying and Love Economics*, http://culturehive.co.uk/wp-content/uploads/2013/10/Measuring-Intrinsic-Value-Hasan-Bakhshi-Alan-Freeman-Graham-Hitchen-2009_0_0.pdf [accessed 16 March 2019].

Brokensha, P. & Tonks, A. 1986 *Culture and Community: Economics and Expectations of the Arts in South Australia*, Sydney: Social Science Press.

Caust, J. 2003 "Putting the 'Art' Back into Arts Policy Making: How Arts Policy Has Been 'Captured' by the Economist and the Marketers", *The International Journal of Cultural Policy*, 9(1), 51–63.

Caust, J. 2018a *Arts Leadership in Contemporary Contexts*, London: Routledge.

Chin, W-K. & Yun, S-W. (2013) "The Predicament of Competition for Cultural Resources among Hong Kong Art Troupes", *LEAP Magazine*, 23 May, quoted in Caust, J. (ed.) *Arts and Cultural Leadership in Asia*, London: Routledge.

Connolly, S. 2015 "Film Funding: Just Who Will Be Walking the Plank", http://dailyreview.crikey.com.au/film-funding-just-who-will-be-walking-the-plank/11507 [accessed 16 March 2019].

DeVereaux, C. 2011 "Arts and Cultural Policy", in Brindle, M. & DeVereaux, C. (eds) *The Arts Management Handbook*, Armon, NY: M.E. Sharpe, 219–251.

Eltham, B. 2013 "Evidence-based Policy: The Minefield of Cultural Measurement", *A Cultural Policy Blog*, 17 August http://culturalpolicyreform.wordpress.com/category/evidence-based-policy/ [accessed 16 March 2019].

Enoch, W. 2014 *Take Me to Your Leader: The Dilemma of Cultural Leadership*, Platform Paper No. 40, Sydney: Currency House.

Frey, B. S. 2008 "What Values Should Count in the Arts: The Tension between Economic Effects and

Cultural Value", in Hutter, M. & Throsby, D. (eds) *Beyond Price*, Cambridge: Cambridge University Press, 261–269.

Hayes, D. & Roodhouse, S. 2010 "From Missionary to Market Maker", in O'Reilly, D. & Kerrigan, F. (eds) *Marketing the Arts: A Fresh Approach*, London: Routledge, 40–53.

Hewison, R. & Holden, J. 2011 *The Cultural Leadership Handbook*, Farnham: F Gower.

Lindqvist, K. 2012 "Effects of Public Sector Reforms on the Management of Cultural Organizations in Europe", *International Studies of Management and Organization*, 42(2), 9–28.

Morganti, I. & Nuccio, M. 2011 "Towards an Enhanced Framework for Impact Evaluation of Cultural Events", Antwerp: 11th AIMAC International Conference.

Mullen, M. 2012 "Taking Care and Playing it Safe: Tensions in the Management of Funding Relations", *Journal of Arts & Communities*, 4(3), 181–198.

Potts, J. 2013 "You've Got $7 billion – So How Will You Fund the Arts?", *The Conversation*, 4 November, http://theconversation.com/youve-got-7-billion-so-how-will-you-fund-the-arts-18839 [accessed 16 March 2019].

Schultz, J. 2014 "The Fourth Pillar", *Griffith Review*, Brisbane, 44, 7–9.

Throsby, D. 1992 "Artists as Workers", in Towse, R. & Khakee, A. (eds) *Cultural Economics*, Berlin: Springer Verlag.

Throsby, D. 1994 "The Production and Consumption of the Arts: A View of Cultural Economics", *Journal of Economic Literature*, 32, 1–29.

Throsby, D. 2010 *The Economics of Cultural Policy*, Cambridge: Cambridge University Press.

Van den Born, A., van Klink, P. & Witteloostuijn, A. 2011 "Subsidizing Performing Arts: between Civilization and Addiction", Antwerp: AIMAC International Conference.

Walmsley, B. 2012 "Whose Value Is It Anyway? A Neo-institutionalist Approach to Articulating and Evaluating Artistic Value", *Journal of Arts and Communities*, 4(3), 199–215.

White, J. 2017 *Culture Heist: Art versus Money*, Blackheath, NSW: Bandl & Schlesinger.

Notes

1 Not a typo.

2 After writing this in the 1st edition of this book in 2015, I played exactly this role at Chunky Move Dance Company in 2018/19.

3 Second in command.

4 As it turns out, other writers such as O'Toole, Galbraith and Lawler (2002) had been writing positively about co-leadership in the business community some years earlier.

5 We were joined a couple years later by Sarah Reynolds.

6 For the list of companies, see www.ampag.com.au/

7 Chief Operating Officer.

8 Participants were kept anonymous and labelled by role (Artistic Director – AD; General Manager/Executive Director/Managing Director – GM) and a randomly allocated number.

9 For example, Dwyer, J. 2015 *Communications for Business and the Professions: Strategies and Skills* (6th ed), Sydney: Pearson.

10 As it turns out, there is someone. Jim Volz (2017, 16) recommends having the door open but only for a short, consistent time each day, along with getting out of the office and walking about.

11 For more myths about creativity see Coffee (2013).

12 Named after the founder of the Union Theatre Repertory Company which turned into MTC, John Sumner.

13 Named after Ray Lawler, writer of the iconic Australian play *Summer of the Seventeenth Doll*.

14 For more detail see *Leadership*.

15 I was on the Board of the company for a number of years but not during the time of the Ganesh story.

16 I am writing days after the massacre of staff and visitors at Charlie Hebdo in Paris.

17 https://backtobacktheatre.com/projects/ganesh/

18 For example: www.hinduccv.org.au/news/45-clarification-re-ganesh-play-controversy [accessed 20 February 2019].

19 E.g. Assassination of Juliano Mer-Khamis, co-Artistic Director of the Freedom Theatre in Jenin.

20 Produced in 1996.

21 You can find fascinating insight into this tension in Salman Rushdie's autobiography *Anton Joseph*.

22 Kenneth Branagh's version: www.youtube.com/watch?v=A-yZNMWFqvM

23 And "investing" tends to be the word these days rather than "subsidising".

24 Australian Major Performing Arts Group.

25 I admit to being a founding member.

26 But also in other countries adopting neoliberal economic approaches to government spending, e.g. Vietnam.

D

Decision-making

Making decisions will be part of your every day as an arts manager but there is no one simple formula to help you make good decisions.

Decisions can be made based on analysis or intuition, evidence or experience. They can be rational or political, quantitative or qualitative. You might have a sense about the outcome or no idea at all. In the process of making decisions it helps if you understand how you prefer to make decisions, what sort of decision you have to make and even whether you should be the one making the decision.

Brousseau et al. (2006) point out that we make decisions in different ways. Some of us are maximisers who mull over realms of data and just can't rest until we've found the right answer whereas others of us are satisfied with just the key facts to check a hypothesis we've already established. Another aspect of decision-making is whether the information you've gathered will lead you to one decision or many. Brousseau et al. (2006) divide people into four categories:

1. Decisive – little information, one course of action
2. Flexible – little information, many options
3. Hierarchic – lots of data, one course of action
4. Integrative – lots of data, many options.

The decisive decision maker values action, speed, efficiency and consistency. Once a plan is in place, they stick to it. They come across as action-focused and task-oriented. The flexible decision maker is focused on speed as well but they also value adaptability. They make decisions quickly and change course just as quickly in a style that comes across as highly social and responsive. The hierarchic decision maker doesn't rush to judgement because they analyse lots of information and expect others to contribute. Brousseau et al. (2006) describe this as a complex style that comes across as highly intellectual. The integrative decision maker is equally happy to explore a wide range of views and decision-making becomes a process of collecting input. This creative style comes across as highly participative.

Brousseau et al. (2006) conclude that managers' decision-making styles change as they progress through organisations. At first, when they are in line positions, they have to act quickly, often with little information. They develop a decisive form of leadership and a single focus to their thinking (get the job done). Later, in middle-management positions they need to be creative, floating ideas upstairs which can be selected (or not) for further development. Their style and their thinking become more open and multi-focused. Later still, in senior positions, there is a cross-over: outwardly, in terms of leadership style, senior executives are open and multi-focused, encouraging others to supply them with what they need: high-grade information from the coal-face. But their thinking narrows and becomes more analytic. Inwardly, they become single focused again, trying to identify the correct decision or decisions that will set their organisation on the right path.

I shared Brousseau et al's (2006) article about decision-making with my management team at MTC because I thought that understanding each other's preferred style might improve our collective work. We discussed what this analysis meant for arts organisations. Our conclusion[1] was that Artistic Directors and Managing Directors in arts organisations will always find themselves bound up in "line" decisions (the art), middle-management decisions (product development) and senior executive decisions (programming and organisational issues). They will need to be decisive in the first, creative in the second and open-in-appearance-but-single-minded-in-reality in the third. The stress that this places individuals under is enormous, not simply because the workload is so large, but because the different kind of decisions that face managers of the arts on a daily basis are likely to be extraordinarily heterogeneous.

While we might have a particular preference towards a decision-making style, we may also have to adopt a certain decision-making strategy depending on how much time or information or pressure that we're facing. Golensky (2011, 88) list six different strategies:

1. Optimising which is similar to Brousseau et al's (2006) maximising where one embarks on a rational process trying to get all the relevant information and carefully weigh all the alternatives. Of course, the basic problem with this approach is that it's difficult to attain perfect rationality and it ignores intuition and wisdom.
2. Satisficing which accepts that perfect rationality isn't achievable and that reaching an acceptable decision may be all that one can realistically achieve.
3. Incrementalism, where you take a gradualist approach, making small decisions and small changes as pieces of information come to light. Golensky calls this "muddling through".
4. Garbage-can is a less orderly process where one is forever adapting and responding to outside pressures or inside constraints.

5. Mixed scanning is a decision-making strategy where you optimise (as best you can) the big decisions and use an incremental approach for small decisions. A flexible approach that probably sounds familiar to most arts managers.
6. Consensus is as it says: an inclusive and participatory strategy of group decision-making where compromises might be needed but the participants feel engaged in an egalitarian process.

Another approach to decision-making is delightfully described by people working in a German creative space: "We have a decision structure that we label 'do-ocracy'. That's not grass-roots democracy – but deciding by doing … It is important that we have progress and not that everybody agrees with everybody" (quoted in Kirchberg 2019, 233). Alvesson and Spicer (2016, 49) also value what they call practical intelligence – "the kind of everyday knowhow that people use in order to get things done".

So what sort of decisions do we have to make? Golensky (2011, 91) divides decisions into three categories and provides labels for each:

1. Familiar-constricted: comparatively well-known subjects
2. Vortex-sporadic: weighty and controversial subjects
3. Tractable-fluid: unusual but not controversial subjects.

She advises on the approaches one should take for each type of decision. For example, for unusual but noncontroversial topics, Golensky describes a fluid process which (as it name suggests) flows smoothly, with regular meetings, few delays or impediments, where experts are consulted but not an endless array of them. That was the way we went about setting up the process for our first capital campaign at MTC. We consulted experts, set up a Board committee and had regular meetings with an effective reporting back process.

It's not that one has to divide every decision that needs to be made into categories but it's useful to consider the nature of major decisions so that one can activate the right process. For example, if a decision isn't precedent setting or has limited consequences, then why not delegate to an expert within the organisation? If a decision is going to require the contribution of outside stakeholders and more particularly politicians, then be prepared for the decision-making process to be very stop-start and take years. That was the nature of the decision to build MTC's new theatre. My predecessor had got very close to getting approval and financing for the project and then the economy changed. I also got close a number of times but each time an external stakeholder derailed the process. Thinking of this decision as "vortex-sporadic" simply means that you'll never be discouraged as you go about trying to get a decision on a major project although you may be disappointed along the way.

Another equally useful approach to decision-making – called the Cynefin Framework – is a reminder to think about the context. Is it a simple situation where there's clear cause and effect? Then the answer may be just to apply best practice. Complicated situations might have a number of right answers so getting experts involved might be helpful. If it's a complex situation, the process of getting to a decision may involve many people and letting an answer emerge. However, in a chaotic situation a more rapid decision-making approach may be required where you need to act first and then work out what's happened (Snowden & Boone 2007). For example, choosing the right company to tender for a café is a complicated but not complex situation. By getting some experts on restaurants onto a panel, you can make a good decision. At a time of crisis and chaos, such as when the Southbank Theatre was flooded, we acted quickly on the day and then as the different impacts of the flood emerged, we developed plans and strategies to deal with in a more strategic manner than that initial response.

Regardless of what sort of a decision you have to make, there will be pressure to make a rational one based on evidence. This is an interesting challenge for arts organisations. Shortly after I started at MTC, a new Board member joined who had a quantitative bent. It was a time of financial stress for the company so he wanted to be convinced that we knew what we were doing when it came to the key decision-making of the company – the annual program of plays. He wanted to see our decision-making model. New to the industry, I rang the Artistic Director of another company and asked what analytical tools he used to choose plays. He laughed dismissively and said "just tell them it's magic". Clearly that advice wasn't going to work for me. I embarked on a process which, as it turns out, fits in with some of the decision-making processes described in an article called *Deciding How to Decide*. Although I didn't use the language of Courtney, Lovallo and Clarke (2013), I did ask myself the same questions that they propose in a toolkit for executives.

Did I know (or did anyone in the company know) what it would take to have a successful season of plays, both artistically and financially? The answer was no. There was no successful commercial company producing subscription seasons of plays. There were no theatre companies that were successful year in, year out. And my company hadn't been particularly successful for a few years.

Could I predict the range of outcomes? Yes, I could. Based on financial and ticketing history plus information about the artistic team from writer to designer, I could place an upper, lower and most likely ticket sales result for each show.

Did I need to aggregate information? Yes, I needed information about past ticket sales for different types of shows; from the artistic team about who they had in mind for each play and their preferred venue for each; budget information for the likely salary costs of actors and creatives and past production costs of particular Directors and designers. Putting all this together, I created a model that delivered a likely box office result plus a risk scenario for each play.

In some ways, this is what the company had been doing through gut feel for years but by spelling it out, we provided comfort to a Board more used to analysis than intuition. It also meant as managers, we were more exposed. Our best guess was on the line and when we failed miserably (which we did occasionally), we could be held to account.

Of course, the decision-making process about what was to be in the season each year also involved taste and intuition, wisdom and serendipity (such as the availability of actors and creatives). Pfeffer and Sutton (2006, 42) call for more evidence-based management rather than relying on "hope, fear, dearly held ideologies, what others are doing, and what they have done in the past". They challenge managers to look for facts and beware of their own preconceived ideas and assumptions and adopt what they call an attitude of wisdom in which you act with knowledge while doubting what you know. In other words, you strike a balance between arrogance (assuming that you know more than you do) and insecurity (believing that you know too little to act).

However, what's missing from this approach is intuition. Sadler-Smith and Shefy (2004, 87) define intuition as "a composite phenomenon that incorporates expertise and feeling". They demonstrate how one can move from intuition to rational analysis in a validation process of checking your "gut feeling" with data or proceeding from rational analysis to intuition through what they call an "incubation process" where intuition provides feeling or expertise-based validation to your initial judgement. If you're uncomfortable with the idea of knowledge obtained through intuition rather than analysis, Dörfler and Ackerman (2012) offer some devil's advocate questions to differentiate intuition from the more ad hoc decision-making processes that Pfeffer and Sutton criticise such as: are you mixing intuition with easily remembered events, or looking for confirmatory evidence in what you hope is true and ignoring contrary evidence, or are you mixing up intuition with wishful thinking? Rationality, feeling and experience all feed into good decision-making.

There are a multitude of ways to make poor decisions such as leaving decisions to the last minute, making the obvious decision rather than the considered one, failing to ask the right question in the process, getting distracted by irrelevant facts, not collecting enough information or consulting the right people. However, the two problems that regularly come up in conversation with my post-graduate students when discussing their experience with poor management are managers who don't make decisions or take too long to make decisions. There is never going to be the perfect time to make the perfect decision and part of the challenge of being an effective leader is to have the self-confidence to make the hard decisions. This reminds me of a senior manager in the ABC who had a completely clear desk, a rather shocking and curious phenomenon. Every time you provided a written report, the manager would handwrite appropriate action on it and hand it straight back. I'm not sure I'm convinced about it as a technique because everything gets done in the order it arrives rather than in priority order and nothing is mulled over and thought about. However, if the opposite is never making a decision and sitting on reports forever than the purity of the clean desk does appeal. Another side to this story is deciding on when to do the important and when to do the urgent. Managers often prefer to make the urgent decision because it feels exciting but although decisions are urgent, they may not always be important. And the important decision, which may be complex, requires more consultation and/or be about values, gets postponed (Hagoort 2005).

Some techniques to help make decisions in addition to gathering facts and reflecting on past experiences are to gather opinions, brainstorm and imagine. Szulanski and Amin (2001, 541–542) recommend a "disciplined imagination" decision-making paradigm where one might generate imaginative options and then use rational methodologies to explore them. This became the process we used at MTC to develop the annual play program. The process of thinking about possible plays and creative teams was an imaginative one but along the way, we would regularly and iteratively analyse the possible combinations of audiences and budgets to see which was going to make the most sense to fulfil our mission and for the financial survival of the company. The final decision was in the hands of the Artistic Director, but the process involved a group of people with a range of different skills and experiences – the Casting Director and the Finance Director, the Marketing Manager and the Production Manager. As Bakke (2005, 75) says, "[w]hen bosses make all the decision, we are apt to feel frustrated and powerless, like overgrown children being told what to do by our parents" and being involved in the process avoided this feeling and added to our collective commitment to the year ahead.

Groups need to be involved in decision-making when you need group acceptance, when the decision will affect the group directly, when the group wants to be involved and when the group has relevant knowledge or experience (George and Cole 1992). The potential advantages of group work are that you have a larger pool of data, different perspectives, intellectual stimulation from the different views and more commitment to the final outcome (Dickie & Dickie 2011). Such processes can be slow and difficult with either too much conflict when people are only thinking of their own self-interest or not enough conflict where people are loathe to disagree with each other. But in organisations where you want to facilitate team work and a sense of community, where you want people to use their individual talents and skills cooperatively, then group decision-making should be part of the mix.

Another approach is to let the smart people you've employed make the decisions for you. Each week at MTC, I would have individual meetings with my key staff. I might have new tasks and ideas for them but most of them time I just wanted to hear what decisions they'd made and be a sounding board for decisions they were thinking about making. After all, I'd chosen these people because of their skills and intelligence, I'd encouraged their care of the organisation, they

were specialists in their areas whereas I was a just a generalist, so why wouldn't I let them make decisions? On reflection, I can see the times when I didn't trust someone's decision-making. For them, I would have an agenda; I would double check to make sure what they'd done; I would insist on written reports and proposals. And usually, I was relieved when that person left the organisation.

One staff member who didn't report directly to me used to come to me a couple of times a year with a particular question about giving complimentary tickets as a thank you to special service providers. At the beginning, I simply approved her decisions. Then I suggested that I was perfectly happy to let her make the decisions. But she kept coming back. In some ways, I was grateful because this allowed us the chance to catch up and have the sort of informal chat that didn't necessarily happen as we were in different parts of the building. But it always worried me that she didn't feel that she could make such decisions. I suspect the answer was a combination of factors: that she also enjoyed the chance to have a catch up but that as this was a decision that wasn't part of her day-to-day work, she felt more comfortable having a "boss" make it.

That story is a reminder that ultimately it's you as the leader or the CEO or the manager who has to make key decisions. Apart from the processes for making a good decision mentioned above, Woiceshyn (2009, 308) suggests a variety of principles that help avoid bias in decision-making such as "evading facts, following someone else's conclusions blindly or pretending that facts are other than they are". We need to apply critical thinking skills and avoid giving weight to the first information we receive, to remember to consider both positive and negative factors, to focus on facts not just what someone was suggested, and to make sure you have enough resources to implement a decision once it's made.

Decision-making within any organisations can be political but the tensions can become more obvious and challenging within arts organisations. Should one spend money on commissioning new work or the education program? Should staff be given a pay increase or should the money go to increase the contract payments to directors and designers? Should we spend more on sets or marketing? As Cray, Inglis and Freeman (2007, 306) say, "[r]ecognizing these differences and dealing with them through negotiation and coalition building helps emphasize common concerns while acknowledging that legitimate differences exist".

McCann (2008, 15) makes a good point about decision-making:

> There are no set rules about decision making – except to appreciate the ambiguity and the tensions at play and to appreciate the tremendous paradox surrounding the really big decisions. Tensions apparent in any organization include: the established in conflict with the new; the need for form and the drive toward openness; critical standards and the need to experiment – to fail; the security of the familiar and the lure of the unknown; discipline in tension with freedom and autonomy; expertise in tension with freshness.

Dehler, Welsh and Lewis (2004, 172) say that complicated understanding involves increasing the variety of ways things can be understood. Viewing the organisation from multiple perspectives should help in that process. Parker (2010, 110) finds a way of describing this using a metaphor which will be familiar to those who work in the performing arts. She calls it an improvisational mindset that requires "we acknowledge there are myriad possibilities and choices, and that we are open and curious enough to not dismiss these out of hand because they do not fit with our rigid world view of how something should be".

One of my favourite books on organisations is called *The Stupidity Paradox* (Avesson & Spicer 2016). They conclude that the only way to stop doing stupid things i.e. making poor decisions, is to use critical thinking and reflection. The three aspects of functional stupidity are:

- Not thinking about your assumptions; taking things for granted; not questioning dominant beliefs and expectations
- Not asking why you're doing something
- Not considering the consequences of your actions.

To help us get over these weaknesses they recommend being more observant, getting other people's perspectives on problems and asking questions – about whether something is correct, is it ethical, will it cause difficulties for people? In other words, don't take your initial observations and solutions at face value. Have post-mortems but also pre-mortems (imagining what it might be like a couple of years after you've made that decision), get opinions from outsiders and newcomers. To which I would add – read their book.

Decision-making is risk-filled but we make big and small decisions at every point in our lives – who to marry, which movie to watch, what car to buy, which political party to support. Each of us will do it slightly differently but we will use a combination of rationality and intuition based on evidence, experience and reflection. Sometimes the decision won't be the perfect one but as long as you've bought skill, thoughtfulness and honesty to the process then that's the best you can do.

See also: Delegation, Intuition, Problem Solving, Strategic Plan

References

Alvesson, M. & Spicer, A. 2016 *The Stupidity Paradox*, London: Profile Books.

Bakke, D. W. 2005 *Joy at Work*, Seattle: PVG.

Bolman, L. G. & Deal, T. E. 2013 *Reframing Organizations* (5th ed), San Francisco, CA: Jossey-Bass.

Brousseau, K. R., Driver, M. J., Hourihan, G. & Larsson, R. 2006 "The Seasoned Executive's Decision Making Style", *Harvard Business Review*, 84(2), 110–121.

Courtney, H., Lovallo, D. & Clarke, C. 2013 "Deciding How to Decide", *Harvard Business Review*, 91(11), 64–70.

Cray, D., Inglis, L. & Freeman, S. 2007 "Managing the Arts: Leadership and Decision Making under Dual

Rationalities", *The Journal of Arts Management, Law and Society*, 36(4), 295–313.

Croggon, A. 2013 "The Perfect Storm: Playwright vs. Director", *ABC Arts*, www.abc.net.au/arts/blog/Alison-Croggon/playwright-versus-Director-130731/ [accessed 23 January 2015].

Dehler, G. E., Welsh, M. A. & Lewis, M. W. 2004 "Critical Pedagogy in the 'New Paradigm'", in Grey, C. & Antonacopoulou, E. (eds) *In Essential Readings in Management Learning*, London: Sage Publications, 167–186.

Dickie, L. & Dickie, C. 2011 *Cornerstones of Management* (2nd ed), Melbourne: Tilde University Press.

Dörfler, D. & Ackermann, F. 2012 "Understanding Intuition: The Case for Two Forms of Intuition", *Management Learning*, 43(5), 545–564.

George, C. S. & Cole, K. 1992 *Supervision in Action*, Sydney: Prentice Hall.

Golensky, M. 2011 *Strategic Leadership and Management in Nonprofit Organizations*, Chicago, IL: Lyceum Books Inc.

Hagoort, G 2005, Art Management: Entrepreneurial Style (5th ed), Delft: Eburon.

Kirchberg, V. 2019 "Managing Real Utopias: Artistic and Creative Visions and Implementation", in DeVereaux, C. (ed.) *Arts and Cultural Management: Sense and Sensibility in the State of the Field*, New York: Routledge, 226–246.

Krug, K. & Weinberg, C. B. 2004 "Mission, Money and Merit: Strategic Decision Making by Nonprofit Managers", *Nonprofit Management and Leadership*, 14(3), 325–342.

Parker, D. 2010 "The Improvising Leader: Developing Leadership Capacity through Improvisation", in Kay, S. & Venner, S. (eds) *A Cultural Leader's Handbook*, London: Creative Choices, 106–112.

Pfeffer, J. & Sutton, R. I. 2006 *Hard Facts, Dangerous Half-Truths, and Total Nonsense*, Boston, MA: Harvard Business School Press.

McCann, J. M. 2008 "Development: Leadership as Creativity", *Arts Management Newsletter*, No. 82.

Sadler-Smith, E. & Shefy, E. 2004 "The Intuitive Executive: Understanding and Applying 'Gut Feel' in Decision-making", *Academy of Management Executive*, 18(4), 76–91.

Snowden, D. J. & Boone, M. E. 2007 "A Leader's Framework for Decision Making", *Harvard Business Review*, November, 85(11), 68–76.

Szulanski, G. & Amin, K. 2001 "Learning to Make Strategy: Balancing Discipline and Imagination", *Long Range Planning*, 34(5), 537–556.

Woiceshyn, J. 2009 "Lessons from 'Good Minds': How CEOs Use Intuition, Analysis and Guiding Principles to Make Strategic Decisions", *Long Range Planning*, 42(3), 298–319.

Delegation

Years ago, Robbie Macrae and I were volunteers together at a community radio station. Now (2019), he's the CEO of Auckland Live, the organisation that manages and programs most live entertainment venues in New Zealand's biggest city. In an interview with Jo Caust he talked about the importance of delegation. She said: "he keeps a hand on the 'big picture' but expects those underneath them to do their job without his interference" (Caust 2015b, 158). Management writer Patrick Lencioni (2000, xiii) says that leaders have to focus on a "reasonable number of issues that will have the greatest possible impact on the success of your organisation, and then spend most of your time thinking about, talking about, and working on those issues" (Lencioni 2000, xiii). Both these comments imply that there are going to be tasks that you either shouldn't spend too much time on or that are more appropriately done by someone else. They are good reasons to delegate.

An even better reason to delegate is because you're not being fair to good staff if you don't delegate some important work (De Pree 1997). One way to motivate people is to give them the chance to undertake and to succeed in doing new work and meeting new challenges. Benson Puah, CEO of the Esplanade in Singapore, describes the role of leader as "a teacher who is there to encourage staff to take more responsibility and be confident enough to make their own decisions" (Caust 2015b, 159).

You can delegate general functions such as budget control, people management, purchasing, strategies around service and performance (Hudson 2009) and you can delegate particular tasks or projects or new initiatives. What you can't delegate are the big ticket items such as policy making, crisis management, serious people management issues and of course both the rituals and requirements of leadership.

By delegating, you are making better use of your time, giving people development opportunities and using people's skills effectively. As Drucker (1990, 117) says, everyone believes in delegation, so why is it seen to be one of the hardest management tasks? There are specific reasons why it's hard in arts and cultural organisations. Managers are especially dedicated, believing in the cause, willing to work long hours and so the temptation is just to work that extra hour or two each day and get the job done. There usually aren't enough staff anyway and they're overloaded already. Sometimes there is only one or two other people in the office so who can you delegate to? All of those points may be true but there are ways around them. For example, in a small arts company, there's always the Board. You can delegate upwards. Even if you and your staff are stretched, then delegating will help you to do your job more effectively and potentially make someone else's job more interesting. And perhaps you can get a volunteer in to do some of the more mundane tasks.

In general, people avoid delegating because they fear that the person won't be able to complete the task, that they won't want to take on extra responsibilities, that by delegating one loses control, that the staff member will take longer than you will to do the task. Again, all of these points may potentially be true but the trick to delegation is the set up: choose a good person, explain the task clearly, arrange to get regular reports and provide feedback (including praise) and make sure they have the relevant information. Don't dump the boring or unpleasant jobs on people and don't overburden them. It requires clear understanding from both parties about expectations and a joint commitment to the task.

I suspect that that the main reason why people don't delegate is that they are still accountable for the results even though they haven't done the work. That's scary – but you can't do everything and so trust is a necessary part of the work environment.

See also: Empowerment, Management, People, Trust, Volunteers, Upward Management

References

Caust, J. 2015b "Different Culture but Similar Contexts: Leadership of Major Performing Arts Centers", in Caust, J. (ed.) *Arts and Cultural Leadership in Asia*, London: Routledge, 148–162.
De Pree, M. 1997 *Leading Without Power*, Holland, MI: Shepherd Foundation.
Drucker, P. F. 1990 *Managing the Nonprofit Organization*, New York: HarperCollins.
Hudson, M. 2009 *Managing without Profit: Leadership, Management and Governance of Third Sector Organisations in Australia*, Sydney: UNSW Press.
Lencioni, P. 2000 *The Four Obsessions of an Extraordinary Executive*, San Francisco, CA: Jossey-Bass.

Diversity

The argument for organisations to become more diverse has been based on a business case unlike equality and discrimination demands which tend to be based in legislation. The business case includes beliefs in outcomes such as:

- Access to a wider labour market if you have a reputation for effective diversity management
- Access to new markets and improved understanding of customer groups
- Creativity with a diversity of perspectives challenging traditional ways of working
- Improved problem solving
- System-flexibility with more questioning and challenging of accepted ways of doing things
- Decreased workplace friction and turnover
- Improved employee relations
- Increased innovation and responsiveness
- Improved public image (Kumra & Manfredi 2012; Sinclair 2005).

I've never been convinced that the dollar value of the business case is the most important part of the argument. It seems to me that it has been developed to help organisations get over the hump of employing the "other". My position is that it's the social justice and fairness arguments that are important and if the result is that it costs the organisation a little more, so be it.

When *Harvard Business Review* asked 24 global leaders why diversity was important in their organisations, their answer was twofold:

> They believed it was a business imperative because their companies need it to stay competitive and they believed it was a moral imperative because of their personal experiences and values.
>
> (Groysberg & Connolly 2013, 70)

The authors provide a quote from Paul Block of the US sweetener manufacture Merisant who points out that "[p]eople with different lifestyles and different backgrounds challenge each other more. Diversity creates dissent, and you need that. Without it, you're not going to get any deep inquiry or breakthroughs" (Groysberg & Connolly 2013, 70).

Amanda Sinclair (2004, 221) is somewhat blunter on the subject:

> The basic justifications for managing diversity seem obvious to the point of being banal. Seeking to accommodate differences in organizations in the interests of organizational health, individual rights and social justice, particularly in a globalizing context, seems like an eminently sensible thing to do.

However, Sheehan, De Cieri and Holland (2013) note that there is still ambivalence amongst Human Resource professionals. Should diversity be encouraged if it only has societal benefits and not direct financial benefits to the company? As arts organisations, exploring new ways of looking and experiencing the world, I think that the social and equity arguments win and that we should actively search for and facilitate a diverse workforce. The starting point has to be management commitment to a policy of diversity. An organisation can become diverse if diversity becomes visible and management sets a good example.

I had the privilege of working in South Africa as a consultant shortly after the first democratic elections in 1994. My job was to review the national English language radio station and make recommendations for change so that it could reflect the reality of a mixed-race country. Radio South Africa as it was then known was a BBC clone but a clone from the 1950s. There was the obvious fact that no-one of colour was on air ("they have their own radio stations"; "they don't speak English properly"). The programs were also fixed in their vision of not just a white past, but a white male past. There was a particularly strange program of what I called "lift music" or "muzak" that lead up to the 7pm news. When asked what it was for, the answer was so that the husband could relax when he got home from work and have a drink with his wife! (I did say this was 1994, not 1954.)

Obviously, any change implementation was going to require finding and/or training people of colour to produce and present programs, but also to help the remaining white staff to embrace the change in a way that provided support for the newcomers. In particular, management needed not only to be seen to accept the change but to actively and positively engage with it. While I was creating my recommendations, a similar process was going on with the national Afrikaans language station.

The difference between the managers of the two stations was fascinating. In the new world, the English speaker was less tarred with suspicion than the Afrikaans speaker but it was the Afrikaner manager who made the transition and become a trusted advisor in the new world. Why? Because he examined his heart, offered to give up his power and authority for the less experienced people of colour, and remained willing to serve them.

I joined the Australian Broadcasting Corporation because of someone who believed in diversity. Roger Grant was appointed to run Radio National and ABC-FM after years of working for the ABC overseas. He came back to face a room full of his peers who all looked the same: male, straight, long-term ABC employees mainly from the news or rural divisions. He was two of those things but the third was the one that drove him to look outside the organisation for new faces, new ideas, new skills. As he undertook his first work tour of ABC state branches, he used his networks to ask for names of people with radio and management experience and mine came up. I was running a community radio station at the time and had no desire to leave. Roger asked if he could stay in touch and every time a management position came up, he'd let me know. Finally, I succumbed, applied and was appointed as the first Station Manager of Radio National. Through this active search for different talent and experience, Roger gathered a team around him that was reasonably diverse. There were three women and two men; three straight and two gay; some religious, some not. The team didn't represent a complete set of diversity (we were white with only modest physical handicaps) but we were different enough to the dominant culture and different enough from each other to enable rich debates, synergistic decision-making, out of the box answers and new strategies. And the lesson I learnt was about the strength of diversity in a team.

In 2018, the Victorian Government in Australia started to consider a Gender Equality Bill which would see gender targets prescribed in legislation (Minister for Women 2018). They are considering, for example, a 50% target for women executives and 50/50 representation on paid public Boards. The rationale for these mandatory quotes is that it places the burden of recruitment on those who control the process, rather than on individual women.

Arguments for quotas include the pressure to act quickly or face penalties; prioritising gender equality action; creating a critical mass of women in an organisation; increasing the talent pool. The arguments against quotas are that women will be viewed as "token", that merit is undermined as a recruitment principle; that there aren't enough suitable women; direct and indirect costs to the business.

Voluntary targets, by comparison, are seen as being able to be set by the companies in a way that's relevant to their business; increase the likelihood of buy-in; and create a positive bias to women within the organisation. On the other hand, they are seen as token and ineffective and take a long time to see positive results.

Regardless of whether you believe in compulsory quotas or voluntary targets, it is still worth using the question of which approach is best as a starting point to examine the openness of your organisation. Because the first thing you have to do is to "measure" your workplace to check your diversity and then be mindful about how to increase it.

Gender

I clearly have opinions informed by experience on the subject of equality and diversity based on gender. I first became conscious of discrimination against women in the work force when my mother talked about the men who managed building society branches and could choose what suit to wear whereas although she'd opened the first suburban branch she was only ever described as a supervisor and had to wear the same uniform as all the other "girls".

In an article on gender diversity in non-profit organisations in the USA, Mastracci and Herring (2010) tested three hypotheses about women's participation in non-profit organisations. The questions were if the proportion of women in core occupations increases if (1) there is greater use of innovative work processes, (2) greater use of formal Human Resource Management practices, (3) more benefits are provided. The first two hypotheses were well supported by their data and the third was supported but not well. The first hypothesis was based on evidence that non-profits provide an environment conducive to exploring and developing new ways of working and that non-profits don't view labour as human capital in the same way as the for-profit world.

However, what's of more interest to me is that the use of explicit Human Resource policies can increase female and minority participation in organisations. For example, transparent employment processes such as publicly listed vacancies, written position descriptions and formal job evaluations all serve to empower employees. "And even if the hiring and promotion decisions did not go their way, women felt at least the process was fair" (Mastracci & Herring 2010, 159).

The starting point can be the development opportunities you offer even before people can access full-time work. I was reminded of the importance of this when reading Michelle Obama's (2018) autobiography and her description of her work for Public Allies, a non-profit organisation encouraging young people to work on social issues in non-profit groups and government agencies. You can't solve the problems of the education system or the department stores that still divide boys into blue and girls into pink, but without those initial opportunities for internships or mentorships, getting jobs on one's own merit – which is what people really want – will be harder than it needs to be. For example, when MTC created a number of associate Director opportunities a few years ago, I insisted that of the four roles, two had to be for women. I also pushed for commissions to be equally allocated.

The next stage is employment. I am into a form of quotas at the beginning of the recruitment process but not the end. If you've advertised a job for a carpenter, then make sure at least one woman makes the short list. If you've advertised a job for a public relations coordinator, then make sure at least one man makes the short list. This way, you actively consider the contribution that someone from an under-represented gender might give your organisation. A way of ensuring that consideration is given to this idea is if the selection committees consist of people of both genders. I'm also into quotas when there isn't just one skill set that's required in a group of people playing the same role. For example: Boards. Given that you require a range of different skills on a Board, there's no reason why you shouldn't be able to get a gender balance. What about casts or orchestras or an opera chorus? I can imagine having a 50% quota for an orchestra on the same argument that I used for Boards, but isn't a chorus a matter of the voices for whom the music was written? With a cast, the question is more open. Are you going to stick to the requirements of the written script or change the rules for all or some of the parts?

However, I'm not a fan of employment quotas *per se*. If you have a Finance Department with six people with a gender balance, and one female resigns, does their replacement have to be a female? No. In fact, it would be illegal in Australia to just advertise for a female.

Within Australian arts organisations, most of the non-artistic positions are openly advertised but many of the creative positions aren't. Artistic Directors want to work with a team they know but the result can often lead to scenarios such as the (in)famous Belvoir St Theatre 2009 Season Launch photo of 11 male Directors and one female Director. The response was an outpouring of anger and grief from women directors and playwrights and a series of forums resulting in a report on women in theatre by the Australia Council (Lally & Miller 2012) with recommendations for companies to help improve the participation of women theatre artists.

There is research to show that women can get career advancement through access to training and selection for high visibility projects, interpersonal influence such as powerful mentors, and self-confidence built through early structured experiences offered by organisations (Kumra & Manfredi 2012). And one could add to this list, role models within companies. When I applied for the first time to be General Manager of 6UVS-FM, I didn't get the job. It might have been because the selection committee saw a young woman or it might have been because they saw a young person with no management skills. I'm convinced it was the latter because the position had been held by a woman. On returning, MBA in hand, two years later, I did get the job.

Arts organisations tend to assume that they treat women well because there are usually women working at all levels of the organisation. But sometimes, assumptions need to be checked. Because MTC employed more than 100 workers it had to report to the Workplace Gender Equality Agency. As part of that report, we had to collect statistics on the number of women in each level of the company, the average wage differentials between women and men at each level, turnover and its reasons, as well as report on active policies to support women at work.

In comparing the organisational structure of MTC between 1993 and 2019, it's interesting to note what had changed (as well as what hadn't). Not that a survey of one proves anything, but it does raise some interesting points:

- Stage Management had continued to be female dominated
- The co-leaders had shifted from two men to one man and one woman
- Production and theatre operations remained male-dominated but some women were now in the department and in management positions
- Sets and props remained a mainly male preserve and costume making remained a mainly female preserve
- The Finance, Marketing and Development departments were slightly more female dominated
- The mix of regular staff hadn't shifted over the 20 years with the company employing more women than men and although there were more women supervisors and managers by 2019 than in 1993, they still aren't in the same proportion as the gender staff balance.

Through doing the analysis for the Gender Equality Agency in the early 2010s, we discovered, for example, that there were wage differentials between set and costume making which may have come about over time because there were more women in the latter department. We were reminded that the gender balance in the management team had shifted and to consider what this might mean for the company. And because each year we had to review the impact of our gender policies, we had to talk about the number of women directors and the number of women playwrights in our season of plays. Talking doesn't deliver a 50% hit rate and it's unlikely to meet that figure for playwrights when a company such as MTC does classic as well as

contemporary work. But it meant the balance of contemporary writers was front of mind. The issue of directors was more complex when you have a male Artistic Director who directs because that builds in a bias but we did set ourselves targets and I continually argued the case for Associate Director positions to be shared on the basis of gender – another example of applying a "quota" to a development opportunity.

Lally and Miller (2012, 54) conclude their report on *Women in Theatre* with the following advice which I think should be kept in mind in all diversity discussions:

> We need to make people more aware of unconscious prejudices, and this applies to everyone, no-one is immune. We need to be aware that we all have these limitations and that it's unhelpful to respond with defensiveness when the limitations of our perspective is pointed out. We all need to take personal responsibility for making decisions that will make a difference to equity in access and representation.

Ethnic and Language Diversity

In a country like Australia that is made up of many immigrants, one would think that a diverse workplace would be a given. Stone (2013, 592) says that "the majority of [Australian] workers are well intentioned in their approach to dealing with those who are different from them in terms of race, gender, age, physical ability and sexual orientation". But this is also a country that had a "white Australia" policy up until 1973 when race was finally eliminated as a component of its immigration policy. So there are plenty of people still in the workforce who may have been bought up to believe that "white is best". One can't assume that one has a diverse organisation unless there are practices and measures around diversity.

While measuring gender bias is easy, measuring other aspects of diversity is not so easy. Assuming people's ethnicity or religion from their name is no longer feasible in increasingly multicultural societies. Self-identification is the only way but do we ever ask? And if we do, will people tell us? Having taken a number of measures about gender at MTC, I decided I should also do more than a visual head count on ethnic diversity. I rang the Victorian Human Rights and Equal Opportunity Commission to get a suitable question (do you ask for languages spoken at home or nationality of parents or racial identification?) and they couldn't help. So I just asked an open-ended question about how people identified themselves: which was stupid really because 90% of those who answered said "Australian".

Even if you could successfully measure the ethnic diversity of your workplace, what numbers do you use to check whether your organisation is out of line with the general community? In Australia, the basic number could be 26% born overseas or 19% if the measure was a language other than English spoken at home. Or should religion be a focus in which case the target might be 6% who identify as Non-Christian. For a measure of Indigenous people, the situation is even more complex with an average of 2.8% of the total population but a range between 1% in Victoria and 29% in the Northern Territory (Australian Bureau of Statistics, 2016 Census of Population and Housing). In other words, I don't have a clear sense of how diversity quotas would work in such a richly diverse country as Australia.

What makes the discussion more problematic is that while I can write strongly about women in the workforce because I have felt exclusion, I can only imagine what it's like to be a person of colour and I bring what Williams (2010) would call a "white gaze" to my analysis of the situation. As a black and minority ethnic worker is quoted as saying in Kumra and Manfredi (2012, 101):

> If you're a white man (sic) who's always worked with white men and who has always been in a position of power, you've got no reference points and you've never had the need to take the perspective of other people into account.

I have seen the white gaze a couple of times. The first time was when I was holding the hand of an Aboriginal actor in the emergency ward of a hospital when the police came into the cubicle. They ignored me – and the fact that the man was clearly very unwell – and started to harass him about what had happened in a tone totally inappropriate to a sick bay and clearly because he was black. The second time was having dinner in an upmarket restaurant with the new Indian head of the South African Broadcasting Commission's Radio Division in Johannesburg two weeks after the 1994 elections that saw the ANC swept to power. I was uncomfortable without knowing way until I suddenly caught the glare of a middle-aged woman – and glanced at the rest of her party. They were clearly talking about us in a disapproving tone and I realised that we were the only mixed-race table in the place. To live with that gaze day in, and day out is something I can only imagine.

Taking my lack of experience as read, I will still offer some comments on diversity in the arts world. I remember, for example, an arts worker criticising MTC for employing Frankie J. Holden and Steve Bisley to play Roo and Barney in the iconic Australian drama *Summer of the Seventeenth Doll*. Why he asked, didn't we employ actors who weren't Anglo to play those roles? There were, after all, immigrants working in Queensland cane fields in the 1950s which is when the play is set. True, but Ray Lawler didn't write about them. Then, in 2018 in a production by Black Swan Theatre Company in Perth, the lead was played by an Indigenous actor, Kelton Pell, with Mr Lawler's blessing.

One can write plays with diverse characters. One can take classic plays and cast them with the diverse faces on our streets. But sometimes, a play only makes sense if the cast member matches the intention of the writer. So no, I don't believe in performance quotas based on cultural diversity. But we must ensure diverse faces on our stage and in our orchestras and on our television. A friend told a story of a young African Muslim man whose family she had supported when she lived in France. After moving to the

USA she brought him across for a holiday and, amongst other things, took the teenager to a local circus. He was in tears by the end of it because of a clown. Not because of the reason you're thinking – an irrational fear of clowns – but because the clown was black. Like him. He had no idea that he could even dream about becoming a clown. So I know that we have to get different faces on our screens and on our stages but it has to start at the beginning with children of diverse backgrounds believing that they can be artists, having the opportunity to enter our training institutions and then making sure that our doors are open to them.

In my experience, both the Artistic Directors I worked with at MTC did colour blind casting. The first time I saw Tony Briggs (writer of *The Sapphires*) on stage was not playing an Indigenous character but in Shakespeare. Bert LaBonte, one of Australia's most versatile actors who is of Mauritian background, played Henry Bolingbroke, the future English King Henry VII as well as Martin Luther King. Jamaican-born Australian actor Zahra Newman played an aviatrix (based on Amelia Earhart) in MTC's *The Drowsy Chaperone* as well as African American roles. Landon-Smith (quoted in Westwood 2013) takes the view that colour blind casting isn't the answer because it seems to erase cultural difference but when the difference shouldn't matter, such as a dancer or a musical chorus member, in Shakespeare or with a contemporary Australian character, I think it does work.

In an article about African American classical ballet dancer Misty Copeland when she was in Australia to play Odette/Odile in *Swan Lake* for the American Ballet Theatre (Verghis 2014), there was a discussion not just about offering scholarships to students of colour but also the need to educate audiences (to accept a black swan) and to broaden our audience base so that they will see their faces on stage as our diversity increases.

Like other countries with an Indigenous population, Australia has particular challenges in facilitating their artistic voice in a culturally appropriate way. The Australia Council has been particularly good in producing protocols for working with Indigenous artists that are important to read before embarking on projects with them and I'm sure that there's similar forms of advice available in other countries. However, the starting point is as Indigenous writer "Jacinta" says:

> Let those who have been the ones whose voices have been silenced tell their stories. It is only when we start to hear and understand different ways of thinking and being will we be able to comprehend being whole – honouring all tilts of spin.
>
> (Quoted in Stevens 2014, 243)

So sensitivity and care are called for in ensuring that your workplace is a safe place for people of diversity to work.

Disability

I was on the Board of Back to Back Theatre for many years, a company for intellectually disabled actors that has toured the world and won awards for the originality of its work. During that time, I learnt a lot through working with people with intellectual disabilities. But what made that organisation so effective was that the company was *for* the actors. Therefore, there was no question of disabled workers having to adapt to a standard workplace with a standard way of doing things. The organisation, its processes and its structures had to be designed to suit their needs. However, most organisations don't start from such an open-hearted position.

In his farewell speech in 2014, the Federal Disability Discrimination Commissioner Graeme Innes said that organisations should have targets for the employment of people with disabilities. He said that 15% of Australians have disabilities but it's certainly not obvious that that figure is reflected in our workplace. For example, even in government employment the number is 2.9%. However, how do you know who is disabled? Is it about having depression? Is it about having diabetes? Is it a disability that is obvious or one that someone wants to keep secret? Once again, I'm not convinced about the efficacy of quotas. But I'm aware that we need to be better at creating opportunities for people with disabilities and an appropriate work environment for them.

I had thought that MTC was an organisation open to diversity so it was a salutary reminder that we weren't as good as we thought when I read Kumra and Manfredi's (2012, 163) list about the adjustments that employers should make at the recruitment stage to help open the door to disabled people such as:

- Provide application forms in alternative formats such as large print or braille
- Provide disability awareness information for staff involved in recruitment
- Provide help with communication at interviews, e.g. sign language interpreter
- Check at the interview whether an applicant would need workplace adjustment if appointed
- Guarantee disabled applicants an interview.

For years, MTC didn't even have a building that people with wheelchairs could easily access. Now both the company's headquarters and theatre are accessible. And in the case of the theatre, not just accessible for audiences but for performers as well. One can wheel from front of house to back of house without a step and so companies such as Restless Dance Company can perform at the Southbank Theatre because of that stage access plus wheelchair accessible dressing rooms.

During my time at MTC, the only time we employed a person with a specific physical disability was for the play *Tribes*. The company undertook an Australia-wide search for a deaf actor, provided a signer for him and also gave training about deaf awareness to all staff. Another example of a "performer" with a disability is Nas Campanella, a news reader for ABC's Triple J radio who is blind. As she says,[2] although her CV looked good, most employers weren't prepared to make any accommodations in the work place to employ a person with vision impairment, but the ABC did.

One aspect of diversity that is harder than others for employers to deal with is mental illness. Whereas people with physical handicaps may cause logistical challenges for organisations, these can mostly be overcome with money. With mental disability, the challenge is more emotional. Once again, it's a combination of educating staff about mental illness, providing support and having flexible leave arrangements (Stone 2013). MTC's response was to use a local support organisation *beyondblue* to provide training for managers about supporting people with depression and to pay for the first couple of sessions at a local counselling service for anyone who needed psychological help. In general, we were reasonably good at supporting people with disabilities who were in our workplace but we didn't actively search for disabled people to join our workforce.

Sexuality

Research shows that what lessens discriminations against Lesbian, Gay, Bisexual, Transgender and Intersex people is the presence of similar others and support from dissimilar others (Kumra & Manfredi 2012).

I don't know whether it's true in all art forms, but the world of theatre seems always to have been populated by people with a range of sexualities. The first gay people in my life were friends my parents had met during their time in amateur theatre groups in the 1940s and 1950s. Perhaps I've been lucky in the cultural and educational institutions that I've worked with over the years but I've always viewed them as places were LGBTI people could find employment with no concern about their sexuality and work safely and comfortably with their straight colleagues.

In the first edition of this book I ended this section saying "I hope I'm right". Then Australia had a plebiscite about Marriage Equality – whether gay people should be allowed to marry. An overwhelming majority of people voted "yes" and most arts organisations came out with public expressions of support. But not all. Sydney Symphony Orchestra (SSO) initially took a "neutral" stance until public pressure and intervention from the incoming CEO and the musicians forced the Board to change its position (Galvin 2017). One can imagine the feelings of LGBTI members of the SSO when the initial stance was publicised. Having a diverse workplace means supporting the rights and social preferences of your staff.

Summary

Mindfulness is much more useful when thinking about diversity than divisive debates about quotas. The starting point is education. Getting kids to experience art and seeing that it could be for them both as audience members and participants. The next stage is to make sure that training providers don't make the sort of assumptions they did in my day ("people don't want to listen to women's voices on radio so there's no point in accepting many into the course"). Then as employers we have to be mindful about diversity in all its forms and be active about ensuring that our doors are open, we have quotas and targets when they are appropriate, and ensure that every person of skill and talent has an equal chance of getting a job in an organisation that is going to be supportive of difference. Once they are in our organisations, we have to make sure that they aren't going to experience any harassment, discrimination or barriers to be able to be their best.

In Plas and Lewis' (2001) case study about a non-profit care organisation in the US, they make the point that one of the organisation's perceived weaknesses was that there was little tolerance for lack of tolerance. Is it acceptable to only employ people who are comfortable with diversity or who can adapt positively to your organisational culture if it's one that supports diversity? My answer is yes.

And parallel with this, we simply need more investment in the arts so that there can be more companies like Back to Back and Restless,[3] Ilbijerri and Bangarra[4] to ensure that people can make and manage their own journeys.

See also: Gender, Human Resource Management, Mindfulness, People

References

Galvin, N. 2017 "Sydney Symphony Orchestra Board's Dramatic U-turn on Same-sex Marriage", *Sydney Morning Herald*, 1 October, www.smh.com.au/entertainment/music/sso-boards-dramatic-uturn-on-samesex-marriage-20171001-gys1it.html [accessed 20 February 2019].

Groysberg, B. & Connolly, K. 2013 "Great Leaders Who Make the Mix Work", *Harvard Business Review*, 91(9): 69–76.

Innes, G. 2014 *Press Club Speech*, 2 July, Canberra, www.abc.net.au/news/2014-07-02/national-press-club-graeme-innes/5567150 [accessed 19 January 2015].

Kumra, S. & Manfredi, S. 2012 *Managing Equality and Diversity*, Oxford: Oxford University Press.

Lally, E. & Miller, S. 2012 *Women in Theatre*, Australia Council, Sydney, http://australiacouncil.gov.au/workspace/uploads/files/research/women-in-theatre-april-2012-54325827577ea.pdf [accessed 20 February 2019].

Mastracci, S. H. & Herring, C. 2010 "Nonprofit Management Practices and Work Processes to Promote Gender Diversity", *Nonprofit Management & Leadership*, 21(2), 155–175.

Minister for Women 2018 "Australia's First Gender Equality Bill: Have Your Say", 21 August, www.premier.vic.gov.au/australias-first-gender-equality-bill-have-your-say/ [accessed 20 February 2019].

Obama, M. 2018 *Becoming*, New York: Crown Publishing Group.

Plas, J. M. & Lewis, S. E. 2001 *Person-Centered Leadership of Nonprofit Organizations*, Thousand Oaks, CA: Sage Publications.

Sheehan, C., De Cieri, H. & Holland, P. 2013 "The Changing Role of Human Resources Management in the Employment Relationship", in Teicher, J., Holland, P. & Gough, R. (eds), *Australian Workplace Relations*, Cambridge: Cambridge University Press, 103–117.

Sinclair, A. 2004 "Teaching Managers about Masculinities: Are You Kidding?", in Grey, C. & Antonacopoulou, E. (eds) *Essential Readings in Management Learning*, London: Sage Publications, 218–236.

Sinclair, A. 2005 *Doing Leadership Differently*, Melbourne: Melbourne University Press.

Stevens, R. 2014 "White Ears and Whistling Duck", Brisbane: *Griffith Review*, 44, 231–243.

Stone, R. J. 2013 *Managing Human Resources* (4th ed), Milton, QLD: John Wiley & Sons.

Verghis, S. 2014 "Black Ballet Superstar Misty Copeland on Swan Lake and Racial Prejudice", *The Australian*, 9 August, www.theaustralian.com. au/arts/review/black-ballet-superstar-misty-copeland-on-swan-lake-and-racial-prejudice/ story-fn9n8gph-1227017793784 [accessed 19 January 2015].

Westwood, M. 2013 "Curtain Slow to Rise on Multicultural Theatre", *The Australian*, 12 July, www.theaustralian.com.au/arts/stage/curtain-slow-to-rise-on-multicultural-theatre/story-fn9d344c-1226677904294 [accessed 20 February 2019].

Williams, J. 2010 "Black Leadership and the White Gaze", in Kay, S. & Venner, K. (eds) *A Cultural Leader's Handbook*, London: Creative Choices, 41–45.

Notes

1 Led by the special insights of Professor Julian Meyrick, then Associate Director at the company.
2 www.abc.net.au/triplej/hack/stories/s3821747.htm
3 Companies for disabled performers.
4 Companies for Indigenous performers.

E

Economics

As an arts manager you don't need to know the language of physics (although hopefully the set designer and the person hanging the exhibition do) but you will have to learn the language of economics. It was described by Thomas Carlyle in the 19th century as "the dismal science" and after four years of studying it at university, that's exactly how I felt – dismal. It informs the language of policy making and funding, the language of finance and business, and so whether you're trying to decide on the price for your show or arguing the case for more funding with a government bureaucrat, words like supply and demand, externalities and elasticity will pop up.

There are two major types of economic discussion: micro- and macroeconomics. While supply and demand of products underlie the logic of both types, microeconomics focuses on the operation of business and what gets produced and covers topics such as consumer behaviour, how price mechanisms operate, the cost of production, competition, wage determination, the role of government when markets fail and on questions about how income should be distributed (Jackson & McIver 2007b[1]). You can see from the topics why it's important to an arts business as we do make decisions about prices and wages, we do want to know how our audience behave, the impact of competition and so on. Macroeconomics is concerned about the larger picture, the conglomeration of all the businesses in measurements like the national accounts, government budgets, fiscal policy and public debt, the banking system, monetary policy, inflation, growth and exchange rates (Jackson & McIver 2007a). Again, you can see how all these topics potentially impact on an arts organisation.

Enoch (2014, 24) claims that after the 1980s stock market crash,

> a new type of economic speak crept into the cultural language. The arts went from being the voice of a nation and started to be seen as an economic powerhouse for the country … We started to see papers on economic impact and multipliers, and we moved from an artistic community to an industry. Our language changed and the reasons we gave for support from the government also changed.

I have to confess that in the 1980s, that's exactly what I was doing: economic impact studies. In 1984, at the request of the South Australian State Government, Peter Brokensha and I undertook one of the first economic impact studies of the arts in Australia – firstly of the Adelaide International Arts Festival and then of the arts more generally in South Australia.

There are a number of ironies surrounding that fact. At that time, South Australia had one of the most supportive and culturally committed state governments in the country. Although the generator of much of this commitment, Premier Don Dunstan, had resigned in 1979 and a liberal government had followed, by 1992 the Labor party was back in power under John Bannon and Dunstan's legacy continued. Economic impact studies and talking about "arts and cultural industries" are now viewed as the marker where government policy shifted from embracing their intrinsic value to those that required instrumental values to be at the forefront. But at that time in South Australia, the idea of measuring the economic value of the arts was seen as just another way of supporting a positive cultural policy.

The other irony is about the authors. I was someone who'd trained as an economist but who had turned my back on the ideology of the discipline. Peter Brokensha (2007) was someone who had reached the top of the corporate ladder and had turned towards the arts, running the Argyle Arts Centre in Sydney, living with and researching the craft of the Ptjantjatjara people in the Australian desert, and finally becoming the Director of the post-graduate Arts Administration program at what was then the South Australian Institute of Technology. So although we could both bring the required analytical skills to an economic impact study, we were both suspicious of the underlying economic arguments for supporting the arts. Although we did the research and wrote the reports, we spend the first chapter of *Culture and Community* (1986) critiquing those economic arguments. It's interesting to go back over 30 years later and see that questioning like ours is still going on (e.g. Meyrick, Phiddian & Barnett 2018; Walmsely 2016).

A final irony of that work is that economic impact studies don't help improve the case for government support of the arts. For example, an economic impact study of a festival and a sports event will probably deliver the same dollar figures in terms of tourism, employment and so on. But which one contributes more to society? If you don't believe that the arts have any intrinsic value, then the answer may well be sport because although the instrumental value of both events may be the same – encouraging participation, improving health and well-being – there may be more evidence about the health benefits of sport than art. Belfiore (2018, 102) captures the frustration of those of us who have tried, with all the good intentions in the world, to use economic language to argue for more funding for the arts:

> 25 years of economic value discourse have done very little to justify public spending on the arts: "making the case" is still as problematic now as it was then, and the vast amounts of impact statistics produced since that time to prop up economic instrumentalism have not taken the sector to a place of financial stability.

What are economic arguments for governments to fund the arts? Some arts and cultural organisations operate quite effectively in the for-profit world such as popular entertainment where demand is strong (musicals, rock concerts, books) and where financial motives dominate over artistic values. So why is it that organisations such as heritage and art museums, opera and dance companies can't survive from the box office alone? The arts are particularly susceptible to market failure because they are unable – outside books, films and recordings – to reproduce their creations in sufficient numbers to exploit their success beyond a certain level. Nor can the arts easily achieve economies of scale. "You cannot downsize an orchestra or reduce the numbers of notes in a concerto, and nor can you build a bigger auditorium without radically altering the audience experience" (Hewison & Holden 2011, 124–125).

The arts also can't necessarily be priced properly because some of the benefits can't be traded. There can be collective benefits which even people who don't go to the arts can experience such as national pride and identity. These are described as non-use benefits and include existence value (e.g. one values the Louvre even though one may never get to Paris), the option value (one day, your children might go) and the bequest value (a cultural asset that will be enjoyed by future generations) (Throsby 2001). People can't necessarily make rational choices about how much to pay for art because they don't know enough about it (e.g. an innovative new experience) or they can't translate the value into money (e.g. the emotional or aesthetic effect). For the most part, arts and cultural goods are described by economists as "mixed" goods. To use an example from Throsby (2001, 23), a painting by Van Gogh can be bought and sold as an art object whose private-good value accrues only to those who own or see it; at the same time the painting as an element in the history of art brings wide public-good benefits to historians, art-lovers and the general public.

Another problem faced by the arts industry is chronic excess supply – meaning that more people want to be artists and are making art than people who want to buy/attend/experience it (van den Born, van Klink & Witteloostuijn 2011; Colbert 2009). The result is that the "price" for most artistic labour is low. Regardless of whether the problem is supply or demand, labour or ticket prices, most traditional art such as theatre and opera, classical music and art museums can't survive without some unearned income in the form of donations or grants.

The defensible arguments for public funding of the arts according to mainstream economists are the result of such market failures. The externality argument says the free market fails to register all the benefits and costs associated with the production and consumption of arts and cultural goods because, for example, some of the benefits accrue to people other than the actual buyer and seller or when there may be social or collective wants that aren't reflected in the price (Jackson & McIver 2007b). Another argument is that of the "merit good" which posits that there are some goods and services that a community should have, regardless of an individual's wiliness to pay. This is the idea that art is good for society. If one believes that the arts contribute to the betterment of common life, then the public interest is served by making art accessible,

preserving it, cultivating the understanding of art and encouraging artistic practice (Stover 1984). However, the "art is good" argument is viewed by some economists as simply a political value judgement. Although those of us who chose to work in the arts industry believe and can demonstrate the intrinsic value of the arts to both individuals and society, in the world of economic argument we end up competing for economic resources with our peers from the health or education sectors making similar arguments.

Back in the 1980s, Peter Brokensha and I joined with Ridley (1983) in concluding that the case for public funding of the arts put by economists was so limited that "those who believe culture to be an essential element of a civilized nation may well be advised to avoid an alliance with economists altogether" (Brokensha & Tonks 1994, 15) But we did join the alliance. Caust (2003, 54) noted that "there is no doubt that the desire to legitimise the 'arts' by describing it in economic terms was based on good intentions" which was certainly our case but some might criticise us for joining the discourse of economics in the first place.

However, we can't escape the language of economics being imposed upon us because the dominating influence of economic thinking has meant that public policy and economic policy have become almost synonymous (Throsby 2001). Simon Longstaff, Director of the St James Ethics Centre in Australia, challenges the way we've bought into the use of economics arguments. He gives examples where governments have only taken notice of arguments about social issues such as petrol sniffing and child abuse where they were rephrased as arguments about economic costs. He believes we have a problem when things only have value if measured in economic terms (Longstaff 2014a). While at heart, I agree with Longstaff and wish for a world where ethical arguments and arguments about truth and beauty dominate, I'm a pragmatist when it comes to arguing for government support of the arts. Sadly, governments and bureaucrats value quantitative measures above qualitative measures and if that means we have to talk about the size of the "arts industry", show how important it is as an employment sector, measure its impact on the tourism industry and so on, then so be it – but at the same time we have to keep arguing for the intrinsic benefits of the arts. As Burnside said:

> The destruction of the library at Byzantium in 1204 and the looting of the national museum of Baghdad in 2004 represent losses which not even the crassest economist has tried to measure in economic terms, because the calculation would be seen by everyone to miss the point completely.
>
> (Burnside 2018)

There are some positive aspects to economic discourse. Most of us operate in organisations or in market places and we do engage in economic processes. We do produce, distribute, market and sell what we make and ideas such as economic sustainability – the means by which an arts organisation uses its assets efficiently to enable it to continue operating over time – offer useful insights into how we should run our organisations. But the reason we have to understand the language of economics is not really to help us in our day-to-day management role. It's because we have no choice given the current world of public policy.

See also: Arts Industry, Cultural Policy, Evaluation, Fundraising, Money, Sustainability

References

Belfiore, E. 2015 "'Impact', 'value' and 'bad economics': Making sense of the problem of value in the arts and humanities", *Arts & Humanities in Higher Education*, 14(1), 95–110.

Brokensha, P. 2007 *Getting to Wisdom Slowly*, Adelaide: Peacock Publications.

Brokensha, P. & Tonks, A. 1994 *Adelaide Festival of Arts 1984: The Economic Impact (interim Report)*, Adelaide: SAIT.

Brokensha, P. & Tonks, A. 1986, *Culture and Community: Economics and Expectations of the Arts in South Australia*, Sydney: Social Science Press.

Burnside, J. 2018 "Why Does Art Matter? Why Should We Support the Arts?", *Daily Review*, 10 May, https://dailyreview.com.au/art-matter-support-arts/74511/ [accessed 22 February 2019].

Caust, J. 2003 "Putting the 'Art' Back into Arts Policy Making: How Arts Policy Has Been 'Captured' by the Economist and the Marketers", *The International Journal of Cultural Policy*, 9(1), 51–63.

Colbert, F. 2009 *Beyond Branding: Contemporary Marketing Challenges for Arts Organizations*, Geelong: Kenneth Myer Lecture, Deakin University.

Enoch, W. 2014 *Take Me to Your Leader: The Dilemma of Cultural Leadership*, Platform Paper No. 40, Sydney: Currency Press.

Hewison, R. & Holden, J. 2011 *The Cultural Leadership Handbook*, Farnham: F Gower.

Jackson, J. & McIver, R. 2007a *Macroeconomics* (8th ed), Sydney: McGraw Hill.

Jackson, J. & McIver, R. 2007b *Microeconomics* (8th ed), Sydney: McGraw Hill.

Longstaff, S. 2014a The Twin Foundations of Leadership, Sydney: St James Ethics Centre, www.ethics.org.au/on-ethics/our-articles/before-2014/the-twin-foundations-of-leadership [accessed 27 February 2019].

Longstaff, S. 2014b Speech at the "Communities in Control Conference", Melbourne, broadcast on Radio National's *Big Ideas*, 28 May.

Meyrick, J., Phiddian, R. & Barnett, J. 2018 *What Matters? Talking Value in Australian Culture*, Melbourne: Monash University Publishing.

Ridley, F. F. "Cultural Economics and the Culture of Economics", *Journal of Cultural Economics*, 7(1), 1–18.

Stover, C. F. 1984 "A Public Interest in Art – Its Recognition and Stewardship", *Journal of Arts Management and Law*, 14(3), 5–12.

Throsby, D. 2001 *Economics and Culture*, Cambridge: Cambridge University Press.

van den Born, A., van Klink, P. & Witteloostuijn, A. 2011 "Subsidizing Performing Arts: between Civilization and Addiction", Antwerp: 11th AIMAC International Conference.

Walmsley, B. 2016 "Deep Hanging Out in the Arts: An Anthropological Approach to Capturing Cultural Value", *International Journal of Cultural Policy*, 24(2), 272–291.

Emotion

Emotion comes into the life of an arts manager in a variety of ways. You will have to deal with other people's emotions and you'll have to manage your own. Your organisation should be able to provide a safe space for emotions – a space where ideas and opinions can be shared and communicated openly and in a straightforward way. This should minimise the need for negative emotions (Ekvall 1996). However, this doesn't mean that emotions won't be expressed at work. As Corrigan (1999, 22) puts it: "It may well be that it would be inappropriate to express many emotions at work, but that does not mean that they are not a major part of the day-to-day experience of managing and being managed."

The best advice I can offer about managing other people's emotions at work is keep tissues handy. As Rosner and Halcrow (2010, 64) say "[s]ooner or later someone will cry". It's not because someone walks into your office with the intention of doing so. And it may not be anything you say that sets them off. But emotions are part of the manager-staff interaction and having tissues at hand also shows that it's ok to cry. I found a wonderful tissue container in Taiwan designed in the shape of a large toothpaste tube with the Mona Lisa smiling toothily on it. Having something that made people smile/laugh as they cried also helped break the tension and embarrassment of breaking down at work.

Emotional intelligence is now an excepted part of a manager's kit bag. I've never done an EQ test so I have no sense on how I might perform in the various categories which are usually defined as self-awareness, self-regulation, self-motivation, empathy and social skills (McShane & Travaglione 2003). Rosner and Halcrow (2010) in a book called *The Boss's Survival Guide* unpack EQ under the following headings:

Intrapersonal

- Emotional self-awareness – recognising one's own feeling and emotions and know what's caused them
- Assertiveness – ability to express feelings, beliefs and thoughts and defend one's wrights in a non-destructive way
- Self-regard – respect and accept oneself
- Self-actualization – ability to realise one's potential capacities

- Independence – self-reliant and self-directed; consider advice but not depend on it; free of emotional dependency.

Interpersonal

- Interpersonal relationships – characterised by intimacy; giving and receiving affection
- Empathy – "emotionally read" others; be attentive to, understand, appreciate the feelings of others
- Social responsibility – cooperating and constructive member of social group.

Adaptability

- Problem solving – identify and solve problems
- Reality testing – assess the correspondence between what is experienced (subjective) and what exists in reality (objective)
- Flexibility – adjust one's emotions, thoughts, behaviour to changing situations.

Stress Management

- Stress tolerance – ability to withstand adverse events without falling apart
- Impulse control – resist or delay in impulse or temptation.

General Mood

- Happiness – ability to feel satisfied with one's life – to enjoy, have fun
- Optimism – look on the bright side; positive attitude even in the face of adversity.

Research confirms what we intuitively know – that positive emotions at work are "consistently associated with better performance, quality and customer service … and negative emotions such as group anger, sadness and fear … usually leave to negative outcomes, including poor performance and high turnover" (Barsade & O'Neill 2015,

60). The evidence about the impact of positive emotions in the workplace includes broadening one's ideas for taking action, enhancing creativity, great goal achievement, improvement in problem-solving performance, better social interaction and mutual understanding (Hoffmann 2015). However, sometimes work itself requires the use of our emotions. For example, our front-of-house staff have to be warm and engaging with our audience members even when they are not in the mood – so-called "emotional labour". There are two versions of this labour. "Surface" acting is where we smile even when we're not in the mood – "controlling one's appearance or behaviour to exhibit the emotions the situation dictates, without changing one's actual underlying feelings" (Hoffmann 2015, 154). "Deep" acting is where we portray the required emotions but we believe in them; where our inner feelings are altered so that we feel what we say/do.

There are different opinions about the impact of surface acting on people – from the stress of pretending to be something we aren't to the idea that we can reduce stress by using a smile to deflect anger. However, most of the research points to surface acting being detrimental to worker well-being and job performance. Deep acting – where your emotions match your behaviour – is clearly better for you.

A young woman who works in retail told me about a recruitment process she went through. Her company does group interviews and picked the people who proactively engaged with strangers. She was very happy in her work place and believed that the company had chosen people who were outgoing but also friendly and supportive. Without knowing anything more about this company, I would say they had successfully found people who could do the required emotional labour in their shops in a way that wasn't always surface acting.

An interesting piece of research on emotions in worker-owned businesses offers some relevant insights to our world. Although most arts and cultural organisations aren't worker-owned, because people actively choose to work for us there is a sense of ownership and

a feeling of family in many of our companies. In Hoffmann's study (2015) she found that people could express more emotions, both positive and negative, at work than they had been able to do in more conventional organisations and this was viewed as a positive change. Even expressing negative emotions such as anger was seen to be useful because it avoided such feelings being built up and leading to worse situations. There was also some "surface" acting as people learnt the emotional rules of their new organisation (e.g. pretending to accept the slow pace of change) but there were also cases where people internalised new emotional reactions such as pride.

Another example of emotional labour that Hoffmann (2015, 161) found in the worker-owned companies, was that even though members had an increased freedom to express negative emotions, they also become more sensitised about offending their co-workers, of "being more gentle and cautious of coworkers' feelings that they would have been in previous jobs".

Hoffmann (2015, 164) noted that many of the people she interviewed described being part of a family or feeling at home and this led her to conclude that

[t]he freedom from management abuse and the liberty to express their emotions freely may be a result of the more relaxed, possibly more home-like, working environment of cooperatives. When at home, people are more likely to address their feeling directly, with less surface acting and more expressions of sincerely felt feelings.

As well as staff doing emotional labour, managers and leaders have to do it too. Managers and leaders have to display a wide range of emotions including friendliness, sympathy, care, warmth but also disappointment and even anger. And they also have to choose which emotion to display. Humphrey, Pollack and Hawverl (2008) give the example of deciding what to do when someone is late. Does one express disapproval (because of the impact on the organisation) or sympathy (because of the personal problems that led to the lateness)?

Another part of a manager's emotional labour is to avoid losing their temper. I'm not a believer in management that involves shouting at people and there's evidence that fear of being yelled at makes it hard for us to think well and act quickly (Barsade & O'Neill 2015). I have been shouted at and little good it did. The inadequate leaders that I most disliked working with were ones who used negative emotions, either deliberately or through lack of control, to communicate their wishes. This is not just a personal belief. There is evidence that amongst other things,[2] the inability to manage one's emotions can lead to leadership ineffectiveness (Pienaar 2010). I've seen many theatre directors at work across Australia and the two extremes were the one that charmed people into working hard and long for them and the other that screamed and abused people to no good effect. I've wanted to lose my temper lots of times – with fools, with idiots, with the slothful or the self-indulgent – but stopping the meeting, or going for a walk, or writing it down rather than responding out loud, all led to better outcomes.

For the most part, I prefer a calm environment, a space where conflicts are resolved carefully and quietly. I don't see the point of screaming and yelling in the workplace because it implies that something is terribly wrong. Verbal confrontations and shouting may be the result of personal lack of control but they may also be the result of lack of satisfaction at work. According to Johnson and Indvik (2001) that lack of satisfaction can lead to "workplace rudeness (such a[s] verbal confrontations, shouting, nasty or underhanded behaviour, and selfish or thoughtless action) which, in turn, fuels conflict and greater dissatisfaction and unhappiness" (quoted in Adams 2007, 180). The research also provides evidence about the impact of this incivility: people leave jobs, lose work time and their productivity is decreased. At the first sign of this type of behaviour in the workplace, the causes need to be explored.

Having a policy about respect in the work place may not prevent the occasional blow up but it will remind people that abuse or aggressive conversation or behaviour is not tolerated. In an organisation where communication tends to be abusive or loud, it's unlikely that anyone is going to hear what really needs to be heard (Adams 2007). One manager I know has given a direction to her staff that if someone starts a meeting with "I'm really angry" then the meeting is to be stopped and reconvened when the person has had time to calm down and reflect. Providing anger management training to anyone who shows signs of not being able to modify their behaviour is also a good investment.

One management writer claims that "a tranquil, harmonious organization may very well be an apathetic, uncreative, stagnant, inflexible, and unresponsive organization" (Heffron 1989, 130), but I haven't seen that. Just because an organisation has an atmosphere without loudness and aggression, doesn't mean that people aren't quietly, efficiently and creatively getting on with the job.

Taking anger out of the workplace can be done by example. If your style is to stay calm, manage your emotions and provide conflict-resolving mechanisms that enable people to see past their differences, then the workplace will be a better environment for all concerned. Stick to constructive emotions that are honest, specific, respectful, genuine and accurate rather than destructive ones that are sarcastic, accusatory, hostile, vengeful or spiteful. People lose trust in a leader who displays such negative feelings (Zineldin & Hytter 2012, 749).

But sometimes, the person feeling angry will be you. It's all a matter of getting the balance right. If you don't feel emotion, you may just be a psychopath,[3] but as a leader you need to control your emotions except when it's absolutely right to show them. As long as you're not going to damage the innocent, then expressing fear or anger or hurt can sometimes be right. Rosner and Halcrow (2010) recommend that you do it by accepting responsibility for your own feelings, using non-destructive ways to express your anger, and tell people how you feel in a clear and controlled way.

There's an interesting tension implicit in such "emotional labour". Can you be an authentic leader if you're expressing emotions that aren't heartfelt? How do you avoid becoming cynical if you're forever acting a role (Gardner, Fischer & Hunt 2009)? There will be times when you need to display feelings of confidence and optimism in order to keep people focused and working effectively, even when they may not be the emotions you're actually feeling. During times of crisis or other negative events, leaders who engage in emotional labour to display more positive emotions than what they are actually feeling will increase their subordinates' feelings of confidence and optimism (Humphrey, Pollack & Hawver 2008). These positive effects will be greater for leaders who use deep acting (attempting to feel the emotion you are displaying) rather than surface acting.

Your organisation's culture will contribute to how emotions are displayed. If laughter and tears are allowed but expressions of anger are discouraged, you'll have an organisation that may be safer for all concerned. Gardner, Fischer and Hunt (2009, 429) give the example of The Body Shop where the feminist norms embodied in the culture lead to what they called "bounded emotionality", where the constrained expression of emotion at work was allowed because it contributed to community building and personal well-being in the work place.

You have to be able to read and manage feelings and emotions, your own and others, in order to be effective in the workplace.

See also: Authenticity, Change, Conflict, Empathy, Laughter, Love, Organisational Culture, People

References

Adams, J. 2007 *Managing People in Organizations: Contemporary Theory and Practice*, Basingstoke: Palgrave Macmillan.

Barsade, S. & O'Neill, O. A. 2016 "Manage Your Emotional Culture", *Harvard Business Review*, January–February, 58–66.

Corrigan, P. 1999 *Shakespeare on Management*, London: Kogan Page.

Ekvall, G. 1996 "Organizational Climate for Creativity and Innovation", *European Journal of Work and Organizational Psychology*, 5, 105–123.

Gardner, W. L., Fischer, D. & Hunt, J. G. 2009 "Emotional Labor and Leadership: A Threat to Authenticity?", *The Leadership Quarterly*, 20, 466–482.

Heffron, F. 1989 *Organisation Theory and Public Organisations: The Political Connection*, Englewood Cliffs, NJ: Prentice Hall.

Hoffmann, E. A. 2015 "Emotions and Emotional Labor at Work-Owned Businesses: Deep Acting, Surface Acting, and Genuine Emotions", *The Sociological Quarterly*, 57, 152–173.

Humphrey, R. H., Pollack, J. M. & Hawver, T. 2008 "Leading with Emotional Labor", *Journal of Managerial Psychology*, 23(2), 151–168.

Johnson, P. & Indvik, J. 2001 "Slings and Arrows of Rudeness: Incivility in the Workplace", *Journal of Management Development*, 20(8), 705–714.

McShane, S. & Travaglione, T. 2003 *Organisational Behaviour on the Pacific Rim*, Sydney: McGraw Hill.

Pienaar, J. M. 2010 "What Lies Beneath Leadership Ineffectiveness? – A Theoretical Overview", *Proceedings of the European Conference on Management, Leadership & Governance*, 280–286.

Rosner, B. & Halcrow, A. 2010 *The Boss's Survival Guide* (2nd ed), New York: McGraw Hill.

Zineldin, M. & Hytter, A. 2012 "Leaders' Negative Emotions and Leadership Styles Influencing Subordinates' Well-being", *The International Journal of Human Resource Management*, 23(4), 748–758.

Empathy

On the one hand, I cry at movies and can't go to scary films because I can't bear the horror. On the other hand, I read murder mysteries for fun. What does this say about my capacity for empathy?

As Scott Rankin (2014, 26), Australian cultural producer, puts it: "Empathy is different to sympathy … empathy is deep, to enter into the life of another. Sympathy … is not so deep. It is still valuable, but it is experienced alongside, rather than empathy, which enters into the experience."

Empathy is important within organisations because if one can identify with the other, one has a chance of understanding their actions in response to yours and building both trust and trustworthiness in the process (Beugelsdijk & Maseland 2011). There are three forms of empathy:

1. Cognitive empathy − the ability to understand another person's perspective
2. Emotional empathy − the ability to read what someone else feels
3. Empathic concern − the ability to sense what another person needs from you (Goleman 2013, 55).

I'm reasonable at #1 and #3 but I can't always tell what people really mean or feel. I get around that by having the open door lolly policy (more about that later) and trying to encourage people to believe that I'm open and accessible (which is generally true) in the hope that they will tell me how they are feeling. In his autobiography, Peter Brokensha (2007) one of my mentors, talks about how he'd come to wisdom over the previous three-quarters of his life. For him, empathy was:

> understanding the expectations of others from your relationship with them. I have found that if I had provided a service, a product, a deed which not only meets the recipient's expectations but exceeds them I have been rewarded twice. I have felt good that I have done something for someone else and in addition, in most cases I have received the gratitude, and perhaps tangible rewards from the recipient (155).

In a *Harvard Business Review* article, the Director of the wonderfully named *Empathy and Relational Science Program* at a US hospital gave advice on how to improve one's empathy:

> Suspending your own involvement to observe what's going on gives you a mindful awareness of the interaction without being completely reactive.
>
> (Goleman 2013, 60)

She goes on to say that one might be able to start a process of improving one's empathy by faking it and proposed a way that might increase your self-awareness and capacity to empathise:

> if you act in a caring way − looking people in the eye and paying attention to their expressions, even when you don't particularly want to − you may start to feel more engaged.

It may seem odd given leadership discussions about "authenticity",[4] to think about faking something as important as empathy but if it helps increase the amount of it going around, then it's worth the effort. There's an entire movement, led by cultural thinker and philosopher Roman Krznaric, to increase our individual and collective empathy. Some of the ideas that he posits include:

- Having meaningful conversations with strangers
- Imagining yourself in other's shoes − not just the poor or the disenfranchised but the wealthy or your enemies as well
- Cultivating outrospection − getting to know yourself by developing relationships with others
- Taking an imaginative journey through films, books − and dare I say it, theatre.

As a leader, you need to develop your emphatic sensibilities, not just for ethical reasons but also because by having a deeper understanding of your staff, your audiences, your Board, your stakeholders, you will be a more effective leader. For example, Walmsley (2011, 5) quotes research demonstrating how

> audiences' anticipation can be enhanced by pre-show activities such as introductory talks, which set the scene, provide a context and create a sense of empathy between the performers and the spectators, drawing them into the action and opening up the "communication loop".

I was reminded of the need to build empathy when I went to a play where the lead actor had had to be replaced at short notice and his replacement was "on the book", that is, holding a script because he hadn't had time to learn his lines. The audience was informed of this by a disembodied voice shortly before the play started. It was obvious that the audience didn't quite hear or understand the announcement and were unsettled at the start of the play which feed their response to the production. I learnt early on that the best solution for actor and audience alike in such situations was to tell a story and get the audience on side. I always went on stage before such a show, explained the situation to the audience, offered them a refund but invited them to stay, to empathise with the actor and have a completely unique experience. No-one ever left and people would often comment positively afterwards about the particular frisson of being in the audience that night. The audience response was always more positive than my most recent experience because I was attempting to build the audience's empathy.

For years I've been saying to students "do as you would be done by" as a way of encouraging them to translate how they would like to be treated into a strategy for treating others. Then someone pointed out that what others do might not be what you actually want. "As George Bernard Shaw pointed out, 'Do not do unto others as you would have them do unto you – they might have different tastes.' Empathy is about discovering those tastes" (Krznaric 2013).

Covey (1992), in talking about principle-centred leadership, says that it's important to listen with our eyes and heart and secondarily with our ears. In other words, we need to understand the intent of the communication without prejudging it and this can take time, patience and objectivity. The result, he says, is not to feel as they feel. That, Covey says, is sympathy. Rather, it means "that you understand how they feel based on how they see the world. That is empathy" (116).

In a speech about the foundations of leadership, strategic vision and moral courage, Longstaff (2015) says that one important aspect of strategic vision is the capacity to "employ a kind of empathetic 'moral imagination' that places a leader in the shoes of key participants including, supporters, allies and foes … to see events as others might see them and to understand the implications of these perspectives". If one can imagine the world of others then one might be able to find ways of understanding what they feel and need and therefore be better placed to communicate your understanding and desires to them.

Not that it's easy work. In a summary of research about empathy in the workplace, Waytz (2016) reminds us that although it's an essential part of people management, it can drain energy and cognitive resources and it's also zero-sum in that the more empathy you devote to your staff, the less you might have to share with family and friends. Waytz proposes that one way of dealing with these challenges is to invest in empathy wisely through getting people to talk about their experiences rather than trying to imagine how they might be feeling:

> Talking to people – asking them how they feel, what they want, and what they think – may seem simplistic, but it's more accurate. It's also less taxing to employees and their organizations, because it involves collecting real information instead of endlessly speculation. It's a smarter way to empathize.
>
> (Waytz 2016, 73)

Empathy is about imagination and communication – and looking after yourself so that you're in a good place to be empathetic. My sister, a drug and alcohol counsellor, uses empathy on a daily basis to build relationships with the people she supports. And she's very smart in making sure that she's in a good place mentally, emotionally and physically to do so. For her, it's cooking and fantasy novels and the cat. Find the processes that will help you apply empathy in the workplace.

See also: Authenticity, Communication, Emotion, Leadership, Listening, Love, You

References

Beugelsdijk, S. & Maseland, R. 2011 *Culture in Economics*, Cambridge: Cambridge University Press.

Brokensha, P. 2007 Getting to Wisdom Slowly, Adelaide: Peacock Publications.

Covey, S. R. 1992 *Principle-Centred Leadership*, London: Pocket Books.

Gardner, W. L., Fischer, D. & Hunt, J. G. 2009 "Emotional Labor and Leadership: A Threat to Authenticity?", *The Leadership Quarterly*, 20(5), 466–482.

Goleman, D. 2013 "The Focused Leader", *Harvard Business Review*, 76(6), 51–60.

Krznaric, R. www.romankrznaric.com/blog [accessed 26 February 2016].

Krznaric, R. 2013 "Six Habits of Highly Emphatic People", www.dailygood.org/story/518/six-habits-of-highly-empathic-people-roman-krznaric/ [accessed 22 February 2019].

Longstaff, S. 2014a The Twin Foundations of Leadership, Sydney: St James Ethics Centre, www.ethics.org.au/on-ethics/our-articles/before-2014/the-twin-foundations-of-leadership [accessed 22 February 2019].

Rankin, S. 2014 "Soggy Biscuit", in Schultz, J. (ed.) *Griffith Review 44*, Brisbane, 12–32.

Walmsley, B. 2011 "'A Big Part of My Life': A Qualitative Study of the Impact of Theatre", Antwerp: AIMAC 11th International Conference.

Waytz, A. 2016 "The Limits of Empathy", *Harvard Business Review*, https://hbr.org/2016/01/the-limits-of-empathy [accessed 4 December 2019].

Empowerment

Empowerment – giving people autonomy and responsibility over aspects of their work – begins with trust. If you don't trust the people you work with, you'll be more likely to want to control them than provide them with power over their work (Covey 1992). Adams (2007, 106) summarises over 20 pieces of research that show the linkages, both positive and negative, between empowerment and control and their impact on employee productivity, concluding that "the perception of control over one's environment is a key factor in reducing stress, and increasing satisfaction with the status quo". There is also evidence that people are more productive and more satisfied when they implement their own plans rather than someone else's because the sense of accomplishment is higher, there's more commitment to doing it well and more room for initiative (Bass 1970).

Ways to empower staff include:

- Involve people in planning
- Communicate extensively with staff
- Remove institutional barriers that prevent people making changes in their areas of responsibility
- Encourage people to determine their own goals
- Provide latitude to people to make decisions regarding collaborators, resources and deadlines
- Ask staff to keep you appraised so you get feedback on your performance
- Increase people's spending limits – indicating confidence in them making good decisions
- Require reports on results, not activities
- Encourage people to come up with solutions rather than presenting problems (Adams 2007; Hudson 2009).

There is the famous Nordstrom department store empowerment rule which was:

Rule #1: Use your good judgment in all situations.

There will be no additional rules.

Please feel free to ask your department manager, store manager or division general manager any questions any time.

(Lebow & Spitzer 2002, 115)

I can't believe that there were no more rules at Nordstrom but an organisation with a culture where people were well trained in their jobs, trust was strong, values were clear and managers were always available to give advice does sound like an attractive place to work.

When I was teaching industrial relations in the 1970s, the favourite topic was "employee participation" – on Boards, in decision-making, in work groups – but that phrase seems to have faded from the management textbooks. The favoured word now is "empowerment". But there is a quality implicit in the old set of words that I think is still worth considering and that is ensuring you hear the voice of your staff. In other words, have opportunities for employees to raise concerns, express their opinions, advance their interests and actively participate in decision-making along with management (Pyman et al. 2013). You may assume that because you're a manager with an open door and an open mind, that this will happen automatically but in my experience that's not always true. You need to set up processes in which the voice of staff can be heard, whether it's through company meetings, specialist gatherings such as occupational, health and safety (OHS) meetings or even encouraging your staff to join unions.

We shouldn't just be concerned with facilitating the actions of people who are assertive, who step up and who actively want more power and responsibility. We also need to help others in our workplaces to become empowered. I've seen the irritation of managers who wonder why people don't take a more proactive stance in both decision-making and self-development. Sometimes people have made a rational decision that they are not paid enough to take on more responsibility or simply don't want to make any more decisions at work than they have to. Sometimes it's about personality as people opt out of putting themselves forward. But often it comes back to diversity, whether of culture or gender. An interesting experience was being part of a training team in a South-East Asian country in 2013. The presentation team consisted of three middle-aged Australian Anglo women. Luckily, my presentation was on Day 3 by which time I could unpack some of the group dynamics. They included:

- Gender – men of the same age or older in the learning group clearly weren't comfortable being taught by women; and in group discussions, the men tended to take control
- Power-distance[5] – whereas group work in a training environment is an accepted part of the process in Australia, it didn't seem as common in the host country
- Age – in the group work, younger people were reluctant to provide ideas let alone challenge older people.

One has to take these differences into account when considering how best to empower people. Part of the process is to encourage people to believe that they have the capacity to take on power and responsibility. In an inspiring TED talk by Amy Cuddy, she demonstrates how our non-verbal body language can govern how we think and feel about ourselves and change our personal empowerment. A two-minute experiment of being in a high or low power physical stance can change testosterone and cortisol enough to have a demonstrable impact on feeling assertive, confident and comfortable.[6]

There will be those who say that my view of people in the workplace is naïve. That not everyone wants to take on responsibility. That not everyone wants to make decisions about how they do their job. That not everyone wants to contribute to the way things are done. That I've spent my life in universities and media/cultural/ arts organisations and that's not the "real" world. But a performing arts company is full of all sorts of employees. There are the artists but there are also the causal labourers loading and unloading trucks. There are Oscar-winning actors but there are also specialised artisans applying centuries-old crafts. There are senior executives and also call centre staff. And I live in the real world and have relatives who are cleaners and neighbours who are plasterers. I've been on building sites and worked in shops and bars and offices and know that when someone is empowered to make decisions and supported by a good boss, the environment is different to when every inch of their work life is micromanaged. Bakke (2005) reminds us that work isn't just about performance, effectiveness and efficiency. The very essence of being human is the ability to make choices and take actions, to actively be part of creating the world we work in and to have at least some measure of control over our lives. Our organisations are better if people are treated like adults at work and given the autonomy to make decisions and take responsibility for the results.

See also: Control, Delegation, Diversity, People, Trust, Unions

References

Adams, J. 2007 *Managing People in Organizations: Contemporary Theory and Practice*, Basingstoke: Palgrave Macmillan.

Bakke, D. W. 2005 *Joy at Work*, Seattle: PVG.

Bass, B. M. 1970 "When Planning for Others", *Journal of Applied Behavioural Management*, 1(2), 1551–1571.

Covey, S. R. 1992 *Principle-Centred Leadership*, London: Pocket Books.

Cuddy, A. 2013 "Empowering through Body Language – Top Tips on Essential Assertiveness", *TED Talk*, www.youtube.com/watch?v=TdU2I0i2Wh0 [accessed on 22 February 2019].

Hudson, M. 2009 *Managing Without Profit: Leadership, Management and Governance of Third Sector Organisations in Australia*, Sydney: UNSW Press.

Lebow, R. & Spitzer, R. 2002, *Accountability*, San Francisco, CA: Berrett-Koehler Publishing.

Pyman, A., Holland, P., Teicher, J. & Cooper, B. 2013 "The Dynamics of Employee Voice in Australia", in Teicher, J., Holland, P. & Gough, R. (eds) *Australian Workplace Relations*, Cambridge: Cambridge University Press, 118–136.

Entrepreneurship

One of the early definitions of an entrepreneur was proposed by Schumpeter in the 1930s (quoted in Beugelsdijk & Masleand 2011, 166). The idea is that an entrepreneur is a leader with autonomous drive who's willing to break through ordinary constraints in order to achieve new outcomes. Schumpeter said "there is the will to conquer: the impulse to fight, to prove oneself superior to others, to succeed for the sake, not of the fruits of success, but of success itself". I don't identify with any of that language although I do like his final point which is that entrepreneurship is "about the joy of creating, or getting things done, or simply exercising one's energy and ingenuity".

In the arts and cultural world, the title of "entrepreneur" has been applied to the impresarios of the past who risked their own money (and that of others) to establish new enterprises. They are the people who start businesses rather than the people who manage them. It's also applied to artists who, through processes of discovery and creation, find ways to make a living. In their survey of artists participating in the Adelaide Fringe Festival, Caust and Glow (2011, 10) describe their entrepreneurial qualities:

> [they]are entrepreneurial; they need to be, just to participate. This is demonstrated here in several ways; the capacity to take artistic risks and innovate, the need to self-manage and promote, and the necessity of presenting something that will attract an audience. The definition of entrepreneurialism that emerges from this picture is a mix of formally and informally acquired skills; the building of complex networks involving support agencies, artist services, peers, venues, and audiences; and making a living that is not primarily driven by the desire for economic outcomes, but shaped by creative and cultural imperatives.

Beugelsdijk and Masleand (2011, 167) summarise a range of research and come up with a list of behavioural qualities for entrepreneurs, including opportunistic, innovative, creative, imaginative, restless, high need for achievement, risk-taking propensity, self-confident, with a preference for energetic and novel activity. They are described as people who want to be free to achieve as well as being comfortable with ambiguity and uncertainty. If one has to have all those qualities, then I'm clearly not an entrepreneur. I simply don't have the appetite for risk that I see in my commercial peers. Obviously, I'm not completely risk-averse because otherwise one wouldn't be able to work comfortably in an arts organisation where every creative activity is risky with the capacity to damage the company financially. I prefer Hagoort's (2005, 214) image on an entrepreneur: someone who has "a lot of energy and a large dose of persistence and imagination which, together with a willingness to take reasonable, calculated risks, enables them to convert something which initially begins as a very simple and unclear idea, into something concrete". That sounds somewhat more like me.

I suspect that a true entrepreneur in Schumpeter's sense would be both bored and irritated by having to work in the framework of non-profit organisations with Boards, rules and regulations and stakeholders to whom one has to be accountable. Perhaps a better approach to entrepreneurship is for the company to be entrepreneurial rather than the leader. Cultural entrepreneurship has a "flavour of the month" feel to it. In 2018, the *International Journal of Arts Management* devoted an entire volume to "Cultural Entrepreneurship and the New Arts Management". However, for a long time, I've found the language around entrepreneurship less than convincing. For example, Leung and Tung (2015 113) describe attributes of entrepreneurship such as "marketing, image building, audience building, e-subscription, e-news, brand building, production cost and time control, partnership and publicity". That just reads like the work of a good General Manager to me.

Carla Walters (2015, 126) has written a whole arts management book with entrepreneurship as a focus. She defines an entrepreneur as "a person who takes the initiative, bundles resources in innovate ways, and is willing to bear the risk and uncertainty of action, with an eye toward creating value for a product of service". She quotes Hausmann's (2010) definition of *culturepreneurs* as "artists undertaking business activities within one of the four traditional sectors of the arts who discover and evaluate opportunities in the arts and leisure markets and create a business to pursue them". But she then stretches this definition too far, in my view, by describing culturepreneurship as "involving or leading a cultural arts organization, producing for a cultural arts audience, and being committed to culturally creative endeavours, based on the cultural value that the entrepreneur desires to create" (Walter 2015, 126). In that case, anyone running a for-profit arts company could call themselves an entrepreneur. Maybe it doesn't matter. Maybe, it is just a matter of words and if people feel better about calling themselves entrepreneurs and governments feel better about supporting entrepreneurs then I should just stop being pedantic.

Varbanova (2013, 20–21) provides eight characteristics of organisations that do seem to link in with the concept of entrepreneurship:

- Evidence of innovation not just in artistic creativity but in strategic innovations that bring value to audiences and clients
- The establishment of teams to work on generation and implementation of innovative ideas
- An experimental "laboratory" climate
- Ongoing financial support for innovative projects
- Generating revenue as a result
- A flexible organisational structure
- Adaptability to change
- Ability to connect and network.

In this type of organisation, according to Varbanova (2013, 19), employees are given "ongoing freedom, encouragement and support, including financially to create and develop new ideas". This sounds to me simply like a well-run arts organisation. Perhaps I'm just trying to excuse myself for not being an entrepreneur at heart but I think there is room for both the more considered servant leader and the more flamboyant entrepreneur in the arts and cultural industry.

See also: Empowerment, Management, Risk, Uncertainty

References

Beugelsdijk, S. & Maseland, R. 2011 *Culture in Economics*, Cambridge: Cambridge University Press.

Caust, J. & Glow, H. 2011 "Festivals, Artists and Entrepreneurialism: The Role of The Adelaide Fringe Festival", *International Journal of Event Management Research*, 6(2), 1–14.

Hagoort, G. 2005 *Art Management: Entrepreneurial Style* (5th ed), Delft: Eburon.

Konrad, E. D., Moog, P. & Rentschler, R. (eds) 2018 "Editorial", *International Journal of Arts Management*, 48(2).

Leung, C. C. & Tung, K. Y. 2015 "Dual Roles: Collaborative Leadership in a Newly Developed Music Ensemble", in Caust, J. (ed.) *Arts and Cultural Leadership in Asia*, London: Routledge, 105–120.

Varbanova, L. 2013 *Strategic Management in the Arts*, New York: Routledge.

Walter, C. 2015 *Arts Management: An Entrepreneurial Approach*, New York: Routledge.

Environment

It's likely that you want your organisation to be "green" because you believe the rich evidence from thousands of scientists that tell us that the earth's climate is warming. Your organisation may not only be "green" in its building and work practices but "green" in its art making. After all: "When politicians disappoint and science is not enough, artistic engagement with climate change can invigorate the issues from a new angle" (Julie's Bicycle 2010, 3). Of course, as Alison Tickell notes in *Long Horizons: An Exploration of Art and Climate Change* (Julie's Bicycle 2010), there's a tension between wanting the arts to actively campaign for action and understanding that art can't be forced to fit a political or social agenda. However, the places in which the arts are created and presented can be made environmentally sustainable regardless of what the art is. Sets can be made from sustainable wood, musicians can record in solar-powered studios, offices can use rainwater and buy renewable electricity.

Greening is usually of concern to people working in the arts industry but it can be a challenge to implement effective policies when resources are tight and the costs, albeit mainly short-term costs, are high. For example, I had visions of water tanks and solar panels over the roof and fly tower of the Southbank Theatre but those "additional extras" disappeared during various cost-cutting exercises. Ultimately, the project was being run by the Victorian State Government and during the mid-2000s, greening clearly wasn't as much of a priority as bringing infrastructure projects in on budget. We did manage to do better in the refurbished HQ with water tanks, recycled furniture, timed and movement sensitive lights,[7] windows that opened with individual air-conditioners which reduced the amount of time they were used plus set, costume, paper, cardboard and bottle recycling.

One of the best sets of resources about greening the arts can be found at Julie's Bicycle (www.juliesbicycle.com), London-based charity that supports the creative community to act on climate change and environmental sustainability. Their website has case studies, riders, advice, benchmarks, impact-measuring tools and industry strategies to improve your organisation to lower its carbon footprint. The starting point is to understand your environmental impact, develop a policy and get staff involved. Whether you're putting an environmental policy in place because you're a passionate environmentalist, or more pragmatically because you want to manage long-term costs or meet funding body requirements, the outcome is a positive one for the environment.

Although the investment in green technology may be higher than standard technology in the first instance, most green ideas – switching to greener lighting, reducing energy consumption, reusing materials – will save money in the medium term. Boris Johnson, when he was Lord Mayor of London, noted that "if all central London theatres challenged the age-old practice of keeping stage lights on and only switched them on half an hour before the performance, they could collectively save over 100,000 pounds a year in energy costs" (Mayor of London 2008, 2).

In *Green Theatre: Taking Action on Climate Change* (Mayor of London 2010, 7–8), a number of suggestions are made that could apply to almost any organisation:

- Work out your carbon footprint
- Write an action plan
- Involve staff
- Designate "environmental champions"
- Keep accurate records
- Write "green" policies into contracts
- Open up your facilities for your partners
- Creative financial incentives
- Ensure that capital expenditure incorporates savings from energy efficient measures
- Buy "green tariff" renewable electricity.

In my experience, many arts companies want to be environmentally sound but haven't done much about it apart from recycling and signing up to low-carbon utility companies, so these suggestions are still relevant. You can get your audience to join in, for example, by putting a surcharge on ticket prices to cover greening costs. You can pay for that initial investment by finding a sponsor who sells green products and wants a public environment in which to show them off or a private donor who shares your passion for the environment. Julie's Bicycle offers practical guides to developing environmental policies and action plans.

The trap is that the green plan becomes yet one more thing that gets put on the backburner because of financial or artistic pressures. As an arts manager working in the access world said to me in a somewhat irritated tone: "if one more person says that they haven't done a disability action plan because they are concentrating on green issues this year, I'll scream." Somehow, you have to make room for the policies and actions on diversity, disability, occupational health and safety *and* the environment.

References

Julie's Bicycle 2010 *Long Horizons: An Exploration of Art and Climate Change*, London: British Council.
Julie's Bicycle 2019 *Practical Guides: Environmental Policy & Action Plan Guidelines*, www.juliesbicycle.com/Handlers/Download.ashx?IDMF=dece678c-682c-4362-80c0-bd8744047213 [accessed 22 February 2019],
Mayor of London 2008 *Green Theatre: Taking Action on Climate change*, London: Greater London Authority.

Ethics

While management has been discussed for over a hundred years, ethics have been discussed for thousands of years so the idea of trying to explore ethics meaningfully in a couple of hundred words feels somewhat arrogant. But as our behaviour as managers and leaders should always be ethical, I had to try. My *Concise Oxford Dictionary*'s definition of ethics includes "moral principles" and "rules of conduct" but the word I like most in their list is "honourable", that is, ethical behaviour is honourable behaviour. There are many more technical words in the study of ethics and it's worth exploring two of them to get a sense of what the conversation is all about.

"Consequentialism is the theory that holds that the 'good' takes precedence over the 'right'. Deontology is the belief that the 'right' is a more fundamental moral concept than the 'good'" (Patel 2010, 74). The consequentialist is someone who makes a decision where the consequences are better than its alternatives. In other words, the process and the action itself aren't as important as a good outcome. The dentologist focuses on the rightness or wrongness of the action and believes that some actions should never be undertaken regardless of the consequences. Can you identify with either of these positions? It's highly unlikely that you'll be exclusively one or the other but the point is that ethical decisions contain these dimensions of action and outcome and both need to be considered.

There are various ways of checking whether your behaviour is ethical. For example, Rotary has an ethics test as a core part of their guiding principles:

- Was the decision truthful?
- Is the decision fair to all concerned?
- Will the actions build goodwill?
- Will the actions be beneficial to all concerned? (Dickie & Dickie 2011, 231).

It covers consideration of both the action and the decision.

Where does our sense of morality, of right and wrong, come from? Like most aspects of management behaviour it is influenced by a person's upbringing and education, personality and national culture and something that isn't always part of management discussions – religion. However, Trevino and Nelson (2011) claim that most people aren't guided by a strict internal moral compass but look outside, to peers, to work, to the environment, for cues about what to do and what to think. Therefore, organisations need to have clear unambiguous organisational policies and an ethical culture to help people make the right decisions. Stone (2013) gives the example of HIH Insurance, a company MTC used to get "key man" (sic) insurance for musicals, which had a culture of fear. As a purchaser of their product, this was not obvious until the service was no longer available because the company collapsed due to cover-ups, incompetence, misuse of company funds and corruption. While some unethical business problems can lead to criminal and civil legal charges, many of the ethical challenges in organisations are on the fringe of illegality involving conflicts of interest, misallocation of resources or inadequate accountability and transparency.

Northouse (2010) describes the principles of ethical leadership as respect for others, serving others, showing justice, being honest and building community which are all great principles, but how do you transfer them into action? If the organisational culture is one of honesty, openness, trust and fairness then you will have an environment in which people are more inclined to make ethical decisions. However, there may be different views of ethical behaviour from management and from the shop floor. In a survey of Australian views on ethical behaviour, top of the list for management was conflict of interest followed by unauthorised use of company assets, conducting private business during working hours, falsifying the organisation's records, disclosure of confidential information and sexual harassment. Management's top concern was at #6 on the employee list which was topped by personal use of company assets followed by falsifying sick leave, conducting private business during work hours, sexual harassment and disclosure of confidential information (Dubrin, Daglish & Miller 2006). I suspect since that survey was taken sexual harassment has moved up the list. Regardless of whether managers and workers agree on the order of ethical behaviours, they did mainly agree about what was right and wrong and there is evidence of a positive correlation between leaders' behavioural integrity and the overall well-being and job satisfaction of workers (Bunting 2016).

Rhode and Packel (2009) summarise research which identifies four crucial factors that influence ethical decisions:

- Moral awareness: recognition that a situation raises ethical issues
- Moral decision-making: determining what course of action is ethically sound
- Moral intent: identifying which values should take priority in the decision
- Moral action: following through on ethical decisions.

There's an assumption that because non-profits are "value-based" organisations that they are also ethical (Nair & Deepti 2011), but that assumption may be just that – an assumption. In the 2007 US National Nonprofit Ethics Survey, slightly more than half of employees had observed at least one act of misconduct in the previous year, roughly the same percentage as in the for-profit and government sectors (Rhode & Packel 2009). What's even more depressing about that survey is that most people didn't bother reporting the misconduct because they didn't think any action would be taken.

Examples of what can go wrong in non-profit companies include where leaders have a passionate commitment to a cause and an equally passionate belief in their own actions, which can lead to ignoring dissent, covering up mistakes and withholding information. I've experienced situations where people tried to disguise what was actually happening because they didn't want to disappoint the management of an organisation they cared for. Other examples are situations where CEOs are paid lavish salaries or where excessive pressure to generate revenue or minimise costs may lead to misleading behaviour or where the organisational habit is for staff to use donated goods and services for themselves. Most people tend to think of theft as an obvious ethical problem (e.g. 660,000 GBP stolen from the London Philharmonic Orchestra by its Finance Director (Saintilan & Schreiber 2018, 247)) but possible ethical breaches extend further than just money.

Rhode and Packel (2010) list six particular areas that have led to problems in non-profit organisations: compensation, conflicts of interest, publications and solicitation, financial integrity, investment policies, accountability and strategic management and, in many cases, the answer to these potential ethical challenges is to have clear policies. For example, having policies around travel issues such as the standard of hotel and use of frequent flyer points solves any sense of unfairness about who gets what benefit. However, in some areas such as financial integrity, a policy won't be the answer. Each offer of money will need to be examined in terms of not just what's required from the organisation in exchange for the donation/sponsorship, but how the relationship will be viewed from the outside.

Why do people make unethical decisions? Bazeman and Tenbrunsel (2011) say that it's because of ill-conceived goals leading to unexpected consequences, conflicts of interest and indirect blindness when the unethical behaviour is carried out by third parties, and the notion of the "slippery slope" where there's a gradual erosion of ethical standards starting with actions where the initial moral cost might be small, and overvaluing outcomes without worrying too much how you get there.

Jeavons (1994, 198) proposes five concepts in the ethical obligations of non-profits:

1. Integrity – what is said is also done or "honesty writ large"
2. Openness – building trust through transparency
3. Accountability – to all the different stakeholders
4. Service – fulfilment of the organisation's mission
5. Charity – caring about the well-being of others.

Bolman and Deal (2013, 220–221) offer some concrete questions for assessing your actions to see whether your decision is ethical:

- "Are you following rules that are mutually understood and accepted?
- Are you comfortable discussing and defending your choices? Would you want your colleagues and friends to know what you're doing? Your spouse, children or parents? Would you be comfortable if your deeds appeared on the web or in your local newspaper?
- Would you want to be on the receiving end of your own actions?
- Would the world be better or worse if everyone acted as you did?
- Are there alternatives you could consider that rest on firmer ethical ground?"

Parker (2012) has written a book called *Ethics 101 Conversations to Have with Your Kids* but it's a book that's equally useful for your management team because it puts all sorts of ethical issues into plain English. For example, there's a great collection of what Parker calls "ethical potholes" which could be used to check the customary behaviour of staff and the organisation. If you use or hear words like those in the list below in your company, then it's worth providing some training on ethical behaviour:

1. Everyone does it – as a justification for behaviour
2. They're too big to notice – if you steal from another organisation

3. If you can't beat them, join them – when you think you'll be at a disadvantage if you don't join in unethical behaviour
4. It's not my fault – and so I've got no responsibility to fix it
5. It's not the worst thing – you should compare wrong acts to right rather than even more wrong
6. It's not illegal – because ethics are wider than the law
7. The letter of the law – always looking for loopholes
8. Poor me – excusing bad behaviour because of stress
9. It's what my heart tells me – not considering the impact on others
10. If I don't do it, someone else will – assuming others are unethical
11. They deserve it – because you've lost respect for a person or institution
12. Eye for an eye – thinking revenge is ok
13. It's too small to count – the slippery slope moment
14. Cognitive dissonance – admiring people who do the wrong things
15. I'm good – and so anything I do is ok
16. The ends justify the means.

I was lucky that early in my time at MTC I participated in a week-long program run by the Cranlana Program[8] in Melbourne. It provides learning experiences to enhance a leader's understanding of the philosophical, ethical and social issues central to creating a just, prosperous and sustainable society. Although it felt like a luxury at the time to immerse oneself in the readings of the great writers and philosophers of our world for a whole week, it wasn't a luxury at all as we shared ideas about how to create an ethical framework in organisations which were as diverse as the police force, banks, government departments and a theatre company. This program bought ethical considerations to the forefront for me in a way that often doesn't happen until there's a problem.

Another ethical theory, virtue ethics, has a focus on integrity with the aim to be a good person. Although Trevino and Nelson (2011) warn that general good character doesn't prepare an individual to deal with complex ethical dilemmas, it seems to me to be a good starting point. However, even if you are "good", you can get caught up in other people's unethical behaviour. For example, in the 1980s in Western Australia, my home state, the Arts Minister, David Parker, was also the Minister for Minerals and Energy. In discussions over the acquisition of a gas company, he inappropriately solicited a promise for a $250,000 donation as part of the deal for Spare Parts Puppet Theatre, a non-profit arts company in his electorate which was looking for a new home. The WA Inc Royal Commission (2000) concluded that the minister acted improperly but the theatre company, which was completely in the dark about the offer, didn't.

Rhode and Packel (2009) say that while no set of rules can guarantee ethical conduct, three steps make it more likely. The first step is to have effective codes of conduct and compliance programs that clarify expectations and establish standards. Second, effective financial management is required including performance measures and transparency through public annual reports. Third, organisations need ethics by leadership, where managers lead with integrity, and values are integrated into day-to-day decision-making.

One good piece of advice in making ethical decisions apart from the obvious steps, such as identifying the stakeholders and the consequences, is to check your gut (Trevino & Nelson 2011). If your decision doesn't feel fair or honest, or is something you wouldn't want your parents to read about in the local paper then it probably isn't ethical.

See also: Fundraising, Money, Sponsorship, Stakeholders, Values

References

Bazerman, M. H. & Tenbrunsel, A. E. 2011 "Ethical Breakdowns", *Harvard Business Review*, 89(4), 58–65.

Bolman, L. G. & Deal, T. E. 2013 *Reframing Organizations* (5th ed), San Francisco, CA: Jossey-Bass.

Bunting, M. 2016, *The Mindful Leader*, Milton, QLD: Wiley.

Dickie, L. & Dickie, C. 2011, *Cornerstones of Management* (2nd ed), Melbourne: Tilde University Press.

Dubrin, A. J., Dalglish, C. & Miller, P. 2006 *Leadership* (2nd Asia-Pacific Ed), Milton, QLD: John Wiley & Sons.

Jeavons, T. H. 1994 "Ethics in Nonprofit Management: Creating a Culture of Integrity", in Herman, H. D. (ed.) *The Jossey-Bass Handbook of Nonprofit Leadership and Management*, San Francisco, CA: Jossey-Bass, 184–207.

Nair, N. & Deepti, B. 2011 "Understanding Workplace Deviant Behaviour in Nonprofit Organizations", *Nonprofit Management and Leadership*, 21(3), 289–309.

Northouse, P. G. 2010 *Leadership* (5th ed), Los Angeles: Sage Publications.

Parker, M. 2012 *Ethics 101 Conversations to Have with Your Kids*, Sydney: Jane Curry Publishing.

Patel, J. 2010 "Doing the Right Thing: The Ethics of Cultural Leadership", in Kay, S. & Venner, K. (eds) *A Cultural Leader's Handbook*, London: Creative Choices, 72–77.

Rhode, D. L. & Packel, A. K. 2009 "Ethics and Nonprofits", *Stanford Social Innovation Review*, 7(3), 29–35.

Saintilan, P. & Schreiber, D. 2018, *Managing Organizations in the Creative Economy: Organizational Behaviour for the Cultural Sector*, Abingdon: Routledge.

Stone, R. J. 2013 *Managing Human Resources* (4th ed), Milton, QLD: John Wiley & Sons.

Trevino, L. K. & Nelson, K. A. 2011 *Managing Business Ethics* (5th ed), Danvers, MA: John Wiley & Sons.

WA Inc Royal Commission 2000, www.slp.wa.gov.au/publications/publications.nsf/inquiries+and+commissions?openpage [accessed 22 February 2019].

Evaluation

The world of organisational evaluation is full of "e" words: efficiency, effectiveness, economy, efficacy. It tends to be a collection of words that either brings dread into the heart of the not-very numerate manager or irritation into the heart of the manager who is more interested in the intrinsic rather than the extrinsic value of the arts. However, one of the best comments I've read on the topic was about an organisation that dropped the "e" and turned the relevant department into one of "valuation" instead (Watkins, Moher & Kelly 2011). Ultimately, what good evaluation should do is to find out the value of what one does.

The benefits of evaluation for an organisation include learning from the past, identifying opportunities to use resources in a way that means you can do more to achieve your mission, making better decisions, identifying strategies to improve the company's operations, working out what's working and what's not (Fishel 2003; Pankratz 2011). But as well as internal reasons, there is an increasing demand from our funding stakeholders to provide evidence in the form of justification for the grants we receive and accountability on how well we used those resources.

Because non-profit organisations are not primarily driven by the financial bottom line, Fishel (2003, 6) says that it's easy to have imprecise objectives and, as a result, "performance can be harder to monitor than in a more commercial environment". In my experience, arts objectives aren't "imprecise" but simply not always easy to measure. How, for example, do you judge the quality of a performing arts production? Is it the opinion of the newspaper critic or the blogger that counts? Is it the amount of money you spend on the production (Gilhespy 1999) or the response of the individual audience member's experience to the event (Radbourne et al. 2009) or the number of people that thought it was worth paying money to see? Is it the intellectual stimulation provided by the artwork or the spiritual value (Hewison & Holden 2010)? What about the experience of the actors or musicians or dancers or when the set design wins an award but the performances didn't? Even something as simple as whether something can be "counted" as an "Australian Play" has caused controversy with arguments for and against the inclusion of adaptations by Australian writers of classic international works (Croggon 2013).

But the starting point isn't what or how to measure, but what would be useful to know? We are often required to measure outputs and outcomes and the dreaded key performance indicators (KPIs) by our funders but if we focus on our needs first, we will come to see the value of measurement. Krug and Weinberg (2004, 326) present a model of three criteria to measure what one does:

1. Contribution to the mission of the organisation – "doing the right thing"
2. Financial contribution – "doing the right thing financially"
3. Contribution to merit i.e. quality – "doing things right".

Concepts such as the "e" words listed above need to be understood in order to think about what to measure and to appreciate their interconnectedness and their validity in debates about how an arts organisation operates and meets its mission.

Zan (2006, 12) provides the following definitions:

Economy is concerned with minimising the cost of resources acquired or used, having regard to appropriate quality (*in short, spending less*).

Efficiency is concerned with the relationship between the output of goods, services or other results and the resources used to produce them. How far is maximum output achieved for a given input, or minimum input used for a given output? (*in short, spending well*).

Effectiveness is concerned with the relationship between the intended results and the actual results of projects, programs or other activities. How successfully do outputs of goods, services or other results achieve policy objectives, operational goals and other intended effects? (*in short, spending wisely*).

Varbanova (2013, 8) defines *efficacy* as the capacity to achieve a final result: the success of achieving a goal rather than only focussing on the resources used.

On the surface, all of those things – meeting goals, spending less or wisely or well – are all

good in themselves but efficiency and effectiveness can sometimes be conflicting notions. For example, reducing either the number of hours a gallery is open or the number of cast members in a Shakespearean play will reduce costs and efficiency will increase, but overall effectiveness may not. In other words, if you're effective but not efficient, goals will be obtained but resources wasted; however, if you're efficient but not effective, according to Dickie and Dickie (2011, 8), your goals aren't attained but no resources are wasted. I find the latter prospect a contradiction in terms because if you haven't reached your goals you must have wasted resources in the process.

It's somewhat easier to prioritise efficiency because its financial focus enables reasonably uncontroversial measurement, and it's been the measurement that has dominated the private sector for decades. However, Jacques (1996, 176) says that as this corporate focus resulted from low-cost, standardised, tangible product making, it is no longer as important in a world where issues such as quality, innovation, flexibility and worker knowledge are of greater concern – a familiar scenario for arts companies. However, effectiveness is more difficult to measure than efficiency. For arts activities, for example, it's not only the output that's important but the outcome which may be something that can only be determined far into the future.

Bonet, Cubelles and Rosello (1997) offer an example of indicators that could be used to measure the artistic process, the results and the impact of a program of a long-term of goal of increasing folk music appreciation and performance amongst children:

- Process indicators: the availability of sufficient number of music instruments per course; the effectiveness of course promotion
- Result/interim indicators: e.g. the number of folk instruments restored; the number of music teachers who can teach folk music instruments

- Impact indicators: the number of school children who can play a folk music instrument after one, two or three years of school lessons; the increase in the percentage of children attending folk music concerts.

This example could easily be transformed into evaluation measures for other arts programs.

Problems with evaluation processes are not just the qualitative versus quantitative question or the timing of when an outcome can be properly measured, but the identification of what indicators one decides to measure because they implicitly involve value judgements. In Australia, major performing arts companies have to submit triennial strategic plans to the Australia Council and their State Government. Key Performance Indicators are a part of what is required and for a couple of years, I got away with a very simple list:

1. Make great theatre
2. Be valued by our major stakeholders
3. Be financially responsible.[9]

Finally, someone said that that wasn't good enough; that we needed to provide KPIs in every subset of the organisation's activities. I did – because I had to – not because such minutiae helped guide the company's operation. I simply invented KPIs that we could meet so that we wouldn't be penalised for failure. The more risk-oriented and boldest parts of our art-making activities weren't put into this straightjacket because I wanted to be able to fail.

Protherough and Pick (2002, 102) have argued passionately against the arts using the language of industry:

No longer do critics search for the quality of the art, instead experts assess the *managerial efficiency* of any organisation which purports to control the distribution and sale of it … Artists are now judged by their *productive efficiency,* their *sales potential,* their *relevance to contemporary needs.* In other words, armament factories, sweetshops and arts centres are all to be judged by the same criteria.

While I agree with their argument, we've lost it. Governments insist on such measures as part of their contract with us. However, this doesn't mean that we should only measure the quantitative and only measure how we operate rather than what we make and share. The point is to measure lots of different aspects of the organisation in lots of different ways. In an article about measuring arts marketing performance, Boorsma and Chiaravalloti (2010) note that measuring financial results and attendance numbers has been the dominant methodology for such evaluation. One could go further and say it's been the dominant evaluation mode for arts organisations *per se* even though the traditional understanding is that arts organisations, like other non-profits, have multiple constituents and therefore should have multiple measures of success.

What you want to be able to do is manage knowledge where knowledge is defined as "the end result of collecting data, organising it into information and presenting it in ways that offer new insights" (Courtney 2002, 221). It's not measurement for the sake of it but measurement so that you can learn to do things better. Gilhespy (1999, 41) provides a long list of all the policy objectives an arts organisation might have and implicit in this are measurements to see if you're being successful:

- Access maximisation
- Attendance maximisation
- Diversity/multiculturalism
- Economy maximisation
- Education
- Excellence/quality
- Innovation
- Revenue maximisation
- Service quality maximisation
- Social cohesion
- Economic importance and impact
- Prestige
- Quality of life.

You can measure these objectives in a variety of ways such as:

- Quantitative – based on numbers and amounts of input and output
- Financial – based on cost
- Qualitative – based on how good the service or activity is
- Process – based on how decisions are made and how people are involved
- Outcomes – what happens as a result of the service or activity
- Social and environment impact
- Comparative (Adironack 2005, 160).

Because of their perceived objectivity, numbers are an inescapable part of the measuring process. My first full-time job was with the Australian Bureau of Statistics so although I wouldn't call them the love of my life, I'm quite comfortable with statistics. I like to play with them, compare them and analyse them, but many people in the arts and cultural industries aren't like that. They had their one exposure to statistics in the first year psychology unit in their arts degree and that ruined them for life. Or they were of the generation where girls did arts and boys did science. As a manager, you don't have to learn to love to statistics but you need to know which ones should be collected and analysed to make sure that both your strategic plan and your annual plan are on track. And if you just don't get it, make sure that you have a Finance Director or a Program Director or a Deputy CEO who does.

Some of these measures will be of inputs (e.g. how many actors did we employ in the education program?) and some of them will be of outputs (e.g. how many school children attended the education program?). Collins (2005) warns that non-profits should concentrate on outputs rather than inputs. He questions the argument that if the Red Cross spends 7% of their total income on administration, overheads and fundraising, does that make them a better organisation than the Cancer Council that spends 10%? But in the case of arts and cultural organisations, we are just as concerned about the artists as we are about the audience and so we need to measure both.

It's easy to collect ticket sales and program costs but sometimes we don't put the two pieces of information together and analyse what's going on. For example, for years a company had been running performing arts classes for the general public. Buried in the accounts were the costs of the program. Sitting in another file were attendances. No-one had looked at two sets of data together for a number of years so it was a shock when management discovered that the classes were losing money. Now that could be a strategy: we'll invest in classes to build interest in our art form. But the company hadn't actively made that decision – they just assumed that classes made money.

Sometimes, the data we collect has to be carefully managed. For example, MTC stage managers knew the number of people who were in the house each night. But they also wanted to know how sales were going so they could tell the cast. When sales were going well it was a fillip to their performance. But what if sales were slow? We developed a process by which each report that was below the average required to hit target was put into a context that would lessen the fear and disappointment of the performers. And the moment an audience target was met, someone from the management team personally delivered a couple of bottles of champagne so that the performance team could celebrate.

The Australia Council has in recent years been requiring the major performing arts companies to measure what they call "artistic vibrancy" as well as financial results. The elements of artistic vibrancy are:

- Quality and excellence of art
- Audience engagement and stimulation
- Development of artists
- Curation and development of the art form
- Community relevance.

They suggest a range of measurement tools including artist and staff surveys, national and international benchmarking, peer panels, awards and nominations, structured interviews or informal discussions with artists and peers. And then there are reviews. Although I have consistently argued for qualitative and arts-focused measures, when it comes to the crunch there can be traps. For example, the main theatre reviewer for one of Melbourne's daily papers consistently gave negative reviews to particular directors we used. Therefore, we couldn't use that information as a reasonable measure of MTC's artistic success. One of the models pushed by the Australia Council was independent external panels to review artistic output. The vision of our Artistic Director sitting in a meeting while people delivered opinions on his work was not one that I was comfortable with. And the idea of finding "independent" people was problematic. Almost everyone in the theatre industry wanted to work for MTC and if they didn't, it was probably because they disapproved of what we did. However, I wasn't going to let this issue get in the way of more funding. So with the support of the Artistic Director, I developed the "Saint Sebastian Group", a collective of people who would make up our Artistic Vibrancy External Panel. It was named after the saint whose image is usually portrayed hung on a crucifix and pierced by arrows – capturing our Artistic Director's response to the idea of such a panel. And the group, a list of very prominent names in Australia's theatre industry, were simply the people with whom he drank and talked endlessly about performance, theatre and art – but in a way that was productive and collaborative, not measurable and judgemental.

Culture Counts, an organisation that provides the technology to measure audience feedback, says that its role is to:

- Standardise the definition of indefinite terms like "quality" so as to create a common descriptive language
- Give control of that language to the sector
- Modernise the means of data collection, analysis and reporting so that it operates in real time and very low cost
- Enable organisations across the world to compare their results and insights, thereby strengthening the combined voice of the sector
- Engage arts funders and investors to ensure that funding decisions are driven by data, thereby ensuring long term sustainable access to those resources. (Culture Counts n.d.)

Morrow (2018, 115) is excited by a process that offers "immediate insights into the cultural experiences of their audiences, participants and peers … using this data to make better cultural programming decisions, focus marketing efforts and grow audiences". It all sounds wonderful but as soon as see "measuring quality" and "standard metrics" in the same sentence, I start to worry. And as soon as I see programming being driven by audience feedback rather than the creativity of artists, I worry. However, we do need to understand our audience's response to our work.

Different stakeholders will judge non-profit effectiveness differently and often important stakeholders aren't clear about their bases for assessing a non-profit's effectiveness anyway. "Like art, they may know effectiveness when they see it, but what do they look for?" (Herman & Renz 2008, 410). You can help them by developing measures that you think are relevant to your goals and ambitions rather than simply using the measures they suggest. Collins (2005, 6) gives a great example of the Cleveland Symphony Orchestra developing measurements based on their aim of becoming a world-class orchestra through artistic excellence. Their three measures of artistic excellence were superior performance, distinctive impact and lasting endurance. For example, for superior performance, they measured the changing demand for tickets but they also measured standing ovations. For distinctive impact, they measured whether other companies were copying their program style but also whether cab drivers talked about the orchestra.

Sometimes the statistics will tell the story for you – for example, when the show sells out – and sometimes you'll have to find ways of personalising the statistics and telling an actual story. MTC ran a scholarship education program for kids experiencing some form of disadvantage. There were various statistical measures: the number of schools that nominate students, the percentage of high schools that applied, the oversubscription of the program by 400 or 500% – but ultimately the number of students in the course was limited to 24. So the statistics don't paint the picture of the impact of that week-long drama course on the kids. That story has to be told in their words, with their passion.

As Meyrick, Phiddian and Barnett (2018, xvii) say: "There is nothing wrong with counting. Counting is an important measurement tool. It's when counting takes the place of judgement that evaluation goes array." They propose the idea of telling parables of value alongside quantitative measurement. The idea is to bridge the gap between "objective" evidence and "subjective" opinion by telling stories that are truthful, apposite, significant, concise, relevant and intelligible (21).

I thought I'd try to write one using those criteria. In the second half of 2018, I was locum CEO/Executive Director for Chunky Move, a dance company based in Melbourne. For 11 years, they'd run a program facilitating the work of emerging choreographers. The impact of that program could be measured by the number of choreographers over the years, the financial investment made by the company, the audience numbers for each season. But none of that speaks to the power of the cultural experience. So instead of the measurements, let's tell the story of a night in the theatre.

On Thursday 8 November 2018, an Indigenous man told a story of a lost ritual through words and dance and music in front of an audience for the first time. The art making enabled him to make contact with his ancestors in a meaningful way and enabled us, a predominantly non-Indigenous audience, to feel the pain of a fractured community as it echoes down the generations.

Isn't that better than saying 96 people saw a new dance work on that date?

Peter Drucker (1990, 62), a famous management writer, said "[y]ou can set goals that are not measurable but [that] can be appraised and can be judged". He gives the example of a research laboratory but it could just as easily be a museum or a dance company. You can't quantify your research (or artistic results) ahead of time. But every couple of years you can ask: what have we done that has made a difference? There are benefits in monitoring and evaluating what your company does over above just because your funders demand it (Fishel 2003, 196–197):

- Learning from experience
- Identifying how far success is being achieved and what impact the organisation's work is having
- Linking individual performance and organisational performance, thorough appraisal processes
- Recognising achievement and creating opportunities for individual recognition
- Averting major problems by identifying them at an early stage, and taking corrective action
- Identifying opportunities to increase efficiency and effectiveness
- Ensuring the organisation is complying with legal requirements.

You then need to make sure that your staff know why you're measuring things and what success looks like. Arts Centre Melbourne addresses this in the booklet they hand to new staff. They use words to provide a framework for the numbers and dollars under the heading "business excellence".

"What we shall do:

- We shall prioritise safety at all times
- Seek out and remove unnecessary bureaucracy
- Build a business platform that is best in call, sustainable and scalable for the future

- Have a clear plan that is well understood and we measure ourselves against it
- Test our competing priorities against our strategy
- Develop a financially sustainable and vital business, with operating reserves, and risk management set at a level that provides resilience
- Engage with your stakeholders in relationships of mutual respect and recognition, always exploring partnerships as our way of business
- Work collaboratively with the Victorian Government in carrying out our legislative responsible and the exploration and leverage of new opportunities

What success looks like:

- We are the benchmark for safety in our industry
- Operating reserves reach target levels and meet the needs of our business
- Our revenue sources are diversified allowing us to invest in our people, community and future business growth
- Our cost base is well managed and flexible to a changing economic environment
- We anticipate and take considered risks without agreed tolerances
- Our systems and processes are robust and flexible – they meet customer needs
- We have strong mutually beneficial business relationships with our stakeholders and partners
- Trusted advisor to government on Creative Industries and broader community issues" (p. 17).

This paints a clear picture of what the organisation wants to be.

In summary, having inputs and outputs that can be measured and tested can help organisations make better informed decisions, use their limited resources more effectively and/or efficiently and be accountable to stakeholders. We can use such informational tactically on a day-to-day basis to check whether we're doing things right and for strategic purposes to check whether we're doing the right things (Grant 2012, 137). But beware of the danger of only focusing on the measurable and taking a short-term view. Beware of measuring just the outputs (how many people came to the theatre?) and not the outcomes (where they emotionally engaged?). Beware of neglecting your cultural aims in order to optimise your KPIs (Zembylas 2019, 143). Keep Protherough and Pick's (2002, 200) comment in mind: it's an illusion to think that the world will be safe "if you reduce everything to numbers". After all, we're making art and that should put the intrinsic aspects of individual experience at the core of what we need to evaluate (Chiaravalloti & Piber 2011).

See also: Arts Industry, Cultural Policy, Economics, Money

References

Adirondack, S. 2005 *Just About Managing?* (4th ed), London: London Voluntary Service Council.

Arts Centre Melbourne n.d. *The Role You Play*, Melbourne: ACM.

Australia Council, *Artistic Vibrancy e-book*, www.australiacouncil.gov.au/ebook/artistic-vibrancy/publication/contents/pdfweb.pdf [accessed 26 February 2019].

Becker, K., Antuar, N. & Everett, C. 2011 "Implementing an Employee Performance Management System in a Nonprofit Organization", *Nonprofit Management & Leadership*, 21(3), 255–271.

Bonet, L., Cubelles, X. & Rosello, J. 1997 "Management Control and Evaluation of Public Cultural Centres", Fitzgibbon, M. & Kelly, A. (eds) *From Maestro to Manager*, Dublin: Oak Tree Press, 85–95.

Boorsma, M. & Chiaravalloti, F. 2010 "Arts Marketing Performance: An Artistic-Mission-Led Approach to Evaluation", *The Journal of Arts Management, Law, and Society*, 40(4), 297–312.

Chiaravalloti, F. & Piber, M. 2011 "Ethical and Political Implications of Methodological Settings in Arts Management Research: The Case of Performance Evaluation", Antwerp: AIMAC International Conference.

Collins, J. 2005 *Good to Great and the Social Sectors*, Boulder, CO: Jim Collins.

Courtney, R. 2002 *Strategic Management for Voluntary Nonprofit Organizations*, London: Routledge.

Croggon, A. 2013 "The Perfect Storm: Playwright vs. Director", ABC Arts, www.abc.net.au/arts/blog/Alison-Croggon/playwright-versus-Director-130731/ [accessed 23 January 2015].

Culture Counts n.d. "5 Key Principles", https://culturecounts.cc/about/ [accessed 22 February 2019].

Dickie, L. & Dickie, C. 2011 *Cornerstones of Management* (2nd ed), Melbourne: Tilde University Press.

Drucker, P. F. 1990 *Managing the Nonprofit Organization*, New York: HarperCollins.

Fishel, D. 2003 *The Book of The Board*, Sydney: Federation Press.

Gilhespy, I. 1999 "Measuring the Performance of Cultural Organizations: A Model", *International Journal of Arts Management*, 2(1), 38–52.

Grant, P. 2012 *The Business of Giving: The Theory and Practice of Philanthropy, Grantmaking and Social Investment*, New York: Palgrave Macmillan.

Herman, R. D. & Renz, D. O. 2008 "Advancing Nonprofit Organizational Effectiveness Research and Theory: Nine Theses", *Nonprofit Management & Leadership*, 18(4), 399–415.

Hewison, R. & Holden, J. 2011 *The Cultural Leadership Handbook*, Farnham: F Gower.

Jacques, R. 1996 *Manufacturing the Employee*, London: Sage.

Kotter, J. P. & Cohen, D. S. 2002 *The Heart of Change: Real Life Stories of How People Change Their Organizations*, Boston, MA: Harvard Business School Press.

Krug, K. & Weinberg, C.B. 2004 "Mission, Money and Merit: Strategic Decisions Making by Nonprofit Managers", *Nonprofit Management and Leadership*, 14(3), 325–342.

Meyrick, J., Phiddian, R. & Barnett, J. 2018 *What Matters? Talking Value in Australian Culture*, Melbourne: Monash University Publishing.

Morrow, G. 2018 *Artist Management: Agility and the Creative and Cultural Industries*, London: Routledge.

Pankratz, D. B. 2011 "Evaluation in the Arts", in Brindle, M. & DeVereaux, C. (eds) *The Arts Management Handbook*, Armon, NY: M.E. Sharpe, 319–347.

Protherough, R. & Pick, J. 2002 *Managing Britannia*, Exeter: Brinmill Press.

Radbourne, J., Johanson, K., Glow, H. & White, T. 2009 "The Audience Experience: Measuring Quality in the Performing Arts", *International Journal of Arts Management*, 11(3), 16–29.

Tusa, J. 2007a *Engaged with the Arts*, London: I.B. Tauris & Co Ltd.

Varbanova, L. 2013 *Strategic Management in the Arts*, New York: Routledge.

Watkins, J. M., Mohr, B. & Kelly, R. 2011 *Appreciative Inquiry* (2nd ed), San Francisco, CA: Pfeiffer.

Zan, L. 2006 *Managerial Rhetoric and Arts Organizations*, Houndmills: Palgrave Macmillan.

Zemblyas, T. 2019 "Why Are Evaluations in the Field of Cultural Policy (Almost Always) Contested? Major Problems, Frictions, and Challenges", in DeVereaux, C. (ed) *Arts and Cultural Management: Sense and Sensibility in the State of the Field*, New York: Routledge, 129–151.

Notes

1 Obviously, there are more up-to-date textbooks on Economics but I want to acknowledge the work of my first Economics lecturer John Jackson. Although I ended up loathing the subject, I valued him.

2 Other issues are the leader's character and their difficulty in managing interpersonal relationships.

3 A fascinating writer on this topic is James Fallon author of *The Psychopath Inside*.

4 In the section on *Leadership*.

5 In high power-distance cultures, people are less comfortable taking an authoritative role unless their position specifically authorises it.

6 Cuddy's initial research was challenged but she's come back with more evidence to support her position: www.forbes.com/sites/kimelsesser/2018/04/03/power-posing-is-back-amy-cuddy-successfully-refutes-criticism/#7e18b4353b8e [accessed 1 September 2019].

7 Although simply typing on a computer wasn't enough to turn them on and so I was often seen madly waving my arms about to get the lights back on.

8 www.cranlana.org.au/

9 I either unconsciously absorbed or accidently did the same as John Tusa who had a very similar set of goals for the Barbican Theatre (see Tusa 2007a, 44).

F

Families

Although the language of arts organisations is full of the imagery of "families" they aren't always good for families. As Mendelssohn (2013a, 4) says "[a]rts organisations do not keep family friendly hours. It is not possible to juggle homework, choir practice and football training with exhibition openings." In Chew and Hello's (2015) examination of the leadership in Singaporean dance companies, they collected demographic information on their interviewees. There weren't many of them so it's hard to extrapolate from their results but one point was particularly telling:

> seven of the interviewees (i.e. 58.3%) are single and only one leader (8.3%) has children. A possible reason for this last result is that leadership roles in these dance companies are time consuming and overwhelming and leave little time for family life (134).

Add into this mix the hours we work and the precarity of the artists we employ and arts organisations may have a particularly challenging time in being family-friendly.

There's evidence in UK workplaces that family-friendly management has a positive impact on productivity and quality but not necessarily on turnover and absenteeism (Wood & de Menezes 2010). Other international research indicates that employees value flexibility and that it impacts on their motivation and commitment to the employer which may in turn impact positively on turnover and absenteeism (Stone 2013). In other words, the evidence of the impact of work-life balance policies is mixed from a business perspective, but I think it's important to have such policies from a human perspective. Sinclair (2007, 134) is critical of the notion behind the phrase "work-life balance" – that somehow there is an equality between the two and that they are distinct – because, as she rightly points out, few people experience work or life like this. I think of my neighbours, one coming home exhausted from a building site, the other stressed after a confrontation with an unhappy customer, and the impact of those experiences on what happens at home shows that the boundaries are very blurred. But any policy that helps people live well in both worlds is helpful. Individuals will benefit from being given the space to handle personal or family problems and find energy and space for life outside of work. Such policies signify "that employees' commitment to the organization is reciprocated by management" (Wood & de Menezes 2010, 1592).

In Australia, the idea of flexible work arrangements is more than symbolic; it's built into legislation as one of the country's National Employment Standards. Employees who have worked with the same employer for at least 12 months can request flexible working arrangements if they are the parent of a young child, a carer, have a disability, are 55 or older, are experiencing family or domestic violence or providing care to a family member who is in that situation. Employers must provide a quick written response to such a request, discuss it with the employee and work to "reasonably accommodate" the employee's circumstances. The business impact has to be considered but equally so does the impact of saying "no" to the employee. This could be a good approach for companies in other countries as well. Examples of flexible working arrangements include changes to hours, patterns and locations of work (Fairwork Ombudsman).

Other examples of flexible working arrangements can include:

- Job-sharing
- Flexi-time
- Staggered hours
- Compressed hours (over fewer days)
- Part-year working or term-time working
- Annualised hours
- Teleworking/homeworking
- Shift swapping
- Self-rostering
- Career-breaks/sabbaticals (Kumra & Manfredi 2012, 186).

Some aspects of the work that takes place in arts and cultural organisations are open to such arrangements but much is not. Shows happen at night and over the weekend. Museums and galleries are open every day of the year except for a couple of religious holidays. Stage managers work for weeks during the day and then have to switch to nights. Freelance directors and designers have to travel to get to gigs. Dancers and musicians will often have to go on tour. The gallery opens at a certain time and guides have

to be in place. Everyone in the cast has to be in the rehearsal room at the same time. The bump-in of the opera has to be done over a series of 18-hour days because of the availability (and cost) of the venue. The dance performance starts at 8pm. These times, often outside of regular working hours, can be particularly challenging for people with young children because, as Mendelssohn (2013b) points out, unless people are in the most senior of positions, people working in the arts tend to have salaries that equate with genteel poverty, most child-care centres close by 6pm and nannies are expensive.

One of the worst challenges for people working with families in the performing arts is the bump-in, that is, moving the set and costumes and actors out of the workshops and rehearsal room and into the theatre, where the long days were remorseless. Every day of bump-in at MTC was a day that we weren't putting the show in front of audiences so the pressure was on to make it happen in the shortest number of days. The truth was that we drove people to work ridiculous hours because of money – rental cost and lost income. Over the years, we did give more and more time to this process but it never seemed to stop the long hours. Luckily, the union recognised this propensity in all performing arts companies and there was a financial penalty built into industrial awards to try and stop people working unless they'd had a 10-hour break – double pay until they did.

Apart from hours and leave, there are other family-friendly work practices that can contribute to a supportive organisational culture. At one point, I had to look after a very young family member at a time when I also needed to be in the office. Admittedly, having a babe in arms in the office is easier than a toddler because they sleep a lot and are often just as happy to be held by a stranger as a relative. However, the experience made me create a policy whereby people could bring children into the workplace. The rules were simple: staff had to have the agreement of their fellow workers and the children had to be safe and supervised at all times. During school holiday periods this was especially useful for parents. Their output for that day may have decreased somewhat but people acknowledged the benefit and worked hard to make up for any loss of time. And the atmosphere in the workplace was usually made a degree lighter by childrens' laughter. Not that this was a particularly innovative policy. At a playreading[1] I attended in 2013 based on the clothing industry in Melbourne in the 1950s and 1960s, the employer not only offers additional money to get the women in the sewing room to come back from home and do overtime, but also let them bring their children into work although this mainly seemed to involve playing soccer in the laneway outside.

Claire Mabey, the Director of New Zealand's LitCrawl, reflected on what a family-friendly arts organisation might look like after having a premature baby in the midst of preparing for her festival. As she said, she was lucky as the CEO of a small arts organisation where she often worked at home with a supportive partner. It's much harder for larger organisations to deal with the flexibility that parents need. Her recommendations are:

1. Talking about babies at work – creating an environment where parents can speak comfortably and what's happening to them and their needs
2. Boobs – having safe spaces for mothers to breastfeed or pump
3. Babies at work – what are childcare options particularly for people on contracts
4. I'll be in at 5, gone by lunchtime – in other words, flexible work hours
5. Your baby looks great on you – seeing babies as a positive addition rather than an obstacle.

As she says: "It doesn't make sense to try and fit work and family life into two straight lines, two square boxes. It makes more sense to be flexible and embrace the chaos." And as a result,

get the best out of committed worker/parents (Mabey 2018).

In a move that some might view as odd, we extended the policy about children in the workplace to dogs with the same rules: work mates had to agree and the dog had to be supervised. It was encouraging when researching this book to find another story about dogs in the workplace. In this case people started bringing their dogs into work when they needed care (the dogs) and to lessen the stress of worrying about them. The staff began to recognise that having dogs around had more positives than negatives. There was some organisation-wide discussion and an informal policy was developed – another example of lived culture driving workplace policies (Plas & Lewis 2001).

I have to confess that while part of the rationale behind developing a policy on dogs at MTC was positive (the happiness that animals can bring into an environment), part of it was also negative. After experiencing the receptionist's barking beagle every time she put through a call and the flea bites I received as a result of another visiting canine, I wanted to have some control over their role in our work lives.

Whether it's children or hours or illness or parents, it doesn't always have to be a formal, flexible work agreement. People will be grateful for time off on an irregular basis for personal needs and in my experience, rarely abuse the privilege. I love the description of working at Oasis, a care service organisation in Tennessee. In the words of Plas and Lewis (2001, 75):

An undisputed reality at the center is that people do not criticize one another for dealing with family responsibilities during regular work hours. Co-workers do not complain, and management does not offer negative consequences. These people routinely bring kids and pets to work, take kids and pets to medical appointments, make personal day time visits to legal and government agencies, and even get the tires on their cars rotated during agency hours when necessary. …. Employees make their own decision about what needs to come first: work or family. If they decide in favor of a family responsibility, they also decide how work at Oasis will be covered in their absence.

It's not always easy to create such an environment because there are often situational tensions that result from work structure and the impact of people's different personal situations. For example, the day-to-day practices such as working from home, flexitime, altering start and finish times need to be negotiated with the team because if the dynamics of the team are badly disrupted or if people develop antagonism towards a member because of a perception of special treatment, then the result won't be positive.

Another area of concern is the difference between those with children and those without. For example, there is evidence from the Netherlands (ten Brummelhuis, Haar & van der Lippe 2010) that the family demands of having young children have a disadvantageous effect on collegiality, whereas having children in itself did not diminish collegial behaviour. For better or for worse, caring for young children takes a lot of time and energy and prevents employees from being fully involved in workplace social networks. So, ironically, you can be trying to develop a family-friendly culture at work but anyone with a young family will find it hard to participate fully. The notion that people with young children aren't as "available" to their colleagues as those without shouldn't come as a surprise to anyone. The main issue is to ensure that any complaints or concerns about staff lack of availability because of these demands are heard and responded to quickly before they become a problem. Rosner and Halcrow (2010) advise that the best way of dealing with this tension between parents and nonparents is to put the focus back on job performance:

if you give people time to deal with their personal lives, it doesn't matter whether they spend that time taking their kids to a soccer game, volunteering at a homeless shelter, or going to an antiques show; it's their business, not yours. Measure whether work is completed on time and done well and don't log every time Jane (sic) comes in late or leaves early (305).

The odds are, even if someone doesn't have kids, they have a partner or parents who will need some care and attention at some time. We now live in a world where many of us are caught between children and elder responsibilities in the "sandwich generation" (Kumra & Manfredi 2012). Before the Australian Government introduced regulations that redefined sick leave as family leave so that it could be used for more than just personal illness, we had such a policy at my theatre company because I'd experienced the need.

In an article entitled "Why are so many arts organisations run by blokes?", Mendelssohn (2013b) gives an example of how to create family-friendly work environments without having to have specific policies. According to her, the Director of the Art Gallery of New South Wales, Michael Brand, is known for his ability to delegate to other staff. This sound management strategy enables him to spend more time with his family. Even when there is the formal right to ask for flexible work arrangements, people may fear what a manager reads into a such a request – you're not committed enough; your family demands will interfere with your work; it's going to cause the company problems; and you don't seem to care. If your organisation is really committed to flexible work practices (and its specific effect on women who continue to bear most family responsibilities) then you need to be more proactive. Leading by example is one way of doing this to create an environment where there's time to care for kids and parents, partners and puppy dogs and still have a productive workplace.

See also: Delegation, Gender, Holidays, Hours, People

References

Chew, S. & Hallo, L. 2015 "On Your Toes: Perception of Leadership Influences in Dance Companies in Singapore", in Caust, J. (ed.) *Arts and Cultural Leadership in Asia*, London: Routledge, 129–147.

Fairwork Ombudsman, *National Employment Standards*, www.fairwork.gov.au/employee-entitlements/flexibility-in-the-workplace/flexible-working-arrangements [accessed 22 February 2019].

Kumra, S. & Manfredi, S. 2012 *Managing Equality and Diversity*, Oxford: Oxford University Press.

Mabey, C. 2018 "What It Really Takes to Juggle an Arts Organisation With Family Life", *Arts Hub*, 8 November, www.artshub.com.au/education/news-article/career-advice/professional-development/claire-mabey/what-it-really-takes-to-juggle-an-arts-organisation-with-family-life-256772 [accessed 22 February 2019].

Mendelssohn, J. 2013a "Déjà vu: Women and Leadership in the Visual Arts", *NAVA Quarterly*, 4–5.

Mendelssohn, J. 2013b "Why Are So Many Arts Organisations Run By Blokes?", *The Conversation*, 10 May, http://theconversation.com/why-are-so-many-arts-organisations-run-by-blokes-13217 [accessed 22 February 2019].

Plas, J. M. & Lewis, S. E. 2001 *Person-Centered Leadership of Nonprofit Organizations*, Thousand Oaks, CA: Sage Publications.

Rosner, B. & Halcrow, A. 2010 *The Boss's Survival Guide* (2nd ed), New York: McGraw Hill.

Sinclair, A. 2007a *Leadership for the Disillusioned*, Sydney: Allen & Unwin.

Stone, R. J. 2013 *Managing Human Resources* (4th ed), Milton, QLD: John Wiley & Sons.

Ten Brummelhuis, L. L., Haar, J. M. & van der Lippe, T. 2010 "Collegiality Under Pressure: The Effects of Family Demands and Flexible Work Arrangements in the Netherlands", *The International Journal of Human Resource Management*, 21(15), 2831–2847.

Wood, S. J. & de Menezes, L. M. 2010 "Family-friendly Management, Organizational Performance and Social Legitimacy", *The International Journal of Human Resource Management*, 21(10), 1575–1597.

Firing

Firing someone is the hardest part of being an arts manager – both because labour laws often make it an extraordinarily long, drawn-out (and not always successful) process and because the emotional impact on both parties can't be underestimated. As Autry (2001, 108) says: "[f]iring people is a violent act … we are taking away someone's livelihood and are often delivering a terrible blow to the employee's sense of identity and self-esteem".

The usual reasons for firing people are redundancy due to economic or structural change or because they aren't contributing to the organisation or their contribution is a negative one. As an arts manager said when asked what were the skills one needed to the job:

> This sounds horrible – but knowing when to fire someone and not live with the pain of a dysfunctional/useless staff member. Most arts managers have staff sizes too small to be able to wear a bad staff member, but when we're young we keep giving them one more chance, to our own and the company's detriment.[2]

Arts organisations are usually too under-resourced to let poor performance continue but they are also the type of organisation where caring about people's well-being is part of the culture. Drucker (1990, 150) says that non-profit executives are always inclined to be reluctant to let a non-producer go because they are seen as a "comrade-in-arms". I've seen scenarios where managers will continue to help someone try to perform better long past a reasonable point in time and scenarios where even though staff object to someone's behaviour, they won't make a formal complaint. In response to this conflict between the need to ensure competence and the need for compassion, Drucker (1990, 150) offers one rule: "if they try, they deserve another chance. If they don't try, make *sure* they leave."

The starting point in the decision to fire someone is to ask whether it's the person's fault or the organisation's fault? Have you provided enough orientation or training or support or information to help someone do their job well? Is it the impact of out of work issues that is causing their work performance to suffer? Is it that they don't match the organisational culture? Are they overloaded and lack guidance about prioritising their work? In other words, are there things that you as a manager should do to see if you can improve their capacity to contribute? Think of it as marriage guidance counselling. If a problem can be identified and acknowledged, both parties may be able to work together to keep the relationship going.

But sometimes, the marriage is doomed. Is one of the parties violent? Are drug and alcohol issues impacting on their work? Are they cheating or using your resources to run another business? Are they verbally abusive or bullying other staff? Are they breaking that vow to "honour and obey" by breaching the organisation's code of conduct? Any of these types of behaviour can potentially be reason enough to want to terminate the relationship.

Because the employment relationship is a contract, there are a number of requirements for a termination based on poor behaviour or performance to be a just process. The language is dense but it's about ensuring that someone has the chance to respond to the "charges" and be treated with respect. Elements in a just or fair termination process include:

- Substantive justice: whether a valid reason exists for the firing
- Procedural justice: whether the employee was given warnings about the employer's concerns, a chance to explain or justify their situation and a reasonable chance to improve
- Distributive justice: where the termination package is perceived as fair and equitable
- Interactional justice: where the people involved in the process are seen as treating the terminated employee with dignity and respect (Stone 2013; Balnave et al. 2009).

At a presentation at the Executive Program for Non-profit Leaders that I attended at Stanford University in 2005, I took down notes about a story told by Dale Miller. In it he gave an example which illustrated the difference between distributive justice (perceptions of the fairness of a particular outcome) and procedural justice (perceptions of whether the process was seen to be fair). Company A lays off staff and gives a good benefit package, outplacement services and so on, while Company B didn't offer such a generous package. With Company A, the result was a number of unfair dismissal legal cases and employee productivity plummeted – but this wasn't the case with Company B. The difference was that Company B's senior management explained the strategic purpose of the redundancies a number of times before they happened, were available to answer any questions and expressed regret to those who lost their jobs. In Company A, the layoffs were never explained, they were handled by the HR department and many staff heard about it on the news as they drove home. Unlike the employees at Company A, those at Company B believed that they had been treated fairly.

Part of being fair if the issue is bad behaviour is to respond to it straight away and don't wait for an annual performance review.

> Except for the most egregious infractions, involuntary terminations are hardly ever spontaneous. The termination should never be a surprise. Anyone who is fired should have seen it coming a long time again – and should have been *given the chance* to see it coming a long time ago.
>
> (Sartain & Finney 2003, 220)

Other practical advice is to document every part of the process and if an investigation is required, get an external expert. You can't be both investigator and judge of someone's behaviour.

Even when you think that you have a watertight case, expect the union (if there is one in your industry) to come in to support their member. In one scenario where someone was under investigation for downloading and distributing pornography via the company's computer system, I thought the evidence was perfectly clear. The union representative started to make the case that as I was clearly a middle-aged woman and the staff member was a young man, that we would have different definitions of pornography, implying that I was over-reacting. I simply laid page after page after page of the evidence on the table. I haven't seen a man blush so brilliantly and the conversation quickly drew to a satisfactory close.

Mind you, I may not be able to do that with such gay abandon now. In an industrial case in 2013, Australia Post was forced to reinstate two people they'd fired for having pornography on their work computers. Although Australia Post had a "'zero tolerance" policy to sending sexually explicit material, the Federal Court decided that sending or receiving pornography was like any other workplace misbehaviour and that the length of service of the men had to be considered. Even more importantly, there was a general absence of monitoring and enforcing work policies in the particular part of the organisation where the offences took place and the Court concluded that it was harsh to dismiss employees without any prior warning for breaches of policy of a type where such breaches had been widespread and unaddressed for an extended period (Robin 2013).

This is what Balnave et al. (2009, 446) call "condonation" – where employers condone or accept certain behaviour. At MTC we had great trouble trying to devise a workable policy on alcohol consumption because of the "condonation" trap. There were well known and even brilliant actors who drank before and sometimes during each performance. In the end we came up with a policy focused on people who were in charge of equipment or had the capacity to put others at risk and they weren't allowed to drink or use drugs before shows.

Whether you're firing someone because of poor performance or bad behaviour or because you can no longer afford to pay them, it's always a time of high emotional drama for both the employee and the person giving them the news. I have never followed the "clean out your desk and leave" approach to termination unless someone has done grievous harm to the organisation or the people in it. If they are being fired because

they failed to do their job, then like Autry (2001), I think they should be given time to say goodbye to friends and colleagues and leave with some semblance of dignity. The organisation should also be willing to provide support for the staff member in these cases because even if you're extremely happy to see them walking out the door, they deserve some help in re-establishing themselves in a more suitable employment environment. It may be just a few extra weeks' termination pay or it may be paying for them to go to a careers counsellor, but it's a way of acknowledging the impact of losing one's job.

Occasionally you can avoid firing someone by helping people to see that the best thing to do is to leave. This is often the case when it's about a mismatch of skills rather than behavioural issues. Rosner and Halcrow (2010) quote one of their readers who tells how to let someone fire themselves. The process was to call them into a meeting, give specific examples of the performance problems, offer them a day off to write down 20 ways to improve, told that if the problems continue they'll be terminated and also told that if they choose not to return they'll get special termination pay and what's owing to them. "Every time I used this system, the employee chose not to return … The employee was given a way out, with the option of retaining their dignity and having enough money to make a transition" (428).

Sometimes firing someone isn't about their behaviour but rather because of the needs of the organisation. Usually for arts organisations, such redundancies are caused by a loss of income, the completion of a program or a change in structure. There is never a good way to fire people but firing people who have contributed positively to an organisation is the worst case scenario. If such redundancies can be made voluntary, at least the people concerned may benefit from a new life (both financially and career-wise) but the organisation may suffer if the best people, the people with the most capacity to get another job, decide to leave. It then becomes an ethical choice about the organisation's requirements compared to the needs of individual workers.

Procedural fairness can often be hard to implement in such cases because trade unions may take a different view about redundancies to management. In the 1990s, the Australian Broadcasting Corporation (ABC) had a collective agreement with the Media Entertainment and Arts Alliance (MEAA) which included a clause to the effect that management had to discuss any possible redundancies with the union first. While in principle, this may have given the union an opportunity to argue against the terminations, in practice it meant that news leaked quickly and people heard on the grapevine that their department was to be closed or their jobs lost. As you can imagine, it's hard enough to hear that news directly, but agonising if it comes unofficially via the rumour mill. During my time with the ABC, we had to make a number of budget-based terminations and I'd seen the damage caused by the formal process. I got approval from my manager to break the rules and tell a group of impacted staff face-to-face at the same time that the union was being told. The situation was such that I had to tell the group the day after they'd received an award for the quality of their work. As you can imagine, a hideous piece of timing and a dreadful process with people in considerable distress. Although the redundancy packages were generous, that wasn't the point. These situations are never just about a job; they are about people's lives and their deepest emotional states. All I could do was to offer support such as help with resumes as well as a stiff drink. At the time, I was seen as both the bearer and the creator of the bad news and my offers of help weren't particularly appreciated. However, in the weeks that followed, people did ask for (and received) my help. I remember one particular phone call months after people had left to thank me for giving the news personally and for being available to help make the transition as bearable as it could be at the time.

The ABC went through another redundancy process in 2014/15 and the headlines weren't pretty. The organisation grouped people with similar skills and they basically had to prove how good they were with the least skilled person losing their position. It was described as the "Hunger Games" and "cruel and inhumane" (Knott 2015; Patty 2014). In my experience there is no "good" way to fire people, particularly when it's for economic and not performance reasons. All one can do is show compassion and concern and accept that this may not be seen or believed at the time.

I've only heard of one positive story about redundancies. It was told by the CEO of a not-for-profit organisation and it's about being taken out to lunch along with his senior management team by the people they'd sacked.

> [The employees] knew that the fact that the funding [that covered their salaries] had dried up in their area wasn't actually our doing. [They also acknowledged] that we had supported them in every way through the process of redundancy. We had brought the HR people in to help them write job descriptions and had done everything we could to make it really work for them in the life after.

The manager quoted one person: "I've been sacked seven times, but never as nicely, so we just wanted to take you for lunch" (Sarros et al. 2006, 35). This is a (rare) example of where working hard to be fair and just had a positive outcome.

In a 2018 example, Arts SA, the state government department of the arts in South Australia, was closed and the staff were told their contracts hadn't been renewed by letter without a manager being available in person to explain why. The response in the arts industry to both the closure and the way people were treated was outrage. Former Artistic Director of Opera Australia, Moffat Oxenbould argues that he used to deliver bad news to artists face-to-face but the he changed to writing a letter followed up by a face-to-face meeting within 48 hours so that people could have time to think and respond and not be blindsided and react purely emotionally (Saintilan & Schreiber 2018, 182). I confess that I don't see the difference between blindsided by a letter and blindsided by a person but I do think that managers need to be seen and available in these difficult times.

On the same day I was told the Arts SA story, I heard about an even more insensitive approach to firing people on ABC's Radio National station – being fired by a computer. The story was that when someone's contract mistakenly had not been renewed, the "system" cancelled his access card, generated emails to the HR department to stop his pay, and to the security department to escort him off the premises – and his boss was powerless to stop it. At that point, one doesn't know whether to laugh or cry. Perhaps the impersonal letters sent to the Arts SA staff were also computer driven. What's happened to the "human" part of HR management?

I've discovered that my belief in facing up to the people you are going to fire and not doing it via text or email or letter now has a name: "compassionate firing" (Barsade & O'Neill 2016, 66). One could also just call it "decent" or "ethical" but when dealing with people, this should always be the process. And part of the process should be looking after you and the remaining staff. I've been stalked and threatened after firing people and I've also cried when the departures were driven by economics and not performance. Whether it's with a mentor, a support person or just a friend, being able to debrief after difficult people-related actions is useful. For staff, even if they wanted someone to leave, the process can make them feel vulnerable, and so managing the emotional impact of terminations on those still in the organisation is also important.

The best advice I can offer about firing anyone is to be tough but fair, get legal advice – and moral support.

See also: Bullying, Ethics, Industrial Relations, Performance Appraisal, People, Unions

References

Autry, J. A. 2001 *The Servant Leader*, New York: Three Rivers Press.

Balnave, N., Brown J., Maconachie, G. & Stone, R. J. 2009 *Employment Relations in Australia* (2nd ed), Milton, QLD: John Wiley & Sons.

Barsade, S. & O'Neill, O. A. 2016 "Manage Your Emotional Culture", *Harvard Business Review*, 94(1/2), 58–66.

Drucker, P. F. 1990 *Managing the Nonprofit Organization*, New York: HarperCollins.

Knott, M. 2015 "ABC Maternity Leave Workers Vie for Jobs in 'Hunger Games-style' Redundancy Process", *Sydney Morning Herald*, www.smh.com.au/federal-politics/political-news/abc-maternity-leave-workers-vie-for-jobs-in-hunger-gamesstyle-redundancy-process-20150117-12r808.html [accessed 22 February 2019].

Patty, A. 2014 "ABC Staff Reject 'Cruel and Inhumane' Approach to Redundancies", *Sydney Morning Herald*, www.smh.com.au/nsw/abc-staff-reject-cruel-and-inhumane-approach-to-redundancies-20141204-11zvtd.html [accessed 22 February 2019].

Robin, M. 2013 *Australia Post Employees Who Sent Porn at Work Reinstated by Fair Work Commission with Back Pay*, www.smartcompany.com.au/people/industrial-relations/34744-australia-post-employees-who-sent-porn-at-work-reinstated-by-fair-work-commission-with-back-pay.html# [accessed 22 February 2019].

Rosner, B. & Halcrow, A. 2010 *The Boss's Survival Guide* (2nd ed), New York: McGraw Hill.

Saintilan, P. & Schreiber, D. 2018 *Managing Organizations in the Creative Economy: Organizational Behaviour for the Cultural Sector*, Abingdon: Routledge.

Sarros, J., Cooper, B. K., Hartican, A. M. & Barker, C. J. 2006 *The Character of Leadership*, Milton, QLD: John Wiley & Sons.

Sartain, L. & Finney, M. I. 2003 *HR from the Heart*, New York: AMACOM.

Stone, R. J. 2013 *Managing Human Resources* (4th ed), Milton, QLD: John Wiley & Sons.

Fundraising

As I flip-flopped between writing under the heading of *Philanthropy* or *Fundraising* in the first edition of this book, I found the following definition which solved my dilemma:

> Philanthropy is the art of giving; fundraising is the art of getting.
>
> (Conte & Langley 2007, 305)

The result was that I only had a section on *Fundraising*. However, since then, I've started teaching a course with "philanthropy" in the title, so I decided I should have a separate section on obtaining money from donors and foundations. This section will focus on lots of other things you can do (apart from selling tickets, applying for government grants and negotiating sponsorship deals) to raise money. But a confession is required first.

When it comes to events and products, I'm a failed fundraiser. With two exceptions, every idea I ever had to raise money for MTC failed to reach budget. Because theatre is so ephemeral and until very recently wasn't rarely recorded, the only thing apart from the memories that people take home are programmes. Therefore, every so often I'd get a bee in my bonnet about capturing something of what we did in a tangible form. And in every case, it was a financial failure. I tried calendars and diaries, key rings and T-shirts, baseball caps and badges. And even the product that I was sure every subscriber would want – a beautiful collection of production photos in a book – didn't sell (Meyrick, Phillips & Tonks 2004). I was the laughing stock of every Finance Director I ever employed. In the end, when money wasn't so tight, I stopped pretending to myself that such ideas would make money and just did it because *I* wanted that beautiful book of photos (Phillips & Tonks 2012).

None of my ideas lost a fortune. My heart was in the right place but I'm not a good shopper so, not surprisingly, I couldn't pick the things that people really wanted to buy. Luckily, I was surrounded by people who were much more focused on experiences than goods and had great ideas so we did have some fabulously entertaining fundraising events such as trivia nights and gala musical dinners. However, I will publicly claim my two successful fundraising ideas. I took a group of MTC subscribers to experience theatre in Canada (the Shaw and Stratford Festivals and some musicals in Toronto) and built a donation into the fee. Twenty-five enthusiasts joined me as novice tour guide and they managed to have such a good time that most of them wanted to repeat the experience. My second success was a series of "garage sales" where MTC sold off its old props and costumes. Hundreds of people would queue for hours to get unique bargains. My strongest memory is a couple of women holding a costume that had been worn by Hugo Weaving, sniffing at the sweat-stained neckband, obviously wanted to make sure they really were buying "essence" of "Tick Belrose"[3] or "Agent Smith".[4] Garage sales appealed to people's sense of getting a bargain *and* of getting a souvenir.

How many ways can your raise money? It depends on your inventiveness. You can run auctions and put on balls, you can sell raffle tickets or sell art, you can put on special events and even run non-arts-related activities such as sports events. Years ago, the Shaw Festival used to receive money as result of theatre lovers putting on boxing matches. The most regular fundraising activity of many arts companies are "galas" which usually provide arts content, dinner and sometimes an auction.

Unlike dance, opera and music companies that usually have artists on their payroll and can use them to make wonderful contributions to fundraising events, theatre companies don't. And while people are happy to listen to a song, watch a duet or talk through a musical interlude, excerpts from plays aren't usually as exciting at a gala. Having said that, I do remember one exception. The University of Melbourne held a 'town and gown" evening with representatives from the business and political world of Melbourne dining with the academics, managers and students from the university. Usually, wonderful student musicians provide the artistic element of the event but one year, the Vice Chancellor asked MTC's Artistic Director to provide the program. He chose an extract from the play he was rehearsing – *Festen* – which involved nudity and explicit language. The extract was enjoyed by some more sophisticated members of the audience but not surprisingly it wasn't exactly the tone the Vice Chancellor desired for the night.

Galas are, in Kaiser's (2013) experience, a chance to gather your supporters together, get a second gift from a donor, influence potential new donors and create the impression of a vital arts company. But he also advises not to have too many non-paying guests or boring events and not ask the same people to too many events. While we had some effective (i.e. made money and built relationships) events at MTC, Sydney Theatre Company has a much stronger tradition of spectacular galas, including one memorable event when the Prime Minister arrived on an elephant. Interestingly, one of the most effective arts fundraising activities in Melbourne was when MTC, Opera Australia, The Australian Ballet and the Melbourne Symphony Orchestra, the major hirers of Arts Centre Melbourne, joined together with the venue and created a series of events including lunches, art sales, a major gala and auction and collectively raised more than the companies usually did on their own through such events.

In discussing the range of opening activities that were held for the Royal Opera House including a royal-hosted gala at Windsor Castle, Kaiser (2008, 120) claims that such events are not elitist. Of course, technically they are – it was a fundraising exercise for the people who could afford to attend. But what he means is that arts organisations rely on a variety of funding sources and have to able to respond to all their needs: "One has to be open and accessible to the general public but also be available to cater to the needs of those who will help pay for this accessibility."

If the purpose of a gala is fundraising and not just profile raising, you have to work to a budget and ensure that you sell enough tickets to do more than just cover costs. For example, a glittering party put on by Sydney's Powerhouse Museum (now called the Museum of Applied Arts and Sciences (MAAS)) and attended by (amongst other important VIPs) Australia's Foreign Minster lost $140,000. The museum spokesperson claimed that event was a success because it enhanced the reputation of MAAS as the leading public centre for fashion in Australia (Boland 2018) but I'm sure that size loss wasn't the budgeted outcome. The point is if you're going to invest weeks if not months of people time and the net result of your fundraising event is modest, I wouldn't repeat the event.

One way of keeping strong relationships and to facilitate fundraising by people other than you and your staff is to have some sort of members' group or friends' organisation. These people may not be personally wealthy but they may be willing to volunteer time and goods and connections to create effective fundraising activities. The trick is to make sure that their focus is your focus. Such groups can also be costly in terms of benefits and privileges and can become unfriendly if you decide to take the organisations in a new direction (Hewison & Holden 2011). When I started at MTC, there was an MTC Society which held regular fundraising activities but the funds were allocated to projects of their choice and not necessarily one's most useful to the company. Interestingly, the President at the time was conscious of this problem and under her leadership, the friends' group was wound up and replaced by a membership group controlled more directly by the company.

In a more recent example of tensions between membership organisations and arts companies, Judith White (2017) tells the story of the Art Gallery of New South Wales' attempts to exert control over the Art Gallery Society of NSW of which she was the CEO for a number of years. The society as an organisation was structurally separate from the gallery, had members, ran fundraising events, provided volunteers to the gallery and donated money to the gallery. Although I sympathised with many aspects of her book, I confess that like the Art Gallery's management, I too would have wanted more control over this body. But what I wouldn't have done was replace well-trained, highly educated, computer-literate volunteers providing free ticketing services with paid staff at a time of financial stress (White 2017, 118–119). I also wouldn't have put out a "year in review" document that didn't make any reference, let along offer thanks, to those volunteers (122).

Volunteers can be key to successful fundraising. They were part of all the effective events we put on at MTC – serving drinks at trivia nights; selling costumes at garage sales; collecting gifts to sell at auctions; selling tickets to galas. This is one way of engaging "friends" of your company and giving them a real chance to contribute to the financial well-being of an organisation they care about.

In conclusion, for every fundraising activity you undertake, do a cost-benefit analysis, because the point is you're trying to make a real profit. You may put on galas or print books or create key rings to reward relationships or capture your company's history but without a clear economic analysis, you can't assume that you are going to make money.

See also: Boards, Cultural Policy, Ethics, Money, Stakeholders, Volunteers

References

Boland, M. 2018 "Powerhouse Museum Uses Public Money to Prop Up Fashion Fundraiser, FOI Reveals", www.abc.net.au/news/2018-07-25/powerhouse-museum-uses-public-money-to-prop-up-fashion-party/10026264 [accessed 22 February 2019].

Conte, D. M. & Langley, S. 2007 *Theatre Management*, Hollywood, CA: EntertainmentPro.

Hewison, R. & Holden, J. 2011 The Cultural Leadership Handbook, Farnham: F Gower.

Kaiser, M. M. 2008 The Art of the Turnaround: Creating and Maintaining Healthy Arts Organizations, Waltham, MA: Brandeis University Press.

Kaiser, M. M. 2013 *The Circle*, Waltham, MA: Brandeis University Press.

Meyrick, J., Phillips, S. & Tonks, A. 2004 *The Drama Continues*, Melbourne: MTC.

Phillips, S. & Tonks, A. 2012 *Play on: Melbourne Theatre Company 2000–2013*, Melbourne: MTC.

White, J. 2017 *Culture Heist: Art versus Money*, Blackheath, NSW: Bandl & Schlesinger.

Notes

1 *The House of King* by Sioban Tuke.
2 Australian arts manager, email to author, 7 January 2014.
3 In *Priscilla, Queen of the Desert*.
4 In *The Matrix*.

G

Gender

My particular interest in gender is (for obvious reasons) women in management. More general issues about women in the workplace are discussed in the section on *Diversity*. In my years of teaching graduate courses in arts management, female students have always exceeded males to the point that in one recent class of 20, there were no men to be seen. This is not solely an Australian phenomenon. Cuyler (2013, 101) says that "[a]rts management [programs in US Universities] have done an excellent job attracting able-bodied, heterosexual, upper-middle class, young white women". He quotes a past president of the Association of Arts Administration Educators as saying "the make-up of our student bodies appears to me to reflect, in large measure (except younger), the make-up of arts audiences: upper-middle class, white, and female" (98). My classes have much more diversity with students from Asia, South America and Europe as well as Australia, but the bias towards women is still there.

There are certainly more women in management or executive leadership roles in Australia's major theatre, opera and dance companies than 25 years ago with an increase from 43% to 72%. In the arts at least, it appears that there is no longer any avert prejudice about women in positions of power – on the management front. The statistics are certainly better than in private companies with only two women in *Harvard Business Review*'s 2018 list of the 100 top CEOs (HBR Staff 2018). However, the percentage of women in artistic leadership roles in those same performing arts companies has decreased from a low base of 18% to 13%. After reviewing the gender divide in leadership in these companies. Caust (2018a) concluded that "[i]n a sector where women represent the majority audience as well as the majority of its participants, the low level of female artistic leadership is significantly out of tune with contemporary expectations" (Caust 2018b, 6[1]).

The debates around women in management and leadership have continued all my working life and include questions such as whether we have special qualities that make us different leaders, whether we tend to underachieve, whether we're perceived differently as leaders and whether socialisation and the responsibility of families will mean that the statistics will never balance out.

Underachievement

Women are often blamed for underachieving, for not being as bold as men at putting themselves forward. For each example that we can offer up where that has happened, we (women) feel guilty about blaming our sisters for such weakness. A woman recently turned the idea on the head. She said that it's not that women are unambitious but that men irresponsibly put themselves forward when they are underprepared or not up to the task.

Perhaps I was lucky having a convent education where education per se was highly valued. I had teachers who were nuns and married women; who left to do a PhD at the Sorbonne; who already had PhDs; who taught science subjects. There was never any sense that we couldn't be whatever we wanted to be. While at points in my career, I might have undervalued my skills, I certainly didn't undervalue them because I was female. In fact, I left the comfort of the Australian public service because someone else did think that women couldn't achieve. On reflection, I was extraordinarily lucky in that first full-time job. It was in the public service and within 12 months I was given the opportunity to be a supervisor in an unusual situation – processing the 1976 Population Census. Due to the financial situation at the time, the processing had been delayed for 12 months and in order to find staff, we had to test and interview anyone who was on unemployment benefits at the time. This meant that not only was I a supervisor who was younger than 95% of my staff, I was looking after people from a much wider range of social, economic, cultural and class backgrounds than I'd been exposed to. With a supportive manager, I learnt some quick and hard lessons about managing people and teams. I'd be challenged by staff because I was young, because I was female, because I was university educated. However, I didn't see any of those points preventing me from doing a good job. But then someone did. An older male manager pulled me aside and advised me not to apply for a promotion because those jobs "weren't for women". He'd come up through the ranks during the days when women had to resign from the public service when they got married and that may have explained his misogyny even if it didn't excuse it. My response was to resign. I didn't want to stay in an organisation where people – even if it was just one person – thought I couldn't be a manager because I was a woman.

Clearly because there are more women studying arts management than men, they believe that they can be leaders. But while there are more women than men in management leadership roles in performing arts companies in Australia, this is not the case in the visual arts. The majority of Australian's state art galleries haven't had a female Director since their exception (Caust 2018b). There is similar evidence from US research in a study called *The Gender Gap in Arts Museum Directorships* by the Association of Arts Museum Directors (Watson 2014). When asked why, Kay Campbell, the Executive Director of the Australian Centre for Contemporary Art, is quoted as saying:

> [T]here's a lot of entrenched thinking on the part of trustees and head-hunters based on who's had the post before, who is already running state galleries elsewhere and who they are comfortable with. And that's a man every time.
>
> (Watson 2014)

However, it's not just the decisions of male Board leaders. The voice of under-confidence is still to be heard. Major and Gould-Lardelli (2011, 52) said that "confidence was a major issue for female arts managers in developing their career". Rentschler and Jogulu (2012) explored whether passion and ambition were enough to ensure satisfactory career paths for female arts managers. It's an article that contains no feminist or gender theory so it could just as easily apply to men apart from the quotes from women managers who believe that they face more challenges than men. One of their respondents says:

> I would like to think in this century gender is not such an issue, however, with most major gallery Directors being men, and something like 90% of the general manager roles (as well as CEO) in my local government organisation being filled by men, one has to admit gender appears a factor, even if it only dampens a woman's confidence of the likelihood that a senior management role will ever be hers.
>
> (Rentschler & Jogulu 2012, 152)

Different Form of Leadership

According to Eagly and Carli (2007), women are associated with communal qualities such as concern for the compassionate treatment of others, being affectionate, helpful, friendly, kind, sensitive, gentle, softly spoken. Men, on the other hand, are associated with qualities which convey assertion and control such as being aggressive, ambitious, dominant, self-confident, forceful, self-reliant, individualistic.

The trap is that leaders have traditionally been men and therefore the masculine qualities or traits are seen to be those of effective leaders. If this is true, does this mean that women can't be good leaders unless they adopt those masculine qualities? Or if it isn't true that those qualities make for good leaders in the 21st century, does this mean that women have the potential to be better leaders than men? But then that position is based on the belief that the "feminine" qualities are innate to women. What if they are simply socialised qualities and as societies become more open to women's participation in the workplace and public life, those qualities change? Part of the perception about men and women having different leadership styles relates to assumptions that differences in biology create gendered minds. However, there's an increasing amount of research that sex doesn't create male and female natures but rather it's a mixture of sex, hormones, culture and evolution and the differences aren't nearly as much as we might have thought. If you're particularly interested in this subject, read Cordelia Fine's (2017) book, *Testorerone Rex.*

In other words, it's a merry-go-round of unresolved questions. Eagly and Carlie (2007) say the evidence would seem to indicate that if women are too assertive, then they are not feminine enough, but if they are too communal, they're not assertive enough to be effective leaders. Men who are helpful get acknowledged more, but women who disagree don't get away with it as much as men. It appears that men can be both friendly and dominant with no penalty either way. Eagly and Carli (2007) conclude that

female leaders are somewhat more transformational than male leaders – and that transformational leadership is more suited to the modern corporation. As discussed in the *Leadership* section, transformational leadership is valued in arts organisations as well, but the point is still based on the assumption that women manage differently to men.

An interesting American business thinker, James March, boldly added to the debate about socialisation. In a *Harvard Business Review* interview, March (2006) claims that there are more interesting women than interesting men in the world. And he sees this as a development issue. Girls are told that they can do things for no good reason because they are girls. "They can be unpredictable, inconsistent, illogical" says March (87). But once she goes to school she has to learn to be consistent and analytical. "In the process, she develops a very complicated value system – one that adapts very much to context." Whereas boys have to be straightforward, consistent and analytical from the get go, which March describes as having "the goals of a two-year old". While this view might appeal to the women reading these words, the situation isn't quite that simple.

Billing and Alvesson (2000, 144) conclude that

> [c]onstructing leadership as feminine may be of some value as a contrast to conventional ideas on leadership and management but may also create a misleading impression of women's orientation to leadership as well as reproducing stereotypes and the traditional gender division of labour.

In other words, if women are seen to be mainly managers of feelings and relationships, they may be defined out of having the qualities for the tough or the top jobs. The authors conclude (hopefully, I think) that by de-masculinising leadership, the result may not be a feminisation of it, but rather a loosening-up of management from traditional male stereotypes.

Bolman and Deal (2013, 352) reach a slightly different conclusion:

the available evidence suggests that men and women in comparable positions are more alike than different as leaders in the eyes of their subordinates … When differences are detected, they often show women scoring somewhat higher than men on a variety of measures of leadership and management behavior … But the differences are not large, and it is not clear that they have practical significance.

The debate about whether women bring a different form of leadership style by virtue of being women or whether it's simply socialised outcomes may never be resolved. I prefer to think of it from another perspective. What are the qualities that are required to lead or manage a complex creative organisation? That's what a Board needs to look for when they create a leadership regime in an arts company.

Gender in Arts Management

In their *Cultural Leadership Handbook*, Hewison and Holden (2011, 31) say:

> Although we do not believe that gender is a significant factor in being a leader, we have noticed than women are often better at silent leadership than men. That is because they are not just thinking about themselves in relation to the organization, they are ready to enable and empower people by genuine delegation, and they are ready to nurture other people's talent. This is why, when they want to achieve change, they also produce general agreement about the need for change and the direction to go in. The result is a much more stable organization, where people do not just feel proud of the success of the organization, they feel they own it. Whereas a transformational leader is definitely seen as being out in front of the organisation, the relational leader will be at the centre of it.

When Kate MacNeill and I (2009) interviewed the artistic and management leaders of Australia's major performing arts companies, we discovered that the General Managers/Managing Directors required a sophisticated set of management skills and qualities that were both "masculine" and "feminine" in order to have a successful co-partnership with an artist and manage a complex organisation.

Because we were exploring co-leadership relationships, the language of marriage came up regularly as a metaphor:

> you end up being Mum and Dad in an organisation and I'm possibly the more nurturing, encouraging, more access to … and AD's much less effusive with his praise but when it comes, it's more important and meaningful. [GM7]

Bilton, Cummings and Wilson (2003, 213), in discussing the relatively high proportion of women in senior positions in arts organisations, talk about stereotypes where the "disorganised creator and omniscient manager take on a Freudian dimension, with the boy-child's artistic ego protected from reality by the indulgent and controlling mother". Another gendered approach is to think of the Artistic Director as "dad", off at work in the rehearsal room leaving problem solving and relationship building to "mum", the GM/MD, at "home" looking after the kids. However, although the mum/dad metaphor might help explain the co-partnership model, it's a very modern marriage with a disconnect of feminine and masculine roles and functions from the biological sex of the person in the specific position:

> I don't think that gender really plays a part in it – it might provide a convenient psychological paradigm for the rest of the company who might like to refer to "mum and dad", but in the theatre of course one could have same-sex parents and it wouldn't be that surprising. [GM2]

As evidenced by the quote above which reminded us that families are not restricted to the male dad and the female mum, many of our interviewees rejected gender stereotypes. Our female interviewees did not necessarily consider themselves to be the "mother", or even the "mothering" type. But when the women did talk about gender (which they didn't do unless pressed) they had an active preference to work with reconstructed, that is, not traditional, men. The intelligent, well-educated women under discussion may choose to work in arts organisations because of the nature of the people they are likely to find there as well as because they have a passion for the output. Men who choose to work in arts organisations aren't necessarily people who are chasing power or money, and the men that women get to work with are more likely to be collegial rather than competitive:

> I guess you'd say that they're fairly ideologically sound men or politically reconstructed men or feminist men or what have you. [GM6]

Many of the men whom we interviewed either described themselves, or were described, in words that imply that they are pro-feminist.

The male and female leaders we talked to were in co-leadership relationships and that may mean they require different qualities to men and women working alone as CEOs. The binaries of masculine and feminine qualities were absent in the way the interviewees discussed their co-leadership arrangements. This is not to say that the interviewees were unaware of the manner in which attributes are assigned to each gender, but rather revealed a level of self-awareness and knowingness around questions of gender. There is a wealth of literature that supports the view that at heart there is little difference in management style between men and women, with both sharing similar aspirations, values, personality traits and behaviours (Billing & Alverson 2000). However, this literature also notes that in leadership positions the attributes, skills and behaviour that both men and women exhibit remain "masculine" and a number of our interviewees, whether men or women, described their management

strengths with words that fit within a more masculine management set such as rationality and analysis. However, their leadership style also had to be focused on relationships, a perceived female leadership strength according to Benko and Pelster (2013) because of the organisational structure in which they worked.

Getting More Women to the Top

Sinclair (2005, 19) lists various stages in how an executive culture responds to the absence of women in the workplace:

1. Denial – not seen as a problem
2. Problem is women – women have to learn to adapt to (male) norms
3. Incremental adjustment – organisations acknowledge that there is a problem but adjustments are only made at the margins, e.g. one or two "safe" women targeted
4. Commitment to a new culture.

When it comes to "fixing" the women, the belief is that everyone has equal access to opportunities and if women aren't taking up senior roles it's that they don't know the rules of the games and need special training to become more assertive or confident. In considering how arts and cultural organisations might increase female representation at senior level, Ladkin (2010, 14) rejects the idea of "topping up women with some additional skills", including ideas such as women-only training,

> Whilst I agree that "fixing the women" isn't the only solution, I'm actually a supporter of women only training. I had a personal experience of such training (in running meetings) that I found particularly empowering as a young manager. Another example I can give is running a training program for women leaders in radio in the Asia-Pacific region. These women, who'd already achieved much by having such roles particularly in patriarchal cultures, loved the freedom to share problems and insights and support in a safe space. So when I read research articles written in 2010s which indicate that women still

feel insecure about leadership, then perhaps we need a *range* of ways to empower them and if working together and apart sometimes does the trick, why not?

Another approach to helping women achieve leadership roles is to ensure that opportunities really are equal by the introduction of flexible working arrangements, generous maternity and paternity leave and creating childcare provision (Ladkin 2010). In reality the informal expectations set for senior managers can prohibit their use and the working hours of arts organisations can also work against such polices, but there is increasing evidence that in companies where all roles can be flexible, including management roles, women's participation overall has increased as has work-life balance with no obvious negative impact on companies' bottom line (Roderick 2018).

Ladkin's (2010) solution to getting more women into arts leadership is for management teams to work on the "aesthetic" they create through their habitual ways of interacting and the extent to which it includes or alienates. By "aesthetics" she means the sensory experience of perception, "an instinctual, rather than rational, response conveying information about our surrounds and those people we meet" (Ladkin 2010, 35). I can remember clearly one of those aesthetic moments. In my MBA studies, I was occasionally the only female in the class. One day, the class was held in the Board room of an international marketing organisation. I was feeling, for no obvious reason, slightly uneasy in this environment. It wasn't until I reached across to get a glass of water that I realised that I simply didn't belong. I was wearing a brilliant emerald green top and all around me were men in grey and charcoal suits. The room had been designed with soft apricot and gold colours to enhance their look and I simply clashed with the environment. I tried to describe that feeling to the men in my group later but they just looked at me with confusion and/or disbelief.

Examples that Ladkin (2010) gives to create an aesthetic environment of inclusivity include changing the physical environment when all the images around you are of men (which takes me back to my initial interview for the MTC position in a room full of paintings of past male Vice Chancellors) and work practices, formal and informal, that tend to exclude women.

Perhaps no matter what we do there will always be barriers. Sinclair (2005, 161) notes that if there's one thing that unites feminists and liberal female managers it is in the desire to avoid the label "feminine", because it defines one as ineffective and frivolous and yet being labelled as "feminist" is also problematic. She further points out that simply being "seen" as a woman can diminish one's leadership:

> Behaviours which draw attention to sex – such as displays of overt femininity, being pregnant, references to family, wearing colourful or expressive clothes, lobbying for women or adopting explicit feminist stances – typically diminish a woman's leadership potential in the eyes of observers.
>
> (Sinclair 2005, 178)

I'd like to think that 15 years on from Sinclair's research, things have changed but I still hear stories that underpin her belief. Sinclair (2005) is also strong on the importance of female role models both as early influences and in the workplace in playing a role to stop women feeling constrained by the social stereotypes of what women can do. And this can come not only from the obvious source of mothers but also fathers who provide their daughters with self-confidence and female teachers, family members and early bosses who are determined and self-reliant. In my case, I can see that pattern clearly. I was the eldest of two daughters, educated in single sex schools, with a mother who went to work as soon as my younger sister was in kindergarten because she was bored by being a housewife. And in the process, the father/husband supported her return to the workforce and supported our dreams of higher education and careers. I was also lucky to have female role models through my working life. My first boss in the public service in the mid-1970s, shortly after the rule about women having to resign when they married, was a woman. The manager of the community radio station which I first joined as a volunteer in the late 1970s and then eventually ran was a woman. The person who established Australia's first post-graduate arts management program was a woman. I know that individual cases are only part of the story, but that they were part of my story meant that I could become a manager.

Once we get to the top, there's yet another challenge: the pay gap. In Australia, that gap is around 18% but in comparing some of the country's major arts institutions, it's 38% (Taylor & Ting 2016). Women need to be responsible for arguing our value case but Boards also need to be conscious not to exacerbate this gap.

Conclusion

Because the argument around women in management and leadership is so complex and the glass ceiling or "labyrinth" (Eagly & Carli 2007) of stereotypes, conflicting expectations, social and familial demands and discrimination are all still there, I believe that we have to apply all sorts of approaches, including mentoring and training, changing attitudes and changing aesthetics, and even targets and quotas to ensure that a diversity of women get a chance for leadership in our organisations. The main gap in Australia at least is women in artistic leadership roles. Those of us who are management leaders can study an arts management course or an MBA but it's much more challenging for women artists to both learn and demonstrate their leadership capacity. This may mean women's-only training as well as active nurturing of potential women leaders, ensuring opportunities for women artists to experience our organisations, and creating a work culture where difference is celebrated and valued.

See also: Arts Management, Arts Leadership, Diversity, Families, Harassment, Leadership, Management, Passion

References

Benko, C. & Pelster, B. 2013 "How Women Decide", *Harvard Business Review*, 91(9), 78–84.

Billing, Y. D. & Alversson, M. 2000 "Questioning the Notion of Feminine Leadership: A Critical Perspective on the Gender Labelling of Leadership", *Gender, Work & Organization*, 7(3), 144–157.

Bilton, C., Cummings, S. & Wilson, D. 2003 "Strategy as Creativity", in Cummings, S. & Wilson, D. (eds) *Images of Strategy*, Oxford: Blackwell Publishing, 197–227.

Bolman, L. G. & Deal, T. E. 2013 *Reframing Organizations* (5th ed), San Francisco, CA: Jossey-Bass.

Caust, J. 2018a *Arts Leadership in Contemporary Contexts*, London: Routledge.

Caust, J. 2018b "To Fix Gender Inequity in Arts Organisations we need more Women in Politics and Chairing Boards", *The Conversation*, 12 June, https://theconversation.com/to-fix-gender-inequity-in-arts-leadership-we-need-more-women-in-politics-and-chairing-boards-97782 [accessed 22 February 2019].

Cuyler, A. C. 2013 "Affirmative Action and Diversity: Implications for Arts Management", *Journal of Arts Management, Law, and Society*, 43(2), 98–105.

Eagly, A. H. & Carli, L. A. 2007 "Women and the Labyrinth of Leadership", *Harvard Business Review*, 85(9), 63–71.

Fine, C. 2017 *Testosterone Rex: Unmaking the Myths of our Gendered Minds*, London: Icon Books.

HBR Staff 2018 "Best Performing CEOs in the World", https://hbr.org/2018/11/the-best-performing-ceos-in-the-world-2018 [accessed 18 January 2019].

Hewison, R. & Holden, J. 2011 *The Cultural Leadership Handbook*, Farnham: F Gower.

Ignatius, A. 2014 "Leaders for the Long Term", *Harvard Business Review*, 92(11), 48–56.

Ladkin, D. 2010 "Creating an Aesthetic of Inclusivity: A New Solution to the 'Problem' of Women Leaders", in Kay, S. & Venner, K. (eds) *A Cultural Leader's Handbook*, London: Creative Choices, 32–39.

MacNeill, K. & Tonks, A. 2009 "Co-leadership and Gender in the Performing Arts", *Asia Pacific Journal of Arts and Cultural Management*, 6(1), 291–404.

March, J. G. 2006 "Ideas as Art: interviewed by Diane Coutu", *Harvard Business Review*, 84(10), 83–89.

Major, S. & Gould-Lardelli, R. 2011 "Becoming an Arts Manager: A Matter of Choice or Chance?", Antwerp: 11th AIMAC International Conference.

Rentschler, R. & Jogulu, U. 2012 "Are Passion and Ambition Enough to Support the Career of a Female Arts Manager?", in Hausmann, A. & Murzik, L. (eds) *Anthology of Cultural Institutions HRM and Leadership*, Frankfurt: Springer Verlag, 143–155.

Roderick, T. 2018 *Does This Job Make My Desk Look Big?*, University of Sydney, https://sydney.edu.au/content/dam/corporate/documents/sydney-policy-lab/all-roles-flex-report.pdf [accessed 18 January 2019].

Sinclair, A. 2005 *Doing Leadership Differently*, Melbourne: Melbourne University Press.

Taylor, A. & Ting, I. 2016 "What Arts Bosses in Australia Earn, and How Women Get Less", *Sydney Morning Herald*, 10 June, www.smh.com.au/entertainment/art-and-design/what-arts-bosses-in-australia-earn-and-how-women-get-less-20160603-gpahfn.html [accessed 18 January 2018].

Watson, T. 2014 "Women Hit Glass Ceiling in Gallery Jobs", *ArtsHub*, 20 October, http://visual.artshub.com.au/news-article/features/museums/women-hit-glass-ceiling-in-gallery-jobs-246170 [accessed 26 February 2019].

Note

1 It's worth reading Jo Caust's chapter on women in arts leadership including a discussion by art form in her book *Arts Leadership in Contemporary Contexts*.

Harassment

It would be impossible to write a book about management in 2019 and not consider the #MeToo movement. So many of the public cases that have resulted from people speaking out about sexual harassment have come from our industries. I know people, both accused and accuser, who have been deeply affected not just by the harassment experience but by the public discussion and ongoing legal cases.

As a sign of how quickly the language in the workplace has changed around this subject, in 2018, Saintilan and Screiber discussed sexuality as a means of influence in the creative industries. The marketing of many performers, but particularly women, is based around their sexual appeal to fans. They also discuss sexual influencing in the work place which they define as ingratiating behaviour designed to increase one's attractiveness and thus influence people. In a case study about a female musician, the authors ask the question: "How might organisational leaders deal with what can often be perceived as questionable sexual harassment issues, but may be simply someone using strategic sexual performance to garner favourable influence over others?" (161). This seems to me to be looking at it from a very masculine point of view. I wonder how a woman writer might have discussed sexuality as a workplace influencer in the post-#MeToo world? Where's the discussion about someone using power to demand sexual favours rather than using sexual favours to obtain power or influence?[1]

A basic definition of sexual harassment is "any form of unwelcome behaviour of a sexual nature, which could be expected to make a person feel offended, humiliated or intimidated" (LPA 2018). This feels stronger to me that the definition offered by Saintilan and Screiber (2018, 242) who use the words "awkward, embarrassing and humiliating". What their definition misses out is what many speakers at the #notinmyworkplace summit[2] in 2019 pointed out – that sexual harassment is just one aspect of gendered violence caused by gender inequality in the workplace and that it's as much about the misuse of power as sex. Of course, men can be the victims of sexual harassment as well and the LGBTIQ community is also vulnerable to such abuse. At the beginning of the summit, participants were asked to respond to the question: How do you feel about sexual harassment? The dominant words were "angry", "frustrated" and "unacceptable".

Live Performance Australia (2018) provide a detailed list of the actions and circumstances that could be considered sexual harassment:

Sexual harassment can be physical, spoken or written. It can include, but is not limited to:

- Staring or leering at a person or parts of their body;
- Excessive or unwelcome familiarity or physical contact, such as touching, hugging, kissing, pinching, massaging and brushing up against someone;
- Suggestive comments, jokes, conversations or innuendo;
- Insults or taunts of a sexual nature or obscene gestures;
- Intrusive questions or comments about someone's private life;
- Displaying or disseminating material such as posters, magazines or screen savers of a sexual nature;
- Making or sending sexually explicit phone calls emails or text messages;
- Inappropriate advances on social networking sites;
- Accessing sexually explicit internet sites in the presence of others;
- Unwelcome flirting, requests for sex or repeated unwanted requests to go out on dates;
- Inappropriate or unwanted gifts; and
- Behaviour that may also be considered to be an offence under criminal law, such as physical or sexual assault, indecent exposure, stalking or obscene communications.

LPA (2018) also responds to a number of points people make to try and justify such behaviour – "other people weren't offended", "I didn't mean to intimidate them", "we've always done that in this workplace", "it was only once", "it happened at the bar after work"– and makes the clear point that none of that stops an act from being harassment.

In a 2017 survey by the Media Entertainment and Arts Alliance (MEAA) (Neill 2018), 40% of respondents had been sexually harassed in the live performance industry but most incidents weren't reported. The only time an issue was reported to me was over 10 years ago on the last preview night before the show. The stage management team had worked to protect the actor concerned from the director but neither they nor the actor wanted the show to be stopped. By leaving it to the last minute, I had to accept their position that the actor didn't want anything done, that the stage management team had managed the situation effectively and as the director was departing the country the next day, the problem was solved. All I was left to do was to tell the director that we were never going to employ him again.

Now I wonder how many other moments like that were there that I was never told about? I thought we had an open, honest culture and one that was supportive of performers but I didn't spend much time in the rehearsal room and sexual harassment is a very hard topic to talk about.

The MEAA survey, along with a series of cases that were still working their way through the Australian Court system in 2019, led to action particularly in the live performance and screen industries. For example, Live Performance Australia (LPA), the employers' representative body, in consultation with the MEAA developed a code of conduct, policy drafts and complaints procedures. Venues and production companies leaned in to support the presentation of seminars and training programs to help organisations develop best practice policies and procedures to manage issues of sexual harassment, discrimination, harassment and bullying. Other organisations such as the Screen Producers Association of Australia have also developed resources to help their members.

I've attended a number of seminars about the codes and have implemented them in a company but the issue still remains – will people report problems? For the performing arts industry, the rehearsal room is a particular challenge where it can be hard to draw the line between intimacy and harassment (Davidson 2018). Virginia Lovett, who followed me as Executive Director at Melbourne Theatre Company, made a thoughtful comment about this space:

intimate scenes can be choreographed, with measures in place to ensure the safety of those involved without compromising the playfulness or impact of those moments – the key is communication and respect.

(Neill 2018, 9)

Saintilan and Screiber (2018, 262) claim that the prevalence of alcohol in the creative industries can mean that people are more at risk of sexual harassment in our workplaces than others. But again, they aren't looking deep enough into the causes. For example, employment for artists in the entertainment industry is based for the most part on personal referral and relationships and this means that the potential employer has even more power than in a standard workplace.

One of the results of the publicity around the issue of harassment has been the creation of an organisation, Safe Theatres Australia, specifically set up to help companies develop guidelines to reduce the possibility of sexual harassment, bullying and discrimination in theatres. The word "safe" is the key to the way we need to think about sexual harassment. We want a workplace that is safe for our employees. Most countries have legislation requiring employers to provide safe workplaces. If your industry or your country hasn't responded to the challenge of #MeToo in this way, you may find LPA's guidelines useful to adapt to your circumstances – because every arts organisation should have a policy that spells out how people can behave respectfully in the workplace.

Such a policy or code of conduct should cover more than just sexual harassment. The LPA (2018) Guidelines cover discrimination, bullying and more general harassment as well which they define as "unwelcome and unsolicited behaviour that a reasonable person would consider to be offensive, intimidating, humiliating or threatening".

For such a policy to be meaningful, every person who works for you needs to sign up to respectful behaviour. As well as running training programs for staff, literally signing a form through which you commit to the policy brings the issues to the forefront of people's minds. This can be particularly important for casual staff or artists on short-term contracts to know what your expectations are and also what they can do if they are harassed or bullied. Such a document can spell out very clearly what you expect:

Standards of Behaviour

Company Name workers are responsible for promoting a safe, respectful, inclusive and flexible workplace environment by:

- Treating all workers and audience members/patrons/customers with dignity, courtesy and respect
- Respecting cultural, ethnic, religious, gender and sexual orientation differences
- Behaving in a professional, fair and courteous manner at all times
- Following the Drugs and Alcohol policy when at work
- Promptly reporting any breaches of this Code of Conduct, whether it is against you or another person, to as appropriate manager
- Maintaining confidentiality when complaints are made and/or under investigation; and
- Abiding by all applicable laws and regulations.

Unacceptable Behaviours

Company name workers *must not*:

- Abuse or threaten to abuse (verbally, physically or in writing) another person
- Physically or sexually assault another person
- Discriminate against or treat someone less favourably because of their race, sex, age, sexual orientation, disability or other personal characteristics
- Intimidate, threaten or harass another person

- Sexually harass another person with unwanted, unwelcome or uninvited behaviour
- Bully, isolate or humiliate another person
- Victimise, unjustly treat or threaten someone because they have raised a complaint or are a witness in an investigation; or
- Behave improperly or unethically (LPA 2018).

As well as codes of conduct and occupational health and safety polices, we also need to consider gender equality in our workplaces. Are there male-dominated areas with a subculture that isn't supportive of women? Are there patterns of socialising and behaviour that work against women? Are there parts of our workplace where LGBTIQ people don't feel comfortable? You need to understand what's happening in your workplace and you can't rely on complaints to measure what's happening because this is an area that is consistently under-reported.

For those companies with Human Resource managers or departments, we need to think about what role they play in the implementation of our policies around people's behaviour. At the #notinmyworkplace summit, examples came up time and time again where HR staff were conflicted about where their responsibilities lay — to the victim, to ensure fairness for the alleged perpetrator, to the organisation. In some companies, people go straight to the CEO because they don't want a convoluted investigation process, they just want the behaviour to stop. Organisational leaders need to talk to and hear their staff, be clear and public in their attitudes and those attitudes need to be supportive and victim-focused.

The word that comes up time and time again when considering workplace relations is respect. As managers, we have to set an example and create a culture where respectful relations are the standard and people are safe in our companies.

See also: Diversity, Gender, Human Relations, Organisational Culture, People, Unions

References

Davidson, H. 2018 "Q&A on #MeToo: actors use sexual energy to connect, Neil Armfield says", *The Guardian*, 30 October, www.theguardian.com/australia-news/2018/oct/30/qa-on-metoo-actors-use-sexual-energy-to-connect-neil-armfield-says [accessed 27 February 2019].

LPA 2018 Australian Live Performance Industry Code of Practice: Discrimination, Harassment, Sexual Harassment and Bullying, http://members.liveperformance.com.au/uploads/files/Combined%20-%20LPA%20Discrimination.H.SH.B%20resources%20-%20Consultation%20Draft%2023.02.2018-1519365284.pdf [accessed 27 February 2019].

Neill, R. 2018 "New Rules of Engagement", *The Weekend Australian*, 8–9 December, 8–9.

Safe Theatres Australia, www.safetheatresaustralia.com [accessed 27 February 2019].

Saintilan, P. & Schreiber, D. 2018 *Managing Organizations in the Creative Economy: Organizational Behaviour for the Cultural Sector*, Abingdon: Routledge.

Volz, J. 2017 *Introduction to Arts Management*, London: Bloomsbury Methuen Drama.

Hiring

If most of your time and money is going to be spent working with and managing people then it's worth investing time and money to find the right person for your organisation. Every Human Resource textbook will give you a checklist of recruitment and selection processes but there isn't one agreed approach. Balnave et al. (2009, 237) provide an interesting set of questions comparing traditional and "strategic HRM" approaches to recruitment and selection:

- Should the emphasis be on technical skills, education and experience or should the emphasis be on personal characteristics (desire to achieve, social skills, work ethic)?
- Should you rely on interviews or use techniques such as psychological testing?
- Should you seek people with differing viewpoints and value systems or people with viewpoints and values compatible with the organisational culture?

My response to these questions is:

- People need relevant skills and experience but they also have to have the capacity and desire to step up to do something different which could be part of their personal qualities
- Interviews are important but sometimes testing is required too
- You want people who share your vision and your values but this doesn't mean that they all have to be the same.

The first part of the hiring process is to think about the type of position you need. The tradition of repertory theatre companies (and this is still the case in many European companies) was to have actors, directors and designers on staff. For reasons to do with economics (cost of under-utilised resources) and audiences (wanting to see the new as well as the familiar on stage), most Australian theatre companies now employ artists on a project basis. This is an interesting lesson for arts organisations in other staffing areas. Do you always need to create a new full-time ongoing position? Would it be better as two part-time positions so that you attract more specialist skills or more highly skilled parents wanting to work less standard hours? Would it be better filled by a casual or a contractor? The short-term cost may be higher but not the long-term cost. Maybe you can get a high flyer for a short period of time, like a star actor who can make more money in the movies but loves theatre.

The second part of the hiring process is to have a position description that both accurately describes the job (in words that the applicant will understand), details the skills and experience required (that will help people to "select out" of applying) and the selection criteria that you're going to use to make your final choice (criteria that are relevant to the job but not too restrictive that you can't justifiably make a brave appointment). What follows are some reflections on getting it right and getting it wrong.

Recruitment

I have always said (because I read it somewhere) that recruitment is about opening the door as wide as possible and that the selection process is working out who gets to stay in your house. One of the best versions of opening the door was a national manager of a media company with a great social life. Wherever he went in the country – whether it was a bar, a show, a dinner party or a work meeting ––he asked people to tell him about interesting managers in their town. And he'd follow up every suggestion. This was before LinkedIn and even before Facebook made finding people easy. He'd talk to people and encourage them to think about working for his organisation. In my case, he stayed in touch for nearly two years until a job came up in the ABC that was right for me. I had to go through the standard selection process but probably wouldn't have applied without his encouragement.

In talking about best practice recruitment, Stone (2013, 208) notes that leading US companies, and he gives Microsoft has an example, "have created an 'employment brand' to convey their values, policies, systems and culture in order to create a differentiated image in the minds of potential employees and attract top talent". Arts and cultural organisations have an implicit brand due to the public nature of their product. While companies might find it hard to recruit in some specialist areas,[3] generally there is an attractive pool of candidates willing to work for modest wages in exchange for the prestige and thrill of working in the arts industry. When you advertise for a marketing coordinator or receptionist, you'll generally be overwhelmed by candidates of high quality.

Cappelli (2013) thinks that having a glut of people applying for jobs is poor recruiting because screening candidates is expensive. He recommends head-hunters to help with the screening process and because he thinks that recruiters are good at finding "passive" applicants, that is, people who aren't actively looking for a job. However, in my experience that simply means the head-hunters ring people like me for lists of people to go on their lists. No head-hunter has done as much searching as that internal recruiter who eventually convinced me to apply for an ABC position.

My policy has been that unless there's an extraordinarily good reason (and I'm hard pressed to think of any), all positions should be advertised externally and internally. Most small to medium arts organisations have little opportunity for internal promotion but large organisations should consider the benefits. Compared to external recruitment, you have a person who understands the organisation and its culture and who has demonstrated capacity and commitment to date. The risk is less than taking on an external candidate. However, the downside of opening up positions to internal candidates is the impact on their morale if they don't get the position and the challenge for their new manager who has to deal with a potentially disgruntled staff member. The trick is to only encourage people to apply who have a seriously good chance of getting the job and to have a realistic conversation with the candidate who doesn't have a chance. Having said that, in one case I was involved in, an external appointment to a new position was made without the job being advertised internally and there was a ruckus. In principle, the current staff agreed that there was no-one in the team who could have done the job but they at least wanted to be able to consider the possibility of applying. Even the process of preparing for and going through an interview process may be a good training exercise for someone as long as they have a realistic view of the chance of promotion.

Given that advertising will attract everyone from the "must fill my Centrelink quota"[4] to the complete outsider, it's sometimes tempting to assume that you know who's out there rather than to advertise every position. Advertising is more work, but it's worth being open to the unexpected. When I applied for the position of General Manager at MTC, there was an "industry list" of the likely candidates that everyone was talking about. I wasn't on the list because I didn't come from the arts industry in Melbourne or even the performing arts industry in Australia.

Many large arts organisations put the task of looking for a new CEO into the hands of head-hunters and let them do the initial shortlisting and sometimes even the final shortlisting. Boards are often time-poor and only want to see the two or three most recommended candidates. While this may be a useful process when employing a specialist such as a Finance Director or a Development Manager, it's a mistake in the search for the leader or co-leader of an arts organisation. When it comes to the most important appointment in an arts organisation — the artistic leader — neither Boards nor head-hunters (unless they are specialists in the cultural industries) are well placed to unpack the requirements for the job, let alone be able to choose the right person without help. There is a risk that head-hunters won't spot the wild card in the pack and they'll be looking for the safe candidates. They don't want to run the risk, reputationally or financially, of getting it wrong. In a recent experience when asked for ideas for an arts position, I provided a head-hunter with a considered list which included a couple of outsiders for interest. They clearly hadn't thought of, or in most cases even heard of, most of the people on my list, outsider or not. When the decision was announced it was at the extreme end of "safe".

In a recent case, I encouraged a Board to consult with a group of informed, interested and diverse people from the arts in order to develop a list of people who should be considered for a leadership role. This provided a great checklist that enabled the Board to encourage appropriate people to apply. What made that process different to that of the head-hunters' ring around of the usual suspects was that the selection committee had the chance to engage with industry representatives and discuss the requirements of the role as well as who were the most exciting artists in the marketplace.

Sometimes help for the Board in making artistic leadership appointments will come from other senior artists; sometimes that help will come from the Managing Director who usually has a good overview of the available talent. In a dual leadership model, the Managing Director will have a better sense than any Board member about appropriate new Artistic Directors but it can't be about picking the person they most want to work with. It has to be about who is the best artist for the job with the risk that that artist may not want to work with the current Managing Director. Boards may find that slightly uncomfortable, particularly if the Managing or Executive Director reports to the Artistic Director, but as the result has to be an effective partnership, the management leader should be part of the process. Sometimes, it will even be appropriate for the outgoing Artistic Director, if they are leaving on a positive note, to express a view on shortlisted candidates. Technically, an outsider might be concerned that someone was actively involved in appointing their successor but people within corporations are always grooming potential successors.

Another interesting model for recruiting the artistic leadership of a company was used by Chunky Move dance company in 2018. Their Executive Director had resigned and their Artistic Director was planning to leave at the end of the year. Normally, the process would be to appoint the AD first and then involve them in appointing the ED but instead, the Chunky Move Board put out an expression of interest that enabled individuals or teams or groups or even another small dance company leadership to put up their hands to run the company. The selection committee met with six candidates, three of which were individuals and three of which were teams. The outcome, greeted overwhelmingly positively by the dance community, was a combination of Artistic Director, Executive Director with a Touring and Program Producer in the mix as well.

A final point on the short-listing process: it's worth having a wild card in for an interview just to open the doors beyond the expected. It's worth interviewing a range of different people because if you ask the right questions, you'll find out a lot about how your organisation is perceived as well as gathering some interesting opinions about change and challenges. Unless you're going to have diversity quotas for positions if the shortlist ends up with only one gender then pick the man or woman who is at the top of their list and add them into the mix. It doesn't matter that they might be six or eight or ten on the combined list. You're still going to appoint by merit because if they do get the job, they would have had to beat all the others but at least you'll be considering someone with a different background or experience by definition of their gender.

Selection

The selection process is always a challenge. Too many applicants or not enough. Too many who fit all the criteria or not enough. The applicant who falls apart in the interview or that one that shines at that, but only that, time.

You can make the whole process somewhat easier for both you and the potential candidate by providing relevant selection criteria. This way, they can tell their story well and you have a chance of developing a good short list of candidates. For a period of time I was sharing advice with a neighbour about job applications and both of us ended up being irritated and bewildered by jargon-ridden selection criteria to which we had to respond. For example (and this is by no means the worst but simply one to hand):

1. Extensive experience in sponsorship management
2. Demonstrated ability to deliver complex projects including project plans, associated strategy, objectives, budgets, resource plans and communication strategy
3. Strong influencing and negotiation skills with demonstrated experience in achieving effective business outcomes
4. High-level experience in developing and maintaining strong commercial-based relationships with key stakeholders at all levels
5. High-level communication skills (verbal/communication) with the ability to use strong discretion and judgement in a complex business and political environment

6. Strong skills in building relationships with key stakeholders including commercial organisations, high-profile business leaders and educational institutions
7. Demonstrated experience in leading a team of people to achieve high performance outcomes with strong coaching skills to develop team capabilities and the ability to effectively manage conflict and underperformance
8. Ability to be flexible and adaptable within a changing environment and delivering high-volume outcomes
9. Ability to demonstrate and display the organisation's values – accountability, integrity, courage, respect for self and others, and striving for excellence.

For example, could there be people with the potential to be really good at the job but who didn't have sponsorship experience? Why have criteria 3, 4, 5 and 6 when they all seem to be saying more or less the same thing? What are high-volume outcomes? How do you sell your "values" on paper? In response to a similar question for a different job I wrote: ask my referees. The feedback from the head-hunter was that this was inappropriate and I needed to provide examples of when I was "ethical" and "honest" and "respectful". The answer is – every day. But I suspect that wouldn't have been an appropriate answer either. The point is to be clear about the skills and experience you require but also to consider what can reasonably be argued in a written application. Then use the other selection processes to dig deeper into the character, qualities and values you require.

There are a number of techniques you can use to get from a shortlist to the final choice. You've already used resumes to cut out the people who can't spell or haven't addressed your selection criteria or are lying (because the arts industry is usually so small, you can tell). The next processes are interviews, tests and references. Given that most of us use interviews for the majority of our selection decision-making,

it was comforting to find that there is strong evidence that how candidates perform in structured interviews is a good predictor of how someone will perform on the job (Van Iddeking, McFarland & Raymark 2007). Structured interviews are where everyone gets asked the same questions and the questions are specifically connected to the selection criteria. I prefer a structured interview because it keeps the interviewing team focused on asking questions rather than making statements and it also allows for more effective comparisons. This doesn't mean that you can't unpack the answers and ask for more details; nor does it mean that you can't ask questions that are specific to the applicant. But it does provide a useful framework for the process.

Another process that is recommended and often required by some recruitment agencies is that people craft their response to selection criteria and interview questions using the STAR approach. This means telling a story that covers the Situation, the Task, the Action and the Result. Regardless of which question approach you use, the point of an interview is to get the potential candidate to tell stories about what they've done and how they've behaved in previous work places. This turns the words on a resume into action.

An important point to keep in mind during interviews is bias. The temptation is to employ people you think you'll like. Yes, of course you're smart enough to know that they have to have the skills to do the job as well, but it feels safer to choose people with whom you feel most comfortable. But that's not always the best answer. We all have in-built biases but gender-related ones have been well researched. For example, Moss, Callanan and Wilson (2012, 157) say that "[m]ale executives tend to recruit attractive, rather than unattractive, female employees – especially if they intend to work closely with these candidates. Thus many extraneous factors, such as red clothing, will bias the selection of employees."

During an extended recruitment process that involved a number of groups working in teams of two to interview a large number of people, I realised that the person I was teamed with was jumping ahead of the other groups to pick attractive women to interview. I wasn't clear whether he was just getting a short-term kick out of the process or actively trying to ensure that such people were employed in his team or, worse still, getting contact information from the application form for future personal use. Whatever the reason, I wasn't comfortable but as the only woman manager in the group, no-one else saw this as a problem. Then one day, his behaviour got the better of him. We interviewed a tall, elegant woman whom I knew. I kept this knowledge to myself and tried to be as professional as possible. She was skilled and appropriate so got the job. My interview partner was thrilled and insisted that she go into his work team and then boasted to the other supervisors about his "good luck". I remember smiling sweetly and saying how pleased I was that we'd put our diversity policy into practice with the employment of a transgender person. Needless to say, he couldn't cope and I ended up with her working very successfully in my team. Whether it's prejudice for or prejudice against, you can end up missing out on good candidates.

I confess I didn't know about the "red" research when I applied for the MTC position but as I do "colour" rather than "power" dressing, I did wear red glasses and take a red and white spotted briefcase to the interview – and a member of the selection committee still talks about it.

A good HR book will give you a list of dos and don'ts for interview processes but some of mine are:

- Always have someone of both genders on the selection panel
- Even if you only want to talk to three or four people, don't say "no" immediately to the next six candidates because you never can tell what's going to result from those first interviews
- Make sure that you have a balance on your committee – if you are intuitive, get a rationalist to listen as well

- Make sure that you leave enough time to explore all the questions you need to have answered so that the next interview starts on time; candidates are going to be nervous enough and if you're trying to judge their likely job performance then minimise their stress
- Encourage the candidate to do most of the talking by briefing the rest of your team to keep their contribution to precise questions rather than rambling introductions
- Putting the candidate at ease is important particularly if interviews are being done by phone or skype where visual signals are missing or not as clear as in a face-to-face scenario
- The point of the interview is that you're hiring the person, not the resume. It's the person you need to consider in the interview process – particularly how the person works with others
- Get the candidate to tell stories – about good times and bad; that way, you hear their "voice" and get to "see" them in the workplace
- Remember all the research that shows that men oversell themselves and women undersell themselves.

I'm nervous about the use of psychological tests in the selection process. Perhaps I was put off by a story I read years ago where a company was desperate to poach the CEO of another corporation for his perceived skills in the market place. On first approach he said no. On second approach he said yes. He was offered a contract and part of the process was that he had to undergo psychological testing. On getting the results, the hiring company was horrified. I can't remember his qualities exactly but let's say he was an aggressive egoist with a messiah complex. The new employer terminated the contract but the qualities that came out in the test were exactly the ones that had attracted them to hire him in the first place. However, once his behaviour had a psychological label, the negative connotations underlying his effectiveness were no longer seen to be desirable.

Arts Centre Melbourne used to do testing for front-of-house positions (Masanauskas 2006). This practice received coverage in a local newspaper because someone applying to be an usher wasn't happy that his experience working in other venues didn't seem to be nearly as important as his skill at making paper planes and, after looking at cartoon ants, using "ant" to make other words. An Arts Centre spokesman defended their process this way:

> Our brand personality is being welcoming, committed, energetic, adventurous and confident. How do you get that out of a resume of a phone interview? Getting the job should be based on merit, not where you've worked in the past.

I agree with some of these points. After all, I'd never worked at a theatre company before I got the job at MTC. And yes, it is hard to find out about people's styles and personalities and capacities out of an interview alone. But I'm not sure that paper planes and word games will give you particular insight into someone's "welcoming personality" and their ability to deal with the young and old, the smart and the frail.

There are various aspects of potential performance that you can't pick from an interview. Sometimes, there are job requirements that can be simply tested. For example, if an administrator is expected to craft, type and proof letters then check that they can. Not everyone, even with a university degree or two, is good at grammar or spelling. In other cases, there will be tasks that need to be learnt and done before they can be tested and you may not know how someone really performs until they start doing it. That's why probation periods are important. The person who charms you and their peers and therefore may look good as a front-of-house usher may not be good at dealing with older people. By having a probation period of three or six months, you can test their performance and give them all the necessary training, advice and practice to do

the job. If they still can't do it well, one can have a not-too traumatic and perfectly legal separation.

It's rare to find the perfect candidate for a position so now you are down to a short list of two. In discussing hiring a new leader, Drucker (1990, 16) says he would look for strengths not weaknesses, match the strengths with the key challenges of the organisation and look for character or integrity because people, particularly young people, will model themselves on the leader. Volz (2017, 133) advises that when there are candidates of equal strength, give it to the one who's most enthusiastic about the company.

The needs of the company can be forgotten in the mix when one focuses on the standard skills and experience for a particular job. For example, in one case there were two candidates who were capable of doing the job. One was clearly ahead on skills but another was ahead on cultural fit. Each candidate's strength matched different aspects of the organisation's strategic plan but the company had been through recent turmoil and needed some healing before forging into the future. In the end the choice was the person with the smaller skill set but with the most chance of providing the focused care that was required. In a couple of years, the higher skilled, more outwardly focused candidate would be a better choice.

It's hard to put these subtleties into a position description and it's hard to describe the outcome to the unsuccessful candidate. Sometimes, it's not always perfectly clear what you want until you have the candidates in front of you. And when you choose the person with capacity rather than the perfect set of qualities, you have to provide them with support whether it's through mentoring or coaching or specific training opportunities. The thought that your new staff member, particularly if they are the CEO, can't hit the ground running can be challenging for a small to medium-sized company but that's often the outcome and can be managed.

So you've made your final choice. The rational and intuitive sides of the selection committee have come together and agreed on a candidate. But you still have to do that last box to tick: the referees. It's extremely important to check references, but they are full of pitfalls. There's the glowing reference because someone wants the person to leave their organisation. There's the written reference that is so bland it's meaningless. There's the referee who's scared to tell the truth. A *US News & World Report* quoted by Jim Volz (2017, 133) noted that "80% of all employers are reluctant to give bad references, and 47% are leery of doing so even when they have proof of employee wrongdoing". There's also the referee who can't really remember the candidate and the referee that didn't know they were a referee. Sometimes the advice to referees is to be factual and only talk about what can be substantiated in order to avoid lawsuits (Lawrence 2003) but as a reference checker, you do want impressions and insights as well as confirmation that the candidate really was head of the project that raised $1 million.

On the day before I was going for a job interview, I received a request to bring a written reference. As I don't think that generalised references are worth the paper they are written on, I didn't have one to hand. Luckily, a good colleague who I'd worked with knew I was searching for other work (to escape from our mutual boss) and was willing to write something quickly. It arrived by fax as I ran out the door and it wasn't until I was sitting waiting for my interview that I read it properly. It was glowing until the last line which read: "Please do not employ this person under any circumstances. We want to keep her." I had no choice but to hand it over and I'm afraid the serious men on the selection panel didn't get the joke … and I didn't get the job.

What do you do when a colleague is a referee for someone who turns out to be a problem employee? You have to tell them. Regardless of whether it was because they didn't know (and therefore should stop being a referee) or whether because they were misguidedly trying to help the applicant knowing they had problems, their reputation was tarnished by the employee's behaviour.

There is an ethical issue about whether you should talk to people who aren't listed as referees, particularly if the candidate doesn't provide anyone from their current workplace. Of course, people may reasonably not want their employer to know that they are looking elsewhere, but such a gap on a referee list always makes me nervous. One way around it is to ask the candidate why and if the issue is only about privacy, to suggest that you will make them the offer but that it will be conditional on a final positive reference from their current employer. If the issue is about a personality conflict then you still need to find someone who can comment on both sides of the story. Speaking to corporate managers after the 2015 Myer Australia experience where the company appointed a senior manager with a fake resume,[5] they recommended not to use the contact information provided by the candidate but to go through the main switchboard of a referee's organisation to ensure that they are talking to the real person. This may seem somewhat paranoid but if the person is completely unknown to you, it may be worth being circumspect when it's a senior position.

You've made the final choice and now you have to tell the unsuccessful candidates. You should be letting the shortlist know how the process is going as the weeks pass but avoid promising that you're going to tell them the result by a specific date, let alone a date that's within days of the interviews. If you're carefully considering the candidates, doing proper referee checks and preparing a process to let the unsuccessful candidates know, then the days can turn into weeks, leaving candidates uninformed and unhappy.

It's very hard to get the timing around informing the successful and unsuccessful candidates right. Often the unsuccessful hear before you get to them and this is particularly true in a small industry like the arts. I experienced one of those moments in the process of getting a job at the Australian Broadcasting Corporation. I travelled from Perth to Sydney for the interview and received a phone call at the end of the day to say I was going to be recommended for the position. My flight was first thing next morning, four to five hours across the Nullarbor Plain. My

Chairman knew that I had applied but my staff didn't, so as soon as I got off the plane in Perth, I went to his office to let him know and then went to my workplace. As I walked down the passage to my office there was a pile of furniture blocking the doorway and on it, a large sign saying "what's short and red and doesn't want to work here anymore". The over-enthusiastic person recruiting me in Sydney got approval for my appointment and because it was a media organisation, immediately put out a press release. So while I was on the plane for the journey back to Perth, anyone who heard the radio news that morning knew before I did that I had the job. As did all my staff.

Steven Libman (2014) has written a plea for better recruitment and selection processes in arts organisations. He's experienced the "Dear Applicant" letter, the "I'm sorry our servers were down and we didn't get your application", the "oh, haven't the search committee got back to you yet?" and there's the scenario of finding out online that someone else got the job before the company gets back to you. I agree with Libman that poor treatment of job applicants is a metaphor for poor management per se. He proposes an Applicant's Bill of Rights which is so straight forward and reasonable that I'm appalled to think that it doesn't happen as a matter of course:

1. Every person who applies for a job is told that his or her resume has been received and is informed of what the search process will be
2. Candidates not selected to advance to the interview stage are informed of that fact via a letter or email
3. Candidates not advancing beyond a phone or personal interviews are told via phone and told why (6).

No matter how good your recruitment and selection processes are, it's still a hit and miss affair because it involves people and opinions and biases. I can think of some spectacular failures where I appointed talented people into the wrong job or teamed them up with the wrong boss. For example, I gave a charming, bright, enthusiastic young woman the job of receptionist ahead of a quieter person with less knowledge of the business we were in. But deep down, the bright young thing didn't want to be a receptionist. She wanted to use the position to meet artists and to get a more creative job opportunity from the people she met in the role whereas the blander soul wanted to be a really good receptionist. I matched two people up who individually were spectacularly good at their jobs but spectacularly unsuccessful as boss and subordinate. I said no to someone because they seemed just a little too boringly corporate for my organisation. I chose the brighter, livelier version. Luckily my "grey suit" candidate applied again a few years later, we appointed him and he turned into a brilliant asset for the organisation. I've also chosen the second-best candidate because I couldn't find the best one rather than spending time going back to the market.

There is research to say that the notion of the perfect candidate is largely a myth and that getting the best performance from someone usually depends on them getting the right job and the right boss (Cappelli 2013), so trying hard to make a good match between position, person and organisation is all you can do.

In my time at MTC, I had ten people called various titles around the theme of "administrator" who worked with me as a personal assistant. The job combined the boring (filing, coffee making) and the sublime (negotiating international contracts, liaising with artists). None of these people were similar. What I wanted were smart, independent people who were also happy to serve. I worked with men and women. People with PhDs and those who went on to get them. There was a 20-year age range. Some were straight. Some gay. Some married. Some single. My point is there is no one particular person who can do a job. Be open to possibilities. There was only one person I finally couldn't work with. It was partly to do with capacity but mainly to do with trust. You may wonder why I had so many in that position over 18 years. If you chose the brightest and the best, you'll probably only be able to keep them for a limited time in a poorly paid job or one where the challenge eventually wears off. And yes, it does cost time and money to find their replacement but that's outweighed by the benefit of their great work when you have them.

You need a robust selection process not just for the organisation's sake, but also for the sake of the successful candidate. If there's a poor fit between the person, their job role and the surrounding environment and between their interests and the opportunities inherent in their new positon (Adams 2007) then the result is going to be unhappiness, stress, underperformance – and a new hiring process.

Induction and Probation

What happened on the day you started a new job? Were you introduced to people but couldn't keep track of their names? Shown around the office but not where the toilets were? Told about when you could expect to get paid but not where the nearest bank was? Given information but too much to absorb on one day? Introducing a new employee to the company is a key part in the hiring process and the beginning of their training and development process. I call it induction but that's somewhat old-fashioned. The new term is "onboarding" or "organisational socialisation" through which new employees learn about the organisation, how to do their job and are introduced to workmates. Having an organisation-wide document with all the things that need to happen for a new employee within the first couple of days, weeks and months helps the direct supervisor or manager provide an effective orientation.

One of the concepts that is often left out of an induction or onboarding process is to give a new staff member some insight into the history, culture and mission of the company. Even if the person has a casual ticketing job or does the accounts, you want them to be part of the team. Helping them understand the context of their job will help them contribute to your organisation.

Induction doesn't stop after the first day or even the first week. Assuming that you've put a probation clause into the employment contract, the next three to six months are when you continue to invest time and training, advice and help into your new recruit and at the same time that you're being supportive, you are also being analytical and check to see whether they really do have the four aptitudes that Collins (quoted in Fitzgerald 2008, 7) says that you need to consider when choosing people to work with you:

1. They must share your vision and core values. "It's hard to teach people core values … having the right skills for a job is one thing but understanding and committing to the organisation's core values is equally important."
2. People should be self-motivated and "do" without being asked
3. People must be in the right jobs with the potential to excel
4. "People should have a broader responsibility to the organisation rather than just to their job."

Arts organisations are under-resourced at the best of times and can't afford to carry people who don't have those qualities. More positively, with that "potential to excel", you may bring someone into your organisation who has the capacity to create new opportunities not just for themselves, but for the company as well.

Other areas: Diversity, Firing, Gender, People, Training

References

Adams, J. 2007 *Managing People in Organizations: Contemporary Theory and Practice*, Basingstoke: Palgrave Macmillan.

Balnave, N., Brown J., Maconachie, G. & Stone, R. J. 2009 *Employment Relations in Australia* (2nd ed), Milton, QLD: John Wiley & Sons.

Cappelli, P. 2013 "HR for Neophytes", *Harvard Business Review*, 91(10), 25–27.

Drucker, P. F. 1990 *Managing the Nonprofit Organization*, New York: HarperCollins.

Fitzgerald, S. (ed.) 2008 *Managing Independent Cultural Centres: A Reference Manual*, Singapore: Asia-Europe Foundation.

Lawrence, S. 2003 "Recruitment Agencies Must Be Vigilant", *Australian Financial Review*, 11 April.

Libman, S. 2014 "The Dignity of the Job Search", *Arts Management Newsletter*, Issue No. 118, February, 4–7.

Masanauskas, J. 2006 "Ushering in a New Era", *Herald Sun*, www.heraldsun.com.au/news/victoria/ushering-in-a-new-era/story-e6frf7kx-1111112605388 [accessed 27 February 2019].

Moss, S., Callanan, J. & Wilson, S. 2012 *The Moonlight Effect*, Melbourne: Tilde University Press.

Stone, R. J. 2013 *Managing Human Resources* (4th ed), Milton, QLD: John Wiley & Sons.

Van Iddeking, C. H., McFarland, L. A. and Raymark, P. H. 2007 "Antecedents of Impression Management Use and Effectiveness in a Structure Interview", *Journal of Management*, 33(5), 752–773.

Volz, J. 2017 *Introduction to Arts Management*, London: Bloomsbury Methuen Drama.

Holidays

"Australians are developing into a nation of 'time poor', 'stress rich' individuals. It is estimated that 40% of Australian workers do not take annual holidays, only 18% take their full entitlements and about 20% have not had a holiday in the past two years" (Macken 2000 2). Although that comment is now 20 years old, does it sound familiar, wherever you live?

In arts organisations, people resist going on holiday because they feel indispensable. "There aren't enough people to do the work at the best of times and who can possible do my job?" they say. You don't have to be a manager to feel that way. Some of the hardest people to get out the door on leave at MTC were skilled craft workers. But it's never true. Someone else can always do your job. They may not be as good. They may do it differently. They may need more support. But they can do it.

Westman and Etzion (2001) suggest that the proper use of holidays helps reduce workplace stress with corresponding reductions in absenteeism and burnout. As this is true for all staff, as a manager you have to set a good example and go on leave. It may be at a time that doesn't really suit you personally. It may be that it can only be a week at a time. But

you have to do it in order to encourage others to use their leave and refresh themselves. And in the process you'll benefit because as Leigh and Maynard say (2003, 46): "[le]isure and holidays are essential for sustaining leadership energy".

When I started at MTC, people had huge amounts of accumulated leave. In some organisations the policy is that if you don't take your leave within a set period of time you lose it, but this always felt unfair to me and can be illegal. People do value holidays so I had to find out why they weren't taking them. The reasons were mainly the predictable ones ("no-one to replace me", "too much work to do"), but an underlying issue was money. Although Australia has a tradition in some parts of the arts industry of paying a 17% leave loading to make up for lost overtime payments, people in many arts jobs are at the lower end of the pay scale. Not because they have low skills but simply because the arts doesn't pay well. And having a holiday that is anything more than sitting at home is expensive, particularly if you have a family. Put simply, people couldn't afford to go on holidays. Once I realised this, the company developed a policy which enabled those with extensive leave balances to cash out some of them in exchange for committing to go on holiday. They still needed to take leave but now they might be able to enjoy the time off. Different countries will have different legislation around the capacity to cash out leave. It's worth knowing the legal requirements, having a policy that covers it and regularly checking people's leave balances.

Once people agree to go on holiday, the UK Families and Work Institute recommends that "employers should discourage workers from taking work on vacation ... Holidays should allow employees to feel rested and recharged so it's important that work is reallocated when a person is on vacation so that they will not waste their holiday dreading the pile of working for them on their return" (quoted in Adams 2007, 44).

Haywood (2001, 127) suggests that for a vacation to be successful in reducing the outcomes of workplace stress, it has to involve:

- Having no contact with the workplace
- Leaving work tools such as laptops and mobiles behind
- Wrapping up duties efficiently before leaving
- Effectively delegating duties to others for the duration to avoid workload on return.

Obviously, that list was written before mobile phones became an integral part of our lives but you can still create rules around when and who can ring people when they are on leave and what the work expectations during this time might be. For example, just before I typed that sentence, a staff member went on leave. Because it's a small organisation in transition, she's the only person who can approve some bank transfers. We agreed that this was the only work communication she should expect from us.

While sometimes it's the challenge of making someone take holidays, sometimes it's the opposite situation where an important member of the team wants to take holidays at a challenging time. If you value them, you just have to say "yes". The temptation is to say "no" – but I've seen what that means. People resign. Instead of a short-term challenge you have a long-term one to replace them.

There are a variety of other "leave" entitlements that aren't always in the form of "holidays" but which can still contribute to creating a positive work culture. In Australia, "sick leave" is now "personal leave" that can be used by people with sick children or dependents or parents as well as themselves. As someone who has experienced the need for such leave, having a generous personal leave policy does build company loyalty and commitment. Different countries will have different legal provisions for leave but if you're free to develop your own, an interesting example in the UK was a company that contracted staff to work a given number of hours per year with a reserve of 160 hours to take account of problems such as sickness, medical appointments and peak production times (Adams 2007). This acknowledges the different needs that people will have for leave but also that the organisation may need more from people on occasional too.

Sometimes it's easy to be generous with leave that may not be called on very often. For example, after seeing people experiencing travel delays through volcanic ash or cyclones and the stress this caused, it made sense to develop a new policy to give people some paid leave for catastrophes. It didn't cost the organisation much and the attitude of care behind the gesture was valued by employees. Similarly, companies will often have a day or two days' leave for death in the family, but sometimes the death of a friend can be just as catastrophic and one can't organise a funeral, let alone grieve, in a couple of days.

Often it's a small gesture that can make a difference to people's motivation and commitment to the organisation. Growing up with a birthday on the last day of the year meant that as a child I always had a holiday on that day. Last year, I had a day off for my birthday just to do some relaxing, enjoyable "me" things. I commented to my sister that she should also take a day off on her birthday just to be able to treat herself on this special day. A couple of days after this conversation I discovered the story of a one firm, Millennium Bright Kid Company, that was singled out by the UK Department of Trade and Industry for their efforts at improving work-life balance in a profitable way. There sitting amongst the list of strategies they'd implemented was giving each staff member a (additional) day off on their birthday (Adams 2007). What a simple idea to give people pleasure. Ironically, when discussing this idea within an Australian company that already did this, there was some ambivalence amongst staff because people wanted to be able to celebrate the day with their work colleagues.

Although it's not exactly a holiday, staff can benefit from taking time off to volunteer for community service. In Australia, that's embedded in National Employment Standards for emergency work such as firefighting and helping with natural disasters. In an organisation I'm involved with, this goes even further to cover work in other volunteer capacities. That leave is unpaid but it contributes to the community, the individual's well-being and the company's reputation as a thoughtful employer.

Whether it's actively encouraging the taking of annual leave or giving the occasional day off as a reward, there's plenty of evidence that providing flexible strategies to improve work-life balance increases productivity. And, once I'd learnt to take holidays, I also discovered that they are usually wonderful, life-changing experiences.

See also: Hours, People

References

Adams, J. 2007 *Managing People in Organizations: Contemporary Theory and Practice*, Basingstoke: Palgrave Macmillan.

Haywood, C. 2001 "Wish You Weren't Here", *Financial Management (CIMA)*, July/August, 42–45.

Leigh, A. & Maynard, M. 2003 *Perfect Leader*, London: Random House Business Books.

Macken, D. 2000 "Desperately Seeking Holiday", *Australian Financial Review*, 2–3 December.

Westman, M. & Etzion, D. 2001 "The Impact of Vacation and Job Stress on Burnout and Absenteeism", *Psychology & Health*, 16(5), 595–606.

Hours

Arts organisations are often schizophrenic about hours of work. On the one hand, there will be the unionised part of the workforce (musicians, dancers, actor, ushers, guides) and on the other, the mainly white-collar workers with individual contracts. The work hours of the unionised people will be measured down to the quarter hour with overtime payments and penalty rates. The workers in the marketing or finance sections of the organisation may have a contract that says 38 hours a week but a work culture that expects somewhat more. Un-unionised artists such as directors and designers will usually be paid a flat fee and may work at a ridiculously low hourly rate although if the show is a success or tours and they have a royalty payment based on box office

built into their contract, all those long hours may be well rewarded. And of course, managers are expected to work all the hours required to get the job done, usually in exchange for a higher salary than others in the company.

The challenge is to get the balance right: to ensure that although no-one is going to be happy with their arts salary, that the hours they work are not so excessive as to cause health and safety issues What has to be avoided is what's described by a theatre director in Quigg's book on *Bullying in the Arts* (2011, 163–164):

> there can be a sense that normal rules do not apply, probably engendered by the sense that it is hard to get work in the arts, and that we are *very* lucky to do something we love, so a sense of perspective in terms of work-life balance, health and safety, pay for work, doesn't seem to apply?

If, for example, there are regular "extra" hours for non-unionised staff, then pay for them or build them properly into the base salary. If there is a flexitime system, then have limits to how much people can accrue but let them/make them take the hours off regularly. If excessive amounts of overtime are being worked in a particular department, it will probably be cheaper to temporarily or permanently employ more staff.

In a fascinating piece of research on stealing minutes of time, Holmquist (2013) starts with the following point:

> For accounting purposes, work done is measured not by performance, but by the clock (2221).

This reminds me of walking into MTC on the first day and discovering that there was an old-fashioned factory time clock with punch cards that a number of the staff used. As a new manager, I wanted to demonstrate my trust of these workers, many of whom had been with the company for over a decade, and so I suggested to the Head of Production that it be removed. He gently reminded me that it wasn't a machine for management but a machine for workers, so that they could claim every last minute that they worked. They may have been committed to the company but their part of the industry had been unionised for years and they had been taught to assume that management would underpay them even if there was no evidence that this had ever happened. After all, if time is money, it can be stolen by either party. If a worker feels that they have been underpaid or exploited by management, ethical considerations against theft of time may weaken. Even in our organisations there will be people who count every single minute and those who give generously. If people aren't being regularly exploited, they may be more willing to give a few more minutes of their time.

Australians prefer to work the standard eight-hour day because hours beyond this are seen as making it difficult for dual income and single parent households (Stone 2013).

> Nearly two-thirds of the extended hours workers felt that they missed out on regarding aspects of being a parent, 47% felt that working left them with little time or energy to be the kind of parent they would like to be, and 37 per cent felt that their long working hours made their family life less enjoyable and more pressured.
>
> (Teicher, Holland & Gough 2006, 422)

The authors also quote research which shows that long hours can have a negative effect on family relationships, children and the community as well as individual health and safety at work. In some ways it's bizarre that, whether reluctantly or not, we all seem to work longer hours than our parents. There are some beautiful banners still hanging in the Victorian Trades Hall in Melbourne celebrating the achievement of the eight-hour day, a battle won in the 1850s in Australia and lost by the end of the 20th century.

Another perspective about hours worked, and this is particularly relevant to creative and management work, is whether in this day and age "face time" is still the most appropriate way to measure productivity (Adams 2007). How

many of us get caught up with the need to be seen to be working longer hours? For some of the time I was writing this book I had a part-time position as a Research Fellow with the University of Melbourne and during this time I was religiously keeping track of the hours I spent at the desk or in the library in order to avoid any sense that I was wasting the university's money. Obviously, that didn't take into account dreaming time, sitting on the tram thinking time, cultural engagement time, discussing work and life with friends time.

I have management colleagues who work 12 hours a day, six days a week. I know others who are sending texts and emails from 6am to midnight. My approach wasn't perfect but I did have some rules:

- If I had to work long hours then I did them at work rather than at home
- I kept the mobile on at home when a show was on (in case of emergencies) but didn't send emails or texts after hours
- When I went on holidays, I went on holidays – I either got someone in to replace me, had someone internal act in the job or delegated power to the management team to make decisions.

How do you get over the idea that you have to work longer hours than any of your subordinates? When offered a CEO role recently, a peer who didn't want to buy into the endless hours of work yet again and said "no" unless she could work less than five days a week. The Board was shocked but wanted this person enough to say "yes". This person said that the shorter working week made them more effective but less consultative. But for their management team, while they were consulted less, they were empowered more with real delegated authority. An interesting outcome.

In a "real life" side bar in a management textbook, an executive is described thus:

> [Karen Stanton's] aim is to create a friendly environment so that people will want to come

to work. She does not expect employees to work long hours, but while they are there she expects them to work hard, smart and efficiently … She works hard to create a positive culture where each staff member is valued.

Examples are given of birthday cards and notes honouring achievements (Dalglish & Miller 2011, 3). While saying thank you and recognising important moments in people's lives is easy (and I have no idea why more managers and leaders don't do it), I've never managed to resolve the work hard versus work long dilemma.

Perhaps it's because I've spent most of my life as a leader in organisations producing products that people cared passionately about but also organisations that were under-resourced. And so we relied on people's goodwill and commitment over and above 38 hours per week. I remember as a public servant, I counted every minute and was out the door as soon as it was legal. But if I found someone counting minutes in the same way in an arts or cultural organisation, I'd be asking why they wanted to be there. However, there's a difference between counting minutes and working ridiculous hours or even expecting people to be at work at difficult times. I know this makes it hard for parents and I have and will restructure meetings and work hours to enable parents to drop off and pick up their children from day care or school. Admittedly that more flexible approach to life came when I had to pick up a child by 6pm at the absolute latest and when I had to drop a teenager off to school and then fight peak hour traffic. So we stopped having early morning or late night meetings as a regular part of MTC operations.

It's not just the management team that tend to work excessive hours. If they aren't setting a good example, then most of their team will also feel the need to stay on. Autry (2001) describes the idea that working long hours is a sign of loyalty as a myth. He made sure that he sent "clear signals that working nights and weekends was not a key to success in our group" (209). If someone is working excessive

hours, Autry (2001, 210) said you need to ask two questions. What's wrong with the person that they can't accomplish their tasks in the time given and/or what's wrong with the job structure that it can't be done during regular hours? However, he's also realistic about organisational needs acknowledging that sometimes extra hours have to be worked but "[i]f someone took extra time and accomplished a special project of merit, that person would be appreciated and rewarded" (210).

In an article about a report on work-life balance in Australia called *Walking the Tightrope* (Baker, Johnson & Denniss 2014), a manager from a training and consulting company gave a variety of examples to prevent people from working overtime such as phones automatically switched over to voicemail at 5pm, people being allowed to work from home, a rule that you can't send someone an email after 5pm and emails disabled when people go on holiday so they don't monitor them while they are away (Patty 2014). In this same report, there was mention of something that had completely escaped my attention even though I regularly used the words as I wandered through the building before I went home, saying it to people who were still sitting at their desks. Apparently in 2009, The Australia Institute launched a "National Go Home on Time Day" as a light-hearted way to start a conversation with employees about the important of work-life balance (Baker, Johnson & Denniss 2014).

There are elements of the arts industry where flexibility is extremely limited – performance times, number of shows a week, gallery opening hours, weekend work. But there are also work patterns where tradition and budgets drive decision-making. Why, for example, did MTC have rehearsals from 10am to 6pm and also on Saturdays? Why do the days of moving a show into a theatre involve 18-hour days? It's not just the number of hours that can be difficult, but when those hours are worked. Part of what contributes to health issues in our industry is the issue of hours. In an Australia survey of entertainment industry workers (Entertainment Assist 2016), the high levels of mental health problems and suicidality was working unpredictable hours with 43% working mainly in the evenings, 42% working on weekends and 30% working unpredictable hours resulting in workers suffering sleep disorders seven times greater than the general population.

An example of the tension between art making and hours, the needs of an arts organisation and an arts worker, is the story of a back-of-house technician who'd signed up for a job that involved working six nights a week, had a change in family circumstances and wanted to reduce the number of nights worked. This would have meant bringing in a casual technician for one or two nights. Both the director and the stage management team were fiercely against this proposal because of the chance of mistakes that could be made by a casual worker who wasn't in the rhythm and pattern of the show. And mistakes backstage can have a serious impact given the implicit danger of the performance space.

Although it's hard to change working hours in the face of government legislation, union agreements, tradition and the behaviour of peer companies, sometimes it's worth stepping back and asking why we do some things that potentially impact negatively on the well-being of the people who work with us. Admittedly, for some people in the arts, working long hours is an active choice although with this desire to spend time in artistic practice, sometimes more hours are worked than might be considered healthy. Paul Saintilan and David Schreiber (2018) quote a UK survey about satisfaction in the creative industries from 2014 (70). The result was that a clear majority were satisfied with the jobs and didn't feel overworked even though traditional hours are long. Saintilan and Schreiber thought this may be because "their 'work' feels more like a glorified hobby" (71).

I find that comment somewhat offensive and lacking insight about the nature of arts practice as a vocation which, combined with the evidence that artists often fail to differentiate their work from their lives, means that we have to proactively look after their well-being.

Many of the strategies that companies can implement to promote work-life balance are based on hours of work and where those hours are worked. Examples that could be used in arts organisations include the use of flextime, practices that provide spatial flexibility such as working at home and videoconferencing, part-time and shared work, but the most important strategies are ones that stop us demanding excessive hours from people and where we, as leaders and managers, set a good example.

See also: Delegation, Families, Holidays, People

References

Adams, J. 2007 *Managing People in Organizations: Contemporary Theory and Practice*, Basingstoke: Palgrave Macmillan.

Autry, J. A. 2001 *The Servant Leader*, New York: Three Rivers Press.

Baker, D., Johnson, M. & Denniss, R. 2014 *Walking the Tightrope: Have Australians Achieved Work/life Balance?* Canberra: The Australian Institute.

Dalglish, P. & Miller, C. 2011 *The Leader in You: Developing Your Leadership Potential*, Melbourne: Tilde University Press.

Entertainment Assist 2016 *Working in the Australian Entertainment Industry: Key Findings*, EA Melbourne.

Holmquist, J. P. 2013 "Workplace Ethics at the Time Clock: Fudging Time With Respect to Western and Eastern Views", *The International Journal of Human Resource Management*, 24(11), 2221–2236.

Patty, A. 2014 "Work-life Balance is Getting Worse for Australians: New Report", *Sydney Morning Herald*, www.smh.com.au/nsw/worklife-balance-is-getting-worse-for-australians-new-report-20141118-11otw6.html [accessed 27 February 2019].

Quigg, A. M. 2011 *Bullying in the Arts*, Farnham: Gower.

Saintilan, P. & Schreiber, D. 2018 *Managing Organizations in the Creative Economy: Organizational Behaviour for the Cultural Sector*, Abingdon: Routledge.

Stone, R. J. 2013 *Managing Human Resources* (4th ed), Milton, QLD: John Wiley & Sons.

Teicher, J., Holland, P. & Gough, R. 2006 *Employee Relations Management* (2nd ed), Sydney: Pearson Education Australia.

Human Resources Management

Human Resources Management (HRM) emerged in the 1980s as a higher level strategy task than what had previously been called Personnel

Management. Legge (2003, 86) says that "HRM represents the discovery of personnel management by chief executives and their elevation to being designers of 'the machine' rather than merely the oil that greased the cogs on it." There are also political divisions with HRM with "hard" and "soft" positions on what's required. "Hard" HRM approaches are focused on increasing efficiency and reducing labour costs whereas the "soft" approach is about developing a return to the organisation in the form of increased commitment, quality and flexibility (Sheehan, De Cieri & Holland 2013). Underlying both definitions, there's a question of whether concern for performance is always compatible with concern for people. "Going to speak to HR" isn't always a good thing if the department is seen as a tool of management and not one that is supportive of employees.

At this point, I have to confess that I hate the phrase Human Resource Management and what it implies. People shouldn't be considered "resources". I think of people as collaborators or contributors or partners in the process of creating art and cultural experiences. Working with people is the most important aspect of the job. Stakeholder management is really people management. Project management is about time but also about people management. And even Finance Management involves people spending money and collecting and analysing data. I'm not alone in wanting to avoid HRM as a phrase. When Libby Sartain joined Southwest Airlines, she was initially embarrassed that they wanted to rebrand the HR function as the People Department but eventually learned to appreciate the symbolic meaning underlying the change (Sartain & Finney 2003).

Regardless of what the department or the role is called, most small to medium-sized arts organisations don't have an HR specialist. Even in a comparatively large organisation such as MTC, I didn't have one. What I did have was a number of people whose work was about people:

- A personnel administrator who managed all the paperwork involved in employing people

- An artistic coordination team who negotiated contracts for actors and creatives and looked after their well-being while they were with the company
- An occupational health and safety officer who developed policies and training programs for staff.

I "managed" the HR side myself: heading the negotiation team when dealing with unions; re-writing employment contract templates when Australia's National Employment Standards were introduced; creating recruitment and selection policies; devising polices on topics such as performance assessment, sexual harassment and respect in the workplace. Taking on these strategic HR functions may have been arrogance on my part because I had taught industrial relations and personnel management in the past or it may have been cost consciousness given the delicate financial state of the company. I don't know whether the company would have been better off if the decision-making on these HR issues had been pushed further down the hierarchy or whether the company would have been better off with an HR manager.[6] I just knew that if people were the most important aspect of the organisation, then I wanted to be hands on in many of the areas that impacted on them.

Bakke (2005) tells of doing away with the HR department at Applied Energy Services (AES) within six months of founding the company with all but a few of the administrative functions being handled by work teams. Recruiting, reviews, compensation, hiring, discipline, firing and benefits were "handled by people who had direct responsibility for the quality of their work". Even if you have a good HR manager or department, as CEO I think that you still need to be across the policies and decisions that are going to contribute to your organisation's culture.

The other problem with HR managers is the paradox implicit in their role. On the one hand, they are there to provide strategic advice about employment issues from salaries to performance appraisal and, on the other hand, they are seen by staff to have an employee advocacy role (Sheehan, De Cieri & Holland 2013). This can create a scenario where staff will use them as a confidential sounding Board but not make a formal complaint. The HR person is then stuck in the difficult position of not being able to resolve the issue. So most serious HR problems will end up on the CEO's desk anyway.

Even if you don't have an HR manager, you'll still need to make sure that you have their traditional roles and activities covered. For example, do you have access to counselling services for staff or industrial relations advice or legal advice? Do you have up-to-date policies about occupational health and safety and complex areas such as bullying and harassment? This can be a challenge for small to medium-sized companies but there are often industry or professional organisations that offer support, and ensuring that you have an HR specialist on your Board can be helpful.

You also have to consider how many of the aspects of HRM will apply to the artists with whom you work. Eikhof and Haunschild (2007) raise an interesting question about why standard HRM practices that get applied to core staff in arts organisation, don't get applied to creative staff.

> For non-artistic theatre staff, the usual HRM portfolio from recruitment to appraisal, training and development and flexible working hours is brought into play. Quite the contrary, HRM practices concerning ensemble actors are basically limited to recruiting, contract negotiations and staff decisions (534).

Any performance appraisal happens in the rehearsal room, through the director's notes, critics and the audience. There is no formal offer of training and development, no clear discipline policies if things go wrong, no standardisation of how to resolve artistic incompatibilities. Most appraisal and training for artists such as actors – and one could add creatives and visual arts and writers – happens at the industry rather than the organisational level (Haunschild & Eikhof 2009).

Regardless of whether you have an HRM team or whether it's just you and regardless of whether you call the function HR or People Management, you need to have a shared philosophy around employment with appropriate policies and practices for everyone you employ. Your managers may all be different people but they need to bring a consistency of practice to how they motivate, evaluate and develop their staff. After all, people are at the heart of arts and cultural organisations and as Fishel (2003, 98) says, "providing appropriate and equitable policies and procedures is essential for organisational harmony and motivation".

Bolman and Deal (2013, 140) propose a simple list of important things to do when managing people:

- Hire the right people: know what you want; be selective
- Keep them: reward well; promote from within; share the wealth
- Invest in them: invest in learning; create development opportunities
- Empower them: provide information and support; encourage autonomy and participation; foster self-managing teams, promote egalitarianism
- Promote diversity: be explicit and consistent about the organization's diversity philosophy; hold managers accountable.

To which one could also add, look after their well-being.

All of which are covered in other parts of this book.

See also: Diversity, Empowerment, Firing, Hiring, Organisational Culture, Organisational Structure, People, Training

References

Bakke, D. W. 2005 *Joy at Work*, Seattle: PVG.
Bolman, L. G. & Deal, T. E. 2013 *Reframing Organizations* (5th ed), San Francisco, CA: Jossey-Bass.

Cappelli, P. 2013 "HR for Neophytes", *Harvard Business Review* October, 2–13.

Eikhof, Dr & Haunschild, A. 2007 "For Art's Sake! Artistic and Economic Logics in Creative Production", *Journal of Organizational Behaviour*, 28, 523–538.

Fishel, D. 2003 *The Book of The Board*, Sydney: Federation Press.

Haunschild, A. & Eikhof, D. R. 2009 "From HRM to Employment Rules and Lifestyles", *German Journal of Human Resource Research*, 23(2), 107–124.

Legge, K. 2003 "Strategy as Organizing", in Cummings, S. & Wilson, D. (eds) *Images of Strategy*, Oxford: Blackwell Publishing, 74–104.

Sartain, L. & Finney, M. I. 2003 *HR from the Heart*, New York: AMACOM.

Sheehan, C., De Cieri, H. & Holland, P. 2013 "The Changing Role of Human Resources Management in the Employment Relationship", in Teicher, J., Holland, P. & Gough, R. (eds) *Australian Workplace Relations*, Cambridge: Cambridge University Press, 103–117.

Humility

Managers and leaders can have many good characteristics but I want to spend a couple of minutes on humility because one of my favourite writers on management, Chris Grey (2005), recommends it as a useful quality. Why? Because the world is an uncertain place and if we take on the responsibility of managing people, we need to have care for them and not believe that our voice is the only one that should be heard. Sinclair (2007, 30) makes the often-unstated point that while conventional wisdom is that leadership is a good thing, it can also be a bad thing. Humility may help overcome tendencies to the dark side such as narcissism and grandiosity.

Humility in the workplace can be defined as:

> a capability to evaluate success, failure, work, and life without exaggeration … humility enables leaders to distinguish the delicate line between such characteristics as healthy self-confidence, self-esteem, and self-assessment, and those of over-confidence, narcissism and stubbornness.
>
> (Vera & Rodriquez Lopez 2004, quoted in Sarros et al. 2006, 99)

To have a humble approach is to acknowledge your limitations and to be willing to seek the views of others to help understand the world. In their analysis of effective leaders in the US corporate world, Collins and Porras (1994) came up with a list of qualities that were somewhat unexpected given the traditional view of leadership. Their successful leaders were described as softly spoken, gentle, good listeners, modest, thoughtful, serious, rather shy – and humble.

The qualities of a humble person can be divided into three – relational, emotional well-being and a focus on learning – and each of these categories is relevant to achieving good outcomes for organisations (Nielsen & Marrone 2018). For example, humility is clearly going to provide a positive orientation towards relationships which in turn will promote meaningful interactions at work. Someone who is confident without being narcissistic will be open to the contributions of others because their ego won't get in the way. Bunting (2016) describes a survey of over 3,000 executives which found that the most innovative leaders share five mental traits: associating (connecting the dots), questioning, observing, experimenting, networking (meeting new people who are not like them). Bunting's (2016, 88) concludes that: "While each of these traits is vital, underlying them, I believe, is an even deeper attribute that it the foundation … humility. Staying humble is the most important thing we can do as leaders."

Servant leadership is a model which seems to fit well with mission-driven, non-profit organisations. The characteristics of such a servant leader include

> asking questions in order to seek solutions, rather than giving orders; earning respect and understanding through engagement; acting as a broker or match-maker, rather than being at the central point of all decision-making; and seeking to find real common understanding between people rather than just wanting consensus to deliver outcomes.
>
> (Norbury 2010, 53)

Being a servant to others takes considerable humility. Even if that's not your preferred management style it's still worth noting one of Drucker's (1990, 23) leadership competencies: "willingness to realize how unimportant you are compared to the task".

One of the managers I enjoyed working with in the past, Peter Brokensha (2007), talked about humility as a quality, along with empathy, that had helped him come to wisdom over three-quarters of a century. He learnt this initially through his mother who was always humble and considerate of the needs of others and then through his first job at a petrol refinery:

> Although I had just finished a university degree in engineering I soon realised I didn't really know much at all about the important things; about people and work and getting things done. I soon found that I could always learn something from everyone no matter what their position was (155).

In Sarros' et al.'s (2006) book on the character of leadership, a corporate director offers good advice on putting humility into practice:

> I think humility is really important. I know that I don't know it all, and I know that for all the things I get right, I'll get an equal number of things wrong, and stuff them up. You can learn from your mistakes, and that comes back to the importance of honesty. You can be honest when you stuff up and say, I didn't quite get that right or I didn't quite understand what you said (106).

You can improve your humility by facing up to your weaknesses, acknowledging your failings, taking feedback graciously and remembering that you are there to serve the stakeholders and the arts makers.

See also: Empathy, Leadership, Listening

References

Brokensha, P. 2007 *Getting to Wisdom Slowly*, Adelaide: Peacock Publications.
Bunting, M. 2016 *The Mindful Leader*, Milton, QLD: Wiley.
Collins, J. C. & Porras, J. I. 1994 *Built to Last: Successful Habits of Visionary Companies*, New York: HarperBusiness.
Drucker, P. F. 1990 *Managing the Nonprofit Organization*, New York: HarperCollins.
Grey, C. 2005 *A Very Short, Fairly Interesting and Reasonably Cheap Book about Studying Organisations*, London: Sage Publications.
Nielsen, R. & Marrone, J. A. 2018 "Humility: Our Current Understanding of the Construct and its Role in Organizations", *International Journal of Management Reviews*, 20, 805–824.
Norbury, C. 2010 "Relationships Are at the Heart of Good Cultural Leadership", in Kay, S. & Venner, S. (eds) *A Cultural Leader's Handbook*, London: Creative Choices, 50–57.
Sarros, J., Cooper, B. K., Hartican, A. M. & Barker, C. J. 2006 *The Character of Leadership*, Milton, QLD: John Wiley & Sons.
Sinclair, A. 2007 *Leadership for the Disillusioned*, Sydney: Allen & Unwin.
Vera, D. & Rodriquez Lopez, A. 2004 "Strategic Virtues: Humility as a Source of Competitive Advantage", *Organisational Dynamics*, 33(4), 393–408.

Notes

1 Saintilan & Screiber (2018, 242) spend less than 100 words talking about sexual harassment compared to a couple of pages on "Strategic Sexual Performance".
2 www.notinmyworkplace.org
3 Usually when they can't afford to pay the market rate for positions such as Development and Finance managers and IT specialists.
4 In Australia, each unemployed person has to demonstrate that they have applied for 40 jobs per month in order to keep their unemployment benefits.
5 http://risqgroup.com/myer-fires-new-recruit-andrew-flanagan-fake-resume/ [accessed 27 February 2019].
6 MTC did appoint an HR manager after I left.

Industrial Relations

Industrial relations (IR) involves the activities of governments, industrial tribunals, employer associations, trade unions and the impact of industrial law, awards, terms and conditions of work, grievance procedures, dispute settlement, advocacy and collective bargaining in determining the rules about employment relationships (Stone 2013) – but apparently, it's a phrase that writers over the last 10 years have tended to ignore. When writing about these issues, the catch-all is either "Employment Relations" (e.g. Balnave et al. 2009; Bray, Waring & Cooper 2009) or "Workplace Relations" (e.g. Teicher, Holland & Gough 2013). "Industrial relations" is considered to have negative ramifications because of sensationalist media reporting of employer/employee conflict and the role of unions that is seen to be at the heart of it (Bray, Waring & Cooper 2009). But as my particular focus in this section is about the impact of government legislation and unions on Employment Relations rather than other aspects of people management, it still feels appropriate.

There are different approaches to industrial relations – unitarist, pluralist, radical or Marxist – although you don't hear much of the latter these days. In the unitarist world (which is often the world of the Human Resource expert), workplace conflict is a temporary aberration. Life is about teamwork and mutual cooperation, with direct communication between management and employees based on common objectives. If conflict does occur it's because of poor management or workers that don't fit in or trade union interference. It's a view to be found on the right wing of politics and ironically (because many arts workers tend to be left-voting), it's a view that most arts managers would rather like to think was the case in their organisation. Because people actively choose to work in an arts organisation, there are shared values and shared objectives, teamwork and mutual cooperation. And sometimes it does feel as if unions interfere with the smooth running of the company. However, just because employees are committed to the art form, doesn't mean that they feel they have power in the relationship or are comfortable without the support of a trade union.

The truth of the matter, in countries like Australia with a democracy, a strong (if fading) tradition of trade unionism, a legal structure that supports the rights of unions, facilitates group bargaining and provides conciliation and arbitration processes, we have a pluralist system where trade unions are legitimate representatives of employee interests and managers have to learn to negotiate with a collective rather than individuals with the state as the umpire.

A radical perspective is that industrial conflict is class conflict and while unions try to rectify the imbalance implicit in the employment relationships, the state actively seeks to support the interests of capital (Balnave et al. 2009). There would seem to be some evidence for this view in countries like Australia where, in the last couple of decades, right wing governments have introduced legislation designed to reduce the power of unions both directly and through a decreased role for government industrial instrumentalities (Pittard 2013).

Managerial prerogative, which is the watch cry of employer associations, means the right of managers or business owners "to make unilateral decisions about all aspects of their business without interference from government, workers or unions" (Balnave et al. 2009, 5). The list of such "aspects" includes to hire and fire, to promote and demote, allocation of work (hours, rostering, shift work, overtime, leave, use of outside labour), introduction of new technology, design and monitoring of work, OHS, management communication and consultation with employees (Balnave et al. 2009). I'm hard pressed to think of any part of that list of so-called managerial prerogatives that isn't impacted by some form of government regulation in Australia. Clearly, different countries will have different industrial laws but the point is that most countries will have some rules that cover the employment relationship. Therefore, arts managers need to understand the legislative environment and how it impacts on employment.

Often if you are in a small arts organisation, you may be able to ignore or avoid collective bargaining or trade union involvement but you will never be able to ignore or avoid laws about the employment of people. One of the best ways of ensuring that you have this knowledge is to join a relevant employers' association. This doesn't automatically mean that you are anti-union but rather that you'll be well informed about unions and industrial relations generally. The next best thing you can do is find an employment law expert that you can call on when required.

The most effective way to ensure that you are compliant on issues to do with employment and linked legal minefields such as occupational health and safety, equal opportunity and harassment is to have written employment contracts and policies that spell out what the organisation expects from staff and what staff can expect from you. And if what they expect is a right to get the support of a union, so be it.

See also Harassment, Hiring, Human Resource Management, Occupational Health and Safety, People, Policies, Unions

References

Balnave, N., Brown J., Maconachie, G. & Stone, R. J. 2009 *Employment Relations in Australia* (2nd ed), Milton, QLD: John Wiley & Sons.

Bray, M., Waring, P. & Cooper, R. 2009 *Employment Relations*, Sydney: McGraw Hill.

Pittard, M. 2013 "Australian Employment Regulation", in Teicher, J., Holland, P. & Gough, R. (eds) *Australian Workplace Relations*, Cambridge: Cambridge University Press, 81–100.

Stone, R. J. 2013 *Managing Human Resources* (4th ed), Milton, QLD: John Wiley & Sons.

Teicher, J., Holland, P. & Gough, R. 2013 *Australian Workplace Relations*, Melbourne: Cambridge University Press.

J

Job Satisfaction

Sartain and Finney (2003, 60) say that the best organisations to work for:

- Are always the ones that demonstrate through word and deed that each individual employee is highly and equally valued
- Have a high degree of employee involvement
- Have a culture that values the individualism of others, respecting the need for people to be themselves
- Have very little hierarchy, distinctions, elitism and bureaucracy
- Have practices and programs that reflect equal, consistent and employee-oriented policies
- Provide their employees with significant opportunities to develop, grow and learn, both professionally and personally
- Recognise that quality-of-life issues for their employees are important components of the business agenda.

If your organisation reflects these qualities in its policies and culture, then some (and hopefully most) of the time, people will get satisfaction from their work.

Two main theories that help explain job satisfaction are about discrepancy, where the level of satisfaction is determined by the gap between what people expect to receive and what actually happens at work, and equity, which is when we feel unhappy if what we receive is less, proportionally, to what others get for the same effort (McShane & Travaglione 2003). This is a useful reminder that even if we have a positive organisational culture, it's people's perceptions that define whether they are satisfied at work or not.

Various studies conclude that non-profit organisations attract people for whom money isn't the main or sole driver, where there is more motivation and commitment because of the meaningfulness of their work, and that they tend to be more satisfied and loyal than people in the private sector (Nair and Bhatnagar 2011). However, there is older research which found that non-profit white-collar workers were not more satisfied with their jobs than their public or private counterparts because of the impact of shortage of resources, intensification of work and increased scrutiny from outside agencies (Mirvis 1992). Given that those issues are still part of the lives of non-profit workers, there is the still the capacity for dissatisfaction.

There is a wide array of research on what leads to job satisfaction. For example, Kim (2002) found that job satisfaction was high among employees who had supervisors with a participatory management style and good communication skills. Employees who could participate in strategic planning processes were also more satisfied, presumably because they had a high sense of engagement with the organisation. A person's perspective of organisational support and whether someone finds meaning in their work also contribute to job satisfaction (Adam 2007). The "support" idea means that if an organisation is seen to reward action and initiative, then in response workers will reward the organisation with their loyalty – and in the process, feel good about their role at work. Most people we employ have chosen to work with us because we're a museum or a dance company rather than because the job is for an accountant or a ticket seller and to a degree they have already made a decision to align their interests with the organisation. However, we can't afford to ignore the second part of the equation – giving people a sense that they are supported by the organisation. Adam (2007) says that this involves:

> the belief … that the establishment has his or her best interests at heart, manifest in timely, appropriate feedback from supervisors, clear communication of goals, an understanding, combined with underlying flexibility, of the job role, and a strong sense of meaningful relations at work (xxi).

Looking from another perspective, there is correlation between negative job satisfaction and health although it's stronger between psychological problems such as self-esteem, anxiety and depression than physical illness. To build psychological well-being, an individual needs to feel good and have a sense of purpose (Zineldin & Hytter 2012).

Adams (2007) reviewed 600 academic papers on job satisfaction and organisational productivity and concluded:

when employees are encouraged to work autonomously, and are given greater control over their tasks, resources, time, interactions, and goals, they will perform substantially better, resulting in greater organizational performance. Consequently, managers need to learn how to encourage employee development by acting in a supportive, coaching or mentoring role, rather than as an overseer or administrator (xvii).

Other researchers collected data from workers in 100 manufacturing plants in three countries and they also concluded that the closeness of the relationship between the employees and their supervisors was a significant enhancer of employee morale, an important factor in worker satisfaction and productivity (McKnight, Ahmad & Schroeder 2001). By "close", this doesn't mean that you have to be your staff member's best friend. But you do have to have an open and honest communication pathway and be capable of playing the role of mentor and advisor as well as boss.

One outcome of a lack of job satisfaction is absenteeism – why bother going to work if you hate it? Absenteeism tends not to be a problem in arts and cultural organisations because there is high commitment to the company. There will always be areas where some absenteeism occurs more often such as casual workers in more mundane jobs where the emotional connection with the company may not be as strong. But if you start to see unexplained absenteeism amongst regular staff, then you need to investigate.

While not every job is rewarding every day, creating an organisational climate and culture in which people want to come to work and get satisfaction from their job seems both ethical and practical.

See also: Ethics, Organisational Culture, People

References

Adams, J. 2007 *Managing People in Organizations: Contemporary Theory and Practice*, Basingstoke: Palgrave Macmillan.

Kim, S. 2002 "Participative Management and Job Satisfaction: Lessons from Management Leadership", *Public Administration Review*, 62(2), 231–241.

McKnight, D. H., Ahmad, S. & Schroeder, R. G. 2001 "When Do Feedback, Incentive Control, and Autonomy Improve Morale? The Importance of Employee-management Relationship Closeness", *Journal of Managerial Issues*, 13(4), 466–482.

McShane, S. & Travaglione, T. 2003 *Organisational Behaviour on the Pacific Rim*, Sydney: McGraw Hill.

Mirvis, P. 1992 "The Quality of Employment in the Non-profit Sector: An Update on Employee Attitudes in Non-profits Versus Business and Government", *Nonprofit Management and Leadership*, 3(1), 23–41.

Nair, N & Bhatnagar, D 2011 "Understanding Workplace Deviant Behaviour in Nonprofit Organizations", *Nonprofit Management and Leadership* 21(3), 289–309.

Sartain, L. & Finney, M. I. 2003 *HR from the Heart*, New York: AMACOM.

Zineldin, M. & Hytter, A. 2012 "Leaders' Negative Emotions and Leadership Styles Influencing Subordinates' Well-being", *The International Journal of Human Resource Management*, 23(4), 748–758.

K

Knowledge

Knowledge can be described as a "dynamic collection of information and skills" and wisdom as a combination of knowledge plus experience and good judgement (Sommerton 2010, 155).

Arts managers in Ireland came up with the following list of skills they needed to do their job (in order):

- Ability to effectively schedule time, tasks and activities, to organise resources and to establish a course of action to accomplish specific goals
- Ability to express confidence and to be decisive
- Ability to listen to others' viewpoints, negotiate sensitively and take account of other's needs
- Ability to quantify and organise needed financial resources and to monitor their expenditure accurately
- Ability to make effective written presentations to others
- Ability to make effective verbal presentations to others
- Ability to develop and maintain networks and formal channels of communication with the outside world
- Knowledge of funding resources
- Ability to influence people and "win the day"
- Ability to stick to a plan and not get side-tracked
- Ability to assign tasks to others and to monitor their performance
- Ability to conduct effective group meetings
- Ability to keep abreast of relevant local, national and international political, economic and cultural developments
- Knowledge of local, national and international structures
- Knowledge of legal issues (Clancy 1997, 360).

These are mainly pragmatic skills which can be gained through formal learning and experience. And experience is a good teacher. At various points in the arts management subject I teach, I ask students to reflect on their positive and negative work experiences about, for example, the leaders and managers they've had or the elements of the environment that have motivated or depressed them. After getting the resulting key words on the whiteboard, I suggest that they take a photograph of them: because that should be the document that accompanies them into their employment future. People know from their own experience what makes a good leader, what motivates them, what a good cultural climate feels like, the results of working in an effective team. And equally they know what's wrong and what doesn't work.

A word that has permeated the world of recruitment and training is "competency". Behind this notion is the idea that skills have to be effectively applied and so behaviour and capacity are also part of knowledge building. Leicester (2007, 15) quotes from an OECD essay *Competencies for the Good Life and the Good Society* about four constellations of competencies for the 21st century:

- Perceptive competencies – able to see the wood from the trees, common sense
- Normative competencies – ability to tell right from wrong
- Cooperative competences – ability to work with others, empathy, trust
- Narrative competencies – ability to make sense of what happens in life.

Plus, he adds the capacity to handle higher levels of complexity and uncertainty than we've been used to. Leicester (2007, 3) says that this tolerance for "unknowing" can only be developed through experience.

Pfeffer and Sutton (2006, 52) say that wisdom means

> striking a balance between arrogance (assuming you know more than you do) and insecurity (believing that you know too little to act). This attitude enables people to act on their present knowledge while doubting what they know. It means they can do things now, as well as keep learning along the way.

To help develop such wisdom, they recommend joining communities of smart people rather than just relying on limited knowledge built on old ideas.

Knowing what you don't know is also an important management quality. Amanda Sinclair (2004, 15), a wonderful writer on leadership, gives the example of Christine Nixon, the first woman to lead a large police force in Australia. Apparently when asked in her job interview by the Premier of Victoria what her vision for the police was, she answered that she didn't know and that she would have to talk to police members, the community

and other stakeholders first. Volunteering that she didn't have the answer to the inevitable vision question is an example of her integrity.

One of the wrap-up statements to my arts management students is to tell them to keep learning because that's the way to build knowledge and wisdom. But one of the other statements is to be sceptical. Read the most recent theories about management but don't just accept them. Think about the research on which the conclusions are based and the context in which it was done (Grey 2005). But here's an even larger point to consider – learning isn't always "benign and beneficial" (Langley 2010, 66). Think of all those little boys learning to hate in all those madrasas; the cultural revolution students in China taught to hate their parents; Australian kids not taught well or enough about the country's First People. This doesn't mean that all management training is fraught but rather it's a useful reminder about context. For example, what you learn about unions won't be the same if the course is presented by a union or an employer's association, an academic from the history department or a business school.

Sometimes our knowledge, if it's the kind based only on rational, logical, linear processes, will constrain us rather than enlighten us (Godfrey 2010). We need to add to self-knowledge about what and how to learn into the mix. And there's another element required as we build our knowledge. Once upon a time I was in a student production of Shakespeare's *The Merchant of Venice*. I played Nerissa, maid and companion to Portia, and early on in the play[1] I said these lines:

> *If to do were as easy as to know what were good to do, chapels had been churches, and poor men's cottages princes' palaces. It is a good divine that follows his own instructions. I can easier teach twenty what were good to be done than be one of the twenty to follow mine own teaching.*

It's a reminder that as arts managers we have to work at acquiring knowledge and then learn how to apply it. As one of the proverbs says "knowledge without practice makes half an artist" (Fergusson & Law 2000, 102).

See also: Decision-making, Humility, Mindfulness, Leadership, Learning, Uncertainty

References

Clancy, P. 1997 "Skills and Competencies: The Cultural Manager", in Fitzgibbon, M. & Kelly, A. (eds) *From Maestro to Manager*, Dublin: Oak Tree Press, 341–366.

Fergusson, R. & Law, J. 2000 *Dictionary of Proverbs*, London: Penguin Reference.

Godfrey, C. 2010 "Working with Uncertainty", in Kay, S. & Venner, K. (eds) *A Cultural Leader's Handbook*, London: Creative Choices, 78–85.

Grey, C. 2005 *A Very Short, Fairly Interesting and Reasonably Cheap Book about Studying Organisations*, London: Sage Publications.

Langley, D. 2010 "Leadership Development: A Critical Question", Kay, S. & Venner, K. (eds) *A Cultural Leader's Handbook*, London: Creative Choices, 64–70.

Leicester, G. 2007 *Rising to the Occasion*, International Futures Forum, March.

Pfeffer, J. & Sutton, R. I. 2006 *Hard Facts, Dangerous Half-Truths, and Total Nonsense*, Boston, MA: Harvard Business School Press.

Sinclair, A. 2004 "Journey around Leadership", *Discourse: Studies in the Cultural Politics of Education*, 25(1), 8–19.

Sommerton, J. 2010 "The Place of Practical Wisdom in Cultural Leadership Development", in Kay, S. & Venner, K. (eds) *A Cultural Leader's Handbook*, London: Creative Choices, 114–119.

Note

1 Act 1, Scene 2.

L

Laughter

A volunteer once asked for an appointment to speak to me and her demeanour was so serious that I thought she was going to leave us. But her story was much more of a shock. She wanted to tell me that in all her working life until now, she hadn't been in an organisation where laughter was the norm – as it was at MTC – and how much pleasure she was getting out of the experience. I find it hard to imagine a workplace without laughter. Admittedly, I have often worked for organisations which manufacture comedy as part of their output but that doesn't guarantee laughter off stage.

In a *Harvard Business Review* article, Beard (2014, 130) says that workplaces need laughter: "Laughter relieves stress and boredom, boosts engagement and well-being, and spurs not only creativity and collaboration but also analytic precision and productivity." Research on care-focused service non-profits in Great Britain also provides examples of what makes employment experiences positive amongst the stress of such work. When asked why an employee loved her organisation, it was because of the laugher. "For her, employee satisfaction manifests itself in the fact that they work and play well together. The staff has fun" (Lewis & Plas 2001, 68).

Even the UK Department of Trade and Industry in a survey exploring the influence of inspirational leaders focused on the importance of fun:

> Employees are able to have fun at work and the importance of a light-hearted attitude is paramount. Business is seldom effective when everything is taken excessively seriously, and employees who work in a relaxed, more fun-filled environment are less stressed and more productive.
>
> (Quoted in Adams 2007, 226)

There are pragmatic ways to engender happiness according to researchers. For example, Cropanzano and Wright (2001) believe that because it's such a subjective state, as long you're providing people with a sense that their work is meaningful, that they're supported and that their work makes a difference, then you've at least contributed some of the precursors to happiness. Of course, those researchers were interested in exploring whether happiness at work results in more productivity. As a manager, one does want people to be more motivated and thus contribute to the needs of the organisation, but it's also just nicer to work with people who are happy. I've even found an organisation that lists laughter as part of their way of working. In their manifesto, the non-profit service organisation Our Community Group states that they believe laughter is good (Our Community Group, n.d.).

In a discussion with a successful and caring arts manager, they talked with pride about the good organisational culture they'd help create. To do this, the organisation had a staff workshop and simply asked what would make for a happy workplace. The answers were wonderfully pragmatic and included things like making sure that time accrued was taken off, regular as well as annual performance appraisals, giving everyone a pay increase (even if it was modest), promising and trying to deliver honesty and transparency and good HR practices. Laughter wasn't on the list but I'm sure it was another organisation where it could be heard.

If happiness can be generated by good work practices and organisational culture, what is the actual role of humour in the workplace? First, it depends on what sort. Some research has concluded that liberating humour and controlling humour relate significantly to organisational creativity, the former positively and the latter negatively, while stress-relieving humour was not found to relate significantly to such creativity (Lang & Lee 2010). The researchers defined the different sorts of humour as:

- Liberating humour: facilitates the freeing of old mindsets and the seeing of things in a new light
- Stress-relieving humour: helps to ameliorate tension and reduce stress in the workplace
- Controlling humor: acts as veiled commands or reprimands, exerting subtle control over the behavior of others (Lang & Lee 2010, 47).

The most surprising part of their research results is that stress-relieving humour doesn't contribute to creativity – but as it contributes to stress relief *per se*, that's an asset in itself.

Beard (2014, 171) says that self-depreciating stories shared between peers, light teasing among long-time colleagues and even privately poking fun at outsiders who prompt the same reaction from the team are all acceptable. I would add as long as those "outsiders" haven't been set up because of issues around gender, sexual orientation or cultural background. I worked with a person who had what I can only describe as a wicked sense of humour. It was particular, accurate, occasionally vulgar, but it was never a controlling humour. His intention was always to lift the mood and create bonds. And they are just a couple of the roles that humour can play. It can also release latent tensions, mirror shared values and beliefs, function as a social lubricant, be an acceptable way to raise sensitive issues, reveal new perspectives and help people cope in stressful situations through being a channel for expressing fears and anxieties (Lang & Lee 2010; Sarros et al. 2006).

Of course, humour is a classic device to create distance (laugher at someone else's expense) and forms of teasing can cover up bad behaviour ("lighten up, I'm just kidding") or lead to bullying. But it also draws people together. Humour "integrates, expresses scepticism, contributes to flexibility and adaptiveness, and lessens status differences … establishes solidarity and facilitates face saving" (Bolman & Deal 2013, 263). As Sarros et al. (2006, 22) say: "good leaders are good communicators and understand the management of meaning; the use of appropriate situational humour is an important tactic". There's also evidence that effective leaders, particularly transformational ones, use humour in a positive way. "Possessing a sense of humor is the essence of knowing oneself and sharing one's authentic self, transparently, with followers" (Hughes 2005, 95). And if one uses humour directed at oneself, one may be seen as more approachable and thus promote relaxation and openness in the person listening to you (Craumer 2013).

I have to confess that I'm not a great joke teller. My humour is better expressed through storytelling. I still blush with shame at telling a gender-related joke at work and being pulled aside by one of the young men in the team to say that he felt excluded from the group because of its content. So I'm not sure I'd ever be brave enough to recommend particular forms of humour to use in the workplace but I do recommend finding ways of sharing laughter.

To quote Ekvall (1996, 99): "Those who were more playful and who worked in climates in which humor and light mood were fostered were also more innovative." We work in organisations that should be creative and innovative and we need to do everything in our power to see that they are. As A. C. Grayling, philosopher and playwright, says in *The Good Book*:

Laughter is sunshine in a house.

See also: Job Satisfaction, Leadership, Motivation, Organisational Culture

References

Adams, J. 2007 *Managing People in Organizations: Contemporary Theory and Practice*, Basingstoke: Palgrave Macmillan.

Beard, A. 2014 "Leading with Humor", *Harvard Business Review*, 92(5), 130–131.

Bolman, L. G. & Deal, T. E. 2013 *Reframing Organizations* (5th ed), San Francisco, CA: Jossey-Bass.

Craumer, M. 2013 "When the Direct Approach Backfires, Try Indirect Influence", in Hill, L. A. & Lineback, K. (eds) "Managing your Boss" in *HBR Guide to Managing Up and Across*, Boston, MA: Harvard Business Review Press, 185–188.

Cropanzano, R. & Wright, T. A. 2001 "When a 'Happy' Worker is Really a 'Productive Worker': A Review and Further Refinement of the Happy-productive Worker Thesis", *Consulting Psychology Journal: Practice & Research*, 53(3), 182–199.

Ekvall, G. 1996 "Organizational Climate for Creativity and Innovation", *European Journal of Work and Organizational Psychology*, 5, 105–123.

Grayling, A. C. 2011 *The Good Book*, London: Bloomsbury.

Hughes, L. W. 2005 "Developing Transparent Relationships through Humour in the Authentic Leader-follower Relationship", *Authentic Leadership Theory and Practice: Origins, Effects and Development, Monographs in Leadership and Management*, 3, 83–106.

Lang, C. & Lee, C. H. 2010 "Workplace Humor and Organizational Creativity", *The International Journal of Human Resource Management*, 21(1), 46–60.

Our Community Group n.d. "Our Community Manifesto", www.ourcommunity.com.au/ [accessed 27 February 2019].

Plas, J. M. & Lewis, S. E. 2001 *Person-Centered Leadership of Nonprofit Organizations*, Thousand Oaks, CA: Sage Publications.

Sarros, J., Cooper, B. K., Hartican, A. M. & Barker, C. J. 2006 *The Character of Leadership*, Milton, QLD: John Wiley & Sons.

Leadership

Introduction

Thousands of research articles have been written about leadership along with self-help books, biographies and textbooks but I rarely recognise myself in any of them.

It's a world full of "ors". Are leaders born or made? Is it a role or a process? Is it about behaviour or skills? Should one be a hero or a servant? Who's better, the charismatic leader or the relational leader? Do you need one style or many? Is it about you or is it about the people who follow you? Should the focus be on people or tasks?

There is an endless array of definitions of leadership and most current writers give a few and then give up. The standard definition usually refers to getting things done through other people. A leader has to have a follower; a follower has to accept or believe in the leader; the leader has to encourage/facilitate/direct people to achieve some sort of goal. As someone once said, the leader's job is to get the job done. Hewison and Holden (2011, 24) define leaders as "people who know where they want an organization to go, who can communicate that vision to other people, and who are able to influence others to help them fulfil that vision".

An Australian Artistic/Festival Director Wesley Enoch (2014, 10) says that the qualities of effective business leadership are "listening, offering guidance, collaboration, building personal ownership and pride while driving to deadlines, creating outcomes and being efficient". He then goes on to say: "God knows that making art has these elements in spades and leadership in the arts is more than our cousins in the business sector will ever have to deal with."

Managers or Leaders?

We'll explore all the "or" questions but let's start with the one that puzzles me the most. Are you a manager or a leader? None of us have "leader" in our title but all of us "lead" teams or organisations. Or do we? Are some of us doomed to be "just" managers?

In discussing the difference between management and leadership, Rowe and Dato-on (2013, 88) say:

> Leaders … are described as those who are more visionary about the organization's future, emphasizing direction (instead of planning), organizational change (instead of custom), inspiration, and risk taking (instead of careful and prudent adherence to normative routines). In that vein, leadership is more reliant on purpose, vision and mission, while management relies on short-term objectives, efficiency and control.

Another pair of writers, Plas and Lewis (2001), make a similar point saying that leaders are about vision and inspiration and managers are about the pragmatics of planning and guiding an organisation towards achieving its goals. They conclude that "a leader quite possibly does not need to necessarily manage, and a manager does not necessarily need to lead" (23). This does make some sense in the world of arts co-leadership models where the artist creates the vision and then disappears into the studio or the rehearsal room to make the art, leaving the business in the hands of a manager. However, given Hewison and Holden's definition of leadership, arts managers working with or even for an Artistic CEO, who is usually the person perceived by the outside world to be the "leader", can be a leader too.

Are you a manager of a leader? Odds are you will be both but maybe at different times. Dym, Egmont and Watkins (2011) argue that as someone is moving up through an organisation they are developing management skills such as budgeting and planning, but when they become

a CEO, they will have to focus on the future and therefore use visionary skills to manage change and evolve the organisation. The roles can also shift on a daily basis as well. Whatever one's role, leadership will occur when one is in the process of developing new visions and goals and management is the process when they are being implemented (Plas & Lewis 2001). So while the Artistic Director might be providing the artistic vision for the company, the Managing Director will be providing vision and inspiration to the marketing or development or financial teams.

Adair (2005, 62) claims that leadership is "added value" to management, describing leadership is an "art form" and management as a "science". In another attempt to differentiate between management and leadership, Caust (2005, 154) quotes Daft (1999) who proposed that "[w]here as management calls for keeping an eye on the bottom line and short-term results, leadership means keeping an eye on the horizon and the long-term future". If this definition is correct then arts managers, in my experience, are leaders as well.

Bolman and Deal (2013, 345) quote Gardner's (1989) argument that one shouldn't spend too much time contrasting leadership with management because "leaders may end up looking like a cross between Napoleon and the Pied Piper, and managers like unimaginative clods". Adirondack (2005, 35) is slightly more polite but still makes the same point:

> A manager without leadership qualities might get work done efficiently, but the organisation and the individuals within it are likely to become stagnant. A leader without managerial skills might inspire a loyal following or generate brilliant new ideas, but may create an organisation that doesn't achieve agreed outcomes or is too dependent on the leader.

Mintzberg (1989) proposes a number of roles for the person in charge or an organisation or a major subunit, regardless of what their title is. He collects the roles under three headings:

- Interpersonal: figurehead (with a ceremonial character); leader, (responsible for people and work); liaison (contacts outside the direct hierarchy)
- Informational: monitor (scanning the environment); disseminator (sharing information with others); spokesperson (to the world outside the unit)
- Decisional: entrepreneurial (harmonize the organisation with its environment); disturbance handlers (reacting to external pressures); resource allocator (of work, time, money etc.); negotiator (to obtain results) (Hagoort 2005, 196).

In other words, he used "leadership" as just one aspect of what a "'manager" does. I think the argument about what makes a leader and what makes a manager is rather academic. Sure, being a leader does sound more "sexy" than being a manager (Alvesson & Spicer 2016, 116), but as the CEO of an organisation or the leader/manager of a team, you have to have the capacity to think about the future as well as the present and apply skills to organise people as well as to motivate them. You have to be both manager and leader.

Born or Made?

In my arts management class, I use a particularly Melbourne example to illustrate a point about leadership. The Melbourne Cricket Ground (MCG) is a famous sports field and an iconic institution in Australian life. The members of its Board are by definition leaders in the community. I check the list each year and this is the 2018 list of family names: Bracks, Carson, Chatfield, Costello, Duarte, McKenna, Monteith, Ray.

What will be obvious to Australian and British readers, but not so obvious to those from other countries, is that the majority of those names are Anglo-Celtic. Where are the names of from Australia's 20th-century streams of immigration – from Poland or Latvia, from Italy or Greece, from Vietnam or China? There is a name of Portuguese origin and one that was probably changed to fit into Australia when the person's family moved from Lebanon. But most of the names are "white". It may be that people from other backgrounds don't like sport (Australian Rules football is played at the MCG as well), but the truth is that if you are born white and from British heritage you are more likely to be able to become a leader in contemporary Australia.[1]

I saw another example of the born v. made argument in play when I worked in South Africa. At the beginning of 1994, all the leaders in the South African Broadcasting Corporation were white. By the end of 1994, after the democratic election of the African National Congress, most of the new SABC leaders weren't white. Politics and history determined who was seen to be a "leader".

The more traditional argument is that leadership requires a particular collection of traits and while some of them (e.g. self-confidence) can be developed, the assumption is that a number of them are innate. Dubrin, Dalglish and Miller (2003) group leadership traits into general (trustworthiness, extroversion, assertiveness, emotional stability, self-confidence, high tolerance for frustration, warmth and sense of humour) and task-related (passion, courage, locus of control, flexibility and adaptability).

However, there are arguments for and against these traits and biographies are full of contrary stories. George et al. (2011, 49) interviewed 125 leaders and concluded "people did not identify any universal characteristics, traits, skills, or styles that led to their success". On the topic of introversion versus extraversion, which is often a worry for my quieter students when they read the trait theory of leadership, there is research which shows that introversion can be an effective leadership quality too. For example in Grant, Gino and Hofmann's (2010) study, they conclude that when employees weren't very proactive, extroverted leadership was associated with higher profits but where workers offered ideas and introverted leaders listened and made employees feel valued, the introverts got better results.

Reflecting on personalities, I have seen leaders with all sorts of different traits being effective. I've seen the inspiring speaker and the bumbling one; I've seen the quiet achiever and the charismatic charmer. Putting issues of competence to one side, the only personalities that I can't imagine being good leaders long term or leaders that I would want to work with are the narcissists and the bullies, the people who genuinely don't like or aren't comfortable with others, and people who are fearful of change and challenge.

Davis (2008, 1) says that as children mature, they recognise "natural leaders", someone who emerges from the pack. I was never one of those people – often the last to get picked for teams, never putting myself forward, never someone who was asked to lead. When I was finally asked by my peers to take up a leadership role it was on the basis of my knowledge about the art form and my availability rather than any innate "leadership" qualities. To this day, I still don't know why people suggested it.

Davis (2008, 3) compares the sets of required leadership qualities proposed by a number of writers and only two appear on all three lists: intelligence/cognitive ability and self-confidence. He concludes that "using these traits, we can predict that someone lacking intelligence or self-confidence is unlikely to be a leader" but I would say that I did – and still sometimes do – lack self-confidence so again, I'm not fitting into the trait explanation of why people become leaders.

Sinclair (2007, 57) somewhat cynically notes that the idea people are born leaders doesn't fit in with our democratic and meritocratic ideas and that it undermines every course that attempts to teach leadership. She also makes the pertinent point that childhoods, families and school experiences "shape people's appetites for and vulnerabilities in leadership" (Sinclair 2007, 59). In the end, Davis (2008, 10) concluded "leaders are made not born, but principally by chance and circumstance". McCann (2008) also doesn't believe that leaders are born: "The ability to be a leader is the result of a lifetime of effort constantly improving communication skills, reflecting on personal values and aligning one's behaviour with those values, learning how to listen and appreciate others and their ideas."

So although you don't have to be born with specific traits to be a leader, life's circumstances will have an impact. Bolman and Deal (2013) tell the story of Steve Job's return to Apple in 1997 and make the point that his character hadn't changed. He was still "demanding and charismatic, charming and infuriating, erratic and focused, opinionated and receptive". The difference, they say, was in how he thought, how he interpreted what was going on around him, and how he led. "To his long-time gifts as magician and warrior, he had added newfound capacities as organisational architect and team builder." In other words, regardless of traits, one can still continue to learn and become a better leader.

People or Tasks?

Another way of looking at leaders is whether they focus on managing tasks or managing people. Rowe and Dato-on (2013) discuss the shift from the trait/born/great leader approach to the perspective that compared leaders who had a focus on concern and respect for their followers with those who were focused on structure and roles. Decades of research have basically supported a model in which "the task-oriented leader is more effective in very favorable or very unfavorable situations, while the more interpersonally-oriented leaders are more effective in moderately favorable situations" (Goethals & Hoyt 2011, 113–114). As we're likely to experience all of those conditions, perhaps the best leaders, as Jack Welch, former General Electric believes, are those who work successfully with people and on tasks. He famously differentiated between four types of manager/leaders he'd experienced:

1. The ruthless, who focused on the numbers regardless of the people costs
2. The people managers, who thought people and their needs were infinitely more important than any numbers
3. The incompetent, who achieved neither the financial nor the people goals
4. And then the only managers he wanted to keep: the ones who met the numbers through excellent people leadership (quoted in D'Aprix 2011, 260).

In discussing the task-relationship continuum and the impact of context on leadership style, Norbury (2010) says this has ramifications for cultural leaders because the people we employ care deeply and while elements of what we do is process driven (such as getting a set up on stage or hanging an exhibition), most of what we create isn't and comes from applied endeavour, thought and reflection. In this case, "a leadership style which is based on empathy and understanding and which nurtures individuality (and maybe even eccentricity) is going to be more productive than one driven by the need to 'task and finish'" (52).

One Style or Many?

Another approach to leadership is to describe the styles which people use to lead: participative, sharing decision-making with others; consultative, looking for ideas from others but making the final decision; democratic, letting the group decide; and the more traditional autocratic style. It is argued in what are called contingency theories, that management styles need to be modified depending on the organisational environment. For example, a directive leader will be effective when the task is unclear whereas the supportive leader will be better when people are unsure of themselves. Participative leaders are best suited for improving the morale of well-motivated employees and achievement-oriented leaders work well with achievement-oriented teams (Dubrin, Dalglish & Miller 2006).

Hay/McBer, a consulting firm, propose six basic leadership styles:

- Coercive – do what I tell you
- Authoritative – come with me
- Affiliative – people come first
- Democratic – what do you think?
- Pacesetting – do as I do, now
- Coaching – try this (Rosner & Halcrow 2010, 81).

In my first successful interview for a management position, I was asked about my leadership style. This was before I'd had much chance to put any ideas into practice and was based on what I'd read about leadership in 1980s textbooks. I hadn't found anything in those books that reflected that way I worked and my self-analysis was that I would have an adaptive approach depending on the circumstances, the people and the needs of the organisation. For example, the leadership styles may vary depending on the age and gender makeup of the team to be managed. I learnt this in the process of teaching a group of smart women from countries in Asia and the Pacific who explained about the different approaches they needed to use as leaders in often strongly patriarchal societies. Looking at the Hay/McBer list, I would say that "affiliative" is probably my natural starting point but I'd add "democratic" into the mix and certainly at times of stress and tension, I've adopted the "authoritative" style when one needed to mobilise people toward a vision or a cause.

Rosner and Halcrow (2010, 76) recommend varying your leadership style to get results:

> Good leaders need different styles of leading, demanding and mobilizing, harmonious and consensus-building, driven and developmental. Good leaders know when and why to use each style. One style works best in a crisis, and another helps forge a new vision; one helps heal, and another builds competencies for the long term.

A great example of leadership styles was played out in the political sphere in Australia in the 2010s. Kevin Rudd was an effective leader in opposition but his leadership style didn't work as Prime Minister. In an article by journalist Paul Kelly (2014) about Kevin Rudd,[2] his replacement Julia Gillard is quoted as saying:

> Kevin's operating style was dysfunctional. It was a great pity. Kevin is a highly intelligent man. If you wanted to talk to someone over dinner about the geopolitics of the region for the next 20 years, then you couldn't have a better companion than Kevin Rudd. But Kevin's fatal flaw was that he couldn't

delegate, he couldn't manage his time, he couldn't plan strategically as opposed to plan tactically. Under pressure he was a great prevaricator (15).

Rather than Kevin Rudd's style, I prefer the style of Glinda, the Good Witch, who is the favourite leadership role model of management consultants Rosner and Halcrow (2010):

> Not only did Dorothy get home, but ultimately she figured out how to do it. Along the way she found strength and resourcefulness in herself she had never seen. She learned from her mistakes. She aced challenges with courage, and relied on friends for support. Yes, Glinda got results, but she was no micromanager. She simply pointed Dorothy in the right direction ("Follow the Yellow Brick Road"), gave her the resources she needed (the Ruby slippers) and removed a few obstacles (such as the Wicked Witch of the West's sleeping spell) when it was judicious to do so (83).

Character or Skill?

In the section on *Knowledge* there's a list of skills that arts managers think are required to do the job well and you'll find similar sets in any textbook on leadership. But learning how to coach or plan, to run meetings or assess performance, to inspire followers or motivate staff is only one part of the leadership story. Such skills can be used to dark as well as light effect.

Longstaff (2014) says that the requirements for leaders are personal in character. He believes that an effective leader is also an ethical leader who requires:

- a well-formed (and informed) conscience
- a well-formed (and informed) intuition
- the virtues of moral courage and humility
- respect for the intrinsic dignity of others
- a capacity for discernment (including strategic vision and empathy)

- a capacity to project and maintain the ethical tone of an organisation, even under conditions of extreme stress
- the ability to identify new opportunities
- the willingness and capacity to challenge "unthinking custom and practice".

Bakke (2005, 133) takes a similar view. He believes that a leader's character is more important than their skills. His view is that leaders don't have to be visionaries or strategists or even good communicators. The first two can be done by others, he says, and good communication won't serve you if one's character isn't good. Bakke's preferred character traits for leaders are humility; the willingness to give up power; courage; integrity; and love and passion for the people, values and mission of the organisation.

Transactional or Transformational?

Transaction and transformation are a set of leadership descriptors amongst the most currently discussed although they seem to me to be simply a more sophisticated take on the people versus tasks approach. Based on the work of Bass and Avolio (2000), the styles can be defined as:

- Transactional leader: motivates people to perform tasks and achieve stated objectives
- Transformational leader: motivates and inspires people to go beyond their normal work behaviour.

The idea is that transformational leaders transform their subordinates in such a way that motivation (and therefore presumably productivity) is increased. They do this through

> a combination of ascribed charisma, inspirational motivation, intellectual stimulation, and individual consideration, motivating individuals to do more than they initially expected they could do, and raising their awareness of the signification of a given

outcome (such as the long-term success of their organization).

(Adams 2007, 211)

On the other hand, transactional leaders are seen as less attractive and from Adam's perspective transactional leadership is simply a more exalted way of describing management rather than actual leadership, with a focus on getting the most out of staff in terms of productivity rather than developing them.

Given that transformational leadership is seen as better than transactional leadership, people can get worried that they don't have the charisma or the charm or the inspirational skills to become transformational leaders and that therefore by definition, they can't be a good leader. I think that the job of leading arts organisations is much more complex than simply inspiring greater motivation in people and there is evidence that transformational leaders don't necessarily lead to innovation in non-profit organisations (Howell & Avolio 1993, quoted in Rowold & Rohmann 2009). Rowold and Rohmann also found that both transactional and transformational leadership contribute to positive emotions and reduce negative emotions in the non-profit arts organisation they examined. But more to the point, they couldn't prove their hypothesis that positive emotions contribute to performance; only the opposite, where negative emotions can undermine or lessen performance.

Rowe and Dato-on (2013, 89) have a different view and believe that transformational leaders are effective in non-profit organisations because of "the leader's ability to convince followers – both formally and informally – to see their own goals as consistent with those of the organisation". But in my view, this attribute is usually not a high priority task for arts leaders. People usually choose to work for arts and cultural organisations *because* they share their goals to start with.

Interestingly, the transformational theory was developed, in part, from research on prominent political leaders (Rowe and Dato-on 2013) and this could be the reason that I'm not entirely

comfortable about its application in the non-profit world. I prefer the Bakke (2005) approach – that by facilitating people's capacities to make decisions and control their destiny, they'll make good decisions for the organisation rather than being "led" to do so.

Heroic or Servant?

The traditional leader has been seen as the hero, out front, alone, decisive, action-oriented and through his (sic) own special unique genius, saving the world. But as many contemporary leadership writers say, leadership isn't an individual pursuit. It's about relationships, doing things together. "Among the thousands of books written on the meaning of leadership, there is grudging agreement that leadership is a process of influence between leaders and followers" (Sinclair 2007, xvi).

Even though we have people in our industry called conductors and directors who seem to fit the heroic model, Wadman and Kolping (2009, 32) remind us that's it not quite true:

> A conductor can't unilaterally decide how an orchestra will sound – the interpretation of a musical piece is a shared process; it's a group idea that develops in the interaction between the conductor and the orchestra members. Similarly, the script and the intentions of the director notwithstanding, the film team has to rely on improvisational processes, where the action and decision-making take place while the team is searching for a means of expression.

Mintzberg (2009, 2) suggests that it's time to wean ourselves off the heroic leader "and recognize that usually we need *just enough leadership* – leadership that intervenes when appropriate while encouraging people in the organization to get on with things". Dalglish and Miller (2011, iv) say that followers are the leader's strength because it's the hard work of non-leaders that turns a profit or enables goals to be reached, but Enoch (2014, 15) doesn't like the language of "followers" saying that "it makes leadership a kind of popular fashion". Dalglish and Miller (2011, 4) quote a leader in a case study who is also ambivalent about the word:

> Karen doesn't like the term "followers", and does not think of others in this way. She leads people by showing them what she expects and setting an example for them. No-one is seen as being below or above her. Karen sees her role as supporting those who run the day-to-day operations of the business. She sets the direction and the targets, and then monitors the progress of the whole organisation. Karen sees it has her responsibility to align the values, goals and ideas of the staff with solid business goals.

Regardless of whether "follower" is the right word, leadership is a relational practice and there has to be a high degree of mutuality and goodwill between the parties for a leader to be effective. Because it's essentially about relationships, Parker (2010, 108) reminds us that in the process of cultivating and nurturing relationships and sharing and exchanging knowledge and ideas, leaders have to be willing to be changed in the process, "to learn from others and from personal experience".

In 1977 Robert Greenleaf created a description of leadership that has particular resonance with the non-profit world: servant leadership. He started with the idea that leaders should put service before self-interest. In practice, this translates into the following practices:

1. Listening – capturing and refining the will of the group plus self-reflection
2. Empathy – being sensitive to what is unique in others
3. Healing – helping people solve problems and relationship conflicts
4. Awareness – staying in touch with what is going on with others and with one's self, getting better understanding of ethics and values in the process

5. Persuasion – relying on convincing arguments rather than coercion to build consensus
6. Conceptualization – thinking beyond present needs, with the capacity to create a long-term vision
7. Foresight – ability to anticipate the likely consequences of decisions
8. Stewardship – holding the institution in trust for the greater good of society with an obligation to help and serve others
9. Commitment to the growth of people – because they have intrinsic value beyond their contributions as workers
10. Building community both within the organisation and amongst other institutions (Golensky 2011; Spears 1995).

Bakke (2005, 133) says that servant leadership isn't about being passive or hands off. "Good servant leaders are engaged in every aspect of an organization's life, from suggesting radical new ideas and strategies to teaching the organization's principles and values." However, rather than directing people what to do, in the servant leader paradigm the leader encourages and coaches. The servant leader role has two important elements – the leadership component (which involves creating and communication the vision) and the implementation component (which is about helping people achieve their goals) (Daglish & Miller 2011). Norbury (2010) describes the servant leader as the nurturer of relationships but regardless of whether one is a servant leader or another sort of leader such as a transformational or transactional one, the process of leadership is about collaborative relationships and collective actions which in the best situation are grounded in shared values (Inglis & Cray 2011).

Research indicates that there are both obvious differences and less obvious similarities between leaders from different cultural backgrounds. In a project that's been going on for over 25 years, academics have been exploring different leadership styles in different countries. To date, they have concluded that out of six leadership styles – charismatic/value-based, team-oriented, participative, humane, self-protective and autonomous – the first two are seen to contribute to outstanding leadership in all cultures (Globe Foundation 2014). In another example, a survey of leadership in Indonesia and Australia, Pekerti and Sendjaya (2010) found that notwithstanding the egalitarian culture of Australia and the paternalistic culture of Indonesia, self-sacrificial leaders who put other people's needs over and above those of their own are perceived to be effective leaders in both countries. Travelling to work in another country will require you to consider what the most effective leadership styles might be in the new culture, but clearly core leadership capacities such as team building and nurturing are always going to be valued.

Authentic or Not (Always)?

Earlier in this book, there is a discussion about a current popular leadership theory, *Authenticity*. In summary Walumbwa et al. (2008) present four components of authenticity:

- self-awareness
- balanced processing of information
- relational transparency and
- internalised moral perspective.

In an article about authentic leadership, the authors say that there have been more than 1,000 studies trying to determine definitive styles of leadership. They conclude, first, that the research has failed and, second, it's good that that it has failed because you can't be authentic trying to copy someone else (George et al. 2011). However, people still clearly value the qualities of "authenticity". Words such as self-awareness and the importance of honest and respectful relations came up time and time again in the research that I did with Kate MacNeill and Sarah Reynolds on co-leadership in the performing arts (2012).

Nicholass and Erakovich (2013, 183) propose the following definition of authentic

leaders: "they know themselves, what they value and believe, and they operate based upon those beliefs and values". Of course, the assumption is that their values are good ones but one can equally see people like Hitler and Stalin being described in these terms.

An interesting insight comes from Ibarra (2015) who looks at the paradox implicit in this desire to be authentic. What happens when, in the process of being transparent, people are disconcerted by your honesty or confused by your confession that you don't know everything? Ibarra suggests that authenticity can sometimes get in the way of effective management and Sinclair (2007) has raised similar points. For example, when one is being true to oneself, which self? Not only do we have different selves as we play different roles in our communities, but we also change over time. What if your self is uncertain and unclear at a particular time? Another example is the coherence between what you feel and what you say and do. Sometimes, you have to control your emotions and not say what you're feeling out loud. Ibarra (2015, 56) quotes a manager who experienced difficulties when she was transparent to staff: "Being authentic doesn't mean that you can be held up to the light and people can see right through you." The challenge is to manage the tension between authority and approachability, both qualities that are required by leaders (Ibarra 2015).

What Do Employees Want from Leaders?

As an assignment in my arts management course, I sometimes ask students to review the qualities and actions of a leader they had worked for. The idea is for them to examine various theories about leadership, see which one/s help make sense of their leader and to discuss what the takeaway lessons might be for them as future leaders. A recent group who did the assignment consisted of 25 students from six countries (although just over half were Australian). Their work experience ranged from being interns or working in casual jobs as students through to middle management. Their industries included fashion and food, publishing and museums, cultural centres and art galleries. Obviously this is not a scientific study, but there were some interesting insights from their analysis.

For example, in every story where there was charismatic founder or CEO, there was also a need for someone to look after the processes or the detail or the planning or the execution. While people generally loved working with such leaders, there was an equal awareness of their weaknesses and a desire for more order and more structure. In most stories where participatory leadership was valued, there was also a desire that the same leader should be authoritative when required, such as in a crisis. One could say that I was dealing with highly educated people who have different needs as employees to those who might work in more prosaic jobs or in more regulated workplaces but consistent in all the stories was their desire to be nurtured, encouraged, supported, motivated and inspired.

In a report by the UK Department of Trade and Industry called *Inspirational Leadership* (2004), which explores the influence of such leaders, employees report feeling listened to, involved, able to have fun at work, trusted, appreciated, valued – and valuing themselves, their workmates and their customers as well (quoted in Adams 2007, 225–226). In a 2007 survey about the most important characteristics of admired leaders by Kouzes and Posner (2007), the top five qualities were:

- Honest 89%
- Forward-looking 71%
- Inspiring 69%
- Competent 68%
- Intelligent 48%

What I find most informative about this list is that "competent" and "inspiring" are almost equal, that is, employees want a manager *and* a leader. Other valued qualities in order were being fair-minded, straightforward, broad-minded, supportive, dependable, cooperative, courageous, determined, caring, loyal, imaginative, ambitious, mature, self-controlled and independent.

What Effect Do Leaders Have?

There's irony implicit in any conversation about leadership because some writers say that leaders actually don't make much difference at all. Pfeffer and Sutton (2006) claim that leaders may make only a small difference in how well a company does for a range of reasons such as having to operate within existing constraints that aren't easy to change (e.g. existing people, products, markets, general economic conditions) and because people who get leadership positions tend to be similar to each other so there isn't much difference when leaders change. Moss, Callanan and Wilson (2010) also agree that leaders don't have as much impact as we might imagine. This is because we overestimate the contribution of leaders, we discount the impact of external forces and we overestimate the merit of such traits as charisma and confidence. Because everyone expects leaders to matter a lot, they act as if they are in control and in the process can sometimes believe that they actually are. Pfeffer and Sutton (2006, 200) suggest that leaders can avoid this trap with "an attitude of wisdom and healthy dose of modesty". They also suggest that "effective leaders must learn when and how to get out of the way and let others make contributions. So sometimes the best leadership is no leadership at all."

However, whether leaders have an impact on the output of the company, they certainly have an impact on the people inside it. There is research which demonstrates that 60–75% of employees in any organisation report that the most stressful part of their job is their boss – and so abusive and incompetent management can create billions of dollars of lost productivity (Pfeffer & Sutton 2006).

In the arts world, the short-term[3] effect of artistic leaders is usually very easy to see very quickly. Does the show work? Does the audience come? Do the critics agree? On the other hand, a poor Managing Director can disguise their weaknesses (at least for a while) in an organisation when the art is delivering the goods.

Organisations with dual leadership have an in-built checking mechanism because if one of the team isn't working, then at least a peer is in a position to "call out" the problem.

Bad Leaders

Because the idea of being an effective leader is so fluid and that there is no one set of traits or qualities or experiences that can guarantee a good leader, I'm interested in what makes a bad leader. If I can advise students how to avoid such behaviour they may find their way to be a good leader. In a foreword to a book on the character of leadership, Hendrix (quoted in Sarros et al. 2006, ix) says:

> when one looks at the failures of leaders, they are not usually due to lack of leadership skills and behaviours: most often they are due to character-related issues. Look at the news. Executives who lose their jobs are frequently dismissed because of theft, embezzlement, insider trading, sexual harassment or other behaviours of poor character.

Life's too short to be bullied or mismanaged or undermined. I've left organisations because of bad leaders. What makes leaders "bad" in my view is usually related to qualities such as self-obsession, insecurity, incompetence, incapacity to listen (and learn) and arrogance. There are people who yell, who want the limelight, who never thank you, who claim credit for your work, who are misogynist and who can't be trusted. They might be smart; they might be good at managing stakeholders; but eventually, they'll poison an organisation.

Bolman and Deal's (2013) examples of ineffective leaders are:

- Petty bureaucrats who manage by detail
- Tyrants who manage by fiat
- Weaklings who simply abdicate
- Con artists who work through manipulation and fraud
- Fanatics and charlatans who use smoke and mirrors.

Bunting (2016, 101), a consultant and writer on leadership and mindfulness, says that he has met too many leaders who act out of either "fear-based niceness or with a heartless 'professional' aggression". I recognise elements of my behaviour in the "nice" leader who might be so fearful of disapproval or not being liked that they end up tolerating things they shouldn't.

Holden and Hewison (2011) have an interesting section in their book on the dark side of cultural leadership. For example, because cultural work is neither reliable nor predictable, the transactional leader may focus too much on tasks and not enough on trust. The transformational leader may turn out to be a narcissist who doesn't listen to people and can't be bothered with the details. The relational leader may worry too much about relationships and not about the productivity of the organisation.

A story about poor cultural leadership played out in the Australia media in 2018. The Managing Director of the Australian Broadcasting Corporation Michelle Guthrie was sacked by the Board and shortly afterwards, the Board Chair Justin Milne resigned. One of the reasons offered by Milne for Guthrie's sacking was the result of a leadership skills survey of her staff: "Her score for parameters such as arrogance, autocracy, criticism and distance were in the 90th percentile (above 90%). Her score for integrity was only in the fourth percentile, meaning only 4% of those questioned scored below her" (Meade 2018). I have to say that if I'd received such scores I would have resigned instantly and found myself a mentor or a coach.

Kellerman's typology of bad leadership (quoted in Erickson, Shaw & Agabe 2007, 28) is:

1. Incompetent – lacking the will or skill to sustain effective action
2. Rigid: unwilling to adapt to change
3. Intemperate: lacking self-control with followers who are unwilling to intervene
4. Callous: uncaring or unkind leaders who ignore or discount the needs and wants of followers

5. Corrupt: who lie, cheat, and/or steal
6. Insular: those who minimise or disregard the welfare of those for whom the leader was not directly responsible
7. Evil: people who commit harm and atrocities, which might be physical, mental, or both.

And if that list wasn't depressing enough, the result of Erickson, Shaw and Agabe's (2007) survey about what people thought of their leaders was the mean of good leaders that participants had experienced was only 24.2% compared to 37.6% average leaders and 37.4% bad leaders. And to add insult to injury, only 23% of the bad leaders were forced out with 45% of them promoted and nothing happening to the rest. The actions that caused someone to be classified as "bad" was (in order) unable to deal effectively with subordinates, poor personal behaviour, poor ethics/integrity, poor interpersonal behaviour, excessive political behaviour, poor at communication, lack of strategic skills, inconsistent/erratic behaviour, inability to use technology, micromanagement and autocratic behaviour.

The response of staff to these leaders was emotional – words such as angry, frustrated, lowered self-esteem, embarrassed, feeling helpless, confused. The impact of such leaders included motivational loss, decrease in performance, increased stress and negative effects on home life. As well as the impact on individuals, there was also the impact on the organisation such as increased turnover, performance loss and a bad organisational culture. Other interesting insights from this research covered gender (not much difference with a fairly universal perception of bad leaders) and examples of positive behaviours such as "walking the talk", recognising employees as people and understanding their strengths and weaknesses. Employees have their own theories about effective leadership and laziness, absence, indecision, taking the credit for the work of others, scapegoating and harassment aren't part it.

Autry (2001, 20–21) offers a list of what we should avoid:

- Leadership is not about controlling people, it's about caring for people and being a useful resource for people
- Leadership is not about being boss; it's about being present for people and building a community at work
- Leadership is not about holding on to territory; it's about letting go of ego, bringing your spirit to work, being your best and most authentic self
- Leadership is less concerned with pep talks and more concerned with creating a place in which people can do good work, can find meaning in their work, and can bring their spirits to work.

It's also not doing what a lot of managers Alvesson and Spicer (2016, 122) have come across: people having coffee with subordinates, engaging in small talk and being respectful and thinking that they were "doing" leadership.

While some of the qualities and behaviours on the list of bad leaders can be fixed through individual training and development, some of it may be created accidentally or deliberately by the places where they work. People with great operational skills but without leadership skills required for the next rung of the hierarchy may be promoted. This is a common phenomenon, for example, within universities where academics are promoted to run departments and not provided with adequate training to help them in their new role. People often have to work under excessive pressure in under-resourced organisations which can lead to displays of inappropriate behaviour. The challenge is to pick up on bad leadership early and whether it's through training, mentoring, coaching or firing, solve the problem.

What Do [Good] Leaders Do?

As I've been writing this section, I have been reading a Swedish detective story (as I often do for relaxation) and there was a quote about leadership, a reminder that the qualities of effective leadership aren't hard to pinpoint. It's just the practice that seems to be the challenge.

Linn Magnuson was stressed. She was stuck in a traffic jam on her way in from Stocksund. In less than half an hour she'd be standing on the podium at the Swedish Association of Local Authorities and Regions to talk about "Good leadership" in front of a large number of intermediate managers from all over the country. Luckily she knew exactly what she would talk about. Clarity, communication, and dealing with relationships.[4]

Sinclair (2007, xix) proposes

> the purpose of leadership should be to liberate. Good leadership aims to support people … to make thoughtful choices about what to do and how to influence … Rather than being used as a means to compel compliance and conformity, to dominate or prescribe, leadership can invite us to imagine, initiate and contest.

She notes that more effort has gone into studies on how to do leadership rather than what leadership is for, but luckily for those of us who work in the world of art and culture, we know what our leadership is for – to ensure that artists have the chance to make work and audiences the chance to experience it.

Yong Kwan Lee, CEO of the Daejeon Culture and Arts Centre in South Korea, reminds us

> leadership of non-profit sectors such as the arts requires much more professional expertise and sensitivity than profit oriented areas. That's because arts sectors need to focus on the missions for art promotion and maximizing the enjoyment of arts and culture by people.
>
> (Quoted in Caust 2015, 156)

Holden and Hewison (2011, 26–27), exploring leadership in the cultural industries, conclude that a leader has to:

- Make sure the organisation knows what its mission is

- Be a figurehead for the organisation as a whole
- Represent the organisation to the Board of Directors
- Represent the organisation to external partners, investors, funders and the rest of the world
- Allocate the organisation's resources, in terms of money, people and time
- Make sure the organisation's structure makes the most of those resources
- Keep an eye on how the organisation is performing – in how it is meeting its mission, and how it is managing its money, people and time
- Make sure all members of the organisation are able to do, and are doing, their best
- Make sure the right people join the organisation – and the people who are not right leave it
- Be able to resolve disputes within the organisation – personal and professional
- Plan the organisation's future.

All of this may be done by leaders with different styles – charismatic or humble, strategic or detail-oriented – as long as the cause is placed above our egos.

Conclusion

The question of what makes a good leader is both complex and straightforward. The straightforward bit is: don't do the things that bad leaders do. The complex bit is that leadership is mixture of qualities and attitudes, traits and behaviours. It's relational – it's all about people. But it's also about vision and getting things done. Authenticity theory tells us that a good leader is someone who is self-aware and genuine, mission-driven and focused on results, who leads with their heart, not just their minds and focuses on the long term. Some other good advice is to be found in a book on the leadership practices of effective non-profit organisations (Crutchfield & Grant 2008, 178). The authors remind us that leadership isn't just about you. Sharing power with your executive team and giving them real authority and accountability will add to the effectiveness of your leadership and therefore your organisation.

The theory that I love most about leadership isn't a 21st-century one. It goes back hundreds of years and describes "the king-becoming graces", that is, the qualities that a person needs to be a good leader:

> As justice, verity, temperance, stableness,
> Bounty, perseverance, mercy, lowliness,
> Devotion, patience, courage, fortitude.
> (William Shakespeare, *Macbeth*, Act IV, 91–94)

See: Arts Leaders, Arts Managers, Authenticity, Co-leadership, Empathy, Humility, Management, Power, Trust

References

Adair, J. 2005 *The Inspirational Leader: How to Motivate, Encourage and Achieve Success*, London: Kogan Page.

Adams, J. 2007 *Managing People in Organizations: Contemporary Theory and Practice*, Basingstoke: Palgrave Macmillan.

Adirondack, S. 2005 *Just About Managing?* (4th ed), London: London Voluntary Service Council.

Alvesson, M. & Spicer, A. 2016 *The Stupidity Paradox*, London: Profile Books.

Autry, J. A. 2001 *The Servant Leader*, New York: Three Rivers Press.

Bakke, D. W. 2005 *Joy at Work*, Seattle: PVG.

Bass, B. & Avolio, B. 2000 *The Multifactor Leadership Questionnaire* (2nd ed), Redwood City, CA: Mind Garden.

Bolman, L. G. & Deal, T. E. 2013 *Reframing Organizations* (5th ed), San Francisco, CA: Jossey-Bass.

Bunting, M. 2016 *The Mindful Leader*, Milton, QLD: Wiley.

Caust, J. 2005 "Does It Matter Who Is In Charge? The Influence of the Business Paradigm on Arts Leadership and Management", *Asia Pacific Journal of Arts and Cultural Management*, 3(1), 153–165.

Caust, J. 2015 "Different Culture but Similar Roles: Leadership of Major Performing Arts Centers", in Caust, J. (ed.) *Arts and Cultural Leadership in Asia*, London: Routledge, 148–162.

Crutchfield, L. R. & Grant, H. M. 2008 "Forces for Good: The Six Practices of High-Impact Nonprofits", San Francisco, CA: Jossey-Bass.

Daft, R. L. 1999 *Leadership Theory and Practice*, Fort Worth, TX: Dryden Press.

Dalglish, P. & Miller, C. 2011 *The Leader In You: Developing Your Leadership Potential*, Melbourne: Tilde University Press.

D'Aprix, R. 2011 "Challenges of Employee Engagement", in Gillis, T. L. (ed.) *The IABC Handbook of Organizational Communication* (2nd ed), San Francisco, CA: Jossey-Bass, 257–269.

Davis, G. 2008 *The Leaders and the Gang: Reflections on Leadership*, Victoria: Leadership Victoria, 5 June.

Dubrin, A. J., Dalglish, C. & Miller, P. 2006 *Leadership* (2nd Asia-Pacific ed), Milton, QLD: John Wiley & Sons.

Dym, B., Egmont, S. & Watkins, L. 2011 *Managing Leadership Transition for Nonprofits*, Upper Saddle River, NJ: Pearson Educational.

Enoch, W. 2014 *Take Me to Your Leader: The Dilemma of Cultural Leadership*, Platform Paper No. 40, Sydney: Currency Press.

Erickson, A., Shaw, J. B. & Agabe, Z. 2007 "An Empirical Investigation of the Antecedents, Behaviors, and Outcomes of Bad Leadership", *Journal of Leadership Studies*, 1(3), 26–43.

Gardner, J. W. 1989 *On Leadership*, New York: Free Press.

George, B., Sims, P., McLean, A. N. & Mayer, D. 2011 "Discovering Your Authentic Leadership", *Harvard Business Review*, 85(2), 129–140.

Globe Foundation 2014, *Globe CEO Study 2014*, https://globeproject.com/study_2014 [accessed 28 February 2019].

Goethals, G. R. & Hoyt, C. L. 2011 "What Makes Leadership Necessary, Possible and Effective: The Psychological Dimensions", in Harvey, M. & Riggio, R. E. (eds) *Leadership Studies – The Dialogue of Disciplines*, Cheltenham: Edgar Elgar Publishing, 101–118.

Golensky, M. 2011 *Strategic Leadership and Management in Nonprofit Organizations*, Chicago, IL: Lyceum Books Inc.

Grant, A. H., Gino, F. & Hofmann, D. A. 2010 "The Hidden Advantages of Quiet Bosses", *Harvard Business Review*, 88(12), 28.

Hagoort, G. 2005 *Art Management: Entrepreneurial Style* (5th ed), Delft: Eburon.

Hendrix, W. H. 2006 "Foreword", in Sarros, J., Cooper, B. K., Hartican, A. M. & Barker, C. J. (eds) *The Character of Leadership*, Milton, QLD: John Wiley & Sons, ix–x.

Hewison, R. & Holden, J. 2011 *The Cultural Leadership Handbook*, Farnham: F Gower.

Howell, J. M. & Avolio, B. J. 1993 "Transformational Leadership, Transactional Leadership, Locus of Control, and Support for Innovation: Key Predictors of Consolidated-Business-Unit Performance", *Journal of Applied Psychology*, 78, 891–902.

Ibarra, H. 2015 "The Authenticity Paradox", *Harvard Business Review*, January–February, 52–59.

Inglis, L. & Cray, D. 2011 "Leadership in Australian Arts Organisations: A Shared Experience?", *Third Sector Review*, 17(2), 107–130.

Kelly, P. 2014 "The Tragedy of Kevin Rudd Can Be Traced to a Personality Flaw", *Weekend Australian*, 23–24 August, www.theaustralian.com.au/opinion/columnists/the-tragedy-of-kevin-rudd-can-be-traced-to-a-personality-flaw/story-e6frg74x-1227033724468 [accessed 30 January 2015].

Kouzes, J. & Posner, B. 2007 *The Leadership Challenge* (4th ed), Hoboken, NJ: Jossey-Bass.

Longstaff, S. 2014 *The Twin Foundations of Leadership*, St James Ethics Centre, Sydney, www.ethics.org.au/on-ethics/our-articles/before-2014/the-twin-foundations-of-leadership [accessed 27 February 2019].

MacNeill, K., Tonks, A. & Reynolds, S. 2012 "Authenticity and the Other", *Journal of Leadership Studies*, 6(3), 6–16.

McCann, J. M. 2008 "Development: Leadership as Creativity", *Arts Management Newsletter*, No. 82.

Meade, A. 2018 "Sacked ABC Boss Michelle Guthrie Was Seen as Arrogant by Colleagues, Inquiry Told", 30 November, www.theguardian.com/media/2018/nov/30/michelle-guthrie-was-pressured-to-reprimand-abc-presenter-jon-faine-inquiry-told [accessed 27 February 2019].

Mintzberg, H. 1989 *Mintzberg on Management*, New York: The Free Press.

Mintzberg, H. 2009 "Rebuilding Companies as Communities", *Harvard Business Review*, July–August.

Moss, S., Callanan, J. & Wilson, S. 2012 *The Moonlight Effect*, Melbourne: Tilde University Press.

Nicholass, T. W. & Erakovich, R. 2013 "Authentic Leadership and Implicit Theory: A Normative Form of Leadership?", *Leadership and Organisational Development Journal*, 24(20), 182–195.

Norbury, C. 2010 "Relationships Are at the Heart of Good Cultural Leadership", in Kay, S. & Venner, S. (eds) *A Cultural Leader's Handbook*, London: Creative Choices, 50–57.

Parker, D. 2010 "The Improvising Leader: Developing Leadership Capacity Through Improvisation", in Kay, S. & Venner, S. (eds) *A Cultural Leader's Handbook*, London: Creative Choices, 106–112.

Pekerti, A. A. & Sendjaya, S. 2010 "Exploring Servant Leadership Across Cultures: Comparative Study in Australia and Indonesia", *The International Journal of Human Resource Management*, 21(5), 754–780.

Pfeffer, J. & Sutton, R. I. 2006 *Hard Facts, Dangerous Half-Truths, and Total Nonsense*, Boston, MA: Harvard Business School Press.

Plas, J. M. & Lewis, S. E. 2001 *Person-centered Leadership of Nonprofit Organizations*, Thousand Oaks, CA: Sage Publications.

Rosner, B. & Halcrow, A. 2010 *The Boss's Survival Guide* (2nd ed), New York: McGraw Hill.

Rowe, W. G. & Dato-on, M. C. (eds) 2013 *Introduction to Nonprofit Management*, Thousand Oaks, CA: Sage.

Rowold, J. & Rohmann, A. 2009 "Transformational and Transactional Leadership Styles Followers' Positive and Negative Emotions, and Performance in German Nonprofit Orchestras", *Nonprofit Management & Leadership*, 20(1), 41–59.

Sarros, J., Cooper, B. K., Hartican, A. M. & Barker, C. J. 2006 *The Character of Leadership*, Milton, QLD: John Wiley & Sons.

Sinclair, A. 2007 *Leadership for the Disillusioned*, Sydney: Allen & Unwin.

Spears, L. C. (ed.) 1995 *Reflections on Leadership*, New York: John Wiley & Sons.

Wadman, M. S. & Koping, A. S. 2009 "Aesthetic Relations in the Place of the Lone Hero in Arts Management: Examples from Film Making and Orchestral Performance", *International Journal of Arts Management*, 12(1), 31–43.

Walumbwa, F. O., Avolio. B. J., Gardner, W. L., Wernsing, T. S. & Peterson, S. J. 2008 "Authentic Leadership: Development and Validation of a Theory-based Measure", *Journal of Management*, 34(1), 89–126.

Learning

Learning should be part of every organisation. As a leader and manager, you should be taking up training opportunities to improve your skills and knowledge. And if that's true for you, it's also true for everyone else in the organisation. In 1990, the Australian Government introduced the Training Guarantee Levy. This scheme operated until 1996 and required Australian enterprises with payroll costs of over A$200,000 to spend at least the equivalent of 1.5% of their payroll on the provision of "structured" training for their employees or pay an equivalent levy to the Australian Taxation Office (Smith & Billet 2005). This seems to me to be a good aim for even a small organisation. For example, if your turnover is $300,000, this means investing $4,500 in training. Training and learning experiences could include induction, OHS, Equal Opportunity, Respect in the Workplace, attendance at conferences, contributions to the fees for people doing external courses, the provision of formal mentoring and coaching and so on. And if even this seems too much to spend, you might be able to negotiate access to a relevant training program provided by a sponsor or a donor.

The point is that we can all be better at our jobs.

There are three parts of the learning process in organisations:

1. Knowledge-based: building knowledge and thinking skills
2. Behavioural: bridging the "knowing-doing" gap – turning knowledge into behaviour
3. Cultural: embedding values and standards of behaviour in the organisation (Ferres 2011, 111).

Some of that learning will happen by example: when new staff go through an induction process, when staff see the way values are "lived" by management, or when new managers learn from the behaviour of senior managers. Some of the learning will happen through formal training courses presented by outside experts either within the organisation or outside it. Some of the best training processes at MTC weren't at MTC but rather when the carpenter and the marketer, the costume maker and the manager all went off and did computer training together. The process was not only effective skill development, but also one that contributed unexpectedly to relationship development.

Cappelli's (2013) research shows that employers who offer tuition reimbursement attract better applicants and have lower turnover than other firms. Reimbursing fees at MTC didn't

lead to either result. In fact, I had the opposite experience – staff who received support to do courses, particularly university or vocational courses, often moved on to other companies. But that's not a bad thing if one thinks how your organisation contributes to the ecology of the arts industry. As a major performing arts organisation, my view was that MTC had a responsibility to the industry and not just to its own survival and so I was happy to invest in the learning experience of staff even if the result was that they left.

One of the most innovative examples of training opportunities came not from an arts or cultural organisation, but from the superannuation fund for people in the printing, media and arts industry. As well as offering tuition reimbursement to staff for work-specific training, the company also offered reimbursement for art courses. So if you wanted to learn photography or have singing lessons, the company was willing to support you because that might increase your appreciation of the lives and needs of your customers.

Plas and Lewis' (2001, 77) comment that "[g]rowth must always be a personal choice. If growth is extrinsically mandated, people are not likely to respond positively … times exist in which people need to remain within the perceived safety of the familiar." This is a lesson that I should have remembered when I kept encouraging people to take supervision or management courses and they failed to take me up on the offer. They were usually already in such positions and I thought, naively, that they would leap at the chance to learn more. There were two things going on which led to their resistance. First, as new managers or supervisors, they'd already taken a step away from their peers. Going to a course on management would confirm that they had moved across to the other side of the fence, leaving their friends and colleagues behind. Another reason, usually for the more experienced people, was at that point in their lives and careers they didn't want to take the extra responsibility of learning more, knowing that as a result of such training, I'd expect their performance to improve. Or course there may have been less negative reasons for them not wanting to do training – family or other obligations – but the point is that not everyone wants to take on the responsibility of learning.

Learning takes place within a social context and not all training or learning will be good. As Langley (2010, 66) asks

> Who has ever been on a course over which they felt they had little choice? Who has been part of a "sheep-dip" process that seemed to take little account of their existing skills, experience and knowledge? Who has brought some great learning back to their organisation only to be told that, "This is not the way we do things around here"?

Learning can be disruptive for both the participants and the people they share their learning with as old learning is overtaken and work patterns are challenged. The point is to try and match the learning experience with the needs of the individuals and the organisation.

It's not just the needs of your staff – it's your learning needs too. William J. Byrnes (2019), author of a well-known arts management textbook, pondered on how you can stay tuned to cultural management theory and research when you're in the middle of a project. For people like him (and me), teaching provides the context for that learning but for the practitioner immersed in putting on an exhibition or a show, it's hard to find the time to reflect on your own processes and management beliefs. But you need to find a way of doing exactly that.

Apart from formal training, the most common learning experiences for managers these days is through mentorships or coaching. Mentoring is described as a process by which a new professional or manager can express their feelings, emotions or concerns about their role and workplace and receive advice and guidance from a senior colleague in a confidential way (Paquette 2012, 208). Whereas mentors use their own experience to enable you to develop, coaches are described as people who help you to get better at what you already do (Hewison

& Holden 2011, 54). Coaching is more self-directed and Assheton (2011) provides an interesting example of Generation Y retail store employees who reported being disengaged with being told what to do but who responded positively to a coaching model.

In one of my co-leadership research interviews, a US participant spoke about the corporate CEOs on their Board. Every one of them had private coaches that they kept on a regular retainer and used to help them prepare for challenges. In his commentary, the participant concluded:

> It was all about the fact that there was not a team around these men. That these men didn't trust their lieutenants … That they needed someone they could be open and frank with and ask advice and show vulnerability.

He told the story to explain that he didn't need such a coach because he had a co-leader, a co-partner in the company and had qualities of sharing and openness and trust with that partner.

In a discussion with an academic colleague we were pondering why universities are particularly bad in creating environments that enable people to become good leaders. First, there's a group of people who don't think they need to be led, let alone managed. Academics work without many of the constraints that the rest of us have such as time or place. There are specific performance criteria for research and publication but as for day-to-day behaviour, there aren't any or many controls. Second, many academic leaders are chosen because of their academic skills and not their management skills. And they don't necessarily have mentors to oversee the implementation of their management practice. I've seen such academics be bad leaders with no support or chance to improve. There are elements of this scenario that are also true in arts and cultural organisations. When the curator becomes the manager. Where the artist who's never actually worked full time in an organisation or experienced being a manager becomes an Artistic Director. In some cases, the organisation will anticipate this outcome and provide formal training but in other cases, someone is appointed because of their artistic skills alone. Mentoring can help the transition to leadership.

I've had good managers, supportive Chairs and mates to whinge to, but I've never had a formal mentor. Having informally advised people for years, I did take on a more formal role for a time and found it an interesting learning experience. As an experienced arts manager you're likely to be asked to be one too. The role is what one wants it to be but the key point is that the mentee or protégé determines the nature of the relationship and how it's going to function. Another important part of the relationship is that there is an "ethics of care where both parties need to be supportive, responsive and caring of each other" (Ehrich 2011, 14).

There has been lots of discussion around the notion of "learning organisations". I find such language suspect because organisations don't "learn", individuals do. Langley (2010, 67) goes further and says that she gets a shiver of discomfort every time someone uses the phrase "learning organisation" because "[n]o one really knows what it means, but it has a plausible and desirable ring to it". However, I am an absolute believer in providing learning and training opportunities to help people reach their potential and in taking up such opportunities so that I can keep learning too.

See also: Empowerment, Hiring, Knowledge, People

References

Assheton, D. 2011 "Coaching at Hitchinson 3", in O'Toole, S., Ferres, N. & Connell, J. (eds) *People Development: An Inside View*, Melbourne: Tilde University Press, 58–64.

Byrnes, W. J. 2019 "Foreword", in DeVereaux, C. (ed.) 2019 *Arts and Cultural Management: Sense and Sensibility in the State of the Field*, New York: Routledge, ix–xi.

Cappelli, P. 2013 "HR for Neophytes", *Harvard Business Review*, 25–27 October.

Ehrich, L. 2011 "Mentoring", in O'Toole, S., Ferres, N. & Connell, J. (eds) *People Development: An Inside View*, Melbourne: Tilde University Press, 7–16.

Ferres, N. 2011 "Leadership and Management Development (LMS)", in O'Toole, S., Ferres, N. & Connell, J. (eds) *People Development: An Inside View*, Melbourne: Tilde University Press, 107–123.

Hewison, R. & Holden, J. 2011 *The Cultural Leadership Handbook*, Farnham: F Gower.

Langley, D. 2010 "Leadership Development: A Critical Question", in Kay, S. & Venner, K. (eds) *A Cultural Leader's Handbook*, London: Creative Choices, 64–70.

O'Toole, S., Ferres, N. & Connell, J. (eds) 2011 *People Development: An Inside View*, Melbourne: Tilde University Press.

Paquette, J. 2012 "Mentoring and Change in Cultural Organizations: The Experience of Directors in British National Museums", *Journal of Arts Management, Society and Law*, 42(4), 205–216.

Plas, J. M. & Lewis, S. E. 2001 *Person-Centered Leadership of Nonprofit Organizations*, Thousand Oaks, CA: Sage Publications.

Smith, A. & Billett, S. 2005 "Myth and Reality: Employer Sponsored Training in Australia", *International Journal of Training Research*, 3, 16–29.

Listening

Arts managers spend a lot of time talking – to staff, to peers, to Board members, to stakeholders. But they probably spend – and should spend – just as much time listening. Management writer Peter Drucker has listening as his first leadership competency and describes it not as skill but as a discipline. "Anyone can do it," he says. "All you have to do is keep your mouth shut" (Drucker 1990, 21). Witty though that comment is, active listening is a somewhat more sophisticated process. Listening is both hearing what is said and a psychological process in which we attempt to make meaning from experience (Archee, Gurney & Mohan 2013).

Bovee and Thill (2010) describe four different types of listening. The first type is "content" where the goal is to understand and retain the speaker's message regardless of whether you agree or disagree, approve or disapprove. The task is to overlook the presenter's style and focus on the information because the task is to understand. The second type of listening is "critical" where you're trying to understand and evaluate the speaker's message on a number of levels such as logic, strength of argument, validity of conclusion, plus their intention and motivation. Their third type is "empathic" listening. This time (or as well as) you're trying to understand the speaker's feelings, needs and wants so you can appreciate their point of view even if you don't agree. The final type is "active" listening where you make a conscious effort to turn off your filters and biases to try and hear and understand. In challenging situations you may need to try and apply all these forms of listening.

According to Archee, Gurney and Mohan (2013, 189), "75% of oral communication is ignored, misunderstood or quickly forgotten". By actively listening to people, you should be able to improve that statistic. Through the process of listening you will receive the information you need to make better decisions, you'll learn more about the people you work with, they in turn will feel appreciated because they will have been heard, and your capacity to anticipate and resolve problems will be strengthened. Rosner and Halcrow (2010, 62) claim that "If employees feel you're a good listener, you'll be seen as confident, compassionate, aware, and fair. If you're seen as a poor listener, employees will describe you as arrogant, mean, out of touch, and unfair." Some of the reasons that make us poor listeners include assuming that the topic will be boring, being put off by the speaker's presentation or even character, having a short attention span and poor comprehension (Archee, Gurney & Mohan 2013). One could add to this list the endless distraction that our electronic devices provide. Geirck (2018) claims, rightly I suspect, that social media is taking away our listening time.

Bunting (2016) points out that we spend a lot of time pretending to be listening but not actually doing so because our minds are either immersed in the past or the future rather than being in the moment. There can also be times when there's so much organisational noise that we can't hear people, literally (where people are talked over) or metaphorically (when we want people to agree). We should be willing to hear other opinions and not silence different or dissident voices (Sigurjónsson 2019). Being open to different perspectives and opinions can leave you open to challenge if as a result, you change your mind because listening isn't just about hearing, it's about seriously considering other points of view. I remember a particular meeting with a group of senior staff talking about strategy. I had a view on what I wanted as the outcome of the meeting but I listened to all the views put forward and was persuaded by one of the participants to adopt their approach which was different to mine. One of the other members of the group was furious that I'd both (1) changed my mind and (2) not changed it to agree with him. We had to spend a lot of time in a side meeting as I unpacked my reasons for the change before he was calm enough to buy into the new idea. He thought I'd been weak to change my mind even though secretly he wanted me to change – but to his point of view. You can manage these situations if you're confident you've integrated all the relevant information, have made the right decision and can explain your reasoning.

Part of the research on empowerment, an important element in job satisfaction, is about listening to ideas and suggestions that people have about their jobs. During a social occasion, I was listening to a person talking about their job. They clearly loved it even though it was emotionally and physically demanding and badly paid. However, there was one thing they wanted that couldn't get: the chance to debrief with a trained person after a difficult day at work – in other words, to be listened to. Senior people within the hierarchy had access to this service but not at this person's level in the organisation. It was in a non-profit environment so, like the arts, I assumed that resources were tight. But it seemed ironic that this person was not being listened to about their need to be listened to.

Effective listening takes effort and I do remember the embarrassment of almost dozing off on a sunny afternoon in a meeting listening to someone who was neither an inspirational speaker nor a smart contributor to the organisation. But every person who has an idea or an opinion that can potentially improve your organisation deserves to be listened to with respect.

See also: Communication, Empowerment, Job Satisfaction, Leadership, Management

References

Archee, R., Gurney, M. & Mohan, T. 2013 *Communicating as Professionals* (3rd ed), Melbourne: Cengage.

Bovee, C. L. & Thill, J. L. 2010 *Business Communication Today* (10th ed), Upper Saddle, NJ: Pearson.

Bunting, M. 2016 *The Mindful Leader*, Milton, QLD: Wiley.

Drucker, P. F. 1990 *Managing the Nonprofit Organization*, New York: HarperCollins.

Gierck, M. 2018 "Take Your Time to Really Hear Others", *The Age*, 6, 30 January.

Rosner, B. & Halcrow, A. 2010 *The Boss's Survival Guide* (2nd ed), New York: McGraw Hill.

Sigurjónsson, N. 2019 "Silence in Cultural Management", in DeVereaux, C. (ed.) *Arts and Cultural Management: Sense and Sensibility in the State of the Field*, New York: Routledge, 205–225.

Love

Bolman and Deal (2013, 401) say that love is largely absent from modern corporations. It's certainly wasn't in many indices of management textbooks when I wrote the first edition of this book. Since then, I have found it in a *Harvard Business Review* article. Barsade and O'Neill (2016, 61) note that a number of companies such as PepsiCo, Southwest Airlines and Zappo all list love ... or at the very least caring as part of their corporate values. To be honest, I find it hard to image how "love" would play out in such corporate settings but I'll leave my cynical hat at the door for the moment. Barsade and O'Neill (2016, 62) use the phrase "companionate love" to describe a positive workplace emotion and they define it as "the degree of affection, caring and compassion that employees feel and express towards each another". In companies where this "love" was expressed and felt, employees were more committed, felt more job satisfaction and, also, more accountability for their work.

Love does come up in the arts management research regularly along with words such as family and friendship (Fitzgibbon 2001). People talk about their love of the organisation, of the art form, of their artistic or management partner. The interviews we conducted for our research on leadership in the performing arts (MacNeill & Tonks 2009, 397) were full of the word:

> You're working for love basically, so you actually have to enjoy what you're doing. [GM7]
>
> I think the motivating force is a general love of [name of organisation] [GM6]
>
> I can't work with anyone I don't love in this business. If I'm not in love with my Artistic Director I can't do it. And so there is automatically a relationship that is deeply personal and deeply respectful. [GM5]\

In Hewison, Holden and Jones' (2013, 148) article on the Royal Shakespeare Company, they call the leaders regular and explicit reference to emotions "remarkable". They quote a speech by Michael Boyd in which (along with words like terror, daring, fear, empathy and compassion), "love" was used ten times.

The reasons that Bolman and Deal (2013) offer for love's absence from the corporate world is because of the power and risks inherent in its meaning. Love, they say, means vulnerability, being open to others. However, there is evidence to prove that love *should* be part of organisations. Moss, Callanan and Wilson (2012, 37) quote research evidence that "Images of love, but not sex, enhanced the capacity of individuals to solve conundrums. These images of love highlighted the potential of a stable future, which in turn improved the insights of participants."

Gail McGovern (2014, 38), President and CEO of the American Red Cross, has said that looking back at her time in the corporate sector, she should have been more willing to embrace the "heart". Her perspective now is that as a leader your job is to tap into the higher purpose of your organisation which you can't do by retreating to the analytical. "If you want to lead, have the courage to do it from the heart." Bunting (2016) has written a book about mindfulness and leadership. He coins the phrase "lovingkindness" which is about thinking of the welfare and happiness of all the people in the organisation:

> It is to deeply and sincerely care about your people, to be emotionally invested in their progress and success. And it is to show how much you care about them by regularly and consistently expression appreciation for their efforts (105).

In a sterner directive of why love is important in organisations, Elsner (2001, 5) quotes Thomas Merton, Trappist monk and poet (1971):

> He, who attempts to act and do things for others or for the world without love, will not have anything to give others. He will communicate to them nothing but the contagion of his own obsessions, his aggressiveness, his ego-centred ambitions, his delusions about ends and means and his doctrinaire prejudices and ideas.

Adams (2007, 223) notes that "[e]mployees that feel that their work (and by extension life) is meaningless will have little love for their boss". But on the other hand, do you want to be/should you be loved by your employees? Isn't it about love for the organisation, for the output and love of the people who make it rather than wanting love for yourself? Even friendship is an awkward issue when you're the CEO. People often used to say to me "how lucky you are, to be friends with all those famous people". But, of course, I'm not. Because, ultimately, I'm the boss. I'm the one that signs their employment contracts, approves their salaries and potentially fires them or fails to re-hire them. Respect, yes. Parties, of course. But friendship isn't an automatic part of the mix.

The situation is the same with staff. One manager had a habit of telling staff about his weekend sexual conquests on the basis that this was what friends shared. Not appropriate. Another manager was desperate for her staff to like her and so never said "no". Not appropriate.

However, this doesn't mean that warmth, care, openness, empathy, compassion aren't part of the employer/employee relationship. When you leave, you want people to come to your farewell and say "she was a good boss" or even "he was a good person" but not "I'm losing my best friend". Even in organisations where the environment is very family-like and socialising goes on inside and outside, there will still be times when the caring leader has to be authoritative. Another trap for companies that have a culture of love is that when "everyone feels like a family, employees might struggle to have honest conversations about problems" (Barsade & O'Neill 2016, 63).

However, it is very hard to stay in an organisation where the culture isn't a warm one and where you as a manager are continually under attack. The hardest examples that I've heard of in the arts have come from symphony orchestras where there appears to be a tradition that management is the enemy. I have heard managers talk about their unwillingness to go to work because the aggression from staff is so strong. So if not loved, then at the very least you want to be valued and respected.

So, love is a powerful concept and should be part of your organisation but it's not about you being loved. Watch out for dysfunctional love and when the love dies, it may be time to move on.

See also: Communication, Emotion, Empathy, Leadership, Passion

References

Adams, J. 2007 *Managing People in Organizations: Contemporary Theory and Practice*, Basingstoke: Palgrave Macmillan.

Barsade, S. & O'Neill, O. A. 2016 "Manage Your Emotional Culture", *Harvard Business Review*, 94(1/2), 58– 6.

Bolman, L. G. & Deal, T. E. 2013 *Reframing Organizations* (5th ed), San Francisco, CA: Jossey-Bass.

Bunting, M. 2016 *The Mindful Leader*, Milton. QLD: Wiley.

Elsner, P. A. 2007 *Authenticity and Leadership: Integrating Our Inner Lives with Our Work*, Iowa State University: Leadership Forum.

Fitzgibbon, M. 2001 *Managing Innovation in the Arts*, Westport, CT: Quorum Books.

McGovern, G. 2014 "Lead from the Heart", *Harvard Business Review*, 92(3), 38.

Hewison, R., Holden, J. & Jones, S. 2013 "Leadership and Transformation at the Royal Shakespeare Company", in Caust, J. (ed.) *Arts Leadership*, Melbourne: Tilde University Press, 144–158.

MacNeill, K. & Tonks, A. 2009 "Co-leadership and Gender in the Performing Arts", *Asia Pacific Journal of Arts and Cultural Management*, 6(1), 291–404.

Merton, T. 1971 *Contemplation in a World of Action*, New York: Doubleday.

Moss, S., Callanan, J. & Wilson, S. 2012 *The Moonlight Effect*, Melbourne: Tilde University Press.

Notes

1 When I first started checking the Board membership, there were no women but in 2018 there were three.
2 Australian Prime Minister from 3 December 2007 to 24 June 2010, and for 11 weeks in 2013.
3 The long-term effect may take decades to be seen.
4 Cila and Rolf Norjlind, *Spring Tide*, Hesperus Press, 2014, Chapter 11.

M

Management

I found a very simple definition of management somewhere which I use at the beginning of each semester teaching arts management. A manager:

- does things (plans, organises, staffs, leads, controls)
- with things (humans, money, physical resources)
- to achieve things (organisational goals).

I like it because it's action-oriented and straightforward – but the one thing I don't like is calling people "things". To make up for that and on the next PowerPoint slide in the lecture, I ask "what is the most important thing that you have to manage?" – and the answer is people, people, people, people, people, money, buildings. And if you don't like people very much, I suggest you find another career.

The original meaning of "management" was to "take care of something" (Kirchberg & Zembylas 2010, 2) which feels like a good definition for arts managers to keep in mind. Management can be thought of in a number of ways – as a function, as a set of activities and as a team of people. From the functional perspective, the traditional definition is that it's about:

- Planning – thinking ahead, designing a future, setting goals
- Organising – identifying the work to be done and coordinating it
- Directing – focusing people's skills, time and energy on the goals that need to be achieved
- Controlling – working out the best things to do and the best ways to do them (Baird et al. 1990, 8–14).

However, as I've commented on these four activities in different sections of this book, what's left to talk about? We could talk about management as opposed to leadership. But if you've been reading this book in alphabetical order you already know that debate. To restate it, some writers view management as the pragmatic part of the job with leadership as the inspirational part. Others see leadership as one aspect of management. In some ways I was lucky. My first cultural management position was as CEO of a small organisation. I didn't have time to develop a set of habits that were about "management" rather than "leadership". I had to do both – which is why I've never been fussed over the differences between the two.

There is some ambivalence about the use of managerial language and practices in arts and cultural organisations. For example, Beirne and Knight (2002, 75) warn against "the folly of conceptualising management too narrowly" and highlight the need for caution when receiving managerial advice. I can understand the latter warning having experienced a number of external reviews by corporate and government consultants, all of which missed the point most of the time. However, sometimes a well-informed external eye can contribute useful insights to the managerial effectiveness of an organisation. One just has to be careful to pick the right question as well as the right person to answer it.

A more important consideration is Beirne and Knight's (2002) implication that "management" *per se* is bad. They are not convinced that the social processes of directing resources and staff are the same in the arts as in manufacturing or retailing. Of course, context is important, but there are some underlying principles and management skills that apply in all industries. Many aspects of people management such as empowerment, feedback, communication, recruitment and selection and payment may be done differently across organisations but all need to be done. The authors provide a series of examples that appear to suggest a difference but which could have been solved by some very traditional management processes. For example, Beirne and Knight tell of the problems created when people don't know to whom they should be reporting. Decades ago, Henri Fayol suggested that people should have clear reporting lines (Skringar & Stevens 2008). Another example was of lots of informal conversation happening at a bar after a show and people feeling left out. A principle of good management no matter where it's practised is to ensure effective communication throughout an organisation. In other words, I'm in the camp that says that good management practices can contribute to the health of art organisations.

What Does a Manager Do?

The first thing you do when you become a manager is to take responsibility − for the people, the money, the buildings. But the practice of such responsibility may not always take place in a straightforward logical manner. Years ago I read a piece of research about school principals that I haven't been able to track down. The researcher followed principals around all day and concluded that whatever they did, it was never more than five minutes on one thing. The vision of the rational, controlled, organised manager sitting in their office heroically making brave and effective decisions is simply not the way it works. As Zan (2006, 1) says, managerial work is "characterized by fragmentation, limited periods of solitude and continuous interruptions, brief contacts, questions, and exchanges of words and ideas".

In presentations that I've made to community groups, I'd list the issues I'd had to deal with at MTC over the previous couple of days. The purpose was to give people a flavour of the work of an arts manager. It usually went on for a couple of PowerPoint pages which is symptomatic of the normal busy life of any manager and it was always a rich and varied list. I've taken one of those lists and tried to match what I did in that few days to the roles that Mintzberg (1989) proposes for managers:

Interpersonal roles:

- Figurehead − being out in the community telling the world about the company
- Leader − a combined meeting and individual meetings with my managers
- Liaison − ringing peers to get items from other arts companies that we could use for a fundraising trivia night.

Informational roles:

- Monitor − reading reviews and social media to see that help understand why a recent show has sold badly; checking the daily sales reports
- Disseminate − starting to write elements of our Annual Report; prepare Board papers
- Spokesperson − respond to an external OHS audit.

Decisional roles:

- Entrepreneur – exploring options for a play to tour with an international agent; discuss filming options with a variety of parties
- Resource allocator – reviewing financial reports
- Disturbance handler – managing a disciplinary process
- Negotiator – negotiating contracts for senior artists; finalising a contract for a show that MTC was bringing into Melbourne.

That particular week must have been quite internally focused without much of the visionary, long-term activities that are also part of the job, but Mintzberg's list is a useful reminder that the work of a manager is complex and layered and the key aspects of it are about information, people and decisions. Bolman and Deal (2013, 307) describe the life of a manager as hectic,

> shifting rapidly from one situation to the next. Decisions emerge from a fluid, swirling vortex of conversations, meetings, and memos. Informational systems ensure an overload of detail about what happened last month or last year. Yet they fail to answer a far more important question: What next?

And while you're doing all this, you are being watched. Corrigan (1999, 14) makes the point that "[a]t every moment staff watch how their managers cope with all aspects of management, from their ability to listen to staff to the way in which they make major decisions". Part of being watched is following the old adage of managing by walking around. You need to be in contact with your staff and your audience. Although I rarely socialised with staff out of the office, I was at every company event. I didn't walk around the building everyday but regularly took time out to take visitors around praising staff as I introduced them. I always attended previews and closing nights as well as opening nights of

shows and was somewhat surprised when actors were surprised to see me so often. But as they were the reason for our existence, I needed to show them I cared. And as for audiences, I was often the warm up act for directors or Artistic Directors at Directors' briefings or subscriber launches and became known to people that way. Even after leaving the company, people still find me – in shopping centres and swimming pools – and want to express an opinion about the company. As a manager you have to be visible and accessible.

Peter Drucker (2004, 59), a famous management writer who generally offers insights that make (common) sense, says that great managers may be "charismatic or dull, generous or tightfisted, visionary or numbers oriented" but they need to follow eight simple practices:

- They ask "what needs to be done?"
- They ask "what is right for the enterprise?"
- They develop action plans
- They take responsibility for decisions
- They take responsibility for communicating
- They are focused on opportunities rather than problems
- They run productive meetings
- They think and say "we" rather than "I".

Just as important as what a manager does is how a manager thinks. Gosling and Mintzberg (2003) propose a collection of five management mindsets:

- Managing oneself: the reflective mindset – being able to stop and think
- Managing the organisation: the analytic mindset – understanding both hard and soft data
- Managing context: the worldly mindset – exploring the world in order to understand home better
- Managing relationships: the collaborative mindset – managing relationships rather than seeing people as resources
- Managing change: the active mindset – remaining curious, alert and experimental.

These are qualities that I keep talking about to students. Knowing yourself but also the world. Thinking analytically but also mindfully. Working with people as well as data.

Context

Does what a manager do differ depending on whether they are working in a company or for an artist? In a large organisation or a small one? The answer is yes and no.

When I wrote the first edition of the *A to Z of Arts Management*, it had been a long time since I worked in a small to medium-size (S2M) company. I'd been on Boards of such organisations, I'd worked with management and Boards on consultation projects, but I hadn't worked *in* a company for an extended period of time. As I updated the book, I was doing a locum CEO gig in an S2M contemporary dance company. Some aspects of the company are ones I remember: everyone helping out in times of stress and challenge; being hands on as a manager; the impact that one person who isn't happy can have on the whole team. However, it's been a long time since I had to do the payroll or get behind a bar to serve drinks at an opening. Some aspects of the company are the same as you see in large companies: financial constraints; managing the Board's expectations; the need to find audiences; the pressure of production week; feeling guilty because the only people without on ongoing salary are the artists. But there were some insights that were new (although not a surprise): how hard it is to find cash sponsors when you're not performing all the time; continuing to run programs without question because you haven't got time to do the financial analysis; finding it hard to prioritise as a manager because you're managing everything. Regardless of scale you still have to create art and share it with audiences, find money and report on how you've spent it, employ people and help them do their best.

I haven't managed artists directly and so I'm not the best person to reflect on what the required skills are for that job. Check our Guy Morrow's 2018 book if you want some more insights. He focuses on "agile management" which is characterised by feedback from audiences that provides an iterative loop into the product development process. Another quality of agile management is small groups working autonomously in a flexible way. There are a lot of cross-overs between managing people within organisations and being an artist's manager and here's one piece of advice from a Scottish band manager that contains points that will be familiar to managers of companies:

> You *have* to love the band's music, and it certainly helps if you love the people too. Put their interest first at all times. Try to get them to agree what to do and don't hang around. Try not to let others down and apologise if you do. Get agreements in writing, and don't be afraid to tell people who deserve to be told to fuck off to do so, even if you don't use those words. Make great art, but realise that you live in a market economy, so try to get a good sense of your market value, then increase it.
>
> (Cloonan 2015, 234–235)

If you accept Brkić's (2019, 83–84) definition of arts management then you can see that all the elements play out in some form or other regardless of the type of organisation or industry sector:

- Managing structures (being part of the management structure of an arts/cultural organization);
- Managing processes (working on arts productions/events);
- Managing careers (taking care of the career of an artist/arts collective);
- Managing messages (creating, promoting, and monitoring the story of an arts organization/events/artists).

Bad Management

People will survive an ordinary manager but they won't survive a bad manager. A friend, who has been a manager, described his recent experience with a new manager this way:

> It's Management 101 – you get to know your team, given them guidelines and expectations. But she doesn't. She doesn't have time for conversation – "I'm snowed under" – even when I'm there to say "do you have some work for me?" There are no processes or structures for the way we're supposed to work. Decisions aren't explained. She talks over me or down to me in front of others.

He felt bullied, but more importantly, he didn't feel that the organisation got value from him because he was badly managed and that's what worried him most. In the end the manager was fired but he still lost sleep, felt under-minded and worried about his future. Bad management hurts people.

Gilley et al. (2015, 71) explored the idea of "development leaders", which they describe as a manager who has the "knowledge, skills and abilities they need to develop their employees so that employees can be more effective". The opposite of this is a manager you don't want in your company and who you don't want to work for. You need to avoid:

- Hiring/promoting ineffective managers
- Hiring/promoting people because they are "best performers" rather than for their interpersonal skills
- Wasting time trying to fix ineffective managers
- Retaining managers who can't get other people to contribute good results
- Failing to reprimand or fire managers who are ineffective or incompetent (Glley et al. 2011, 76–77).

Apart from bosses who are bullies or simply ineffective, the next worst complaint that I regularly hear about is the micromanager. This is a manager who is fearful and doesn't trust people. Ambile and Kramer (2011) say that micromanagers get four things wrong:

1. They fail to provide autonomy to get the work done
2. They frequently ask subordinates about their work without providing any real help
3. They apportion personal blame when problems arise so subordinates hide problems rather than honestly discuss them
4. They hoard information and in the process, handicap the work being done.

I've never heard a story of when a micromanager was valued by a staff member or was seen as an effective manager. However, this doesn't mean that you don't have to care about the detail. Tony Sweeney (2012), ex-CEO of the Australian Centre for the Moving Image, said:

> whatever level of work you're doing look at the detail of your work and look at the big picture of your work and leave the middle ground to the people who work for you … the detail is where the standards are set. The power, the precision, the checking that things are really as good as they can be, comes from the detail. But details without being in service of a bigger picture is normally fairly futile.

I'm not a micromanager but I do worry when the details aren't right – when a website design isn't easy; when the drinks aren't properly poured at the bar; when the receptionist takes too long to answer the phone. There are all the experiences that the consumer has and I want their connection with the company to be the best that it can be.

Other behaviours that you find in lists of poor management include lack of consideration, self-serving managers, tolerance of poor performance, resistance to new ideas, failing to make decisions, blaming others, not delegating, having favourites, lacking enthusiasm, seeing people's weaknesses instead of the strengths – and the problems go on (Adams 2007; Hudson 2009; Rosner & Halcrow 2010).

Sometimes, managerial problems aren't the result of unskilled or unethical managers. Grey

(2005, 29–30) takes the view that management is a continually failing exercise. Not because all managers are bad but because there are always unintended consequences of one's actions. People aren't predictable and you can't control every aspect of people's work lives. An example of what this means in practice was when, as part of MTC's Environment Health and Safety certification, we had to "prove" that people were competent to do their job and use the relevant equipment even if they had been doing the work for 20 years. Obviously, people were going to be irritated, even upset, that their skills were under analysis. We had to do it so we decided to make it beneficial for people. Instead of just having someone tick a box, at the end of the process people could be awarded with a Trade Certificate qualification which recognising their prior experience. I thought this was going to a great opportunity for people to obtain qualifications but instead it was seen as a deep insult. People didn't want to have to explain or justify their work to strangers who they thought wouldn't appreciate it. The intended outcome was a positive result for staff. The unintended outcome was that people saw this as an even greater threat to their status and history than the original "tick the box" process. They didn't need a qualification. They already had the job.

Grey's (2005) point is that you can't assume that people are simple passive receivers of your action as a manager. Rather, they are actors who can and do respond differently to events, interpret them in different ways and can deliberately or unwittingly obstruct or subvert your actions.

What Makes a Good Manager?

Managers are a little like real estate agents and politicians. You rarely find stories of good managers in literature or on film. However, given that we work in the industries that create such images, maybe we can start telling stories about good managers?

Tusa (2014) separates leadership from management with the management list containing all the functions (finance, people management, building management, marketing, fundraising and so on) with his leadership list full of personal qualities such as being authentic and passionate, possessing courage and being flexible, inspiring trust and articulating vision. He claims that leaders and managers are different in quality and temperament but I think the arts need people who embody the capacity to do all the management tasks in a leader-like manner. Whether you're a CEO or a managing Director who's a co-CEO, you need a combination of functional skills and positive personal qualities.

Of all the lists about management that you find in standard textbooks, the one that feels most based in reality is Hamlin's (2004). It's the result of analysing a large number of critical incidents in companies and so it's more than just one writer's feelings or a single story. If you can develop the skills and capacities on his list, you are on your way to becoming a good manager. He suggests that you need to be good at planning, proactive, supportive of people, effective at empowering and delegating, be inclusive in your decision-making, communicate and consult widely and have genuine concern for people.

Matthew Stewart, author of the amusing and insightful *The Management Myth* (2009, 132), makes an important point about management. He says that if you ask anyone to talk about a great manager, while they will recognise their technical skills, "the discussion will almost always take place in the language of moral obligation: respect, consideration, fairness". Stewart is someone who started as a management consultant and ended up as a philosopher which is probably why I like his thinking so much – informed but critical. So here are his words on what makes a good manager:

> A good manager is someone with a facility for analysis and an even greater talent for synthesis; someone who has an eye both for the details and the one big thing that really matters; someone who is able to reflect on facts in a disinterested way, who

is always dissatisfied with pat answers and the conventional wisdom, and who therefore takes a certain pleasure in knowledge itself; someone with a wide knowledge of the world and an even better knowledge of the way people work; someone who knows how to treat people with respect; someone with honesty, integrity, trustworthiness, and the other things that make up character; someone, in short, who understands oneself and the world around us well enough to know how to make it better. By this definition, of course, a good manager is nothing more or less than a good and well-educated person (303).

And if that list seems too daunting, some of the best managers I've worked with had a simple set of qualities. They were smart and good at the core technical requirements of their job, but in addition, they were positive about life, open to new ideas and directions, polite (sounds old-fashioned but it makes a difference) and inspiring – not always in a charismatic way (although that too sometimes), but in way where their passion for the organisation inspired one to work harder/longer/better.

See also: Control, Human Resource Management, Leadership, Manners, Motivation, Organisational Culture, Organisational Structure, People, Uncertainty

References

Adams, J. 2007 *Managing People in Organizations: Contemporary Theory and Practice*, Basingstoke: Palgrave Macmillan.

Ambile, T. & Kramer, S. J. 2011 "The Power of Small Wins", *Harvard Business Review*, May, https://hbr.org/2011/05/the-power-of-small-wins [accessed 27 February 2019].

Baird, L., Post, J. & Mahon, J. 1990 *Management: Functions and Responsibilities*, New York: Harper & Row.

Beirne, M. & Knight, S. 2002 "Principles and Consistent Management in the Arts: Lessons from British Theatre", *International Journal of Cultural Policy*, 8(1), 75–89.

Bolman, L. G. & Deal, T. E. 2013 *Reframing Organizations* (5th ed), San Francisco, CA: Jossey-Bass.

Brkić, A. 2019 "Death of the Arts Manager", in DeVereaux, C., *Arts and Cultural Management: Sense and Sensibilities in the State of the Field*, New York: Routledge, 75–88.

Cloonan, L. 2015 "Managing the Zoeys: Some Reminiscences", in Beech, N. & Gilmore, C. (eds) *Organising Music: Theory, Practice and Performance*, Cambridge: Cambridge University Press, 226–235.

Corrigan, P. 1999 *Shakespeare on Management*, London: Kogan Page.

Drucker, P. F. 2004 "What Makes An Effective Executive", *Harvard Business Review*, 82(6), 58–63.

Gilley, J. W., Shelton, P. & Gilley, A. 2011 "Development Leadership: A New Perspective of HRD", *Advances in Human Resource Development*, 13(3), 386–405.

Gilley, J. W., Gilley, A. M., Jackson, S. A. & Lawrence, H. 2015 "Managerial Practices and Organizational Conditions that Encourage Employee Growth and Development", *Performance Improvement Quarterly*, 28(3), 71–93.

Gosling, J. & Mintzberg, H. 2003 "The Five Minds of a Manager", *Harvard Business Review*, 81(11), 54–63.

Grey, C. 2005 *A Very Short, Fairly Interesting and Reasonably Cheap Book about Studying Organisations*, London: Sage Publications.

Hamlin, R. G. 2004 "In Support of Universalistic Models of Managerial and Leadership Effectiveness: Implications of HRD Research and Practice", *Human Resource Development Quarterly*, 15(2), 189–215.

Hudson, M. 2009 *Managing Without Profit: Leadership, Management and Governance of Third Sector Organisations in Australia*, Sydney: UNSW Press.

Kirchberg, V. & Zembylas, T. 2010 "Arts Management: A Sociological Inquiry", *The Journal of Arts Management, Law, and Society*, 40(1), 1–5.

Mintzberg, H. 1989 *Mintzberg on Management*, New York: The Free Press.

Morrow, G. 2018a *Artist Management: Agility and the Creative and Cultural Industries*, London: Routledge.

Morrow, G. 2018b "Distributed Agility: Artist Co-management in the Music Attention Economy", *International Journal of Arts Management*, 20(3), 38–48.

Rosner, B. & Halcrow, A. 2010 *The Boss's Survival Guide* (2nd ed), New York: McGraw Hill.

Skringar, E. R. & Stevens, T. 2008 *Driving Change and Developing Organisations* (1st ed), Melbourne: Tilde University Press.

Stewart, M. 2009, *The Management Myth*, New York: W.W. Norton & Co.

Sweeney, T. 2012 "Creative Talk with ACMI's Director, Tony Sweeney", *Creative Foyer*, www.artnewsportal.com.au/art-news/creative-talk-with-acmi-s-Director-tony-sweeney [accessed 27 February 2019].

Tusa, J. 2014 *Pain in the Arts*, London: I.B. Tauris.

Zan, L. 2006 *Managerial Rhetoric and Arts Organizations*, Houndmills: Palgrave Macmillan.

Manners

Maybe it's because I was brought up to be a polite young girl by the nuns. Maybe it's because I have an allergy to being yelled at. Whatever the reason, I think "please" and "thank you" and "sorry" all have currency in the work place. As Grayling says in his version of the Epistles (2011, 579): "[n]o less necessary than either ancient or modern knowledge therefore, is knowledge of the world, manners, politeness and society". If you are nice to people, they will usually be nice back. Stewart (2009, 131) notes that this insight is "a timeless precept, grounded in ethics, barely rising about tautology, and emerging naturally from the experience of being a human surrounded by other humans" but that doesn't guarantee that people are always nice to each other in the workplace.

The starting point is respect amongst people in the workforce. You don't have to be friends but you should acknowledge and value each other's contribution to the organisation. Adams says that you win people's respect if you say what you mean, do what you say, are good at what you do and inspire confidence (Adams 2007, 159). An Australia Board Chair says that she will not work with people who don't respect people, "no matter how brilliant they are, if they treat people poorly, if they are rude or if they have bad manners" (quoted in Sarros et al. 2006, 37).

Technically if you're the boss, you can direct someone to do a task but why not say "please" in the process? What starts as an order turns into a request. The answer may simply be "sure" but it gives the receiver a sense that at the very least, communication can be two way with the possibility to ask questions about the requirement. The result could be a better defined task or a clearer sense of the timing of the outcome which lead to a better result for both parties.

One of the most profound tools in the manager's kit is a well meant "thank you". James Button (2012, 65), in a book about working as speechwriter for Kevin Rudd, the Australian Prime Minister in the 2000s, tells stories about the man who said thank you and the man who didn't. Rudd's Departmental Secretary regularly said "thank you" if he liked someone's work, whereas the Prime Minister's habit seemed to be one of being "rude and contemptuous" towards his staff. This, presumably, was one of the reasons why Rudd was removed as Prime Minister by his own political party.

And it's not just because it's polite to say "thank you". There's evidence that when someone expresses appreciation for the work we've done, there are chemical changes to our brain. "Recognising others trips the reward circuits ... which reinforces the behaviours we want to see in them" (Bunting 2016, 114). There's also evidence that the more positive comments compared to negative comments a team receives, the more effective they will be (Bunting 2016, 116). In a study of call centre employees, their effort increased by 51% after a single visit from a manager to thank them for their work (Anon 2011). Our organisations don't usually have the negative organisational cultures of call centres but some of us do have the potential for similar environments in our ticketing and subscription departments. The old-fashioned model of management by wandering about is part of the process of people seeing that their work is noticed, understood and valued. Gestures of appreciation don't have to be expensive, just heartfelt. I was in the habit of finding a gift for everyone in the company at Christmas. That meant over 100 items so it was obviously never an expensive gift. One year it was a small diary, next year it was a book from my collection. But each gift was given with a personal note because without all of them, I didn't have a job worth doing.

Dan Ariely (2016) has done some fascinating research on motivation and included in some of the studies is a comparison of productivity when someone acknowledges another person's work which is a way of saying "thank you". He concludes: "Acknowledgement is a kind of human magic – a small human connection, a gift from one person to another" (27). Underlying please and thank you is the virtue of being kind. As Andrew Baker, an independent Australia producer, said in piece of career advice to young producers:

> Everyone knows that getting a show up takes time … And throughout the process be respectful, professional and kind. Mainly because that's just a good way to live, but also because your team will walk away with a fun, valuable and worthwhile career experience, even though they may not be getting paid very much.
>
> (Watts 2018)

I like the idea that kindness is a "good way to live". Think about the times when people have been kind to you – when you've made a mistake, when you're nervous, when you're unhappy. A kind workplace doesn't mean that you don't work hard and that you don't face pressure – but it makes hard work and pressure bearable.

The other important word is "sorry". Because you will make mistakes. But you'll also have to take responsibility for other people's mistakes. When you delegate tasks, the results are still your responsibility. And when things go wrong for your organisation due to external pressures that you can't control, you are still going to have to say "sorry". "Accept your role as apologist-in-chief," say Rosner and Halcrow (2010, 70). "You're the boss, which to your employees makes you the voice of the company. That means you'll be called upon to apologize for things you have had nothing to do with."

I was rather stunned by an article about incivility in the workplace in the *Harvard Business Review* (Porath 2016). First, because research indicated that 98% of surveyed workers had experienced uncivil behaviour and 99% had witnessed it at work. And second, because the author placed most of the responsibility on individuals – they were expected to steel themselves to deal with it. Confronting the rude person was seen to make things worse and only 15% of employees thought their employer had managed the problem effectively. Porath's advice is that you build your resilience through techniques such as continual learning, being healthy and finding excitement inside and outside of work. Of course, those strategies are good at any time but where's the manager in all of this? Where's the CEO? What sort of organisation lets rudeness rule? Yes, there'll be moments when we lose our cool and are rude to a co-worker but the next step should be an apology rather than more toxic behaviour.

One of Drucker's (1990, 115) "don'ts" in his list of what to avoid when managing non-profit organisations is:

> Don't tolerate discourtesy … manners are the social lubricating oil that smooths over friction … One learns to be courteous – it is needed to enable different people who doesn't necessarily like each other to work together. Good causes do not excuse bad manners.

The times when I felt the most belittled in the workplace were when I've been yelled at. Apart from the fact that each time I wasn't at fault and each time someone else was trying to cover up their own inadequacies, the point is that it didn't improve my work or my attitude. And in most cases I left the company. Not everyone can do that. People may stay in an environment with an aggressive boss because alternative jobs are seen as worse quality, the perceived cost of leaving is too high and that people feel that they have invested heavily in their current workplace (e.g. years of service, good friends) (Madlock & Dillow 2012). So they stay – and are increasingly negative, unproductive and dissatisfied. Another reason why management should address issues such as bad manners.

As a manager, the best thing you can do is to polite in the good and the bad times, control yourself and in Grayling's (2011, 579) words:

To be well-mannered without ceremony, easy without negligence,

Steady and intrepid with modesty, genteel without affectation,

Cheerful without noisiness, frank without indiscretion, and able to keep confidences;

To know the proper time and place for whatever you say or do, and to do it with an air of condition.

See also: Delegation, Emotions, People

References

Adams, J. 2007 *Managing People in Organizations: Contemporary Theory and Practice*, Basingstoke: Palgrave Macmillan.

Anonymous 2011 "The Problem with Financial Incentives − and What to Do About It", *Knowledge@Wharton*, http://knowledge.wharton. upenn.edu/article/the-problem-with-financial-incentives-and-what-to-do-about-it/ [accessed on 27 February 2019].

Ariely, D. 2016 *Payoff*, London: TED Books.

Bunting, M. 2016 *The Mindful Leader*, Milton, QLD: Wiley.

Button, J. 2012 *Speechless: A Year in My Father's Business*, Melbourne: Melbourne University Press.

Drucker, P. F. 1990 *Managing the Nonprofit Organizations*, New York: HarperCollins.

Grayling, A. C. 2011 *The Good Book*, London: Bloomsbury.

Madlock, P. E. & Dillow, M. E. 2012 "The Consequences of Verbal Aggression in the Workplace: An Application of the Investment Model", *Communication Studies*, 63(5), 583–607.

Porath, C. 2016 "Managing Yourself: An Antidote to Incivility", *Harvard Business Review*, 94(4), 108–111.

Rosner, B. & Halcrow, A. 2010 *The Boss's Survival Guide* (2nd ed), New York: McGraw Hill.

Rudd, K. 2008 "Kevin Rudd's Sorry Speech", *Sydney Morning Herald*, 13 February, www.smh.com. au/news/national/kevin-rudds-sorry-speech/ 2008/02/13/1202760379056.html [accessed 27 February 2019].

Sarros, J., Cooper, B. K., Hartican, A. M. & Barker, C. J. 2006 *The Character of Leadership*, Milton, QLD: John Wiley & Sons.

Stewart, M. 2009 *The Management Myth*, New York: W.W. Norton & Co.

Marketing

After analysing articles in academic journals, Rentschler (1998, 2002) summarised three stages of marketing in arts organisations: the foundation period when companies needed to become "open" to marketing (1975–1984), the professionalisation period when Marketing departments became more established (1985–1994) and the discovery period as a marketing orientation became more embedded (1995–2000). I find the timing of the first stage somewhat curious because the archives of MTC were full of marketing material and questions about how to find audiences are in almost every chapter in the founder's autobiography (Sumner 1993). In the 1950s and 1960s days the communication mechanisms tended to be flyers and posters and advertisements and editorial articles in newspapers so neither as complex nor strategic as marketing in the 21st century but still an important part of making and sharing art.

Some of the early proselytisers of arts marketing Kotler and Scheff (1997, 31) define marketing as "the process by which an organization relates creatively, productively, and profitably to the marketplace, with the goal of creating and satisfying customers within the parameters of the organization's objectives". Some years later, Boorsma and Chiaravalloti (2010, 305) defined arts marketing as "the stimulation of exchange with selected customers, by offering service-centered support for the co-creation of artistic experiences and by building and maintaining relationships with these customers for the purpose of creating customer value and achieving the artistic objectives simultaneously".

I'm not going to spend pages on marketing theory because there are plenty of textbooks (including arts-focused ones) which do that well but I will spell out the "traditional" approach to marketing defined as the four Ps:

- Product – programs and services
- Price – money, time, payment, perceived value
- Promotion – communicating the benefits through advertising, public relations, special events, publicity, communications
- Place – location, getting there, access.

While the last three Ps lie in what O'Sullivan (1997, 142) calls the "secular domain", there are differences of opinion about how involved an arts marketer should be in first P – the product. In the for-profit world, the marketer will be actively involved in the process of defining the product, that is, giving the customer what they want, but in our world, the "product" or art is usually seen as more sacred and its creation lies in the hands of the artist. Hayes and Roodhouse (2010, 40) claim that arts marketers have "tended to pursue customer satisfaction by focussing on adaptation to the augmented product (pricing, packaging, delivery) rather than run the risk of challenging the core product's aesthetic values or creative process". The accepted model is that artistic quality and programming choices should be in in the hands of the Artistic Director but at MTC, the Marketing Director was part of the repertoire development process, bringing both a personal aesthetic but also a more traditional approach ("that will sell", "they won't attract an audience", "price will be an issue") into the conversation. Equally, Artistic Directors in my experience will want to be intimately involved in the marketing, particularly the visual look, of shows and the company.

Varbanova (2013, 159) proposes that the strategic objectives of arts marketing should be:

- Assisting the core artistic programming
- Fundraising from outside sources
- Generating revenue and profits
- Educating and engaging audiences and communities

- Increasing accessibility and participation
- Creating, improving or changing the public image
- Contributing to a social cause.

If you are managing a small to medium-sized company, these will be *your* goals because you'll probably be the marketer as well as the General Manager or Managing Director. In a larger organisation, you may have an expert or even a team to do the work. In a 2014 *Harvard Business Review* article, the authors described three attributes of a marketing team in what they called the Orchestrator Model:

1. Think: focus on data and analytics
2. Feel: focus on consumer engagement
3. Do: focus on content and production (De Swaan Arons, van den Driest & Weed 2014, 60).

If your marketing team is missing any of these capabilities, you'll need to find them. The balance will depend on the task, but you need all three approaches for marketing to be effective.

In the for-profit world marketing is defined as "the management process that seeks to maximize returns to shareholders by developing relationships with valued customers and creating competitive advantage in the long term" (Doyle 2003, 336). While profitability and return to shareholders isn't the language for non-profit companies, building audiences usually is and so is building reserves for the future. So if Doyle is right, what measures are important? What's our equivalent to shareholder value? Future value? The capacity to invest in the art form now and to build reserves? He defines marketing assets as:

1. Marketing knowledge
2. Brands
3. Customer loyalty
4. Strategic relationships (338).

Developing an effective brand is the focus of many arts marketers. As Hewison and Holden (2011, 169–170) say:

Whether you are communicating to individuals … or to the public at large, you need to be able to project an image of the whole organisation – its mission, its values and what it actually does – in a completely accessible way that is known in the commercial world as "the brand".

The brand tells your audience what they can expect from you and how you're different from other cultural organisations. When someone thinks about buying a ticket or walking through your door, they'll recognise the value of the institution from the public face of the brand which is usually the logo. Tusa (2007b, 3), an interesting manager and writer on the arts, says that it is a

great mistake to create a logo without first defining what the brand values are, or for what you stand. The worst error is to define the organization's brand values without consulting those who work for it to see if they do represent the organisation.

When I worked for Radio National, we tried to develop a logo to reflect the station's unique qualities amongst the endless blue boxes that were used as logos by the other ABC radio stations. Triple J, the ABC's youth network, had always stood separately to the standard brand portfolio but Radio National had no real differentiation. Although the ABC had a strong marketing team, we decided to go to an outside agency with a reputation for innovative work. To be honest, I don't remember the process but I do remember the day when the preliminary image was presented. It had potential but there were elements about it that were simply wrong for us and we had the temerity to ask for changes. It was a classic example of two creative organisations in conflict. We (initially) valued the creativity of the other, but they didn't value our creativity in return. All I can remember from that day is the senior agency representative screaming at us and storming out in response to our temerity in questioning his choices.

The lesson I took from that experience is that when using marketing experts, you have to build a relationship in which your expertise – your unique understanding of your audience, your company and your brand – will be valued rather than dismissed by your marketing partner. At MTC, we went through a tender process that was as much about working out our compatibility and whether both parties heard each other clearly as the cost. As a result, the company had a positive relationship with the winning agency for many years with the process of brand development involving a sophisticated interaction between our key artistic and management staff and their creatives.

Brands are more than just logos or tag lines or the "look" of a company's marketing material. Branding is about organisational fundamentals such as "recognisability, integrity, continuity, creativity and quality" (Hackley 2015, 133). Schumann (2011, 394) says brands "capture the essence of the relationship between organizations and stakeholders – customers, investors, employees, communities – as they articulate the fundamental value that relationships deliver". He suggests that for a brand to be successful it has to journey through five stages: it must be seen and heard, inspire or motivate someone to do something, must be experienced, must be shared and even if times are tough, must still be valued.

This raises an interesting question for arts organisations about the value proposition implicit in a brand. Varbonova (2013, 181) says that marketing is about making promises and implementing a marketing plan is about "keeping the promises that you have made to your audiences, communities and clients". There is a delicate network of promises strung between the vision of the art, what's actually delivered and the marketing message. For example, at MTC the marketing team had to "sell" a performance long before the play was cast, let alone designed and directed.

For the organisation that is presenting art such as a museum or gallery, the quantity and quality of the art is known but the promise will be broken if the event has been oversold. In an article on the origins of the blockbuster exhibition in Australia, Berryman (2013) compares the success of the first two such exhibitions presented by the Australian Arts Exhibitions Corporation Ltd in the 1970s. The first, *The Chinese Exhibition*, was described as a remarkable success generating a net profit of over half a million dollars. The next exhibition presented by the AAEC was *El Dorado: Colombian Gold* with gold artefacts from the Museo del Oro in Bogota. It incurred a loss of $300,000. While part of this loss was a result of ineffective budgeting, Berryman questions whether the collection lent itself to a "block-buster style of treatment" (165). While the Chinese collection was described as containing monumental and spectacular artefacts, the Colombian exhibition was described as "a jewellery exhibition that was brought into the country in two suitcases". This feels like an event that was over-promised.

The ethics of marketing promises are that you believe that you are going to create a masterpiece. It's just that you make art and so sometimes it doesn't work out that way. The star actor who you hope will attract the audience may not be as good on stage as they are on TV. The new commission that was going to be a comedy turned very black. The serious classic just didn't work in the current zeitgeist. And sometimes, the initial marketing message under delivers. MTC commissioned the original play *The Sapphires* that was later turned into a charming movie directed by Wayne Blair starring some of Australia's greatest Indigenous performers. The play was written by Melbourne actor Tony Briggs and was about his mother and her sisters. When we programmed it, Tony hadn't even finished writing it. We just knew that it was going to be a great story and took the risk. But this meant that we didn't have any cast or design or images that we could use in the season subscription brochure. Because the story was based on real people, we used them in the marketing image. But no matter how much we want to believe that our brand was enough to sell an unknown show and to believe that middle-aged women, even attractive

middle-aged women, would work as a communication device, they didn't. *The Sapphires* was amongst our worst-selling shows to subscribers for that year. And, of course, the show itself was brilliant. Directed by Wesley Enoch, it was full of music and laughter, wit and humanity. I felt sorry for every subscriber that failed to include it in their package of plays for the year. And the image for the single ticket campaign had the shining, familiar faces of young Indigenous actors such as Deborah Mailman and Ursula Yovich dressed up to the nines in brilliant sapphire sequins with the result that single tickets sales were much stronger than subscription sales.

When it comes to the logo as brand representative, arts organisations are rarely going to have the marketing budgets to make sure their logos become memorable and instantly identifiable, but one can develop a public visual style that defines the company. Design is an important part of marketing and if we can't get it right, who can? Kaiser (2013, 43) captures these needs well:

> As arts organizations, our marketing materials should be beautiful and creative and well designed. They also need to be readable – especially by our target audiences – and convey a spirit of excitement and artistic accomplishment.

MTC tried a variety of different ways to create artistic marketing material. When I joined the company in the mid-1990s, the tradition was to commission local artists to paint a response to a play and this became the marketing image. While the results were brilliant original art, they suffered from being one-off unconnected pieces which, while reflecting the artist's response to the play, didn't always capture the director's vision of the play or reflect the company's brand. The next approach was to use specifically briefed cartoonists and graphic designers to create the play image. While the marketing message was implicit in the image, there was still a lack of coherence across the season of plays and the actors were still missing from the marketing story except by name. When Simon Philips, a Director with a strong visual aesthetic, joined the company as Artistic Director he decided to create a new visual language for company. Although the logo changed, the most powerful change was moving to the simple consistency of black, white and a single colour with strong photography as the aesthetic driver. The only point of potential conflict between Simon and I was over the colour. He was torn between a brilliant yellow and a vibrant red. My office was an airless, lightless pit and the only way to make it bearable was to cover the walls with the company's posters. I love red but yellow is one of those colours that I can only take in very small doses. I would have had to resign if he'd chosen yellow but luckily my preference won out. The process of developing the images for each play was one that involved the Artistic Director, the photographer and the company's graphic designer but it also involved the whole Repertoire Committee in the search for an image, metaphoric or literal, that would tell the story of the play. With Earl Carter as our photographer during most of this time, our posters and ads were striking and began to be emulated by other Australian arts organisations. I still go into houses and find framed posters from that period on people's walls.

We revisited our brand as part of the process of moving into the Southbank Theatre which in itself responded to our visual language with its use of black, white and red. The tweak to our visual imagery was modest, changing the logo from a round font to one reflecting the white lines of light of the building, and this black and white core enabled Brett Sheehy, who was the next Artistic Director, to find a strong new language that reflected a change of regime but still managed to hold on to some of the company's history.

One of the most complex marketing processes MTC went through was the transitional year between Artistic Directors when three artists were invited to co-program the 2012 season. Each artist was multi-skilled (actor/directors and writer/directors) with a deep understanding of the company. One had been

an Artistic Director of two theatre companies. Another was a current Associate Director of MTC. The third knew the stresses and strains of the job through marriage to an Artistic Director. So their knowledge of the art form and the art of programming was deep. They also had three very different aesthetics when it came to the visual aspects of marketing which terrified the Marketing Department. They were fearful about the team's capacity to agree on a "look" for the season, let alone one that would work to sell the season. It was also hard for the team because they wanted to create a different persona to the previous AD but at the same time not create too much of a disjuncture between the past and the future, given the shortness of their tenure. By using the same marketing company to provide advice and the same in-house graphic designer to provide a visual framework, we successfully negotiated an outcome that was elegant and strong. I'm sure both the artists and the marketing group would have preferred to do things that were slightly more oriented to their personal desires and needs, but the conversations were open and honest and the compromises beautifully realised.

Another one of Schumann's marketing assets is customer loyalty. Relationship marketing is a key part of the activities of any art organisation with a subscriber or member base. O'Sullivan (1997, 145) provides a useful reminder that the key to relationship management is the key to everyday human relationships such as "mutuality, emotion investment, trust, concern for the other's long-term interest, giving priority to the other's needs". Kaiser (2013, 2) makes the good point that creating great art is not enough for an arts organisation to be successful. "Healthy organizations excel at creating visibility for their art among large numbers of constituents." There is nothing more depressing than sitting in an audience of five or six for an artistic work that demonstrates craft, enlightenment and entertainment. Kaiser advises that companies pursue "strong, sophisticated programmatic marketing campaigns", designed to get people to participate but also to create institutional marketing activities that "create a sense of enthusiasm and focus around the organization" (2).

The point of institutional marketing is to create what Kaiser (2013, 2) calls the "family" – donors, Board members, volunteers. While this is a very American approach with their focus on individual giving and Board membership based on donations, the notion that you have an increasing and diverse group of people who support you is important in any country. They provide the positive digital word of mouth that is increasingly replacing the public relation stories printed in newspapers which used to be the core of arts companies' marketing activities.

Before you can build loyalty, you need to entice someone to experience your art. Beautifully designed, strategically crafted marketing materials can't create demand where there is no interest so the search is always for the marginal buyer who will need just a little more convincing. For each work we produce there are hundreds, sometimes thousands of people who are on the cusp of coming. What holds them back can be money or time, fear of a new experience or no-one to go with, a sense that the work is elitist or not relevant to them/their community, risk aversion or not enough information. The challenge of what Kaiser calls "programme marketing" is to allay as many of those concerns as possible. You may also need to attract current members of your audience to new or experimental work. Kaiser (2010, 65) calls this "missionary marketing" required when the work is unfamiliar or the artist unknown. In this case, the potential audience member needs more information than usual such as extracts and explanations on an array of media platforms. This is one time when those beautifully designed posters won't have any impact because with an unknown title or actors, they won't work to help a buying decision.

Colbert (2009) offers a really depressing perspective on finding audiences. He claims that the arts market is saturated and his advice in order to survive in such a market is to get your positioning right, build customer service and capitalise on technology. These are similar to the marketing "assets" proposed by Schumann (2011). By "position" Colbert means have a good understanding of the value of your arts offer, the market segments that might hold potential audience members and the strength of your competitors. Customer service, as I've discussed in *Audiences*, is crucial to turning audience members into Kaiser's "family" members. Our audiences don't come in response to expensive marketing campaigns. Most of them come because a friend or colleague or family member tells them about the event and recommends it.

Capitalising on technology is unavoidable in these days of iPads and Tumblr, Facebook and Instagram. First, because the most powerful of marketing communication techniques, word of mouth, takes place this way. The moment the curtain goes up or the person experiences the exhibition, they turn into a marketer, updating their Facebook page, tweeting the world or texting their friends to go/not go. Second, digital technology in all its forms is important because the power of the traditional media used by the arts – print – is in an ever-increasing race to no readership.[1] Third, there is now more possibility for direct connection between artist and audience, providing opportunities for the access and dialogue that used to be mediated by our companies. We communicate with our audiences more than ever before even though, ironically, we have less direct communication with the potential audience. Even five years ago, one could be a non-arts consumer and still stumble across arts-related stories and advertisements in your local newspaper. Now it's hard to find that information "accidentally" on the paper's online version and we need our audiences to send the word (and the image and the clip) out into the digital sphere for us. Every communication has the possibility of being a two- or three- or thousand-way conversation – an even stronger reason to focus our marketing on building relationships and loyalty.

These marketing communication opportunities also offer us new challenges. I've just come back from a meeting with 25 young volunteers for a community dance project which is going to include another 400 people. We've had to negotiate with these volunteers how and when they use their social media to tell the story – what hash tags to use; the stage at which what happens in the rehearsal room should be shared; the language they use now that they are representatives of the company. Another challenge is when to allow the audience to take photos. In some recent experiences, I've seen shows where people could and did use their phones to take pictures without having a negative experience on the performers or the audience. In New Zealand's Globe Shakespeare Pop-up, I saw young groundling girls taking selfies after they'd been splattered with fake blood during a battle scene in *Henry V*. It was a show which deliberately reached out to the audience and where the actors wandered through the crowd engaging physically and emotionally with the audience. In this case, taking photos seemed appropriate. Taylor Mac's *A 24-Decade History of Popular Music* was a completely immersive piece with audience involvement at every level. Taking photos of one's friends and lovers participating in the show made sense and with all the colour and movement, a few people taking photos didn't interfere with the nature of the work. On the other hand, I can think of shows when taking photos would be appalling for both actor and audience, for example in intimate production of a small cast work or even dangerous for the performer, for example flashes during a circus act.

Another challenge is trying to get people's attention given the proliferation of digital communication technology (Besan et al. 2018). How do we cut through in what sometimes feels like an excessive world of choice? Not just excessive in terms of what's on but excessive in terms of all the competitive messages that people are getting minute by minute about the world. Baxter (2017b) challenges us to lift our game and offers the example of the Art Institute of Chicago's Van Gogh campaign when they created an actual bedroom based on one of his paintings that audience members could walk around and sleep in. The result was a massive viral campaign and the largest

number of visitors for years. One could imagine that a small to medium-sized arts organisation could be just as inventive but one suspects that the Art Institute had a large audience to start with.

With all the two-way communication that digital media offers, another point of difficulty for arts organisations is that along with positive word mouth comes (potentially) endless criticism. Every audience member is now a critic. Every artist's Facebook or Twitter account is open to commentary. Even your own staff may comment negatively about the company in the public realm. While one can attempt to manage the latter scenario via a Social Media Use policy, it's harder to decide what to do about negative reviews. One can ignore them, engage with them or delete them (where possible). In research about consumer perceptions of arts organisations' responses to online reviews, Wiggins et al. (2017) found that altering or quoting from reviews generated distrust and scepticism whereas providing access to full reviews was viewed more positively. It's impossible to stop people telling their stories so perhaps all one can do is engage when the facts might be wrong but accept that opinions will differ.

While our Marketing department will always be focused on communication, I rather like the metaphors that Ryan, Fenton and Sangiori (2010, 227–228) use to describe the arts marketer as they move from a focus on delivery to a more collaborative mode. They describe them as "collectors and sharers of stories", as "guide" and as "network facilitators" because they look externally towards the audience and internally towards the organisation.

See also: Audiences, Economics, Media, Money, Technology

References

Baxter, L. 2010 "From Luxury to Necessity: The Changing Role of Qualitative Research in the Arts", in O'Reilly, D. & Kerrigan, F. (eds) *Marketing the Arts: A Fresh Approach*, London: Routledge, 121–140.

Baxter, A. 2017a *How Marketing Can Help Influence Philanthropists to Give to Your Not-for-profit Cause*, www.andrewbillybaxter.com.au/blog/2017/9/15/how-marketing-can-help-influence-philanthropists-to-give-to-your-not-for-profit-cause [accessed 27 February 2019].

Baxter, A. 2017b "Performance Pressure: Arts Companies Need to Lift Their Game When it Comes to Reaching Out and Growing Their Audiences", www.adma.com.au/resources/performance-pressure-arts-companies-need-to-lift-their-game-when-it-comes-to-reaching-out [accessed 27 February 2019].

Besana, A., Bagnasco, A. M., Esposito, A. & Calzolari, A. 2018 "It's a Matter of Attention: The Marketing of Theatres in the Age of Social Media", *International Journal of Arts Management*, 20(3), 20–37.

Berryman, J. 2013 "Art and National Interest: The Diplomatic Origins of the 'Blockbuster Exhibition' in Australia", *Journal of Australian Studies*, 37(2), 159–173.

Boorsma, M. & Chiaravalloti, F. 2010 "Arts Marketing Performance: An Artistic-Mission-Led Approach to Evaluation", *The Journal of Arts Management, Law, and Society*, 40, 297–312.

Colbert, F. 2009 *Beyond Branding: Contemporary Marketing Challenges for Arts Organizations*, Geelong: Kenneth Myer Lecture, Deakin University.

De Swaan Arons, M van den Driest, F& Weed, K. 2014 "The Ultimate Marketing Machine", *Harvard Business Review*, July–August, 55–63.

Doyle, P. 2003 "Strategy as Marketing", in Cummings, S. & Wilson, D. (eds) *Images of Strategy*, Oxford: Blackwell Publishing, 331–335.

Hackley, C. 2015 "Branding and the Music Market", in Beech, N. & Gilmore, C. (eds) *Organising Music: Theory, Practice, Performance*, Cambridge: Cambridge University Press, 127–134.

Hayes, D. & Roodhouse, S. 2010 "From Missionary to Market Maker", in O'Reilly, D. & Kerrigan, F. (eds) *Marketing the Arts: A Fresh Approach*, London: Routledge, 40–53.

Kaiser, M. M. 2010 *Leading Roles*, Waltham, MA: Brandeis University Press.

Kaiser, M. M. 2013 *The Circle*, Waltham, MA: Brandeis University Press.

Kotler, P. & Scheff, J. 1997 *Standing Room Only*, Boston, MA: Harvard Business School Press.

O'Sullivan, P. 1997 "Marketing the Arts: from Paradigm to Plan", in Fitzgibbon, M. & Kelly, A. (eds) *From Maestro to Manager*, Dublin: Oak Tree Press, 139–181.

Ryan, A., Fenton, M. & Sangiori, D. 2010 "A Night at the Theatre", in O'Reilly, D. & Kerrigan, F. (eds) *Marketing the Arts: A Fresh Approach*, London: Routledge, 214–230.

Rentschler, R. 1998 "Museum and Performing Arts Marketing: A Climate of Change", *Journal of Arts Management, Law and Society*, 28(1), 83–96.

Rentschler, R. 2002 "Museum and Performing Arts Marketing: The Age of Discovery", *Journal of Arts Management, Law and Society*, 32(1), 7–14.

Schumann, D. M. 2011 "The Engagement of Brands", in Gillis, T. L. (ed.) *The IABC Handbook of Organizational Communication* (2nd ed), San Francisco, CA: Jossey-Bass, 393–403.

Sumner, J. 1993 *Recollections at Play*, Melbourne: Melbourne University Press.

Tusa, T. 2007b "The New ABC of the Arts", *Arts Education Policy Review*, 108(4), 3–6.

Varbanova, L. 2013 *Strategic Management in the Arts*, New York: Routledge.

Wiggins, J., Song, C., Trivedi, D. & Preece S. B. 2017 "Consumer Perceptions of Arts Organizations' Strategies for Responding to Online Reviews", *International Journal of Arts Management*, 20(1), 4–20.

Media

Newspapers, free to air TV, and radio, the "mass media", used to be the place arts companies turned to for publicity and editorials, reviews and advertisements. Sometimes it was a case of begging (for that free news story); sometimes paying (for listings or ads); sometimes it was welcomed (the page three story); sometimes it was loathed (the bad review from the person who just didn't understand your work). By covering arts news, season launches, feature stories about our work and our industry as well as providing critical reviews, the media contributed to our capacity to find audiences and also created a more educated audience (Kaiser 2013). It's curious to go back to Radbourne and Fraser's book on arts management, published in 1996 when, in talking about the media, they say that "the arts organisation, usually seen to be a *producer* of goods, is in this scenario a *customer* or *consumer* who has minimal control over what is being broadcast to the public" (89). How the world has changed. Arts and cultural organisations are now actively creating communication via a range of digital platforms.

Newspapers used to be the main source of communication for arts organisations, but that world is changing. In the first edition of this book, I checked the circulation of my local Melbourne newspaper, *The Age*. Between 2011 and 2013, it had lost a third of its circulation which was down to 142,050 out a population of 4.25 million. For this edition, I checked again, and by July 2018, the print version circulation was down to 74,360. The definition of news has changed with the ever-increasing number of television and online channels and what Mathews (2011, 302) called "do-it-yourself" online media.

As social media is inescapable, it is more useful than traditional marketing tools? I think the answer is yes and no. There are many more media channels but each is designed to narrow cast to our current interests. While there are many more options to communicate with the people we know, it's much harder to find and talk to the people we don't know. While it's easy to reach across the world, target a campaign to a specific group, interact with the audience, measure the impact, go viral – and of course digital media is cheaper – it's harder to find the person who might, given the right message, be willing to engage with you. People have to already have an interest in your work to search you out, to "friend" you, to follow your hashtag. It's now a much more complicated world than just placing an ad in the local paper.

An arts management student was collecting views on social media from managers in 2017 and asked me the question about whether it was good for arts marketing. It's not a matter of whether it's good or bad – it's inescapable. You have to use it. If you're not out there, you're not real to most people.

You can divide social media into two groups or platforms, one that allows for discovery and one that allows for communication. If you want your work to get noticed, you should focus on platforms that allow for discovery. By focus, I mean you should be creating work and posting at those websites consistently. Consistency is the key. For discovery, there's Tumblr, Instagram, YouTube, Flickr, Pinterest for example, and

for communication there's platforms such as Facebook, Google+ and Twitter (Cave 2016).

The distinction is important. If people don't already know that you exist or your name, it will be almost impossible to find you on a communication-type website. However on a discovery-type website, even if they don't know your name, your work can still be found provided you have tagged it appropriately (Chie 2015).

The most important shift in the media for arts organisations is not so much the increase in forms and the need to create one's own news but the use of the media for critical discussion. Australia has never had powerful reviewers such as Frank Rich *New York Times* theatre reviewer in the 1980s and 1990s who was known as "The Butcher of Broadway", but press reviews from the major reputable papers did have a demonstrable impact on audience numbers. However, now that every audience member can be a reviewer, the power of critics and authoritative experts has lessened (Thelwall 2007, 51) but this doesn't mean that criticism has waned.

At the end of 2014, the Artistic Director of Opera Australia Lyndon Terracini, refused to provide complementary tickets to two arts critics because of website pieces on the company. In a newspaper article about the story, arts journalist Peter Craven compared the old and new style of arts coverage:

> in traditional newspaper arts journalism, there is the sympathetic puff piece, the review which is no-holds-barred and written in full consciousness of the larger readership and the influence the critic wields, and there is the "think" piece, which may well be analytical and critical of a general direction. Opinion pieces are characteristically measured in style, tempered by the seriousness of the occasion. Online talk, by contract, is likely to conflate criticism and analysis and mouth off with a fair bit of colour and looseness.

The policy for artists and companies used to be not to respond to bad reviews or critical pieces, a policy that annoyed me when confronted with reviewers who regularly demonstrated a cavalier disregard for an artist's work or the experience of the rest of the audience. Now there are a multitude of voices with tones from the polite to the rabid. Do you still stay silent when critics review your work, knowing that it might be retweeted endlessly? And how do you respond to the general public who use social media to express opinions that might be supportive but equally might be uninformed drivel? If a negative comment is inaccurate or not factual, you can respond, but opinion is opinion.

When I was at MTC I didn't tweet about our shows or anyone else's. My opinions would have read as those reflecting the company's position. Now, I'm free to comment – but only do so when I have something positive to say. Artists face too much criticism, often uncalled for or politically motivated, to need negative comments from me. And in the face of these many voices all an arts company can do is to create its own "news" and be part of all the conversations.

In traditional media, the arts rarely got out of the entertainment pages and into news except when there was a crisis. And this hasn't changed. All that has changed is the speed at which the story about a crisis spreads due to the ubiquity of digital media outlets and the 24-hour news cycle. Having a policy about your relationship with the media, about who gets to represent the company and how staff are allowed to comment about the company on their social media will help in such circumstances.

Media is important not just as a marketing tool. You need to use the media for every aspect of your role as an arts leader. Although I find the business pages somewhat dry, they are the source of information about potential sponsors, about the wealth of your donors, about the viability of that overseas tour, about the possible returns on your financial reserves. What's happening in China or Greece or the USA will provide inspiration for the artists you work with, impact on the government arts budget, provide an opportunity for a partnership and create a conversational opening at an opening.

In other words, read, listen, watch and contribute to the media.

See also: Crisis, Marketing, Technology

References

Cave, J. 2016 *Digital Marketing vs Traditional Marketing: Which One is Better?*, Digital Doughnut, 14 July, www.digitaldoughnut.com/articles/2016/july/digital-marketing-vs-traditional-marketing [accessed 27 February 2019].

Chie, T. Y. 2015 *The Best Social Media Site to Promote Your Art?* Parkablogs, 19 October, www.parkablogs.com/content/imfa-13-best-social-media-site-promote-your-art [accessed 27 February 2019].

Craven, P. 2015 "Reacting to the Sting of Critics Casts Light Where One Might Prefer Shadows", *The Weekend Australian*, 10–11 January, 17, www.theaustralian.com.au/arts/opinion/reacting-to-the-sting-of-critics-casts-light-where-one-might-prefer-shadows/story-fn9n9z9n-1227180052396 [accessed 8 February 2015].

Kaiser, M. M. 2013 *The Circle*, Waltham, MA: Brandeis University Press.

Mathews, W. K. 2011 "Media Relations", in Gillis, T. L. (ed.) *The IABC Handbook of Organizational Communication* (2nd ed), San Francisco, CA: Jossey-Bass, 301–313.

Radbourne, J. & Fraser, M. 1996 *Arts Management*, Sydney: Allen and Unwin.

Thelwall, S. 2007 *Capitalising Creativity: Developing Earned Income Streams in Cultural Industries Organisations*, London: Proboscis, 14.

Meetings

Love them or hate them, meetings are unavoidable. As Mankins, Brahm and Caimi (2014, 80) say "they are essential for fostering collaboration and making critical decisions". Because I'm a relational/consulting type leader, I'm happy to attend a well-managed meeting but I once worked with a highly skilled and intelligent person who hated meetings with a passion. I tried to run good ones to show them that meetings could be useful but I think I failed to convince. One has meetings to share information about what's happening and going to happen, to consult and collect opinions, to make decisions, because you have to (legal compliance/Board meetings), to learn things, to network and for social and support reasons (Adirondack 2005). Given the necessity of meetings, why are there endless cartoons about bad meetings which suggest, in Tropman's rather witty words (1996, xix), that they are made of up of "groups that take minutes to waste hours"? What creates this negativity towards meetings?

Tropman (1996, quoted in Dwyer 2009, 337) says that part of our dislike of meetings is cultural – in countries like the USA and Australia compared to countries with a more community ethos, individual action is prized over collective action. Another point is that meetings are ubiquitous – they are everywhere and there can be too many of them. Perlow (2014) describes a company with an overly collaborative culture in which too many employees were involved in every decision. People only found time to do their work outside of normal office hours. The problem was partly solved by having a meeting-free day a week – no face-to-face meetings, no teleconferences, no video conferences. But probably even more importantly, the organisation reviewed every meeting in terms of why, who should be there, how long they should be and their agenda. As a result, "meetings became smaller, shorter, more focused and less frequent" (Perlow 2014, 25).

Another point made by Tropman (1996) is that we don't have enough training for work in groups. How many times have we been in meetings that are badly run with a Chair that lacks the skills to control and direct the group, let alone encourage participation and facilitate useful discussion? I was extremely lucky that in the 1980s, I attended a course run by the Australia Council about how to chair meetings. Not only was it a very practical program, it was also a women-only weekend that had been developed in response to the lack of women on Boards of arts organisations. This course enabled skill building amongst the participants but more importantly built confidence. Hewison and Holden (2011, 149) provide an excellent description of a good Chair who can make people feel both relaxed and disciplined:

> the key to good chairing is good listening and good looking: glance around the room when someone is speaking, and use eye contact to gauge reactions and see when people want to speak … summarise what has happened and make sure everyone is clear about the outcomes and actions that flow from the meeting.

To which I would add the skill of encouraging the quiet to speak, the chatterers to focus and the cynical to contain themselves.

The worst meetings I have ever attended were part of a multi-stakeholder process where one of the stakeholders wanted to discount the views of another stakeholder. Although the former was the facilitator of the meetings, they failed to provide agendas, a Chair or minutes. The result was that decisions could be avoided in the context of the meeting as time and energy usually ran out in this blancmange of inefficiency. What was worse, when decisions were made that didn't suit the organiser, there was ultimate deniability. No formal record of the decision existed. Although I couldn't take on the role of Chair, I did informally become the minute taker, agenda creator and action recorder. And slowly, the meetings became more useful and effective as the facilitator was embarrassed into slightly better behaviour.

Another problem with meetings, particularly regular ones, is that they become boring and the result of boring meetings are bad decisions and wasted time. When people lose interest they fail to "hear" crucial ideas or issues and don't properly evaluate opinions. Lencioni (2005) recommends deliberate conflict generation but I haven't tried that approach. My solutions have been to mix up the format, provide opportunities for different sorts of presentations and invite special guests to talk to the group.

As meetings are necessary, Mankins, Brahm and Caimi (2014, 80) propose four simple norms to make them work:

1. An agenda with clear objectives
2. Advance preparation so, for example, information sharing is reduced because people already have it
3. Starting on time

4. Ending early, particularly if the meeting is going nowhere.

Fishel (2003 147) provides a deeply depressing list of 20 ways to disrupt a meeting and the top of the list is "arrive late". Getting that last person through the door is a challenge. I used to sit there with the early birds and then watch them nip out for a coffee or a quick catch up rather than sit passively waiting for the last person to arrive. Which meant that when they did, they were no longer the last person to the meeting – the early bird was. I tried various techniques such as starting meetings at 10am so that people could drop off kids to school and/or avoid peak hour traffic but even that didn't always work. One slightly more effective response was starting on time regardless of who was there. Another idea is to not let latecomers join but I'm afraid I wasn't ever bold enough to try that one. Part of the reason people are late is because it's a not a meeting that's important to them so only inviting who really needs to be there may be the answer. Sometimes the person who leaves the meeting early is equally as irritating as the person who arrives late because they will probably miss out on that crucial piece of information or being part of that final decision. The only way to solve this problem is to follow up with them and brief them on the outcome – and try and keep your meetings short so that no-one is tempted to leave early.

Another problem with meetings is when no-one is actually clear about why they should attend and what they are going to get out of it. Judith White tells of meetings held by the CEO of the Art Gallery of New South Wales. He clearly had an agenda – he was trying to reach out to all his staff through a serios of informal Monday morning stand-up meetings at various locations in the gallery. He invited staff to join him for a few minutes' chat followed by a visit to the café. White (2017, 86) says that she "found them awkward occasions; he was trying hard to connect but more people were reluctant to speak frankly, and attendance tended to drop off". If the meeting is voluntary, and you're not sure what you're going to get out of it, why go?

I don't think the CEO did himself any favours by calling these meetings "the mosh pit".

One of the most frustrating parts of meetings, particularly Board meetings, is when it becomes clear that people haven't done their homework. As a CEO, there's not much you can do to get Board members to prepare in advance apart from making sure that your reports are concise and interesting and timely and suggesting to your Chair that rather than talk about what's in the report at the meeting, you simply have to take questions about its content. Another weakness of meetings when the point is to make decisions rather than simply share information is that ideas aren't really thought through and people take the easiest decision. Covey (1992) suggests that for decision-making meetings people should be given work to do beforehand and if that doesn't produce a good result, someone should be given the task to explore an idea in depth, identify alternatives and make a recommendation to the next meeting.

Lencioni recommends four different types of meetings:

1. The Daily Check In – five minutes of the team standing around reporting on their activities that day
2. The Weekly Tactical meeting which consists of:
   - "The Lightning Round" – everyone indicates two or three priorities for the week for one minute each
   - "Progress Review" – reporting for no more than five minutes on four to six pieces of critical information or measures that are important for success
   - Real-time agenda – picking up from the first two processes what is really worth talking about in what he calls "disciplined spontaneity"
3. The Monthly Strategic meeting which needs work in advance to successfully debate and decide on critical issues
4. The Quarterly Off-site Review to check the strategic plan.

My "daily check in" was more in the form of wandering about and checking in with the management team rather than a team meeting per se. The off-site meeting is something that I should have done more often. I resisted it not in terms of the content but in terms of the cost of hiring a space somewhere else. Usually it only happened on Board Strategic Planning Days. Finally, when there was enough money in our reserves for me to justify paying for a conference centre, overnight accommodation and a facilitator, the MTC management team had an off-site review and, on reflection, it was one of the most bonding, honest and effective meetings we ever had.

Sometimes, having meetings that aren't specifically about work but which might help inspire or re-invigorate people or simply add to their knowledge about the world or each other is a good thing. For example, one organisation I know has a staff "salon" every couple of weeks. A staff member presents something of interest to the team. It may be personal. It may be political. It may be about art. And as well as sharing knowledge, it also builds the public presentation and case-making skills of people in the team.

Bolman and Deal (2013, 293) say that while "[m]eetings may not always produce rational discourse, sound plans, or radical improvements … they serve as expressive occasions to clear the air and promote collective bonding". Your role is to make sure that each meeting has a clear purpose, is interesting enough to keep people awake, has documented, action-oriented outcomes and is attended by just the right number of people for just the right amount of time.

See also: Boards, Decision-making, Groups, Strategic Plan

References

Adirondack, S. 2005 *Just About Managing?* (4th ed), London: London Voluntary Service Council.

Bolman, L. G. & Deal, T. E. 2013 *Reframing Organizations* (5th ed), San Francisco, CA: Jossey-Bass.

Covey, S. R. 1992 *Principle-Centred Leadership*, London: Pocket Books.

Dwyer, J. 2009 *Communication in Business* (4th ed), Sydney: Pearson.

Fishel, D. 2003 *The Book of The Board*, Sydney: Federation Press.

Hewison, R. & Holden, J. 2011 *The Cultural Leadership Handbook*, Farnham: F Gower.

Lencioni, P. 2005 *The Five Dysfunctions of a Team: A Field Guide to Managers, Leaders and Facilitators*, San Francisco, CA: Jossey-Bass.

Mankins, M., Brahm, C. & and Caimi, G. 2014 "Your Scarcest Resource", *Harvard Business Review* 92(5), 74–80.

Perlow, L. 2014 "Manage Your Team's Collective Time", *Harvard Business Review*, June, 23–25.

Tropman, J. E. 1996 *Effective Meetings: Improving Group Decision Making* (2nd ed), San Francisco, CA: Sage Publications.

White, J. 2017 *Culture Heist: Art versus Money*, Blackheath, NSW: Bandl & Schlesinger.

Mindfulness

"Mindfulness" is a word that has its roots in Eastern spiritual practice, became used more recently in clinical psychology and psychiatry, and is now one that appears in the language of leadership and management. Langer (2014, 68) defines mindfulness as "the process of actively noticing new things" because when you do "it puts you in the present. It makes you more sensitive to context and perspective." Sinclair (2007b, 260) says:

> Being mindful means learning how to observe and detach from extraneous thought, allowing a stiller, clearer consciousness that leads to less distraction and more presence.

She says that it can improve our ability to deal with stress as well as our insight and creativity, self-awareness and quality of life. In her view, it also reduces the likelihood of depression and anxiety and the tendency to blame and bully. Sinclair provides a number of examples and stories about mindfulness in her great book on *Leadership for the Disillusioned* (2007). As she rightly says, too many things come through our doorways than we can reasonably cope with and so leaders have to develop the capacity to give their attention to the things that really matter and in ways that aren't prematurely judgemental

(Sinclair 2007b). Being mindful can help that process.

Bunting (2016), who has written a book on leadership and mindfulness, says that to be our best as leaders we need to be calm not anxious, we need to be relaxed not frantic, we need to be open not closed. And as he also says, we can't control the world around us but we can control how we respond to it (18, 35).

I've also used the word "mindfulness" (and found it useful to do so) in a different way, more connected to the standard dictionary definition of "mindful" – taking heed or care of. What I mean is that capacity to remember to think about the broader implication of one's actions. It became a phrase that I used often when there was a major debate in Australia around the role of women directors and writers in theatre. For many women, quotas were an answer to try and lift the number of female artists to 50% within theatre companies. But for many artists, female and male, quotas were not acceptable. The funding bodies encouraged companies to increase the number of opportunities for women but didn't build in any penalties. So how, as a female manager, was I to encourage the generally male artists I worked with to choose women? Mindfulness. I became the person to take heed of, to have the responsibility for, the organisation's gender balance: I was the watcher, the counter, the reminder:

M: I want you to draw up some commissions for writers

F: But there's only one woman out of four on the list. We can afford another commission but can you think about giving it to another woman?

F: Have you noticed that we haven't employed any female lighting designers for a while? I know there aren't many but we should be able to find one or two for next season.

One of the roles of a leader or manager is to ask questions every time there is an organisational change or a new process or the implementation of different ways of doing things: what does this mean for diversity/health and safety/risk/ stakeholders? The challenge is to think about more than just the project or the change and to think holistically about the organisation.

Another side of "mindfulness" is reflection. It's the practice of stepping back and thinking about what has just happened in order to gain understanding. Sinclair (2007, 171) warns against reflection that is only focused on self-improvement. Through reflecting on a perplexing work situation, you can potentially get a clearer understanding of what's happened and what that means for others as well as yourself. If we only hear the words that are said at the time, we don't necessarily get the whole picture which consists of actions, beliefs and feelings, as well as words (Pässilä 2012).

There are different forms of reflection, all of which can be useful for us as managers:

- Critical reflection: to identify and question taken-for-granted beliefs and values
- Public reflection: to become collectively aware of and transform one's own behaviour
- Productive reflection – to develop work and learning activities that change work practices and personal engagement
- Organising reflection – to take account of emotional and political processes in the workplace (Pässilä 2012, 64).

We can sometimes get so bogged down in a particular project or the day-today demands of challenging jobs that we don't take the time to be in the present, to think more carefully about what we do or to reflect on what we have done. Processes of mindfulness and reflection might lead us to good judgement and better decisions.

See also: Decision-making, Leadership, Listening

References

Bunting, M. 2016 *The Mindful Leader*, Milton, QLD: Wiley.

Langer, E. 2014 "Mindfulness in the Age of Complexity", *Harvard Business Review*, 92(3), 68–73.

Pässilä, A. 2012 *Reflexive Model of Research-Based Theatre*, Finland, provided by author.

Sinclair, A. 2007b "Taming the Monkey", *afrboss.com. au*, http://works.bepress.com/cgi/viewcontent. cgi?article=1020&context=amanda_sinclair [accessed 27 February 2019].

Sinclair, A. 2007 *Leadership for the Disillusioned*, Sydney: Allen & Unwin.

Mission

You may be wondering why there's a heading for *Mission* and not one for "vision". The answer is that there could have been. There are so many contradictory versions of what a "vision" or a "mission" actually is … and whether using such language actually helps organisations. It just so happens that my version of "mission" includes the idea of "vision".

Zan (2006, 21) doesn't like "missions" for arts organisations, seeing it as "an obsession with procedures that do not attend to the substantive characteristics of organisations such as museums and hospitals". Don Watson (2010), an Australian commentator on language (and its misuse), gives a wonderful example of where "mission statements" can serve to obscure the reality of what an organisation does. At St Martins-in-the-Fields in London he noted that their mission included "excellence in hospitality". As he said, "[s]urviving the Black Death, the Great Fire of London all this, they never had excellence, they just gave out soup and bread, they now they provide excellence in hospitality". With a sigh in his voice, he said "it [management language] goes everywhere". Watson's view can be found even in a detective story:

> Challis printed it [a paper about regional policing] out and tried to make sense of the guidelines, a low-level fury burning in his head. Was there a clear distinction between a "mission statement", an "aim" and an "objective"? Words, meaningless words, that's what policing had become.[2]

I do wonder whether arts organisations need mission statements in the same way that private sector organisations require them. The very existence of an arts or cultural company is a reflection of its "mission" whereas the first rationale of a for-profit company is profit and therefore they have to find some other language to capture what they do to make that profit. They need some form of inspirational statement for staff and stakeholders whereas we already have that inspiration built into our conversations about why we do what we do. However, in a world of strategic plans and KPIs, we have to use corporate language – not through choice but because it's required of us by our funders and expected of us by our stakeholders. Your funding body may advise you whether they want a "mission" or a "vision". Your Board may have a preferred set of words they want you to use. The point is that whatever you call it, it can be useful for an organisation to articulate aspects of its operations that help explain it to the outside world and provide a focus as it moves into the future.

To take some simple ideas, you need:

- A statement of "purpose" – what you believe in; why you exist
- A "vision" of what you want your organisation to look like in 5 or 10 years' time
- Beliefs or "values" which underpin your organisational culture
- A method – what you actually do
- A couple of important measurable goals that will give you something against which you can check your progress.

Phills (2005) proposed four elements in a "mission": the purpose and values, which capture the enduring nature of the organisation and vision and goals which propel the organisation into the future. Such statements, according to Kotter (1996, 71), need to have qualities that are desirable (to you and your stakeholders), feasible (because agonising over things that can never be isn't useful), clear (so that you can make decisions based on them) and communicable. The person who's written the most about strategic planning for arts organisations is Michael Kaiser (2013, 166) who says that "an effective mission statement limits activity and makes it easier for staff and Board to separate relevant opportunities from projects that would not further the institution's goals". He adds some other qualities to Kotter's list and says that such statements should be "concise (so it is memorable), comprehensive (inclusive of all major activities) and coherent (so it is believable)".

Starting with the statement of purpose and the values, the idea is that such statements or lists need to be inspirational, credible, durable and distinctive. You have to walk the talk of the values. The "lift" statement[3] needs to be one that staff believe in and are proud to say. This can become difficult if there are lots of other organisations like yours. The other challenge is to find the words that capture your organisation's essence without being too wordy or overburdened with jargon. Cummings (2003, 45) gives a great example of the New Zealand police force pre- and post-consultants. Before the experts came in to help design a mission, the statement of purpose was:

> To work with the community to maintain the peace.

Afterwards:

> To contribute to the provision of a safe and secure environment where people may go about their lawful business unhindered and which is conducive to the enhancement of the quality of life and economic performance.

You can guess which one I think works best.

If you can get the "why we exist" part of your storytelling right, it adds to your capacity to inspire and engage. Some of the statements that my arts management students have chosen as being inspiring include:

- Use our pioneering spirit to responsibly deliver energy to the world
- We're for Dogs

- Exploring Victoria, Discovering the World
- A computer on every desk and in every home
- Where dreams come true.[4]

Usually statements of purpose are longer than these examples but the challenge is to avoid the trap proposed by Scott Adams, the creator of Dilbert cartoons:

> A Mission Statement is defined as "a long awkward statement that demonstrates management's inability to think clearly".
> (Quoted in Cummings 2003, 51)

I wouldn't say that MTC's mission statement was perfect. There was a statement about its purpose embedded in the university regulation that provided its governance framework. It was somewhat dry and so I added a few more words of emotion into it:

> The company's aim is to produce contemporary and classic Australian and international theatre with style, passion and world-class artistic excellence in order to entertain, challenge and enrich audiences in Melbourne, Victoria and Australia.[5]

And words to that effect still sit on the company's website:

> Purpose: Every generation deserves remarkable storytelling to help understand their times.
> Mission: To create excellence in all forms of theatrical storytelling – including existing and new Australian stories, international hits and classics – with imagination and passion in order to entertain, challenge, inspire and grow audiences.[6]

It's short-ish, one hopes it's inspiring, it's certainly durable (I first wrote it in 1995), specific, credible and everyone in the company knew why we did what we did although they probably couldn't say the statement off the top of their head. Mind you, it could apply to many other theatre companies which is why "Melbourne" and "Victoria" were added in to make it distinctive.

If I'd seen the way the Northern Dutch Theatre Company describes itself, I might have stolen some of their words:

> as a producer of theatrical performances that challenge spectators and make them aware of their doubts, angers, prejudices and fears; theater that actually says something about the world and considers theater a perfect means to analyse and unmask human and societal processes.
>
> (Quoted in Boorsma & Chiaravalloti 2010, 303)

The questions to ask about any statement of purpose, regardless of what you call it, is:

- Is it a "lift"[7] statement?
- Do your staff remember it?
- Do they believe it?
- Can you inspire donors and government with it?
- Is it the check point for all your decisions, i.e. does it help you decide what to do and what not to do?

In some strategic planning sessions that I run, I ask the participants, Board and staff, to respond to the following questions:

- What is it about your company that inspires you?
- How do you think your company contributes to the world?
- What's the best experience you've had or you've heard someone tell in their interaction with the company.

Sharing such stories helps clarify purpose and values. Grace (2005) offers another way of getting to your purpose. She proposes getting your Board and staff to complete this sentence: "Our organisation exists because …" But they aren't allowed to use the infinitive form of the verb, for example to inform, to educate – but rather to use the values and express why the organisation exists. She gives a fascinating example of an organisation that helps in the repair of injured hands:

> Next to the human face, hands are our most expressive feature. We talk with them. We work with them. We play with them. We comfort and love with them. An injury to the hand affects people personally and professionally. At Vector Health Programs, we give people back the use of their hands (7).

When students trawl the net looking for short, inspiring statements from arts organisations, regardless of whether they are called vision or mission or purpose or whatever, they usually discard anything that is too long. If the initial sentence was strong enough they might just be interested to explore the rest of the artistic manifesto but they didn't want to read endless paragraphs to work out what the organisation stood for. As well as rejecting length, they also rejected statements that could belong to a similar organisation or ones that just seemed to reflect the need to match government-funding policies. It was usually the short statements that had the most power and also the ones from which you can unpack the company's values. For example, they tended to like the Australian Ballet's "vision" statement from a few years ago:

> To care for tradition while daring to be different.[8]

You can guess from that short statement that their values might include caring (for people as well as tradition), innovation and creativity.

Values[9] are the fundamental beliefs and guiding principles of an organisation. A core value for a university, for example, could be "intellectual freedom" or "innovation" for a technology company (Phills 2005, 197). For Australia's great physical theatre company Circus Oz, their values have included multi-skilled team-work, irreverence and humour, democracy and social justice and you see these values play out in their performances in the big top as well as the range of education and diversity programs they run. They do live their values. And that's the point. One can have important and meaningful words on one's list of values but unless they are experienced positively by staff and stakeholders, then the words are pointless. Some of MTC's values were excellence and loyalty. While many arts companies would aspire to excellence, it has to be translated into action not just on stage, but in every aspect of the organisation's activities – from Finance department processes to the quality of one's website.

The next part of Phills' (2005) "mission" definition is to have a vision of the future. The vision can sometimes be captured in words and sometimes in images. It should be a rich picture of what the world might look if the company achieves its goals. When I first typed the previous sentence, I was sitting in a small to medium (S2M) sized arts company and their future dreams were captured in chalk speech bubbles on the door to their rehearsal studio. MTC's vision was a set model of a new theatre. Fishel (2003, 109) says that a vision can either be expressed as a world you want to realise or a description of how your organisations will look in five or ten years' time. Kotter's (1996, 71) description of an effective vision is one that is imaginable, desirable to all stakeholders, flexible (because the world might change), communicable and, most importantly, feasible.

And if the vision is the destination, then what Phills (2005) calls BHAGs – big hairy, audacious goals – are the dynamic part of the mission that will clarify the path to that future. Another set of words for BHAGs that you'll see in strategic plans are WIGs – wildly important goals. The one that's always quoted but I still think is extraordinary in terms of its combination of concreteness and inspiration is President Kennedy's line:

We will put a man on the moon by the end of the decade and bring him back safely.

Such a major goal applies to the whole organisation, is long term, requires significant time and effort to accomplish, you'll know when you've achieved it, it's energising and inspirational, attainable but ambitious.[10]

Every so often it's worth checking that your purpose and values are still the ones you believe in and that your vision and goals are achievable. There were times when I despaired about whether MTC would ever get a new theatre but by doing a reality check and revisiting the reasons why you exist, you can be re-inspired to go on. Or alternatively, you could save the organisation from stagnation by being willing to adjust or change the mission to reflect new stakeholder demands or new styles of art (Tshirhart 1996).

The point about having some statement that captures the psychological and emotional language about why you do what you do and what you want to do in the future is that you need it as an artistic planning tool. You can check whether the decisions you make about the art you present or create are contributing to the future you dream about. A "mission" creates organisational clarity. It tells your staff and your stakeholders your reason for existence, what's important to you, what business you're in and what you plan to achieve (Phills 2005). What you call that statement is irrelevant as long as you can clearly state why you exist and what your inspirational future looks like.

See also: Organisational Culture, Strategic Plan, Values

References

Boorsma, M. & Chiaravalloti, F. 2010 "Arts Marketing Performance: An Artistic-Mission-Led Approach to Evaluation", *The Journal of Arts Management, Law, and Society*, 40, 297–312.

Cummings, S. 2003 "Strategy as Ethos", in Cummings, S. & Wilson, D. (eds) *Images of Strategy*, Oxford: Blackwell Publishing, 41–73.

Drucker, P. F. 1990 *Managing the Nonprofit Organization*, New York: HarperCollins.

Dym, B., Egmont, S. & Watkins, L. 2011 *Managing Leadership Transition for Nonprofits*, Upper Saddle River, NJ: Pearson Educational.

Fishel, D. 2003 *The Book of The Board*, Sydney: Federation Press.

Kaiser, M. M. 2013 *The Circle*, Waltham, MA: Brandeis University Press.

Kotter, J. P. 1996 *Leading Change*, Boston, MA: Harvard Business School Press.

Phills, J. A. 2005 *Integrating Mission and Strategy for Nonprofit Organizations*, New York: Oxford University Press.

Grace, K. S. 2005 *Beyond Fundraising: New Strategies for Nonprofit Innovation and Investment*, Hoboken, NJ: Wiley.

Tshirhart, M. 1996 *Artful Leadership*, Bloomington, IN: Indiana University Press.

Watson, D. 2010 *The Invasion of Management Language*, fora.tv, www.youtube.com/watch?v=RsVTDz6sunA [accessed 27 February 2019].

Zan, L. 2006 *Managerial Rhetoric and Arts Organizations*, Houndmills: Palgrave Macmillan.

Money

Introduction

Money and art have developed alongside each other from early civilisation. In one of Europe's oldest cultures, the Minoan civilisation in Crete, one can see the development of beautiful jewellery, extraordinary frescoes, fine polychromatic pottery – and coins.

Double-entry book keeping was first brought into business practice in that most art-imbued of cities, Venice. Luca Pacioli, a friend of Leonardo da Vinci, was the first person to write about double entry bookkeeping in his book *Summa de arithmetica, geometria, proportione et proportionalita* in 1494. The practice of debits and credits, journal entries and ledgers had been used by the Venetians for 200 years before his book was published. Pacioli advised that three things were needed for someone to carry on a business effectively: cash or its equivalent, a good bookkeeper, and a system of arranging all transactions so that they can be understood at a glance (Gleeson-White 2012, 93–94). All good advice for anyone thinking of setting up an arts company.

Many arts management students are insecure about accounting and finance. For those who started as artists or came to management via the humanities, financial numeracy can be a challenge. For better or for worse, you have to overcome this fear and learn both the structures and workings of accounts, income and expenditure statements, cash balances and balance sheets, and learn to apply analytical skills in interpreting them. However, it's not that hard. It's basic arithmetic and not differential calculus. Stewart (2009) believes that if you add a three-week mini-MBA to learn spreadsheet skills, basic financial analysis techniques and some business jargon to a Liberal arts degree, you'll make good managers. However, he does note the "scandalous level of innumeracy in our culture". Knowing how to use Excel or Xero is important but not enough. You need to be able to look at a budget or a forecast and test whether it's true. You don't have to be an accountant. But you do have to understand what your Financial Manager is telling you and to challenge their conclusions.

As well as talking to your Finance Manager, you have to be able to talk to your Artistic Director about money because it's your role to manage the tension between art and commerce. As Beard (2012a, 43) found in her research, if the Artistic Director has the most control, they may plan a season and then expect the marketing and fundraising teams to find the resources to pay for it, regardless of whether the revenue budget is realistic. And if the Managing Director has too much control, the artistic team may have to work within financial parameters that don't allow them to make the work they believe in.

In a Norwegian arts case study, Røyseng (2008, 44) summarises the best outcome for art/money discussions: "Financial considerations are valid when it comes to the financial basis of the artistic activities. The artistic priorities made within that framework are considered to be outside the financial domain." In other words, as long as the artistic dreams aren't going to bankrupt the organisation or destroy the health of the staff and the Managing Director believes that the budget, both income and expenditure is acceptable, then the artists can do what they want within that framework.

Although I love him dearly, my Finance Director for many years at MTC, thought (and regularly told me) that I was a complete wimp when it came to managing the financial extravagances of the Artistic Director. Part of the reason that I'd stayed through the first change of Artistic Director at MTC was at the Board's request because of Simon Phillip's reputation for "financial profligacy"[11]. But what Simon also bought was the art of being the best theatre director in the country. My strategy was to make sure that the rest of the financial capacity of the company was strong enough to absorb his blowouts because most of the time, they were more than paid for by the over-budget positive box office results. This led to tensions not only with the Finance Director and occasionally the Board but also with visiting directors who wanted the same blessing to blow budgets as Simon seemed to have. However, they didn't necessarily bring the same capacity for audience upside. I take comfort from James Abruzzo's (2009, 11) quote from an unnamed former General Manager of Covent Garden who said:

> The chap who cares about the artistic quality of the work will certainly sail nearer the wind or come closer to the border of what is financially affordable. He or she is the proper person to decide how close to that limit is right to push. Otherwise, you just get safe play.

Budgets

A well-run arts organisation has to have effective financial operations including accurate financial data, understandable and timely financial statements, regular comparisons between actual and budget figures and an independent audit on an annual basis (McMillan 2010). While financial documents such as Income and Expenditure Statements and Balance Sheets tell the reader what has happened, there has to be a document that shows how an organisation plans to pay for its spending in the current year (Bowman 2011, 49). That statement is a meaningful budget which as McMillan (2010, 99) says is an "educated guess" about future intentions. The point to note in that phrase is "educated". Kaiser (2013, 138) says: "It is unfortunate how many arts organizations develop annual budgets that are not motivated by their strategic plans and that are based on optimism rather than reality."

I'd always taken for granted the need to do a budget and was shocked when I read about a theatre company in India that had worked for 35 years without ever drawing up a budget (Deshpande 2015, 96). However, by the end of the story of how this company raised money to build a studio, even the participant/author was convinced by the notion that goals made concrete were more realisable.

The budget is a financial goal for the future and is the starting point of checking your progress towards reaching that goal. For commercial organisations the goal will be a profit, and for non-profit organisations the goal will be sustainability. The starting point has to be the organisation's mission and the checking point has to be whether your budget is moving you closer or further away from achieving your goals.

The budget process involves the following stages:

1. Discuss desired accomplishments for the coming year
2. Expense projections for proposed activities and basic operations
3. Revenue projections for each proposed activity
4. Comparison of projected expenses and revenues
5. Negotiation and setting of organizational priorities
6. Presentation to the Board for discussion and approval
7. Monitoring and adjusting operations continually throughout the year (Beard 2012b, 13).

One stage that's missing from that list is deciding who is going to be involved in the budgeting process. Varbanova (2013, 42) talks about coordinating activities in an organisation horizontally as well as vertically as "a *spiral* of coordination between different levels of management, department and units". The "spiral of coordination" is a great image and an important one to keep in mind when budgeting. At MTC, our annual planning cycle including budgeting was driven by the artistic programming needs of the main season. When I first got to MTC I was surprised that not only were key non-artistic management staff part of what was called the "Repertoire Committee", they were valued for their aesthetic contributions as well as their practical ones about income and expenditure. This of course did lead to some challenging moments when a Finance Director who loved musicals had to talk himself into risking large amounts of money by programming one. Ultimately, the Artistic Director had the final choice but in the meantime he'd heard views that reflected decades of exposure to and appreciation of the art form from the committee members as arts workers and as audience members. The result was decision-making on the mix, timing, casting, income and cost of plays that was rich in its process and content. The flow on effects of this involvement included buy-in and excitement about the artistic vision. This deeper understanding of the vision helped Finance prepare better budgets, Marketing prepare better campaigns, and so on.

But we couldn't involve everyone in the process. Although the Production Manager was there, decisions were being made on shows before designs were created and often before designers were even chosen. This meant that the impact of our decisions on the set workshop, props, scenic art and wardrobe departments was considerable and there wasn't much they could do to influence the financial outcomes.

In order to create a budget, there are income and expenditure lines which will be reasonably straightforward (an employment agreement based on an annual percentage salary increase; a standard royalty contract for an artist), but sometimes you have to guess:

- We haven't done a musical for 10 years. How many people will come?
- We haven't started a capital campaign before. How much will the start-up costs be?
- We haven't operated a theatre for 20 years. What's the electricity bill likely to be?

But in all cases, you can model outcomes:

- You can look at your audiences for shows that are similar to the musical. You can check the audience numbers for musicals done in other cities by companies like yours
- You can pay for expert advice on setting up a capital campaign. You can cost every aspect of the marketing and communications plan. You can determine whether you have enough internal resources or whether you need to employ more people
- You can benchmark your new building against a number of other like buildings. You can create plus or minus sensitivity budgets to explore the extremes of your income and cost assumptions.

As the role of the Managing Director is to balance support for the artist with reasonable pessimism, part of your job is to find the resources that will enable new strategic visions to be met. But into each budget, you can build just enough negativity to ensure that if the result is a little below expectation, you'll survive to make art another day. However, if you build too much contingency into the budget, there'll be no financial justification to enable you to do the project. I had a Chairman who didn't believe in contingencies. His view was that if people knew there was money there to spend, they would. But I snuck some modest contingencies into my revenue forecasts and delicately padded a couple of administration expenditure lines. Either way, you protect a company whose very output is risky by having some money up your sleeve each year.

An irony about the role of Boards is that although approving budgets is one of their major responsibilities, they often don't really grasp the underlying assumptions. Kaiser (2010, 94) says:

> The Board members who do understand numbers will look for reasonableness: do the increases in annual revenue and expenses seem to make sense? But they quite often make this judgement without a true comprehension of the plans of the organization. Can the programs be created at the expense levels set in the budget? Are the programming and marketing exciting enough to achieve the earned-income budget? Is the growth in fundraising revenue justified by the strategies of the organization?

Part of your role is to help the Board understand the budget. At a stage when MTC was in financial difficulties, we invited a couple of members of the Board Finance Committee to participate in discussions about revenue projections and costs of shows. This exposure built their understanding of our budget assumptions and calmed their nerves when it came to signing off on the annual program.

Income

Phills (2005, 49), who has taught in a number of executive programs for non-profit leaders at Stanford University, says: "[a]sk any group of nonprofit leaders what their greatest challenges and concerns are … the most common response is 'securing adequate funding'". We have the artistic passion and skill, we have the managerial expertise, we have dedicated staff committed to the mission – we just never have enough money to do all the things that we want to do.

In the for-profit world such as film making or musicals, you're looking for investors before you can create your art and sell tickets to it. And in the non-profit world, you're also looking for "investors". They may not want a financial return but they will be looking for some sort of return whether it's a contribution to urban renewal or

social cohesion or corporate image building or public acknowledgement. Even the audiences, who one might hope are giving you their money because of the intrinsic value of the art, also usually want a chance for an entertaining day/night out with friends and family.

Money isn't free.

You'll need to complete a grant application, develop a sponsorship relationship, hold donor thank you events, host a government minister. Every aspect of raising income for your organisation will come at a cost of time and attention (Taylor 2013). Sometimes we forget to measure the actual cost of our income-raising activities not only in terms of staff and time but also in terms of overheads and processes. It is rare to receive money that comes unencumbered. Governments and foundations and corporations and even donors want something in exchange.

Some of the best stories I've heard about money are where a company analysed all the costs of a new income stream and decided against it. For example, fundraising and sponsorship positions are amongst the best paid in arts organisations because it's a hard skill to develop relationships and ask for money and there are many other non-profit organisations (universities, hospitals, charities) trying to do the same thing. The chance of a small to medium-sized arts company in Australia getting more than a 20–25% return on their investment is low. So some companies have decided (regardless of government pressure) that corporate sponsorship is not for them. Others have decided that given the grantmaking process and its contractual requirements, they'll raise money through crowdfunding rather than trying to get a government or foundation grant. Others focus their development plan on foundation grants rather than individual donors. As one of my former Finance Directors pointed out, be careful of the trap of being seduced by the availability of money for a purpose outside your core mission. Much time can be wasted fabricating new programs just to qualify for a grant. At the end of the day it's a distraction. The point is to measure the literal cost and the strategic cost of the money you're trying to obtain.

Preece (2015, 465) provides a useful model about income sources and the core competency you need to be able raise revenue:

- Earned income: managing the complete experience including marketing, ticketing and servicing the audience
- Government & foundations: responding to policy and meeting all the bureaucratic requirements
- Private sector: having the managerial language to talk to corporates about their needs
- Individual donors: building a relationship on the back of your vision.

It depends on what art or cultural form you're making as to your earned income options. There's the arts sector where the outputs are unique moments, not made to be replicated (even a repeated performance is not the same as last night) and what one might call the cultural industries where exact replication is the point (such as film, recorded music, video games) (Colbert 2007, quoted in Boeuf, Darveau & Legoux 2014). The next challenge is how to fill the gap between earned revenue and expenses, and the solutions are limited: put on popular rather than innovative shows, increase ticket prices, find profit-making auxiliary activities, get government or philanthropic grants, build new strategic relations with corporations, raise money from donors.

Arts organisations in Australia generally earn more of their income than their peers in Europe (who get more government support) and the USA (who get more philanthropic support). Although earned income can free one from the reliance on the policies of others, there is a trap that innovative or riskier programming may be diminished and that community members may be disenfranchised as ticket prices increase (Vernis, Sanz & Saz-Carranza 2004). Another risk of relying on box office income has been explored by Nilsson and Stokenstrand (2014). They compared a British orchestra with 60%

self-generated income to a Swedish orchestra with 17% income from box office. Because of the funding pressure on the British orchestra it had to focus on a "safe" repertoire. Because its strategy was focused on cost, it didn't have goals such as improving quality and innovation. The musicians, for example, were replaceable and so they missed out on the opportunity to learn from each other. An organisation with long-term, stable funding is able to afford a strategy based on quality with a looser management system compared to an organisation with less stable funding which was to focus on minimising costs with a tighter control system (Nilsson & Stokenstrand 2014).

And of course, what we really need to acknowledge is that the principal funders of the arts aren't government, corporations or philanthropists. "First come the artists, then the volunteers and supporters, finally the benefactors. The gift economy, where art and ideas circulate *gratis* dwarfs the money economy where culture turns a buck" (Meyrick, Phiddian Barnett 2018, 65).

Ticketing

In Melbourne, there's a well-known vegetarian restaurant *Lentil as Anything*[12] that doesn't put prices on their menus. They rely on people's good will and generosity to pay an appropriate amount. Unfortunately, in the summer of 2014/15, people lacked both qualities and on one particularly busy day, 1,500 people ate at the café which lost $4,000 as a result (Worrall 2015, 8). The point of this story is that few of us are funded well enough to provide free tickets to our arts events and although there is evidence that people would willingly pay more taxes to support the arts, we can't rely on their generosity to pay an appropriate ticket price that would actually cover the cost of the books or exhibitions or shows or art we produce.

There are five methods for planning prices:

- Cost-based: direct and indirect costs plus expected profit

- Competition-based – what's everyone else charging? Can you afford to be the price leader?
- Demand-based (or consumer-based): prices increase when consumers' requests and attention increase
- Advanced – where you can charge a higher price when a unique characteristic is involved, e.g. a star performer
- Subsidised – where the majority of your income is coming from state subsidies (Varbonova 2013, 170).

At MTC, we used all of these methods for determining prices. The starting point was the average ticket price we needed to generate for our main stage shows because these activities needed to cover not only the variable costs of each individual show, but also a considerable part of our overheads given our low government funding. Yet each year we would check the subscription and single ticket prices of our competitors; we'd work out just how low we could put our concession and youth prices and still keep our average ticket price at the right level; we'd calculate a premium if we were doing a particularly expensive show such as a musical or a large cast/big frock show; and miraculously, every so often, we could break the rules and charge a price that would actually generate a profit when demand was particularly high.

Each year when it came to budgets, I would have an internal debate as well as an external one about how high we could – let alone should – push ticket prices. On the one hand, every dollar on the price could deliver between 70 and 80 cents and with an audience of over 200,000 that was a lot of extra money to spend on the art. On the other hand, each increase made it harder and harder for people with low incomes or high-risk thresholds to take the plunge and come to see MTC's work. Each year, I would succumb to the pressure and put up prices above inflation but each year, I'd try and find a way to help the new and the poor get to the theatre.

On the surface, with the poor it's easy. A cheap ticket. But of course it's not. First, who

is poor? It might be the student but what if they have wealthy parents? What about the senior citizen with a self-managed superannuation fund when interest rates have sunk to rock bottom? What about the young person who's perfectly happy to pay a couple of hundred dollars to go to a rock concert but not $40 to go to theatre?

In my first year at MTC I introduced what we called a Day Seat. For every show, no matter whether it was sold out or not, there were a handful of cheap seats available at the box office from 9am. They weren't the best seats in the house but they were the same price as a movie ticket. The idea was that the people who had the time – students, the unemployed, pensioners – would be able to go to the theatre box office at that time of the day and take advantage of the cheap prices. We didn't actually insist on proof that the purchasers were on some form of pension, we simply assumed it. But of course, what happened over time as word got out, a coterie of non-concession folk – usually retired, often from wealthy suburbs – started to buy the tickets. When we realised this and changed the rules, the outrage was loud and vociferous. In other words, never assume that your discounted ticket is going to your desired audience member.

At the other extreme, you are never going to get the risk-averse attender coming to see your show with discounts unless they are large and/or the person is dragged along by a passionate friend. Similarly, discounting tickets for a show with poor word of mouth or bad reviews won't sell tickets either. As Kaiser (2010, 96) said: "When one can buy a computer[13] for the price of two tickets to a major opera company performance (as one can today), it becomes increasingly attractive to stay home and watch YouTube."

And of course, if someone really wants to see your show, they'll probably pay more than your top price because you weren't brave enough to really push the envelope. According to Kaiser (2010, 69) there is research to suggest that arts tickets are subject to a kinked demand curve. This means that audience members who pay the highest price are less price sensitive than those who buy the lowest price tickets and if this is true, you can raise the highest price tickets more than you expect. The last play that Simon Phillips directed as Artistic Director of MTC was a reprise of a brilliant production of *The Importance of Being Earnest* he'd done as a young associate with the company 20 years earlier. In addition, he cast one of Australia's best character actors, Geoffrey Rush, as Lady Bracknell. We could have put the production into a large theatre but Simon wanted to have his last show for the company in the theatre which he'd been so responsible for – the 500-seat Sumner Theatre. We let subscribers buy the tickets for the same price as all the other shows in their package to recognise their loyalty to the company but I increased the top single ticket price by 40%. And underestimated demand badly. Within days the season was sold out and tickets were being scalped at twice my top ticket price. Having learnt the lesson, we started to use what John Tusa (2007, 88) calls EasyJet pricing for other shows: start cheap when booking opens – which is where subscribers come in – and then "ratchet up the price, as the plane fills up".

For those organisations that have subscribers or members, their ticket prices usually sit at the lower end of the range even though price discounting isn't the only or even the major reason for their subscription. The reasons they subscribe or join are varied but for many it's simply about getting organised. In busy lives, putting the date into the diary to go out with partner/friend/child is an important part of fulfilling people's social and cultural desires. From a financial point of view, such members and subscribers provide advance cash flow, reduce marketing costs and ensure that even the most risky show sells tickets in advance.

Kaiser (2010) offers wise words about ticket pricing. We have to be careful not to raise them so high that we disenfranchise whole groups of people because "[a]rts attendance is a habit … If we lose audience members today, we may lose them forever."

Expenditure

Expenses can be estimated by using either an incremental approach (taking last year's expenditure and adding a percentage such as one based on inflation) or using a process called zero-based budgeting. Instead of just adding a couple of percent on to what you spent last year, you go back to the basics. You get new quotes for your electricity service. You look back to see the impact of those posters you produced. You question "the real value and contribution of any activity or factor used" (Zan 2006, 48). This means that you understand what's going on in your organisation and that budgets are prepared with more detail and accuracy, limited resources are allocated in a more thoughtful manner and programs are checked against goals and maybe even eliminated (McMillan 2010, 183). However, it does take more time and cutting out expenditure items altogether is hard.

Another important part of the expense budgeting process is getting as many of the people who do the work and spend the money involved. There will of course be the temptation for staff to continually fight for their patch and their budget but if the process is transparent, the goals are clear and there's trust in management as the umpire, then people can behave altruistically when it comes to the allocation of resources.

Profit

Non-profit arts organisations live in a continual tension between income and expenditure. The artist will usually want to spend as much as possible. The manager will want to squirrel away a reserve. The major funder will at least want to see a balanced budget. Zietlow, Hankin and Seidner (2007, quoted in Beard 2012a, 87) say that many non-profit managers are "philosophically reluctant to earn or plan for a surplus – preferring instead to take a 'breakeven' approach". As well as the capacity to build net worth through a surplus budget or maintain it through a breakeven budget, there is a third alternative which may be appropriate at times of business model renewal or simply the result of putting on risky art, and that is to invest (deplete) net worth through a deficit budget. "Any one of these could be the right decision for financial health depending on the missions and state of the organization" (Bell 2010, 469).

As income is more variable than expenditure, the odds of achieving a balanced budget are low unless there is some contingency built in. But it's more important to argue the case that you should plan to make money each year. "But it's a non-profit organisation" is the cry. Yes, but it's a "cultural non-profit" which means it's an organisation that by definition takes risks and making a surplus and adding it to a reserve creates capacity for both investing in future artistic risk and surviving environmental risk. As Hewison and Holden (2011, 1) say, "[w]hat 'not-for-profit' really means is 'not-profit-*distributing*', where the profits that are made are ploughed back into the organization in order to sustain and develop its creative activity. It is the result of that creativity … which is the true profit".

The Council of Cultural Ministers in Australia[14] recognised this when they accepted two recommendations from the Nugent Inquiry (1999). The first was that the country's major performing arts companies should aim to reach a reserve of at least 20% of annual turnover and the second was that the State and Federal Governments should provide a system of matching grants to help companies reach that level of reserve. For MTC, this meant that in a couple of good years, each surplus dollar was matched with two dollars from government.

The urge to expand is a challenge for non-profit companies. Unlike profit companies which can fund growth through debt, the capacity of non-profits to repay interest, let alone the principal, is not strong. Therefore, the primary source of new money for growth is either going to be philanthropic donations or reserves. Taylor (2013, 851) makes the point that growth has to be fully funded because otherwise

> the impact of growth is generally to stretch organizational and financial capacity more

and more thinly … leading to systemic under-funding of areas as facilities maintenance, funded depreciation, working capital, staff development, competitive salaries, or training – all of which are required to support programs.

Although the Southbank Theatre was nearly totally funded through the Victorian Government and the University of Melbourne, we had a funding gap as was the case for MTC's new headquarters. We used our reserve to fund the initial stages of a capital campaign designed to raise philanthropic funds to fill the gap and also to fund a number of one-off operational costs focused on planning, staff and training to make the move into the two buildings effective.

Forecasts

I've always been deeply suspicious of organisations that don't start providing forecasts of financial outcomes within a couple of months of the beginning of a financial year. As Kaiser (2013, 139) says:

> [e]arly detection of problems can lead to solutions; when one waits too far into a fiscal year to adjust expenditures or pursue new revenue generation strategies, it can be too late to cut the budget, solicit emergency funding, or develop a strategy for addressing a cash-flow shortfall.

There are a variety of financial measures that non-profits can use to see if they are on the right path. Of those proposed by Keating and Frumkin (2001), the ones we regularly used at MTC included peer benchmarking, trend analysis, comparisons in relation to the budget, measures of profitability, cash flow analysis and activity reviews. Added to this list were regular reviews of contractors, detailed program budget to actual analysis, earned to contributed income ratio comparisons, detailed audience analysis. In other words, one needs to measure inputs and outputs in a variety of ways to make sure that your financial performance is effective.

Sustainability

In an article about how non-profit organisations can structure themselves financially to survive hard times, Zietlow (2010) talks about the transition from an organisation that is only worried about breaking even or having a modest surplus to organisations that have enough financial flexibility to survive the tough times. He discusses solvency (the amount of assets an organisation holds relative to its liabilities) and liquidity (the ease in which assets can be sold) which combined with things such as reputation and the ability to tap a credit line all contribute to an organisation's financial strength. Zietlow's financial paradigm moves from the organisation that just worries about the breakeven budget and has the capacity, in his terms to "muddle" through, to Phase II where the organisation wants a cash-positive outcome as well ("survive"), to Phase III which involves the measuring, managing and forecasting of cash flows ("progress"), to Phase IV ("thrive"). At this point

> organisations manage cash position, cash flows, and also financial flexibility sources such as large donors with latent ability to give much more than they normally give (and which can be called on in a deep recession to give some of that additional money) and previously untapped grant sources and contractors (246).

Organisations on that journey have what Zietlow (2010) calls two mindsets: thinking that equally values the current services (mission mindset) and that the organisation survives and thrives (sustainability mindset).

Having cash reserves is important for unexpected expenses and times when income coming in and going out don't match and Zietlow (2010) recommends having three to six months of operational costs in this reserve. This recommendation of between 25% and 50% of turnover is higher than the Australia Council's recommendation of 20% but the point is to decide on a reasonable reserve level. One can also have reserves for new program initiatives, venue renewal, repair and replacement reserves. The trick is to balance the conservatism implicit in a reserve with the desire to spend more money on the art. Zietlow (2010) quotes research that found that almost 30% of non-profit organisations in the USA, including those in the arts, didn't have any reserves and this isn't a good position to be in.

Another perspective on building sustainability is the idea of endowments. Although I am deeply in favour of reserves, I'm less enthusiastic about endowments. Unites States companies tend to focus on endowments where part of the interest can be used in the annual expenditure cycle. My view is that while cash reserves are an important stabilisation mechanism, you're simply locking money away for a future that may not come by putting excess cash into an endowment when you could be using it to make art now. However, that's probably a minority view as the standard position is that they are "a powerful tool for values-centred management because it permanently subsidizes goods and services below their cost of production, thus severing production from profit" (Bowman 2011, 46). And for conservative donors, it gives them a sense of security that a large donation will have a lasting effect.

Mutz and Murray (2010) note that endowments took a big hit on both principal and interest as a result of the GFC in 2008 and with it, the operational budgets of non-profits were also affected. However, they still consider that with the right characteristics (if you've been around for a while, have a reasonably guaranteed constituency and your mission is broad enough to last), then building an endowment is probably worthwhile. Kaiser (2013, 134) is slightly more negative about endowments arguing that:

> Arts organizations should only pursue endowment campaigns when the annual effort is strong enough to sustain a period of reduced gifts, the art is strong enough

to withstand a potential cut in budget and the family is large enough to suggest the campaign will be successful. Nothing saps the energy out of a not-for-profit organization more than a failed campaign that never seems to end.

Another consideration in discussing sustainability is investment. As policy makers in Australia encourage the recipients of government grants to build reserves of at least 20% of turnover, the question is what to do with the money? The world has been in a low interest environment for a number of years. For example, in Australia as I write, the interest rate on business saving accounts are in the 0.4–1% range with year-long term deposits are attracting 2–2.75%. Only some bank deposits are keeping up with the cost of living so how else do you invest your money?

Arts companies in the USA have more experience in this area than many other countries because of their focus on endowments that are designed to generate annual financial contributions. In Australia, the Australian Ballet is viewed as one of the more successful arts companies in terms of investment. For example, one of their more astute investments was to add a car park and rentable offices to their headquarters in Southbank.

It is likely that most arts companies will have a Board member who has a financial background and is a donor and therefore who might be willing to chair an Investment Committee but that depends on whether the organisation has the appetite for risk. In a book on *Nonprofit Asset Management*, Rice, DiMeo and Porter (2012, 188) offer three takeaway messages:

1. Align the non-profit's mission to the investment objective
2. The asset allocation strategy is important to get right first before finding an appropriate investment manager
3. Quality help is available if the non-profit doesn't have the time or the resources to oversee fund assets.

The asset allocation strategy is about understanding the likely returns on different classes of investment (stocks, bonds, real estate, art for example), the risk around those returns and the relationship between different classes of assets. If you're not a natural investor, then getting advice is the best advice that can be offered.

Tough Times

When I applied for the job at MTC in May 1994, the industry gossip was that the company was $1 million in debt. When I was interviewed for the job and asked the Board in July, they said $2 million. Once I got into the company and unpacked the financial statements and projections in September, the answer was $4 million.

People often asked what we did at MTC to get out debt. It was a combination of all sorts of activities but the starting one was dealing with creditors, that is, the University of Melbourne. We had to convince them to give us enough time to turn the organisation around financially. This meant that they had to agree to let us keep operating rather than closing us up in order to sell the assets and recover the debt. Another aspect of the debt problem was that the University charged interest on the debt which simply led to ever-increasing debt so the next stage was to ask for interest relief. The final stage was to get agreement that we could keep running a modest operational deficit for another year or two until we could make the relevant changes to revenue and expenditure.

Not every arts organisation is going to have such ultimately supportive bankers but the starting conversation is always going to be with your key financial stakeholders such as your government funders, major donors and your bank. The next stage isn't going to be about cutting budgets per se. For MTC it was about analysing the underlying strengths and weaknesses of the company in order to get a new strategic direction. Did we in fact deserve to continue in existence? Where there other and better models to produce mainstream theatre in Melbourne? Was there another way of structuring or outsourcing our operations to make us efficient? While we were having those strategic conversations we also explored every aspect of our operations to see where we could improve our financial performance. We looked at programming to see if we could find some (to put it crudely) cash cows that would increase our subscriber numbers and our single ticket income and enable us to continue to do new Australian work and innovative overseas plays. I was brutal and completely restructured the sponsorship and fundraising departments which had been underperforming. We started selling a new vision of the company to the media so that every article about us didn't start with "the debt-ridden MTC". It's hard to attract sponsors and donors to a company that's perceived to be failing.

On the expenditure side, we did look for new, cheaper suppliers, restricted expenditure on optional extras, improved budgeting and expenditure review processes, and restricted non-core activities to profit making ones. One traditional area of expense cutting in difficult times is staff salaries. Kaiser (2010, 97) has had this conversation a number of times and believes that "[s]lashing salaries or eliminating raises demoralizes hard-working staff members and may force them to evaluate other career options". I reached a very similar position very quickly and while other expenses were being cut and we were still accruing deficits, we gave staff a modest pay increase. Their salaries had been frozen for a long time and we hoped the increase would be seen as a sign that we believed in them and their capacity to help us reverse the fortunes of the company. On the artistic side, we kept doing things like commissioning new plays, presenting an education program, going on tour but tried to do all these things either with new money or within a policy framework that made them self-sufficient.

Kaiser is one of the few arts managers who has written extensively about his experience in running companies, usually ones in crisis. He says the question is not about cutting budgets (because usually you have to) but about where you cut. "Too many arts organizations cut budgets where it's easiest – where we don't not have to fire anyone or eat into an established infrastructure. This means cutting discretionary spending: typically, art-making and marketing" (Kaiser 2013, 139). As he points out, cutting these areas is potentially very damaging because it makes it harder to develop revenue in future years. He suggests cutting unneeded staff (a hard one in generally under-resourced organisations), support expenses, travel and entertainment budgets.

This might be when a zero-based budget approach could help make you make the best decisions. It's a tool that not only facilitates the allocation of resources in the most appropriate way, if you have to do what Zan (2006) calls "negative incrementalism", that is, cutting into existing budgets, it enables you to have a clear understanding of what each figure is based on.

The language around budgets is also important. In those financial challenging times at MTC, there were departments reluctant to look at or change their financial operations. They said that they were "on budget". Technically that was correct in terms of their expenditure. But as the income wasn't on budget, the point was moot. And it's usually that side of the equation which is the hardest to judge.

At MTC, I did cut both the artistic output and the marketing budget. And it was a last resort. The decision about cutting the number of plays the company produced was as much about art as it was about money. The company was presenting between 16 and 18 shows in two subscriptions seasons a year. The opinion was that the company was stretching itself too far and thus not doing artistic justice to the work it was putting on. By reducing output to 11 or 12 shows a year, we could have one rather than two subscription "seasons" per year and this reduced the marketing budget, enabled us to increase ticket prices, cut expensive casual production labour and focus on doing only the plays we wanted to do really well.

Although people were made redundant during this time at MTC, it was to enable the restructure of key income-focused departments such as fundraising and sponsorship. No-one else lost their job during this period. Moss, Callanan and Wilson (2012, 36) give a simple starting point for an organisation in financial crisis: don't think about retrenchments first; instead ask employees to identify novel and creative ways to save money. Encouraging all departments to work out what they could reduce, share or get cheaper didn't necessarily mean that the organisational culture got tighter and meaner although sometimes I went too far. For example, I was wrong to worry about the comparatively minor expense of business cards. Only those who dealt with outside suppliers and stakeholders got one. But on reflection, everyone should have been offered one even if all they did was give it to their family and friends, to show that they were part of a meaningful organisation of which they were proud. It's always the staff that pull you out of the mire. When MTC was in particularly dire financial straits, we couldn't afford to put on lavish Christmas parties. In fact, we asked people to make a cash contribution. But we also handed the parties over to staff with an interest to create a great event and that enthusiasm lead to more pleasurable outcomes than spending a fortune at a local restaurant.

At the time I joined MTC it operated out of a building that was fabulous in terms of space and medieval in terms of conditions. One day I went to a meeting with another state-based performing arts company. They had offices in a comparatively new corporate office block with all the standard elements of such a building: doors that closed, floors that were flat, blinds on windows, desks that were office furniture and not re-used props. I was suitably jealous. But the one image that I took away with me was a huge floral display on the receptionist's desk. I remember thinking "that must be worth hundreds of dollars a month" compared to the modest vase with flowers on our front desk that our receptionist bought in from her garden. A short time later, the company collapsed financially and had to close. I look back and breathe a sigh of relief that MTC survived.

Sometimes, the tough times are a result of nothing you've done. The Global Financial Crisis hits. Governments change and reduce their investment in the arts. A major donor changes focus. The strategies to find new funding sources and manage expenses remain the same. For example, Bagwell, Corry and Rotheroe (2015) reviewed the impact of UK government cutbacks on heritage and cultural organisations and concluded that they had been reasonably effective at replacing government grants with money from charities and trusts. Once again, it's working out what's the most cost-effective source of funding.

Financial Leadership

If you're running a small to medium-sized arts organisation the people who are worrying most about money are likely to be you, your part-time book keeper and the Board Treasurer. If you're running a major arts company you need an effective Financial Manager because you want to be able to produce the right financial data. But it also helps if that person also has great financial leadership skills to help you analyse that data, make good decisions based on it, and thus strengthen your organisation's financial position. I was lucky enough (with one exception) to have financial managers who were also financial leaders. In Bell's (2010, 462) words, financial leadership is:

- ensuring that the nonprofit's decision makers have *timely and accurate* financial data
- using financial data to *assess* the financial condition of your activities and the non-profit organization overall
- *planning* around a set of meaningful financial goals
- *communicating* progress on these goals to your staff, Board and external stakeholders.

However, the responsibility for the financial outcomes of the company isn't just in the hands of the Finance Manager. You have to understand the financial plan even if you didn't design the quantitative model that underlies it. For example, MTC had a sophisticated financial model to cost productions that had been developed over time. In its first iteration, it was a fairly simple if detailed excel spreadsheet which I could use just as easily as my Finance Director. As it became more integrated into other overhead models such as salaries, I lost the ease of use but still understood its nature. When we had an acting Finance Director who obviously had to take time to learn how to use it, I could pick up problems not because I knew the intricacies of the model, but because I could estimate the financial outcomes. This meant that I could spot accidental errors in the early stages of budget development.

A healthy culture of money requires transparency and good quality data. It also requires people to have budgets they can manage and to be truthful about what's happening financially in their department. It also has to mean that there's a sense of shared responsibility. People have to feel that if they are responsible and spend modestly, so will others. If they save money, it won't automatically be allocated to the profligate.

Non-profit organisations are concerned with more than just the bottom line, the financial outcome. As Bell (2010, 463–464) succinctly puts it:

> Effective leaders do not allow a mission *or* money culture to take root but insist instead on a mission *and* money culture.

Knowing and caring what is happening financially day-to-day to your organisation is important. I was told that my predecessor at MTC checked the sales reports a couple of times a day. But he wasn't the only one. I also found small handwritten notebooks going back to the 1950s in which the company's founder John Sumner, wrote down the daily ticket sales and income.

Finding good financial staff can be hard. Obviously, such a person (like your marketing and development manager) can be earning two or three times more in the corporate world. They, like you, have to care about the art that is being made. That care will keep them with you for a while but sometimes you'll have to stretch yourself to make sure they stay. One of my Finance Directors wanted to take six months' leave without pay during a period which included our annual budgeting process. I could have said "no" and they would have resigned. But instead, I took on the angst of a temporary replacement in the belief that I was investing in their long commitment to the organisation. And that was the result (although I could have done without the extra stress!).

Finally, the numbers on a page are there to help you decide what to do about expenditure or staffing or buildings or growth, but it's you who has to decide what those numbers mean for the short- and long-term future of the company. If you want the organisation to continue, its economic sustainability is important. You want to be able to use your organisation's assets well to enable you to continue operating over time and keep producing great art.

See also: Audiences, Buildings, Cultural Policy, Evaluation, Fundraising, People

References

Abruzzo, J. 2009 "Arts Leaders and Arts Managers", *Arts Management Newsletter*, 94, 10–11.

Bagwell, S., Corry, D. & Rotheroe, A. 2015 "The Future of Finding: Options for Heritage and Cultural Organisations", *Cultural Trends*, 24(1), 28–33.

Beard, A. 2012a "Dual Leadership and Budgeting in the Performing Arts: A Tale of Two Organizations", in Beard, A. (ed.) *No Money, No Mission – Financial Performance, Leadership Structure and Budgeting in Nonprofit Performing Arts Organisations*, PhD, New York, 9–54.

Beard, A. 2012b "Financial Performance in Arts Organizations – An Empirical Look at Its Relationship to Leadership Structure", in Beard, A. (ed.) *No Money, No Mission – Financial Performance, Leadership Structure and Budgeting in Nonprofit Performing Arts Organisations*, PhD, New York, 55–96.

Bell, J. 2010 "Financial Leadership in Nonprofit Organizations", in Renz, D. O. (ed.) *The Jossey-Bass Handbook of Nonprofit Leadership and Management* (3rd ed), San Francisco, CA: John Wiley & Sons, 461–481.

Boeuf, B., Darveau, J. & Legoux, R. 2014 "Financing Creativity: Crowdfunding as a New Approach for Theatre Projects", *International Journal of Arts Management*, 16(3), 33–48.

Bowman, W. 2011 *Finance Fundamentals for Nonprofits*, Hoboken, NJ: John Wiley & Sons.

Colbert, F. 2007 *Le Marketing des Arts et de la Culture*, Montreal: Gaetan Morin Editeur.

Deshpande, S. 2015 "The Studio Safdar Story", in Caust, J. (ed.) *Arts and Cultural Leadership in Asia*, London: Routledge, 91–101.

Gleeson-White, J. 2012 *Double Entry*, Sydney: Allen & Unwin.

Hewison, R. & Holden, J. 2011 *The Cultural Leadership Handbook*, Farnham: F Gower.

Kaiser, M. M. 2010 *Leading Roles*, Waltham, MA: Brandeis University Press.

Kaiser, M. M. 2013 *The Circle*, Waltham, MA: Brandeis University Press.

Keating, E. K. & Frumkin, P. 2001 *How to Assess Nonprofit Financial Performance*, Washington, DC: Aspen Institute.

McMillan, E. 2010 *Not-For-Profit Budgeting and Financial Management* (4th ed), Hoboken, NJ: Wiley.

Meyrick, J., Phiddian, R. & Barnett, J. 2018 *What Matters? Talking Value in Australian Culture*, Melbourne: Monash University Publishing.

Moss, S., Callanan, J. & Wilson, S. 2012 *The Moonlight Effect*, Melbourne: Tilde University Press.

Mutz, J. & Murray, K. 2010 *Fundraising for Dummies* (3rd ed), Hoboken, NJ: Wiley Publishing.

Nilsson, F. & Stokenstrand, A. K. 2014 "Funding Strategies and Management Control Systems: Empirical Evidence from Two Chamber Orchestras", in Jannesson, E., Nilsson, F. & Rapp, B. (eds) *Strategy, Control and Competitive Advantage*, Berlin: Springer, 213–234.

Nugent, H. 1999 *Securing the Future: Major Performing Arts – Final Report*, Canberra: Department of Communications, Information Technology and the Arts.

Phills, J. A. 2005 *Integrating Mission and Strategy for Nonprofit Organizations*, New York: Oxford University Press.

Preece, S. B. 2015 "Acquiring Start-up Funding for New Arts Organisations", *Nonprofit Management & Leadership*, 25(4), 463–474.

Rice, M. R., DiMeo, R. A. & Porter, M. P. 2012 *Nonprofit Asset Management: Effective Investment Strategies and Oversight*, Hoboken, NJ: Wiley.

Røyseng, S. 2008 "Arts Management and the Autonomy of Art", *International Journal of Cultural Policy*, 14(1), 37–48.

Taylor, A. 2013 "All Revenue Comes at a Cost", *The Artful Manager*, 22 July, www.artsjournal.com/artfulmanager/main/all-revenue-comes-at-a-cost.php [accessed 27 February 2019].

Tusa, J. 2007a *Engaged with the Arts*, London: I.B. Tauris & Co Ltd.

Varbanova, L. 2013 *Strategic Management in the Arts*, New York: Routledge.

Vernis, A., Iglesias, M., Sanz, B. & Saz-Carranza, A. 2006 *Nonprofit Organizations, Challenges and Collaboration*, New York: Palgrave Macmillan.

Worrall, A. 2015 "'Pay As You Feel' Eatery Hit by Lack of Largesse", *The Age*, 9 February, 8.

Zan, L. 2006 *Managerial Rhetoric and Arts Organizations*, Houndmills: Palgrave Macmillan.

Zietlow, J. 2010 "Nonprofit Financial Objectives and Financial Responses to a Tough Economy", *Journal of Corporate Treasury Management*, 3(3), 238–248.

Zietlow, J., Hankin, J. & Seidner, A. G. 2007 *Financial Management for Nonprofit Organizations: Policies and Procedures*, Hoboken, NJ: John Wiley & Sons, Inc.

Motivation

What is motivation? Checking some online dictionaries one can find phrases such as "the act or process of giving someone a reason for doing something" (Merriam-Webster) and "enthusiasm for doing something" (Cambridge English) and "desire or willingness to do something" (Oxford).

You can tell a company that has highly motivated staff. The atmosphere is positive with cooperative staff full of energy and with laughter echoing down the corridors. A demotivated workplace is one with bitching over coffee, politicised groupings of people, conflict and absenteeism.

There's an array of theories about how to motivate people at work. You want motivated staff because of a very simple formula: performance = ability x motivation (Bolman & Deal 2013, 119). Unpacking that equation, the inputs that employees bring to work include time, effort, education, experience, skills, knowledge, work behaviour, and the outcomes they receive in exchange are pay, job security, benefits, paid vacation time, job satisfaction, autonomy, responsibility, feeling of accomplishment, pleasure in interesting work (Dickie & Dickie 2011).

If you haven't done much reading on motivation, here's an instant summary of some of the theories. They come in different packages such as "needs" theories which say that the degree to which people's needs are met or not met at work will influence their motivation to achieve. Some of the more famous theories such as Maslow and Herzberg fit into this category. Another collection is called "process" theories which try to unpack the way people think when they are deciding how to act at work (e.g. Adam's equity theory).

1. Maslow: people have a hierarchy of needs starting from physiological needs such as food through safety, love/belonging, esteem up to self-actualization. The idea is that the satisfaction of each need in the hierarchy will lead to activation of the next need as a motivator. Although all of those needs make sense, the hierarchy doesn't. Just think of people creating art in concentration camps. As Leicester (2010, 22) says: "[w]e do not have to satisfy the need for shelter in order to graduate to the need for love. We are all capacious human beings with capacities for higher purpose." However, this is probably one of the most quoted management motivation theories.
2. Herzberg: 2-factor theory where motivating factors are achievement, recognition, work itself, responsibility, advancement and hygiene factors, which can only mitigate against dissatisfaction rather than contribute to actual motivation, include working conditions, pay, job security, company policies. This is one of the theories that makes sense from my experience as a manager.
3. McGregor: Theory X says that people are inherently lazy, not fond of their jobs and uncooperative so require authoritative management and so motivation occurs through the threat of punishment. Theory Y employees are self-motivated, enjoy their work and will seek out responsibility. They are motivated by the satisfaction of doing a good job. Stewart's (2009, 134) view is that Theory Y is utopian and workers who seem to match Theory X may be rational rather than lazy in resisting the organisation's demands.
4. Adams: social equity theory in which a worker weighs up what it costs (what they have to give, materially and psychologically) to work in a particular job and what they get out of it (such as pay and status). When the balance between benefits and cost is inequitable, they'll feel dissatisfaction and when equitable, they'll be satisfied.
5. Hackman and Oldham: three critical psychological states – meaningfulness of work, responsibility for outcomes, knowledge of results – inform how people behave.
5. Lawrence and Nohria: people have four drivers – to acquire (objects and experiences that improve our status relative to others), to bond (with others in mutually beneficial, long-term relationships), to learn (about and make sense of ourselves and the world around us), to defend ourselves, our loved ones, our beliefs, our resources.
6. Bandura: social learning theory which hypothesises that motivation is influenced not just by the individual's thoughts and beliefs but also by the behaviour of others so if you see someone being rewarded for a particular behaviour, you'll replicate the behaviour (Bolman & Deal 2013; Dickie & Dickie 2011).

And there are more. In other words, no-one knows for sure what motivates people but it's all about responding to the different needs and perceptions they bring to the workplace. I like Dan Ariely's (2016) definition. He's a behavioural psychologist who'd done lots of experiments to try and understand it:

Motivation = Money + Achievement + Happiness + Purpose + A Sense of Progress + Retirement Security + Caring About Others + Your Legacy + Status + Number of Young Kids at Home [squared] + Pride + E + P + X + [All kinds of other elements.].

The reason why there is so much concern and so many theories about motivation is because of studies that demonstrate that generally people aren't happy at work. For example, Stone (2013, 42) quotes a US study that suggests that "only 30 per cent of employees are truly loyal, committed and motivated; the rest are unhappy, prone to quit and less likely to provide satisfactory customer service". In the non-profit environment where one might think that the evidence would be more positive given the importance of the mission of our organisations to our employees, there is still some evidence to the contrary. In reflecting on Australian research about non-profits, Cunningham (2008, 49) notes that the increasing pressure on our organisations to be more efficient may translate into work practices and rewards that are demotivating. In research that compared administrative workers in for-profit and not-for-profit organisations, the result was they were different because the non-profit worker's job is of value to their community and that means it's of value to them; they were the same with similar levels of job satisfaction; and they were different because the non-profit workers were considerably less satisfied with their pay. In other words, money is an equally valid part of the motivation equation for arts workers as for other workers (Townsend 2000).

The major debate around motivation is the importance of intrinsic versus extrinsic (or hygiene) motivators. Intrinsic factors include ideas such as autonomy and purpose plus a sense that work is stimulating, challenging and worthwhile. All of the articles that Adams (2007) reviewed on motivation point to the importance of intrinsic rather than extrinsic motivating forces. In fact, some research demonstrated that extrinsic factors such as pay incentives or promotion could actually work against motivation. For example, a promotion may take people away from the job and the people they enjoy to take on a role for which they have little training (Adams 2007, 231).

Money is an important extrinsic factor and about the only thing that can be said with any certainty is that motivation is always about *more* than money. There's an entertaining TED talk about motivation by Dan Pink (2009) and the impact of financial rewards. His conclusion is that there is plenty of scientific evidence that financial rewards don't lead to better performance except in mechanistic jobs. Pink believes that intrinsic motivation "around the desire to do things because they matter, because we like it, because it's interesting, because they are part of something important" is better. So the motivators that he recommends are: autonomy, mastery and purpose.

- Autonomy: the urge to direct our own lives
- Mastery: the desire to get better and better at things that are important
- Purpose: the yearning to do what we do in the service of something bigger than ourselves.

Those of who work in arts organisations are lucky because purpose is built into our organisations. What is then required from us as managers is to facilitate as much autonomy as possible plus providing people with the opportunity to learn. Hewison and Holden (2011) who have written extensively about cultural leadership, also support Pink's (2010) view on motivation. They conclude that a wise employer will pay people enough so they don't have to fret about money and can concentrate on work. Beyond that, they say that high performance is best achieved by making sure employees get Pink's three motivators.

Another interesting TED talk about motivation is by Dan Ariely (2013). Summarising a series of experiments, he demonstrates what to me is a common-sense outcome – that ignoring people's performance is a demotivator. Even simple acknowledgement of people's work can improve their motivation. He makes the point that Adam Smith thought that efficiency was important whereas Karl Marx thought that meaning was important when it came to productivity in the workplace. Ariely concludes that Smith was right in the Industrial Revolution but that Marx might be right in the Knowledge Revolution. He says:

> I think that as we move to situations in which people have to decide on their own about how much effort, attention, caring, how connected they feel to it, are they thinking about labour on the way to work and in the shower and so on, all of a sudden Marx has more things to say to us. So when we think about labour, we usually think about motivation and payment as the same thing, but the reality is that we should probably add all sorts of things to it – meaning, creation, challenges, ownership, identity, pride, etc.

Ariely's conclusion is that if these elements are added into the workplace, then we'd be happier and more productive. Sartain and Finney (2003) agree with Airely that recognition is important but note that it has to be sincere. Sartain says rewards and fun are more powerful motivators than money and the act of "[s]howing that you care on a daily basis" is both effective and cheap. Her list covers everything from sending flowers to talking to people face-to-face more often (178). MTC is a semi-autonomous department of the University of Melbourne. No-one could tell me what this meant when I joined so I took it to mean that where university policies were good (e.g. paid maternity leave), we should adopt them and when they weren't appropriate to our industry or our organisation, I'd ignore them. One example of the latter was flowers.

The University had a very clear policy that you couldn't spend money on flowers for staff. However, on theatre opening nights, dressing rooms are full of flowers. It's part of the culture. And if it was part of the culture for actors, why shouldn't it be part of the culture for staff? So we used flowers for thank yous, for special occasions and for family members at times of sadness. The University auditors never pulled me up on this modest expenditure but I would have fought to keep spending. Buying flowers wasn't designed to motivate those individual people but to add to a culture of care which in itself supported a productive environment.

Important points to remember about motivation are captured by Carlopio, Andrewartha and Armstrong (2005, 408):

- Everyone is different and needs to be motivated in a different way
- Individual perception determines what is satisfying
- Rewarding performance skillfully is hard
- Motivators vary over time and context
- Simple recognition and acknowledgement are very important
- The importance of saying "thank you".

Even in cash-strapped arts organisations where pay is never going to be good, one can find ways of acknowledging the work that people do. It may not be a pay increase but if may be a small investment in a course or a conference. However, with rewards, one has to be both careful and consistent because an unfair allocation of rewards can be a demotivator. Another thing to watch is that co-workers may not be motivated by the same thing. MTC implemented Tessitura as its CRM system and even though it was expensive exercise, I tried to send between three and four people to the annual conference held in the USA. For people on very average wages, this was a great opportunity to travel and learn plus it built a sense of commitment to the company because people came back full of good ideas and new skills and wanted to apply them. One of my best staff kept resisting the offer to travel and finally confessed that they hated flying. Sending them to the conference was torture, not motivation.

Another point of difference in what motivates people may be different across age cohorts. How much do arts organisations need to worry about the needs of Baby Boomers compared to Gen Y? Is it true that Gen Y finds working with Baby Boomers a chore? Is it true that Gen X dislike close supervision and that Gen Y are spoilt and selfish (Stone 2013, 68)? In terms of well-researched generalities these statements are probably true but people need to be viewed as individuals and not categories. I've seen Gen X bond with boomers; I've seen Gen Y's with the qualities of optimism and self-confidence and loyalty that are supposedly boomer qualities. You can't have different employment policies for different generational categories but you can have development and performance management policies that enable tailoring to individuals and their specific motivational needs.

While most commentators stress intrinsic motivators, some extrinsic ones are important too such as one's relationship with others at work and with your manager. No matter how good you feel about the job itself, it's performed in a context of other people. When you are surrounded by unmotivated people, that has an impact. Sometimes people are motivated by all the wrong things – guilt because they don't want to let the organisation down or fear that they won't find another job (Adirondack 2005). Sometimes people are working for arts organisations just because it's convenient or they need an income. Collins' (2005, 15) conclusion is that great companies concentrate on getting the right people, those who are self-motivated and self-disciplined to start with.

When a manager takes on a role closer to that of a mentor or coach, sharing knowledge and expertise and creating a mutually rewarding relationship, this can impact positively on motivation (Adams 2007). Moss, Callanan and Wilson (2012) encourage managers to undertake a least one role in which they had acquired limited experience or which may seem lowly such as if 1,000 letters have to be stuffed, then do the first 100. "After the initial phase is completed, employees often feel more committed to the task" (145). Put simply, when managers demonstrate interest in a task, employees become more engaged. I've done this a number of times ranging from participating in really boring tasks (such as cleaning up after an event) to getting training on software that I didn't have to use, but staff appreciated that I cared enough about their jobs to want to help them and understand it.

Non-profit arts organisations do seem to be ahead when it comes to motivational factors such as meaningful work and purpose. However, one of the most depressing statements I've read about motivation was about that sector:

> The nonprofit sector survives because it has a self-exploiting work force: wind it up and it will do more with less until it just runs out.
> (Light 2004, 7)

Often arts managers assume that the care and commitment to the arts is enough to balance those other more practical factors; that you can substitute the value of the mission for hygiene factors. And you can, *but only to a limit.* Years ago when I was studying arts management I wrote down what someone said about those limits but unfortunately I haven't been able to track down the reference. Put simply, they were:

1. The level of commitment of the individual
2. The salary – if you can't eat or pay the rent, you can't stay in the job
3. The environment e.g. is there something that is cross-subsidising your work such as living with parents or other opportunities to make money or a cheap rental market?

Don't think that because people have chosen to work in the arts that they don't care about their pay, their security, their work environment, their hours of work, their need for information and participation. Dancers from the WA Ballet Company went on strike in 2008. Staff from the National Gallery of Victoria, Museum Victoria, the Arts Centre, the Australian Centre for the Moving Image, and Film Victoria threatened industrial action in 2012 over a pay increase. Musicians from the Chicago Symphony went on strike over contract negotiations in 2012, the San Francisco Symphony went on strike in 2013, musicians from the Pittsburgh Orchestra went on strike and singers from the English Opera nearly did so in 2016, and Chicago Lyric Opera musicians did so in 2018.

Adams (2007) says that motivating people isn't as hard as we think it is, although I'm not entirely convinced. If we focus on creating good conditions at work, including empowerment and autonomy to build up the intrinsic motivators and solve the hygiene factors so that issues such as pay don't undermine people's feelings about the workplace, then we're a long way towards having a hard-working and motivated workforce. However, it's a subtle process of implementing combinations of all the things that can potentially motivate people. Siber (1999, 199) provides a great list for motivating creative people:

- Money
- Recognition
- Career advancement
- Winning
- Being part of a team
- Responsibility
- Knowledge
- Respect
- Usefulness
- Time off
- Food
- Job Security
- Challenge
- Growth
- Comfort
- Open Bar (although he does add "just kidding").

And he's right about one thing – you can motivate people with food. I recommend chocolates and jelly beans.

See also: Hours, Industrial Relations, Job Satisfaction, Manners, Pay, People, Trust, Unions

References

Adams, J. 2007 *Managing People in Organizations: Contemporary Theory and Practice*, Basingstoke: Palgrave Macmillan.

Adirondack, S. 2005 *Just About Managing?* (4th ed), London: London Voluntary Service Council.

Ariely, D. 2013 *What Makes Us Feel Good About Our Work*, TED Talk, www.ted.com/talks/dan_ariely_what_makes_us_feel_good_about_our_work.html [accessed 27 February 2019].

Ariely, D. 2016 *Payoff*, London: TED Books.

Benson, J. & Brown, M. 2011 "Generations at Work: Are There Differences and Do They Matter?", *International Journal of Human Resources Management*, 22(9), 1843–1865.

Bolman, L. G. & Deal, T. E. 2013 *Reframing Organizations* (5th ed), San Francisco, CA: Jossey-Bass.

Carlopio, J., Andrewartha, G. & Armstrong, H. 2005 *Developing Management Skills*, Sydney: Pearson Education.

Collins, J. 2005 *Good to Great and the Social Sectors*, Boulder, CO: Jim Collins.

Cunningham, I. 2008 *Employment Relations in the Voluntary Sector*, London: Routledge.

Dickie, L. & Dickie, C. 2011 *Cornerstones of Management* (2nd ed), Tilde Melbourne: University Press.

Hewison, R. & Holden, J. 2011 *The Cultural Leadership Handbook*, Farnham: F Gower.

Leicester, G. 2010 "Real Cultural Leadership: Leading the Culture in a Time of Crisis", in Kay, S. & Venner, K. (eds) *A Cultural Leader's Handbook*, London: Creative Choices, 16–22.

Light, P. C. 2004 *Sustaining Non-profit Performance: The Case for Capacity Building and the Evidence to Support It*, Washington, DC: Brookings Institution.

Moss, S., Callanan, J. & Wilson, S. 2012 *The Moonlight Effect*, Melbourne: Tilde University Press.

Pink, D. 2009, *On Motivation*, www.ted.com/talks/dan_pink_on_motivation.html [accessed 27 February 2019].

Pink, D. 2010 *Drive: The Surprising Truth About What Motivates Us*, Edinburgh: Canongate.

Sartain, L. with Finney, M. I. 2003 *HR from the Heart*, New York: AMACOM.

Siber, L. 1999 *Career Management for the Creative Person*, New York: Three Rivers Press.

Stewart, M. 2009 *The Management Myth*, New York: W.W. Norton & Co.

Stone, R. J. 2013 *Managing Human Resources* (4th ed), Milton, QLD: John Wiley & Sons.

Townsend, A. M. 2000 "An Exploratory Study of Administrative Workers in the Arts", *Public Personnel Management*, 29(3), 423–433.

Notes

1 Although we keep being told that traditional media is dead in a 2018 survey of a contemporary dance audience that I did, the go-to source for news was still traditional newspapers and TV but the dominant sources for information about arts events were social media, direct communication from companies and, somewhat surprisingly, the good old rock poster.

2 From *Snapshot* by Garry Disher (2005, ebook).

3 What you say about your organisation when some asks you in a lift or at a barbeque where you work and what your company does.

4 (1) ConocoPhillips – US based energy company; (2) Pedigree; (3) Museums Victoria; (4) Microsoft; (5) Walt Disney Corporation.

5 www.unimelb.edu.au/Statutes/pdf/r81r1.pdf, [accessed 3 March 2014].

6 www.mtc.com.au/discover-more/about-us/the-company/ [accessed 27 February 2019].

7 An Elevator Statement for American readers.

8 This statement has disappeared from the Australian Ballet's Strategic Plan: https://australianballet.com.au/corporate/five-year-strategic-plan but is still to found in their history: https://australianballet.com.au/our-story [accessed 27 February 2019].

9 See the section on *Values* for further discussion.

10 Executive Program for Non-profit Arts Leaders handout, 2005, Stanford University.

11 This is not a defamatory statement but one that Simon would smile at!

12 www.lentilasanything.com [accessed 27 February 2019].

13 Maybe these days you'd be buying a mobile phone or a tablet for the same price.

14 State and Federal Arts Ministers.

N

Negotiation

We negotiate every day. Whose turn it is to do the dishes? Where we will go on holidays? What Netflix series shall we watch? Negotiating is "any form of discussion, formal or informal, designed to reach agreement" (Balnave et al. 2009, 182). So all of us have the capacity to be effective negotiators – but it doesn't always feel that way in the workplace. In fact, it's because we negotiate everyday that we don't prepare enough and consider the consequences of more formal negotiating environments.

A tougher definition of negotiation is "the process we use to satisfy our needs when someone else controls what we want" (Maddux 1989, 7). We might want access to a painting for an exhibition, rights to a play, avoidance of industrial action, a pay increase. And to get them, we need to negotiate. There are lots of online lists of the top ten books (mainly American) on how to negotiate. The reason I'm pointing you to other experts in the field because I'm not a good negotiator.

Of Dwyer's (2009, 134) list of psychological barriers to negotiation, I suffer from a number of them: fear of being taken for a ride, guilt about wanting to be assertive, wanting to be liked, the need to be "nice", fear of conflict or confrontation and lack of self-confidence. I can't work out whether I'm not good at negotiating because I'm not good at poker or vice versa but the skills required for the two are very similar: "a strategic focus, the imagination to see alternatives, and a knack for assessing odds, reading people, understanding others' positions, and bluffing when necessary" (Brooks 2015, 64). I know this about myself and have developed strategies over the years to manage (although not always successfully) this weakness. As a nervous negotiator, I try approach such situations in the ways that Brooks (2015, 60) recommends – "train, practice, rehearse".

Many artists and creatives have worked out that they are much better served in a negotiation if an agent does it for them. Yes, they have skin in the game, but they're not likely to be as emotional as the actor who just wants the gig and will accept whatever monetary offer is on the table. When I started at MTC, I discovered that my predecessor had been a very effective and enthusiastic negotiator. Worried that actors' agents would expect the same behaviour from me, I got on a plane and travelled around the country to introduce myself and to describe my somewhat more lowkey negotiating style so there would be no surprises. Only one company didn't believe me and stuck to their particularly aggressive approach to negotiating. There is some evidence that men are better negotiators than women (Balnave et al. 2009, 207) but I can't use that as an excuse because the aggressive negotiators in this case were also women.

The basic stages of negotiation are preparing the background, imagining alternatives (the "what if" part of the process), reviewing options and reaching an agreement. In my experience, the skills required to do this well are a combination of confidence, managing your emotions, being lateral, understanding boundaries and enjoying the challenge. Other pieces of advice that have resonated over the years include focusing on both your interests and theirs and not just taking a position, bargaining in good faith, trying to find options for mutual gain (increasing the size of the cake rather than just cutting it up) and trying to build common ground early in the process. In some negotiations, you'll think that it's a straight-forward division of the pie – you've only got so much money in the budget to pay a set designer and your negotiation with their agent will be defined by that limit. But it may be that giving a little more to a different designer might lead to a production that sells more tickets than you've budgeted and therefore everyone is better off. Negotiation is not always a zero-sum game.

A couple of the most famous writers on negotiation, Fisher and Ury, the authors of *Getting to Yes* (1991) remind us to separate the people from the problem by which they mean that you have to disentangle substantive issues (such as terms, conditions, fees, dates, etc.) from the relationship issues around emotions, communications, trust and understanding.

Writers on negotiation usually focus on strategy and tactics: how to frame a first offer, identifying alternatives, making counteroffers and so on. More recent research has focused on the impact of emotions – how our feelings influence our capacity to reach agreement and get a good deal (Brooks 2015). For example, not surprisingly, there's evidence that anxious negotiators made deals that were 12% less financially attractive than those who weren't. The only time Brooks (2015) recommends the use of anger (or fake anger) is if it's a transactional negotiation with no further relationship required such as buying a car from a stranger. Two other pieces of advice that Brooks (2015) offers that I think are worth keeping in mind is don't let your

excitement make the other team feel that they've lost and don't let your excitement increase your commitment to a strategy that might actually be wrong.

The most challenging negotiating experiences for me have been with unions. I've never experienced a negotiation round where the union tried to build common ground at the beginning. Rather the starting point has been to attack management in order to look good to their members. Balnave et al. (2009, 201) quote an Australian study from 2005 where the majority of companies that had been through a bargaining round negotiating with unions reported that the results failed to deliver any productivity gains. I'm deeply comforted to know that I was not the only one who failed.

The difference between negotiating with unions and more occasional buyers or sellers is that you have to have an ongoing relationship with the former but not the latter. I remember reminding myself of this fact when I was called a liar by a union representative in one negotiating meeting. In any other forum, the relationship would have been broken off. Bolman and Deal (2013, 218) make the point that if you expect to work with the same people in the future, using scorched-earth tactics that lead to anger and distrust are not worth it. Regardless of whether it's negotiating with a union or an agent or venue or another arts company, you can't afford to have a reputation for being untrustworthy or manipulative because even if you don't have to deal with them again, our industry is small enough that other companies will hear about it and may not want to deal you as a result. And usually you do have to deal with them again. Negotiating venue deals were the bane of my life because of the power imbalance. There were no other theatres that we could use and so technically, the Arts Centre Melbourne could impose whatever conditions they wanted on us – and sometimes they did. Our only strategy was to hold out as long as possible in the hope that they might change their minds, but this could only work up to the day when our tickets had to go on sale because they couldn't go on sale without a signed contract. The lesson I took from these negotiations was that even when you have the power, use it fairly if you want the ongoing relationship to be a cordial one.

Although the best outcome in negotiations is supposed to be "win-win", there is an art to reaching a compromise which doesn't have to be a betrayal of values or lead to a sense of failure. If the compromise is ethical and results in an agreement where both sides end up with something they like, then the outcome can be positive (Baldoni 2010). A successful negotiated outcome is one where most of your interests are met, is viewed as fair by both parties, is implementable and will last, is better than the alternatives, didn't absorb too much of your time and energy and leaves both parties willing to do it again (even if there's relief that it doesn't have to happen again for a couple of years).

See also: Industrial Relations, Trust, Unions

References

Baldoni, J. 2010 *Lead Your Boss*, New York: American Management Association.

Balnave, N., Brown J., Maconachie, G. & Stone, R. J. 2009 *Employment Relations in Australia* (2nd ed), Milton, QLD: John Wiley & Sons.

Bolman, L. G. & Deal, T. E. 2013 *Reframing Organizations* (5th ed), San Francisco, CA: Jossey-Bass.

Brooks, A. W. 2015 "Emotion and the Art of Negotiation", *Harvard Business Review*, December, 57–64.

Dwyer, J. 2009 *Communication in Business* (4th ed), Sydney: Pearson.

Fisher, R. & Ury, W. 1991 *Getting to Yes* (2nd ed), New York: Penguin.

Maddux, R. B. 1989 *Successful Negotiations* (3rd ed), San Francisco, CA: Crisp Publications.

Networks

There are networks which help you develop your career. There are networks which enable you to learn. There are networks through which you can find advice and support. There are networks of women managers and gay managers. There are networks which in Hewison and Holden's (2011, 16) words make an organisation "healthily porous". Every email from LinkedIn reminds one of the importance of networks. Networking is defined as "the voluntary collaboration and exchange of information among individuals, groups and organizations, [that] enhance access to knowledge, and promote trust, norms and reciprocity or social capital, and incentives for further knowledge sharing" (Adams 2007, 253). Networking is a task that is seen to be a lifelong project "requiring consistent effort and commitment" (Stone 2013, 409).

Networking creates a "fabric of personal contacts who will provide support, feedback, insight, resources and information" (Ibarra & Hunter 2007, 40).

There are three sorts of networking:

- Operational – building relationships with people who can help you do your job
- Personal – building your personal development through coaching and mentoring
- Strategic – which can help you think about new directions and what stakeholder support you need (Ibarra & Hunter 2007).

The latter makes sense particularly when it comes to funding bodies. Although bureaucrats in systems with arm's length funding processes may not be able to directly influence your funding, it helps if you're regularly briefing them, asking their advice and building their relationship with your company.

In the best case, networking is about maintaining relationships and staying visible although Stone (2013, 409) uses the word "friendships" rather than the cooler "relationships". I prefer the latter because I'm not comfortable using friends or trying to turn people into friends just to get the benefit of their influence. However, I can't decry the people who do it well. I've seen it work. I've seen people with plans and ambitions strategise their relationships and work the room. I'm always impressed but it's just not me.

If you do have an aversion to networking (and Ibarra and Hunter (2007, 40) call it "one of the most dreaded development challenges that aspiring leaders must address"), Casciaro, Gino

Kouchaki (2016, 105–107) offer four strategies that might help:

1. Focus on learning – change your mindset to think about "networking as an opportunity for discovery and learning rather than a chore"; concentrate on the positives of what the event can bring you
2. Identify common interests through serious research
3. Think broadly about what you can give back even if it's just gratitude
4. Find a higher purpose – don't just thinking about what it means to you.

Ultimately it's about learning how to read the room, find out what's being talked about and having the courage to talk to people you don't know (Watts 2018). I prefer networking in different ways than schmoozing the influential and the important. As part of your job, you should attend industry conferences, join professional bodies, alumni organisations, trade and commercial associations and this will provide a way to meet people who may be important to you in terms of advice and contacts along the way. In any management job that I've had, I have tried to join a relevant industry network. Other people will join personal network organisations which can also be useful but I've preferred to be part of organisations that act as lobbyists, information clearance houses and support mechanisms so that I can both benefit from knowledge sharing *and* contribute back to the industry I care about.

In reflecting on her work as an arts executive, Louise Mitchell (CEO of the Colston Hall in the UK) talks about the "importance of building and maintain good relationships". She said that

> she is always trying to network, even without an immediate purpose or agenda, and always helping others if you can … It's important take a long-term view and not to expect an immediate return, while also simply being a reasonable person to deal with.
>
> (Mitchell & Russell 2015, 215)

Because I've always been insecure about how much – or rather how little – I know, I have never been afraid of asking for advice. When I joined MTC I'd never worked for a theatre company. It was a terrifying first year because the company was in serious debt and under threat of closure. I had three senior managers reporting to me. One of them thought that they should have got my job and actively worked against everything I tried to do until they left 18 months later. A second initially believed in the views of the first and was of little positive help. The third, on the other hand, was a wonder to work with. She was extraordinarily supportive, offering me knowledge, wisdom and experience. Without her, I wouldn't have survived those first couple of years. Learning from her generosity, I tried to exhibit those same characteristics every time a new person joined the network of performing arts companies in Australia and was looking for help. While we were competitors in many ways – for donations, for grants, for sponsors, for audiences – we were all in our jobs because we believed in the arts. And a robust arts community can only be built by sharing information and skills.

Eagly and Carli (2007) say that one of the traps for women in leadership is the demands of family life which are still mainly a female responsibility. Therefore, women often don't have enough time left to network and so can underinvest in social capital. Ironically, one of the benefits that arts companies can offer sponsors is a space where couples, families and single females can all network comfortably – at the ballet or orchestra or gallery opening or theatre.

Whether it's building your career or supporting others through networking it's an important part of skill building and sharing.

See also: You

References

Adams, J. 2007 *Managing People in Organizations: Contemporary Theory and Practice*, Basingstoke: Palgrave Macmillan.

Casciaro, T., Gino, F. & Kouchaki, M. 2016 "Managing Yourself – Learn to Love Networking", *Harvard Business Review*, 94(5), 104–107.

Eagly, A. H. & Carli, L. A. 2007 "Women and the Labyrinth of Leadership", *Harvard Business Review*, 85(9), 63–71.

Hewison, R. & Holden, J. 2011 *The Cultural Leadership Handbook*, Farnham: F Gower.

Ibarra, H. & Hunter, M. 2007 "How Leaders Create and Use Networks", *Harvard Business Review*, 85(1), 40–47.

Mitchell, L. & Russell, D. S. 2015 "Organising Music Festivals", in Beech, N. & Gilmore, C. (eds) *Organising Music: Theory, Practice, Performance*, Cambridge: Cambridge University Press, 213–217.

Stone, R. J. 2013 *Managing Human Resources* (4th ed), Milton, QLD: John Wiley & Sons,

Watts, R. 2018 "Three Tips for Emerging Producers", *Arts Hub*, 5 November, www.artshub.com.au/education/news-article/career-advice/professional-development/richard-watts/top-3-tips-for-emerging-producers-256759 [accessed 27 February 2019].

Non-profit

Whether it's non-profit or not-for-profit, unfortunately the phase that defines so many arts and cultural organisations is a negative one (Drucker 1990). It describes what it's not rather than the rich panoply of what it is. Peter Brokensha, a great teacher and adviser on arts management, described why he moved out of the corporate world to the world of the arts in his biography *Coming to Wisdom Slowly*:

> I had come to realise that I wanted to contribute to the society something that was distinctively mine. In the corporate world there is rarely very little of a lasting nature that any executive can point to as his or her personal achievement. A brilliant chief executive can turn a company around from disaster to profit but this can be illusionary as non-controllable external factors can wipe out the achievements overnight … The lubricant that enables most organisations and large corporations in particular not only to run but to be successful is the ambition

of its supervisors and managers. This drove me as I climbed the ladder of success from plant foreman to Director but when I got there I found that the god of success I had worshipped for so long turned out to be a false idol … one soon learns that ambitions can be realised and rank and success achieved only by conforming to the rules and traditions of that particular organisation or company … What finally dawned on me was that I was becoming very narrow and inwardly focussed and that my creativity and imagination were being inhibited by being narrowly focussed on my work at Caltex (81, 83).

It's reasons like that which lead many of us to make active choices about working in the non-profit world.

The United Nations defines non-profits as "organisations that do not exist primarily to generate profits, either directly or indirectly, and that are not primarily guided by commercial goals and considerations" (quoted in Bowman 2011, 3). This doesn't mean that in some years, perhaps every year, non-profits don't make surpluses. It's just that those surpluses aren't distributed to trustees or directors or shareholders; rather, they are accumulated and reinvested in the process of achieving the mission of the company. Bowman (2011) says that social values are the business of non-profits and Drucker (1990, xiv) says that the non-profit's "product" "is neither a pair of shoes nor an effective regulation. Its production is a *changed human being*."

Other differences that writers point to between the for-profit and the not-for-profit world include the pre-eminence of the mission, a multiplicity of stakeholders with conflicting needs and expectations, the difficulty in judging performance due to often intangible outcomes, high accountability and the complexity of resource generation (Tshirhart 1996; Courtney 2002; Inglis & Cray 2011). In terms of the people who work for them, there is the tradition of unpaid Board members, a higher proportion of women leaders, and worker commitment and motivation which isn't primarily about money (Nair & Deepti 2011).

Bowman (2011, 3) says that non-profits practice "value centred management" and Courtney (2002) describes the culture and values of such organisations as more participatory and egalitarian than for-profit companies. However, it's not all sunshine and light. Non-profit arts organisations face a number of challenges such as never having enough money, paying people poorly, having to deal with politicians, bureaucrats and the wealthy, operating in a risky business with long lead times, inflexible deadlines and uncertain demand. Having said that, a number of for-profit managers would say they have to deal with many of the same challenges and we do share some qualities with for-profit companies. Although non-profits are not in the business of making money, they are in *business* because they are hiring, organising and directing people to produce goods and services (Bowman 2001).

Another difference between the for-profit and non-profit world is what Beech and Gilmore (2015, 3) call a "a blurring between competition and collaboration" and I agree. At the same time one might be competing with a nearby theatre company for audiences, one could also be sharing information about those audiences and working to put together a co-production.

I think that the most important difference between the two types of organisations is the motivation of the people who choose to work for them. In the non-profit company, people are usually working for love and not particularly for money. They choose to work for us because they want to contribute in some way to the making of a rich and vibrant community. Their motivational rationale will have an impact on the operation of our organisations because they'll want to participate, to be inspired, to have meaningful relationships with their peers and their leaders.

Having said that, one of the most inspiring art companies I've been involved in was a for-profit company with a focus on song and dance for young girls. The company was established by and is run by women and has an organisational culture that reflects their values of respect, collaboration, integrity, innovation and excellence in real and practical ways. Yes, they make a profit but they share part of that profit with staff and have a non-profit wing that contributes to the education of Indigenous girls.

Some would say that non-profit companies behave like for-profits in their search for new income sources, for example establishing cafés or bars or shops or parking lots. But the purpose of these ancillary activities is to feed excess income back to fund the core artistic mission, and the values and culture of the company should be the same in all its aspects.

Another example of blurred boundaries is the low-profit, limited liability company model in the USA where the primary purpose is a social mission such as the arts with profit as a secondary purpose. This model enables companies to not only obtain philanthropic donations, but also more traditional forms of investment (Walter 2015, 243).

When starting a company, you need to consider what legal structure is going to be best for you. For most art forms in the 21st century (but certainly not all), it's likely to be a non-profit company. Because of the non-profit's multiplicity of funding sources, stakeholders and outcomes, as an arts manager you need to be able to deal with diversity, complexity, uncertainty and risk. In 2019, DeVereaux says the current challenges for non-profit arts organisations – or what she calls "discontents" – are:

- increasing managerialism
- apparent diminishing value of the arts by the general public
- decrease in available funding
- aging of audiences
- insufficient policy action and support (2019c, 187).

In other words, there's a lot to deal with as a manager of a non-profit company but ultimately you are there to serve the artist and the audience first and the financial stakeholders second.

See also: Arts organisations, Gender, Money, Motivation, Organisational Culture, Uncertainty

References

Beech, N. & Gilmore, C. (eds) 2015 *Organising Music: Theory, Practice, Performance*, Cambridge: Cambridge University Press.

Bowman, W. 2011 *Finance Fundamentals for Non-profits*, Hoboken, NJ: John Wiley & Sons.

Brokensha, P. 2007 *Getting to Wisdom Slowly*, Adelaide: Peacock Publications.

Courtney, R. 2002 *Strategic Management for Voluntary Non-profit Organizations*, London: Routledge.

DeVereaux, C. 2019c "Cultural Management and Its Discontents", in DeVereaux, C. (ed.) *Arts and Cultural Management: Sense and Sensibility in the State of the Field*, New York: Routledge, 187–204.

Drucker, P. F. 1990 *Managing the Non-profit Organization*, New York: HarperCollins.

Inglis, L. & Cray, D. 2011 "Leadership in Australian Arts Organisations: A Shared Experience?", *Third Sector Review*, 17(2), 107–130.

Nair, N. & Deepti, B. 2011 "Understanding Workplace Deviant Behaviour in Non-profit Organizations", *Non-profit Management and Leadership* 21(3), 289–309.

Tshirhart, M. 1996 *Artful Leadership*, Bloomington IN: Indiana University Press.

Walter, C. 2015 *Arts Management: An Entrepreneurial Approach*, New York: Routledge.

Occupational Health and Safety

At the end of one of my first weeks at MTC, we were sitting around having a drink (it was the 1990s) when a white-faced designer dripping blood walked towards us. He had decided, after the set builders had knocked off work and gone home, that he just needed to add some finishing touches to the set. So alone, he grabbed a router and started work. And injured himself in the process.

These days, even though he made the decision and took the action without consultation, it's likely the company would have been found responsible for his injuries. In Australia, occupational health and safety (OHS) is a serious business with an array of legislation and punishments. The legislative starting point is worker participation and consultation through health and safety committees. Such committees are useful forums for unpacking not just OHS issues but the structural and communication issues of the company as well.

Accidents are generally considered events that are unexpected, unforeseen or random. But through an effective risk analysis process one can anticipate most "accidents" and thus reduce their likelihood. You can do this through what's called a hierarchy of control:

1. Elimination of the hazard
2. Substitute the hazard with a safer alternative
3. Engineer interventions to isolate the hazard
4. Administrative controls
5. Use of personal protective equipment (Balnave et al. 2009, 391).

The theatre stage is a very dangerous place with the capacity for things to fall from heights, for stage machinery to move, for traps to open unexpectedly, for costumes to get in the way, for electrical equipment to blow up. When I reflect back to the on-stage accidents over my time at MTC, it's interesting to judge what might have been anticipated and prevented. The spanner wouldn't have fallen from the fly grid if there'd been rules in place about securing tools when working at height. Tripping on the edge of a long frock an actor had worn for weeks of performances leading her to fall off the stage might not have happened if they or someone else had commented that she was still sometimes catching on the hem. One of the best OHS strategies we put in practice at MTC was to report everything that went wrong. Australian culture tends to avoid "dobbing in" but if the company culture means that it's all right to say if a mistake has been made or a near accident happened then it helps an iterative process of refining safety processes and that in turn means that the big accidents are less likely to happen.

In many ways, I was lucky at MTC. The University of Melbourne, our owners, was a self-insurer and as such had a rigorous process of internal and external audits to ensure that all departments were OHS compliant. We were one of the most challenging departments for the University (along with the Veterinary School) but we worked hard to make sure that we had safe work practices. We employed an OHS officer long before we employed an HR manager. We had policies and committees, documentation and training, processes and practices, to ensure good work practices.

Each part of the arts and cultural industry will have its own health and safety challenges. The fumes of paint. The spark of metal welding. The physicality of dance. The high wire work of the circus. Film stunts. And for almost everyone these days, the ergonomics of using digital equipment. The challenge is to get everyone on the same page about the importance of OHS. This is particularly hard with contract or temporary workers who may not be as imbued with the OHS culture as ongoing staff. Unlike companies with a permanent ensemble of performers who usually also have specialist medical staff to support them, MTC had to find different ways of ensuring that contract actors could access advice and help them to use preventative processes to reduce risk. Even so, the University insurance staff did get some surprise claims such as the muscle strain of the middle-aged actor who, working on a rake in high heels, had to climb onto a table and then onto a chair on the table and stand on it playing a trombone. The main difficulty we faced was around differences of opinion on "risk". Directors and designers often wanted to stretch the boundaries. For example, a designer had created a wonderful "house" and wanted real glass to be used in "skylights". The production team was very concerned about the safety of putting glass in at a height with people working underneath it. On the basis that the aesthetic impact of using plastic rather than glass was negligible compared to the risk, I said "no" to the use of glass.

At MTC, while the commitment to OHS was generally strong and positive, our problem was the same as many under-resourced companies that have a culture of "doing". We always seemed to be behind on the OHS paperwork. Our processes and training were good but documenting everything was not our strength and it took a while before I simply threw money at the problem to get us over the hump of producing safe work material statements, training matrices, inspection checklists, hazardous chemical documentation, and so on. When I think about the amount of work MTC had to do to ensure it was OHS compliant, the challenges for small arts organisations are enormous because so much of it is about administration and paper work. This may be a scenario where a small company needs to get the support of a larger one or where an industry organisation can provide advice on OHS policies and procedures.

Underhill (2013, 192) argues that in the general workplace, with the push towards labour flexibility, deregulated labour markets and intense competitive pressures, there are increased OHS risks and the capacity of workers to respond to such risks has eroded. I haven't seen that in the major performing arts company in Australia where there's been increased attempts to improve OHS. But there is still the potential with time pressure and budget stress for corners to be cut, for people to take on hazardous tasks and for hours of work to be excessive. If rules are regularly broken or training isn't up to date or if people don't feel comfortable in saying "stop", then all the paperwork in the world won't create a safe work environment.

Apart from physical issues, people in our companies also may face psychological problems. A pilot study by Victoria University concluded that Australia's entertainment industry workers are more likely to have mental health issues and higher rates of suicide than the general population (Hawthorn 2015). The creative people in the survey described a work environment that could often be divisive, competitive, and lacking social support. "Further, they have to hide their 'weaknesses' – their injuries, health issues and mental health issues – because to disclose these would mean they would not gain work" (Victoria

University 2015). Lead researcher Julie van den Eynde said that coping issues include drug and alcohol over-use and so having both preventative and supportive policies in place for these issues is necessary.

Having confessed to post-work drinks at the beginning of this section, I have to acknowledge that the organisational culture around alcohol and drugs has changed in Australia over 30 years. When I started at MTC, I was told of the very recent culture which was drinks at lunchtime at the pub down the road and drinks before (and sometimes during the intervals of) plays. That was just starting to fade (although the damage of that culture amongst actors and theatre workers continues to play out). By the time I left MTC, there were practices around the serving of alcohol at company events including the serving of food, the availability of non-alcoholic drinks, a limit to the number of drinks served and the presence of someone who wasn't drinking to enforce the rules. Policies which forbade the consumption of alcohol and drugs not only during a performance but in the lead up to it were also in place along with support processes and counselling services for people deemed to have a drug or alcohol problem. It wasn't a "wowser" culture, rather one that enabled people to enjoy but not risk themselves, and certainly not risk others.

For such policies to work, they have to be designed in consultation with staff. There is evidence that worker involvement helps in the development of a healthy workplace (Underhill 2013, 203). Whether that is the collective work of an OHS committee with worker representatives or the power that staff feel they have in speaking up because they have a union to support them, the voice of the staff has to be heard because they are the ones who know more about hazards than most managers.

Summarising their research on the mental health of the Australian entertainment industry, Van den Eynde said:

"[d]espite the challenges of the risk of mental health problems, and regardless of the unhealthy work environment, these creative workers in the entertainment industry share a deep passion and commitment for their work. An actor felt their work was a "privilege", another said the interaction with the audience was almost a spiritual experience.

(Victoria University 2015)

Our role as managers is to make sure that we don't exploit this passion to the point where people are damaged.

See also: Diversity, Harassment, Hours, Industrial Relations, Risk, Unions

References

Balnave, N., Brown J., Maconachie, G. & Stone, R. J. 2009 *Employment Relations in Australia* (2nd ed), Milton, QLD: John Wiley & Sons.

Hawthorne, M. 2015 "Study Sashes Myth of Roadie Lifestyle", *The Age*, 23 February, 8.

Underhill, E. 2013 "The Challenge to Workplace Health and Safety and the Changing Nature of Work and the Working Environment", in Teicher, J., Holland, P. & Gough, R. (eds) *Australian Workplace Relations*, Cambridge: Cambridge University Press, 191–208.

Victoria University 2015 *Researching the Rock 'n Roll lifestyle*, 24 February, www.vu.edu.au/news-events/news/researching-the-rock-n-roll-lifestyle [accessed 27 February 2019].

Offices

... a workplace environment that is stimulating, but not stressful, and that embodies ergonomic principles (or example, the effective use of lighting, colour and temperature to increase cognitive functioning and physical health) is more likely to be both motivating and enjoyable.

(Adams 2007, xxii)

I spent 15 of my 18 years working for Melbourne Theatre Company in an environment that many would (and did) call "shocking". Towards the end I had rat bait in a corner, an asbestos monitor above the door frame, carpet stuck together with gaffer tape, a floor with a ten-inch height difference between the corners and the centre of the room and a door that wouldn't close because of building movement. And that was just my office. I solved that problem eventually (more about that later) but as I type, I'm sitting in an arts organisation where only one office has a window (not mine), one of them is actually a passage way to a noisy plant room, and the architects gave more space over to the area around the staircase than they did to any staff amenities.

Finally, at MTC we managed to find the resources to modify a car showroom and workshop into a new headquarters and worked with a great architectural company that understood "poor" aesthetics. By this I mean they had the capacity to create a colourful, artistic, warm environment on the cheap. And colour does make a difference. Years ago, the community radio station I ran had to move to a different building on the campus of one of the universities that owned it. Similar to the MTC story, we were going from a ramshackle space to a new building and we were grateful for the change. But there was one battle that I had with the interior designers. We were taking up an entire floor in this new building and the university standard was cream walls with dark wooden doors and architraves. Which was all very well for serious, quiet academics but we were a lively, volunteer-run radio station. Our logo colours were simple: black and white and red. This was the way we thought of ourselves (the black of LPs, the red for our passion for music) and we wanted this reflected in the new station. So after a long, hard fight, we got white walls, shiny, black gloss doorframes and brilliant red doors.

If you're running an arts organisation, then you've probably focused on making a creative environment in the theatre or the gallery. But why not do the same for the people who work in administration or marketing? In the case of MTC's new headquarters (HQ), artists were commissioned to create stained glass structures that were installed in the public reception space *and* the offices. If you can afford to have carpet,

it doesn't have to be beige or black. Walls have to be painted so why not provide people with a selection of colour choices so that their space reflects their desires? We did this in the new MTC HQ but the only trouble was in my office. I was too busy consulting about everyone else's desires and so forgot to submit my choice of colour. During a building inspection, I walked into my new office space and discovered a wall of powder blue and another of olive green. I love colours but these are not two of them. The architects, to tease me, repainted the walls … grey. Needless to say, that paint job didn't last long either.

A couple of years later I was reading some research about colours in offices. In a review of the psychological effect of colours Baughan-Young (2001) concluded:

- People who are naturally cautious work better in cool colours, e.g. blues and greens
- More outgoing people respond better to warmer colours, e.g. red and orange
- Cool colours provide a calmer environment better suited to high levels of concentration because they "speed time"
- Warm colours "slow time" and are better suited to work that requires stimulation such as creativity and brainstorming, e.g. meeting rooms
- Colour breaks are required at regular intervals
- All-white environments understimulate the eye, leading to ocular fatigue.

It seems that a combination of architectural wisdom and common sense had led us to the same conclusion as Baughan-Young. MTC's colour scheme at the time was red, black and white and although this meant that red had to be a key theme in the building, we also provided a choice of cooler colours for people to work in.

Another point of choice was in air temperature. We did a very old-fashioned thing in the building: we put in louvre windows and individual air-conditioning units. It wasn't to save money (although it didn't cost us any more) but rather to give as many people as possible the chance to decide on the temperature of their work space. There was an added "green" result as well: people didn't use the air conditioning much, preferring the fresh air and windows to modify the climate first.

As well as colour, one has to consider the nature of the workspace. There are experts in how to lay out offices, feng shui practitioners, ergonomists, architects – but sometimes you can't afford them, don't believe in them or they've created the problem in the first place. So what can one do to ensure that people are connected and have the right type of space to facilitate their work? Waber, Magnolfi and Lindsay (2014, 72) propose three keys to successful communication which impact on how you lay out your offices:

1. Exploration – interacting with people in many other social groups
2. Engagement – interacting with people within your social group
3. Energy – interacting with many people overall.

Work spaces can be designed to favour any of these factors. For example, high engagement is accomplished with tight, walled-off workstations and adjacent spaces for small group collaboration and interaction rather than open social spaces which favour exploration more than engagement. The authors provide a "beginner's guide to space design" with quadrants of assigned seating, flexible seating, private offices and open plan offices. Assigned seating in private offices enables individual productivity and deadline work and at the other extreme, open plan and flexible seating facilitates silo busting and more innovation (Waber, Magnolfi & Lindsay 2014).

MTC's headquarters from the 1980s to 2000s was in a collection of interconnected buildings that were sinking into the ground at different rates. For all the problems I've listed, it still had some wonderful qualities. The positive aspects of the building complex made visitors jealous. For most theatre companies, the administration staff are in offices in the city; the actors work in a rehearsal room in the theatre; and the artisans – the set and costume makers – are in a workshop usually in an industrial suburb. But Ferrars St had room for all of us. And in the centre of the building was a café. Originally created because there wasn't a decent cup of coffee to be had for kilometres around, it became a subsidised restaurant where people could get a good, fresh, hand-cooked meal every day. No chips, but the best home-made sausage rolls in the country and it was a daily source of freshly baked cakes and muffins as well as fresh fruit.

Enough ranting about the food. The point is that it was a meeting place. The artistic coordinator would meet the payroll clerk. The publicist could bump into the actor they wanted to use in a photo. The production manager could find the stage manager at lunchtime without bothering them in the rehearsal room. The designer would have to walk past the scenic artists to get there. There were birthday celebrations and welcome morning teas for new casts; meetings with insiders and outsiders; games of chess and staff meetings.

When we finally got the chance to move into another building, closer to the arts precinct and with access to coffee shops, I was told to save money and delete the café from our plans. I refused because the company still needed a physical heart. There were issues with the placement of the café in the new building. The workshop folk had further to walk. The administration staff no longer walked through the workshop to get there. The connection dynamics were different. And by then, a percentage of the staff lived in a different building. But it was still the daily gathering place. There will always be people who don't join in the socialising potential of such a space, who just order their coffee and head back to the office so each floor or area had their own small space for making cups of tea or storing shopping or microwaving lunch. But I do recommend a space that enables the entire organisation to connect.

Another aspect of office layout that you have to think about is open plan or offices. Open plan seems to be embraced by architects and cost planners but disliked by staff. In an article about balancing privacy and connection in the workplace, Congdon, Flynn and Redman (2014) say that it has remained the dominant workplace design because it fosters collaboration and learning and nurtures a strong culture. The only advantages I see for open plan offices are democracy (although someone always gets a better position), ease of communication and cost saving. Yes, you can pick up information in them. Yes, it enables a quick catch up. But there is no quiet time or private time. How do you ever get work done in such spaces when surrounded by the noise and potential interruption of others?

A survey of 40,000 workers concluded that workers in open plan offices felt "more stressed, distracted and unproductive than those in more traditional work settings" (Blair 2017, 19). The main complaints were the traditional ones – lack of privacy and noise – and the benefits were increased ability to collaborate and socialise. Interestingly, a survey of Finnish millennials thought that this trade-off – collaboration versus noise – was worth it. Blair's (2017, 19) response to this result was that "may be that this generation, who have grown up surrounded by multiple information streams, can screen our distractions more easily". As I read this I was reminded of walking into the open plan office of an arts company where all the people in the open plan section were wearing headphones.

Congdon, Flynn and Redman (2014) provide a more scientific response to open plan spaces than my ambivalence. The authors discuss the neuroscience of attention and how it impacts on privacy needs. They list three different types of attention:

1. Controlled attention – working on tasks that require intense focus such as writing or thinking deeply
2. Stimulus-driven attention – switching focus when something catches our attention because when doing routine tasks such as emails or admin work, we may tolerate or even welcome interruptions or distractions
3. Rejuvenation – periodic respites from concentration with time out for brains and bodies and a chance to engage socially with others or express emotions (53–54).

They conclude that we need a range of different workspaces as well as personal strategies for privacy such as using headphones to indicate "do not disturb" and spaces for privacy. Another example I've heard from an arts company is people have flags they can "fly" on their open plan desk to indicate that they don't want to be interrupted. In the design of MTC's new headquarters, we had to have some open plan administration offices because of space and cash limitations but on the architect's advice, we gave them the best part of the building – with the most light and a street view. Not a perfect trade-off for the lack of quiet privacy but a reasonable one. Congdon, Flynn and Redman (2014, 57) conclude that open plan offices aren't inherently good or bad.

The key to successful workplaces is to empower individuals by giving them choices that allow control over their work environment. When they can choose where and who they work, they have more capacity to draw energy and ideas from others and be re-energised by moments of solitude.

In 2018, the Australian Ballet did a major refurbishment of their building and created a large, open plan space. Not surprisingly, some people weren't happy to begin with but the feedback now is that it's a better working space than the old version. But it's not just open plan – it's light and white and airy and spacious, with meeting rooms and a great cafeteria. If the alternative to an open plan is small, noisy, rooms without light or good airflow, then maybe open plan would be better. Blair (2017) concludes that "[f]lexibility is the key. Offices will need to reflect this by providing some desks for individual work, soundproof spaces for confidential discussions, meetings rooms – and of course, a coffee shop."

There are some CEOs who have their desks in amongst the open plan. There are some CEOs who have a semi-office (walls but no doors). And some argue that managers shouldn't have offices at all because they're always off at meetings somewhere else. But I confess I like an office with a meeting layout and a door.

In Michelle de Kretser's novel *Questions of Travel* (2012, 474), one of character is reflecting on offices:

> Tyler had once heard Helmut Becker say that a German manager's notion of earning respect was to keep his office door shut. You know what is really tragic about this idea? It works. In Australia, where everyone was equal except for their salaries, managerial doors stood wide. It followed that a closed door switched the office to alert. It was simply amazing thought Tyler, how often the human factor caused the theatre to come undone.

Although Tyler is right, I'm still of the view that open doors are better than closed doors. However, I do like a door. I have worked in the open and even in a passage way but I like both a door and enough room for a quick meeting. Most of the time the door is open. But it can be closed – usually for the benefit of a staff member who wants to have a private conversation. Yes, of course we could book a meeting room but that requires foresight. Yes, of course we could have a meeting off-site but that implies weighty seriousness before the meeting has even started. People need to be able to come in at any time and close the door if that's what they want.

In Ferrars St, my open door policy worked by default because the structural movement of the building meant that the door couldn't be properly closed. However, for years I've had a technique to encourage people to call by my office on a regular basis. It's called lollies.[1] At some time in the afternoon, people tend to crave a sugar hit … and they could always find something sweet

in my office. However, even something that is designed as a gesture of largesse towards the staff (I always paid for them personally) may cause problems. Perhaps I hadn't thought to buy someone's favourite sweet. Perhaps someone had a nut allergy. Perhaps people wanted the lollies but were too scared to go into the boss's office when I was there.

Research shows employees who work on different floors interact 50% less than those who work on the same floor – and it's even worse if they are in different buildings (Gigerenzer 2006). There's a name for this phenomenon – the Allen Curve. There is strong negative correlation between physical distance and frequency of communication. For example, we're four times as likely to communicate regularly with someone sitting two metres away compared to 20 metres away and almost never communicate with colleagues on separate floors or in separate buildings. The thought was that as new technologies meant an office could be anywhere, the Allen curve would disappear, but according to Congdon, Flynn and Redman (2014, 73) it still holds true. They even provide evidence of people who are close to each other, emailing and staying in touch digitally more often than with those who are more distant.

In Ferrars St, every department except one was on the same level. We couldn't do that in the new HQ. We were stuck with a three-story office block and part of the workshop space was two-tiered. One of the techniques to overcome this division was designed by the architects 6 Degrees. They created a short-cut stairway which ran next to the ordinary staircase but which was skinnier and steeper and cut five seconds off the travel time. It may not sound like much, but if you can make travel between floors quicker, people will be more inclined to do it rather than send an email or pick up a phone.

Our other strategies to ensure communication and effective relationships were the obvious ones – make sure production is near the rehearsal room; that marketing is next to fundraising. But there were also attempts to ensure that unlikely people were near each other – because otherwise they might never meet. For example, we put the creative team next to the Finance department. Of course, different people will make different decisions. We put the Artistic Director on the top floor so that even if everyone didn't go up to his office, he would pass each floor on the way up to his. Because the Artistic Director and I had worked together for years, we didn't feel the need to live in each other's pockets and so we spread ourselves about the building. However, his replacement felt too removed at the top and so moved down to the middle floor next to the new Executive Director so that they could bond more effectively. Hewison, Holden and Jones (2013) tell of a new leadership team at the Royal Shakespeare Company breaking down silos by creating open plan offices and putting themselves at either end of the new main floor in order to be both seen and more accessible.

When I first arrived at MTC, the furniture in my office was terrible: an office desk that had been a stage prop and so had drawers that didn't open and wasn't the "correct" OHS height along with mangy blue chairs with rapidly failing stuffing. However, spending money on my comfort wasn't the point at that early and critical stage in the financial fortunes of the company. Finally, after spending a fortune at the physiotherapist and with complaints from the management team about the comfort factor of the chairs during meetings and when enough time had passed to demonstrate that we had turned the financial corner, I decided it was time to get new furniture. And there are management lessons to be learnt out of that simple decision.

I didn't actually have a personal budget line. My expenditure whether on travel or magazines, entertainment or stationery, was part of a more general administration fund so I explained my intentions to my Finance Director – second hand desk; $400 budget; I'd check out the local furniture stores. I had a cursory look the following weekend but because everything at that price was bland and boring, it was hard to get excited even though my aching arms reminded me that I needed a proper desk. The next week, the Finance Director rang from the city to tell me that she'd just been at an auction and bought me a desk. "But," I protested, "what if I don't like it?" She replied: "I'm better at bargaining than you so whatever I've got will be better than what you might have found." She was right: a manager who understood my skills, her own strengths and felt empowered to make decisions.

The result is hard to describe. She'd been to the auction of furniture owned by a mining company that was upgrading their head office and she'd bought me the CEO's desk. A magnificent handmade desk of Tasmanian blackwood, 275cm wide and created with a curve. The most impressive desk I'm ever likely to sit behind – and all for $400. It was completely over the top – I literally had to roll from end to the other – but each day I was reminded of the skills of the craftsperson who had lovingly created it.

The next challenge was the chairs. Again, I wanted to be respectful of the artists and not spend too much on the management team who were going to be the main users. This time the question wasn't about my capacity to get a bargain but my aesthetic sensibility. The room itself was horrible – no natural light, walls covered with posters to hide old marks and cracks and worn blue carpet. The logic might have been to simply replace blue chairs with blue chairs but I wanted some colour and movement so I chose a style of chair where colour was an option – and suddenly everyone had an opinion. That's the trouble when you encourage your team to express their views in a forthright fashion. In the end, the easiest thing to do was to give everyone a choice. The result was a liquorice allsorts array of colours, some of which (orange) I would normally avoid but everyone had ownership of the decision and the management meetings that followed felt livelier and more productive as people were both more comfortable and happy in their choice of chair.

You may never get to move into new offices. You may not be able to do anything much to change the layout of your current building. But think of how simple things like colour and carpet, lighting and furniture can not only make the environment pleasant to be in, but they can also contribute to peoples' creativity.

See also: Buildings, Communication, Creativity, Empowerment

References

Adams, J. 2007 *Managing People in Organizations: Contemporary Theory and Practice*, Basingstoke: Palgrave Macmillan.

Baughan-Young, K. 2001 "The Color of Success", *Journal of Property Management*, 66(5), 68–70.

Blair, L. 2017 "Hate Your Open-plan Office? Join the Club", *The Age*, 26 October, 19.

Congdon, C., Flynn, D. & Redman, M. 2014 "Balancing 'We' and 'Me'", *Harvard Business Review*, 92(11), 51–57.

De Kretser, M. 2012 *Questions of Travel*, Sydney: Allen & Unwin.

Gigerenzer, G. 2006 "Follow the Leaders, Breakthrough Ideas for 2006, #13", *Harvard Business Review*, 84(2), 58.

Hewison, R., Holden, J. & Jones, S. 2013 "Leadership and Transformation at the Royal Shakespeare Company", in Caust, J. (ed.) *Arts Leadership*, Melbourne: Tilde University Press, 144–158.

Waber, B., Magnolfi, J. & Lindsay, G. 2014 "Workplaces That Move People", *Harvard Business Review*, 92(11), 69–77.

Organisational Culture

Put simply, organisational culture is the "feel of things" in a company or as someone might say to a new comer, "the way we do things around here" (Deal & Kennedy 1982, 4). It's not written in a policy manual but has a profound impact on the way organisations operate and how people within them connect and behave.

More technically, organisational culture is defined as "deeply rooted value or shared norm, moral or aesthetic principles that guides action and serves as standards to evaluate one's own and others' behaviors" (Hofstede 1994, 68). Such norms and beliefs are established through leadership, personal example, organisational history, management policy, the role of unions, what money is spent on, recruitment and promotion criteria and what's happening in the general culture.

As Bolman and Deal (2013, 263) say, organisational culture is both a product and process:

> As a product, it embodies wisdom accumulated from experience. As a process, it is renewed and re-created as newcomers learn the old ways and eventually become teachers themselves.

Although organisational culture isn't concrete, it is easy to sense. Think of an organisation you've worked for and find some adjectives to describe it. Was it warm or cold, caring or heartless, people- or task-oriented, closed or open, fun or focused? Skringar and Stevens (2008, 96) use the phrases "strong and weak" and "thick and thin" to describe cultures. For example, a strong culture is one with a system of informal rules spelling out how people behave and as result people feel better about what they do and so are likely to work harder. On the other hand, a weak culture is where employees waste a good deal of time working out what to do and how to do it. In a thin culture, staff don't share common values, whereas in a thick culture, values are shared, communication is effective and there's less social distance between staff and managers.

Sometimes, arts companies are described as families and this can be a thick, positive culture where people feel that they are in a safe and friendly environment. However, families can be dysfunctional too. A family culture could create conformity where divergent thinking is discouraged (Alvesson & Spice 2016) or where "parents" abuse or bully staff. Saintilan and Schreiber (2018) make the clever point that sometimes you don't want a happy family, but rather an effective sports team if you're in a fast-moving industry needing to get optimal output from the best people.

Understanding organisational culture is important because it provides the underlying ethical framework for how people relate and behave. A positive, shared culture brings people together, forges a common identity and sense of purpose, creates a good place to work and hopefully leads to great outcomes. A negative culture does the opposite and in such environments people end up being hurt.

Golensky (2011, 70) says there are three levels of organisational culture:

1. Observable artefacts – for example physical layout, dress code, the annual report, overt staff behaviour
2. Espoused values – expression of personal convictions to explain or justify expected behaviour
3. Deep-seated assumptions – guides to actual behaviour that have become so ingrained that they don't require conscious thought.

The observable culture at MTC was very casual. After one day in the job, our quite formal Finance Director took off his tie except for Board meetings. And even then, because the meetings were on a Friday, some of the Board members took advantage of "casual Fridays" to dress down. When you are sitting down having morning tea or lunch with people who are carpenters in overalls or actors in leotards, one looks slightly foolish if overdressed. Another type of observable artefact is noted by Plas and Lewis (2001, 66). They give the example of how informal and seemingly insignificant symbols can tell a story, and in their case it was an in-house telephone directory. Just like MTC's, it was alphabetised by first names rather than family names – "reflecting the personal touch that is so important to the culture".

I always wondered what impression visitors had of MTC when they came into a building that was falling down: at those moments when I tripped over the gaffer tape holding the carpet together under my desk; or when they started to roll away from the meeting table because of the slope of the floor. Did they think that we didn't care about our environment? That we were slack? I hope they believed us when we said we'd rather spend money on the art than on our surroundings, although of course eventually occupational health and safety issues meant that we had no choice but to find a new home with flat floors.

In the old HQ, the Wardrobe Department was physically removed from the rest of the organisation because it was upstairs. The only reason to go upstairs apart from designers wanting a word or actors needing a fitting was to visit the props storeroom, the Board room or the library and one got to the latter two rooms by a different set of stairs. Whether distance was the only reason, I'll never know, but Wardrobe lived in a world of their own. They had their own birthday parties, their own morning teas, their own champagne moments. This physical and emotional divide meant that they developed their own culture and their own world view of what was happening in the company that wasn't necessarily informed by the same experiences as other staff. At times that difference became a problem.

The trick of Golensky's second level of organisational culture, espoused values, is that one has to believe in them and display them as well as say them. If the company policy says that it supports training opportunities for staff, then you have to do so. If you have a code of responsibility that says people have to be respected, then you can't let people get away with bullying others. If you want people to help others, then you have to check in that this is happening.

An occasional tension can be found in performing arts companies when people who aren't artists have the permanent jobs and the (sometimes) higher salaries. But as we're only there because of the artists, we have to find ways of making them feel valued and having an organisational culture that reflects this. At MTC this happened in a number of formal and informal ways. They included welcome morning teas, preventative OHS processes, champagne when audience targets were met and explanations when they weren't, time off for births and funerals even when shows had to be cancelled. From what I was told, the company was particularly good at making actors feel at home with its culture of inclusiveness, care and protection.

A way of thinking about Golensky's third category of culture, deep-seated assumptions, is the phrase "but we've always done it this way". Sometimes this is great because it means that a particular ethical behaviour or approach is embedded in the organisation. But sometimes it can be a barrier that stops change and innovation and sometimes that behaviour isn't ethical.

Another way an organisation's culture is revealed and communicated is through its symbols. Bolman and Deal (2013, 256) describe these as myths, visions and values, heroes and heroines, stories and fairy tales, ritual, metaphor, humour and play. Hewison, Holden and Jones (2013) tell of the use of "ensemble" as a metaphor applied to an entire organisation not just in a rehearsal room in their story of organisational change at the Royal Shakespeare Company. The ensemble principles were described by the company as "collaboration, trust, mutual respect, and a belief that the whole is greater than the sum of its parts" (quoted in Hewison, Holden & Jones 2013, 146).

An example of ritual, a routine that has layered purposes and meanings, was MTC's morning teas to welcome casts. On one level, they were a gathering of actors, creatives and staff. On another level, it was a way of saying to the actors "you're very important". It was also a time for the Artistic Director to re-inspire the company about the next bout of hard work. For some staff it was simply a free feed. For others it was a way of understanding what the company did. And for some, it was a chance to rub shoulders with a famous (or about to be famous) actor. But its key message was that theatre making was the focus of our lives and not just accounting or carpentry or marketing.

Organisational cultures will also reflect the norms of different countries. Australian companies will probably be more relaxed than Japanese companies. A European artist recently described the Australian rehearsal room as more collaborative than German ones. A number of my arts management students are young women from Asia. They talk about the cultural differences between Australia and their countries in similar ways to the performance arts centre managers interviewed by Jo Caust (2015). For example, Yong Kwan Lee from the Daejeon Culture and Arts Center in South Korea described Asian

work places as being "more hierarchical and collegiate in their structure and behavior" (quoted in Caust 2015, 159–160). However, for many of my students, this was viewed as a problem with dominating leaders and a forced collegiality that lead to long hours of work and harassment.

Organisational culture is considered to be important because it has an impact on the capacity to recruit staff, staff retention, morale and motivation, productivity, the capacity to successfully introduce change, the customer experience and there is even evidence about a positive link with the financial bottom line (Bolman & Deal 2013, 264). A recent Australian example from another industry offers insights into the impact of cultural change. One of the issues that came up time and time again in the 2018 Royal Commission into Banking, Superannuation and Financial Services in Australia was poor organisational culture: cultures that led to dead people being charged fees, to people being charged for services they didn't receive, to people putting profit before customers. Lorsch and McTague (2016, 98) argue that putting new processes and structures into place will create cultural change but I'm not convinced that's enough. My sense of culture is that it's a result of history and current leadership and not just business processes or structures. Yes, one can tackle the profit versus people challenge by redesigning bonus systems but, equally, the organisation's leadership has to walk the talk of customer service.

The Chairman of one of the banks under scrutiny said that it would take ten years to change the culture (Dancert & Yeates 2018) but this person lost their job as a result of the Royal Commission and the more general belief is that change can happen quickly if, for example, the Board says that particular conduct is no longer acceptable.

It's important for a new leader to come to grips with an organisation's culture quickly. Some writers question whether managers can change organisational culture or whether they are shaped by it (Bolman & Deal 2013; Walmsley 2013), but sometimes you just have to try. You may be lucky to step into an organisation with a positive culture in which case you just need to understand and honour it. Sometimes it may be about negotiating around the edges and trying to change it subtly. But sometimes the change can't afford to be subtle. I was told a story about an organisation where people were encouraged to compete with each other, to withhold information from each other, to view each other as impediments to success. The result was an organisational atmosphere of fear and loathing. You have to change that type of culture.[2]

Sometimes, a problematic culture can be created by new leadership. In 2017, a series of articles in the online *Daily Review* and the cultural magazine *Limelight* discussed a supposed "toxic" work culture at the Queensland Symphony Orchestra. A couple of elements in the stories told in the media give insights about how such cultures can develop and actualise. For example:

- Scenes of "backstabbing, gossip and shouting matches"
- A gap between the orchestra and administration because of physical distance (on different floors of the building)
- So-called "ineffectual leadership" including not being "in synch with the 'Australian way' of working"
- New leader with a strong personality.

The result was high turnover with 27 people leaving over 21 months out of a staff of 37 and a couple of unfair dismal cases settled out of court (Gill 2017a; Gill 2017b, Wanchap & Litson 2017), all of which would have been costly for the organisation. The Chair of the orchestra denied there was a problem and provided rational explanations for both the extensive staff turnover and the use of external consultants to improve cohesiveness (Wanchap & Litson 2017). Regardless of who was right, there would have been a serious impact on the remaining staff and the organisation's efficiency and output. We'll never know the truth but as one commentator on the *Daily Review* said, there can be two reasons for losing such a high percentage of your human

capital – change agents at work or dysfunctional management.

When I started at MTC, there might have been a similar story about me. I cleared out the entire sponsorship and fundraising department because of their failure to meet targets as well as their obfuscation about that fact. The result was four unfair dismissal cases settled out of court. Needless to say, I would claim that I was a change agent and not a dysfunctional manager but the staff concerned would probably disagree.

In a world of social media, stories about toxic cultures are more likely to come out and it can be very difficult for a company, particularly a small to medium-sized company with no HR resources, to deal with both the public debate and the internal ructions. As the General Manager of Red Stitch theatre company in Melbourne said in response to accusations of shouting, rudeness and aggression, they

> had a large and devastating effect on the company. We are a company whose ongoing existence depends upon our reputation, upon the willingness of artists to work for us and for philanthropic support … Allegations of this kind are hurtful and damaging and undermining to the morale of the company.
> (Cuthberson 2018)

The Banking Royal Commission has got Australian organisations, for-profit and non-profit, focused on organisational culture in 2019. One can ask how can bad behaviour in banks apply to our organisations which, on the surface, don't appear to have the same issues? But we do have some regular challenges to an effective culture: for example, silos – divisions between the creative department and the finance department; divisions between permanent and casual staff; divisions between staff in the office and staff on the factory floor. In order to solve these, one needs both processes that bring people together but also leadership that demonstrates the value of all these different groups.

An example that's indicative of how important culture is and how it can be formed happened at the Southbank Theatre. I thought that building a theatre was hard – and it was – but in some ways it wasn't as hard as dealing with the cultural change that was introduced into MTC because of the building. In the days before we got our own theatre, there were always people who spent some of their time in other people's venues – actors and stage managers for the run of a show; production, workshop and wardrobe staff during the bump-in – but they also spent time at HQ. Suddenly we had a group of people – front-of-house and ticketing staff – who didn't spend *any* time at HQ. There had always been people who worked at night while the rest of us worked during the day, but again they usually spent some time during the day at HQ. Now we had people who worked at night, the back of house team, who didn't have any reason to walk down the road to visit HQ.

These new staff started off with an unformed culture in the new building. We were still finding our way physically and artistically and so there was much more impact from the culture they bought with them than the culture they came into. For the young front-of-house people for whom this was just a part-time gig while they studied, their opinions and views of how organisations should work weren't hard and fast but the technical staff who had spent years working in other venues came with fixed views that didn't necessarily reflect those of HQ. The culture they came from contained elements of bullying, of anti-management views, of minute counting, of general negativity. That created a challenge that led to both voluntary and less than voluntary resignations because we couldn't afford to let some aspects of the old-style culture of "mechs and techs" infiltrate the new environment. This was an example where "organisational culture is historically derived, socially constructed, and often resistant to change" (Golensky (2011, 70).

Hudson (2009, 298) says that organisational culture will influence how ambitious change can be, how it should be introduced, how much consultation will be needed and how fast it can be implemented. For example, if you want to introduce more flexibility into the work place

but the culture is highly focused on union rules, it will be more difficult than in a company without a union history. While one might think that creative organisations have positive cultures, there is evidence that some aspects of what we do can create negative cultures, such as when veneration of the art leads to accepting a culture of bullying (Quigg 2011), or excessive commitment to the art leads to overwork and burn out.

How can you change the culture? Sometimes it's easy. Management changes the rules and lets women wear jeans or lets men not have to wear ties. This signals a loosening of control, a casualisation of the environment. Sometimes it happens accidentally. A person is appointed to a management position who has a cheery personality and suddenly the department seems warmer. Sometimes it is about new processes that contribute to better communication and therefore relationships. Sometimes it's new leadership at Board or executive level that demonstrate different behaviour. Sometimes it's a change in mores or rules outside the organisation. For example, when the Australian Government introduced fringe benefit taxes onto food and alcohol consumed as part of the work process, suddenly the number of boozy lunches diminished as did the culture of regular worktime alcohol consumption.

More formally, changing organisational culture requires management to:

- Communicate new environment demands
- Invite participation from employees
- Negotiate preferred and agreed methods of change
- Use formal power as a last resort
- Be an example of the change (Dickie & Dickie 2011, 42).

At the very least, you have to create a culture where people are respectful to each other. A simple definition of respect is to "treat with consideration" (Australian Pocket Oxford Dictionary). Another version is to avoid degrading or insulting or injuring someone. Respect means an environment where staff know their voices are heard and valued and where good manners prevail. For managers, this doesn't mean that you have to be everyone's best friend but "most people respect others who say what they mean, do what they say, are good at what they do, and who inspire confidence" (Adams 2007, 159).

I don't know what it's like to work in the Our Community Group which "provides advice, connections, training and easy-to-use tech tools for people and organisations working to build stronger communities" (Our Community Group, nd) but if their manifesto is anything to go by, it's organisation with a positive culture. For example, some of the elements are:

- We believe treating people with respect gains respect
- We believe that laughter is good
- We believe that women have equal rights to leadership roles.

Mind you, there is one part of their manifesto that I find somewhat scary:

- We believe mayhem is not only health but critical.

De Pree's (1997) ideas for positive relationships in non-profit companies are:

- Nourishment: where people are constantly learning through taking on new tasks, participating in professional development and are able to learn from making mistakes because they don't fear punishment
- Justice: all people are treated equally and fairly in terms of compensation, workload and opportunities for promotion
- Confidence: every person in the organisation believes that they and those served by the them will enjoy a brighter future, and that their commitment to their cause is making a significant difference to society
- Accountability: where all staff know what is expected of them and are recognised and rewarded for their good work.

Leadership example is a crucial part of this process. Sometimes it's purposeful and sometimes its accidental. If you can control your temper even at the most difficult of times, if you can reward good behaviour in a public way, if you can stop bad behaviour in its tracks, if you can say "thank you" regularly, then you have the beginnings of a positive culture.

In an article about changing organisational culture, Ferrazzi (2014) compares some aspects of behavioural change with the 12 steps of addiction programs. I confess that apart from US movies, I have no experience with such programs but he makes some interesting points. He says that organisations have trouble changing their cultures unless people change their behaviour and that is hard. Twelve-step programs use incentives, celebration, peer pressure, coaching, negative reinforcement and role models to create the willingness and capacity to change and he suggests that organisations can draw on these ideas.

Other suggestions about changing organisational culture relate to organisational structure. For example, Ladkin (2010, 37) says that "[a]n organisation which values creativity, responsiveness and openness might express these through creating space for unstructured thinking and dialogue, conversation, free-flow of thinking and easy communications between layers of the organisation". Ladkin also makes a strong point about the aesthetics of an organisation particularly when it comes to creating a culture that is supportive of diversity. She gives positive examples of where the photos on the wall weren't all of dead white males but live people of diversity; where a male leader got coffee for his secretary; where a male leader in a male-dominated industry actively encouraged the participation of his female managers (2010, 36–37).

Abruzzo (2014) proposes that the characteristics of organisations with a positive culture and ethical values are ones where there's:

- Openness and transparency
- Respect and appreciation of the art

- Risk taking and creativity is encouraged
- Where values are aligned with the mission
- People recruited, evaluated and rewarded based on values
- Low tolerance for breach of values.

And most particularly,

- Where leaders live the values and provide an example.

If our staff respond with words such as respect, open, creative, fair, warmth, fun, trust when asked what the company feels like to work in, then we will have created the core values of a positive organisational culture.

See also: Bullying, Diversity, Ethics, Harassment, Manners, Offices, Organisational Structure, Values

References

Abruzzo, J. 2014 "Creating the Company Culture", *Arts Management Newsletter*, 118, 2–3.

Adams, J. 2007 *Managing People in Organizations: Contemporary Theory and Practice*, Basingstoke: Palgrave Macmillan.

Alvesson, M. & Spicer, A. 2016 *The Stupidity Paradox*, London: Profile Books.

Bolman, L. G. & Deal, T. E. 2013 *Reframing Organizations* (5th ed), San Francisco, CA: Jossey-Bass.

Caust, J. 2015 "Different Culture but Similar Roles: Leadership of Major Performing Arts Centers", in Caust, J. (ed.) *Arts and Cultural Leadership in Asia*, London: Routledge, 148–162.

Cuthberson, D. 2018 "I no longer feel safe working at Red Stitch", *Sunday Age*, 10 June, 6.

Dancert, S. & Yeates, C. 2018 "NAB's Culture Could Take 10 Years to Fix, Chairman Says", *The Sydney Morning Herald*, 26 November 2018, www.smh.com.au/business/banking-and-finance/nab-s-culture-could-take-10-years-to-fix-chairman-says-20181126-p50igk.html [accessed 27 February 2019].

Deal, T. E. & Kennedy, A. A. 1982 *Corporate Celebration: Play, Purpose and Profit at Work*, San Francisco, CA: Berrett-Koehler.

De Pree, M. 1997 *Leading Without Power*, Holland, MI: Shepherd Foundation.

Dickie, L. & Dickie, C. 2011 *Cornerstones of Management* (2nd ed), Melbourne: Tilde University Press.

Ferrazzi, K. 2014 "Managing Change, One Day at a Time", *Harvard Business Review*, 92(7–8), 23–25.

Gill, R. 2017a "Queensland Symphony Staff Churn Prompts Claims of a 'Toxic' Work Culture", *Daily Review*, 15 November, https://dailyreview.com.au/queensland-symphony-staff-churn-prompts-claims-toxic-work-culture/68193/ [accessed 27 February 2019].

Gill, R. 2017b "QSO Chair and Musicians Say Everything is Fine", *Daily Review*, 17 November, https://dailyreview.com.au/qso-chair-orchestra-say-everything-fine-brisbane/68279/ [accessed 27 February 2019].

Golensky, M. 2011 *Strategic Leadership and Management in Nonprofit Organizations*, Chicago, IL: Lyceum Books Inc.

Hewison, R., Holden, J. & Jones, S. 2013 "Leadership and transformation at the Royal Shakespeare Company", in Caust, J. (ed.) Arts Leadership, Melbourne: Tilde University Press, 144–158.

Hofstede, G. 1994 *Uncommon Sense about Organizations: Case Studies and Field Observations*, Thousand Oaks, CA: Sage.

Hudson, M. 2009 *Managing Without Profit: Leadership, Management and Governance of Third Sector Organisations in Australia*, Sydney: UNSW Press.

Ladkin, D. 2010 "Creating an Aesthetic of Inclusivity: A New Solution to the 'Problem' of Women Leaders", in Kay, S. & Venner, K. (eds), *A Cultural Leader's Handbook*, London: Creative Choices, 32–39.

Lorsch, J. W. & McTague, E. 2016 "Culture is Not the Culprit", *Harvard Business Review*, April, 96–105.

Our Community Group n.d. "Our Community Manifesto", www.ourcommunity.com.au/ [accessed 27 February 2019].

Plas, J. M. & Lewis, S. E. 2001 *Person-Centered Leadership of Nonprofit Organizations*, Thousand Oaks, CA: Sage Publications.

Quigg, A. M. 2011 *Bullying in the Arts*, Farnham: Gower.

Saintilan, P. & Schreiber, D. 2018 *Managing Organizations in the Creative Economy: Organizational Behaviour for the Cultural Sector*, Abingdon: Routledge.

Skringar, E. R. & Stevens, T. 2008 *Driving Change and Developing Organisations* (1st ed), Melbourne: Tilde University Press.

Walmsley, B. 2013 "Rethinking the Regional Theatre: Organizational Change at West Yorkshire Playhouse", Bogota: AIMAC International Conference, 224–237.

Wanchap, G. & Litson, J. 2017 "QSO Chairman Responds to Claims of Low Morale", *Limelight*, 17 November, www.limelightmagazine.com.au/news/qso-chairman-responds-claims-low-morale/ [accessed 27 February 2019].

Organisational Structure

Introduction

In university classes about organisational structure, I ask students to "organise" a group of three volunteers who are stuffing envelopes for a mailout.[3] The most common structure is one person folding the newsletter, another person putting it in the envelope and sealing it with the third person putting on the stamp. A more sophisticated version has the three of them changing roles a third of the way through so they don't get too bored. And then an even more sophisticated view is to check how long each task takes because if putting stamps takes half the time of stuffing envelopes, then the stamp sticker can contribute to the stuffing. Another suggestion has the three of them folding and then stuffing and then putting the stamp on. A slightly more tongue-in-cheek version has one of them as the boss managing the other two as does one where the role of "boss" gets shared and/or turned into an entertainment role to keep people happy while doing a fairly routine task. This proves that there is no single – or simple – way to structure a set of tasks, let alone an organisation. After all, a structure is simply "a means to an end" (Saintilan & Schreiber 2018, 189). However, one does want to provide some form of organisational structure in order to make clear who is doing what, who's in charge of whom, who should communicate with whom and making sure that the right number of people are working to achieve the right objectives (Byrnes 2015). An arts organisation can have a clear cultural mission and strategy but as Hagoort (2005) says, if the division and coordination of labour don't work then it's almost impossible to realise the mission.

The traditional approach to organisational structure is that it should follow strategy. This logic is that the organisation of people needs to be based on what you're trying to achieve. Byrnes (2015, 205–207) gives the example of a new opera company with a strategy to build a subscriber base as quickly as possible (so need staff for marketing, PR and ticketing); plus a strategy to use famous guest artists (needing staff to look after them); and want to keep operating costs low and so they rent sets and costumes (small production department). Another example is record companies which have had to completely reshape their business in the face of technological change and are often becoming "a looser federation of diverse skills that coalesce around projects as needed, rather than a collection of people organised into rigid silos" (Saintilan & Schreiber 2018, 200).

However, at their core, most arts organisations have structures that have existed for thousands of years such as music groups, acting ensembles, art collections and public performance spaces (Hagoort 2005). Other impacts on structure include technology, the environment, location, size, people and where an organisation is in its lifecycle. When one is thinking about an appropriate structure one has to think about the types of jobs, the span of control (how many people report to one person), levels of management (hierarchy), formality (how many rules), autonomy (who needs a manager) and working relationships (who needs to connect and communicate with whom).

Job Design

Structure is based on the division of labour and the coordination of activities so the starting point is putting together the tasks that make up a job for one person. This is usually then written up in the form of a job or position description which explains what the person actually does (duties, responsibilities and standards), what's required to do the job (work tools, formal qualifications, knowledge, skills, abilities and personal characteristics) and how the position fits into the organisational structure (Stone 2013).

In Human Resource Management books such as Stone's (2013), there is plenty of criticism of job descriptions, including that they are symbols of an archaic past, yet another attempt by management to control work, and that they have no place in a world of project work and organisational fluidity. In my experience employees like to know what their job is. Some people don't bother with very sophisticated job descriptions and some go into an extraordinary amount of detail. Most of my middle managers were determined to put every last task into a position description whereas my view was to capture the key roles and leave things open for new tasks and new requirements. That's what glorious phrases such as "any other tasks as directed" are for – within reason. That may have had something to do with the fact that I didn't have a position description at MTC for years until I had to write one when we were all required to have them as part of an OHS process. Other elements of the job description such as competencies needed and where the work fits in to the company are also important for both the recruiter and the successful applicant.

I'm not someone who makes good use of a personal assistant so my "helper" was more of an administrator with a portfolio of independent activities as well looking after me. I tried to make that very clear in the job description and included phrases like "mundane and boring work such as filing" and "less creative tasks such as refreshments for guests" so that the successful candidate would know exactly what they are buying into. Occasionally, my lack of concern for detail in position descriptions caught me out. Every so often, my assistant would need to drive me or my car. It wasn't a regular part of the job and my assumption was that everyone would have a driver's licence. So I was completely shocked when, after a couple of months in the job, my assistant said "but I can't drive". Somehow in Melbourne, which has a good public transport system and where arts workers can still afford to live in suburbs close to the city, many young people don't bother to get a driver's licence. So if there are crucial skills that you require, put them in the job description.

"Competencies" or an underlying characteristic of a person that leads to or causes superior or effective performance has become a defining word in the recruitment and training environment but can often be particularly hard to pin down. Competency characteristics include motives, traits, self-concept, knowledge and skill,

but as Stone (2013, 182) says, "knowledge and skill competencies tend to be visible while self-concept, trait and motive competencies tend to be hidden and more central to personality". Even if one can define the required underlying characteristics, one needs to be able to demonstrate that they cause or predict effective performance. In recent times, I've been looking at position descriptions from all parts of the non-profit sector and my response to them is that they are over written, jargonistic and often imply that the job is more exciting and meaningful than is actually the case. I'm not yet taking Bakke's (2005) position which is don't bother with them, but being clear and honest about the nature and the requirements of the position is the best starting point. Another point is well made by Varbanova (2013, 212) and that is when planning positions, it's important to remember that jobs have to motivate the people who perform them and motivating factors include skill variety, the capacity to actually complete an identifiable piece of work, task significance and autonomy.

When looking at what the organisation needs, sometimes the answer is a part-time position and not a full-time position; sometimes it's a casual position and not a permanent one; sometimes the right answer is to contract out the services, particularly in specialist areas such as IT. The short-term cost may be higher but not the long-term cost. Sometimes, you decide on a full-time ongoing position even when you know people won't stay for more than a couple of years. Most of my marketing and development staff at MTC could have earned considerably more working in other industries but loved the company. Eventually they would move on when they wanted to earn enough to pay a mortgage or afford to have a family or simply go on a holiday but if I had their brightness and their ideas and their energy for just couple of years it was worth it.

Another aspect of job design is job titles. I'm not that fussed about titles as long as they make sense. If people want to be called managers and they actually manage staff, then why not. If people don't understand what "development" means in an arts organisational context then make it clear by saying "fundraising and sponsorship". So I was rather amused (in a sardonic way) to read the proposed titles of the positions I was familiar with at the Australian Broadcasting Corporation. The title of manager of Radio National (close to the position I once held) was to be "Ideas Network Lead" and the manager of the Classic FM radio network was to become "Classical Lead". A number of the people I worked with at the ABC who were still there, wrote in 2016 to their Board to complain about "preposterously named executives" (White 2017, 127).

Sometimes when Boards or government bureaucrats are looking at ways of cost cutting in arts organisations, someone will come up with the idea that outsourcing is the answer. In the first place, cost cutting may not be the best approach to improving efficiency and productivity. Adam (2007, 4–6) quotes a range of research showing that when a workforce is reduced, the productivity of the "survivors" is lessened. The downsizing of the 1980s and 1990s has been shown to be ineffective in increasing productivity but there still seems to have been a shift to relying on contracting and outsourcing.

In the performing arts, for example, there is often a push to outsource areas such as set building, costume making, venue management, ticketing and some aspects of marketing. Unless there are some inherent productivity weaknesses, I can rarely see the logic behind this deconstructing of an organisation. White (2017, 144) tells of the installation of 13 mini-cinemas in a gallery to show a work.

> In a previous era the installation would have involved the Gallery electrician working in collaboration with the building, lighting, audio-visual and paint shop teams. They all knew how to work with each other and with Gallery management. But the electrician's job had been outsourced and the other technical teams had been reduced to skeleton staff. Instead of the tried and

tested procedure, there was a scramble to finish with at least nine separate outside contractors hired. It was hard to see how the outsourcing could possibly be saving money.

I agree with her. For example, if a theatre company is only making a couple of shows a year, then it may not make financial sense to have set builders working full time for the company. But if you are working year round, then having an in-house team who works well together is going to be much more cost efficient than paying an external commercial organisation to build your sets. The underlying logic of outsourcing is the one I have trouble with – you're a non-profit organisation but now you're contributing to someone else's profit.

Hierarchy and Span of Control

Span of management or control is the number of staff managers can guide and coordinate. The number of people reporting to a manager and the layers of management and supervision in an organisation provide insight into the aspects such as trust and efficiency. For example, a low trust culture would be very hierarchical with a small span of control because you can only actively control so many people. If you have high trust, the organisation is flat and flexible with large span of control because people are supervising themselves. "They are doing their jobs cheerfully without being reminded because you have built an emotional bank account with them. You've got commitment, and they are empowered" (Covey 1992, 155). Research suggests that the most appropriate number of people reporting to a manager is 4–60 when dealing with routine work and 8–10 in the case of intensive professional work (Hagoort 2005, 141). Issues you need to consider in making the decision about an appropriate span include required interaction, standardised procedures, similarity of tasks, physical dispersion of staff, frequency of new problems and competence (Griffin 1999). Griffin also mentions the impact of CEO preferences. I've seen this in an organisation where the CEO wanted to be across every aspect of the organisation and so had a dozen executives reporting to them. In my view, if someone has 10 to 20 people reporting to them then the conversation with those staff will be minimal, implying either a highly regulated environment, a standardised workforce or lots of autonomy because you can't effectively "manage" that many people. However, if the reason for deciding to have that many people reporting to you is about control, then the result won't be autonomy but simply indecision with the managers not being able to do anything without the approval of the CEO who's too busy to meet with them.

Flatter organisations with reduced "chains of command" give people more capacity to make decisions and to communicate ideas and suggestions and this contributes to an organisation's creativity (Adams 2007). Bakke (2005), the past CEO of a large international energy company, believes that there should be a minimal number of layers between the CEO and the entry-level person. He started off with a goal of two layers but ended up with three or four in a company with over 30,000 people. At MTC, the most extreme distance would be between an usher and the Managing Director, with a Theatre Manager, a Services Manager and a Front-of-House supervisor between them. For most people, there were only one or two people between them and the Managing Director. In 13 organisational charts from some of Australia's major performing arts companies, the largest number of positions reporting to one person that I could see was eight and the average was six. There was very little organisational depth because with one or two exceptions, there are only two to three people between the most junior/casual position and the Artistic Director or the Managing Director.

Another thought about span of control is offered by Clare (2010, 47). He says that a creative organisation will know that good ideas are developed everywhere and aren't just the preserve of the few at the top or "management". In a typical hierarchy, the higher you are up the ladder, the greater freedom you have and the more frequently your ideas are deferred to by those with lower status (Ginther 2010). But if an organisation has values such as "working together", "accountability" and "respect", leadership exists at every level and everyone in effect becomes a leader.

Bureaucracy

As one arts management expert said, if arts organisations are filled with creative people and leaders want their companies to be creative, why do most arts organisations have the same structure as banks or government departments – hierarchies, fixed reporting lines, traditional organisational charts? Most people cringe when they think of bureaucracies having images in their mind from George Orwell's *1984* or the TV series *Yes Minister*. They are seen as soulless and inefficient, a world of rules and forms. Bureaucrats are seen as heartless, inflexible and manipulative. The qualities of bureaucracies include centralised and stratified structures that are control-oriented and governed by rules. Mentioning "bureaucracy" and "arts organisation" in the same breath feels like a contradiction in terms. The argument is that for an organisation to be creative it needs to have a more "organic", fluid structure, dispersed power and less rules and formal processes. While this may be generally correct, there are some elements of bureaucracy in its original conception that can benefit organisations. For example, having rules and policies which mean that people are treated the same and not as individuals who can be favoured because of their gender or their relationship with the boss is a good thing. Having processes which are clear to everyone may mean more efficient task fulfilment and use of limited resources. The assumption is that people prefer loose structures with more choices and latitude but there is research to show that people like clarity of expectations, roles and lines of authority (Bolman & Deal 2013). Even the most flat and organic of organisations will have some form of structure, the "necessary centre" that focuses on problem solving and communication (Ginther

2010, 13). Equally, very large organisations can incorporate structural elements that facilitate innovation and creativity.

In arts organisations, you usually find what Fitzgibbon (2001, 161) calls a creative paradox. On the one hand, arts organisations might be very informal in demeanor, attire and ways of interrelating which may look like disorganisation from a business perspective. But low formality co-exists with the peak performance neces-sary to high innovative output and the "veneer of informality casts a blurred film over the function of both arts and innovative organisations, veiling a firm trellis of discipline and control". Another paradox is that rules are the price you have to pay for avoiding the calamities that happen if you don't have rules (Grey 2005), although the other side of that coin is when a union "works to rules" and everything grinds to a halt.

Departmentalisation

The starting point of an organisation is usually a vertical structure because in all but the leanest and smallest of companies, everyone needs a boss for direction, mentoring and feedback. The next traditional approach is to gather people together who do similar work – in finance or marketing or production or ticketing departments. Another traditional structure is called "divisional" based on geography or programs or products.

Regardless of the departmental structure, communication and coordination in organisations is never just up and down. Clare (2010, 47) says that in successful organisations that encourage innovation and creativity, the structure will usu-ally be a matrix in which "relationships are nourished vertically, horizontally and diagonally". Peer-to-peer relationships exist at many levels in organisations starting with the manage-ment team. While there may be the temptation to compete for resources and to have different perspectives on the needs of the organisation amongst the senior management team, the CEO's role is to encourage collaboration, build horizontal bridges and to manage conflict in a way that leads to more resilient relationships.

Organisations that become too siloed will end up wasting resources through defective communications.

The most difficult but most potentially innovative part of a matrix structure is when communication and collaboration happens in diagonal relationships between departments and levels. Clare (2010, 48) describes it this way:

> A successful matrix exists when line man-agers do not feel threatened by bright ideas from below; when credit is given to the person who makes a difference, rather than their boss; and when reactions to failure and omission are at once pragmatic and supportive. Diagonal relationships release the full potential of a team, triggering solutions and helping to step up the tempo of productivity.

At MTC we had an attempt at a matrix structure between the new theatre team and the produc-tion department and it failed … partly because of personalities, partly because of the timing of the work (night and day), partly because the staff were used to and felt more comfortable with a clear line of authority. However, when we changed the structure back to a more traditional model in response to the staff, we ensured that the new manager was embedded in both worlds and understood the need to work diagonally as well. In other words, you can have matrix thinking without a matrix structure *per se*. Just because there are departments doesn't necessarily mean that there are silos.

Leadership Structure

Another traditional approach to organisa-tional structure is that one has to have "unity of command", to have one boss. This isn't the case at the top of many arts organisations where co-leadership models exist. Kate MacNeill and I (2013) explored this in relation to structure. For example, sometimes the leadership model matches the structure where the parties are joint CEOs. Sometimes the structure will have a sole CEO but the day-to-day operations see the Artistic Director and the Management Director working as equals. Another version has a sole CEO and a sole leader (in Australia, this was seen most often in art museums) and a fourth model was where there was a sole CEO but a form of differentiated dual leadership took place such as in symphony orchestras. In our research, even when staff had dual reporting lines, if the communication between the leaders was clear, regular and trusting, conflicts were minimised.

Organisational Chart

According to Byrnes (2015, 198), an organisational chart should show the division of work, types of work, working relationships, departments or work groups, levels of management and lines of communication and it's usually displayed in a graphic form. For a while I didn't bother with an organisational chart for MTC on the basis that nobody inside wanted one and nobody outside asked for one. Bakke (2005, 283) said that they didn't have either an organisational chart or even job descriptions in his 30,000 staff organisation until someone wanted one. When I created the first one, it was fluid and circular with the Artistic Director and General Manager floating in the middle surrounded by lots of interacting teams and it reflected departments rather than specific jobs. Eventually, a new Board member wanted a traditional version so of course I created one for them but that didn't change the way we worked. This last action does relate to Ginther's (2010, 8) point that sometimes arts organisations structure themselves like corporate bodies in order to be seen to be using "good business practices" and thus reassure funders (and one could add the Board) that all is well with the world.

Environmental Changes

Organisational structures will change not only as a company changes but also as the environment changes. It was interesting to compare the structure of MTC in the year before I started and the year after I left. The company was smaller in 1993 than 2013 even though the number of plays in the main season was greater. The changes on the production front were the increased complexity of all aspects of design. In both years, the company owned a theatre but in 2013, the theatre had two performance spaces, an electronic fly system, a flexible staging system and more computer-based technology than in 1993. This new technology changed the job requirements of backstage staff but it also added to the staff numbers as designers wanted to use more and more of these technologically driven options. By comparison, the more craft-based departments such as set building, scenic art, props and costume making have barely changed in employment numbers or job requirements.

The push for new funding sources meant that the number of Development staff increased by 150%. The shift from print to digital media is reflected in both the change of some titles and the increasing numbers of marketing and graphic design staff. Increased legislation around employment such as equal opportunity, occupational health and safety, discrimination, and so on, meant the creation of an HR department in 2013. Ticketing processes also changed during that period and there are more people with computer competence and specific program requirements built into their position descriptions.

Many artists and producers and arts managers have worked in fluid ways with temporary groupings coming together for projects and small companies using agile project management processes to generate work (Morrow 2018). Changing technology and communication practices will continue to lead us to explore new ways of working together.

Change

Work is done by people not by structures, but structures can prevent people working at their best (Clare 2010). If formal structures get in our way or bury us in red tape, then they need fixing. But a good structure can enhance how people feel at work if it helps to get the job done.

If there's a sense of the former rather than the latter, a careful study of the structure and the processes to see what works and doesn't work in the context of the organisation's goals and strategies and environment will help gain insight into useful changes. Bolman and Deal (2013) recommend experimenting as you go, retaining things that work and discarding things that don't. The only way to get real insight into what's working is by talking to staff. In an organisational review I did, the Board thought that the structure wasn't right with too many silos and inappropriately structured positions. The staff thought otherwise, were positive about the structure and their desired changes were to do with improved technological support.

A good story of change with examples of structural shifts is in Hewison, Holden and Jones' (2013) analysis of the Royal Shakespeare Company when Michael Boyd and Vikki Heywood took over as co-leaders. The hierarchy become flatter with weekly meetings for senior staff and monthly meetings for heads of departments and middle managers. Human Resource tasks and responsibilities were spread throughout with organisation. The organisational chart was expressed with the co-leaders at the centre rather than at the top of the classic hierarchical pyramid. Efforts were made to reduce the "silo" behaviour of departments. There were other changes based on budgets, office layouts and communication but structural changes made a major contribution to the organisation's improvement.

Informal Structure

Within every formal structure, there's an informal structure because people will gather together and create teams for all sorts of reasons such as common backgrounds (ethnicity, religion, education, past work) or interests (hobbies, sport, culture). These "departments" and relationships develop because people value social acceptance, variation from work, support from others and different communication networks (Hagoort 2005). A classic example in the 1990s was the smoking team which I would join on occasion. It gave me access to a network that as a manager I wouldn't have had any other way. Such informal networks can provide people with a way to make the workplace more interesting and even help to get work done more efficiently, but if they turn into negative, gossiping spaces, then they can undermine the organisational culture of the organisation. Being alert to informal networks (without having to take up smoking) is the best approach because they are not easily changed or managed.

Conclusion

Beirne and Knight (2002, 84) write negatively about management processes in the arts, including formal organisational structures. Although I find understanding many aspects of organisational structure important and useful, I tend to agree with their conclusion that "[h]arnessing shared values and expressed interests through cross-functional collaboration is more important than dividing work tasks in a rationalistic manner". I would simply put "overly" in front of "rationalistic" and keep the focus on creating organisations with clear but flexible position descriptions, flattish hierarchies and matrix communication systems to enable them to be effectively creative.

See also: Co-leadership, Hiring, Organisational Culture

References

Adams, J. 2007 *Managing People in Organizations: Contemporary Theory and Practice*, Basingstoke: Palgrave Macmillan.

Bakke, D. W. 2005 *Joy at Work*, Seattle, WA: PVG.

Beirne, M. & Knight, S. 2002 "Principles and Consistent Management in the Arts: Lessons from British Theatre", *International Journal of Cultural Policy*, 8(1), 75–89.

Bolman, L. G. & Deal, T. E. 2013 *Reframing Organizations* (5th ed), San Francisco, CA: Jossey-Bass.

Byrnes, W. J. 2015 *Management and the Arts* (5th ed), Burlington, MA: Focal Press.

Clare, R. 2010 "A Cultural Leadership Reader 47 Leadership in a Matrix ... Or Getting Things Done in More than One Dimension", in Kay, S. & Venner,

K. (eds) *A Cultural Leader's Handbook*, London: Creative Choices, 46–49.

Covey, S. R. 1992 *Principle-Centred Leadership*, London: Pocket Books.

Dickie, L. & Dickie, C. 2011 *Cornerstones of Management* (2nd ed), Melbourne: Tilde University Press.

Fitzgibbon, M. 2001 *Managing Innovation in the Arts*, Westport, CT: Quorum Books.

Ginther, R. 2010 *Making the Case for Change: Challenging Hierarchy in Arts and Cultural Organizations*, Canada: Athabasca University.

Grey, C. 2005 *A Very Short, Fairly Interesting and Reasonably Cheap Book About Studying Organisations*, London: Sage Publications.

Griffin, R. W. 1999 *Management* (6th ed), Boston, MA: Houghton Mifflin Company.

Hagoort, G. 2005 *Art Management: Entrepreneurial Style* (5th ed), Delft: Eburon.

Hewison, R., Holden, J. & Jones, S. 2013 "Leadership and Transformation at the Royal Shakespeare Company", in Caust, J. (ed.) *Arts Leadership*, Melbourne: Tilde University Press, 144–158.

MacNeill, K. & Tonks, A. 2013 "Leadership in Australian Arts Companies: One Size Does Not Fit All", in Caust, J. (ed.), *Arts Leadership*, Melbourne: Tilde University Press.

Morrow, G. 2018 *Artist Management: Agility and the Creative and Cultural Industries*, London: Routledge.

Saintilan, P. & Schreiber, D. 2018 Managing Organizations in the Creative Economy: Organizational Behaviour for the Cultural Sector, Abingdon: Routledge.

Stone, R. J. 2013 *Managing Human Resources* (4th ed), Milton, QLD: John Wiley & Sons.

Varbanova, L. 2013 *Strategic Management in the Arts*, New York: Routledge.

White, J. 2017 *Culture Heist: Art versus Money*, Blackheath, NSW: Bandl & Schlesinger.

Notes

1 For the America reader, I mean candy and the UK reader I mean sweets.
2 For the results, see the *Change* section.
3 For very young students, I sometimes have to describe what a mailout is but it's such a neat practical exercise, I'm loathe to give it up!

P

Passion

Passion is a word that is used by almost every arts manager that I've ever met and the majority of arts managers Kate MacNeill and I interviewed for our leadership research (2009, 2013). Often the word was used about the art made by the company but equally often it was about the job itself. Some examples include:

> … we are both very wedded to the company and very passionate about what we do. [GM, UK]

> I think all arts require a kind of foolish passion which is very hard to justify and explain to people outside of the artistic community, but without it you'd have to really question, you know for the remuneration and the amount of time and all of that stuff, you'd have to question why you're doing it, so you both have to feel confident that the other person has that level of passion. [AD, Australia]

> Q. What enables you to work in this job? A: A passion for the arts I think. If you're going to work in the arts, you need to love what you're doing; an ability to just go with the flow in terms of lifestyle. [GM, Australia]

> I think that artists know I have a real passion for the art we make and that I try to show that to our staff and artist. [GM, USA]

> Q. What makes you an effective leader? A: …. believing passionately in what we do, because 20% of our revenue comes from convincing other people that they too should believe passionately and dig into their own pockets and another 30% for convincing governments that they should do likewise. So I guess it's the combination of believing passionately and being able to juggle lots at once. [GM, Australia]

In international research on the Director's role in art museum leadership, one of the primary and critical aspects of their jobs was passion. "A deep feeling in the heart for the work in hand sustains art museum Directors on a daily basis, as well as contributing to the vision of the organisation. Passion, energy and creativity are baseline competences for leadership roles" (Suchy 1999, 57).

Passion is not unheard of in the corporate management world. Sarros et al. (2006, 145) quote leadership guru Warren Bennis, saying "We are productive when we do what we love to do … If passion or love of your work or vocation is missing, then choose another vocation."

Chris Arnold, Melbourne CEO and lawyer, was equally strong about the need for passion:

> You must have passion and belief in what your organisation is doing, in its goals and its people. There's no point in working for an organisation at a senior level unless you believe in what they're doing … You can't, over a long period of time, kid a kidder about what you don't believe in the organisation. It comes out in the way in which you deal with people. So your own people will recognise you don't believe in what you're doing, and nor will your clients or other people.
>
> (Sarros et al. 2006, 147)

What passion means in all these quotes is the sense of being deeply connected to work which is highly meaningful (Suchy 1999). If this is the way we feel going to work each day, then we're luckier than most. However, Rentschler (2015) is right to warn us that there are some negative aspects of passion. To start with, she notes that the work passion comes from the Latin meaning "to suffer" (20). And suffer we do sometimes – when the artist is a bully or the art doesn't attract an audience or the funding is cut or the capital campaign fails. Constructive passion provides motivation and generates positive emotions but obsessive passion can lead to the destruction of relationships and potentially even the downfall of a company. Passion can mean that you work too hard and burn out. Shared passion means that it's hard to say "no" to the Artistic Director. Rentschler and Jogulu (2012) explore whether passion and ambition are enough to ensure satisfactory career paths for female arts managers and conclude that while passion may keep us in lowly paid arts jobs, it's not enough to ensure career progression. "Other skills need to be developed in order to develop the arts manager's career, such as education earlier on in the career and then mentoring and networking as the arts manager progressed" (153).

Most arts organisations have dreams that are bigger than their resources. This means that as the CEO or leader, you are working long and hard and continually under stress. Passion is an unavoidable ingredient in what makes us want to work in the arts but sometimes it needs to be balanced with that somewhat less thrilling word – pragmatism. Look after yourself and your staff. Avoid excessive hours. Take holidays. Be mindful that passion can lead to joy – and heartbreak.

See also: Holidays, Love, Mindfulness, You

References

MacNeill, K. & Tonks, A. 2009 "Co-leadership and Gender in the Performing Arts", *Asia Pacific Journal of Arts and Cultural Management*, 6(1), 291–404.

MacNeill, K. & Tonks, A. 2013 "Leadership in Australian Arts Companies: One Size Does Not Fit All", in Caust, J. (ed.) *Arts Leadership*, Melbourne: Tilde University Press.

Rentschler, R. 2015 *Arts Governance: People, Passion Performance*, Abingdon, Oxon: Routledge.

Rentschler, R. & Jogulu, U. 2012 "Are Passion and Ambition Enough to Support the Career of a Female Arts Manager?", in Hausmann, A. & Murzik, L. (eds) *Anthology of Cultural Institutions HRM and Leadership*, Frankfurt: Springer Verlag, 143–155.

Sarros, J., Cooper, B. K., Hartican, A. M. & Barker, C. J. 2006 *The Character of Leadership*, Milton, QLD: John Wiley & Sons.

Suchy, S. 1999 "Emotional Intelligence, Passion and Museum Leadership, Museum Management and Curatorship", *Museum Management and Curatorship*, 18(1), 57–71.

Pay

People's pay is a highly emotional topic. It's a measure of one's value to the organisation. It's a point of comparison with others, both one's peers and one's bosses. It's the enabler of all one's out of work activities. Most people would rather their pay was a secret although they are usually desperate to know what others earn. In a recent review of an arts organisations, every person I interviewed was extremely positive about the leadership and the culture and their job and every person gently wished out loud that they could have a pay increase.

Every person I've ever spoken to about pay has a different perspective. There are those who think that because they've been around the longest, they should get more pay. There are those who think that they work harder than their peers and so should get more pay. There are those who think that everyone on the same level (e.g. the executive team) should get the same pay. There are those who think that because their peers in another (better funded, larger) arts organisation get more, that they should too. And then there are union agreements which required that every newcomer starts at a particular level regardless of their skill or experience.

Pay is one of Herzberg's motivational hygiene factors. It has the capacity to make people very unhappy but never to proactively make people happy. Bakke (2005, 75) says that "unfair compensation can make a workplace less attractive, but fair or generous pay will have almost no effect on the quality of the work experience". No matter how much money you have, it's never quite enough and so you are never going to be "happy" because of what you earn. Comfortable maybe. Grateful occasionally. But not happy. Pay is "a reward for work accomplished, not a predictor of future happiness" (Bakke 2005, 119).

For cash-poor arts organisations, the question of how to pay people fairly is a challenge. In some cases, that challenge is added to by the need to negotiate with unions. On the one hand, we do have the benefit of providing important intrinsic motivational factors such as interesting work, but on the other, we usually can't afford to pay the same rates as the private or public sector. On the positive side, Hannan (2005) found that if the company is in poor financial straits then a pay increase is seen as generous with increased feelings of loyalty and productivity; if the company has made a healthy profit, then there was no resulting increase in productivity following a pay increase. This is confirmed by my experience when, after years of a salary freeze at MTC, I initiated a modest increase even though we were in financial difficulties. The positive response to that was overwhelming compared to later periods when we could and did share more generous increases with staff.

Although pay is now accepted by most researchers as a hygiene factor, the belief that people will work harder for money is still around. Not many arts and cultural organisations use incentive-based pay systems but every so often, a Board member will muse about whether such a system would be appropriate for a particular part of the company. In a e-opinion piece by Grant and Singh (2014) summarising research on financial incentives, the authors conclude that although there's evidence to say that, on average, individual financial incentives do increase employee performance, this is usually for tasks that are seen as uninteresting to most employees. In this case, incentives need to be delivered in small sizes and have to be supplemented by major initiatives to support intrinsic motivation. The key to their conclusion as it relates to arts and cultural organisations is that incentives reduce intrinsic motivation – the "over justification" effect. Adams (2007) had reached the same conclusion: that interesting or challenging tasks were seen as less desirable when incentives were applied to them.

Another longstanding belief is that employees will be motivated to work harder if their supervisor has the authority to rate them and either increase their pay or even decrease it. However, this hasn't been proved either (Adam 2007). An important part of the reason why it doesn't work is that staff don't trust managers to provide a fair performance rating because in the words of an Australian public servant (quoted in Teicher, Holden & Gough 2006, 401):

> (1) Managers forget things you've done that meet the criteria (2) Personality differences and differences in style affect manager's decision making regarding ratings (3) Some rely too much on hearsay and no evidence (4) Some managers lack the objectivity and intelligence to apply ratings fairly.

I've had the experience of being punished by a manager in circumstances where additional payment for performance was a structured part of the salary. I was scored down because I'd stood up to what I perceived to be his ineffective management. Another perspective of the management rated pay increase is that many managers are reluctant to differentiate between staff and feel uncomfortable recommending anything other than the standard increase.

So how can one decide on fair wage levels? In some countries and some sections of the arts and cultural industries, wages are determined by negotiation with unions or through government-sponsored conciliation and arbitration systems. In other employment sectors, decisions on wages or fees are made through negotiations with third parties such as agents. However, in organisations where union agreements cover staff, they may not cover all staff and such agreements may provide a minimum and not an actual pay level. Therefore, having some form of salary framework that helps one determine an appropriate salary is required – and that isn't easy if you have a wide range of tasks and skills in your company. How, for example, do you scientifically compare a set builder with 20 years' experience to a recent marketing graduate with two degrees?

Types of pay structures can be based on seniority, merit/performance and/or skill, although all of them have their problems. Seniority has been a traditional model in public services around the world and is often preferred by unions because it's not open to bias. But management usually don't like it because it rewards longevity rather than performance. I can still remember my mild-mannered father, public servant for 37 years, ranting against people getting pay increases and promotions because they'd been around for ever rather than because they'd done any work of value.

Although there's not much evidence that performance-based pay works (Balnave et al. 2009), it's still used in for-profit companies as are skill-based pay systems where pay is decided not just on the skills and knowledge required for the job (which would mean that everyone doing the same job would get

the same pay), but where consideration of *how* staff apply their skill and knowledge and add new skills to their portfolio is part of the decision-making mix.

For all the research and pay systems, in arts organisations pay is likely to be a combination of union minimums, peer company comparisons, more general market pressure, what the organisation can afford and what seems fair given what people do. As MTC was considered to be a large arts company, our rates were above the union minimum and we made regular checks to see how we compared to other elements of the entertainment industry, such as set building for TV or film. For example, when employing a set builder at MTC, there was a union rate but it was usually considerably lower than what carpenters could earn on the open market. However, most of those jobs were on building sites or in factories doing repetitive work and so there were some intrinsic benefits that MTC could offer, such as creativity and being about to make unique pieces of work that balanced the market pressures and enabled payment of a lower rate.

Where there is little difference between some jobs in an arts venue, a commercial theatre or a non-profit performing arts company (such as mechanist or usher or ticket seller or accountant or marketer), instrumental issues such as pay are likely to be more important than social value, unless an organisation has a strong culture and intrinsic motivators. For example, discussing employment with casual front-of-house staff who often worked shifts at the MTC's Southbank Theatre as well as a commercial theatre, the pay difference wasn't much and they preferred our organisational culture, so given a choice, would opt to do a shift with us first. However, when the pay difference was higher, the attractiveness of MTC faded.

People judge the fairness of their pay not in absolute terms but rather in terms of what the people around them earn. This perspective can be based on any of those pay-related elements – does the person have my skills, have they been in the business as long as me, have they worked here for as long as me? Using the set builders as an example, there was always tension when a new person was employed because the existing staff felt that because the newcomer didn't know how the company worked, they shouldn't receive as much pay as the "old hands" but usually given market pressures, new staff wanted even higher salaries. The result, which didn't satisfy either party, was to pay people the same if they were doing the same job.

Another perspective on fairness comes when part of the workforce is unionised and part isn't. Although I supported unions in the workplace, I didn't believe that being unionised should automatically lead to higher salaries. Everyone received the same basic annual pay increase. This irritated the more insightful union members who thought that everyone else was a free rider on the back of their exhausting negotiations. The truth of the matter was that my final position was always the final position for all staff and the union members would have received the same increase even without negotiations.

While the base pay in arts and cultural organisations may be modest, sometimes there will be the capacity to provide a bonus to staff either because of individual or organisational performance. Bonuses can be a contentious issue. Often in organisations, they are only paid to senior staff on the basis of performance outcomes. In most circumstances, such outcomes are the result of shared activity and so I always find such bonuses problematic. I have had endless discussions with well-meaning Board Chairs who wanted to give me a bonus but not the rest of my management team and I have, on most occasions, refused the payment. Occasionally, there will be a standout person who does an amazing and original job and then an individual performance-related bonus may be well deserved. Even if money is tight one can reward such a staffer in other ways through access to a training program or attendance at a conference. The capacity for non-cash recognition to replace cash more generally could be helpful for non-profit companies but unfortunately research concludes that cash and non-cash rewards aren't substitutes, but that

both cash and non-cash were complementary in reinforcing positive performance (Long & Shields 2010).

If a non-profit company has a successful financial year resulting in a surplus, Boards usually want to squirrel money away for the bad times – because there will be bad times. While I agree that every non-profit should have a healthy reserve, one should also share some of the good times with the people who make it possible. Once MTC started to make some surpluses, I convinced the Board to share at least a portion of it with the ongoing staff. Some years the payment was just a couple of hundred dollars each. In one particularly good year it was $2,000 or 6% of the average worker's salary at the time. That was higher than any salary increase we could have budgeted to give and such payments also leave the underlying salary structure intact in case the next year isn't as good.

Board members often asked at this point why I insisted on flat bonus payments to everyone. After all, so the thinking goes, the management team are paid more because they're expected to do more and contribute more to the operations of the company and so any surplus would mainly be the result of their work. However, the impact of a $2,000 payment to someone who is earning $50,000 is considerably more than someone who is earning $100,000 and I'm an egalitarian at heart.

These general bonuses weren't an attempt to motivate people. For rewards to act as positive reinforcement, they need to be connected to specific outcomes and happen in a timely manner. They were more in the form of profit sharing and a "thank you" to staff.

When people earn modest amounts and where each hour has an additional value when converted into overtime or leave, pay slips can be extraordinarily important. In one catastrophic episode, a Finance Director introduced new pay slips which contained more information than ever before in the belief that this would be a positive contribution to the organisation. But the pays lip was issued without notice to staff and the reaction was visceral. The initial response to the new document was that hours had been lost or miscalculated because people didn't know how to read the new document. After a series of seminars, the mood calmed and the pay slips were seen to be a good thing but the lesson was clear. We should have involved staff in a discussion about what they wanted on their pay slips, integrating their ideas if possible and run training sessions *before* the new slip was distributed.

There is some research that will give comfort to arts and cultural organisations that want but can't pay high salaries. Carr and Mellizo (2013) found that voice and autonomy play a much larger role than the wage in explaining satisfaction with work. "Voice" is the idea that workers can express their interests and concerns about work matters to management in a meaningful manner. The researchers acknowledged that wages play an important part in recruiting employees and in people's overall well-being outside the workplace, but increases in autonomy and voice can be made with little or no cost to the company and may have a better impact on performance than wage increases alone.

Although pay may be a hygiene factor, we can't escape from the fact that money is important. In a radio interview, economist Justin Wolfers summarised his research on the link between money and happiness. Unlike Herzberg's hygiene approach, he says that money *is* highly correlated with happiness and although correlation is not causation, money does buy autonomy and agency and these are things that can make us happy. In Wolfer's words "money is probably a marker for the choices you have" and with money, many of us can make use of such choices to live "fairly happy lives". So providing people with a decent amount of remuneration can add to their happiness.

When we think about pay, it's not just about what people receive now but what they are going to be able to live on when they retire from our organisations or when they can't keep working as artists. Many countries have a pension scheme that provides basic support but even when there are more sophisticated retirement

funds, art workers, artists and particularly women artists can lose out.

In Australia, we have a superannuation system in which employers pay 9.5% (or more) of people's salary level into a retirement fund. However, employers only have to do so if someone earns more than $450 per month. This means that a lot of artists or casual art workers, working across of range of different companies, lose out. Under Australian government legislation, companies aren't required to pay superannuation to women on paid maternity leave.

I introduced policies in a small to medium-sized company to get over both of these problems – paying superannuation regardless of the monthly pay cheque and when people were on maternity leave. Yes, it costs more money but if we really believe in the importance of the people who work for us now, we should also be invested in their future well-being.

Arts organisations may never be able to pay as much as for-profit, public sector or large, well-funded non-profit organisations, but they should be able to provide reasonable salaries and a high-quality work place.

See also: Empowerment, Holidays, Hours, Industrial Relations, Money, Motivation, Negotiation, People, Unions

References

Adams, J. 2007 *Managing People in Organizations: Contemporary Theory and Practice*, Basingstoke: Palgrave Macmillan.

Bakke, D. W. 2005 *Joy at Work*, Seattle, WA: PVG.

Balnave, N., Brown J., Maconachie, G. & Stone, R. J. 2009 *Employment Relations in Australia* (2nd ed), Milton, QLD: John Wiley & Sons.

Carr, M. D. & Mellizo, P. 2013 "The Relative Effect of Voice, Autonomy, and the Wage on Satisfaction with Work", *The International Journal of Human Resource Management*, 24(6), 1186–1201.

Grant, A. & Singh, J. 2014 "The Problem with Financial Incentives – And What to Do About It", Knowledge@Wharton, http://knowledge.wharton.upenn.edu/article/the-problem-with-financial-incentives-and-what-to-do-about-it/ [accessed 10 March 2019].

Hannan, R. L. 2005 "The Combined Effect of Wages and Firm Profit on Employee Effort", *Accounting Review*, 80(1), 167–188.

Long, R. J. & Shields, J. L. 2010 "From Pay to Praise? Non-cash Employee Recognition in Canadian and Australian Firms", *International Journal of Human Resource Management*, 21(8), 1145–1172.

Teicher, J., Holland, P. & Gough, R. 2006 *Employee Relations Management* (2nd ed), Sydney: Pearson Education Australia.

Wolfers, J. 2014 Interviewed on *Sunday Profile*, Radio National, 14 December, http://mpegmedia.abc.net.au/rn/podcast/2014/12/spe_20141214.mp3 [accessed 10 March 2019].

People

There are times when you'll be alone in this job as an arts or cultural manager. But most of the time you'll be listening to, talking to, supporting, training, advising and agonising over people. Leung and Tung (2015, 114) developed a word map after interviewing the Artistic Director and General Manager of the Hong Kong New Music Ensemble and the dominant word was "people".

You've chosen to be an arts manager because you care about the arts and that implies that you want to dedicate your life to supporting the artists who make it. As well as artists you'll be dealing with politicians and philanthropists, carpenters and cleaners, accountants and arts workers, ticket sellers and technicians. Some of them will be like you but most of them won't – they'll be of a different gender or sexual orientation or age or ethnicity or religion or ableness or class. You'll have to live with this diversity and treasure all the benefits that come from different experiences and opinions.

In many ways, people management is the hardest part of the job. In a salutary quote, Deming says:

> In my experience, people can face almost any problem except the problems of people. They can work long hours, face declining business, face loss of jobs, but not the problems of people.
>
> (1982, 137)

I've known good managers who will do anything rather than deal directly with underperformance. Or who are fabulous in their area of speciality but just can't build the team cohesion that will make a difference. Or who aren't comfortable with people of a different gender or ethnicity. Or who want to be friends with their staff rather than be the boss. If people like this are in your team, you have to coach them or provide them with development opportunities to build their skills in managing people. Because ultimately you can't be a really good manager unless you can help people fulfil their potential for the betterment of the company.

Shelly Lazarus, ex-Chairman and CEO of Ogilvy & Mather Worldwide talks about advice he received from the founder David Ogilvy:

> [n]o matter how much time you spend thinking about, worrying about, focusing on, questioning the value of, and evaluating people, it won't be enough. People are the only thing you should think about, because when that part is right, everything else works.
>
> (Wademan 2005, 107)

It often surprises me that Boards don't have "people" on their agenda – checking in on turnover, company culture, hearing from people other than the CEO.

In "managing" people, you have to play a variety of roles. In talking about managing young people, Drucker (1990, 148) quotes someone who says that they need a mentor to guide them, a teacher to develop their skills, a judge to evaluate their progress and an encourager to cheer them on. In my experience, it's not a matter of age. People appreciate all these aspects of support from their manager.

The only way you'll find out what people need to be productive in the workplace is to talk to them. Autry (2001, 55) tells of working in a large organisation and having a small session with employees once a week. It was morning coffee with a randomly selected group once a week and with 900 people in the organisation it took him a year to cover everyone. The process was simple: people would introduce themselves, Autry would give a report on the state of business and any new projects and then ask for comments and invite questions. His conclusion was that "their sense of involvement and appreciation was palpable". I think about a CEO I knew who was rarely seen by his staff and the impact on that organisation was equally palpable – but for all the wrong reasons. People were unsure of what they were supposed to be doing and so rarely did anything.

I had an interesting reminder about the place of people in our work as managers from a young colleague. He pointed out that people often apologise when they knock on our doors and we're in the middle of something. They feel as if they are interrupting but they aren't. The work you're doing on your computer is no more important or urgent than talking to the people in your team.

There is all sorts of research about what makes people feel engaged at work. The Gallup Organisation, for example, has spent over 30 years asking about people's relationship to the company they work with and concluded that the six most powerful predictors are an understanding of job expectations, the availability of equipment to do the job, the opportunity to contribute one's best at work, praise for a job well done, whether one's supervisors cares about them as a person and whether anyone is encouraging their development (D'Aprix 2011). None of that sounds impossible to put into practice.

People often chose to work for an arts organisation for reasons that are beyond the more traditional reasons of income or status. While this is obvious for the artist, there's differing research as to whether it applies to non-artistic staff. We want to believe that everyone who works for us is engaged (because more companies with engaged staff outperform companies with disengaged staff by a large percentage (Gofee & Jones 2013)) but that's not necessarily true. The results of Guillon's (2017) research were that non-creative people in creative organisations are no more committed to the goals of their organisation than similar people working in other industries. My experience is different. Yes, I've met

administrative and even technical staff who didn't have any interest in the art form but there were also people in the same departments who did. Sometimes people stay in jobs they don't like or they've outgrown because it's too scary to move. But most of the people I've worked with or met in arts organisations have actively chosen to be there. It even applies to those students working for a bit of money behind the foyer bar. They could have chosen to work in the more upmarket bar in the city or the trendy bar in their neighbourhood but they've chosen your company. They have every reason to work productively given that active choice. But this doesn't mean that they will always work hard; that they'll be there for you on the day you really want them; that they'll be happy at work; that they won't complain about aspects of the job and the people around them.

Hagoort (2005) offers an interesting insight into another difference between arts managers and artists and the others who work in our organisations. He says that employees and volunteers "see their organisation mainly as a place where operational activities such as performances, exhibitions and art lessons are carried out". Their view of a successful organisation will be one where procedures (ticket selling, set making, exhibition hanging, film showing) take place smoothly and without too many malfunctions. What they want from management are effective policies and procedures that enable the organisation's vision to be translated into effective operations. In addition, they'll want objectives, feedback, decisiveness, accessibility and honesty from their manager (Bossidy 2007).

A particular challenge for larger organisations is that there will usually be a mix of casual and ongoing staff. Often, the nature of casual work will mean that such people are not as "connected" to the company as regular staff. For example, they may be working in a ticket-selling or donation-raising call centre. They may be working at night-time behind a bar or back of house whereas the majority of staff work during the day. They may only come in for a couple of weeks or months and then disappear only to return a year later. However, you want the casuals to be just as committed and just as productive as your regular staff. There are strategies to help achieve this goal. Adams (2007, 15) gives an example of an insurance company with a call centre and how they reduced turnover from 95% to 50% and increased company profits by 200% in one year:

- Onsite concierge to help staff with personal needs, e.g. dry cleaning, appointments, show bookings
- Coffee cups with lids so that people could drink at their desks
- Signing bonus for staff who introduced friends/family and who then were hired
- Ability to take leave in hourly increments so that people could deal with daily life needs such as doctor's appointment
- Natural light, colour scheme to reduce stress with a chillout area for staff
- Direct mail to the CEO so that staff could voice complaints and concerns anonymously
- Free food once a month in the canteen
- A social club to enable staff to interact outside of work hours
- Offering long-term contracts.

While not all these ideas are necessarily going to work in your organisation, the point is to think about ways to improve the connection of causal staff to the company and to provide ways to help them feel valued at work.

However, even with the best will in the world, work can have a negative impact on people. I've seen people's relationships suffer because of work. I've seen people's health suffer because of work. I've seen people turn to drugs because of work. I've seen people injured because of work. Your job as a manager is to try and minimise the damage that working hard can do even if it's for a company you love. You can:

- Have an effective occupational health and safety program
- Provide training for people in not only the physicality of their job, but also in areas such as depression and mental health

- Insist on work-life balance and send people on leave
- Find a way to help those with kids and ageing parents to take care of them without irritating other people at work who don't (yet) have the same responsibilities
- Encourage people to share moments of laughter and cake, champagne and sunshine
- Have times where people come together – not just at Christmas or Thanksgiving (or your culture's most important holiday), and not just once a year.

Rosner and Halcrow (2010, 118) remind us that we should celebrate people's milestones but it's easy to let some pass without noticing. There were people at MTC who had been there for years – up to and over 30 years. They were employed when record keeping wasn't computer based; where initial employment contracts were non-existent; where paper records from decades ago had been eaten by mice or soaked in a flood. And those amazing milestones like 20 or 30 years' service could slip by without being noticed. Make sure you have a system that is going to tell you when to celebrate people's key employment milestones – and do it generously.

Other gestures of generosity can be modest in scale but profound in impact. A large non-profit organisation with links to the creative industry decided that in addition to encouraging healthy living by making a cash contribution to people's participation in sport and exercise, they would make an even larger contribution to the development of their staff's creative skills. Qualifying activities include formal lessons in singing, playing musical instruments, acting, comedy, public speaking, circus skills, writing, editing, film making, photography, drawing and painting.

However, life as an employee isn't all about celebrations and kind gestures. Managing people is full of paradoxes:

- The need for stability *and* change
- The need to both harness a valuable "resource" *and* exploit a "commodity"

- The need for both "care" *and* "control" of the workforce (Legge 2003, 98).

We have to remember that behind words like "the company" and "the organisation", there are real people having good days and bad, worrying about their kids and their partner, thinking about their future and tomorrow's deadline. They aren't just passive recipients of our actions (Grey 2005).

I'm an optimist at heart. I believe that the people who choose to work for us will, on most days, try hard to ensure the success of the company. Grey (2005) says (rightly) that work isn't everything but it makes up a lot of our lives. And we'll be better off if we care about what we do and that we work in a place where that care is both encouraged and acknowledged.

See also: Manners, Organisational Culture, Organisational Structure, Pay, Performance Appraisal, Work

References

Adams, J. 2007 *Managing People in Organizations: Contemporary Theory and Practice*, Basingstoke: Palgrave Macmillan.

Autry, J. A. 2001 *The Servant Leader*, New York: Three Rivers Press.

Bossidy, L. 2007 "What Your Leader Expects from You – And What You Should Expect in Return", *Harvard Business Review*, 85(4), 58–65.

D'Aprix, R. 2011 "Challenges of Employee Engagement", in Gillis, T. L. (ed.) *The IABC Handbook of Organizational Communication* (2nd ed), San Francisco, CA: Jossey-Bass, 257–269.

Deming, W. 1982 *Out of Crisis*, Cambridge: Cambridge University Press.

Drucker, P. F. 1990 *Managing the Nonprofit Organization*, New York: HarperCollins.

Goffe, R. & Jones, G. 2013 "Creating the Best Workplace on Earth", *Harvard Business Review*, May, 99–106.

Grey, C. 2005 *A Very Short, Fairly Interesting and Reasonably Cheap Book About Studying Organisations*, London: Sage Publications.

Guillon, O. 2017 "Do Employees in the Cultural Sector Adhere More Strongly to Their Organization's Goals than Employees in Other Sectors", *International Journal of Arts Management*, 19(2), 4–13.

Hagoort, G. 2005 *Art Management: Entrepreneurial Style* (5th ed), Delft: Eburon.

Legge, K. 2003 "Strategy as Organizing", in Cummings, S. & Wilson, D. (eds) *Images of Strategy*, Oxford: Blackwell Publishing, 74–104.

Leung, C. C. & Tung, K. Y. 2015 "Dual Roles: Collaborative Leadership in a Newly Developed Music Ensemble", in Caust, J. (ed.) *Arts and Cultural Leadership in Asia*, London: Routledge, 105–120.

Rosner, B. & Halcrow, A. 2010 *The Boss's Survival Guide* (2nd ed), New York: McGraw Hill.

Wademan, D. 2005 "The Best Advice I Ever Got", in *Harvard Business Review on Managing Yourself*, Boston, MA: Harvard Business School Publishing, 103–127.

Performance Management

People are employed to do a job and to do it well. Your challenge as a manager is to make sure that your organisation consists of highly functional people whether they are hanging up art work or developing a marketing plan. Arts organisations are extremely performance-oriented. The curtain goes up at 8pm. The exhibition is opened by the Minister at 6pm. And not only that, the performance of artists is under review by critics, by audiences, by governments, by sponsors and fundraisers. But what about the performance orientation of the rest of the staff? Most people work for us because they have a vocation – to be a costume maker or a curator – or because they love the arts. This doesn't mean that they'll work relentlessly every day. All of us are allowed time when our attention is distracted by family or love affairs or health or financial concerns. But our staff will generally work to create something that they can be proud of and that audiences will appreciate. If there are staff who don't work hard, then our organisations are too thinly resourced to carry them.

Performance management (PM) is about giving both positive and negative feedback in the hope that people's work will improve. When it comes to the performance of staff, the process of managing them in an arts organisations is usually much like what you'll find in a standard company. However, in my opinion there's performance management and there's performance management. There's the day-to-day feedback you give people as you coach and mentor and develop and train them and there's the formal, sit-down-once-a-year performance review. The latter is the focus of most academic writing and I suspect that consultants make a fortune out of creating performance management systems particularly for large organisations. More important than the process itself, it's worth noting Grant's (2012, 115) point: "If you have a de-motivated, demoralised workforce with big management problems, no performance system know or unknown will put things right."

Performance management documentation is made up of the collection of skills, knowledge and abilities required to do a job (inputs or competencies), classification of the required behaviour (the way the inputs are applied/things are done) and the outcomes that are to be appraised (the results). The PM process is a cycle of monitoring, informal feedback, formal assessment or rating, diagnosis of issues, formal review, action planning and learning and development (Becker, Antuar & Everett 2011).

One year when I had a paid fellowship with the University of Melbourne, I had to go through their performance management system which is very similar to the Personal Planning Development process discussed in Becker, Antuar and Everett (2011). It has six sections:

- Objectives
- Competencies, Professional and Skill Development
- Agreement (between the staff member and their supervisor)
- Approvals (of actions to be taken)
- Performance Review Comments
- Career Development Plan.

It's one of those horrible processes which involves points and weights and measurement of tasks and their achievement. One understands why the University had such a process. There are thousands of staff members and to have some form of equitable process is reasonable. Universities also have a history of unchallengeable job security particularly for academics in order to protect academic freedom. So if one was going to have any chance of getting rid of people who were bad teachers or poor researchers, then you need something that provides comparable data.

However, the process doesn't tell you whether someone is a good colleague – something which is equally as important as research, teaching, community engagement or teaching. And of course, the process is infinitely malleable. In practice, one can manipulate some of the initial weights and points required to get the scores that you and your assessor might want. Ultimately, I learnt nothing useful about my contribution to the University from the process. Admittedly, as I was leaving, we didn't talk about the future – and that to me is the main reason for having the conversation. Where am I going? How can the organisation help me? Do my beliefs and values and desires match theirs? Is this the right place for me to stay? More to the point, if I'm being slack and inefficient, is a once a year pep talk from the Head of Department going to help me? And if I'm rorting[1] the system but have permanency, is a series of poor scores over a couple of years really going to put my position in jeopardy?

One of the most depressing but funny takes on performance appraisal can be found in the Australian TV series *Utopia*. Set in a fictional government authority it is full of witty and close-to-the-bone insights into organisational cultural and operations. In Series 1, Episode 4, Damian, a staff member who has only been with the National Building Authority for a month, demands a performance appraisal. His language during the process is full of words like "rewarding and challenging", "results driven", 'team-oriented", "outcome focussed", "the tasks and responsibilities assigned to me are commensurate with my capacity to deliver desired performance outcomes on a consistent basis", "I delegate with clearly defined responsibilities" and one that keeps coming up time and time again: "to identify strategize and solve problems". His supervisor, Nat, stops him and asks him to use his own words to tell her something he's actually achieved and the silence is deafening. But what's worse, when she gives him "needs improvement" as feedback, he's on the doorstep with a union representative who uses language such as "Allegation 1. Verbal Attack on an employee." My favourite part of the dialogue is:

> Union rep: Allegation 2. You failed to take into account all that he has contributed within the workplace setting.
> Nat: He's only been here five weeks.
> Union rep: In which time, he has overseen the drafting of a long-term strategic ….
> Nat: No. He did four bad paragraphs that we had to completely rewrite.
> Union rep: Another attack.
> Nat: When?
> Union rep: Then. Are you not seeing a pattern here?

The result is that Nat rewrites the performance review describing Damian as an "exemplary worker" and not the "lazy, incompetent, scheming, phony" she really thinks he is and so he gets a promotion. One does have to remember that this is a satire and such a result of course would never happen in real life.

I wonder how Damian would go with Samuelson's (2015) proposal of self-evaluation? Adams (2007) also suggests that if the performance standards are clear and specific and people are allowed to self-rate then the appraisal process will work. On the surface, it seems like a better approach to box ticking because you get to tell your story and provide a context for both the positives and the negatives of your output and behaviour. But there are some potential issues. The first problem is whether you feel comfortable about emphasising your accomplishments. This doesn't take into account evidence that women traditionally undervalue their skills and performance compared to men. The second problem lies in the trust relationship with your boss. How are they going to use the mistakes that you admit to? However, if you're feeling bold and if you trust your boss, then why not tell the truth, celebrate the successes and be clear about what you want to help you move forward in the company? If you don't trust your boss then maybe performance management processes are the least of your issues.

My approach to performance management has been to provide regular and clear feedback and direction every day rather than once a year, and to use the annual meeting to look at development opportunities for the future. I was relieved to find some supporting evidence in my local paper on the day I started to write this section. In an article entitled *Performance Reviews: Get Rid of Them*, Professor Samuel Culbert from the University of California, Los Angeles starts this way:

> Ask most managers and employees about the corporate performance review, and the answer probably is the same: it's a pain to give, a pain to get, but a necessary part of modern corporate life.

Culbert then asks "is it"? And his answer is "no" because performance reviews aren't objective, they don't help teamwork by getting people to work together, people don't want to admit to weaknesses and that everyone is different and so shouldn't be measured by the same yardstick. He makes an important point about accountability. The boss is accountable as well as the staff member for getting the job done because if the latter isn't producing results, then maybe the boss shouldn't have given the person that job or should have provided more help. His alternative approach is to do a "preview" rather than a post-review, where the preview is focused on the future and what needs to happen rather than on the past and who's to blame. And such meetings can take place whenever something isn't working well.

There are elements of formal systems that seem to make sense such as the SMART approach to setting goals – specific, measurable, achievable results, time-bound goals. But they only apply to the task aspects of our work and not the equally important relationship requirements. And when reflecting about goal setting, all I can think of is the goal to get a new theatre for MTC that took me 15 years. If my pay and my performance review had been built around that goal, I would have failed year in, year out.

Other evidence that supports my unease about performance appraisal is about the ambivalence of the manager doing the appraisal. According to some research, if managers were agreeable they were more likely to be lenient in their appraisal, giving higher ratings and, if conscientious, they'd give lower ratings (Saffie-Robertson & Brutus 2014). I can't believe that I wasn't conscientious in all those performance appraisals I have given over the years but I do admit to the occasional desire to be liked. In my experience, appraisal of high-performing and low-performing people is easy. It's the people in the middle where it's harder. The people who try hard but don't always produce the best results. The people that want to be good but just aren't creative enough to do the work in a new or more productive way. One of the few positive comments about formal appraisal systems that I endorse is that they provide an opportunity for managers to be trained and learn to be able to discuss performance in a constructive manner (Becker, Antuar & Everett 2011).

My position on performance management matches Sartain (Sartain & Finney 2003) who says that the best annual performance is daily and the best performance review tool is a blank sheet of paper. She says that the questions to ask are:

1. How are you doing and what do you need to improve?
2. Where are you going?
3. As your boss, what do I need to do and know to help you do your job better? (217)

If you're not comfortable about going into a performance appraisal, then Bossidy (2007, 63) also recommends a piece of paper with a few pertinent words on it:

- Name
- Date
- What I like (e.g. team player, innovative, stays current)
- What can improve (e.g. inconsistent communication, often fails to anticipate)
- Comments.

Regardless of whether you use a simple or a complex performance management system, your role as a manager is to get and receive feedback. Regular, useful feedback enables staff to improve their work and to understand the importance of their work to the company. Writers such as Dwyer (2009 155) provide practical advice on what to keep in mind when you're giving feedback such as being timely, constructive (aiming to be helpful not hurtful), specific and empathic. One of her best points is that people can only change something they are responsible for. People can only be accountable for what they can control. They can care about what happens in the rest of the organisation but they can't be held accountable for the actions and decisions of others. Ironically, those who do care and as a result share, may actually lower their own productivity. In exploring the impact that interaction has on productivity, Waber, Magnolfi and Lindsay (2014) conclude that a worker who finds a better way to do her job but never tells anyone improves her performance, but if she takes time out of her day to tell other people, she increases their productivity but not her own.

The reason that most managers find giving feedback a stressor (Stone 2013) is because if you're providing critical feedback you have to keep in mind that you're criticising a key part of people's self-image. Your words, even if delivered with care, can still have a visceral impact. In Drucker's (1990, 107) view "the real difference between managers and leaders is measured by the way these emotionally difficult situations are handled". Every manager needs a box of tissues on their desk for these moments but Rosner and Halcrow (2010) offer a neat piece of advice. One should always give feedback in a private space but they suggest that you praise people in private too. "That way, not everyone who walks out of your closed door will be crying" (188).

Another thing to keep in mind when giving feedback is cultural differences. Luc Minguet (2014), a Frenchman who moved to take over a US company, tells an instructive story about the differences between the two countries. In France, feedback focuses on what's wrong with someone's performance. "It's considered unnecessary to mention what's right. What's good is taken as a given." But in the US, such an approach can be devastating because "Americans tend to sugarcoat one negative with a lot of positives" (78). However, maybe the Americans have the best approach because there is evidence that focusing on people's shortcomings in an appraisal is likely to ensure that the employee won't perform well in the future (Watkins, Mohr & Kelly 2011).

If people have failed, Pfeffer and Sutton (2006, 233) offer good advice: forgive and remember. "Forgive, so that people are willing to talk about and admit the errors that are inevitable in any human endeavour, and remember, so that the same mistakes don't occur repeatedly." I found a great insight into blame in a TED talk by Boston Consulting Group's Yves Morieux. He quoted the CEO of the Lego Group Jorgen Vid Knudstorp, saying that people should not be blamed for failure, but rather for failing to help

or to ask for help. But finally, there will come the time when forgiveness of failure is no longer appropriate.

Collins (2005) advises non-profits to look for and work hard at retaining exceptional performers rather that investing time and resources in trying to fix underperformance. I think of the various people I've had in senior executive teams and the ones that didn't work were lazy, not good at managing teams, lacking inspiration or fond of delegating too much work and not taking responsibility for the outcomes. And their staff knew it more quickly than I did. Luckily, those staff were brave enough and committed to the organisation so they told me what was going on. Such staff are obviously different to the ones that are themselves lazy and unproductive who will complain about a manager who is actively pushing them to achieve. Stone (2013) says that managers must be able to discriminate between those who are contributing the organisation and those who aren't and that a performance-oriented organisation should have no room for egalitarianism when it comes to performance. I was lucky that staff spoke up because it can often be a problem to find real evidence of poor performance or bad behaviour in order to be able to act on it. This may be why researchers found that only 29% of US non-profit executives and staff believed that underperforming staff didn't stay long in their organisations (Meehan & Jonker 2017, 51).

We are all a problem for someone, someday, and one of the tricks is to work out whether someone is performing badly because of a lack of ability or a lack of motivation? Carlopio, Andrewartha and Armstrong (2005) advise that if it's a lack of ability then retrain, reassign or release, and if it's a lack of motivation, establish performance goals, remove obstacles, link performance to outcomes, individualise the reward/recognition and provide feedback. However sometimes it's not about ability or motivation but about personality or ethics, or even home life.

One of the characters in Emily St John Mandel's novel *Station Eleven* is Clark, a corporate coach whose clients include a salesman who made millions for the company but yelled at his subordinates, an obviously brilliant lawyer who worked until 3am but couldn't meet her deadlines, and a public relations executive whose skill in handling clients was only matched by his ineptitude at managing his staff. Clark interviews Dahlia, a late 30s/early 40s secretary, as part of a 360-degree feedback process. She asks if the point is to change her boss. When he confirms this, she says that she doesn't believe in the perfectibility of the individual:

> "These people you coach, do they ever actually change? I mean in any kind of lasting, notable way?"
>
> He hesitated. This was actually something he'd wondered about.
>
> "They change their behaviours," he said, "some of them. Often people will simply have no idea that they're perceived as needing improvement in a certain area, but then they see the report …"
>
> She nodded. "You differentiate between changing people and changing behaviours, then?"
>
> "Of course."
>
> "Here's the thing," Dahlia said. "I'll bet you can coach Dan, and probably he'll exhibit a turnaround of sorts, he'll improve in concrete areas, but he's still be a joyless bastard."
>
> "A joyless …"
>
> "No, wait, don't write that down. Let me rephrase that. Okay, let's say he'll change a little, probably if you coach him but he'll still be a successful-but-unhappy person who works until nine p.m. every night because he's got a terrible marriage …"

In an interview between Peter Drucker and Max de Pree, de Pree says that one should build on what people *are* rather than trying to change them (Drucker 1990). When the problem isn't about organisational fit or lack of motivation and more about personal behaviour, it helps to have written policies about all the things that might go wrong because without a written policy, you can't have a fair and transparent discipline or firing policy. Examples of policy topics include bullying, respectful conduct, conflict of interest, drugs and alcohol, harassment, use of computers, social media and company resources.

Nair and Deepti (2011) have developed an interesting model to help understand deviant behaviour in the non-profit world and it's useful to reflect on the issues that might drive such behaviour in arts organisations. Some of the qualities that differentiate for-profit from non-profit organisations may actually drive counterproductive behaviour in the workplace. Nair and Deepti (2011) offer examples such as the presence of high role ambiguity, the existence of looser organisational structures and weaker accountability because of multiple stakeholders. All of these qualities may allow deviant behaviour such as theft and embezzlement to take place.

On a more positive note, other qualities of non-profits such as an ethical climate and positive role models may serve to mitigate negative behaviour. And there is also the thought that because people who opt to work with us do so because of idealism and commitment, they are less like to behave badly in the work force. The researchers also claim that because there are more women employed in the non-profit world, there is likely to be less aberrant behaviour.

However, this doesn't mean to say that you won't have to deal with problem people. Whether it's personal aggression or theft, drug taking or laziness, at some point in your career as a manager you will have to deal with workplace deviance. Some of the problems may result from the personal characteristics and lives of staff. Some of them may come about because of organisational factors such as reduced trust or pressure to conform or perceived injustices. It's also worth noting that some forms of deviance may actually be constructive. You want people to be able to express opinions on the way things are done. Whistleblowing and principled dissent can serve as a safety valve, uncover wrongdoing, act as a warning signal and challenge assumptions (Nair & Deepti 2011).

My preferred position in life, either due to naivete or stupidity, is to assume that people are decent – and in the work place, this means being hard-working and honest. People have to behave very badly for me to give up on them. Sometimes, I feel this is a weakness. When a staff member has been given a dozen feedback sessions about their performance along with advice, counselling and training, it's time to pull the plug. And of course, I should have done it much earlier. The flip side of this situation is that I'm always amazed when a staff member who has been getting regular negative feedback, who knows that the people around them aren't happy or comfortable with what they do, still doesn't understand why we don't want them to keep working for us. I know that it's about fear of finding another job or lack of self-awareness or an unfounded belief that they'll outlast their manager. After all your efforts to help such a person inside the organisation, your next job is to help them leave.

See also: Firing, People, Policies, Trust

References

Adams, J. 2007 *Managing People in Organizations: Contemporary Theory and Practice*, Basingstoke: Palgrave Macmillan.

Becker, K., Antuar, N. & Everett, C. 2011 "Implementing an Employee Performance Management System in a Nonprofit Organization", *Nonprofit Management & Leadership*, 21(3), 255–271.

Bossidy, L. 2007 "What Your Leader Expects of You", *Harvard Business Review*, April, 58–65.

Carlopio, J., Andrewartha, G. & Armstrong, H. 2005 *Developing Management Skills*, Sydney: Pearson Education.

Collins, J. 2005 *Good to Great and the Social Sectors*, Boulder, CO: Jim Collins.

Culbert, S. 2015 "Performance Reviews: Get Rid of Them", *The Age*, 18 February, 45, www.smh.com.au/comment/performance-reviews-get-rid-of-them-20150217-13gozk.html [accessed 10 March 2019].

Dwyer, J. 2009 *Communication in Business* (4th ed), Sydney: Pearson.

Drucker, P. F. 1990 *Managing the Nonprofit Organization*, New York: HarperCollins.

Grant, P. 2012 *The Business of Giving: The Theory and Practice of Philanthropy, Grantmaking and Social Investment*, New York: Palgrave Macmillan.

Mandel, E. S. J. 2014 *Station Eleven*, London: Picador.

Meehan, W. F. & Jonker, K. S. 2017 *Stanford Survey on Leadership and Management in the Nonprofit Sector*, Stanford, CA: Stanford Graduate School of Business.

Minguet, L. 2014 "Creating a Culturally Sensitive Corporation", *Harvard Business Review*, 92(5), 78.

Morieux, Y. 2013 "As Work Gets More Complex, 6 Rules to Simplify", *TED Talk*, www.ted.com/talks/yves_morieux_as_work_gets_more_complex_6_rules_to_simplify [accessed 10 March 2019].

Nair, N. & Deepti, B. 2011 "Understanding Workplace Deviant Behaviour in Nonprofit Organizations", *Nonprofit Management and Leadership*, 21(3), 289–309.

Pfeffer, J. & Sutton, R. I. 2006 *Hard Facts, Dangerous Half-Truths, and Total Nonsense*, Boston, MA: Harvard Business School Press.

Rosner, B. & Halcrow, A. 2010 *The Boss's Survival Guide* (2nd ed), New York: McGraw Hill.

Saffie-Robertson, M. C. & Brutus, S. 2014 "The Impact of Interdependence on Performance Evaluations: The Mediating Role of Discomfort with Performance Appraisal", *The International Journal of Human Resource Management*, 25(3), 459–473.

Sartain, L. with Finney, M. I. 2003 *HR from the Heart*, New York: AMACOM.

Stone, R. J. 2013 *Managing Human Resources* (4th ed), Milton, QLD: John Wiley & Sons.

Samuelson, M. 2015 "Analysis Group's CEO on Managing with Soft Metrics", *Harvard Business Review*, November, 43–46.

Waber, B., Magnolfi, J. & Lindsay, G. 2014 "Workplaces That Move People", *Harvard Business Review*, November, 92(11), 69–77.

Watkins, J. M., Mohr B. & Kelly, R. 2011 *Appreciative Inquiry* (2nd ed), San Francisco, CA: Pfeiffer.

Philanthropy

Introduction

Although we are probably all generous in our own ways, our task as arts and cultural managers is to encourage the generosity of others to enable art to be made and shared. Given that I'm about to express opinions about philanthropy, I should warn the reader that I wasn't as good at raising money as many of my Australian peers and certainly nowhere near as good as my USA peers. I did manage to run a capital campaign that raised a couple of million dollars (before we hit the wall with the Global Financial Crisis) and MTC did have many generous donors but I always felt that I underperformed in this area compared to (say) the team at the Australian Ballet or Sydney Theatre Company. However, this won't stop me from having in-principle opinions about how to do it better (next time).

The need to raise funds from sources other than governments will vary in importance from country to country. Arts and cultural organisations in the United States of America have had to rely more on private financial support than organisations in Europe, the United Kingdom and Australia, but there is increasing pressure from governments in those latter countries for arts companies to find new corporate and private partners. This pressure increased as governments tried to balance their budgets after the Global Financial Crisis which was somewhat ironic as this was exactly the same time that corporates were reducing their discretionary spend and the returns on foundations and private investments plummeted. The rhetoric of privatising funding of the arts has even spread to Vietnam, a communist country, where I provided training on fundraising and philanthropy in 2013.

In some ways, philanthropy is simply another form of government funding without any democratic control over where money is spent. What do I mean? Philanthropy is tax foregone. People donating to registered charities in countries where that donation can be used as a tax deduction are simply making the decision about what charity gets funded rather than a government department. A Dutch historian made this point very succinctly in a talk at the 2018 Davos conference. Mr Bregman said industry had to "stop talking about philanthropy and start talking about taxes" (ABC News 2019).

In a survey of contributors to a debate about philanthropy in the Netherlands including private patrons, commentators, academics, government officials, consultants, fundraisers, Board members and managers of cultural institutions, van den Braber (2011) found a tension between those who believe that private patronage replacing lost income due to government cuts will lead arts organisations to professionalise and open up to the public and those who feel that the dominance of philanthropy will lead to artistic sell-out and commercialisation. Van der Braber (2011) offers three pieces of advice to those who want to attract private donations:

1. Cultural organisations should professionalise by having sound financial management, a unique brand and clear fundraising strategies
2. Cultural organisations should invest in getting to know their donors
3. Cultural organisations should provide their donors with a way of becoming part of the artistic atmosphere.

Motivation

Van der Braber's last point provides a good starting point to explore the nature of philanthropy in arts organisations. The first question is why do people give to arts and cultural organisations? Fischer (2000, 11) believes that the underlying rationale of philanthropy is to "build and sustain human communities". She uses the idea of clusters of virtues to help unpack the motivation and behaviour of both the giver and receiver. For the giver, the virtues are generosity, compassion and charity and for the receiver, the virtues are gratitude and mutuality. The authors of a slightly more pragmatic book, *Fundraising for Dummies*, provide a list of 20 reasons why people give, including having an emotional response to the cause, wanting a tax deduction, wishing to leave a legacy, personal gain, the influence of peers, wanting to make a difference and the final very practical point: someone asked them (Mutz & Murray 2010). An orientation towards philanthropy will vary from country to country, culture to culture, as will what people give to.

In the Barclay's white paper on philanthropy in the UK (2009), six types of donors are described:

1. Privileged youth who have inherited some or all of their wealth feel an element of guilt because of that and wish to engage, using donations of time to make up for lower donations of cash
2. Eco-givers, mainly women, who are donate to environmental charities and to disaster relief
3. Altruistic entrepreneurs, self-made with a view that the wealthy have a duty to give and to share their wealth
4. Reactive donors, predominately male, high-earning executives who give because it's expected amongst their peers
5. Cultured inheritors often in semi-retirement with social and moral rather than religious beliefs at the heart of their giving
6. Professional philanthropists are large donors but more demanding of charities, given their professional background, who want to know exactly how their money is to be used.

Would this list be similar in your country? Another list is provided by Grant (2012, 55–56) (based on a typology from Beth Breeze (University of Kent)):

1. Agenda setters – humanitarian, human rights and environmental causes
2. Big fish – donating where they live/where their business is
3. Salvation seekers – giving to projects that benefit their own religion
4. Kindred spirits – give to projects that benefit "people like me"
5. Patriots and players – give to establishment/historic institutions
6. Culture vultures – visual and performing arts, museums
7. Big brands – no discernible pattern beyond giving to major charities

8. Secret operators – donating anonymously.

What he doesn't comment on is the fact that there's a huge cross-over between categories, for example, as a donor, I fit into descriptions 1, 2, 5, 6, 7 and 8.

When it comes to donating to the arts, people will usually donate more to other "worthy" sectors. For example, in a 2016 survey of giving in Australia, cultural funding came 4th on the list after social services, education and health (Commonwealth of Australia 2017), and in the USA where religion is the top attractor of donations, arts funding was 10th on the list at 5% of all donations (Charity Navigator). The words of a Hong Kong arts manager will probably ring true to managers from many other countries: "Hong Kong people give generously to charities such as orphanages or hospitals but rarely to the arts. This is because the arts are regarded as a non-essential luxury" (Qiao 2015, 45). So we have our work cut out for us to attract philanthropic donations.

Van der Braber (2011) explores six possible motives for supporting the arts:

1. Getting a (financial) return on investment, e.g. a patron backs an artist and the value of their collection goes up
2. Creating and preserving power or prestige, e.g. receiving special privileges such as special invitations to exhibitions or private audiences with artists
3. Becoming part of the artistic atmosphere
4. Feeling responsible for the development of the arts
5. Increasing public support for the arts, e.g. by serving as an example for other aspiring benefactors
6. Feeling responsible for the community.

Captured in this list is one of the tensions built into the relationship arts companies have with philanthropists. Do they donate because they are motivated by altruism or reciprocity? Rowe and Dato-on (2013, 282) say "both". Fischer (2000) prefers to think of philanthropy as a gift economy, where while reciprocity is important, the return isn't always to the original giver. But at the same time, in her cluster of giving virtues, generosity is seen as compatible with enjoying honour and recognition. Evidence from a survey about donations to museums concluded that for the most part, people weren't looking to make a name for themselves (Szczepanski 2017). Even if the values that drive people to support the arts are self-serving such as public recognition or the chance to rub shoulders with the rich and famous, Grace (2005, 4) doesn't believe they should be criticised. She says: "A person's motivation for giving … as long as it is within the ethical and values framework of the recipient organization, should be the starting point of a relationship."

The form reciprocity takes depends on what each country's tax law allows donors to receive. In Australia, the assumption is that the rationale for giving is altruism and not reciprocity. For a donation to be tax deductible, the main "gift in return" is modest recognition. Up until a point in the 2000s when the Australian Tax Office sent a pointed letter to performing arts companies reminding them that they couldn't regularly give free tickets or glasses of champagne to donors, we all did exactly that. We then had to restructure our giving program so that any special relationship-building activities such as meeting the cast after a show had to be charged for and couldn't, by definition, be restricted to donors. Some of our donors hated this. The reason they donated was to have a special relationship with the company. One could say that their donation was not philanthropic but rather a market transaction, buying access to a personal moment with an award-winning actor for example.

Radbourne and Fraser (1996, 63) argue that "[p]eople are more likely to give to a 'cause' rather than the organisation" but in my experience, arts donors are more focused on the organisation than the cause of culture or ballet or theatre making or the visual arts. While some of MTC's wealthier donors also donated to other local theatre companies and other performing arts and festival companies, most wanted a relationship specifically with MTC.

In addition to individual donors, there are also philanthropic foundations and trusts. They are a non-profit legal form that many wealthy individuals and families as well as corporations establish to distribute philanthropy. One can also find community foundations and foundations formed as a result of a bequest. The history of foundations is strong in the USA and these organisations are often seen as "state replacers" (Katz 2006, 1316). As with individual donors, the legal and financial structures of foundations as well as their motivation and interests will vary from country to country. In Australia, for example, a new form of philanthropic fund was introduced in 2001 – Private Ancillary Funds – which are a platform for the wealthy to distribute money. A minimum of 5% of assets has to be distributed annually and they are growing at a faster rate than other forms of giving (Radbourne and Watkins 2015, 169). Foundations, trusts and forms such as PACs are more likely to be what Grant (2012, 64) describes as the "shoppers" (looking for a particular outcome or product) or "investors" (looking to influence those they fund) than "givers" (expecting little from their gift).

The Ask

While some people will actively search out a relationship with your company, when it comes to a financial relationship usually you have to ask. There is evidence that receiving a direct appeal for help "triggers the underlying motivations that lead to altruistic action" (Breeze & Jollymore 2017, 3). As Weinstein (2009, 3) says: "[s]uccessful fundraising is the right person asking the right prospect for the right amount for the right project at the right time in the right way".

Kelly (1998) gives a history of fundraising and talks about three different approaches to asking for money: the emotional appeal, giving truthful information and using scientific research to identify the most persuasive forms of appeal. She considers each to be inappropriate because they feel like a form of manipulation of a passive donor. She believes that donors don't give because they've been convinced or persuaded but for their own reasons, some of which might be self-interested, but all of which have some connection to the organisation's mission.

Grace (2005, 13) suggests that if you see asking for a donation as way to let "potential donors act on the things they value, then asking no longer feels like begging". Under the heading "accepting that you have to talk about money", Mutz and Murray (2010, 142) offer two tips. First, you have to remember that money is an exchange mechanism; that you're helping your donor participate in a cause they care about and both your organisation and the donor get something out of the gift. Second, they suggest thinking about the other person and focusing on helping them give rather than on taking their money. There is no getting away from the fact that successful fundraising, particularly for major gifts, is conducted on a very human level and requires appealing to the heart, the head, the ego and the wallet. And if it feels awkward to ask, one has to remind oneself that it's about the organisation, not about you.

There are many people who earn considerably more than you and not all of them give to anyone, let alone the arts. For example, a large proportion of Australia's wealthiest don't donate to any charitable cause (Fulton 2011). Dick Smith, a successful entrepreneur, said in 2011 that 2,000 Australians who declared that they earned over $1 million claimed no deduction for charitable donations which means that they didn't give back to their communities. However, in an interview on ABC TV News[2] another wealthy Australian, Sam Walsh CEO of Rio Tinto (and Chair of Black Swan Theatre Company at the time), said: "Wealthy Australians are reluctant to donate because they don't like to be seen as 'too rich' and artists and producers seem to be too shy to ask for money for their projects." So you have to ask the wealthy but you can also ask the not-so-wealthy. One of the simple techniques that Australian arts organisations are using to ask people to donate is a tap and go machine that sits on their box office counter, or their reception desk, or their bar which enables people to donate a couple of dollars just by waving a credit card. However, most donations will come from a more personal interaction than proximity to a machine.

Interestingly, as an arts manager you are not necessarily the person to whom the potential donor wants to talk. They usually want to meet, to know, to be connected to the Artistic Director. In Beard's (2012c) research she discovered that if the Managing Director is committed to fundraising while the Artistic Director avoids it, contributed income will decrease or not be fully realised because of a failure to connect donors and potential donors to the artistic product. On the other hand, the arts manager's role is to provide an appropriate environment for effective fundraising and so if the Artistic Director is willing to fundraise but the Managing Director is averse, the Artistic Director won't have sufficient access to donor information or administrative support.

Marketing plays an important role in philanthropy because you have to find the words and the story to make your art and your organisation more compelling than all the other companies in the marketplace. There are three communication points:

1. Creating awareness about your cause
2. Reassuring the donor that they've spent their money wisely through content and stories
3. Highlighting the results (and saying thank you) (Baxter 2017a).

American choreographer Bill T. Jones offers an interesting insight into Baxter's first point. If you're rich, you can just buy an artwork or commission an artist but with dance, he says, "what's the thing a rich person gets? You've got to find a way to connect with their sense of adventure and the notion of art making in the world of ideas" (Lissy & Beard 2015). Nick Mitzecivh,

CEO of the National Gallery of Australia (Turner 2018), has "the philosophy that money follows good ideas. You have to have the conviction and the confidence and the resilience to keep advancing those ideas. It's about purposefulness and connecting and harnessing a collective achievement." You have to find the right words to tell your story. Grace (2005, 9) gives a great example of an advertising executive responding to an ask from his old university. Apparently, the donation request was over intellectual and wasn't emotional enough. He encouraged them to evoke "images that stirred nostalgia … the smell of a campus grove after a rain, the sound of the stadium … the taste of coffee hastily drunk between classes with friends". We have to find the equivalent emotional call for our potential donors.

While finding the right words for a potential donor is important, sometimes it's giving them an experience that counts. In my early days at MTC, I was approached by an artist who worked on our Education program. She pointed out that while the program content was great, it was only accessible to those whose parents could afford to pay. So we came up with a workshop for disadvantaged teenagers. We wrote to every high school drama teacher in the state and asked them to nominate a student. They weren't necessarily to be the best student in the class but the one who would benefit most from such a program. We were very open about what sort of disadvantage was relevant: geography and poverty, social and sexual/gender challenges – and sometimes it was all of it. One participant that I meet was a gay boy in a single parent family from a tiny country town. The results of this one week of drama on the kids was extraordinary. Family and company members were invited in on the last day and year after year, I left that room with tears in my eyes.

Each year for our tax appeal,[3] we'd ask an artist to tell a story of why donating to a particular program was important. In my final year in the company, the fundraising team asked if I'd be the voice of the company and I chose to focus on this education program. I told the story with all the passion that I could in a letter to subscribers and past donors and we had the best outcome for a number of years. In the past for this campaign, lots of people donated modest amounts so we also said that we'd invite anyone who donated more than $1,000 to the education presentation on the last day. Of these donors, only one could attend but the emotional impact on her was the same as on me – tears plus an instant extra donation and a long-term commitment to the program.

That story is also a reminder that small donations are just as important as big ones. People with modest means may have exactly the same passion for your art as the wealthy. Their small annual donation may not increase much over time but the donation they give every year means that a student's ticket can be subsidised or a pair of pointe shoes can be bought. Watkins (Radbourne and Watkins 2015) describes the "giving catalogue" the Australia Ballet produced which started at A$25 to print a lighting plan for a ballet to $3,500 to hire a truck to move scenery from Sydney to Melbourne. And as people's circumstances change, if they are a committed donor, valued by you and valuing the relationship with you, that donation may grow and turn into something larger now or a legacy in the future.

Relationships

Breeze and Jollymore (2017) interviewed a number of fundraisers in the UK and Canada and concluded that there were three important factors that resulted in successful "asks" and each was about the human connection:

- The ask was made within a relationship of trust
- The fundraiser was an "honest broker" between the donor and the company
- The fundraiser had to find the alignment between company's needs and the values for the philanthropist.

In the story of a capital fundraising campaign in India, the author/participant who was engaged in this type of activity for the first time reached the same conclusion that you'll find in any good textbook on philanthropy – that people can't give unless they're asked and that you have to spend time asking, that is, building the relationship. As Sudhanva Deshpande (2015, 100) said:

> [a] beautifully designed brochure is nice, but really, at the end of the day, anybody can produce a brochure that says all the right things, but nobody can substitute you when it comes to conveying your sense of passion, vision and commitment to your values. In other words, you are your best advertisement.

You have to build a relationship with the donor or the foundation to ensure that the money you receive isn't a one-off exchange of goods. The best arts philanthropy relationship builder that I've met is Kenneth Watkins from the Australian Ballet. If you want some examples of how, based on a value-focused approach to relationships, he goes about it, read his stories in Radbourne and Watkins (2015).

In the USA the importance of philanthropy and fundraising is such that most of the Managing Directors I met during a philanthropy fact-finding tour in New York in 2012 had held the role of Development Director[4] before their promotion to CEO. And most of them saw relationship management of both their wealthy donor Board members and other financial supporters as the most important part of their job.

Going back to Fischer's virtues, gratitude is an important part of the relationship with donors with its expression of appreciation. Van der Braber (2011, 5) says that there is a universally acknowledged tendency that arts and cultural organisations demonstrate a shocking lack of attention to patrons. I suspect that this may be a European experience rather than an American one, but even in US publications there seems to be recognition that failing to say "thank you" is the unforgiveable point when many donor/company relationships break down. As Mutz and Murray (2010) ask, how can something as simple as saying thank you be overlooked? Their answer is:

> Easily – organizations often focus on receiving and not on giving. Recognizing your donors by saying thank you, sending cards, making phone calls, or planning a luncheon needs to comprise about 20 percent of your fundraising time. Seems like too much time? Well, it isn't if you recognize that your primary goal is building relationships with your donors, not raising money (128).

Fischer (2000) proposes a cluster of virtues around the relationship between donor and receiver: respect, honesty, fairness, cooperativeness – to which I would also add trust. Donors trust you to treat them with all those qualities but they also trust you to use the gift as expected (Tshirhart 1996). In *The Complete Community Fundraising Handbook*, three simple qualities for an effective relationship with donors are proposed: recognition, respect and rewards. I've been through an interesting process over the last couple of years as the executor of a will through which a donor gave six-figure donations to two universities. The difference between the two is captured in those three words. One provided annual updates; the other didn't unless pushed. One provided a public opportunity for the donor to be specifically acknowledged; the other didn't. One regularly sent out invitations to donor events; the other didn't. Of course, neither organisation really has to do anything because the money isn't going to be withdrawn and I don't have the capacity to be a major donor in the future, but I don't hesitate in telling the story to others who might be thinking about donating to either university.[5] Van den Braber's (2011, 5) conclusion after collecting advice from donors and arts managers was in order to build a good relationship one needs to invest in "more enthusiasm, more courtesy, more respect, and less arrogance, lassitude, reticence and scrupulousness".

The most depressing story I read about relationships was this one: after 10 years of giving to a gallery, no-one bothered to ask the philanthropist for anything more (White 2017, 141). You may not like them very much. They may be looking for glory rather than simply being an altruist. But unless there's something terribly wrong with the source of their money and their public persona, why wouldn't you continue to work on this relationship? The key to any donor relationship is communication and what Radbourne and Watkins (2015, 44) call the principles of values-driven cultivation:

- See every donor as an individual
- Build a meaningful partnership
- Know when to ask for a gift
- Build the capacity for maintaining simultaneous relationships with a variety of donors
- Use storytelling as a means of engagement.

It's often hard for small to medium-sized arts companies to run successful philanthropy campaigns because they lack the resources to fund a development position and so relationship building becomes one of the multitude of things that the CEO has to do. In Australia, most S2M companies will have a couple of passionate donors but most of their non-government money will come from foundations and trusts because it's easier to write a good application than to source and solicit people of wealth.

A new form of philanthropy is called "venture" or "strategic" philanthropy. In this model, the relationship is about more than just Fisher's virtues. It's where individuals or foundations/trusts want to get more deeply involved in the operations of the organisation. The investment is longer term, often providing expertise as well as cash, focused on capacity building and looking to achieve specific outcomes (Grant 2012). However, most of these "new" philanthropists are focused on issues such as poverty alleviation or other forms of social change rather than the arts. Although cultural organisations are interested in capacity building and improving the instrumental aspects of their output such as education, they're more interested in obtaining philanthropic funds to make more art. A philanthropist who wanted to influence or control the choice of art or artists wouldn't necessarily be a welcome one. Mind you, depending on their level of wealth they could just as easily create their own arts organisation to fulfil their interests.[6]

Crowdfunding

Much of the discussion to date has been based on the experience of working in large arts organisations with staff and structures to support the building and maintaining of philanthropic giving. For small project teams without this resource, crowdfunding whereby one attracts donors via online solicitation has been a boon since it started in the 2000s. Many of the same principles of motivation, asking and thanking apply. For example, Cohendet and Simon (2014, 4) note that people pay for the production of the idea rather than buying the final output and this is what many traditional donors also do. They go on to say "these models rest on the idea that the intrinsic value of an artwork or a scientific project does not come from its actual consumption but instead lies in the creative process and/or creative experience". Governments may not really believe in the intrinsic value of the arts but it would seem that crowdfunding investors and arts donors do.

Most projects seeking crowdfunding will offer material rewards of some form such as a copy of the product (CD or tickets to previews), creative mementos (signed posters and a credit in the program), creative collaboration (appearing in the work) and/or creative experience (communication from the artist). All of these examples can be found in more traditional fundraising relationships. However, there is evidence that support in such a public context is negatively affected by the offer of material or monetary rewards in exchange for donations whereas public acknowledgement increases the motivation to give (Boeuf, Darveau & Legoux 2014). In research on donating via Kickstarter to theatre projects, the authors concluded that when a material reward is offered the amount drops 33% compared to when the reward is just public acknowledgement. So it seems that saying "thank you" through public recognition is just as important in the online world as in the real world.

There are drawbacks to crowdfunding because unless you're lucky enough for your ask to go viral, you are usually asking the same group of people year after year – your Facebook friends and the people following your Instagram account. You run the risk of "exhausting their funds and patience" (Thompson 2016, 80) and the advice tends to be that you still need a plurality of funding sources to survive (Davidson and Poor 2015).

Boards

The driving force in philanthropy in most US arts organisations is Board members. Of a wide range of US non-profit Boards surveyed in 2015 (Larcker et al. 2015), 58% had a "give or get off" policy – where you can't stay on a Board unless you donate money – and 45% required Board Directors to fundraise on their behalf. For S2M companies with a turnover of under $5 million, the mean ask of Directors was $5,609 and the maximum $30,000. For large companies, the mean was $11,706 but the maximum was $100,000 (21). In addition to these annual donations by Board members, they may also be asked to make an even larger contribution to a capital campaign as well as to ask their peers to donate and attend fundraising events. This is not a common pattern in other countries, although there is an increasing shift towards expecting Board members to contribute more than just their time.

When I first joined an arts Board in the 1980s, there was never any question that part of my role would be donating or asking for money. As a post-graduate student at the time, if that had been a prerequisite I wouldn't have been able to donate anything more than cents. I admire those Board members who have worked hard, made a good living, and have some money that they are prepared to spend on the arts rather than on themselves or their family. However, in Australia even those people are often reluctant askers of their friends and networks for understandable reasons. If you ask, you may be asked back. And when it comes to fundraising events, how many charity balls or gala dinners or special auctions do you really want to go to each year? There is subtle pressure from governments in countries like Australia to push us towards the American model of Board philanthropy. In a conversation with an arts CEO who was managing a capital campaign, she said unless Boards are part of the process, the chance of success was low. Her challenge was to find people who want Development jobs. Most of them are young and inexperienced and simply don't have access to people with money. The introductions have to come from more senior people – which means the Board.

However, in my performance reviews of Boards and conversations with Board members in Australia, many of them are not convinced that a "give or get off" policy is appropriate. It may be decades or generations before a cultural change occurs in countries shifting them to the USA model where it's acceptable that you can only be on a Board on condition that you both donate and ask others for money.

Problems

Almost any aspect of philanthropy can have its challenges. We know all the things that we can do wrong – failing to ask; failing to thank; failing to be bold. But there can also be problems that donors create and the biggest problems come with the biggest donors. Providing naming rights to public buildings can lead to negative publicity if the names are not ones universally appreciated by audiences. When the Lincoln Centre accepted $100 million from David H. Koch,[7] libertarian and anti-Obama businessman, to modernise their State Theatre building and in exchange named it after him, some public response was negative, and there were demonstrations outside the Metropolitan Museum of Art in response to a plaza being named after Koch as a thank you for a $65 million donation.

A more important issue is the one that some of van den Braden's (2011) recipients were frightened about – the impact on what art is made and presented. Do major donors either directly or by subtle self-censorship on behalf of management have an impact on the mission of an arts or cultural organisation? Although I haven't had that experience, I have met managers who have. For example, a US theatre company in a large city decided that their community needed to hear alternative voices and put on a play with gay themes. It wasn't a particularly "out there" or "graphic" play and was one that had been produced in many other parts of the world to great artistic effect. But in this case, one of the company's Board members who was also a major donor took exception to the production and withdrew his funding, encouraging other donors to join him. The financial impact was profound and the CEO was directed not to program such plays again. At the time I heard the story, he was still considering his position, wondering whether he could stay at a company with such donor-led constraints.

Part of my ambivalent attitude to philanthropy was informed by the role of Richard Pratt, a powerful Melbourne businessman who had a history with MTC. As a young man, he studied at the University of Melbourne, became involved with the Union Theatre Repertory Company (the original name of MTC) and was cast in the international touring production of an iconic Australian play, *Summer of the Seventeenth Doll*. Pratt carried a love of the performing arts into the business world (including singing songs such as *If I Were a Rich Man* from *Fiddler on the Roof* at public events) as well as a positive attitude towards philanthropy. When I arrived at MTC he wasn't donating to the company but he was generous to many other Melbourne arts organisations.

At the time, he was also Chair of the Victorian Arts Centre[8] and had a problematic relationship with the CEO. His biographers call his style a technique of provoking people to see what they really thought (Kirby & Myer 2009, 114) whereas I would use less complimentary words. This relationship was so difficult that the major hirers were concerned for the well-being of the CEO and the effectiveness of the organisation and went to the Premier of Victoria to ask for Pratt to be removed from the role. We failed in that attempt but those who were receiving annual donations from Pratt were, not surprisingly, punished for their audacity and the grants were not renewed. MTC didn't suffer directly but when, a couple of years later, a generous six-figure cheque from the Pratt Foundation arrived unexpectedly in the mail, I treated it as a one-off donation and didn't build any expectation of its repeat into the budget. And I was right to take this approach. A couple of years later, arts leaders were asked by a Pratt advisor to make positive statements to the press in the face of a media storm about Pratt and a mistress. Most declined to comment because his private, now public, life was not their concern. Shortly afterwards we were all told that donations were no longer going to the arts but to community services. His biographers claim that this was already being planned (Kirby & Myer 2009), but companies that usually received a donation hadn't been told of any change in policy and saw it as a response to their refusal to engage with the media on Pratt's behalf. As a result, programs had to be cancelled.

Fischer (2000, 102) makes an interesting point that the desire to seek win-win situations with donors, which on the surface would appear to be enacting the qualities of mutuality, cooperativeness and respect that are so important in philanthropy, can also lead to moral slippage when win-win becomes a cover for keeping everyone happy. She tells a story about a non-profit company being offered a large donation – but the donor was notorious for some of his business practices so the non-profit declined the offer even though technically it was win-win: money for the organisation and profile building for the businessman.

While people who leave money to arts companies in their will clearly aren't expecting any personal return (unless their religious beliefs lead to them to think such an action might deliver a heavenly reward), some large donations made this way are given to ensure their name is carried forward into the future. If such legacy donations are given without ties, they can be of great benefit but if the will specifies certain desired outcomes that have not been discussed with the company, the money may be a diversion rather than a benefit. And a large donation that hasn't been discussed within the donor's family can also create a problem. In one case I know, the company gave the money back rather than be the cause of a family dispute.

Capital campaigns, when a company needs to buy or renovate a new building, for example, can be a reason to build the depth and breadth of a company's philanthropic capacity. Current donors can be asked to give more. New donors can be sourced through appropriate research. But such campaigns can also undermine funds that would come in annually to cover operating expenses. When MTC launched its capital campaign, we took that into account and looked for other sources of funding to make up the short-term gap as donors made larger donations but for a rehearsal room fit out rather than the rehearsal itself. In the early 2000s, when the Australian Ballet was actively building its philanthropic capacity, they made a decision not to accept major capital gifts at the expense of an annual gift. The result of this policy was that annual gifts increased as "donors became aware of the importance of each gift" (Radbourne & Watkins 2015, 120) and after a couple of years, the company was better placed to manage capital gifts.

Another challenge facing arts organisations is getting the balance right between government support and private support. Evidence from the USA is that government grants can crowd out donors (Hughes, Luksetich & Rooney 2014). That happens because a donor might feel that they don't need to donate at all or as much if an organisation is getting government support and it could also result in the company feeling that they didn't have to fundraise as much because of that support. However, arts managers in other countries facing a push towards the American model of philanthropy have the opposite fear.

In Australia, the conversations I've heard have been focused on the likelihood of governments reducing their commitment to the arts because of increasing donations. There are various facets to this discussion. Perhaps it's harder in countries with a strong tradition of government support to attract potential donors *because* they know that the government provides grants to arts and cultural organisations. And yet a further part of the prism is that government grants could enable crowding-in with donors feeling more comfortable about the stability and effectiveness of the company because the government was willing to invest. It depends on whether government funding and private funding are complementary or substitutes for each other. And the answer could be both – with a positive complementary effect at low levels of funding and a substitution effect as government support increases (Hughes, Luksetich & Rooney 2014).

The results from an analysis of US symphony orchestras from 2004–2007 (Hughes, Luksetich & Rooney 2014, 460) concluded that the outcome was "complex" with a crowd-in effect for individual giving, crowding out for foundation grants and no significant effort on business philanthropy. My conclusion from this is as long as the crowding-out effect isn't dollar for dollar, then you should continue trying to raise money from a diversity of sources.

Conclusion

There are people and foundations who want to support our art making and cultural institutions and we should search them out and build relationships with them. We can't rely on or even expect governments to fund all our activity.

Generous donors, whether of small or large amounts, deserve to be treated with respect, recognised for their support and rewarded where appropriate regardless of whether they are making their donation for reasons of pure altruism or in search of some reciprocity related to their passion for the art form. However, one should bring ethical thinking into one's philanthropy policy. Are there donors from whom you will not accept money? What are the reasonable and legal obligations you have towards donors? Are you willing to compromise your work to get more money? I agree with van den Braber (2011) who concludes that we should be more tolerant towards patrons pursuing honour or status or public recognition than those seeking to shape or manipulate the production and distribution of art.

See also: Boards, Cultural Policy, Ethics, Fundraising, Money, Stakeholders

References

ABC News 2019 "Dutch Historian Rutger Bregman Goes Viral After Challenging Davos Panel to Talk about Taxing the Wealthy", 31 January, www.abc.net.au/news/2019-01-31/dutch-historian-rutger-bregman-goes-viral-after-davos-tax-speech/10766504 [accessed 10 March 2019].

Barclays 2009 *Philanthropy: The Evolution of Giving*, wealth.barclays.com/content/dam/bwpublic/global/documents/wealth_management/Philanthropy-The-Evolution-Of-Giving.pdf [accessed 10 March 2019].

Baxter, A. 2017a *How Marketing Can Help Influence Philanthropists to Give to Your Not-for-profit Cause*, www.andrewbillybaxter.com.au/blog/2017/9/15/how-marketing-can-help-influence-philanthropists-to-give-to-your-not-for-profit-cause [accessed 10 March 2019].

Beard, A. 2012c "Revenue Structure in Nonprofit Arts Organizations – Do Dual Leadership or Budgeting Matter?" in *No Money, No Mission' - Financial Performance, Leadership Structure and Budgeting In Nonprofit Performing Arts Organizations*, New York, 97–140.

Boeuf, B., Darveau, J. & Legoux, R. 2014 "Financing Creativity: Crowdfunding as a New Approach for Theatre Projects", *International Journal of Arts Management*, 16(3), 33–48.

Breeze, B. & Jollymore, G. 2017 "Understanding Solicitation: Beyond the Binary Variable of Being Asked Or Not Asked", *International Journal of Nonprofit and Voluntary Sector Marketing*, 22, e1607. https://doi.org/10.1002/nvsm.1607 [accessed 11 December 2019].

Charity Navigator n.d. *Giving Statistics*, www.charitynavigator.org/index.cfm?bay=content.view&cpid=42 [accessed 10 March 2019].

Cohendet, P. & Simon, L. 2014 "Financing Creativity: New Issues and New Approaches", *International Journal of Arts Management*, 16(3), 3–5.

Commonwealth of Australia 2017, *Giving Australia 2016*, www.communitybusinesspartnership.gov.au/wp-content/uploads/2017/04/giving_australia_2016_philanthropy_and_philanthropists_report.pdf [accessed 10 March 2019].

Davidson, R. & Poor, N. 2015 "The Barriers Facing Artists' Use of Crowdfunding Platforms: Personality, Emotional Labor, and Going to the Well One Too Many Times", *New Media & Society*, 17(2), 289–307.

Deshpande, S. 2015 "The Studio Safdar Story", in Caust, J. (ed.) *Arts and Cultural Leadership in Asia*, London: Routledge, 91–101.

Fischer, M. 2000 *Ethical Decision Making in Fund Raising*, New York: John Wiley & Sons.

Fulton, A. 2011 "Smith Threatens to Out Rich Who Don't Help Others", *Sydney Morning Herald*, www.smh.com.au/executive-style/smith-threatens-to-out-rich-who-dont-help-others-20110909-1k1sy.html [accessed 10 March 2019].

Grace, K. S. 2005 *Beyond Fundraising: New Strategies for Nonprofit Innovation and Investment*, Hoboken, NJ: Wiley.

Grant, P. 2012 *The Business of Giving: The Theory and Practice of Philanthropy, Grantmaking and Social Investment*, New York: Palgrave Macmillan.

Hughes, P., Luksetich, W. & Rooney, P. 2014 "Crowding-Out and Fundraising Efforts: The Impact of Government Grants on Symphony Orchestras", *Nonprofit Management and Leadership*, 24(4), 445–465.

Kaiser, M. M. 2013 *The Circle*, Waltham, MA: Brandeis University Press.

Katz, S. N. 2006 "Philanthropy", in Ginsburg, V. A. & Throsby, D. (eds) *Handbook of the Economics of Art and Culture*, Oxford: Elsevier, 1300–1321.

Kelly, K. 1998 *Effective Fund-Raising Management*, Mahwah, NJ: Lawrence Erlbaum Associates.

Kirby, J. & Myer, R. 2009 *Richard Pratt: One Out of the Box*, Milton, QLD: John Wiley & Sons,

Larcker, D. F., Meehan, W. F., Donatiello, N. & Tayan, B. 2015 "2015 Survey on Board of Directors of Nonprofit Organisations", Stanford, CA: Stanford Graduate School of Business & Rock Center for Corporate Governance.

Lissy, D. & Beard, A. 2015 "Life's Work: An Interview with Bill T. Jones", *Harvard Business Review*, November, 93(11), 156.

Mutz, J. & Murray, K. 2010 *Fundraising for Dummies* (3rd ed), Hoboken, NJ: Wiley Publishing.

Our Community 2007 *The Complete Community Fundraising Handbook*, ourcommunity.com.au, Melbourne.

Qiao, L. 2015 "Re-negotiating the Arts in China", in Caust, J. (ed.) *Arts and Cultural Leadership in Asia*, London: Routledge, 26–38.

Radbourne, J. & Fraser, M. 1996 *Arts Management*, Sydney: Allen and Unwin.

Radbourne, J. & Watkins, K. 2015 *Philanthropy and the Arts*, Melbourne: Melbourne University Press.

Rowe, W. G. & Dato-on, M. C. (eds) 2013 *Introduction to Nonprofit Management*, Thousand Oaks, CA: Sage.

Szczepanski, J. 2017 "Understanding Donor Motivations", *Museum Management and Curatorship*, 32(3), 272–280.

Thompson, C. 2016 "Are We Done Crowdfunding?", *Dance Magazine*, January, 80–82.

Tshirhart, M. 1996 *Artful Leadership*, Bloomington, IN: Indiana University Press.

Turner, B. 2018 "I Will Change Everything", *Good Weekend*, 9 June, www.smh.com.au/entertainment/art-and-design/i-will-change-everything-the-assured-ambition-of-new-nga-Director-nick-mitzevich-20180605-p4zjij.html [accessed 10 June 2018].

Van den Braber, H. 2011 *Pushy Patrons or Selfless Philanthropists? The Debate on Private Support for the arts in the Netherlands 2001–2010*, Antwerp: 11th AIMAC International Conference.

Weinstein, S. 2009 *The Complete Guide to Fundraising Management* (3rd ed), Hoboken, NJ: John Wiley & Sons.

White, J. 2017 Culture Heist: Art versus Money, Blackheath, NSW: Bandl & Schlesinger.

Policies

Bureaucracies are known and often criticised for the endless array of policies that attempt to regulate every aspect of work life and decision-making. Policies are seen to stifle creativity and prevent initiative taking. Sartain (Sartain & Finney 2003) is not fond of policies because she thinks they stop managers making decisions that are appropriate to the time and the place. She gives examples from when she was the HR Head at Southwestern Airlines of being asked for policies about riding scooters in the hall, bringing dogs to work and having bare feet in the cafeteria. "Any adult," she says "can see that scooters, bare feet, and dogs are usually inappropriate in the workplace. Why make a rule about it?" (192). Having created policies on dogs and bare feet, my response is that sometimes people need to be protected from themselves (when they are wandering around in bare feet in an environment where nails were being used) and sometimes we need to be protected from their pets (at least barking and flea-ridden ones).

I'm of the view that with clear policies, one creates an environment of fairness, transparency and predictability and takes the stress out of some decisions. Having policies means there isn't continual debate about how things should have been done or who's in the right. This doesn't mean that there's a detailed procedure for everything because we still want to have an environment where people are trusted to do both their jobs and come up with new and better ways of helping the organisation meet its goals. Typical policy areas will include:

- Objectives and priorities
- Participation and decision-making – authorities, accountabilities, conflict resolution
- Services, activities and facilities – work procedures, complaint resolution, opening hours, recruitment and selection, volunteers
- Difficult situations – occupational health and safety use of drugs and alcohol, violence, racism, sexism, harassment, bullying (Adirondack 2005, 195–196).

At Southwest Airlines, Sartain reduced the policy document from 350 pages to 35 pages, keeping only the ones that were necessary by law or that reflected the key elements of the organisational culture. Her managers were trained and encouraged to use their own good judgement and common sense with a culture of trusting people to do their jobs and to think for themselves. I like her advice about keeping policies simple in language and concept. That's not always possible in heavily legalistic areas but if you want people to understand and value policies, then get staff to participate in developing them and get feedback on drafts.

It's not only large companies that need and use policies and procedures. Some of the best documentation I've seen has been in small to medium-sized companies. Often there are only two or three staff members but at peak times when employee numbers increase having policies, for example, about occupational health and safety, petty cash and respect in the workplace provide guidelines for the casual or contract staff. You don't have to reinvent the wheel and write every policy yourself. I often borrowed good policies from other companies and adapted them to fit my company's organisational culture.

A policy that sits in a drawer is no use in these circumstances. It has to be turned into an active document through training, either as part of the induction process or as a special one-off exercise for staff when a new policy is introduced or guidelines modified in a major way. At MTC, we had regular training on OHS issues but some of the best training was when we all got together to learn about harassment and bullying and to translate the legal requirements into a policy about respect in the workplace that was in our language.

Rosner and Halcrow (2010, 110) summarise the use of policies well:

> On your grumpy days you may have been tempted to burn your own handbook. The rules can seem overbearing, arbitrary, silly, or even counterproductive. But don't do it. Whether brief or voluminous, elegant or imperfect, the handbook is your friend. It enables you to be consistent, to treat people equitably, to avoid managing on a whim, and to keep out of court.

The best policies are ones that use common sense and clear language, that help people know what their responsibilities are and when they may have to get advice or help in making decisions. In my experience, people like some rules, the ones that enable fairness and take the stress out of decisions. And if you want an organisational culture to change, then putting those changes into policies as well as putting them into practice will help the process.

See also: Decision-making, Occupational Health and Safety, Organisational Culture, People, Performance Appraisal

References

Adirondack, S. 2005 *Just About Managing?* (4th ed), London: London Voluntary Service Council.
Rosner, B. & Halcrow, A. 2010 *The Boss's Survival Guide* (2nd ed), New York: McGraw Hill.
Sartain, L. & Finney, M. I. 2003 *HR from the Heart*, New York: AMACOM.

Power

Power is a topic about which I feel some ambivalence. I don't see myself as powerful but I have held roles in which others would see me as powerful. As a woman, I don't look like the people that traditionally hold powerful roles in Western countries but I do have what Sinclair (2007, 89) calls the privilege of both whiteness and of working in my native tongue. I don't feel comfortable about holding power if DeSteno is right when he says (2014, 113): "increasing status and power go hand in hand with decreasing honesty and reliability". However, having chosen a leadership role, I have to exert power because having power means that you can make things happen, create possibilities for others and attract resources.

Power is the ability to direct or influence the behaviour of others or the course of events. Authority is socially sanctioned power that comes when you are, for example, the CEO or the Board Chair of a company. Influence is one of the means by which power is used. In addition to the legitimate power that you have in a senior role where you are legally allowed to make a decision and expect people to comply, you also have the coercive power to reward people and to punish them.

One can obtain power or the potential to influence people in a number of different ways in addition to simply being in charge. For example, power can be found through one's position in an organisation. Other people may depend on your work (criticality) or you may have information that people need (centrality). One of the most powerful people I experienced early on in my work life was the personal assistant to a senior government bureaucrat. She had power over information and access. I've seen the power of a designer when they can't make up their mind over the final finishes on a set and thus holds up the whole process and I've seen a junior staff member with great relationship skills getting more things done than a senior manager.

Other sources of power are personal qualities such as expertise, attraction, effort and legitimacy (Carlopio, Andrewartha & Armstrong 2005). My Finance Manager had power because of his deep understanding of the underlying structure of the budget spreadsheets. A producer had power because of her personal warmth and her capacity to attract friends. A marketing manager had power because not only was she knowledgeable about her area of expertise, but because she put in a higher than expected effort. People who exhibit behaviour consistent with organisational values can gain power simply by being good examples. Sometimes one can gain power by being close to power (Dubrin, Dalglish & Miller 2006). One way of understanding power is to think about how an orchestra conductor uses different types of power:

- Expert power – the conductor's mastery of the music and capacity to communicate their message will clearly have an impact on the motivation and performance of the orchestra members
- Referent power – the conductor as a positive role model with shared values about the music
- Reward power – where the conductor provides attention and recognition to the musician
- Coercive power – where the conductor blames or shames the musician in front of their peers
- Legitimate power – a conductor is recognised as the leader of the group

- Informational power – when the conductor explains the context or history of a piece of composition (Krause 2015).

In her research about the use of power by conductors, Krause (2015) concluded that expert power and referent power had the strongest positive impact on artistic quality even though all the other forms of power were used. The reason offered for this result is that the orchestra members see themselves as artists, following a calling and not just doing a job. Even though the conductor has, by definition, legitimate power, what the musicians are looking for is someone with professional competence (expert power) and social competence (referent power). This conclusion fits neatly into the conversations I've had over the years with orchestral musicians and the stories they tell of working with conductors they didn't value or trust and simply ignoring the person at the front and playing their own way.

In organisational life, individuals and groups are interdependent, they need things from each other and power relationships are multidirectional, not simply from the top down (Bolman & Deal 2013). The power at the top can sometimes be constrained until one is empowered by others. A particular example that comes to mind is a staff member who intimidated fellow workers, particularly women, but who had a team of supporters, particularly men, and who in my attempts to manage him out of the organisation was protected to some degree by employment law. The result was that I had very little power until the staff decided that he wasn't as powerful as he looked and that I had the power to remove him if they denied him his power. By finally making formal complaints, they returned power to me to solve the problem.

While I've seen arts leaders who technically had power but who seemed to have little capacity to influence others, I haven't seen much coercive power used in arts and cultural organisations. The only time I personally experienced the use of such power I simply left and this fits in with Covey's (1992) argument that leaders who try to control others through fear or coercion will find that their power is temporary as people learn to resist, work around them or depart. When Hewison and Holden (2011) propose that leadership should not be about power but rather be about the ability to influence others, they are really talking about coercive power. Power is inescapable in any organisation because it's basically about the capacity to make things happen, but if applied by inviting people on the journey with you rather than directing them which bus to catch, then you'll find yourself in a much more positive organisational culture. One can influence people in a range of different ways including rational persuasion, exchanging favours, building networks, inspiration, forming coalitions, having a reputation as an advisor or expert (Dubrin, Dalglish & Miller 2006), but one of the most powerful forms of influence is through example. In a wonderful film *Moolaade* made in Burkina Faso, a woman refuses to let her daughter undergo circumcision and saves a number of other girl children from the same fate. She lives in a tribal, patriarchal and Islamic community where the power of women is limited but she influences her community through example. To influence people, "you need to make a difference not only to what they do but also in the thoughts and feelings that drive their action" (Hall & Lineback 2011, 127). Another film which is a fascinating example of influence at work is *12 Angry Men*.

Often, we assume that rational discourse will be the most persuasive technique to influence people either providing facts or appealing to principles but it doesn't always lead to the desired outcome. Hill and Lineback (2011) provide two other influence strategies. The first is based on the principle of liking. People like those who like them and so uncovering real similarities and offering genuine praise may get people to do what you want. Another principle is that of reciprocity where people repay in kind so that if you offer help or exchange then people will feel obligated or may simply wish to give you something back. Of course, you can influence people through threats or intimidation but like the use of coercive power, unless you're running

a dictatorship, it's likely to backfire. Hill and Lineback (2011) recommend trust as the best influence strategy. If people believe and trust in your competence (that you know what to do and how to do it) and your character (that your motives are good and you want people to do well), then you will have the capacity to influence them.

Covey (1992, 122) takes a similar approach. He says that the best way of "powerfully and ethically influenc[ing] the lives of other people" is to model by example (others see), build caring relationships (others feel) and mentor (others hear). As well as influencing subordinates, one also needs to influence superiors, peers and clients. Based on her search on women leaders, Sinclair (2005) proposes a range of influence strategies including focusing on making a contribution, being a trusted ally, being persistent and building networks, and one that's somewhat out of the box: surprise, shock and challenge. After all, if you've got a really good idea and can present it in a persuasive way that uses both logic and emotion, you will be able to influence others.

Saintilan and Schreiber (2018, 149) propose a number of ways of checking whether you are using power ethnically. For example, if you do have to use coercive power, make sure that people know the rules, that you warn before punishing and that the punishment is administered consistently. If you're using reward power then make reasonable requests and offer credible and desirable rewards. Even when we're using legitimate power, we should be respectful, consistent and aware of the needs and concerns of our staff. The other side of the power coin is powerlessness and if that's how our employees feel, the organisational culture won't be a positive one.

Power does not have to be negative or coercive. If its application is based on positive influencing strategies and if it's used for a mission that is shared and valued by people inside and outside the organisation, the result will be an organisation where people work collaboratively to get things done.

See also: Decision-making, Leadership, Organisational Culture

References

Bolman, L. G. & Deal, T. E. 2013 *Reframing Organizations* (5th ed), San Francisco, CA: Jossey-Bass.

Carlopio, J., Andrewartha, G. & Armstrong, H. 2005 *Developing Management Skills*, Sydney: Pearson Education.

Covey, S. R. 1992 *Principle-Centred Leadership*, London: Pocket Books.

DeSteno, D. 2014 "Who Can You Trust?" *Harvard Business Review*, 92(3), 112–115.

Dubrin, A. J., Dalglish, C. & Miller, P. 2006, *Leadership* (2nd Asia-Pacific ed), Milton, QLD: John Wiley & Sons.

Hewison, R. & Holden, J. 2011 *The Cultural Leadership Handbook*, Farnham: F Gower.

Hill, L. A. & Lineback, K. 2011 "Are You a Good Boss or a Great One", *Harvard Business Review*, 89(1/2), 124–131.

Krause, D. E. 2015 "Four Types of Leadership and Orchestra Quality", *Nonprofit Management & Leadership*, 25(4), 421–447.

Saintilan, P. & Schreiber, D. 2018 *Managing Organizations in the Creative Economy: Organizational Behaviour for the Cultural Sector*, Abingdon: Routledge.

Sinclair, A. 2005 *Doing Leadership Differently*, Melbourne: Melbourne University Press.

Sinclair, A. 2007a *Leadership for the Disillusioned*, Sydney: Allen & Unwin.

Problem Solving

It's almost tautological to have a section on problem solving in a book on arts management because most of the time, that's what the job is all about. Adirondack (2005, 2) starts her wonderfully titled book *Just About Managing?* with a depressing list of problems that non-profit organisations can face:

- Lack of clarity or unwillingness to set goals and priorities
- Unwillingness to think realistically about resources
- Confusion about boundaries between Boards and employees
- Unconfident Boards
- Over-committed Boards
- Unconfident managers
- Over-committed managers
- Misfit between ideas and reality
- Badly planned, badly run and badly minuted meetings.

I'm sure that you can add to this list. Although this is not the place to "solve" each of those challenges, there are some good insights about problem solving from a variety of different perspectives that are worth sharing. For example, Bolman and Deal's (2013) book on organisations proposes looking at problems from different perspectives (frames) – structural, personal, political and symbolic – and that connects with my experience of trying to problem solve. And anyone who has a chapter entitled 'Organization as Theater' attracts my interest. They give a fascinating case study of a new principal in a dysfunctional school and walk the reader through the use of each different frame asking two simple questions:

1. From this perspective, what's going on?
2. What options does this angle suggest? (417)

Their advice is that managers fail when they take a narrow view and don't look at an organisation from multiple perspectives. This isn't always easy because we become comfortable in the "frame" that suits us best. Do we tend to look at things from an analytical perspective or an intuitive one? Are we political animals or reflective people? Bolman and Deal (2013, 434) admit that this layered thinking is challenging: "To see the same organization as machine, family, jungle, and theatre requires the capacity to think in different ways at the same time about the same thing." As problem solving is about insight into possible futures, different perspectives add richness to the list of possibilities.

In a recent example of problem solving, my approach was to help the person concerned go through a process of analysing all the possible options and what each meant for them, whereas for someone else working on the same problem, the strategy about how the problem was to be addressed was more important than the options. As it turns out, both approaches were necessary but it was a useful reminder that problems can be considered and solved in different ways from different viewpoints. As Beech et al. (2015,

14) note, how you frame a situation will impact on how you see and deal with it. Is it a problem or an opportunity? A disaster or an acceptable mistake?

Most advice on problem solving combines pragmatic strategies such as analysis and scenario generation with more creative processes such as reflection and sensing because most serious problems don't have solutions where the alternatives are easy to define let alone judge. To add some creative thinking into the mix means that you need to give yourself some relaxing time in a quiet space but, equally, you may need to talk to other people and get their views on your problem (Carlopio, Andrewartha & Armstrong 2005).

The common trap in problem solving is that the focus is on allocating blame rather than finding a solution – blaming the bureaucracy, blaming the Board, blaming the customer, blaming staff. It's all about someone else's personality or stupidity or incompetence or attitude. But sometimes it's about us and time and processes and not people at all. I had a staff member who caused considerable grief to the people around them and of course it was the individual that was at fault. But if one unpacked the story, it was probably my fault. Why? Because we had to bring a project forward, we needed to make some quick appointments. Which meant that although the person was far from perfect, they could do the job so we employed them rather than repeat the recruitment process and find a better fit for the organisation. If I had been more effective at anticipating the start date of the project, we wouldn't have had to rush, we wouldn't have employed the person, and the rest of the staff wouldn't have suffered. One of the original writers on organisations, Herbert Simon (1987) advises that solving a problem should take priority over looking backwards but when it comes time to look back, although determining blame may be part of the process, the primary focus should be on working out what can be learned to prevent similar problems in the future.

Equally important is to create a workplace where innovation is fostered and other people solve problems for you. Part of your role as a manager is to get people to shift from bringing you a problem to providing you with a solution. In *Six Ways to Get People to Solve Problems Without You*, Morieux (2011) focuses on large, complex organisations but there are some insights that would work in smaller and non-profit organisations as well. The rules are divided into two groups. The first set is about *enabling*, providing the information needed to understand where the problems are and empowering the right people to make good choices. The second set involves *impelling*, motivating people to apply all their abilities and to cooperate. The enabling rules are ones that feel particularly useful, including making sure that you actually understand what your staff do and empowering them to use their judgement and their intelligence so that problems are solved where they happen and not in your office. Another important part of the process is to give people feedback so that they know the outcome of their decisions.

Ultimately, the big problems will and should end up on your desk. I can still pinpoint those moments: when I was told the university was going to defund the radio station; when we had the first meeting about which programs on Radio National had to go because of funding cuts; when the Ministerial Advisor said MTC would never get a new theatre. All you can do is bring your rationality, your intuition and your creativity to bear on the problem, collect the wisdom and insight of others, develop and test alternatives and take a deep breath and make a decision. It's hard but it's a key part of the job. One of the most simple but difficult pieces of advice about problem solving comes from Adirondack (2005, 159). And it is: eat properly and get enough sleep. "The situation may be horrendous, but it will seem even worse (and you might actually make it worse) if you are exhausted and living on caffeine, doughnuts and alcohol."

Taylor (2013) says that the problems we face aren't independent of each other but part of dynamic and complex systems. He calls these situations "messes" with problems being abstractions extracted from messes by analysis.

He says that we don't solve problems but rather manage messes. Although arts managers do actually resolve problems every day, often in smart and original ways, it's still a mess which is changing all the time because of external forces and because of the consequences of your problem solving. Some may find the metaphor of *messes* depressing but I find it a relief as it's a reminder about the complexity of the job, the need to enlist others to help and an acknowledgement that the world doesn't end if I don't solve every problem perfectly. It also fits in with another approach to management called Appreciative Inquiry (Cooperrider, Whitney & Stavros 2005). From that perspective, an organisation is viewed not as "a problem to be solved" but rather as "a mystery to be embraced" (Faure 2011, 275). The cycle of problem solving consists of discovering the best of what is (appreciating), "dreaming" about what it could be (envisioning), designing how it could be (co-constructing) and determining your destiny or what it will be (sustaining). It's a useful framework when it comes to solving long-term challenges and developing meaningful strategic plans.

See also: Conflict Management, Creativity, Decision-Making, Strategic Planning

References

Adirondack, S. 2005 *Just About Managing?* (4th ed), London: London Voluntary Service Council.

Beech, N., Broad, S., Cunliffe, A., Duffy, C. & Gilmore, C. 2015 "Developments in Organisation Theory and Organising Music", in Beech, N. & Gilmore, C. (eds) *Organising Music: Theory, Practice, Performance*, Cambridge: Cambridge University Press, 1–24.

Bolman, L. G. & Deal, T. E. 2013 *Reframing Organizations* (5th ed), San Francisco, CA: Jossey-Bass.

Carlopio, J., Andrewartha, G. & Armstrong, H. 2005 *Developing Management Skills*, Sydney: Pearson Education.

Cooperrider, D. L., Whitney, D. & Stavros, J. M. 2005 *Appreciative Inquiry Handbook*, Brunswick, OH: Crown Custom Publishing.

Faure, F. 2011 "The Emergent Organisation", in O'Toole, S., Ferres, N. & Connell, J. (eds) *People Development: An Inside View*, Melbourne: Tilde University Press, 272–284.

Morieux, Y. 2011 "Smart Rules: Six Ways to Get People to Solve Problems Without You", *bcg perspectives*, Boston Consulting Group, www.bcgperspectives.com/content/articles/organization_design_engagement_culture_hbr_smart_rules_six_ways_get_people_solve_problems_without_you/ [accessed 10 March 2019].

Simon, H. A. 1987 "Making Management Decisions: The Role of Intuition and Emotion", *Academy of Management Executive*, February, 57–64.

Taylor, A. 2013 "Managing a Mess", *The Artful Manager*, www.artsjournal.com/artfulmanager/main/managing-a-mess.php [accessed 10 March 2019].

Notes

1 An Australianism for taking advantage of a system or a service to get the most personal benefit while still remaining within the letter of the law.
2 Friday 18 January 2013.
3 An appeal held just before 30 June which is the close of the financial year in Australia.
4 Development tends to be the summary word that covers philanthropy and fundraising.
5 After complaints about the problem university, they are now responsive and the other has started to fail in their communication and connection.
6 For example, Russian energy tycoon Leonid Mikhelson building a $130 million contemporary art gallery in Moscow: www.bloomberg.com/news/articles/2018-06-14/billionaire-builds-a-big-museum-for-russia-s-tiny-art-market [accessed 10 March 2019].
7 Mr Koch died on 23 August 2019.
8 Now called Arts Centre Melbourne.

Q

Quality

There had to be a section on quality simply because there had to be a Q in an A to Z of arts management. But it's really unnecessary because quality is embedded in every aspect of an arts organisation's activities.

Our artists want the chance to be at their most creative when they work with us so that they can produce art of quality that is valued by their peers and the audience.

Our Artistic Directors want a quality relationship with us that involves trust, effective communications, respect and a shared passion for the company's mission. They want to partner with someone who is thoughtful and cares about quality in all aspects of the organisation (Reid 2013, 106).

Our audiences expect us to provide a quality arts experience. It may a different one from last year. It may be more challenging than last year. But it has to be just as good if not better than last year. As Maifeld (2012, 219) says delivering consistency of quality requires care. He goes on to quote Hewison and Holden (2011): "Organizations demonstrate true care when they view their audience as a 'relationship, not a transaction'."

Our Boards are expected to provide quality governance so that our organisations remain financially resilient, enabling the ongoing creation and sharing of art into a distant future.

Our government funders expect us to produce quality art and to be able to prove that we have done so. For example, consultants to the government in Western Australia proposed the following measures of arts quality:

- Inquisitiveness – the extent to which the funded activity promotes curiosity in artist and audience
- Imagination – the extent to which the funded activity explores new possibilities and views
- Originality – the extent to which the funded activity breaks new ground (modes of practice and content)
- Risk – the extent to which the artist is fearless and negotiates new artistic approaches
- Rigour – the extent to which the funded activity has undergone thorough research and development
- Currency – the timeliness of the creative idea in relation to contemporary events
- Authenticity – the extent to which the funded activity respects cultural tradition or is uniquely Western Australian
- Innovation – the extent to which the funded activity demonstrates an ability to realise creative ideas into real world outcomes
- Excellence – the funded activity is widely regarded as best of its type in the world (Chappell & Knell 2012, 15).

Our staff want us to provide an environment where their quality of life is enhanced rather than damaged. This means adequate pay and benefits, a safe and healthy work environment, the opportunity to develop one's skills, and a reasonable work-life balance. The production of high-quality innovative work involves "real labour and often considerable sacrifice" according to Fitzgibbon (2001, 193) but there is no reason why an arts organisation can't meet these minimum requirements for their employees. They also want quality leadership where values are lived, decisions are made, respect is given and there is a believable vision for the future.

Our stakeholders want a quality relationship with us that includes honesty and transparency and a meeting of minds over objectives and outcomes.

We want to manage quality venues and to produce quality art and cultural experiences; to produce quality marketing materials and achieve a quality financial result.

And we need to be able to measure all these aspects of quality in a way that is rigorous but also that captures not just the numerically measurable parts of the equation but the intrinsic part of quality, whether it's in our art or our relationships.

See also: Economics, Evaluation

References

Chappell, M. & Knell, J. 2012 *Public Value Measurement Framework*, Perth: Government of Western Australia, Department of Culture and the Arts.

Fitzgibbon, M. 2001 *Managing Innovation in the Arts*, Westport, CT: Quorum Books.

Hewison, R. & Holden, J. 2011 *The Cultural Leadership Handbook*, Farnham: F Gower.

Maifeld, K. 2012 "Review of 'The Cultural Leadership Handbook: How to Run a Creative Organization' by Robert Hewison and John Holden", *The Journal of Arts Management, Law and Society*, 42(4), 217–219.

Reid, W. 2013 "Dual Executive Leadership in the Arts", in Caust, J. (ed.) *Arts Leadership: Internal Case Studies*, Melbourne: Tilde University Press, 98–111.

R

Resilience

Whether it's a real crisis or simply the ongoing complexities of a changing world, arts organisations need to be able to survive and managers and staff have to be able to deal with the stress of their job. The list of things that can cause stress goes on for pages. The list of things that management can do to prevent stress isn't quite so long because some things can't be solved. If the train you catch to work is late and dirty, you'll be stressed – but the manager can't solve that problem. If you have a challenging personal life, you'll be stressed – but the manager can't solve that problem (although they could offer family counselling). But if you are particularly sensitive to criticism and your performance review is coming up, your manager may be able to create an environment and a communication process that lessens that stress.

The quality that helps best in managing stress is resilience. According to the *Concise Oxford Dictionary*, resilience is about springing back, resuming original form, readily recovering from depression. In other words, resilience is the capacity to bounce back or recover from challenges. Wilson and Ferch (2005, 48) define resilience as the ability to let go of old ways of thinking and behaving and to create new structures of thought and behaviour. Resilience applies to both people and organisations.

In Walmsley's (2013) paper about the West Yorkshire Playhouse, he describes a process put in place by the Arts Council of England (AEC) to help arts organisations develop their "resilience" by promoting innovation, artistic excellence and robust business planning. He then summarises interviews with AEC staff who define resilience in terms of "artistic ambition; financial stability, effective leadership, management and governance; strategic focus; and situational awareness" (244). Other qualities mentioned include being well networked, entrepreneurial, adaptive and reflective, with "a culture of shared purpose and values rooted in organizational memory" (230). It's a list of good arts management practices. In other words, if your organisation is creating great art that audiences love, has effective leadership along with a committed, hard-working staff and you've got money in the bank, then you can probably weather most crises.

Just as an organisation is stronger if it's resilient, so are individual leaders. Jo Caust (2013), in her study of three artistic leaders of small arts organisations, ponders whether developing resilience and the capacity to fight back are signs of an effective leader. She describes all three individuals as demonstrating great strength of character and having weathered many obstacles in their careers. Moss, Callanan and Wilson (2012, 52) say that resilience enables flexibility and helps leaders to "readily and effortlessly" get over anxiety and distress. They also link resilience with positive emotions and say that, as a result, leaders can "more readily uncover novel and effective solutions to intractable problems" (53).

The reason that I've chosen to write about stress under the heading of *Resilience* is because not all stress is bad and resilience can be developed as a strategy to deal with stress. Bakke (2005, 77) uses the example of sports games where there is lots of positive stress and those of us in the arts know what it's like to be faced with similar high demands of mental and physical energy as the deadline for an exhibition or a show opening looms. He says stress can enhance an outcome-focused experience as long as the person has a certain amount of control over what happens. The people who are most likely to lack this control are people caught in the middle – managers who don't have enough power to make decisions with staff who expect them to do so.

Stress can occur even in a good job if one feels frustrated because there doesn't appear to be hope for more resources or desired change. Carlopio, Andrewartha and Armstrong (2005) describe three strategies to manage stress: eliminate it, use reactive strategies to make the situation more manageable and be proactive by building resilience. Ways to reduce or eliminate stress include effective time management and sorting out priorities along with creating a calm and pleasant work environment and giving people more control over their work (Carlopio, Andrewartha & Armstrong 2005; Adams 2007). Reactive strategies include techniques such as relaxation and deep breathing, rehearsals and reframing which can make situations more manageable.

The starting point in building resilience is to have some psychological balance in one's life so that you have activities related to family or friends, intellectual or physical, in addition to work. Resilience comes in a number of forms. For example, being healthy – a proper diet and exercise – helps resilience. One of the members of the MTC selection committee asked me what I did for relaxation. She was a doctor and so was looking for a response that gave some consideration to the physiological aspects of resilience. Adirondack (2005, 133) recommends long baths, music before bedtime and giving yourself

treats – all of which appeal to me more than serious exercise.

Finally, people will help you build resilience whether it's through supportive social relations, a good team or a mentor or coach (Carlopio, Andrewartha & Armstrong 2005). Wilson and Ferch (2005) list characteristics that contribute to resilience: having a supportive environment in which change can occur, the development of personal autonomy and self-esteem, one's emotional maturity, creative thinking and having a sense of hope for the future. They conclude that caring relationships in the workplace are important contributors to resilience.

The capacity to de-brief, to talk about something other than work, to laugh, to be loved, all help build resilience. I was watching the final episode of a season of a French police television series called (in English) *Spiral* recently. Not surprisingly, as all the story lines came together there was high drama and lots of conflict. But I remember noticing at the time that there were some subtle but powerful moments when team members reached out to support each other with a hug or a held hand. Our resilience is built when we know people care about us and are available to help us deal with the stress of our demanding work lives.

I'm often asked what I do when I get tired or frustrated or exhausted when a problem has blown up. I'd like to say that I do healthy things like yoga or meditation or jogging but my response tends to be much more prosaic: wine and chocolate. Well, that's not quite true. I love the water, so sometimes just swimming mindlessly up and down will help. I've been lucky working for a theatre company for so long because I can always disappear into a dark auditorium and immerse myself into someone else's life. I learnt (eventually) to take holidays. I wasn't very good to start with because of the old fear that the place won't survive without you. But through a series of health challenges faced by friends and family, I learnt that I could be away without the place falling apart. That I wasn't irreplaceable. And in fact, my replacement was often better than me. The break may be about going off to a training course or looking after a sick family member or giving yourself a long weekend doing your favourite thing. But any break will enable you to look at your workplace and its challenges in a new light.

See also: Change, Crisis, Holidays, Knowledge, Leadership, Learning, You

References

Adams, J. 2007 *Managing People in Organizations: Contemporary Theory and Practice*, Basingstoke: Palgrave Macmillan.

Adirondack, S. 2005 *Just About Managing?* (4th ed), London: London Voluntary Service Council.

Bakke, D. W. 2005 *Joy at Work*, Seattle, WA: PVG.

Carlopio, J., Andrewartha, G. & Armstrong, H. 2005 *Developing Management Skills*, Sydney: Pearson Education.

Caust, J. 2013 "Thriving or Surviving: Artists as Leaders of Smaller Arts Organizations", in Caust, J. (ed.) *Arts Leadership: Internal Case Studies*, Melbourne: Tilde University Press, 194–209.

Moss, S., Callanan, J. & Wilson, S. 2012 *The Moonlight Effect*, Melbourne: Tilde University Press.

Walmsley, B. 2013 "Rethinking the Regional Theatre: Organizational Change at West Yorkshire Playhouse", Bogota: AIMAC International Conference, 224–237.

Wilson, S. M. & Ferch, S. R. 2005 "Enhancing Resilience in the Workplace through the Practice of Caring Relationships", *Organizational Development Journal*, 23(4), 45–49.

Risk

Arts and cultural organisations face three types of risk – first, the creation of art; second, the business risks to support that creation; third, the uncontrollable risks of just operating in the world. Every other organisation has to face the second and third type but only our organisations embrace the first. As a reminder of what we mean by the word risk, an insightful American business leader described it this way:

> Risks involve ambiguity and uncertainty.
> Risks result in a kind of learning available in no other way.
> Risks may entail a loss of control and an acceptance of vulnerability.
> Risks accompany abandoning the old, but abandoning the old makes way for the new.
> Risk on the part of individuals are the only way to improve our world.
> Humility invites risk; pride discourages it.
> Risks are inevitable.
>
> (De Pree 1997, 146)

When you work with artists that's what they are doing every day and in a much more profound way than the risks a banker or an engineer might take. Which isn't to minimise their risk – of stockmarket and building crashes – but an artist is trying to create a totally new and unique experience that is going to explore our humanity. Tusa (2007b, 5) says: "Programming art is totally, innately, constantly, gloriously unpredictable." It's the capacity to take personal risk that separates the potential artist from the actual artist (Bilton & Leary 2010, 59).

So as an arts manager, I have to take risks that are going to minimise the artists' risks of failure. I have to risk agreeing to spend more money on the set if there's the chance that it's going to make for a better production – but not if it's simply going to change the angle of the floor and add to the chance of injury. I have to risk not recovering the cost of that actor from another part of the country if they are the best actor for the part – but not if they are only as good as a local. I have to risk commissioning some new writers even if the historic odds are that two out of three commissions don't work because the one that does may be the one that tells us all something new about our world.

There is a paradox built into the nature of non-profit arts organisations. On the one hand, they take risks with every show and every exhibition. However, restraints imposed by government and private funding may see management trying to play it safe. Shea and Hamilton (2015) have done some interesting research about the risk orientation of different non-profit stakeholders. They explored the idea that the less diversified a stakeholder's interests were, the more risk they might be willing to take. For example, donors and government-funding entities have diversified risks. As a donor giving to several non-profits, you're not reliant only on one company to get your reward for giving. On the other hand, if you're the non-profit manager you're reliant on the organisation's survival and so may be more inclined to take strategic actions that reduce risk and entrepreneurial activity.

A classic requirement from government which would reinforce that risk aversion is often a balanced budget which can make it a challenge to take artistic risks. However, risk taking is essential. Sometimes the artistic risk pays off and even if it doesn't one hopes that ultimately audiences and funders would prefer to support an organisation that is innovative and exciting than one that isn't (Maifeld 2012, 217). The way to solve the challenge of risk is to give attention to risk, to monitor it, measure it and not be afraid of it.

In an example of financial risk management, Fox (2013) tells the story of the Atlanta Symphony Orchestra's (ASO) attempt to increase its net income in the face of ever-increasing revenue pressures. The ASO clearly had visionary management and a Board with a taste for risk because they bought two for-profit organisations – a telemarketing company and a 12,000 seat amphitheatre. These were both "treated as separate, outside ventures, funded independently and fully staffed with new but experienced personnel". These were risky undertakings because not all for-profit businesses survive within volatile markets. Not every Board is going to want to take such risks. Fox says that the components for success are "a sufficient capital base, a committed and highly capable management team, a healthy appetite for benchmarked risk, and a knowledgeable and supportive Board willing to think and then step outside the box". The amphitheatre is now operated by Live Nation with rental payments supporting the core mission of the orchestra (Woodruff Arts Center 2016).

The first point that I take from this example is the phrase "*benchmarked* risk". If you are taking on a risky project, then analysing income possibilities and costs are essential. For example, when creating a financial operations model for the Southbank Theatre, I asked all the managers of similar buildings to provide me with their costs for everything, from electricity to toilet paper. And because of the cooperation that one finds in the arts, they did. On the income side, there was no single answer to how many tickets we might sell and at what cost, but for each income line, one could develop a sensitivity analysis based on history and intuition. The result was a series of income and expenditure summaries which, with an informed narrative, helped the MTC Board understand the depth of the risk and test their willingness to buy into it.

The second point is that if one is venturing outside one's core business, there is no point doing it unless one has a good chance of making a profit. For years MTC ran a costume hire department in competition with a number of for-profit companies. However, we were doing it at a time where we had no financial capacity to invest in the business and after moving the business out of a leased commercial space back to our HQ, our profile decreased along with our profit. After a couple of years of losses, we pulled the plug on the public shop part of the business. We continue to rent costumes but with no expectations beyond breakeven and on a different model, hiring to film and TV companies in order to subsidise hires to the small to medium-sized theatre industry.

The third point worth reflecting on from Fox's story is the idea that the businesses were run separately with their own skilled managers. This is a lesson worth taking when it comes to the non-core parts of operating a venue. There are plenty of examples in which an arts company ends up with a loss-making catering operation and/or poor quality bars and cafés. In my experience, the best bars are run by theatres but the best cafés and catering are run by commercial operators. Theatre bars are unique. Where else (except during the infamous Melbourne 6 O'Clock Swill[1]) do you find the need and the skill to serve hundreds of people a drink within 15 minutes but in a theatre? Yet café and catering skills aren't unique.

Every mission statement of arts organisations will probably have what Phills (2005) calls Big Hairy Audacious Goals and by definition each of them will inherently have risks built into them. The point is to analyse and understand the risk. What's the likelihood of something going wrong and what is the cost if it does? Not many symphony orchestras would be in a position to take on the risks that the ASO did but clearly they examined the risks and decided they were acceptable.

Leigh and Maynard (2003) note fear of failure, of losing control and of criticism usually lie behind the inability to take risks. As an arts manager there will be a time when you need to step out of your comfort zone and try new things in the same way an artist does. This may mean acting without knowing all the likely outcomes but if you have done your research and evaluated the risks then sometimes you just have to commit to action. Tusa (2014, 96) captures what's required well:

> Leaders must always know what the risks are. Being unaware of risk or indifferent to it – especially reputational risk – is unforgivable … But taking risks is not the same as being rash or foolhardy or reckless.

The Institute of Community Directors Australia offers a sensible list of how to deal with the risks that are implicit in running a business. They call it 10 Steps to a Safer Organisation:

1. Take risk seriously
2. Have a legal structure that limits liability for individuals (except if there's a breach of duty of care)
3. Put someone in charge of thinking about risk
4. Work out the likely hazards and their consequences
5. Evaluate and prioritise the risks
6. Fix what you can fix
7. Shift what you can shift (e.g. disclaimers about the nudity or gunshot noise in a play)
8. Insure what you can insure
9. Get ready for the worst (e.g. have an evacuation procedure)
10. Build all this into a policy and train people.

For example, MTC's operational risk processes included:

- Environment Health and Safety Committee
- Production meetings
- Fortnightly staff meetings
- Weekly management meetings
- Daily stage management reports
- Daily sales reports
- Weekly Marketing and Development meetings
- Monthly Financial Reports to the Board and the University.

We also created what some call a risk register which is the result of thinking of all the things that could go wrong in terms of governance, management, operations, finance and external factors.[2] Some of it will be what Tusa (2007b, 5) calls the "blindingly obvious" such as the risk of failing to sell enough tickets but the next stage is the important one: prioritising them into likelihood (from miniscule to high) and financial impact (negligible to extreme). As a manager, this helps you focus on managing the most challenging risks.

No – you can't predict a hail storm. No – you can't predict when your Finance Manager is going to leave. No – you can't predict what art is going to appeal. But you can have strategies and plans and approaches to problem solving in place to deal with each risk. For example, make sure you have comprehensive insurance that will cover the hail storm, an evacuation plan for your building and resilient staff who can deal with emergencies. As long as you've got robust financial systems, the world isn't going to end when the Finance Manager leaves. You can get an external contractor in as a locum and advertise for their replacement as quickly as possible.

If you don't sell enough tickets for the current exhibition or show, did you have contingency built into your budget? Do you have reserves? And it's a good time to review both your decision-making processes and your forthcoming production budgets.

Another strategy that's important for an organisation to have is a plan for business recovery – what you do if something did go seriously wrong. In an article about business recovery in arts organisations, there's a terrifying list of all the types of disasters that have the potential to affect us (Kirchner, Mottner & Ford 2013). I checked it to see how many I'd had to deal with over time and out of the 29 possibilities, I'd experienced half of them … and I could add some more to the list. So the starting point is – make sure you have insurance.

What did I have to cope with?

Storm/thunderstorm: a year after the Southbank Theatre was opened, Melbourne experienced a spectacular hailstorm and the building was damaged with water flowing in via box gutters that were jammed with hailstones. It was a Saturday afternoon and we had two shows that had to be cancelled. The theatre team were fantastic in handling the challenge and continued to be during the weeks of work replacing carpets and wooden floors, damaged wiring and walls. We had to close the building initially for a week to get the temporary work done and then for six weeks to finish the building repairs. This was a shocking experience as it came only 12 months after this beautiful building we'd fought so hard to get had opened. The hail also damaged the equally new HQ and I remember splashing around in the dark trying to move set pieces to safer ground. We survived the storm because of insurance, a dedicated theatre manager and resilient staff.

Flood: MTC's Ferrars St headquarters was regularly prone to flooding no matter how much patch-up work was done on the roof and the gutters, but the final indignity came when the water flowed in from below as well as from above and the poor Finance Manager's office was like a swimming pool in the rain. Temporary repair work was helpful in the short term but, eventually, we had to find a new building.

Fire: luckily none of the fires we experienced at MTC were anywhere else but in rubbish bins or light fittings or in the café kitchen, and with an amazingly effective Fire Brigade, no major damage was caused. Moving into two new buildings meant that we had lots of false callouts as systems were bedded down but the fire brigade people liked coming to us because they always received an apology in the form of fresh muffins hot from the oven (as long as that hadn't been the cause of the call out).

Heat wave: Australia regularly suffers heatwaves which can lead to power outages and the near impossibility of putting on shows. While Arts Centre Melbourne has a back-up generator, the Southbank Theatre and Melbourne Recital Centre (which share infrastructure) don't, but with enough planning, one can self-insure by hiring one as a heatwave gathers momentum. One could assume that in such appalling weather people won't venture out but theatre goers are dedicated and most will still make their best effort to see a show, so the least one can do is to make sure the show goes on.

Drought: Melbourne suffered an ongoing drought for four or five years in the 2000s where water restrictions meant that you couldn't water your lawn or your garden, wash your car or your driveway, or build a new swimming pool. On the surface, this shouldn't have had a major impact on a theatre company but in 2003 we decided to bring American Director Mary Zimmerman and her design team to Australia to remake her beautiful production *Metamorphoses* with a young Australian cast. One of the magical elements in her production is that the storytelling takes place in and around a swimming pool. Not only did we have the challenge of building one inside a theatre, we then had to go through the process of getting special permission to fill it with water. I suspect that the water control people were so surprised by our application, they couldn't come up with a precedent to say "no".

Pandemic: we all feared that the SARS epidemic in 2003 would have a major impact on people's desire to spend time in an enclosed space with lots of strangers. But surprisingly, we didn't see a major drop off in numbers. The government was considering closing all public spaces but, in the end, didn't. The major impact on the company was that I had to provide plastic disposal gloves for people who wanted sweets from my lolly jar but didn't want to risk too many germs.

Information systems outage: there was always one moment every year when we held our breath to see if the computer system would crash and that was immediately after the launch of the annual subscription season. One can test the website and ticketing system, be well prepared, have back-up systems and contingency plans, but you never quite know until the subscribers race to go online whether the system will survive that first surge. There were a couple of years where the system crashed for a short period but detailed planning and an experienced Ticketing/IT team saw us through the bumps. All I could do was hang around, be supportive, get people food and drinks if they were going to be stuck there all night and thank them when we came through the other side.

Industrial accidents: I was told by an experienced production manager that theatre is the most dangerous workplace after the construction industry. It feels that way – with traps in the floor and flying scenery, sets moving in all directions, actors working under bright lights, often doing challenging movements including working at height, with guns and rapiers, sand and water, raked stages and flying bodies. Australia has strong occupational health and safety standards but, equally important, MTC had a strong internal culture of care and concern linked to very detailed and practical polices about the safety of staff. So although the designer did cut himself, and the actor was nearly killed by a falling spanner, and the electrician was electrocuted and the actor did trip over her long frock and fall off the stage, all lived to tell the tale.

Economic crisis: over my 18 years at MTC we faced a number of downward turns in the economic cycle and as each deepened, one could see the impact on ticket sales. Subscription theatre companies have a two-year cycle from starting to think about the next season to the end of it and the cycle for opera and classical music is even longer, so the capacity to program in anticipation of a downturn is almost impossible. This is where insurance such as a reserve fund will help you through the bad times. Although the Global Financial Crisis hit MTC particularly hard because we were half way through our first capital campaign to fund the outstanding elements of the new theatre and HQ, we were lucky because people kept coming to the theatre.

Strike: although the actors union in Australia, the Media Entertainment and Arts Alliance (MEAA) did occasionally threaten to "hold the curtain" and had done so in the past, my period at MTC was reasonably quiet industrially. This was not the case when I worked at the ABC. The organisation faced major funding cuts from the Federal (Labor) Government in the early 1990s and as the majority of the Radio Division's budget was spent on people, it was people who lost their jobs. In the process of trying to control or reduce the redundancies, the ABC staff union went on strike and formed picket lines on a number of occasions. Having always seen myself as left-of-centre and having taught industrial relations with a strong pro-union bent, I was perturbed to find myself on the wrong side of the fence. My manager was extremely sympathetic and handled my dilemma well. He told me to stay away, think about what I wanted to do, and not to cross the picket line until I was ready. I had to accept the fact that I'd chosen to be a manager, and unless I wanted to give up that position, I had to act with the other managers. However, that was only one part of the equation. The other was the content of the dispute. Was management being wrong or unethical? And the answer was no. Without the money to pay everyone, some people, unfortunately, had to lose their jobs and the decisions about who those people were being made in a rational and considered way. If I hadn't been comfortable about both those aspects of the situation, I would have had to resign.

Debt: well, as you know if you've already read the section on *Money*, MTC had lots of it — and found ways to solve the problem. It's also important to be realistic about debt. We're arts organisations. We take risks. Sometimes, the outcome is a deficit. Hollywood studios lose money all the time and this is seen as part of the business. Just because we lose money one year, isn't necessarily a sign of mismanagement as long as we learn from that experience (Tusa 2000)

Public Relations Disaster: disaster is probably too strong a word for it but there were moments when one's inability to control the media was frustrating. Whether it was the phrase "the debt-ridden MTC" which was used for a number of years or the reviewer who took a personal dislike to an Artistic Director, as a major company one was always going to be a more interesting target than a small company. A good communications team is the best form of insurance in this situation.

Withdrawal of stakeholder support: the most spectacular version of this crisis, when the University of Western Australia decided to withdraw its funding from 6UVS-FM, is described in *Leadership*.

Legal action: during the period of the Balkans War in the 1990s, MTC put on a play *Miss Bosnia*, set in Sarajevo, written by an Australian writer. We thought it was important to explore this political crisis but some members of the Bosnian community saw the play, which was a satire, as inappropriate and worse, a form of racial vilification. We were taken to the Equal Opportunity Tribunal and a court case dragged out for years over whether this was the case. Eventually, the Tribunal found in our favour but it was a costly and stressful time for the company and the playwright.

The *Miss Bosnia* crisis was made even more stressful by another set of manmade disasters that aren't on Kirchner, Mottner and Ford's (2013) list: bomb and gun threats (see *Crisis*). Other elements missing from the list are poor building construction and rodents (see *Offices*).

We didn't imagine that a hail storm would so severely damage the theatre. We thought that putting on a play with political themes would generate conversation but not bomb threats. But while we weren't prepared for the detail, we were prepared in terms of communications, resilience, insurance and organisational capacity. And the upside about all these disasters is that it brings people together. Kirchner, Mottner and Ford (2013, 393–394) provide a sensible list of propositions that will help make arts organisations more capable of recovering from the risks that you can't control:

- Existence of documented policies and procedures
- Communication capabilities
- Risk assessment
- Appropriate insurance
- Frequency of information systems and date off-site back ups
- Appropriate investment in financial and human resources
- Strategic planning
- Organization-wide business continuity plan and regular testing of the plan
- Recoverability of critical functions and date
- Previous experience with disasters/outages.

In their survey of arts organisations about whether they had a disaster recovery and/or business continuity plan, some indicative answers received by Kirchner, Mottner and Ford (2013) were:

> Someday, when we have time, that would be a good thing to do.

> That hasn't been a focus for us — we're just trying to make next week's payroll.

> Not yet. That is something that we need to do, but the problem is finding the time to do it (400).

I can imagine that for a small organisation, the challenge of yet another set of policies and processes is exhausting just to think about and you can hear that in the quotes. However, a simple risk analysis plus insurance will provide the beginnings of a policy and for a large arts organisation there is no excuse not to analyse risk and have processes and policies to deal with it.

See also: Artists, Buildings, Crisis, Money, Problem Solving Resilience, Strategic Planning

References

Adirondack, S. 2005 *Just About Managing?* (4th ed), London: London Voluntary Service Council.

Bilton, C. & Leary, R. 2010 "What Can Managers Do for Creativity? Brokering Creativity in the Creative Industries", *International Journal of Cultural Policy*, 8(1), 49–64.

De Pree, M. 1997 *Leading Without Power*, Holland, MI: Shepherd Foundation.

Fox, D. F. 2013 "New Ventures to Support your mission: Financial Diversification in Arts & Cultural Institutions", December, *Arts Insights* www.artsconsulting.com/pdf_arts_insights/insights_dec_2013.pdf [accessed 23 February 2015].

Institute of Community Directors Australia, *Risk Management: Ten Steps to a Safer Organisation*, Our Community Melbourne, www.communitydirectors.com.au/icda/tools/?articleId=1363 [accessed 10 March 2019].

Kirchner, T. A., Mottner, S. & Ford, J. B. 2013 "Business Continuity/Disaster Recovery Readiness of Nonprofit Arts Organizations?", Bogota: 12th AIMAC International Conference, 394–403.

Leigh, A. & Maynard, M. 2003 *Perfect Leader*, London: Random House.

Maifeld, K. 2012 "Review of 'The Cultural Leadership Handbook: How to Run a Creative Organization' by Robert Hewison and John Holden", *The Journal of Arts Management, Law, and Society*, 42(4), 217–219.

Phills, J. A. 2005 *Integrating Mission and Strategy for Nonprofit Organizations*, New York: Oxford University Press.

Shea, M. & Hamilton, R. D. 2015 "Who Determines How Nonprofits Confront Uncertainty?", *Nonprofit Management & Leadership*, 25(4), 383–401.

Tusa, J. 2000 *Art Matters*, London: Methuen.

Tusa, J. 2007b "The New ABC of the Arts", *Arts Education Policy Review*, 108(4), 3–6.

Tusa, J. 2014 *Pain in the Arts*, London: I.B. Tauris.

Woodruff Arts Center 2016 "Woodruff Arts Center and Live Nation Reach New Operating Agreement at Verizon Wireless Amphitheatre", www.woodruffcenter.org/news/new-operating-agreement-at-verizon-wireless-amphitheatre/ [accessed 1 September 2019].

Notes

1 www.emelbourne.net.au/biogs/EM01379b.htm
2 For a great but depressing list, see S. Adirondack 2005 *Just About Managing?*, 4th Edition, London: London Voluntary Service Council, 151.

S

Sponsorship

Sponsorship is a contractual relationship between two organisations where one receives cash or in-kind support in exchange for a range of benefits such as profile building or marketing. In the cultural industry, the relationship is usually between a for-profit or non-profit company presenting an exhibition or a festival or show and a for-profit corporation although it can also be with a government department or statutory authority.

What a corporation is usually concerned to determine before it signs up to become a sponsor is the prestige of the institution, the number of people expected to view the event or work and their demographics, the marketing plan for the event, the amount of product identification or endorsement allowed and the benefit to employees and clients (Simpson Solicitors).

In the mid-1980s, I wrote a student essay on Sponsorship and in it I was deeply cynical about the relationship between arts organisations and corporations. Although I've had many good financial relationships with private sector companies, I retain that cynicism. It wasn't that sponsorship was a new idea to me. I'd found in-kind support from local companies for arts activities in the 1970s and been a volunteer at a community radio station that relied heavily on sponsorship in the early 1980s. But deep down I distrusted the underlying logic of the relationship and that was in the days when at least some sponsorship was based on philanthropy. Fischer (2000 185–186) summarises the history of corporate giving in the USA, moving from social responsibility in the 1960s and 1970s (what is a corporation's responsibility to society?) to enlightened self-interest in the 1980s (how can serving society benefit the corporation?) to strategic philanthropy and corporate social investing in the 1990s. In the 2000s and 2010s, the focus turned to marketing and corporate profiles. There is debate about whether this shift is a loss in philanthropic intent (Fischer 2000) and I would say "yes" but at the same time acknowledge that corporate giving has probably always been self-interested. There's a curious tension currently about whether or not to develop sponsorship relationships. There would be very few arts organisations in countries like Australia, the UK, Europe, Canada and the USA that don't have corporate partners and of the few that didn't, most (although not all) would be desperate to find some in a world of ever-decreasing real government support for the arts. However, there are also companies that are actively choosing not to have sponsors with some suggestion that sponsorship is on the wane for arts bodies in the UK at least (Anonymous 2015).

The benefit to the arts organisation of sponsorship is obvious – an additional income source. But as I've said before, money is never "free". Some companies don't believe that price of this new income is worth the cost. For example, Janam Theatre Company in India does political theatre and avoids accepting grants or sponsorships from governments as well as corporates (Deshpande 2015). Other arts organisations are becoming much more rigorous in their analysis of whom they'll take money from. And others (particularly S2M companies) often don't have enough appeal to attract a sponsor.

The benefits of sponsorship to the corporation on the surface seem obvious – new forms of access to markets and an improved corporate profile. But there are always problems lurking below the surface and they lie imbedded in the motivation of corporations. Kirchberg (2003, 3–4) describes these motivations under four headings:

1. Neoclassical – raising profits, promoting sales, symbolising and extending the market position of company
2. Ethical – corporate social responsibility; promulgates image of "good corporate citizen"; moral obligation; personal satisfaction gained from helping; wish to have connection to a vital, creative world outside business
3. Political – the means to create and preserve corporate power and autonomy
4. Stakeholder – means for companies to profit from the positive influence their corporate behaviour (support of an arts organisation) has on the outside world.

Lewandowska (2015) would add increasing creativity and learning in the sponsoring organisation to this list, Proteau (2018) would add increased staff loyalty when they feel pride in the company's support of cultural organisations and Eltham (2018) would add influence on governments. One anonymous commentator to Eltham's (2018) piece about corporate leaders on arts Boards claimed that corporate support is "crassly transactional":

> I recall one lauded "philanthropist" who openly stated that he had absolutely no interest in the performing arts, but found that funding them paid dividends because it would win favour with the Minister (who usually holds some other useful portfolio!).

Severino (2014) provides a list of sponsorship tools used by companies including arts events that facilitate contact with customers, branding and PR, product testing and sales promotion, staff volunteering and the services or product of an artist. However, it's hard to imagine justifying arts sponsorship compared to sponsoring sport, for example, in terms of audience size or other returns on investment. The arts are seen as "as less lucrative, deemed exclusivist and inaccessible by some firms, and thought to preclude mass participation" (Severino 2014, 115). Because of this corporate sponsorship of our companies tends to be slightly more "philanthropic" along with other rationales such as passion and engagement. For example, Credit Suisse supported the education program of the Sydney Symphony Orchestra and their CEO explained that the program resonated with him because of his own childhood experience (Carroll 2018).

However, companies are still going to want to be able to demonstrate some real return on their sponsorship and marketing is usually the key. Volz (2017, 156) offers examples of US companies offering deals to arts companies, for example,

> Delta Airlines offers free seats in exchange for mailing list access; Coca-Cola trades contributions for pouring rights and logo displays; Toyota donates cars for raffles in exchange for prime car display access outside a theatre's front doors; and Del Taco, Pepsi, and Evian water spend sponsorship money for food-service access outside concert halls.

Another rationale is brand alignment where there's a connection between the company's staff and their clients. I remember giving a pre-opening speech to a group of car dealers, their partners and clients. Apart from having a night out, they weren't clear why they were there but I managed to link the values and creativity of my organisation with their's in a way that clearly resonated. I suspect the company had made a strategic decision about the sponsorship but hadn't really thought through how to explain it to their stakeholders. Luckily, I managed to do it for them.

A good example of staff involvement is sponsoring LGBTI activities such as Pride

Festivals that provide an opportunity for a company to demonstrate its commitment to diversity. For other corporates it might be about improving their brand by being connected to edgy creative organisations. "The message here is 'We may be serious accountants, but look how cool and sophisticated we can be'" (Carroll 2018). Carroll (2018) concludes: "they'll still want measureables and deliverables and audience synergy with simpatico brand values, but they'll also want some of your charisma and cultural capital".

There are lots of books that can tell you how to sign up a sponsor and case studies about "good" sponsorship relations. My favourite recent story is a partnership between a dance company and furniture making company in Lemington Spa in England. The arts company was used by government as part of the pitch to encourage the furniture company to relocate there and the result was a relationship which lead the creation of a rehearsal studio in the furniture factory. High ceilings and light, ventilation are all the things that you'd hope for in a dance studio but what makes it even more special is that it's an open space. So when the company is rehearsing to music, so are the workers. Usually one expects arts companies to be bold but this is an example of a corporate partner demonstrating just as much courage (Richards 2018).

I've had lots of positive relationships with sponsors (from chocolate tasting as performances of *Pride and Prejudice* to serious cash investments) but I'm more interested in discussing the ethical issues that arts managers face in such relationships.

Radbourne and Fraser (1996, 83) say that an alliance between arts organisations and business makes sense because cultural excellence suggests corporate excellence. But does it? There is no guarantee of cultural excellence because there's a risk involved with every new event. What happens if a play gets a bad review? How does the corporate sponsor feel about the brand linkage then?

What if the art you're producing is challenging in terms of topic or nudity or language or politics? This means that sponsorship is easier for traditional art forms such as classical music or historic art because there's less reputational risk for the sponsor. In one case, MTC provided corporate entertaining for the sponsor of another arts company because having created the relationship, none of the work of the original company was deemed "safe" enough for the corporation to take its clients or staff to. New York's Public Theater lost financial support from Delta Air Lines and Bank of America in response to their production of *Julius Caesar*, which depicted the assassination of a Trump-like Roman ruler (Stack 2017). MTC had sponsors who would only support comedies and in one case, only if the comedy contained no swear words. The tension all the time is whether you modify your programming to try and attract another sponsor. In an Australian example, the WA Opera Company received funding from a health promotions organisation with anti-smoking strategies and as a result said that they wouldn't produce *Carmen* during the length of the sponsorship because some of the opera is set in a tobacco factory. Interestingly, the Australian Prime Minister called the decision "political correctness gone crazy" (Ducey 2014), but one can appreciate the logic of the opera company. From their position, it wasn't about censorship but just postponing a production in order to get cash to do other shows. But it does feel like the beginning of a slippery slope.

The answer to the programming challenge is either to accept that there will be some companies you can't build a relationship with or shows or events that will never attract a sponsor. When MTC programmed Edward Albee's *The Goat*, my Sponsorship Manager was very proud when he announced that he'd "sold" it to a company. "But," I asked, "do they know what it's about?" "Well they've read the subscription brochure," he replied. "Come back to me when they have read the entire script and if they still want to sponsor us, I'll buy you champagne" was my reply. The play is about a man who falls in love with a goat and it was the type of show I knew would generate walk-outs every night. They read the script, declined to sponsor the play but were grateful for the warning and signed up for another show. If the relationship is going to work it has to be absolutely transparent.

Thinking back to Radbourne and Fraser's (1996) comment, how do you know whether the corporation you're partnering with is excellent or ethical? Most arts companies do think about the values of the companies they partner with but such decisions tend to be based on what a company does rather than how it does it. For example, companies may decide to avoid companies that mine, process or distribute fossil fuels or manufacture weapons. Most will accept sponsorship from a bank or a retail chain or an airline but what if a problem occurs such as exploited workers or a plane crash? Many Australian companies would have readdressed their relationship with banks or wealth management companies after the 2018 Financial Services Royal Commission which exposed a range of unethical behaviours in the banking industry. What if your sponsor has business policies or practices that may not be unethical per se but which don't appeal to your stakeholders? In 2014, a group of artists objected to a particular company that sponsored the Sydney Biennale. In summary, the Biennale had been originally created by the Belgiorno-Nettis family with a family member chairing the Board and sponsorship coming from a family-owned company Transfield Holdings. Transfield Services, of which Transfield Holdings was a shareholder, bid for and won a government contract to provide services to the offshore processing of refugees, an extremely divisive topic in Australia. Cultural commentator Ben Eltham describes the time line this way:

> As the campaign snowballed, the Biennale tried unsuccessfully to hose down the scandal, first with dead-bat statements in support of artistic freedom, then by organizing a forum on the issues, and finally with warnings that the Biennale would cease to exist if its major sponsor exited. [The Chairman] … alternately pleaded and then remonstrated with the boycotting artists, before angrily pulling the plug.

The response ranged from the Federal Arts Minister who demanded to know why the Biennale (or any arts organisations) should continue to receive government funding if they refused corporate support (Artshub News 2014) through to commentators who said that there is no such thing as "clean" corporate money (Eltham 2014). Eltham (2014) goes on to say that sponsoring the arts is a symbolic gesture for many corporations that enables them to "burnish their public image and present themselves as 'good corporate citizens'".

However, if marketing rather than philanthropy is at the heart of a sponsorship relationship, then one can ask why would a corporation bother, particularly with small to medium-sized arts companies or even large-scale companies that still can't deliver a football stadium's worth of audience? This is why commercial musicals, coming into town with a risk-free proven product, likely to play for months to hundreds of thousands of people are much more likely to attract sponsorship than a contemporary dance company playing in a 500-seat venue for three weeks. A sponsor logo on the front of an opera program just doesn't have the same impact as a logo on a TV advertisement or a banner at the Australian Tennis Open. But if sponsorship is also about money in exchange for reputation then we may have more to offer than violent or drug-ridden sports codes. What we do have is a highly educated and often opinionated and influential audience who may not be accessible any other way and we do have access to senior political figures. In one case that I'm aware of, a company sponsored an event with only one proviso: a guarantee that they would have private time on the opening with the State Premier.

If the requirement from sponsors is profile building, who are the companies we're ready to do what some might call "corporate image laundering" for (Eltham 2014)? Arts Manager Philip-Harbutt (2009) offers an interesting analysis of applying ethical principles to a sponsorship question in an arts organisation. First, she differentiates between ethics and morals.

Ethics she says, start with the idea of do no harm whereas morals is more about doing good. Ethics, therefore, is in our head, what we think, and morals is in bodies, what we do. Her scenario is this: "We need a new [income] source to maintain our current program. A new avenue for sponsorship opened up through the local mining boom. A multi-national corporation is offering community grants." She asks:

> What good could it do? It could give us a new income stream for a number of projects that currently can't occur and a new and very different partner in our cross sector work. What harm could it do? The multi-national corporation's track record is not squeaky clean in relation to work in third world countries and there have been complaints about their environmental practices. This could mean our good reputation could be tarnished by association. A number of our members are activists and it could compromise us in their eyes.
>
> (Philip-Harbutt 2009, 508)

By doing an analysis of the potential sponsorship relationship which is more than about logo placement or cash return and which takes into consideration other stakeholder concerns, one can potentially make a better quality decision. Wesley Enoch (2014), an Indigenous writer/Director, tells a constructive story about dealing with such conundrums when he was Artistic Director of Queensland Theatre Company. His general conclusion is, like Eltham's, that there is no such thing as "clean" money and the question that needs to be asked is what can one feel comfortable justifying to one's stakeholders – staff, audience, other donors. He made the decision to accept money from a company that mines sand on his community homeland, Stradbroke Island. After discussion with his community elders and his own family experience of employment and advancement with the company, he decided that the creation of the work (*Black Diggers*) was important enough to take the money.

[The elders] advice was to accept the money and use it to promote the stories, people and spiritual and cultural values that the project was attempting to celebrate (49).

When it comes to sponsorship such as that of Transfield Holdings where stakeholders are divided, Enoch (2014) sees the options as:

1. Boycott or deny participation as artist or sponsor/donor
2. Accept support from the sponsor; but at the same time create a critical environment within the work or in a discussion about the work that promoted alternative views to those of the donor
3. Adopt a "it has nothing to do with me I just make Art" position.

He doesn't support Option 3 but he worries about Option 1 because it has a component of censorship built into it. He believes that an artist should be allowed to reject a sponsor but thinks that it's an extreme position and more likely to silence debate than promote it. Usually the artist doesn't get a say until too late because the relationship may have been contracted long before the singer is cast or the exhibitors are chosen. So it is a rare case when an artist is consulted about a sponsor. For example, a particular corporation wanted to sponsor new work (brave of them) and the new work contained a negative reference to one of their products. The artist was asked whether they had particularly named that product to make a point, in which case the potential sponsor would been politely told "no". But the choice had been completely arbitrary, the artist was interested in engaging in a dialogue with the company, the brand name was changed to an invented one and everyone ended up feeling good about the relationship.

For the most part, sponsorship relations once negotiated are trouble free as long as both sides meet their obligations. But deep down, most of the arts managers I know would rather that they didn't have to participate in what

Michael Williams of the Wheeler Centre for Books Writing and Ideas called on ABC Radio National (19 December 2015) "culture washing" when he said the arts should be "dirty and gritty".

See also: Fundraising, Money, Philanthropy, Stakeholders

References

Anonymous 2015 "The Sponsorship Files: Who Funds Our Biggest Arts Institutions", *The Guardian*, www.theguardian.com/culture/2015/mar/02/arts-corporate-sponsorship-tate-british-museum [accessed 16 March 2019].

ArtsHub News 2014 "If the Sydney Biennale Doesn't Need Transfield's Money, Why Should They Be Asking for Ours?" *ArtsHub*, 13 March, www.artshub.com.au/news-article/news/trends-and-analysis/-if-the-sydney-biennale-doesnt-need-transfields-money-why-should-they-be-asking-for-ours--198432 [accessed 16 March 2019].

Carroll, D. 2018 "What Sponsors Want from the Arts", *ArtsHub*, 14 May, www.artshub.com.au/news-article/features/grants-and-funding/diana-carroll/what-sponsors-want-from-the-arts-255672 [accessed 16 March 2019].

Deshpande, S. 2015 "The Studio Safdar Story", in Caust, J. (ed.) *Arts and Cultural Leadership in Asia*, London: Routledge, 91–101.

Ducey, L. 2014 "PM Calls Opera Decision Crazy", *The Age*, 9 October, www.theage.com.au/it-pro/tony-abbott-calls-wa-operas-carmen-ban-crazy-20141009-113mc8.html [accessed 23 February 2015].

Eltham, B. 2014 "Biennale Boycott Backlash: Vicious Ingratitude or Valid Critique?", *ArtsHub*, 12 March, www.artshub.com.au/news-article/opinions-and-analysis/trends-and-analysis/biennale-boycott-backlash-vicious-ingratitude-or-valid-critique-198405 [accessed 16 March 2019].

Eltham, B. 2018 "Why the Australian Arts Sector Could Be in for a Major Reckoning", *Crikey*, 26 April, www.crikey.com.au/2018/04/26/australian-arts-major-reckoning-governance/ [accessed 28 December 2018].

Enoch, W. 2014 *Take Me to Your Leader: The Dilemma of Cultural Leadership*, Platform Paper No. 40.

Fischer, M. 2000 *Ethical Decision Making in Fund Raising*, New York: John Wiley & Sons.

Kirchberg, V. 2003 "Corporate Arts Sponsorship", in Towse, R. (ed.) *A Handbook of Cultural Economics*, Cheltenham: Edward Elgar Publishing.

Lewandowska, K. 2015 "From Sponsorship to Partnership in Arts and Business Relations", *The Journal of Arts Management, Law and Society*, 45, 33–50.

Philip-Harbutt, L. 2009 "Am I An Ethical Arts Worker?" *Asia Pacific Journal of Arts and Cultural Management*, 6(2), 504–511.

Proteau, J. 2018 "Reducing Risky Relationships: Criteria for Forming Positive Museum-corporate Sponsorships", *Museum Management and Curatorship*, 33(3), 235–242.

Radbourne, J. & Fraser, M. 1996 *Arts Management*, Sydney: Allen and Unwin.

Richards, L. 2018 "Part of the Furniture", *Arts Professional*, 8 November, www.artsprofessional.co.uk/magazine/319/case-study/part-furniture?utm_source=Weekly-Good-Reads&utm_medium=email&utm_content=nid-209836&utm_campaign=8th-November-2018 [accessed 9 November 2018].

Severino, F. 2014 "Cultural Sponsorship and Entrepreneurial Mistrust", in Aiello, L. (ed.) *Handbook of Research on Management of Cultural Products*, Hershey, PA: IGI Global, 113–125.

Simpson Solicitors (2019) "Sponsorship", http://simpsons.com.au/wp-content/uploads/chapter-21-sponsorship.pdf [accessed 16 March 2019].

Stack, L. 2017 "Et Tu, Delta? Shakespeare in the Park Sponsors Withdraw from Trump-Like 'Julius Caesar'", 11 June, www.nytimes.com/2017/06/11/arts/delta-airline-trump-public-theater-julius-caesar.html [accessed 16 March 2019].

Volz, J. 2017 *Introduction to Arts Management*, London: Bloomsbury Methuen Drama.

Stakeholders

Every book on non-profit organisations talks about the number of stakeholders that managers have to deal with and the challenge of balancing their interests. The reason there are so many of them is that a stakeholder is defined as "any group or individual who can effect or is affected by the achievements of the organisation's objectives" (Freeman 1984, 46). Tshirhart (1996), who has done the most detailed work on arts stakeholders to date, provides a stakeholder map for non-profit arts companies which includes internal stakeholders (Board, employees, volunteers), resource providers (funders, media, suppliers), political environment (legislators, lobbyists), community (interest groups), arts industry (associations, competitors, collaborators) and customers (patrons, advertisers). And if that wasn't enough, she defines each group more finely:

- Patrons: audience, clubs, study groups, commissioners of works, contractors of performance
- Funders: members, individual donors, corporate donors, foundations, government
- Associations: professional and technical associations, unions, industry alliances
- Interest groups: chambers of commerce, developers, tourism bureaus, businesses, public
- Suppliers: publishing houses, playwrights, performance spaces, exhibit sites (65).

When we analysed MTC's stakeholders, we also added artists as suppliers and consumers.

Of course, not all stakeholders are equal even though one does have to address the needs and expectations of all them in some form or other. Donaldson and Preston's (1995) theory seems intuitively sensible in that stakeholders vary in:

1. Their power to influence
2. The legitimacy of the relationship
3. The urgency of their claim.

We want a legitimate relationship with our stakeholders particularly if we're getting income and resources from them but also because having a good relationship with them might reduce demands for accountability, allow increased room for artistic movement, build loyalty and, as Tshirhart (1996) notes, advance our own personal interests such as career development and social acceptance.

An example of applying Donaldson and Preston's (1995) theory can be found in an article by Boerner and Jobst (2011) which examines how a German theatre company balanced the competing needs of their stakeholders. Stakeholders for such a company include:

- Funding agencies (local government, sponsors)
- The audience
- The public (media, critics)
- Suppliers (authors, workshops)
- Competitors (other regional cultural organizations, television
- Theatre itself (theatre management, artistic employees).

The stakeholders were prioritised in order with local government (the main funder) first followed by theatre management, audience and artistic employees. Boerner and Jobst (2011) then mapped the various interests of these stakeholders which included artistic excellence, education functions, entertainment, economic efficiency and other concerns. Obviously, there are potential conflicts between these interests such as entertainment (the cost of using TV stars) versus economic efficiency, or artist excellence versus entertainment. The exercise for arts managers is to make good trade-offs between the interests of stakeholders in a way that will "maximize the interests of all relevant stakeholders and simultaneously minimize the loss of support" (77).

Using the development of an annual theatre program, Boerner and Jobst (2011) explored a variety of strategies the theatre company management used to manage stakeholder interests. First, they set priorities. For example, in Germany, government grants are a much higher proportion of income than box office and so local government interests are more important than the audience. Second, management looked to find a way of combining interests. In an annual theatre program, that's possible because one can do shows that are entertaining as well as shows that are serious, new work and classic work. A third approach was to look at goals that would positively impact on some stakeholders without negatively impacting on others. For example, by adjusting when various elements of the season program occurred, management could fulfil the audience's leisure-time preferences (comedy in summer, tragedy in winter for example) without hurting any other stakeholder. The final approach was a long-term one. In order to balance the conflict between the company's own desire to pursue artistic excellence and the audience's preference for entertainment, they also invested in audience development. This example provides a useful model for considering the importance of stakeholders and responding to their needs.

Tshirhart (1996, 7) describes four possible problems between organisations and stakeholders:

1. Interest clash – where the activities or outcomes of an organisation and stakeholder are incompatible and interdependent. An example was when MTC and the Arts Centre Melbourne, which managed the venues we wanted to hire but which also had its own programming stream, both wanted the same "best" dates for performances
2. Organisational legitimacy problem – when an organisation violates a stakeholder's values or norms. A classic example is where audience members are offended by the content of the art we make, regardless of the warnings we post
3. Stakeholder legitimacy problem – where a stakeholder's purposes, activities or outcomes are not congruent with organisational values or norms. An example would be a current wine or beer company wanting to sponsor a performance or festival designed for teenagers
4. Latent conflict – lack of congruence of values; the problem is latent until one party violates the other's values or norms through its actions and then it becomes a problem of legitimacy. This can occur on Boards if members represent or think they represent another set of stakeholders and a clash of interests arises.

Two general approaches to addressing problems with stakeholders according to Tshirhart (1996) are to try and improve the congruence between the two parties or attempt to reduce the negative consequences of the problem. Another approach might be to ignore the problem such as complaints from subscribers or audience members about content. Losing some subscribers may be the price of innovation which in turn may attract new replacement subscribers.

The strategies that Tshirhart (1996) proposes to manage stakeholder relationships include adapting the organisation's activities or outcomes; attempting to change the stakeholder's understanding, values or norms; compromising; misrepresenting the organisation's activities or outcomes or cutting or weakening ties to the stakeholder.

For example, organisations will adapt if management believes that stakeholders are important and have authority. A classic example would be the impact of funding bodies. In the 2010s, the Australia Council was concerned with the lack of women directors and playwrights in theatre companies. Although they didn't provide a directive to companies to change their policies on the employment of women, they provided research and information papers and encouraged companies to do so. And for the most part, companies responded positively.

A stakeholder's understanding or values could be changed by putting a positive spin on what the organisation does or providing more information, but it could also be changed, as the German theatre company did, by putting effort into audience development.

Compromise can be harder work because it's about changing both organisations but it can be worth the effort. An example is that MTC worked with Arts Centre Melbourne in the late 1980s to improve what can often be a conflictual relationship between producer and venue through modification of rental agreements and developing more flexibility on hiring dates.

Misrepresenting or concealing information isn't a strategy that I'd recommend although it might be useful if, for example, providing accurate information would be harmful to the organisation. I confess to doing it – but only in a response to the stakeholder doing it first. When the Vice Chancellor of the University of Western

Australia decided to withdraw funding from the community radio station I managed, he told the Board Chair but gave specific instructions that I wasn't to be told. An instruction which, thank goodness, the Chair ignored. Given the Vice Chancellor's position, I certainly did not tell him that I was working to have his decision reversed although it became perfectly obvious very quickly as a media and community campaign to save the station got into gear. Another more benign example of concealing information might be keeping donor lists secret so other arts organisations can't approach your donors.

Sometimes, one doesn't want to keep dealing with a stakeholder, either because they actively threaten the mission of the organisation or because they are no longer as important as they used to be. And sometimes, outside influences can cause the relationship to be broken. The story of the Sydney Biennale and their sponsor Transfield Holdings (see *Sponsorship*) is an example of how a perceived value clash led to a cutting of ties.

How arts organisations deal with stakeholders depends on the importance of each of them in terms of income that they can provide, their decision-making authority, their access to information about the company and their relationship with the staff (Tshirhart 1996). Stakeholders that control major parts of a company's resources such as governments in places like Australia and Europe or major donors in the USA will be treated differently to minor income contributors. Losing one audience member is not the same as losing a sponsor. Obviously, Boards and managers have a profound capacity to influence an organisation because of their decision-making roles, but sometimes funding bodies do too. Traditionally, decisions about what is artistic quality has resided with intellectual experts or critics but as government funding retracts and funding bodies have to decide where to make cuts, these stakeholders are impacting on artistic output as they decide what art is good enough to keep funding.

For arts organisations in countries where government funding is key to survival, managing government stakeholders is particularly

important. It's not just the relationship with the Arts or Cultural minister that has to be managed. There is a collection of stakeholders – other ministers, politicians from different parties, ministerial advisors, bureaucrats. The CEO of a lobbying organisation pointed out that politicians are by definition natural connectors of social and economics networks. Therefore, they are potentially an arts organisation's natural ally but you have to understand them. This stakeholder management expert wasn't quite so positive about some other parts of government and provided my students with the following quotes from stakeholders who had the potential to impact companies funding:[1]

> The Arts needs to stop being so rarified and precious. They need to link with the rest of the community, put in more and make the dollars go further – Bureaucrat

> They are kidding themselves if they think the Arts are really on the radar screen. We do what we have to, but it's hardly top of mind – Bureaucrat

> The ones who do well have friends in high places – Ministerial advisor

> Arts organisations can be their own worst enemies. If they can't make a quid that's the market at work, isn't it? – ex Junior Minister

The perception of arts managers and leaders as lobbyists has even made it into popular literature. In Shane Maloney's amusing murder mystery, *The Brush Off* featuring arts politicians, funders and organisations, a new advisor to the Arts Minister is being given advice by an old hand:

> Sproule: A word to the wise, Murray. Those wogs you've been duchessing at Ethnic Affairs have got nothing on the culture vultures. Tear the flesh right off your bones, they will.

> Ken had climbed into the ring with some hard-nosed bastards over the years, and he spoke with genuine awe.

I said: Going soft?

Sproule: The first thing you should know about this job, pal, is that in this town the arts are a minefield. Everything from the pitch of the philharmonic to the influence of landscape painting on the national psyche is a matter of public debate. We've got more experimental film-makers, dramaturges and string quartets than you can poke a conductor's baton at. And every last one of them has a direct line to the media. You've never seen so much colour and movement in all your life. Tell you, pal it's more than a can of worms, it's a nest of vipers.

Advice from experts about managing government stakeholders include:

- Align your objectives with government
- Demonstrate connection with "the real world"
- Form alliances
- Foster advocates amongst key influencers
- Don't identify government as the enemy
- Understand government priorities – unless there's a crisis, you're probably not it
- Keep written briefs to one page and dot points
- Be professional, passionate, innovative, clever – and feed them information
- Link the arts to other policy areas.

We do have a great advantage in our work of influencing government stakeholders – brilliant events. Inviting politicians and officials to experience the art helps them to understand your work and have a good time in the process. And for companies that have existed for a long time, our very history can help us influence stakeholders. Some other results of Tshirhart's (1996) research were that the more one interacts with stakeholders, the more likely one is to understand and respect each other's values and interests, and the older the organisation, the less likely they were to adapt and the more power they had to change stakeholders.

There can be conflicting opinions and actions between an organisation's stakeholders which can have a negative effect on the organisation. As an example, at one stage in developing the plans for the Southbank theatre, the University of Melbourne was in discussion with the State Government. The University reached a particular conclusion and put out a press release to that effect. The Government believed that the conclusion was slightly different and that they should have made the announcement. The result was a very unhappy Premier who responded by attacking me loudly at an arts event and in front of the media. There weren't any long-term consequences because I copped the abuse on behalf of the company and spent the next couple of days calming everyone down and worked with the parties to find a more coherent agreement. That story is a reminder that you can't control your stakeholders but if I'd been more effective at wangling my way into the original conversation between them, I might have been able to prevent the conflict – and the public dressing down.

One shouldn't only dwell on the negative aspects of stakeholder management. Stakeholders can be extraordinarily helpful too. Without the listeners and the staff, the volunteers and other media outlets, community partners and sponsors, we would never have been able to save 6UVS-FM (see *Leadership* for more detail). In 2014, the announcement that the San Diego Opera would shut down after 50 years caused an outcry from patrons and company members alike who had no advance warning of the company's escalating financial troubles. This is a fascinating example of Kotter's (1996) prescription that organisations need a sense of urgency if anything is going to change, plus an example of where your stakeholders can help you at a time of crisis. Within days of the announcement, a faction of the Board had called for a postponement of the closure and 20,000 people had signed an online petition to keep the organisation going. The next stage in the company's turnaround was to start a crowdfunding campaign to raise $1 million to prevent the close and mount a 2015 season, but a season that would be substantially different to past seasons.

The company met its $1 million crowdfunding goal 10 days early and in fact raised $2 million. This money plus some large one-off donations and a 10% salary cut meant that the 2015 season could go ahead (Boehm 2014; Ng & Boehm 2014).

One has to work hard to manage stakeholders, particularly those important for the financial health of your organisation such as governments, philanthropists, sponsors and audiences. The key is to remain continually in touch with them, understand their needs and try, within the range of potential clashes of interests and priorities, to meet those needs.

See also: Audiences, Cultural Policy, Fundraising, Leadership, Sponsorship

References

Boehm, M. 2014 "San Diego Opera's Crowdfunding Campaign Has Strong Start", *Los Angeles Times*, 29 April, www.latimes.com/entertainment/arts/culture/la-et-cm-san-diego-opera-emergency-fundraising-campaign-20140429-story.html, [accessed 11 March 2019].

Boerner, S. & Jobst, J. 2011 "Stakeholder Management and Program Planning in German Public Theaters", *Nonprofit Management & Leadership*, 22(1), 67–84.

Donaldson, T. & Preston, L. E. 1995 "The Stakeholder Theory of the Corporation: Concepts, Evidence, and Implications", *Academy of Management Review*, 20(1), 65–91.

Freeman, R. E. 1984 *Strategic Management: A Stakeholder Approach*, Boston, MA: Pitman.

Kotter, J. P. 1996 *Leading Change*, Boston, MA: Harvard Business School Press.

Maloney, S. 2004 *The Brush Off*, Melbourne: Text Publishing.

Ng, D. & Boehm, M. 2014 "Questions roil San Diego Opera in Aftermath of its Decision to Close", *Los Angeles Times*, 5 April, http://articles.latimes.com/2014/apr/05/entertainment/la-et-san-diego-opera-20140405 [accessed 11 March 2019].

Tshirhart, M. 1996 *Artful Leadership*, Bloomington, IN: Indiana University Press.

Strategic Planning

This is another topic around which opinions swirl and language is muddled. Should one have a strategy and not worry too much about a plan? Is a strategy meaningless without a plan? When is a plan not a strategic plan? Does a plan do anything else except sit in a CEO's drawer? Is an annual plan a strategic plan? Do you have to pre-plan before you can plan? Can a five-year plan ever have meaning given how fast the world changes? Do we only create annual and triennial plans because our funders want us to?

There are entire books and courses dedicated to strategic planning. I've attended one presented by Stanford University. My favourite practical resource on planning is Kaiser's *The Circle* (2013) because it's written by an arts manager. The best summary I've read about strategic planning can found, somewhat ironically, in a novel. In Derek B. Miller's *American by Day*, one of his heroes, Sheriff Irving Wylie is trying to solve a potentially catastrophic problem:

> Irv had been taught in a business course once that all strategic action has four components: a goal, resources, you'll use, methods you'll perform, and – at the center of it all – a theory or argument about *why* using those resources a certain way will bring about the desired goal.
>
> (Miller 2018, 266)

Simple, really.

For government-funded arts organisations, strategic plans are now *de rigueur* and arts and cultural departments and ministries will often provide formats and training to help arts managers complete the process (for example, the Australia Council's *Strategic Plan Framework*). Therefore, I'm not going to spend much time on "how to do it". What's more interesting to me is why we do it? After all, as Bilton, Cummings and Wilson (2003, 213) say anyone who has spent time in a non-profit arts organisation will appreciate the endless amount of paper work that's done for others such as business plans and mission statements, action plans and evaluation reports, all of which "bear only a passing, semi-fictional relationship to the real plans and aspirations of the organisation itself". I was reminded of this as I read numbers of beautifully crafted strategic plans as part of a funding process. These documents were the only thing we could use to make decisions on grants because most of the people in the room hadn't seen the work of most of the applicants. This was unfortunate because, to date, I haven't come across any research that links the quality of a strategic plan with the quality of the art.

However, these days an organisation that doesn't have a plan will be seen as ineffective and reactive and that may be the truth. Plans have important symbolic roles:

1. Plans are signs: a signal that all is well or improvement is just around the corner
2. Plans become games: a justification for expenditure where the benefit may lay more in the process than the result
3. Plans become excuses for interaction: they require discussion and therefore increase interest in and commitment to new priorities
4. Plans become advertisements: to persuade funders and donors of the legitimacy of the organisation (Cohen & March 1974).

Mintzberg (1994) said that a good deal of corporate planning is like a rain dance – "it has no effect on the weather that follows, but those who engage in it think it does" (quoted in Bolman & Deal 2013, 294). A more positive spin on planning is that it's the "organisation of hope" (Stephen Blum, quoted in Crosby & Bryson 2005, xx). After all, a lot of our organisations start with "an impractical, illogical, seemingly unattainable dream" but, as Deshpande (2015, 99) says, such dreams will become unattainable if you don't translate them into "concrete, quantifiable, attainable goals".

So, for the less cynical of us, plans are pragmatic tools that provide direction, help to make the right resource allocation, identify potential risks along the way and ensure that everyone agrees with the direction.

There are a variety of different plans – ad hoc, project, action, annual, long term – so let's start with planning before moving on to "strategy". Annual plans are often the action base for arts organisations because their organisational cycle is built around a year's programming and/ or because their funding (and therefore their grant applications) is annual. For organisations with longer planning cycles such as symphony orchestras or art museums, that operational plan may be three or even five years in outlook.

A wonderful metaphor for getting such pragmatic planning cycles to work well is offered by Rosner and Halcrow (2010, 55) They say look at Julia Childs, the famous cookery writer, as a good project manager because every recipe has an effective plan:

• A clear purpose
• All the resources needed are itemised
• The timeline and ideal work environment is spelt out
• The correct tools are specified
• Milestones are identified
• Time frames established
• and there's step-by-step instructions to achieve the desired results.

It's important to remember that an annual operational plan will, by definition, focus on short-term goals and doesn't always capture the richness of future ambitions. It tends to have a conservative effect because it usually takes the existing situation as the starting point. Even a long-term plan is unlikely to anticipate a recession, or a natural disaster or a change in policy or even the resignation of a long-time leader. Such unplanned outcomes "mandate real-time decision making and the leaders who get more of those decisions right rather than wrong are the ones who sustain and grow mission impact over time" (Bell 2010, 472). The action that drives you forward is sometimes a result of the environment and sometimes the result of internal dreams and ideas and so an operational plan may not necessarily be a strategic plan.

When do you need to develop a strategic plan? Kaiser says "[a]nnual strategic planning is an antiquated idea. You can't wait for your normal cycle to change your strategy" (Kaiser 2013, 77). Varbanova (2013, 43) says you should do it when:

- Your organisation is operating well but does not know what its priorities would be in the next four to five years
- There are major economic, political or social changes in your region, city or country which will affect your organisation's future
- You and your team are constantly striving to find financial support and struggling to maintain operations
- You are constantly losing members, supporters or clients, or your audience levels are decreasing
- You sense decreased levels of motivation among your staff, Board members and/or volunteers
- You are uncertain how to balance creative programming with marketing and fundraising.

She comments that there are many different definitions of "strategy" probably because the term is "quite rich" but usually strategy is connected with the long-term objectives of an organisation and is interpreted as a direction or a way by which the objectives can be reached (Varbanova 2013). To illustrate some of the subtle and not so subtle differences in the use of the word, Kaiser (2013) thinks strategy is a plan, Drucker (1990) thinks it's a bulldozer, Stewart (2009) considers it a way of thinking ahead and Wolf (1999) sees it as part of the planning process.

Kaiser's (2013, 176) definition of strategy is "a detailed plan for how to address a problem posed by the gap between requirements for success and the current capacity of the organisation". Drucker (quoted in Fishel 2003, 115) offers a robust image. The mission and plan of an organisation, he says, are the good intentions whereas "strategies are bulldozers. They convert what you want to do into accomplishment." Stewart (2009, 151) simply likes the idea of strategy as "thinking ahead", keeping an eye on the big picture. He goes on to say:

Seeing the big picture means seeing not just what is, but what can be. It is, by its nature, a synthetic activity, not an analytical one. It is essentially creative, not reductive. It happens in an imperfectly knowable world, and it is risky (219).

Wolf (1999, 286–287) sees it as part of the planning process rather than being the main focus. He describes planning as a road map using the following images to capture the process:

1. Purpose or mission – reveals why the organization is making the journey
2. Goals – provides the general direction it is heading
3. Objectives and targets – reveals the destination
4. Strategies – specifically how the organization will get there
5. Actions – the trip itself
6. Evaluation – have you arrived?

If you still feeling muddled, Rosewall (2014, 58) offers a clear example of separating out goals, objectives and strategies, pointing out that goals aren't actions, they are an actuality. If your goal was to increase artistic quality, an objective could be to improve conditions for artists and some strategies to help do that could be to solicit input from artists and provide attractive housing for non-resident artists. A good definition of what strategy formulation means is that it's

> the task of selecting an action-oriented game plan that indicates *how* chosen objectives will be pursued and *what* entrepreneurial, competitive and operational approaches management will adopt to get the organisation in the position it wants to be
>
> (O'Connell 1997, 81)

In arts organisations, this strategic planning process may start with a vision and some major goals (called WIGs or Wildly Important Goals by Drucker (1990) or BHAGs, Big Hairy Audacious

Goals by Phills (2005)) which may have been created in different ways. It could be based on the founder or Artistic Director's passion or dreams. It could come from the Board and management adopting an iterative approach responding to emerging issues and trends. It could also come from a specific analytical or theoretical approach to examining a company's strengths and weaknesses in the environment in which they operate (Rowe & Data-on 2013, 162).

As an example of the latter approach, in the 2000s the Australia Council bought some business academics from Stanford University to run sessions about strategic planning with the major performing arts companies and also sent a number of Artistic and Managing Directors to Stanford for their Executive Leadership Program for Non-Profit Arts Leaders so that we could all start using the same specific model. This was a useful planning tool in that it brought Board and senior management together to start finding a shared language. But other models will have the same learning effect.

The Stanford approach (see Phills 2005 for more detail) proceeded from developing a mission to developing a strategy which needed to be guided by the mission because the strategy is designed to achieve and serve the mission. The strategy is seen as the economic logic that guides the organisation, the logic that helps you make the right choices to achieve your goals. The process is to look at where you sit in the environment – your suppliers and consumers, your competitors and potential new entrants to your market as well as substitute products[2] – to determine why people would buy your product rather than others and what other companies simply can't emulate. This is called a "sustainable competitive advantage" and for MTC at that time, we concluded that it had two factors. We had an advantage over other theatre companies because of our better production values, the high-quality actors we could attract to work for us, the range of international work for which we could get rights, along with the fact that we commissioned the best playwrights in the country plus a 50-year reputation for presenting

great theatre. The second advantage related to our nearest competitor in terms of people's time, money and interest – and that was film. The advantage was that we were live.

We then used this conclusion to check the economic logic of our resource allocation.

For example, major resource allocations that were consistent with this competitive advantage included spending money on artists, finding a new theatre with the best sized performance space for spoken word drama, an experimental studio and increasing production budgets. Examples of major resource allocations that were inconsistent with the competitive advantage included spending large amounts on venue hire, ticketing fees, administration and excessive expenditure on furniture and fitout in non-public spaces.

In other words, the Stanford process led us through a logical exercise that helped us with decisions around resource allocation (both money and time). As Kaiser says (2013, 164), too many strategic plans are simply a set of wishes – we will raise more money by raising more money – whereas the Stanford approach was a more robust way of planning action. There is no strategic holy grail which can be brilliantly conceived, carefully implemented and defended through all time (Montgomery 2008). You will need to keep evolving and changing but always keeping in mind your underlying mission. With all the different types of schools of thought around strategic planning, you have to find the process that delivers the best results for your organisation.

Morrow (2018, 27) questions the use of standard business planning tools in the arts environment which is inherently unpredictable and uncertain. But sometimes it's unavoidable. Your funders, government, foundation or philanthropic will require you to develop a strategic plan so use the one that suits them. And when you doing it, keep Kolsteeg's (2013, 988–989) challenge in mind:

traditional strategy formulation has been a rational and analytical exercise but we're creative organisations after all. Shouldn't we be using more creative processes to find out way into the future?

The creative starting point is what Longstaff (2014) describes as the capacity to "see" at a variety of levels:

- Satellite view – the large picture in which key issues are located
- Submarine view – the undercurrents that shape the operating environment
- Present – being in the "now" so as to deal with issues in an evolving situation.

However, sometimes the very idea of embarking on a strategic planning session with staff and the Board is exhausting given the demands on the leadership team and it feels like a deeply uncreative and repetitive process. That said, Fishel (2003, 109) makes the important point that "[t]he process of generating and confirming the statements of vision, mission and values can be a powerful way of digging into the heart of the organisation, and reminding Board, staff and others why they are doing the work".

For arts organisations with Boards and multiple stakeholders, a strategic planning process should be able to answer the following questions:

- What specifically does our organisation want to achieve in the next few years?
- What have we learned from past experiences?
- How should we allocate resources among different objectives?
- What quality standards should we aim to achieve?
- How can we make better use of our resources? (Fishel 2003, 110)

Most of the time, strategic planning will look like a linear process: starting with establishing/ reviewing the mission and key goals, leading through internal and external checks to formulating objectives, strategy implementation and evaluation processes. But it doesn't always happen that way. In my experience, the difference is determined by the purpose of the planning or what Hagoort (2005) calls the strategic motive. Is it to produce a document for stakeholders? Is it to check that you really are heading in the right direction? Is it to remind and refresh the Board and senior management of why you're doing what you're doing? Is it because a new CEO has been appointed with a vision that they need to share internally and externally? Is it because you want to work out what's going wrong and how to fix it?

Suppose an organisation has a few strong strategic options in mind and people really want to talk about it. Rather than spend too much time evaluating current activities, the most productive approach would be to start with option formulation. Hagoort (2005, 92) gives another example where if the strategic team strongly feels that the most important move is to research environmental trends on account of a lack of knowledge, the process can start with that exercise. Having experienced a multitude of strategic planning processes where it felt that time was wasted on things we already knew or agreed on, choosing the point you want to focus your energy on rather than going through every step of the traditional process makes sense. And as Hagoort (2005, 94) rightly says: "if the organization is in deep financial crisis, mission and continuity are in real danger, and it will be virtually impossible to develop a strategic process. Here, radical crisis management intervention is called for."

While there are sophisticated planning tools available and every external consultant you use will have their own toolkit, sometimes old-fashioned techniques such as a SWOT (strengths, weaknesses, opportunities, threats) analysis plus an environment review covering trends under headings such as culture, social, economic, political, media, technology, international, ecology (Hagoort 2005) are good starting points to try and pinpoint where the organisation sits and what the future might hold. And if thinking about the W and T part is too depressing, you can always do a SOAR – strengths and opportunities, aspirations (a preferred future) and (desirable) results (Cooperrider, Whitney & Stavros 2005, 405). These processes are familiar parts of strategy days or retreats but such days are often better for bonding and sharing than for actually creating a plan. Sometimes too much time is spent trying to wordsmith goals or visions or objectives and other times the result is a document filled with hopes and dreams but lacking detailed strategies and measures (Kaiser 2010).

Martin (2013) differentiates between strategic planning and strategic management. He describes planning as "a process that guides conversations about an organization's purpose, helps integrate perspectives from multiple stakeholders, and provides the steps to develop goals and objectives that will move the organization forward" but points out that a plan is comforting but it's not a strategy. That, he describes, as having two phases: strategy formation (what are we going to do?) and strategy implementation (how are we going to do it?). However, to me that seems like pedantry. A good strategic plan will have the elements of strategy formation *and* implementation in it.

Strategy can be in the form of experimentation, growth, quality enhancement, stability or retrenchment. Courtney (2002, 207–208) provides a more detailed list of the types of strategies that non-profit organisations might adopt. For example:

- Reduce services
- Reduce costs
- Maintain through continuing existing activities
- Improve quality
- Experiment
- Quantitative expansion such as increase audiences over time
- Expand boundary such as touring or international activities
- Switch to new related activity
- Switch to new unrelated activity
- Piggyback such as finding an income earning stream to subsidise core business
- Partner
- Building.

At various times, MTC pursued most of these strategies such as reducing output when trying to reach financial stabilisation, improving quality of stage design and performance and building a new theatre to create a viable financial future. And that's the next point: once the strategy has been formulated, it then has to be implemented. The worst part of every planning session I have ever attended is the implementation discussion. While everyone is in fine form at the beginning of the day, they are tired by the end. While everyone gets an emotional hit from revisiting the vision and the mission, the implementation plan brings you back down to the ground. In some ways, I'd rather have a vision morning, head off to the beach or the yoga room to let the ideas percolate, and then return next day with new energy and insights to work out how the strategic plan can be implemented. Because implementation is more important than writing the plan down.

I left an organisation because my manager didn't understand that point. As part of an Australian aid project to South Africa after the first democratic elections in 1994, I went to develop a strategic plan for the national English language radio station. After a number of weeks, the new Radio Manager for the South African Broadcasting Corporation (ABC) began to trust my process and insights and asked if I'd stay on to start the implementation process. I was eager to do so but my Australian boss wanted me back. "They can sort it out themselves" was his attitude, not appreciating the complex stakeholder environment or the importance of implementation for a plan to be effectively translated into action. He just wanted me back in Sydney to look after his (minor) problems. I didn't last long in the ABC after that.

Stewart (2009, 174) quotes Jack Welch: "In real life, strategy is actually very straightforward. You pick a general direction and implement like hell." The key to implementation is selling the vision and its strategies so once you've created a plan, including how you're going to implement the strategy, don't put it in the drawer. The arts are littered with stories where the vision was brilliant but not shared effectively with staff or stakeholders, resulting in resistance to strategic change. Fishel (2003, 117) says that a good plan is a well-thumbed plan:

> Require the CEO to report against it on a regular basis. Re-read it before the planning retreat. And, most of all, adopt it, even if it has imperfections, rather than honing it and refining it for month after month until everyone is heartily sick of it. You can always make it better next time.

When MTC first tried the Stanford approach, we found words that we believed in for most aspects of the process quite quickly. There was one section that we didn't do well. And looking back at the original document, it still reads awkwardly. But that lack of refinement didn't stop us getting a document that became part of our regular conversations because it captured our collective dream and I used it in a very pragmatic way – as the reporting structure for my monthly Board reports.

In the Turkish film *Winter Sleep*, there's a translated line to the effect that one should live life to the full and not spend a life planning. Another way of expressing that idea is offered by Hill (2014) in her description of successful innovative organisations. She says they act as opposed to plan their way to the future. There is a tension between those who say that strategy precedes action and those who think that "strategy can only emerge through action: by experimentation and responding to operational realities" (Bilton & Cummings 2015, 92). Another approach combines planning and action whereby they take place simultaneously. This methodology has come from the software industry which faces the need for rapid prototyping. Guy Morrow (2018) has written a book about the use of agile management by artists' managers and you can also see this process at work in the rehearsal room where a scene will be played out, the outcome is reviewed and at the end of the day there's a new plan for what's to be done tomorrow. Bilton and Cummings (quoted in Beech & Gilmore 2015, 94) describe the "planning" process of a small

record label and quote the owner as saying he has a "consistent voice" rather than a strategy. What he means is that his values – sincerity, trust, reliability – enable him to be "decisive in uncertain circumstances". He may not have a strategy but he does have a framework in which he can make decisions.

> He understands that his decisions and actions are dependent upon the decision and actions of artists, promoters, CD manufacturers and venues; there is no point in trying to anticipate every possibility, or blaming himself when things don't work out. Leading from the middle, planning by doing … An important lesson from *Song, by Toad*[3] is that there is no perfect strategic recipe. Things go wrong and mistakes are made. One response to this scenario is simply to give up any attempt at planning and follow the next opportunity [but] a flexible adaptive approach to strategy is not the same thing as no strategy at al. *Song, by Toad* has an ethos [aka values] and action is purposeful, not random or opportunistic.
>
> (Beech & Gilmour 2015, 95)

It's easy to get cynical about theories and approaches to management that are linear and logical in a world that's not. In the arts "failure is frequent and can't be prevent by advance planning; … excellence cannot be guaranteed or delivered by detailed planning" (Tusa 2011). Grant (2012) warns that strategic plans can become an internal obsession and lead to inertia rather than change, but there are benefits. If Boards and management can't find a way to agree the vision of a company, they can't develop a strategic plan. But strategic planning can enable a greater sense of focus and a clearer understanding of where we're going, better teamwork because people have been involved in the planning process, better use of resources and a more cohesive organisation and potentially better communications (O'Connell 1997, 72). And as Taylor (2015) says, as long as we recognise that all human processes are "sloppy and slippery" then we might be "kinder and calmer" about our capacity to achieve our visions.

I'm going leave the final words in this section to one of the more insightful writers about strategic planning in the arts, Giep Hagoort. He says that a strategic plan should make a cultural organisation "more capable of being flexible and 'ready for the fray'" (2005, 103).

In a letter that he sent to a theatre company with whom he'd worked on developing a strategic plan, he wisely noted:

> the ultimate success of artistic expression cannot simply be derived from the quality of strategy formulation. Artistic success depends primarily (and sometimes in highly unpredictable ways) on the interaction between individually-minded artists, programmers, designers, theatre producers and their public. Interactive strategy formation does, however, contribute towards fostering a professional attitude in the cultural organization as employer, allowing a structural place for the knowledge of all those involved.
>
> (Hagoort 2005, 230)

See also: Evaluation, Mission, Money

References

Australia Council "Strategic Plan Framework: A Guide for Arts Organisations", Sydney: Australia Council, www.australiacouncil.gov.au/workspace/uploads/files/arts-organisations-strategic-p-54c1867bca7bf.pdf [accessed 11 March 2019].

Bell, J. 2010 "Financial Leadership in Nonprofit Organizations", in Renz, D. O. (ed.) *The Jossey-Bass Handbook of Nonprofit Leadership and Management* (3rd ed), San Francisco, CA: John Wiley & Sons, 461–481.

Bilton, C., Cummings, S. & Wilson, D. 2003 "Strategy as Creativity", in Cummings, S. & Wilson, D. (eds) *Images of Strategy*, Oxford: Blackwell Publishing, 197–227.

Bilton, C. & Cummings, S. 2015 "Creative Strategy: Notes from a Small Label", in Beech, N. & Gilmore, C. (eds) *Organising Music: Theory, Practice, Performance*, Cambridge: Cambridge University Press, 83–98.

Bolman, L. G. & Deal, T. E. 2013 *Reframing Organizations* (5th ed), San Francisco, CA: Jossey-Bass.

Cohen, S. G. & March, J. G. 1974 *Leadership and Ambiguity*, New York: McGraw Hill.

Cooperrider, D. L., Whitney, D. & Stavros, J. M. 2005 *Appreciative Inquiry Handbook*, Brunswick, OH: Crown Custom Publishing.

Courtney, R. 2002 *Strategic Management for Voluntary Nonprofit Organizations*, London: Routledge.

Crosby, B. C. & Bryson, J. M. 2005 *Leadership for the Common Good* (2nd ed), San Francisco, CA: Jossey-Bass.

Deshpande, S. 2015 "The Studio Safdar Story", in Caust, J. (ed.) *Arts and Cultural Leadership in Asia*, London: Routledge, 91–101.

Drucker, P. F. 1990 *Managing the Nonprofit Organization*, New York: HarperCollins.

Fishel, D. 2003 *The Book of The Board*, Sydney: Federation Press.

Grant, P. 2012 *The Business of Giving: The Theory and Practice of Philanthropy, Grantmaking and Social Investment*, New York: Palgrave Macmillan.

Hagoort, G. 2005 *Art Management: Entrepreneurial Style* (5th ed), Delft: Eburon.

Hill, L. 2014 "How to Manage for Collective Creativity?", *TED Talk*, www.ted.com/talks/linda_hill_how_to_manage_for_collective_creativity?language=en#t-7224 [accessed 11 March 2019].

Kaiser, M. M. 2010 *Leading Roles*, Waltham, MA: Brandeis University Press.

Kaiser, M. M. 2013 *The Circle*, Waltham, MA: Brandeis University Press.

Kolsteeg, J. 2013 "Developing the Practice of Organisation Design", Bogota: Session G3, AIMAC, 987–993.

Longstaff, S. 2014 *The Twin Foundations of Leadership*, www.communitydirectors.com.au/icda/tools/?articleId=7458 [accessed 16 March 2019].

Martin, R. L. 2013 "The Big Lie of Strategic Planning", *Harvard Business Review*, 91(1/2), 78–84.

Miller, D. B. 2018 *American by Day*, Boston, MA: Houghton Mifflin Harcourt.

Mintzberg, H. 1994 *The Rise and Fall of Strategic Planning: Reconceiving Roles for Planning, Plans, Planners*, New York: Free Press.

Montgomery, C. A. 2008 "Putting Leadership Back into Strategy", *Harvard Business Review*, https://hbr.org/2008/01/putting-leadership-back-into-strategy [accessed 31 March 2019].

Morrow, G. 2018 *Artist Management: Agility and the Creative and Cultural Industries*, London: Routledge.

O'Connell, A. 1997 "Strategic Planning and the Arts Organization", in Fitzgibbon, M. & Kelly, A. (eds)

From Maestro to Manager, Dublin: Oak Tree Press, 69–84.

Pfeffer, J. & Sutton, R. I. 2006 *Hard Facts, Dangerous Half-Truths, and Total Nonsense*, Boston, MA: Harvard Business School Press.

Phills, J. A. 2005 *Integrating Mission and Strategy for Nonprofit Organizations*, New York: Oxford University Press.

Rosewall, E. 2014 *Arts Management: Uniting Arts and Audiences in the 21st Century*, New York: Oxford University Press.

Rosner, B. & Halcrow, A. 2010 *The Boss's Survival Guide* (2nd ed), New York: McGraw Hill.

Rowe, W. G. & Dato-on, M. C. (eds) 2013 *Introduction to Nonprofit Management*, Thousand Oaks, CA: Sage.

Stewart, M. 2009 *The Management Myth*, New York: W.W. Norton & Co.

Taylor, A. 2015 "The Theory of Strategy", *The Artful Manager*, 6 February, www.artsjournal.com/artfulmanager/main/the-theory-of-strategy.php [accessed 11 March 2019].

Tusa, J. 2011 "Finding a Necessary Language for the Arts", www.theguardian.com/culture-professionals-network/culture-professionals-blog/2011/nov/16/finding-necessary-language-arts [accessed 20 February 2019].

Varbanova, L. 2013 *Strategic Management in the Arts*, New York: Routledge.

Wolf, T. 1999 *Managing a Nonprofit Organization in the Twenty-first Century* (2nd ed), New York: Simon Schuster.

Succession

A succession plan is a plan that helps you survive the almost guaranteed crisis that starts when a CEO or senior manager announces their resignation. Even if they give you six months' notice, there is no guarantee that a perfect replacement will be in place by the time they leave. Landry (2013, 214) describes succession options in a matrix of planned and unplanned, simple or complex change:

> Classic: simple change, planned
> Unexpected: simple change, unplanned
> Crisis: reorganisation, unplanned
> Reorganisation: reorganisation, planned.

Landry (2013) only uses "crisis" for one of the categories, but "planned" is a euphemism for "they've just given notice" compared to "unplanned" which means "they've been run over by a bus". In terms of finding the right replacement, there isn't much difference. An organisation will survive a leadership change if it is resilient and in good financial shape.

Walter (2015, 374–376) proposes three ways of thinking about succession planning:

1. Having the right people in the organisation to start with
2. Having a strategic plan
3. Effective crisis management.

Whether it's an expected or unexpected change, if you have great people in your organisation then there should be enough resilience to keep going forward. In an organisation in transition that I've experienced, although all the staff were nervous about what a change in leadership would mean for both the company and themselves on a personal basis, some were much more open to change than others. For the most part, the latter group were the people who were secure in themselves and knew their own skills were valuable.

Stone (2013, 76) gives an example of how McDonald's succession plan works. Every manager had to have at least two potential successors, one who is "ready now" and one with a "ready future". He goes on to say: "The goal is for McDonald's executives to surround themselves with subordinates smarter than themselves." However, you don't have to have a succession plan to enjoy the pleasure of having a bright group of people in your team.

Most S2M arts companies with little hierarchical depth rarely have the luxury of one let alone two possible successors to a CEO. And in bigger companies, even if you do have such people in place, you run the risk of a disappointed internal candidate if they don't get the gig and what this might mean for the new CEO. However, you should give senior managers a chance to demonstrate their skills in acting roles when, for example, you go on holiday. My approach to succession planning is that you should be succession planning for the entire arts industry rather than one's own organisation. In other words, you train your people to get promotions in other parts of the industry. While you invest in them, they'll feel valued and work hard. And when they leave, you will have delivered a well-trained, experienced person to take up a job in an industry to which you're committed.

Having a strategic plan in place will help you find the best leadership fit for the next stage of the organisation's life but a good practice is to test the vision of the company before you go to the market. This can mean a strategic planning session with the Board but it can also mean consulting with other industry members. In an artistic leadership replacement process I was involved with, the Board invited a group of artists to a conversation to reality check their vision, advise them on the future focus of the company and, therefore, what they should be looking for in their new co-CEOs.

An emergency backup plan means thinking about the crucial management and leadership functions that are needed for the company to continue and then work out how you can make sure they happen. This could mean allocating tasks across your leadership team (and even your Board) or getting a locum manager in for the duration. My most recent work has been in such a role in two S2M arts companies in different parts of Australia. Both companies had a great team of people and my role was to help the Board in their recruitment process and provide a steady hand in the change process.

In a survey on US non-profit governance (Larcker et al. 2015), when asked if Board Directors could immediately name a permanent successor if the CEO left tomorrow, 78% said yes. I found this result surprising – because it was so high. In my experience, most organisations don't have a person specifically in mind and even if they did, they would still want to advertise to see who else might be out there. The Board members in the Stanford survey thought that they could name an appointment in a (median) of 90 days and that's probably about right. That was the timing from the beginning of the recruitment process to naming the co-CEOs in the S2M

where I was locum Executive Director in 2018 although it was another 100 days before the co-CEOs could start full time. This can be a long time to be without leadership in an organisation.

In Australia there have always been a number of arts managers and consultants willing to step into locum management positions and I assume that is true in other countries. Finding "locum" arts leaders may be harder but that simply means one has to be more creative. When Simon Phillips resigned from MTC as its Artistic Director, he gave the Board almost a year's notice which enabled plenty of time for an extensive international search process for his replacement. However, when the Board finally decided on Brett Sheehy, he'd just re-signed for another year as Artistic Director of the Melbourne International Arts Festival. Rather than have the Board lose their preferred candidate and Brett lose his desired next job, I came up with a leadership transition plan which involved asking three valued artists to work together to program the subscription season for 2012 as well as participate in it as actors, writers and directors. The result was a year that honoured the past, didn't make radical changes for the sake of it, brought the skills and interests of some of Australia's greatest artists to the company and, because they were all known by the staff, bought a sense of stability during a period of change.

People are always going to leave and even if they give you months of notice, you'll probably still need to implement a transition plan. A resilient company in an industry full of talented people will survive such a challenge.

See also: Hiring, Learning, People

References

Larcker, D. F., Meehan, W. F., Donatiello, N. & Tayan, B. 2015 "2015 Survey on Board of Directors of Nonprofit Organisations", Stanford, CA: Stanford Graduate School of Business & Rock Center for Corporate Governance.

Landry, P. 2013 "The Succession of Artistic Directors in Cultural Organizations and Organizational identity: A Typological Approach", Bogota: Session B4, 12th AIMAC International Conference, 213–223.

Rothwell, W. J. 2011 "Succession Planning", in O'Toole, S., Ferres, N. & Connell, J. (eds) *People Development: An Inside View*, Melbourne: Tilde University Press, 148–165.

Stone, R. J. 2013 *Managing Human Resources* (4th ed), Milton, QLD: John Wiley & Sons.

Walter, C. 2015 *Arts Management: An Entrepreneurial Approach*, New York: Routledge.

Sustainability

Sustainability is one of the words that has felt "popular" over the last decade without being either well defined or clear about what it should mean to arts organisations. With its origin in discussions about environmental sustainability, the idea is about being diverse and productive but operating in a way that doesn't cause harm. Peter Ellyard (2015), futurist, describes it as doing things with zero net collateral damage.

In a recent conversation with a colleague who works in the area of ethics, I said that "sustainability" was the underlying rationale for all arts managers. What I meant was a sense that they all want their organisation to exist in the future because of a belief in the arts. This is compared, for example, with a for-profit manager who is currently investing in making car parts but if that becomes "unsustainable" they will turn their investment to making computer parts. Having said that, there may be arts groups that only want to come together to do a project and don't want to continue into the future or an organisation that decides to close once its artistic founder has left. So even that simple approach to sustainability as "ongoing survival" isn't true for all of us.

Unpacking organisational sustainability leads to thinking about economic, artistic and audience sustainability. For example, for an arts organisation to be economically sustainable it needs to have sufficient income streams, effective governance, financial management systems and good staff. Artistic sustainability requires being open to new ideas and new artists, investing in risk-taking work as well as building on the past and creating work that excites and inspires audiences, because without them, the sustainability of the art form and the organisation becomes questionable. The idea of artistic sustainability could also be defined as simply ensuring the artistic vibrancy of an organisation (Australia Council n.d.). Audience sustainability is literally wanting more live ones to replace the dead ones! Every Annual Report of an arts organisation is likely to have measures that capture each of these elements although they wouldn't necessarily be defined under a single heading "sustainability". And many of those same Annual Reports would comment on the "greening" activities of the organisation, reflecting their concern with a broader definition of sustainability from an environmental perspective. As the battle to reduce global warming continues, arts companies looking to reduce their carbon footprint will introduce green policies ranging from light globe use to water collection and organisations such as Julie's Bicycle's provide practical guides to help this aspect of arts sustainability (2013).

As the conversation continued with my ethical colleague, he talked about his work with various industries and their desire to measure and share their sustainability. However, much of that seemed to be driven by a perspective that they needed to justify their behaviour in a way that arts organisations don't. For example, the Australian dairy industry clearly feels that they need to demonstrate their credentials because "[o]ur customers and the community are increasingly demanding proof we are doing the right thing by people, animals and our planet" (Australian Dairy Industry Council 2014). The call for arts organisations to demonstrate their sustainability hasn't come from outside but rather from within the industry itself with a concern about environmental issues and an ongoing concern about survivability. Images of Islamic State terrorists destroying historic art works in an Iraqi museum remind us how fragile art making can be.

As early as 2001 Throsby (2001, 161) described "sustainability" as a ubiquitous term "deployed indiscriminately". But he did offer a series of criteria which might be useful measures for the managers of cultural capital such as the contribution of the art to well-being,[4] intergenerational and intragenerational equity (preserving art for future generations), the maintenance of diversity and culture systems and what he calls the precautionary principle. This is an approach to risk management which says that if an action or policy is suspected of causing harm to the public or the environment then the burden of proof falls on the those planning to take the action. In other words, our policies and actions should be determined within an ethical framework, taking into account our staff and our artists, our audiences and our community, our environment and the future.

In an example of how an arts organisation captures "sustainability" in their strategic plan, the Museum of Applied Arts and Sciences in Sydney states that it is one of their four "strategic ambitions".[5] The subheading of "sustainability" is "supporting long term relevance" and the action statements include having sound business modelling, resilience, fiscal sustainability, workforce and stakeholder trust, conserving collections for future generations, continuous improvement in operations and governance, being an employer of choice and well-maintained and safe buildings with an agile and efficient workforce (MAAS 2014). In other words, sustainability is about good management with an eye to the future.

See also: Environment, Ethics, Evaluation, Money, Risk Management

References

Australia Council *Artistic Vibrancy*, www.australiacouncil.gov.au/ebook/artistic-vibrancy/publication/contents/pdfweb.pdf [accessed 16 March 2019].

Australian Dairy Industry Council 2014 *Australian Dairy Industry Sustainability Framework Progress Report – December 2014*, Melbourne: Dairy Australia.

Ellyard, P. 2015 Interview on *The Conversation Hour*, *ABC Radio National*, 26 February, www.abc.net.au/radio/programitem/pgJE6g2bLG?play=true [accessed 11 March 2019].

Julie's Bicycle 2013 *Practical Guides: Environmental Policy & Action Plan Guidelines*, www.juliesbicycle.com/Handlers/ Download.ashx?IDMF=dece678c-682c-4362-80c0-bd8744047213 [accessed 11 March 2019].

MAAS 2014 *Strategic Plan*, Sydney: MAAS.

Throsby, D. 2001 *Economics and Culture*, Cambridge: Cambridge University Press.

Notes

1 Quotes gathered by an arts lobbyist – 2011/12.
2 Based on Michael E Porter's Five Forces model of competitiveness.
3 The name of the company.
4 Interestingly, also one of the criteria measured by the Dairy Industry.
5 The other three are Curiosity, Creativity and Collaboration.

T

Teams

Unless one is an artist who works alone (a writer, a painter, a composer), most of us in the arts and cultural industries work in a variety of teams and groups. Academics differentiate between the two with groups being defined as "two or people who interact with a leader and each other to perform individual tasks for which they are held personally accountable" and teams being "a number of members who work cooperatively to pursue interdependent roles that achieve a common goal which there is a shared responsibility" (Dickie & Dickie 2011, 164). Groups are like the collection of people in the Marketing department who may be at different levels in the hierarchy but who work together and teams are more like individuals from different departments who come together to solve a particular problem. Other examples of teams are temporary groups that manage a project or cross-functional groups such as a management team (Teicher, Holland & Gough 2006). Although the differences are real (for example, there is more personal interdependence in a team), the strengths and weaknesses of working in groups and teams are similar.

We work in groups because we have to. Organisations have hierarchies with a number of people reporting to a supervisor or a manager. As it's highly unlikely that each of those people reporting to the manager will be working completely independently of everyone else, we automatically have a work group. Even in a small to medium-sized arts organisation with only two or three paid staff, they will come together to make some decisions and do some work together. There are benefits in doing so. The main advantage of working in groups or teams is that more information is shared so decision-making is better because there's a wider range of alternatives and opinions to consider (Dwyer 2009). These "better" decisions may also be more creative ones. Bilton and Leary (2010, 57) make the point that "if creativity is seen to result from a set of complementary yet opposing processes, creative thinking requires an engagement with 'the other'; with unfamiliar people and types of thinking" and so coming together with other people can add to the creativity of both the process and the outcome. In addition to making better decisions, there's better buy-in to those decisions because people's opinions have been heard and in the process, people learn and build their knowledge and skills (Dickie & Dickie 2011).

But as any of us who ever suffered through the process of doing a group assignment at school or university know, there are disadvantages to working in teams as well. In fact, the list of disadvantages provided in most management textbooks tend to be longer than the "advantage" list and include a longer time to make decisions, lack of responsibility for the decision, conflict caused by diverse views, the effect of group think, problems with coordination undermining benefits of collaboration, domination by the loudest, trying too hard to find consensus, group process amplifying biases and so on (Dickie & Dickie 2011; Dwyer 2009; Hackman 2009; Sunstein & Hastie 2014).

A manager or a team leader has to manage not only the individuals in the group but the group itself. I know a manager who is so concerned to get both these tasks right that on commencing a new job or work with a new team, he buys all his direct reports a copy of Patrick Lencioni's "leadership fable", *The Five Dysfunctions of a Team*. I'm not fond of fables but this recommendation was enough for me to read it. Lencioni (2005) takes the position that team work is hard to achieve but contributes to fulfilment at work because it gives people a sense of connection and belonging. His five dysfunctions (in other words, the five problems you have to solve) are:

1. Absence of trust
2. Fear of conflict
3. Lack of commitment
4. Avoidance of accountability
5. Inattention to results.

The book is focused on the more competitive and less trusting world of the corporate sector but the notion of creating a safe and trusting environment for the group, of enabling different voices to be heard, of building commitment to shared decision-making, are all important tasks for a team leader. Other roles include managing conflict, identifying the goals for the meeting and keeping track of decisions and their implementation (McShane & Travaglion 2003). However, before all of this, one has to provide that disparate group of people with a reason to be a team. Halvorson (2014, 38) says there are three reasons: kinship, mission or a common enemy. He recommends that providing a compelling mission is best — and luckily for those us in the arts, we have those.

When you start a new management job, you usually inherit a team and Watkins (2016) offers a number of good recommendations. To start with, you need to know what qualities you need in your team — are they competent and trustworthy with good energy, focus and judgement? For example, competence might be the most important value for your Finance Director but energy might be more important for your Marketing Director. This point reminded me of the charming description of a well-balanced management team that Tusa (2014, 97) based on the famous Christopher Robin books by AA Milne:

> Pooh Bear – warm general person with forgeable failings: the Creative Director
> Owl – serious and knowledgeable but can miss the point: finance
> Rabbit – eternally busy but need direction: premises management
> Kanga – the mother figure: human relations
> Christopher Robin – embracing them all and to whom they all turn: the CEO.

You need to get all the people in your team you've inherited aligned to your new ways of doing things and Watkins (2016, 65) recommends that you can do through asking questions such as

- What will we accomplish?
- Why should we do it?
- How will we do it?
- Who will do what?

If that alignment doesn't come about and you don't have the right team, you may want and hope that people will leave the company. If you can't instantly fire people you can:

- Signal your expectation of higher performance and get people to self-select out
- Groom high potential people to talk on extra responsibilities
- Adjust the scope of existing roles (Watkins 2016, 64).

When it comes to trust building, arts organisations are better placed than most because it's not about competition and office politics but about commitment to the creation and sharing of art. Having said that, there can still be competition over limited resources resulting in unhealthy differences. One arts colleague did trust-building exercises as one of the first actions in a new job. On reflection, I tended not to do enough renewal of trust when I started at MTC, taking for granted that each new member of the management team would see how I worked and learn trust along the way. I was reminded of the imperative of trust building when we finally felt financially secure enough to have a planning session out of the office, staying overnight at a pleasant place in Victoria's Yarra Valley. The simple fact of sharing a glass of wine and a family story was enough to rebuild connections and loosen organisational tensions, and that was reflected in the workplace in the months that followed.

When you can or need to start a team from scratch, you should consider the question of diversity. Diversity is not just about gender or race or age but can be found in other forms "such as core assumptions or beliefs, perspectives or habits" (Goffee & Jones 2013, 100). Do you want lots of Kangas or Owls or just one? Homogeneous teams, according to Kurtzberg (2005, 55), "seem to excel at more emotional outcomes such as trust, liking, and positive attitudes, and heterogenous teams seem to excel at more performance-based outcomes such as originality, complexity, and decision performance". My recommendation would be go for diversity and help the team build trust. One of the most interesting exercises I've seen in building a diverse team was not about gender (they were all women) but about age and experience. The company set up what they called a "breakfast and brainstorm team". It was chance for younger staff from a variety of departments to work together with the CEO to come up with ideas that would make the organisational culture better. The results ranged from changing the form of key meetings to bringing dogs to work. The team consisted of people who didn't usually work side by side and provided young people with a voice; a chance to work with the CEO; and it also provided an environment in which the newest members of the company could see how ideas were tested and implemented.

Lencioni (2005, 51) makes a good point when he says that in groups commitment doesn't have to be consensus but rather buy-in to decisions. People in a group need to feel included, that their opinions are valued and their contributions acknowledged and then, hopefully, even if they don't get their own way, they'll back the decision. Some of the best teamwork I've experienced has been when all voices were heard and opinions discussed, a decision was reached that not everyone was comfortable with but which everyone agreed was the right outcome for the company at the time. Getting all those voices heard in a group is the major challenge for team leaders. Often it's the loudest, most confident person who gets the most airtime. Bonner and Bolnger (2014) recommend ensuring that the expertise of each member of the group is brought to the fore early on. Sunstein and Hastie (2014) suggest that the leader should speak last (or not at all) as people will be reluctant to express alternative views if you've already expressed yours.

Lencioni's (2005) best work environment is painted as one where people are passionate but apologise if they do something inappropriate, are willing to sacrifice their resources for the good of the team, are concerned about letting down the team and where each meeting ends with agreed action. The underlying norms of such an organisational culture are ones that support openness, trust, cooperation and a commitment to a shared purpose.

Finally, what is it about those university group assignments that I hated so much? In that process, you are part of a self-managed and autonomous team, responsible for planning, undertaking and completing the project. Technically such self-managed teams are supposed to be good for job satisfaction and productivity. However, when such teams don't work is when, according to Adams (2007), the groups are autonomous in name only, that is, when management decides on the project, the resources, the completion date and the standards. Sounds a lot like student group work to me!

See also: Meetings, Organisational Culture, Organisational Structure, People, Trust

References

Adams, J. 2007 *Managing People in Organizations: Contemporary Theory and Practice*, Basingstoke: Palgrave Macmillan.

Bilton, C. & Leary, R. 2010 "What Can Managers Do for Creativity? Brokering Creativity in the Creative Industries", *International Journal of Cultural Policy*, 8(1), 49–64.

Bonner, B. L. & Bolnger, A. R. 2014 "Bring Out the Best in Your Team", *Harvard Business Review*, 92(9), 26.

Dickie, L. & Dickie, C. 2011 *Cornerstones of Management* (2nd ed), Melbourne: Tilde University Press.

Dwyer, J. 2009 *Communication in Business* (4th ed), Sydney: Pearson.

Goffe, R. & Jones, G. 2013 "Creating the Best Workplace on Earth", *Harvard Business Review*, 91(5), 99–106.

Hackman J. R. interviewed by Coutu, D. 2009 "Why Teams Don't Work", *Harvard Business Review*, 87(5), 98–105.

Halvorson, G. 2014 "Getting to 'Us'", *Harvard Business Review*, 92(9), 38.

Hewison, R. & Holden, J. 2011 *The Cultural Leadership Handbook*, Farnham: F Gower.

Kurtzberg, T. 2005 "Feeling Creative, Being Creative: An Empirical Study of Diversity and Creativity in Teams", *Creativity Research Journal*, 17(1), 51–65.

Lencioni, P. 2005 *The Five Dysfunctions of a Team: A Field Guide to Managers, Leaders and Facilitators*, San Francisco, CA: Jossey-Bass.

McShane, S. & Travaglione, T. 2003 *Organisational Behaviour on the Pacific Rim*, Sydney: McGraw Hill.

Sunstein, C. R. & Hastie, R. 2014 "Making Dumb Groups Smarter", *Harvard Business Review*, 92(12), 90–98.

Teicher, J., Holland, P. & Gough, R. 2006 *Employee Relations Management* (2nd ed), Sydney: Pearson Education Australia.

Tusa, J. 2014 *Pain in the Arts*, London: I.B. Tauris.

Watkins, M. D. 2016 "Leading the Team You Inherit", *Harvard Business Review*, 94(6), 61–67.

Technology

Technology impacts on both our art making and our organisations. For example, Australian smartphone ownership was estimated to be at 90% by the end of 2018 and is the "go to" device for most of us. Preferred ways of consuming news has tipped from papers to digital format and entertainment is almost equally shared in places like Australia between mainstream broadcasting and the internet. People multitask, sending texts or reading emails, browsing the web or social media while watching their favourite entertainment, TV. There's an endless array of data capture capacity through our mobile phones from finance apps to survey programs. The key is to get it right for the scale of the organisation. For example, in one S2M company, they went from using excel spreadsheets to collecting donor data in a large commercial sales software program – so large, that nobody could work out how to use it effectively and, in the process, data was lost from both the old and the new systems.

Gilmore (2011, 2) offers a conceptual framework for looking at the adaptation of new technology in arts organisations:

1. Functionality – technical innovation that improves the efficiency of business operations and management structure
2. Public service – changes in public media through digital channels creating a more visible space for the arts
3. Digital engagement – between audience and artist, consumer and company
4. Digital aesthetics – innovation in art form development created through application of new digital media
5. Strategic relations – use of social networking for arts advocacy.

The use of technology in organisations for business purposes is captured by the phrase Management Information Systems (MIS). One way of thinking about MIS is outward facing (to audience members, supplies, stakeholders) and inward facing (managing people, documents, customer relationships, finance) (Walter 2015). The obvious elements of the former are your website and social media communication processes. The latter are CRM systems, audience and financial performance dashboards, personnel management software. The key to having the right systems, particularly for an S2M company, is to learn from others. For example, a company wanted to design an incident reporting log that linked to their risk management program. A Board member worked for a large organisation that had one. That was too complicated but provided an appropriate framework to enable the small company to create one that suited their purposes but based on sound principles.

We create digital content for promotional and marketing reasons, recording and archival purposes, as part of exhibitions and performance, to create income for the organisation – and because people expect it. We use digital technology to grow new audiences (social media), for audience development (broadcasting online), to increase our ticketing and donor income, to provide audiences the chance to interact with artists, to collaborate more economically, in new commissioned work and to create new work. In 2014, Deloitte reported that buying decisions were based on digital recommendations whether from friends (80%) or strangers (51%). Although that research is now a few years old, I assume that those percentages will have continued to go up. All of these changes have an impact on how people find out about us, communicate with us and experience us.

In talking about Baumol and Bowen's (1996) hypotheses that there is an ever-widening gap between costs and earned revenue in the performing arts because their labour requirements remain the same as they were hundreds of years ago, Throsby (2001, 118) points to ways in which the live performing arts have withstood the pressures imposed by stagnant productivity and of the six strategies that he lists, two[1] are directly linked to technology:

1. Technological change in areas such as venue design, sound and lighting facilities – enabling larger audiences to participate as immediate consumers of live performance
2. Media reproduction technology – more consumption and new revenue sources.

Reproduction technology has been a mixed blessing for many art forms. As people initially pirated and then learned to buy music from the internet, CD sales (and with them, most CD shops) collapsed. There is a growing expectation that performance-based companies will show excerpts of their work on the internet but rights holders, both originators and performers, are still often reluctant to allow this to happen. On a more positive note, musicians can now sell directly to their audience and the arts, having been the poor cousin in terms of mainstream broadcasting, now have access to an increasing number of digital platforms.

MTC's history in filming its own work is an interesting case in point. In the archives, there are a few TV interviews from the 1950s and 1960s and one recording of a play, *Mystery of the Hansom Cab. Summer of the Seventeenth Doll*, was made into a movie but it wasn't based on an MTC production. The *Doll Trilogy*[2] was recorded and played on television in the 1980s but my attempt to turn it in to an Educational DVD failed in the 1990s because Equity, the actors union, wanted more payment up front than could have been justified by likely sales. The next recording and broadcast was of a one-woman show, *Bombshells*, broadcast by ABC TV in the 2000s. Before I left the company in 2012, I made a last-ditch effort to record one of Simon Phillip's productions but failed for two very different reasons. One of the actors said "no" to recording a production and regardless of what everyone else thought, that was the end of the debate. For the second show, there was a brilliant design but in fact it was so strong theatrically that the film producer advised that it would be impossible to film.

And in the meantime, almost every show from the 1990s onwards was recorded for "archival purposes". Which meant that it could only sit in a cupboard, unable to watched by the public under union rules and unwatchable because it was usually a one-camera recording from the back of the theatre. This means that over 600 productions, including 250 new Australian works, exist only in the memories of the audience, in publicity shots and in the costumes hanging in the wardrobe department.

The main constraint for MTC was money. Money to pay for a proper recording. Money to pay the actors and creatives what they wanted.

But equally, there was a sense that theatre is so close to film and TV drama that even a competent recording wouldn't do the art form justice. It's only with the development of digital cameras, mini-microphones and other technological devices that companies such as the National Theatre and the Metropolitan Opera are making good quality filmed versions of plays. But there are still some shockers where the makeup, set and performance style that work on a big stage don't work on screen. On the other side of the coin, more digital technology is making its way onto the stage. Whether it's as part of the set design or the performance intent, artists will always find ways of using new technology to tell old and new stories.

Bianchi (2008, 242–243) offers a fascinating insight into the impact of reproduction technology on time, making it both more productive and more flexible:

1. Durability – improved technology for duplicating, preserving and storying cultural artifacts extends the time horizons to exercise choice and enlarges the menu of available cultural experiences
2. Reproducibility – does the same as (1) but increases accessibility and diffusion of cultural consumption opportunities
3. Modularity in art – we can now create our own digital collections of art, books, music
4. Decomposability – allowing for an active and flexible recombination of cultural goods which in turn allows for an "innovative use of time".

All of which sounds potentially good for the arts. But, of course, the technology of reproduction means that there are many more products competing for our time. And although much technology is time saving, Bianchi also points out that it's more time-consuming. We not only spend more time looking at screens than we used to but we're multitasking and looking at numerous screens. There is a constant source of new substitute products and alternative uses of our time and these are "more readily available and cheaper in terms of time [and so] can easily replace cultural goods that tend to be more complex or novel" (Bianchi 2008, 250).

If technological change is a mixed blessing in attracting audiences, it's also a mixed blessing within individual organisations and sectors of our industry. Think of the impact of video piracy before the introduction of affordable streaming services. Think of the impact of music streaming on how musicians can make a living with more touring and less sales income. Within organisations, we may simply not have enough in-house support of IT or capacity to pay for technological upgrades.

Another challenge is because of the impact of technology on our relationships. There's the belief that the more we're connected electronically, the less we're connected personally. Autry described it well 20 years ago even before the onslaught of social media and emojis:

More good ideas, better understanding and more creativity come from personal contact than from blizzards of email. More is communicated with a smile, frown, shrug, head shake, nod, or wave than from all those cute constructions of smiles and frowns you can devise on the keyboard with punctuation marks.

(Autry 2001, 87)

I've been on the end of teleconferences, telephone interviews, videoconferences and skype conversations and although none of them are as bad as having no meeting, they are usually worse than even a badly run face-to-face meeting. At least in that environment, you can read all the subtlety of the room. However, sometimes there has be a connection across the space and even a teleconference is better than a round robin of emails. I was based in Melbourne for part of my time with the ABC but most of the managers were in Sydney so I was regularly stuck alone in a room with just a loudspeaker phone while people talked over me, around me, often forgetting that I was there. If you're chairing a meeting based on technology, you have to work even harder to make sure that everyone's voice is not only heard but listened to.

The key to the introduction of new technology is to focus on the outcome the technology is set to achieve rather than the technology itself. The iPad was first introduced in 2010 and although I found the idea interesting, I couldn't initially justify either personal or work expenditure on the device. The following year, MTC was in transition with a three-member artistic team creating the 2012 season of plays. Two of the artists were based in Melbourne with one in Sydney. Two were actors performing in different states during the year and all three had directorial roles in different parts of the country as well. The need to easily and effectively communicate via email and skype, to share documents and images both between each other and with me as the CEO was essential – and investing in iPads met all the criteria.

Introducing new technology can suffer from all the challenges of any other change process requiring clear intentions, champions and effective implementation including training. Opinions about technology can vary even within a department with some being eager to take up new systems and others concerned that they will lose control or not be able to deal with the new content. Listening to people's worries is just as important as listening to people's needs. Arts organisations often fall into the same technology trap as many other organisations seeking to create new digital systems and processes from scratch which often results in poor outcomes and cost blowouts. One of the few successes is the Tessitura CRM system, initially developed by the Metropolitan Opera in New York, and now shared by hundreds of owners across the globe in a collaborative non-profit model. Another strategy for successful technology introduction is to have an effective project team using change management techniques that involve end users.

The introduction of new technology is not just about budgets and project teams. It's also about ethics. I'm a baby boomer so I'm not quite as quick as the Xs and Ys and Millennials to take up new technology. And I'm also of the generation which fought hard over privacy issues. In a world of social media, privacy has become somewhat moot. However, it's still an issue in the workplace. For example, in Stone's *Human Resource Management* textbook, he has a section called "Dr HR". One question is "my boss says there's nothing wrong with checking a job applicant's Facebook page. I'm not so sure. What do you think?" (Stone 2013, 104). I still remember the first time that question came up for me. My assistant was putting together all the documents for a group of shortlisted candidates for a job and had done what I had failed to do – an online check. Someone had provided a personal website (pre-the mass adoption of Facebook). I hadn't thought to look at it but she did and was shocked. It contained semi-pornographic photos of the person and various partners. If I hadn't seen it, the person may have got the job because they were personable and had the required skills. But I had seen it and all I could think of was the lack of judgement that it showed to put the internet address on their application. But what if the person doesn't provide the detail – should you go trawling through the internet to see what you can find? The answer from employment headhunters of my acquaintance is an emphatic "yes".

Another ethical issue is around the use of mobile devices and the way this enables us as employers to encroach on people's home life. Are they entitled to overtime if they respond to emails on their iPhone after hours? What happens to work-life balance? People often behave is if they are available 24–7 posting on Facebook or Tumblr or Twitter at all hours. Does this mean that we can expect them to do "digital work" at all hours as well? This a particular issue for arts organisations because dedicated staff often want to donate endless hours to the organisation. And even when they don't, charismatic but not very relational artistic leaders can demand that they do. What if current staff then complain online about their working hours or post images or comments that are inappropriate either in terms of the company or the accepted social niceties of the wider world? Although it will be a work in progress, having policies that cover topics such as social media, out of hours access expectations, use of company technology and respect for others will at least provide a framework in which the impact of ever-changing technology can be managed.

See also: Audiences, Change, Hours, Marketing, Meetings, Policies

References

Autry, J. A. 2001 *The Servant Leader*, New York: Three Rivers Press.

Baumol, W. & Bowen, W. 1966 *Performing Arts, The Economic Dilemma: A Study of Problems Common to Theater, Opera, Music, and Dance*, New York: Twentieth Century Fund.

Bianchi, M. 2008 "Time and Preferences in Cultural Consumption", in Hutter, M. & Throsby, D. (eds) *Beyond Price*, Cambridge: Cambridge University Press, 236–257.

Colbert, F. 2009 *Beyond Branding: Contemporary Marketing Challenges for Arts Organizations*, Geelong: Kenneth Myer Lecture, Deakin University.

Deloitte 2014 *Deloitte Media Consumer Survey 2014 Australia Media Usage and Preferences*, www2.deloitte.com/content/dam/Deloitte/au/Documents/technology-media-telecommunications/deloitte-au-tmt-media-consumer-survey-2014-infographic-031014.png [accessed 11 March 2019].

Gilmore, A. 2011 "Not just CEOs Tweeting: Digital Content, the Arts and the Cultural Politics of Innovation", Antwerp: 11th AIMAC International Conference.

Skringar, E. R. & Stevens, T. 2008 *Driving Change and Developing Organisations* (1st ed), Melbourne: Tilde University Press.

Stone, R. J. 2013 *Managing Human Resources* (4th ed), Milton, QLD: John Wiley & Sons.

Throsby, D. 2001 *Economics and Culture*, Cambridge: Cambridge University Press.

Walter, C. 2015 *Arts Management: An Entrepreneurial Approach*, New York: Routledge.

Trust

Trust is about believing in someone else, believing in the fairness of processes, in believing that what is said will be done. Leadership and organisations depend on trusting relationships for maximum effectiveness (Drucker 1990; Hughes 2005).

Imagine if you're the CEO of an organisation but you don't feel comfortable to leave your door unlocked. Not even the cleaners have a key and so your room just gets more and more dusty. Imagine that you don't feel comfortable having any documents on the company's hard drive. Imagine that you don't have anyone in the organisation you can have an honest conversation with? Can you possibly be happy in such a position? I don't think so. Such behaviour implies a complete breakdown in trust between you and your staff. If I was in such a position, I'd resign. Of course, one keeps *some* documents confidential and under lock and key but that's pragmatism not distrust.

Apart from the obvious statement that one feels safer and happier working with people you trust, trust can deliver a range of positive outcomes for organisations:

- Reduced costs (e.g. less time playing politics and checking up on people)
- More friendly, satisfying and less stressful environment
- Increased motivation and performance
- Reduced turnover
- More effective communication
- Increased creativity when ideas and opinions are openly shared (Covey 1992; Hughes 2005; Stone 2013).

As Corrigan (1999, 102) says: "If staff do not trust you they don't believe you, and if they don't believe you then they cannot be motivated by you, they cannot act on your goals."

There a number of different types of trust. There's trust based on rational calculation, on experience or reputation, and on a sense of connection or similarity (Beugelsdijk & Maseland 2011). There's trust about the organisation, its processes and promises, and the people who are running it. And there's trust about how people are treated and how their needs are met.

Trust can be:

- Perception and interpretation of the other's expected dependability
- The confidence that a partner will not exploit the vulnerabilities of the other
- Expectation of reliability with regard to their obligations
- Predictability in behaviour
- Fairness in actions and negotiations while faced with the possibility to behave opportunistically (Beugelsdijk & Maseland 2011, 183).

Depressingly, Stone (2013, 43) quotes a survey about Australian workers in which most of them have lost faith in their employer and almost half don't believe their company has their best interests at heart. Another survey also found that 80% of Australian employees do not trust information given by their CEOs.

How do you build trust? Shockley-Zalabak and Morreale (2011, 46–47) list five dimensions of organisational trust:

1. Concern for employees – feelings of care, empathy, tolerance and safety
2. Openness and honesty – the amount and accuracy of information and the sincerity and appropriateness of how it's communicated
3. Identification – how connected people feel to the mission of the organisation
4. Reliability – is there congruence between words and action?
5. Competence – is the organisation being managed well enough that it (and my job) survive into the future?

Heenan and Bennis (1999) suggest that if everyone's busy and focused on the task in hand, there's little time for the constant intrigue that breeds mistrust. Adams (2007) says that when people feel that their employer is invested in their well-being, they'll respond with more commitment which demonstrates trust in the organisation. Transformational leadership is seen to lead to trust because the relationship is based on mutual collaboration (Adams 2007). The

authentic leader is also described as a person who can establish trusting relationships (Hughes 2005). A leader's behaviour has to be demonstrably consistent with stated organisational values (Bunting 2016; Caust 2018). The starting points for trust according to De Pree (1997) are truth and respect.

Truth telling however has its challenges. As a leader you can't always tell the truth. What happens if you're exploring various scenarios, one of which might involve staff losing their jobs? When's the right time to tell people? You might be in delicate negotiations with an artist but the rest of team want to know so that they can start work on marketing or costume making. How long should you keep them in the dark? You're about to fire someone. Do you brief your entire management team or just the person most affected? If you have managed to create an organisational culture that is generally open, where people see that your decision-making is usually right for them and the organisation, where people's views are sought and listened to, then in those moments when you have to keep information to yourself, the trust won't be damaged. The key is to be as upfront as possible even if you can't tell the whole story.

Galford and Drapeau (2003) offer a useful collection of other potential enemies to trust which are mainly self-explanatory, such as inconsistent messages and standards, misplaced benevolence, false feedback, failure to trust others, elephants in the room, rumours in a vacuum and consistent corporate underperformance. Misplaced benevolence and false feedback are easy traps to fall into. One doesn't want to be too hard on people but giving good performance reviews when they are not true doesn't help the individual or the organisation. If people see others behaving badly and getting away with it or incompetent people left in place, a sense of cynicism about the organisation, its standards and its values can develop.

The "elephant in the room" image is always one that needs some explaining for non-English speaking readers. It literally means that one can't and shouldn't ignore the big issue that everyone is aware of but that everyone is pretending not to notice. After all, how can you not notice an elephant in a room? This behaviour – ignoring the obvious – can happen particularly when shows aren't selling or the art isn't as good as one hoped or the exhibition didn't get good reviews and, in addition, there'll be an impact on the financial position of the organisation. There is a temptation to keep everyone's spirits high rather than deal with the challenge, but people's trust will be damaged if they can't trust management to deal with the problem.

As for trusting others, I have a long history of believing people until they prove themselves to be untrustworthy or liars. Even though I've been caught out and had some difficult situations to deal with as a result, I prefer to trust rather than not. There's a great quote from Abraham Lincoln: "it's better to trust and be disappointed occasionally than to distrust and be miserable all the time" (quoted in Rosner & Halcrow 2010, 84). It's better to take that view because research shows that our accuracy in deciding whether or not someone can be trusted tends to be "only slightly better than chance" (DeSteno 2014, 113). Apparently, we place too much emphasis on reputation and perceived confidence and don't rely enough on our intuition. Lencioni (2005) talks about the importance of vulnerability-based trust and the importance of building trust by sharing life stories and of phrases such as "I'm wrong", "I'm not sure", "I made a mistake".

You have to:

Trust when you go on holidays.
Trust when you share a secret.
Trust that someone is working hard/well.
Trust that people have the best interests of the organisation at heart.
Trust that they are telling the truth.
Trust that your trust is being returned.

(Lencioni 2005)

Even when you might be trusted as a person for some people, particularly unionised staff, that trust will always be qualified by your role. I remember a constant refrain through the negotiations of my first enterprise agreement at MTC. To paraphrase, it was "You're ok, we trust you, but what about the next person?" As it turned out, I was the only person they had to worry about for the next 18 years and through four agreement negotiations but underlying the line was an implicit lack of trust in "management". And because you are "management", don't be surprised if the things you say – even perfectly innocuous statements – are given deep and sinister meaning. I still remember thanking a director after a preview but hearing later that because I either wasn't effusive enough or detailed enough, they took it to mean that I hated the show. Needless to say, this wasn't the case – I just thought it was appropriate to make a brief comment and get out of their way so they could go and talk to their actors.

Another barrier to trust that is missing from Galford and Depeau's (2003) list is fairness. Organisations need processes to ensure people are treated fairly. For example, is your salary review process transparent? Do only the unionised staff get a pay increase? Do you only enquire about child care needs with women in your selection interviews? Are jobs advertised internally as well as externally?

In summary, you can't demand trust. You can only work to deserve it. Thomas (2008, 54–55) provides a list of "don'ts" that can undermine credibility and therefore trust:

- Don't renege on a promise of support
- Don't leave the door open by being vague
- Don't make open-ended promises
- Don't say you'll do something unless you will
- Don't assume you will remember to do something
- Don't betray a confidence
- Don't make decisions based on what you would personally like to do.

And to this list one could also add "Don't micromanage", the classic example of a lack of trust.

I've heard stories of co-leaders who don't talk to each other. Of Boards that meet without their executive and without reporting back. Of leaders who actively encourage competition (and by definition, secrets) between members of their management team. Of managers who lock themselves away in their office or even another building. I have no desire to work in such environments. Working with people who don't trust you is nearly as exhausting as working with people you don't trust. They're never open about their needs or about their mistakes and so you end up proving their point that people can't be trusted and fail to trust them.

One of the most challenging of times to trust someone is when circumstances might not be in your favour or where you don't have enough evidence to justify trust. Reid (2013, 105) discusses this "emotional or affect-based trust" in relation to a co-leadership case study in a Canadian Theatre Company. She compares it to "cognitive-based trust" which requires regular proof for one partner to trust another. Sometimes you do have to take a deep breath and trust even when there isn't evidence to prove that your trust will be returned.

The main aspects of one's behaviour and character that are seen to be indicative of trust are benevolence, competence and honesty (Hughes 2005). However, Covey (1992) says that competence is required as well as good character. Even if you have faith in my character, if I'm not competent as a manager or a leader then you're still not going to trust me.

What you want is a workplace where people trust each other so that communication is clear, empathy is possible, productive interdependence works and creativity occurs. And equally you want a workplace where people trust management to provide fair employment processes, to be honest about the state of the company and to create an environment where respect and honesty are active values.

In a 2018 survey about financial firms, Milliken, Alstein and Sun said: "Trust is not a campaign, it demands sustained effort" (2018, 7). Although banking may seem worlds away from that of arts companies, that insight into trust is worth noting. Building trust between you

as a leader and your staff, your stakeholders, your audience isn't a one-off event. It requires continuing to act in a way where your promises are kept and that your values are lived.

See also: Co-leadership, Leadership, People, Values

References

Adams, J. 2007 *Managing People in Organizations: Contemporary Theory and Practice*, Basingstoke: Palgrave Macmillan.

Beugelsdijk, S. & Maseland, R. 2011 *Culture in Economics*, Cambridge: Cambridge University Press.

Bunting, M. 2016 *The Mindful Leader*, Milton, QLD: Wiley.

Caust, J. 2018 *Arts Leadership in Contemporary Contexts*, London: Routledge.

Corrigan, P. 1999 *Shakespeare on Management*, London: Kogan Page.

Covey, S. R. 1992 *Principle-Centred Leadership*, London: Pocket Books.

De Pree, M. 1997 *Leading Without Power*, Holland, MI: Shepherd Foundation.

DeSteno, D. 2014 "Who Can You Trust?" *Harvard Business Review*, 92(3), 112–115.

Drucker, P. F. 1990 *Managing the Nonprofit Organization*, New York: HarperCollins.

Galford, R. & Drapeau, S. A. 2003 "The Enemies of Trust", *Harvard Business Review*, 81(2), 88–95.

Heenan, D. A. & Bennis, D. 1999 *Co-Leaders: The Power of Great Partnerships*, New York: John Wiley & Sons.

Hughes, L. W. 2005 "Developing Transparent Relationships Through Humour in the Authentic Leader-follower Relationship", *Authentic Leadership Theory and Practice: Origins, Effects and Development, Monographs in Leadership and Management*, 3, 83–106.

Lencioni, P. 2005 *The Five Dysfunctions of a Team: A Field Guide to Managers, Leaders and Facilitators*, San Francisco, CA: Jossey-Bass.

Milliken, B., Alstein T. & Sun, S. 2018 *Restoring Trust in Financial Services in the Digital Era*, Melbourne: Deloitte Consulting.

Reid, W. 2013 "Dual Executive Leadership in the Arts", in Caust, J. (ed.) *Arts Leadership: Internal Case Studies*, Melbourne: Tilde University Press, 98–111.

Rosner, B. & Halcrow, A. 2010 *The Boss's Survival Guide* (2nd ed), New York McGraw Hill.

Shockley-Zalabak, P. & Morreale, S. 2011 "Communication and the High Trust Organization", in Gillis, T. L. (ed.) *The IABC Handbook of Organizational Communication* (2nd ed), San Francisco, CA: Jossey-Bass, 41–53.

Stone, R. J. 2013 *Managing Human Resources* (4th ed), Milton, QLD: John Wiley & Sons.

Thomas, M. T. 2008 *Leadership in the Arts: An Inside View*, Bloomington, IN: AuthorHouse.

Turnover

Do you really know why someone is leaving your organisation? Do you really want them to leave? If someone is leaving because of a better opportunity, you just have to grin and bear it. If someone is leaving for better pay, then unless you can match it you have to let them go. If someone is leaving because they hate their boss or don't like their workmates, that's probably a good thing because they'll be unhappy and probably unproductive at work – unless the manager is poor and the workmates are bullies, in which case you have to solve that problem. Whatever the reason, make sure you know why people are going.

People's decision to leave an organisation will depend on their level of commitment, which may change over time (Meyer & Allen 1997). If someone has been given training opportunities or the chance to learn new skills or act in a more senior position, then they may have feelings of obligation to the organisation and the manager that provided those chances. If people are embedded in the social fabric of the company, then they are likely to have an emotional attachment which will be hard to break. If someone feels that they are heard in the organisation, that their voice is valued and that they can impact on the way things are done, their job satisfaction is likely to increase with a corresponding decrease in the desire to quit.

Of course, a lack of all these aspects in an organisation's culture can lead to problematic turnover and that costs an organisation time and money to find replacement staff. In 2017, there were a series of media articles about the reasons behind high turnover at Queensland Symphony Orchestra (Gill 2017a; Gill 2017b; Wanchap & Litson 2017). Twenty-seven people had left over 21 months out of a staff of 37. Anonymous staff and ex-staff claimed the high turnover was because of a "toxic culture". The Chairman explained turnover as a natural result of both a new leadership team and people not successfully completing their probation. Regardless of who was right, that amount of turnover requires detailed analysis to find out the reasons why.

Evidence about the impact of pay on job satisfaction and turnover isn't quite so clear as one might expect. For example, Bryson, Cappellari and Lucifora (2004) concluded their study by saying that unlike previous research results, employee compensation was largely unimportant. The most important practice they discovered in reducing turnover was the use of flexible working time arrangements. However, because the arts usually pay comparatively poorly, people do leave because of financial issues. Often they leave reluctantly but when a larger arts organisation or non-profit offers a 20% or 30% salary increase or a corporation offers an 80% or 100% increase then loyalty will rightly give way to pragmatism.

Sometimes people won't leave because the emotional costs of leaving friends and a safe, understood workplace and going into the unknown are hard to calculate. Other times, people won't leave because they have such specialist skills that it would be hard to find a comparable job in the same city. In a review of the MTC staff lists from 1993 to 2019, it's interesting to see that six names out of an original list of 63 were still there. All of these people worked in craft areas such as costume or set making. If one wants to have a full-time secure job making costumes or props, there aren't many opportunities even in city the size of Melbourne.[3]

I have often wondered why some people stay in organisations when it is clear that there isn't a good job fit or where relationships aren't positive or even when someone is under a performance review that is unlikely to have a positive outcome. One would imagine that unless the person is failing to read all the negative signs, the main reason for not leaving is the cost – including the fear – of change. If it's going to be a better outcome for the organisation if the person leaves, then it may be worth investing in their leaving through actions such as paying for career counselling and offering higher than standard termination pay in order to reduce that sense of "cost".

The best way to understand turnover is to ask. An exit interview is good because you'll learn how the company, its policies, its culture and its staff are perceived. Not everyone will tell you the truth but it's better to try and find out than to simply give a farewell speech and wave them out the door.

See also: Hiring, Job Satisfaction, Motivation, Pay, People

References

Bryson, A., Cappellari, L. & Lucifora, C. 2004 "Does Union Membership Really Reduce Job Satisfaction?" *British Journal of Industrial Relations*, 42(3), 439–459.

Gill, R. 2017a "Queensland Symphony Staff Churn Prompts Claims of a 'Toxic' Work Culture", *Daily Review*, 15 November, https://dailyreview.com.au/queensland-symphony-staff-churn-prompts-claims-toxic-work-culture/68193/ [accessed 11 March 2019].

Gill, R. 2017b "QSO Chair and Musicians Say Everything is Fine", *Daily Review*, 17 November, https://dailyreview.com.au/qso-chair-orchestra-say-everything-fine-brisbane/68279/ [accessed 11 March 2019].

Meyer, J. W. & Allen, N. J. 1997 *Commitment in the Workplace: Theory, Research and Application*, London: Sage.

Wanchap, G. & Litson, J. 2017 "QSO Chairman Responds to Claims of Low Morale", *Limelight*, 17 November, www.limelightmagazine.com.au/news/qso-chairman-responds-claims-low-morale/ [accessed 11 March 2019].

Notes

1 The others are performing with simpler sets and smaller casts, use of voluntary labour, rising consumer income leading to some increase in demand, increasing unearned income such as sponsorship.

2 *Kid Stakes*, *Other Times*, *Summer of the Seventeenth Doll* by Ray Lawler.

3 $5 million in 2018.

U

Uncertainty

The challenge of management education according to Dehler, Welsh and Lewis (2004, 182) is "to prepare future managers for complexity, uncertainty, equivocality and value conflicts". Writers often use "complexity" and "uncertainty" in the same phrase but the reason I've chosen to write about both under the latter heading is because, somehow, "complexity" is simply part of day-to-day living in the 21st century but "uncertainty" is a more scary state to be in. Unlike some elements of the manager's role which can be taught (e.g. communication, planning), developing a tolerance for complexity, uncertainty and simply not knowing the answer all of the time, is what Leicester (2007, 3) calls an existential condition – developed through experience.

Godfrey (2010) has written about working with uncertainty in the arts and quotes the work of Stacey (1996) in talking about the "edge of chaos". This is what sits on a continuum between having lots of certainty about the world and agreement about what to do next and having neither of either. Somewhere in the middle is an environment with some chaos (but not too much), some room for risk taking and experimentation, a place of mess and muddle but also a place of creativity.

Management definitions usually contain the word "control" in them but it's probably a myth to help us get over the anxiety of being uncertain in a world of complexity. One way to resolve that anxiety is to network with peers, find a coach or a mentor, or simply have a good circle of friends to talk things through. It doesn't matter whether they work in the arts or not because a lot of the uncertainty is about management issues that can occur in any organisation such as dealing with difficult people. Corrigan (1999) says that a good manager lives with anxiety and continues to act whereas a poor manager either finds the challenge so debilitating that they don't do anything or forgets that they can't control the world and act as if they do.

Another way to deal with uncertainty is a willingness to take informed risks. By definition a risk is a risk but it may be one that's based on research or experience (yours or someone else's). To give a small example, at one point in the development of a year's season of plays at Melbourne Theatre Company we reached the point where the brochure had to go to the publisher but we still hadn't obtained the rights to one play. We could have simply reduced the season by one play and lost the subscription income that made putting on new plays possible. We could have left it in the brochure, gone to print but run the risk of discarding tens of thousands of brochures if the rights didn't come through. Instead, I remembered seeing the subscription brochure of a US theatre company where they advertised a "mystery" play. I don't know whether they were facing the same problem as MTC but I loved the idea of turning the unknown into a positive. We made the unnamed play into a bold adventure in the brochure. And although it was the worst-selling show on subscription, over 10,000 people paid money in advance to see a play about which they knew absolutely nothing.

In her case study on the Druid Theatre in Ireland, Fitzgibbon (2001, 175) describes their strategy for dealing with uncertainty. Rather than depend on structures and mechanisms, the company depended on its capacity to be fluid and to adapt "keeping its compass fixed firmly on its overall vision". Another strategy for dealing with uncertainty is to simply accept that things can't be known in advance. An organisation I know that is for young people and run by young people accepts the fact that because of their youth, they have limited knowledge and experience but a great capacity to learn. Therefore, every strategic decision is one that starts with uncertainty and is worked through with contributions and iterations until finally a decision is reached that feels right. Interestingly, this approach is the opposite of what Corrigan (1999) proposes – that organisations uncertain about their environment need stronger guidance and leadership than those that operate in an atmosphere of certainty. But perhaps that's simply because he was writing 20 years ago and uncertainty has increased in the private, public and non-profit spheres and people have had to find more creative ways of dealing with it.

In Leicester's (2007) article about dealing with uncertainty and complexity, he describes the distinctions between the different spheres for managers. In the private sector, the tensions were between the short and long term with strains on personal loyalty in a fiercely competitive market. In the public sector, the challenges were in coordination between agencies, managing scarce resources and keeping up with the endless new ideas from politicians. And in the arts, it was the "sheer challenge of making ends meet – managing the basics while trying to support creative innovation" (11). His research is based on using a public health consultant and a psychotherapist to shadow a number of CEOs to see how they managed in this uncertain world. Their conclusion was that the CEOs had "to cope with long days, little predictability in their lives, disconnection and fragmentation of their teams in a global working environment, short term concerns crowding out long term ones" (11).

Given this description, perhaps Cleveland (2002, 8) is right in the view that leaders need "a mindset that crises are normal, tensions can be promising, and complexity is fun". Godfrey (2010), who has worked as a venue manager, arts consultant and teacher and has worked helping people in the arts to deal with uncertainty, offers these five thoughts:

1. Pay attention to relationships
2. Learn to have conversations
3. Ask more questions
4. Pay attention to beginnings – and she means both the beginning of the process but also the state that you are in at the beginning
5. Get out of your own way – in other words, don't always use learnt rational, linear approaches to problem solving.

Dehler, Welsh and Lewis (2004) recommend that we need to develop different frameworks to deal with uncertainty and complexity – learning to see the world from other perspectives, to look beyond the professional and intellectual world in which we're most comfortable. This doesn't have to be scary. It just means developing a skill that John Keats, the English poet, described and what the authors of my favourite books on what happens in our organisation, *The Stupidity Paradox* (Alvesson & Spicer 2016b), call "negative capability": "Writing to his brother, Keats described negative capability as the ability to be in 'uncertainties, mysteries, doubts, without any irritable reaching after fact and reason'." In other words, developing the capacity to deal with uncertainty and in the process, allowing new ideas and perceptions to emerge.

For Keats this meant being able to experience, and recognise experiences, and "remain open to the world … [meaning] the ability to face up to uncertainty, paradoxes and ambiguities … and so to allow for 'the emergence of new thoughts or perceptions'".[1]

A number of years ago, I was having a collegial drink with a number of fellow arts managers, all of them woman on that particular day. We were sharing wisdom about how to deal with the complex and uncertain environment in which we all operated and, in the process, discovered that we all had low blood pressure. Not necessarily at that exact time, but in general. I had a sudden vision of why I enjoyed working in the stretching and challenging mad world of the arts: it actually gets me out of bed and gets my blood pressure up to normal. In other words, if you're not comfortable with tension and challenges, complexity and uncertainty, this may not be the right job for you.

See also: Decision-making, Knowledge, Learning, Management, Risk, You

References

Alvesson, M. & Spicer, A. 2016a *The Stupidity Paradox*, London: Profile Books.

Alvesson, M. & Spicer, A. 2016b "Why Smart People Buy into Stupid Ideas: The Stupidity Paradox", *Australian Financial Review*, 17 June, www.afr.com/leadership/why-smart-people-buy-into-stupid-ideas-20160613-gpi56s [accessed 16 March 2019].

Cleveland, H. 2002 *Nobody in Charge: Essays on the Future of Leadership*, Hoboken, NJ: Wiley.

Corrigan, P. 1999 *Shakespeare on Management*, London: Kogan Page.

Dehler, G. E., Welsh M. A. & Lewis, M. W. 2004 "Critical Pedagogy in the 'New Paradigm'", in Grey, C. & Antonacopoulou, E. (eds) *In Essential Readings in Management Learning*, London: Sage Publications, 167–186.

Fitzgibbon, M. 2001 *Managing Innovation in the Arts*, Westport, CT: Quorum Books.

Godfrey, C. 2010 "Working with Uncertainty", in Kay, S. & Venner, K. (eds) *A Cultural Leader's Handbook*, London: Creative Choices, 78–85.

Leicester, G. 2007 *Rising to the Occasion*, International Futures Forum, March.

Stacey, R. 1996, *Complexity and Creativity in Organisations*, San Francisco, CA: Berrett-Keohler.

Unions

Trade unions were formed to provide a collective voice for employees. By banding together and acting as a monopoly, wage earners could combat the power of employers and seek to improve pay and working conditions. By having a union to represent them in the workplace, people could express their grievances safely without the threat of being fired or otherwise punished (Bray, Waring & Cooper 2009). In an article on trade unions in the performing arts in the USA, Moskow (1970) points to a range of reasons for high unionisation from the 1900s:

1. Exploitation by managers and booking agents with shows being cancelled and people not receiving their pay
2. The casual nature of the workforce with people being forced to compete on pay rates and with little incentive for employers to offer benefits such as benefits and welfare plans.

In this scenario, the union played the role of hiring agent, controlling the labour market and offering employers a ready pool of skilled workers. For many years in countries like Australia, the UK and the USA, unions such as Equity, representing actors, worked as a monopoly provider. If you didn't have a union card, you couldn't get employment and so supply was limited; as a result, competition for jobs reduced. In an industry that has always had an oversupply of people wanting to be actors, this created more chance of employment for union members. Unions were also able to negotiate on conditions such as pay, hours of work, travel allowances and other employment benefits.

It's not that performers and technical staff are completely powerless. As Moskow says (1970), a play can't be put on without actors and stagehands and this gives them some power. This is the reason why there was such a union backlash about the use of recorded music on Broadway because suddenly a musical could go on without musicians. But it's a power that many artists have been reluctant to use with threats made more often than enacted.

Unionisation varies from country to country, job to job and workplace to workplace. Musicians, actors, dancers and technical staff tend to have a long history of unionisation in western countries but many performers in small companies may not be union members. Directors and designers will be unionised in some countries and not others. Administration staff, often including managers, are likely to be unionised in government and semi-government organisations but not in non-profit or for-profit companies. Artists and writers usually don't belong to a union but may have a guild or agents to support them. Whatever the pattern, there was been a decline in union membership in Australia. In 1961 membership was at its peak of 61% dropping to 14% in 2016 (Gilfillan & McCann 2018). Union membership in the Australian arts and recreational services are even lower than general union membership with a halving of membership from 17.1% in 2000 to 8.5% in 2016. Cultural unionism in the USA has also been decreasing, although whether it's in parallel with general union patterns (down below 12% by 2011) is unclear (Shane 2013).

Reasons for this decline include the shift from manufacturing to service industries, increasing casualisation of the workforce, the privatisation of government services, macro-economic factors such as unemployment and price levels, decreasing protection of unions by governments and employees either no longer believing that collective action was worth the cost or more people free riding (getting the benefits of union action without paying for membership). There are now many people who have never even been exposed to a union (Balnave et al. (2009). Another reason offered is that young people have less loyalty to employers and are more likely to move if they are unhappy with employment rather than stay and battle it out with the help of unions (Balnave et al. 2009). However, Teicher and Bryan (2013) point out that even so, unions remain one of the largest organised social groupings in Australia and this probably remains true in many other industrialised countries (although less so in the USA). They also put this shift into an interesting conceptual context which they call the "financialisation" of daily life. They argue that "individuals are increasingly being required to treat themselves (and their families) as if they are financial units (or enterprises)

to be risk-managed" (269). Critical changes that account for this include the growing casualisation of employment and the contracting out of jobs through the gig economy, which has a negative impact on unions (98).

People join or don't join unions because of the economic benefits unions provide, their feelings toward unions, the employer's response to unions and information (or lack of) about unions. (Balnave et al. 2009). "Star" actors gain little benefit from union membership because they can always negotiate good conditions, but traditionally they remain members to support the union because of the "sense of family" that exists in this industry (Moskow 1970). Even in a world of decreasing membership, research in Australia proved that at least 36% of employees would prefer to have a union presence – even though membership was only half of that figure (Teicher & Bryan 2013, 271). Feelings about unions can be influenced by the media, family history, union actions such as occasional unethical behaviour, and government policies. Employers' response to unions can vary from the positive to the extremely negative.

The impact of unions on workplaces depends on what position you take but one should start with the evidence before considering the politics. Pyman et al. (2013) say that research shows that unionisation reduces quit rates and turnover but that union membership has a negative impact on the workplace. For example:

- Employees with lower job satisfaction are more likely to join a union to improve their terms and conditions and stay rather than look for a new employer
- Unionised workers are more likely to be dissatisfied because unions raise awareness of management inadequacies, resulting in more negative evaluations of the workplace which impacts on job satisfaction
- Unions encourage people to voice dissatisfaction rather than quitting and their attitudes may impact on other workers (123–124).

Australian statistics show that union members earn on average 15% more than non-members (Balnave et al. 2009, 131) but in industries covered by industrial awards, there is a free rider phenomenon by which non-union members also benefit from improved wages and conditions negotiated by unions. Apart from this cost impost, another impact on employers is that people may receive a pay increase but without any improvement in productively. In every union negotiation I ever participated in, people weren't prepared to trade any conditions but still wanted pay increases. Any changes in productivity such as the introduction of new technology and improved people management processes were implemented outside of the negotiating process and the resulting written agreements. A final perceived negative for employers is that unions curtail management prerogative but as I have commented in the *Industrial Relations* section, just as many restrictions on our "prerogatives" come from government legislation on employee relations.

Many employers see trade unions as an irritation, "an unnecessarily outside presence in the workplace … a barrier to direct communication with their employees" (Balnave et al. 2009, 127). My position on trade unions has been informed by studying and teaching industrial relations, including the history of workers' movements. So in principle, I'm both supportive of the union movement generally and people's desire to join unions. I have always allowed unions' site access, paid for staff to attend union training sessions, enabled direct deduction of union dues and provided facilities for meetings. However, none of this will guarantee a positive relationship with union representatives because ultimately you are "management". And none of this will guarantee that the positive relationship you have with staff on a day-to-day basis won't turn into something else altogether during union negotiations.

I first learned the lesson about being "management" when I worked at the Australian Broadcasting Corporation. Although I was a member of the union, when it came to strike action I had to choose a side. The first time, I was protected by my manager who simply directed me to stay away for the day. This meant that I didn't have to cross the picket line. But, ultimately, I had to take a management role, provide replacement broadcasts during the strike and walk through a crowd of staff waving banners and placards. The strikes during that time were about money, conditions and redundancies and, ultimately, I didn't think that management was in the wrong. The demonstrations should have been in front of Federal Parliament where the reduced funding for the organisation had been decided.

In order to attract members in these days when union membership is no longer compulsory, unions seem to need to create a "battle" with management over wages and conditions. Union representatives traditionally need to show that they are aligned with their constituents and be seen to push hard to achieve goals. That can turn into uncomfortable demonstrations of opposition and anger (Bolman & Deal 2013). Perhaps there are managers in the not-for-profit world that want to underpay their staff. Perhaps there are organisations where working conditions could and should be improved at a reasonable cost. Perhaps there are managers who spend extravagantly on themselves and not their staff. But most of the time, I think that unions waste their energy "fighting" non-profit arts organisations. The outcome can never be more than the organisation's capacity to pay. And after the negotiations are over, as the manager you have to rebuild the relationship with staff who have seen you in a negative light through the process – negative because the union implies that you are holding out or even lying and negative because you seem to be saying "no" to everything that's important to staff.

Simon Burke, then Australian Equity President, said that the most important thing in dealing with producers and other stakeholders was "mutual respect" (Groves 2014). While I would like to agree with him that all parties should show such respect in their negotiations, I've been on the other side of the fence. I've been yelled at, called a liar, had staff told that I wasn't to be trusted and accused of falsifying information. In fact, apart from a couple of really horrible bosses, my worst work experiences have been during union negotiations. This is deeply depressing for someone who has actively supported people's membership of trade unions. I still absolutely believe in them. I just don't like the experience of being seen as the enemy all the time.

I believe in unions because employees don't have as much power as employers. Actors, for example, are vulnerable to exploitation because they are so desperate to ply their craft that they will do it for next to nothing. Witness the number of co-ops where all that artists make financially is a share of a usually very modest box office. There are lots of people who are desperate to get on stage and so the power technically lies on the demand side. Therefore, unions and agents provide a reasonable counter balance to employers. However, managers of non-profit arts organisations[2] are an unlikely source of greed. Savings on salaries don't go to a bottom line to be given to unknown shareholders. If there is a surplus from a year's activities, it's going to shore up the future of the company – and therefore the future employment of other artists. Thus, negotiating openly and honestly is likely to result in a better outcome than defining managers as the devil incarnate and yelling at them.

My most problematic industrial relations have been with musicians who tend not to have agents, who work in small teams and, in the case of musicals, usually work unnoticed behind or under the action. Every individual grievance turns into a collective one. Every time that happened, people would tell me privately that they didn't agree with the complaint or the threat but the practice was a collective one. These artists felt literally on the edge and less connected with the company than the actors. They'd started rehearsals later, hadn't been exposed to the welcome/we love you moments, and weren't as integrated into the show or the company as much as the other artists, and so they needed more delicate management.

However, there were times when even I would support raised union voices, particular in

the face of a powerful employer and anti-union governments. The dispute about filming *The Hobbit* in New Zealand must make it into a book someday but, in summary, Actors Equity sought to collectively bargain and in response Warner Brothers and the New Zealand Government spun a narrative that, by doing this, the movie would be made elsewhere and other people in the film industry would lose work thus dividing the workforce and keeping the film industry non-union (Kelly 2012).

Balnave et al. (2009, 168) say: "Workers are more motivated to help the organisation become productive and efficient when they regard the work environment as fair and satisfying and when they believe a cooperative relationship exists between management and the unions." For each moment when I left a negotiating room frustrated and angry, I took a deep breath and prepared to return to the table in a positive frame of mind. One simply has to accept that sometimes, employees feel they need support in expressing their "voice" in the workplace and unions help them do it. An example of where the Media Entertainment and Arts Alliance (MEAA) in Australia has been strong in recent times has been around issues of sexual harassment and discrimination. Their work on behalf of their members and in collaboration with employers' associations has led to improvements in the working lives of their members.

If you have a non-union workforce, it's still worth remember that no matter how caring the management and how committed the workers, there is still a power imbalance between the manager and employee in moments of conflict. In such situations, even when staff are not unionised it's worth offering them the chance to meet and discuss changes and challenges in groups and the opportunity to bring a friend or support person if meetings concern serious issues such as performance and the person's future. If you have a unionised workforce, you have to find ways to deal respectfully with the union at the same time that you don't let them create a wedge between you and your staff.

See also: Harassment, Industrial Relations, People

References

Balnave, N., Brown J., Maconachie, G. & Stone, R. J. 2009 *Employment Relations in Australia* (2nd ed), Milton, QLD: John Wiley & Sons.

Bolman, L. G. & Deal, T. E. 2013 *Reframing Organizations* (5th ed), San Francisco, CA: Jossey-Bass.

Bray, M., Waring, P. & Cooper, R. 2009 *Employment Relations*, Sydney: McGraw Hill.

Gillfillan, G. & McCann, C. 2018 *Trends in Union Membership in Australia,* Canberra: Parliament of Australia, www.aph.gov.au/About_Parliament/ Parliamentary_Departments/Parliamentary_ Library/pubs/rp/rp1819/UnionMembership [accessed 11 March 2019].

Groves, D. 2014 "Veteran Actor Quits Equity Committee", *if.com.au*, http://if.com.au/2014/ 06/26/article/Veteran-actor-quits-Equity-committee/TKXBFNUWBE.html [accessed 11 March 2019].

Kelly, H. 2012 "How the Hobbit Dispute Was Said to Justify Curbs to the Actors' Union", *The Guardian*, www.theguardian.com/commentisfree/2012/ nov/30/hobbit-actor-union-dispute [accessed 11 March 2019].

Moskow, M. H. 1970 "Trade Unions in the Performing Arts", *Monthly Labor Review*, 93(3), 16–20.

Pyman, A., Holland, P., Teicher, J. & Cooper, B. 2013 "The Dynamics of Employee Voice in Australia", in Teicher, J., Holland, P. & Gough, R. (eds) *Australian Workplace Relations*, Cambridge: Cambridge University Press, 118–136.

Shane, R. 2013 "Resurgence or Deterioration? The State of Cultural Unions in the 21st Century", *The Journal of Arts Management, Law, and Society*, 43, 139–152.

Teicher, J. & Bryan, D. 2013 "Globalisation, Economic Policy and the Labour Market", in Teicher, J., Holland, P. & Gough, R. 2006 *Employee Relations Management* (2nd ed), Sydney: Pearson Education Australia, 11–25.

Teicher, J., Holland, P. & Gough, R. 2006 *Employee Relations Management* (2nd ed), Sydney: Pearson Education Australia.

Tilley, D. 2014 "Moving Sue McCreadie", *Arts Hub*, http://screen.artshub.com.au/news-article/ news/television/meaa-moving-sue-mccreadie-244470?utm_source=ArtsHub+Australia&utm_ campaign=aa98b581ad-UA-828966-1&utm_ medium=email&utm_term=0_2a8ea75e81-aa98b581ad-303971961 [accessed 11 March 2019].

Upward Management

Unless you own your own company or are the Board Chair, there's always going to be someone with authority over you. Understanding how they work will help you do your job better because your relationship with them is one of "mutual dependence between two fallible human beings" (Gabarro & Kotter 2005, 94). It's also a relationship that has to be negotiated efficiently because whether it's a part-time volunteer Board Chair or a CEO with a number of other direct reports, their time and energy for you is limited.

Hill and Lineback (2013, 4) explain why one might have an uneasy relationship with one's boss. First, "a boss plays conflicting roles: supporter and evaluator, which can create confusion" and second, because you bring your past experience with a different boss into the new relationship. They offer some ideas about what you can do to make yourself indispensable to your boss and the organisation such as collaborating with others, putting up your hand to do new/extra tasks, driving your own growth, being positive even in the tough times, ensuring that you're meeting expectations in terms of results and providing relevant information, support and loyalty. Their best piece of advice is that you need to understand your boss's strengths and weaknesses, preferences and foibles. How do they like to work? How do they like to receive information? How do they make decisions? Does your Chair need briefing before the Board meeting or do they just wing it? Does the CEO love or hate meetings? Hudson (2009) suggests that you also need to understand the broader context in which they are working and to find ways of using their skills to help you with your tasks. Your leader is going to expect what you expect from your staff: collaboration and initiative, being proactive and offering solutions to problems. Bossidy (2007) also recommends the importance of staying current and continuing to learn.

Gabarro and Kotter (2005, 96) tell an interesting story of a change in CEOs from one who was informal to the next one who worked best with written reports, formal meetings and set agendas. Instead of just continuing to work in the same way, an astute subordinate worked with the new CEO to identify the kinds and frequency of information and reports that they wanted. The authors quote Peter Drucker who divided bosses into "listeners" and "readers". "Some bosses like to get information in report form so they can read and study it. Others work better with information and reports presented in person so they can ask questions" (98). By working out the most appropriate communication processes to use with your boss, you'll also be working out the best way to use their time and resources. And it's not just what they need to know but how they need to know it. I learnt this the hard way – by being screamed at. The CEO of the ABC at the time I worked there was known as a screamer but because I was in middle management, I wasn't exposed to this behaviour very often. But for a particular period, I was acting as the equivalent of his Chief of Staff and saw him in action. Part of my role was to be up very early, and scan every newspaper in the country for articles about the ABC and put together a media pack which was the first thing the CEO looked at when he came into the office. You have to remember this was the early 1990s so before the joys of digital media.

I was acting in the position after the Easter break and even with extra papers to look at, there were very slim pickings as most journalists seemed to have gone on holiday. While there were lots of minor mentions of the ABC, the top story in my view was that an ABC music recording has just won an international award. That was my pick for the front of the media pack which I popped on his desk. Half an hour later he arrived and within seconds was bellowing for me. Red-faced, he screeched at me that he didn't give a stuff about ABC Records, that he didn't care that they'd won an award, that he didn't want to waste his time on good stories, he only wanted to be prepared for the bad. So for the rest of those weeks, I just searched out bad stories for him. I always included the good so that other people who saw the information pack

after him would find reasons to be proud of the organisation but that wasn't his need.

Another story that illustrates the point is when my Finance Director came in one day and said "the Chairman hates me". I said, "don't be ridiculous. I know that he values your expertise and your contribution to the company turn-around." "But," she said, "he's always interrupting me and talking over me at Board meetings. He doesn't seem to want to listen to what I have to say." I was pondering this dilemma when I came across an article about research on the differences in how men and women communicate in the workforce. The writer's conclusion was that when asked a question, men will give an answer. If the answer's acceptable, the conversation moves on to the next topic. If the answer needs more context, the man will be asked for it to be explained. When a woman is asked a question, she'll provide the information about what led to her answer and then give the answer. And I realised that this is what was happening – both were fulfilling the gender communication stereotypes. The Chairman *did* trust the Finance Director. When he asked a question, he wanted the answer, not the detail. And she was providing all the detail before the answer. I gave her the article to read, we discussed it and decided we'd try a different communication approach. And it worked. If he wanted more information he'd ask for it. And trust was restored.

There's no guarantee that you will always have a good manager or a good leader. Adirondack (2005) has a great approach to management in the non-profit sector. She talks about "good enough management" and provides a range of advice on dealing with "not-yet-good enough management". It may be incompetent management. But it can also be about lack of direction from the Board, or poor processes such as badly run meetings, or unclear objectives or expectations, or lack of good financial management. You can help provide advice and ideas to improve these scenarios even when you're not the boss.

One of the regular whinges from students is about bosses who micromanage them. I'm lucky enough to have avoided such a relationship (to date) so for their sake, I went looking for some advice. Gallo (2013b) provides some useful strategies. The starting point is that it's more likely to be about your bosses' insecurities than it is about your competence. And some micro-management might be good for you. You may simply have a manager with very high standards who pays a great deal of attention to detail. While they are exerting a degree of control, you can probably learn from them.

However, what students are generally talking about are the bosses who give you little independence, are obsessive about what you're doing every minute of the day, don't let you make decisions and seem incapable of focusing on the bigger picture. Gallo's (2013b) advice is not to fight it but rather to try and understand what's behind it – is it fear of failure, pressure, company culture, the only way they know how to be a boss? Understanding will help sort out which strategy is best to use to deal with it, including trying to earn your boss's trust, making upfront agreements about their level of involvement in your work and providing regular and detailed updates about your progress.

The other boss that regularly gets a mention is the one that's simply incompetent – whether it's because they can't make a decision or because they play politics (or computer games) instead of doing work, or because they are focused on their career rather than on helping you. Gallo (2013a) also offers insight on how to deal with this problem. Once again, it's about trying to understand what causes it, asking others for help, finding creative ways of collaborating with them and stepping up and taking on responsibilities and decisions if they can't or won't. Her final point is the most important – take care of yourself. If you find yourself with a manager that isn't good enough, you can and should take it up with someone higher up, formally or informally, if that's possible. As Adirondack (2005) suggests, you can do it in the spirit of asking for advice and guidance rather than complaining.

But what if you feel that the relationship is all one way? Management is not just "not yet good enough" but actually bad. You're doing their work for them; they take all your ideas and don't give you credit; you can't trust them; they can't make a decision – or make bad decisions. You may decide to stay on and put up with a poor relationship because you love the organisation and hope that they will leave soon. But it's important to remember that you won't be able to make significant differences in how they think or operate (Hill & Lineback 2013). So you may have to do what I've done in the past and decide that working for such people is ultimately so demeaning and disappointing that it's not worth staying. It's traumatic and scary to leave but it's better than working for a bad manager even in a good company.

See also: Boards, Management

References

Adirondack, S. 2005 *Just About Managing?* (4th ed), London: London Voluntary Service Council.

Bossidy, L. 2007 "What Your Leader Expects from You – And What You Should Expect in Return", *Harvard Business Review*, April, 58–65.

Gabarro, J. J. & Kotter, J. P. 2005 "Managing Your Boss", *Harvard Business Review*, 83, 92–99.

Gallo, A. 2013a "Dealing with Your Incompetent Boss", in *HBR Guide to Managing Up and Across*, Boston, MA: Harvard Business Review Press, 55–59.

Gallo, A. 2013b "Stop Being Micromanaged", in *HBR Guide to Managing Up and Across*, Boston, MA: Harvard Business Review Press, 47–59.

Hill, L. A. & Lineback, K. 2013 "Managing Your Boss", in *HBR Guide to Managing Up and Across*, Boston, MA: Harvard Business Review Press, 3–16.

Hudson, M. 2009 *Managing Without Profit: Leadership, Management and Governance of Third Sector Organisations in Australia*, Sydney: UNSW Press.

1 They are quoting from Eisold, K. 2000 "The Rediscovery of the Unknown: An Inquiry into Psychoanalytical Praxis", *Contemporary Psychoanalysis*, 36(1), 65.
2 In my experience, as Vice-President of Australia's employer organisation for the live entertainment industry Live Performance Australia, there was a clear difference between managers of commercial and managers of non-profit performing arts companies with the former much more likely to resist union demands.

V

Values

Stating one's values is a way of describing what is important in life. Stating an organisation's values is a way of helping employees know what behaviours are expected and what principles underlie the policies and actions of the company. They help organisations because they encourage consistency, clarity, decision-making and autonomy (Hewison & Holden 2011). Values provide a shared framework within which people can make decisions and act. Phills (2005, 197) gives some simple examples such as intellectual freedom for a university, innovation for a high-tech firm, meritocracy for a professional service firm and aggressiveness for a professional hockey team.

When the major performing arts companies were learning about strategic planning with some Stanford University academics in the 2000s, the direct question we were asked to help us unpack the values of our organisations was:

> Given our purpose or our mission, what are a couple of things – philosophies, guiding principles, things we believe in – that we would never compromise?

Autry (2001, 32) says that you find out what values people want by asking people to finish the following sentences:

> We want to work in an organization that values _____

> We want to work with people who value_____

And then use the same sentences to check congruity:

> This organization values _____

> These people value_____

A more indirect way of finding out about the company's values is to ask people about inspirational moments they've experienced in the company. It's in the heart of stories about how people interact with or experience an organisation that you'll find the enacted values. Because that's what you're looking for – not just words but words that are turned into action in the day-to-day operations of the company. For example, a value such as "concern for others" needs to be turned into a series of policies and actions that ensure a workplace where people are treated with respect and allowed to fulfil their potential (George et al. 2011).

One of the best stories about values in an arts organisation can be found in Hewison, Holden and Jones' (2013) story about a change of leadership at the Royal Shakespeare Company. The RSC has traditionally been an ensemble company of actors and the new leadership team of Michael Boyd and Vikki Heywood used the idea of "ensemble" to guide their decisions. The company understood the qualities of an ensemble as it was experienced in the rehearsal room and on stage and so it was a transparent metaphor standing for the values of trust and mutual respect, transparency and collaboration. What Boyd and Heywood did was apply these qualities to the new organisational structure and culture. They streamlined processes, opened up silos, broke down hierarchies and got people on Board for the change in collaborative and participative ways. There was no dissonance between values and actions.

Where dissonance can occur is not just in the gap between words and action but also between action and belief. As a leader, you're going to be in trouble if the values you express and talk about aren't actually values you believe in. You will eventually be seen by staff as inauthentic but in the meantime, you'll be uncomfortable in your own skin.

Another problem with values is that words get overused and every organisation wants to be "service-oriented" or "respectful" or "honest". After all, because (almost) everyone agrees with values such as fairness, kindness, dignity, charity, integrity, quality, service it would be absurd not to claim these principles and instead try to run a business on "unfairness, deceit, baseness, uselessness, mediocrity or degradation" (Covey 1992, 95). So the task is to find three or four values that are special to your organisation. Most organisations can't resist having long lists but the best values will be those that are lived and recognised as being particular to your company. For example, Circus Oz is an internationally recognised circus whose performances reflect a particularly Australian larrikin sense of humour through the work of multi-skilled teams who also work with disadvantaged communities. One of

their values is "democracy" which is reflected in their organisational structure, their performance teamwork, their focus on social justice and their membership and governance principles.

At MTC our list was far too long even though we could claim that all of the words were important to us. In the last strategic plan that I wrote for the company we listed humour, vigour, excitement, inquisitiveness, family, loyalty, energy and excellence. On reflection, if I had to choose three or four, the values that were most reflected in our work practices and our organisational culture were family, excellence, humour and inquisitiveness. Collaboration and care were important to the company and that is captured well by the metaphor of "family" even though, sometimes, it was a dysfunctional family. Excellence was important in every aspect of the company's operations. Laughter was valued both on stage and off stage. And inquisitiveness captures both that desire for continuous improvement as well the nature of what goes on in the rehearsal room. The question is would others in the company agree with me because that's the point — what are the shared values?

Although I like the concept of organisational values I'm somewhat cynical about them. And this starts from the very first step. For example, if your organisation has published values, do you actually know what they are? I suspect most people, even those who were in the room when they were first articulated, won't remember them. And you won't be alone in this (Bunting 2016). So the next question is are they enacted in your organisation? When you join an organisation it may already have a set of written or unwritten values based on history that may still feel right. Of course, you may want to change those values to help redefine more general change because shared values may not always be positive values. The value of "mateship" in Australia, for example, can mean the boys in the tech crew heading to the pub between shows or it could mean a spirit of caring and looking after each other on tour. Changing an organisational culture isn't easy but the expression and acting out of new values helps the process.

When a new CEO started at Arts Centre Melbourne (ACM) in the 2010s she took people in the organisation through a process which included determining its values. As a result, ACM publishes their values; hands them out to new staff; has them stuck up on noticeboards; and I assume builds their reporting and KPIs on them. Their values are:

- "Leadership: we work with courage and conviction for the good of Arts Centre Melbourne
- Community: we work together with diverse perspectives and act with integrity
- Care More: we create a safe and secure environment for everybody
- Creativity: we use our imaginations and sense of adventure to stay one idea ahead" (Arts Centre Melbourne 2017, 25).

Each value is followed by "we" statements about how people should work and work together. Bunting (2016, 57) suggests that as well as listing behavioural standards that flow on from the values, storytelling (something that we're particularly good at in the arts) helps people understand the linkage. I particularly the following example:

- Value: Integrity
- Behavioural standard: We say it like it is
- Shared stories: "We will not talk behind one another's back ... nor will we go home and complain about others at work if we had not had the discussion directly first. As leaders, we must make it safe for people to be honest ... We cannot leave meetings saying one thing and thinking something else. This will erode trust and ruin our culture .... We need to be constructive, not destructive in the way we say things."

Values provide meaning to people inside the organisation and they also have to make sense and be felt by people outside the organisation. For example, MTC's value of "family" also described the relationship between the company and its donors and subscribers. People felt they were part of the family and that they had a personal connection, particularly, with company leadership. Hewison and Holden (2011, 180) talk about values such as "engagement", where the organisation is genuinely responsive to the needs and opinions of the audience and "service" which means that the organisation cares about and treats its audiences well. The result is a trusting relationship between the company and its stakeholders.

During a strategic planning session with a non-profit organisation, the word "passion" kept coming up – in stories about dealing with customers and clients, in how staff felt about their work and their colleagues – and so not surprisingly it came up when values were discussed. When it came to write the word down, people were somewhat embarrassed, feeling that it was an overused word that wasn't really a value. During the rest of the day people searched for an alternative that would encapsulate the care and commitment, and enthusiasm and energy, and love and belief that were strong themes in the company's operations and failed. Because, ultimately, "passion" was the right word to describe what was important to them.

See also: Change, Ethics, Leadership, Organisational Culture

References

Arts Centre Melbourne 2017 *The Role You Play*, Melbourne: ACM.

Autry, J. A. 2001 *The Servant Leader*, New York: Three Rivers Press.

Bunting, M. 2016 *The Mindful Leader*, Milton, QLD: Wiley.

Covey, S. R. 1992 *Principle-Centred Leadership*, London: Pocket Books.

George, B., Sims, P., McLean, A. N. & Mayer, D. 2007 "Discovering Your Authentic Leadership", *Harvard Business Review*, 85(2), 129–138.

Hewison, R. & Holden, J. 2011 *The Cultural Leadership Handbook*, Farnham: F Gower.

Hewison, R., Holden, J. & Jones, S. 2013 "Leadership and Transformation at the Royal Shakespeare

Company", in Caust, J. (ed.) *Arts Leadership*, Melbourne: Tilde University Press, 144–158.

Phills, J. A. 2005 *Integrating Mission and Strategy for Nonprofit Organizations*, New York: Oxford University Press.

Venues

I've been to venues for the presentation of art in six continents. I've been to ancient Greek amphitheatres and contemporary quarries; brand-new buildings and historic ones; iconic pieces of architecture such as the Sydney Opera House and exhibitions in a friend's lounge room; buildings turned into performance spaces and gardens specifically designed to show off sculpture. Some of the time, my presence was driven by the art itself, but sometimes by the venue itself. If you are only going to be in a place once, you'll go to the national gallery or museum or performing arts centre in that town and see whatever's on.

For the most part, venues for presenting art are bricks and mortar and many of the comments that I've made in the *Building* section are relevant to their management as are comments in the section on *Audiences*. However, it is worth noting a couple of unique aspects about venue management.

Venues stand as representatives of both the art they present and their community. We're proud to have an arts centre in our city. We want to have a large performance space so that the best bands in the world will visit us. We like the idea of a gallery or museum that reflects our culture to visitors. So even if people never visit arts venues, they'll claim them as their own and have opinions about how they are managed and what they present. In her article about leadership in four Australasian performing arts centre, Caust (2015) makes a number of insightful points about the role of such centres in their communities. Major arts centres are more than just buildings in which art happens. They represent a major capital investment by cities and to that degree they are status symbols as well cultural centres. If they are more than just a hall for hire,

they are also organisations that take more risks than most other types of government-funded bodies because arts programs by definition involve risk. And both these points contribute to the complexity of their relationship with their government owners. In this context, art and politics are inextricably linked. Because leadership of a venue is so political and because such venues are important icons in their cities, their leader is more in the public eye than the CEOs of many other arts organisations. As Caust (2015, 159) concludes: "They are continually under review by the press, politicians, powerful individuals and the public."

An example of this is the ruction in Sydney in 2018 when Louise Herron, CEO of the Sydney Opera House was directed, against the House's own policies, by the Premier of New South Wales to run an advertisement for a horse race on the sails of the building (Henrique-Gomes 2018). Ms Herron suffered attacks by powerful media interests but, equally, received support from many individuals in the community.

That story is indicative of the complexity of stakeholders that a venue manager usually has to deal with. There are those who "own" it, those who want to hire it, those who have expectations about what role it should play, the visitors, and even those who didn't want it built in the first place. Arts venues have often been at the heart of gentrification processes which benefit some residents but not all as rent increases, services and shops change and the nature of the community itself shifts.

As well as politicians and the media, audiences and the community, there are staff, unions and other arts companies all with multiple aspirations and attitudes towards the space. All this can lead to conflict between owners, managers, users and participations. For example, even the simple question of who gets to hire a venue and when can lead to clashes of opinion that can spill over into the public realm. There can be multiple and intersecting brands in a venue as the work produced by the venue operator competes with the marketing messages from external hirers. And within the organisation itself there can be differences of opinion about its core purpose, its ancillary activities and expenditure priorities. The best venue managers are jugglers of all these expectations.

Wolff (2017) has developed a model of how performing arts centres have changed over time – from home to place; place to community centre; community centre to nexus. What he means is they often started as a home for the local performing companies; they then became a place which gave life to decaying urban cores; and through that process, they became a centre for the arts interests of local neighbourhoods and communities; and now, they are a nexus for cultural expression and participation through "performance, education initiatives and community outreach programming" (35). Wolff (2017, 39) describes the many roles of this 4th generation of arts centre as: place/brand, showcase, partner, incubator, thought leaders, educator, home, innovation. These roles could also apply to what we expect from galleries and museums as well.

When people do visit our venue, their decision to return will depend not only on the perceived value of the show but also on the value of the place (Martinez, Euzéby & Lallement 2018). Some venues have "star" attraction. For example, I've had people book to see work showing in the Sydney Opera House just because it was there. And colleagues presenting work there have told of audiences that disappear at interval because people can say they've had their "experience" at the Opera House and that was more important than seeing the whole show. While our large and glamorous venues can attract tourists, they might be off putting to locals. There can be an assumption that crossing the threshold of an arts venue requires a special dress or special language or special understanding. People will seek out a space that feels more like them. Grungy inner-city bars compared to concert halls; rough timber and concrete rather than red velvet and gold fittings. In designing our venues, we have to think about the audience that might come as well as those we know will come. The architecture and the personality of a venue along with its reputation are part of the attraction and part of the process of reducing the risk of investing in an arts experience (Martinez et al. 2018).

We know that our audiences want more than just the arts experience in our venues. They want to spend time catching up with friends before the exhibition or show; they want cool-down time after the event; and they want the chance to drink and eat as well as talk. Our venues have to enable what Martinez et al. (2018, 68) describe as a multifaceted experience that covers "hedonic, cognitive, discovery and emotional dimensions, and the opportunity to share an experience with the artist and other audience members".

For this to be a reality, our venues need to be opened for more than just the traditional times and for more than just the traditional ways. We're seeing art museums open late (or even for 24 hours during "White Night" type events). We're seeing the lobbies of venues used for product launches and education activities. We're seeing the informality of someone wandering up to a piano which says "play me" in the car park of an arts centre. In other words, given that so much has been invested in the infrastructure of our venues, our communities expect an atmosphere that is "buzzing and welcoming" (Webb 2017, 57).

However, there is another side to our venues. The events at the Bataclan Theatre in Paris, the Manchester Arena bombing in England, the Afghanistan National Music School in Kabul, remind us that our venues can be a symbol of values that others don't share. The first time I was exposed to this was a bomb threat at Arts Centre Melbourne because of the content of a play my company was putting on. Australia sometimes feels far removed from the world's troubles but venues here as well as elsewhere are having to face the increasing challenge of balancing security with openness.

When managing a venue you have to manage the land, the buildings, the infrastructure, the furniture, the equipment, the fixtures and make sure it's all reliable, safe, secure and environmentally sound in order to attract and keep hirers and audiences.

In writing about operations in a new performing arts centre, Donnelly (2017, 157–159) provides a great insight into what's required and what can go wrong in a "level of care matrix". His topics cover maintenance, service and response time, aesthetics and building systems reliability through to crisis management. The place you don't want to be on customer service matrix, for example, is "consistent customer ridicule", but it's easy to let simple things slip when the art is all-consuming.

As a venue manager, you need to understand the cultural and civic scene in which you're operating as well as all the aspects of building operations. I've learnt how to manipulate air-conditioning units and understand the minutiae of insurance contracts. I've dealt with architects and local government officers, builders and plumbers, restaurateurs and ticketing providers. I've agonised over the choice of art but I've also agonised over the choice of furniture. I've learnt about emergency and event management as well as the importance of well-trained, happy staff. I've tried to appease politicians and audience members. In other words, managing a venue is one of the most complex jobs in the arts and cultural industry.

See also: Audiences, Buildings, Marketing

References

Caust, J. 2015 "Different Culture but Similar Roles: Leadership of Major Performing Arts Centers", in Caust, J. (ed.) *Arts and Cultural Leadership in Asia*, London: Routledge, 148–162.

Donnelly, P. "Managing Venue Operations for a Newly Opened PAC", in Lambert, P. D. & Williams, R. (eds) 2017a *Performing Arts Center Management*, New York: Routledge, 142–162.

Henrique-Gomes, L. 2018 "'It's Not a Billboard': Anger at Use of Sydney Opera House for Horse Racing Ads", *The Guardian*, 6 October, www.theguardian.com/australia-news/2018/oct/06/its-not-a-billboard-anger-at-use-of-sydney-opera-house-for-horse-racing-ads [accessed 11 March 2019].

Martinez, C., Euzéby, F. & Lallement, J. 2018 "The Importance of the Venue in an Information Search: Online Ticket Purchase in the Performing Arts", *International Journal of Arts Management*, 20(3), 60–74.

Webb, D. 2017 "Trends in the Development and Operation of Performing Arts Centers", in Lambert, P. D. & Williams, R. (eds) *Performing Arts Center Management*, New York: Routledge, 45–62.

Wolff, S. A. 2017 "The Evolution of the Performing Arts Centre: What Does Success Look Like", in Lambert, P. D. & Williams, R. (eds) *Performing Arts Center Management*, New York: Routledge, 20–44.

Volunteers

I started off my arts and cultural career as a volunteer presenter and producer in a community radio station and I joined my first arts Board before I'd even finished my post-graduate arts management studies. If you believe that arts and culture are essential parts of our world, then you have to do everything you can to support the artists in their work. So I've been a volunteer envelope stuffer, a donor, a mentor, a committee member, a lobbyist, an adviser – anything to help artists and arts organisations to survive and make our world a richer place.

One finds volunteers in all aspects of the not-for-profit art and cultural world. Board members and interns. Ushers and presenters. Artists and administrators. People volunteer for a range a reasons including:

1. A belief in the importance of the organisation's work
2. Lifestyle needs such as the transition from work to retirement
3. Wanting to make a useful contribution to society
4. Altruism, as an expression of religious beliefs and/or family traditions and upbringing
5. Companionship, as a way to widen one's circle of acquaintances and develop personal connections that may extend beyond the volunteer setting
6. Learning about a field of interest, such as the arts, for personal enrichment
7. Protecting oneself against feelings such as guilt and doubt

8. Developing contacts that may prove useful in one's business or professional life, including within the organisation
9. Getting ahead in a for-profit that expects up-and-coming executives to volunteer
10. Obtaining training and experience that may pave the way for seeking a paying job in the field
11. Social status through associating with those who are part of the community elite (Fishel 2003; Golensky 2011; Macduff, Netting & O'Connor 2009).

My parents came from a generation of volunteers and their reasons included most of those listed above. They contributed to school and church activities, sport and welfare organisations, arts and cultural companies in many ways, from routine administration to chairing Boards. Of course they received benefits out of doing it – public recognition, new networks of friends and personal satisfaction when the organisations went well. But they probably didn't hear the stories that I was told by the arts managers who worked with them about how important their practical and emotional contributions were to the companies they helped.

There is a definition of a volunteer as someone who incurs a net cost because of their volunteerism (Classes 2015, 145). I confess that I found this rather confronting because my assumption (and my experience) had always been that volunteers get a lot out of what they do – otherwise why do it? Classens (2015) attempted a "social return on investment" analysis of people who volunteered with a food bank program in Toronto. He concluded that for every $1 that an average volunteer put in, they got $0.86 back in social value. The inputs were measured by time and a proxy wage and the outputs such as skill development and feeling connected to the community were valued by proxy measures such as the cost of a course or a percentage of their annual expenditure on recreation. Looking at the list of outputs, I suspect that it would be longer for arts volunteers and therefore the social benefits may in fact be higher than the volunteer's "costs".

On the other side of the fence, it's worth noting that using volunteers costs money because you have to manage them. I've only found one measure for how much it costs organisations to "hire" volunteers and that was A$750 per person for the Sydney Olympic Games in 2000 (Van der Wagen 2007, 65). But that's still cheaper than employing a casual usher or guide to work for your organisation. We use volunteers for:

- Establishing an event e.g. many music festivals start from a volunteer base
- Expanding the workforce e.g. finding people to do the work that others don't want to such as filing
- Expanding the level of customer service e.g. volunteer front-of-house staff that you find in many American theatres
- Creating a social impact e.g. expanding the size and scale of an arts event (Van der Wagen 2007).

As I wrote this section in 2019, the company where I was working created a public dance work with over 400 volunteer participants. The artist who came up with the idea wanted to raise the public profile of contemporary dance. By involving that many people of all ages, you also reach out to their friends and families and by using volunteers, you can make it a free event and attract larger audiences. We assumed that people were volunteering simply because they love dance but it may be because they wanted to share an activity with a family member or learn more or add the experience as a volunteer team leader to their CV.

Given the rich range of reasons about why people might want to volunteer for your organisation, you need to understand their motivation in order to effectively manage them.

If the purpose of volunteering time is gain work experience, then putting leaflets into envelopes all day isn't quite "experience" enough. Whereas if the purpose of volunteering is to socialise then spending an afternoon doing that task with a group who share your interest in the arts may be an excellent outcome if you are retired. This raises the question of whether managing volunteers is different to managing staff. There are mixed messages in the literature. Liao-Troth (2001) explored attitudinal differences regarding the psychological contract between paid staff and volunteers in medical centres and concluded there were no significant differences. However, Brudney (2010, 780) says that managing volunteers is different to managing employees because they are much less dependent on the organisation than paid staff who need the wage.

Classen (2015, 151) noted that in his two years of doing research and visiting the food markets run by volunteers as well as other such projects: "I have never encountered a disgruntled volunteer." One of the reasons is that it's easy to move on – if you don't like the work or the boss, it's much easier to leave if you're a volunteer than if you're a paid staff member who has to find another source of income.

This means that non-profit managers don't have as much control over volunteers compared to salaried workers (Brudney 2010, 780). It also means that volunteers can be more fussy about what work they do; may want to work hours that suit them, not the organisation; may not be as good at sticking to the rules because there isn't the same legal structure around the "employment" relationship as there is with staff. The value proposition for volunteers is different to staff. It's not "would you like to join us" but "we need you and here's what we will do for you" (Bryant & Pozdeev 2011, 4).

One of the reasons that I got my first role as a CEO was because I had been asked to apply by my peers – fellow volunteers at a community radio station. When I got the job I had to manage those same peers in a volunteer organisation where no-one *had to come to work*. If the volunteers were happy, enjoyed the experience, were willing to do the job, liked the ambience of the station, like the opportunities the station offered, only *then* would they "work". Therefore, one's management style had to involve participation and empowerment. But that's a style I used with paid staff as well. I believe that managing volunteers requires the same range of people management skills as paid staff but there is

debate about whether you should use the same type of human resource management processes.

In most books about volunteers, there's usually a direction to apply standard HR practices to volunteer management such as recruitment and selection, performance appraisal, supervision, rewards. Hager and Brudney (2015) decided to ask whether this was the best outcome for organisations or whether we'd been induced to take on policies that may not deliver the best outcome. They asked the question because they found evidence that most US non-profit organisations hadn't adopted these supposed "best practices" and instead had fairly undeveloped volunteer management structures.

Their research concluded that the best way to apply these "best practice" policies was to take a contextual approach, that is, what's best for your particular organisation. For example, interviewing for volunteers isn't always the best approach if your organisation is about social change and your volunteers are more like activists (Hager & Brudney 2015, 237). If you've got a group of younger volunteers (usually described as less responsive to supervision and looking for more autonomy), then your communication and management structures might be different to having a more traditional structure with older volunteers.

In other words, check out best practice advice but choose the practices that best suit your volunteers and your organisation – what Hager and Brudney (2015, 252) call a "tool box" approach to volunteer management.

If someone was going to be a regular part of the team, albeit a volunteer, I used the same process as one would for staff such as assessing the organisation's needs, proper recruitment and section, screening and placement, a contract, orientation and training, supervision, performance assessment and recognition. For example, after advertising in MTC's subscriber newsletter for volunteers to help with filing, we found a wonderful person who in exchange for doing this necessary but boring task once a fortnight received theatre tickets and lunch. The exchange was meaningful to both parties and the needs of the volunteer and the organisation were reflected accurately in a volunteer "contract".

In the same way that you have policies and codes for staff, you need to have them for volunteers and this includes creating a safe work place, insuring them, providing clear guidelines about expectations and behaviour, such as respect in the workplace, provide relevant training, effective communication, providing breaks and so on (Van der Wagen 2007).

Problems with volunteers are usually caused if you haven't invested enough time in their training and supervision and whether you've made the mission, the policies and processes of the organisation clear. For example, someone with a long-term commitment to the organisation may be dogmatic and inflexible if an organisation wants to change direction. Someone who is volunteering for social contact may spend too much time chatting and not enough time doing the required work. It's an investment to have volunteers and because they come to you for an array of reasons, they have to managed and motivated with an eye to their personal requirements.

In a list of dos and don'ts from organisations that have won awards for working with volunteers, the "don'ts" aren't unexpected – don't take people for granted, don't provide ineffective communication, don't be inflexible, don't overload volunteers, don't put them in difficult or dangerous situations, don't lose your patience, don't ignore their interests (Van de Wagen 2007, 69).

In professional arts organisations, I think that there is a limited role for volunteers apart from the Board. If you have an ongoing job that needs doing, one should try to find the resources to pay someone. However, there are times when volunteers are a blessing – for the large community art project; for the occasional mundane tasks (filing); for the all-consuming fundraiser that requires more hands than the organisation has to give; for the tertiary work experience student who can bring fresh insights into the organisation in exchange for learning.

Another potential issue for professional companies is that staff may not want to work with volunteers. They may feel overstretched already and not want to take on the responsibility of a volunteer. They may feel irritated that they get a volunteer rather than a paid staff member because they see that as undervaluing their work and support needs. They may not like the volunteer but feel that it's hard to direct them when they aren't being paid. Compared to 6UVS-FM which couldn't have survived without volunteers, MTC didn't have a strong volunteer culture. As a professional theatre company, I was determined to use paid staff whenever possible. But we did have some volunteers: through programs for high school work experience; tertiary performing arts student mentorships; occasional calls for volunteers for one-off fundraising events. When I decided that we could do with some regular volunteers, I consulted staff and only created the "positions" that staff wanted and were prepared to manage.

If firing a staff member is hard, so is firing a volunteer. But it's much more likely that a volunteer leaves because of issues such as lack of respect, isolation from other volunteers, a belief that they are been used and underappreciated (Bryant & Pozdeev 2011, 8). Your job is to make sure that the volunteer leaves as an ambassador for the company because their needs (and yours) have been met.

See also: Boards, Motivation

References

Brudney, J. L. 2010 "Designing and Managing Volunteer Programs", in Renz, D. O. (ed.) *The Jossey-Bass Handbook of Nonprofit Leadership and Management* (3rd ed), San Francisco, CA: John Wiley & Sons, 753–793.

Bryant, P. & Pozdeev, N. 2011 "'Don't Have Time to Drain the Swap: Too Busy Dealing with Alligators': Defining the Governance Skills Sets that Enhance Volunteer Retention and Recruitment in Small Arts and Cultural Organisations", Antwerp: 11th AIMAC International Conference.

Classens, M. 2015 "What's in It for the Volunteers?", *Nonprofit Management & Leadership*, 26(2), 145–156.

Fishel, D. 2003 *The Book of The Board*, Sydney: Federation Press.

Golensky, M. 2011 *Strategic Leadership and Management in Nonprofit Organizations*, Chicago, IL: Lyceum Books Inc.

Hager, M. A. & Brudney, J. L. 2015 "In Search of Strategy: Universalistic, Contingent and Configurational Adoption of Volunteer Management Practices", *Nonprofit Management & Leadership*, 25(3), 235–254.

Liao-Troth, M. A. 2001 "Attitude Differences Between Paid Workers and Volunteers", *Non-profit Management and Leadership*, 11(4), 423–442.

Macduff, N., Netting, F. E. & O'Connor, M. K. 2009 "Multiple Ways of Coordinating Volunteers with Differing Styles of Service", *Journal of Community Practice*, 17, 400–423.

Van der Wagen, L. 2007 *Human Resource Management for Events*, Oxford: Elsevier.

Work

Why have a separate chapter on work when it's the basis of every aspect of this book? Work, paid or unpaid, loved or unloved, is what we do every day. We talk to each other about our work. We read and watch how other people work. Most cultural products contain a reflection about work whether it's the implements we use at work on display in a museum or stories about workplaces in a television series. Every novel will have some reference to work:

> "I think people like him think work is supposed to be drudgery punctuated by very occasional moments of happiness, but when I say happiness, I mostly mean distraction. You know what I mean?"
>
> "No please elaborate." [said Clark, the corporate consultant]
>
> "Okay, say you go into the breakroom," she said, "and a couple of people you like are there, say someone's telling a funny story, you laugh a little, you feel included, everyone's so funny, you go back to your desk with a sort of, I don't know, I guess *afterglow* would be the word? You go back to your desk with an afterglow, but then by four or five o'clock the day's just turned into yet another day, and you go on like that, looking forward to five o'clock and then the weekend and then your two or three annual weeks of paid vacation time, day in day out, and that's what happens to your life."
>
> [And as he leaves the building, Clark wonders whether he's been] "half-asleep through the motions of this life for a while now, years; not specifically unhappy, but when had he last found real joy in his work? When was the last time he'd been truly moved by anything? When had he last felt awe or inspiration?"
>
> (Mandel 2014, 163–164)

I chose this quote because I happen to be reading *Station Eleven* at the same time I was writing this book and because it was a reminder about how lucky we are, those of us who work in the arts. We've chosen to work in this specific industry, trading financial security for engagement and passion. There might be a few people who work with us because they can't find better paying jobs elsewhere but for the most part, we have meaningful jobs even if we're not necessarily happy every day.

In a UK survey, people were asked "Does your job make a meaningful contribution to the world?" and 37% said it didn't. In the Netherlands, the figure was higher at 40% (Graeber 2018). I would like to think that the percentage of people working in the arts who would say "yes" would be considerably higher. However, we shouldn't take this for granted. World leading research by Australia's Entertainment Assist and Victoria University (2016) found that although the majority of Australian entertainment industry workers express an overwhelming passion for their creative work, "[t]here is a powerful, negative culture within the industry including a toxic, bruising work environment; extreme competition; bullying; sexual assault; sexism and racism" and not surprisingly, the result was high levels of mental health problems and suicidality. As managers we have to ensure that this is not a description of our workplace.

It's the passion and the moments of inspiration that balance out the times when the work is boring or frustrating, the people around us are irritating or lazy, the audience members are annoying or not buying, the stakeholders are demanding or unsupportive. And we'll experience more moments like that than most other people experience at work. While not all my days have been inspirational, many have been. I remember going with an outside broadcast team to record the thanksgiving celebration at Orlando Stadium with Nelson Mandela and Desmond Tutu and tens of thousands of South Africans celebrating a peaceful transition to democracy. I remember looking up from a budget to go to a run of a play in the rehearsal room and seeing some of Australia's greatest actors at work. I remember getting the first pressing of a CD of work by Australian composer Peter Sculthorpe that we'd recorded in our modest community radio studio. I remember taking a break from writing a strategic plan to sit in on an education presentation and returning to the work with tears in my eyes and the motivation to keep writing.

Adams (2007, xiv) says "we are at our most effective, psychologically and physiologically, when stimulated by productive activity". But he goes on to say that even though most people would continue to work even if they didn't have to, "most people dislike the work that they do, and cannot wait to leave their workplace at the end of each day". It's useful to be reminded that work can be boring, one can be underappreciated, one can certainly be underpaid. No work place is the perfect vehicle for self-esteem, growth and happiness (Rosner & Halcrow 2010) and not everyone, even in an arts organisation, is going to be happy or productive or cheerful every day. As a manager, you have to create a good workplace but also to enable the balance between work and the rest of life. In a book called *Hard Facts, Dangerous Half-Truths, and Total Nonsense* based on evidence-based knowledge about organisations, Pfeffer and Sutton (2006) discuss a number of assumptions that are held by managers about work life. In a chapter called "Is Work Fundamentally Different from the Rest of Life and Should It Be?", they say the following rules reflect how most workplaces operate:

- Your time is our time, even when you work all the time
- Clothes make the person
- Don't think, you'll weaken the team – just do what you're told
- Display prescribed feelings, not your real feelings – check your emotions at the door
- Love – babe, even friendship – is a dirty word
- Conflict and competition are desirable in the workplace
- Rules of polite, civilised behaviour don't apply at work
- Meaning and fulfilment come elsewhere – work is just about the job.

It's terrifying to think that a majority of organisations might be managed this way; that leaders believe this is what a workplace should be like. It may be just me (and may explain why I've never worked in the for-profit world) but I've never followed any of those "rules". I've turned the phone off after the show's done. Power dressing has never suited my style. I think therefore I am. I have tried to avoid abusive emotions at work but I've felt happy and sad and laughed and cried. I confess I even had a work affair. Politeness is a virtue which I've tried to express. And I've been lucky enough to have worked in organisations where the output was of value to the community.

A US organisation with the ambition to create, study and recognise great workplaces called *Great Place to Work* says that from the employees' perspective, great workplaces are those where they trust the people they work for, have pride in what they do and enjoy the people they work with. Trust is a defining principle created when people are respected and treated fairly, managers are credible and there's pride and authentic connection between people. From a manager's perspective a great place to work is one where they can achieve organisational objectives with employees who give their best, working together as a team in an environment of trust. Other words they use to capture the "great workplace" are thanking and caring, celebrating and sharing, developing and listening.

With good will and skill, we can create such workplaces. What we have more difficulty doing is getting the balance right between home and work. Because our organisations are usually under-resourced compared to our ambitions, there is a temptation to expect people to work longer that the standard work hours and to set the example by doing it ourselves. Of course, you have to work during the day and often at night for shows or donor events or openings but you can create limits around when and how you work. Everyone will find their own way but I, for example, would stay at work until I'd finished rather than take work home, leaving home to be a place of reflection and renewal. But when it comes to finding more personal time, I don't know what I would have done if I'd had to take time out from the company in the early part of my work with MTC. To begin with, I had so much

to learn and the organisation was under threat so for both personal and organisational reasons, I had to be available to everyone. By the time I had to take time off (for dying friends, elderly parents, personal illness) the company was in much better shape, I had a bright, committed team around me and had a fabulous locum that I could call upon. And so I did. Because there are times when you have to put family, friends and even yourself first, not matter how committed you are to the company.

In a *Harvard Business Review* article about work-life balance, management interviewees talked about the need to have a strong network of behind-the-scenes supporters. For a lot of the men, this still means a stay-at-home wife. For women, this often means paid help such as nanny or someone to do the shopping. "Even interviewees without children said they needed support at home when they became responsible for aging parents or suffered their own health problems" (Groysberg & Abrahams 2014, 63). After I'd been at the company for a couple of years I moved into a house with my sister and her child and exchanged baby-sitting for food. When asked in a newspaper puff piece what my favourite kitchen implement was I said "my sister". I survived my time at MTC because at home there was food and emotional nourishment.

The trap can be that you feel proud of yourself when working long and hard. I remember a staff member telling me that she felt the company was in good hands when she saw the light on in my office after hours. This made me feel good but also caused me to ask whether I was staying later than everyone else just so that I would prove that I was working harder than everyone else. Longer maybe, not necessarily better.

The workplace can be inspirational, but not every day. People do want to work hard for us, but they shouldn't be exploited. Art may be both work and life for an artist, but even they need time out to be loved.

See also: Hours, Holidays, Manners, Trust

References

Adams, J. 2007 *Managing People in Organizations: Contemporary Theory and Practice*, Basingstoke: Palgrave Macmillan.

Entertainment Assist 2016 *Working in the Australian Entertainment Industry: Key Findings*, EA Melbourne.

Graeber, D. 2018 "My Bullsh*t Career", *Weekend Australian Magazine*, 12 May, 20–23.

Great Place to Work, *The Dawn of the Great Workplace Era*, www.greatplacetowork.net/storage/documents/Publications_Documents/The_Dawn_of_the_Great_Workplace_Era.pdf [accessed 16 March 2019].

Groysberg, B. & Abrahams, R. 2014 "Manage Your Work, Manage Your Life", *Harvard Business Review*, March, 58–66.

Mandel, E. S. J. 2014 *Station Eleven*, London: Picador.

Pfeffer, J. & Sutton, R. I. 2006 *Hard Facts, Dangerous Half-Truths, and Total Nonsense*, Boston, MA: Harvard Business School Press.

Rosner, B. & Halcrow, A. 2010 *The Boss's Survival Guide* (2nd ed), New York: McGraw Hill.

X

It's rare to find anything under X in a management or leadership book but having promised an alphabet, I decided to make the effort to deliver. After pouring over dictionaries to get inspiration, it suddenly became obvious. X = No. So I should share some of my favourite lists – the list of things not to do. I'd seen the first list in a set of readings years ago but had no idea who created it. But technology being what it is, I've tracked down the author John Durel on a website devoted to a community of consultants serving museums and cultural non-profits.[1] It makes sense that someone who worked in our world would create a more useful list than many of the "must do" lists written from a for-profit perspective. His list is:

- Stop hogging all the work
- Stop managing people
- Stop telling employees how to do their job
- Stop trying to change people
- Stop trying to solve problems
- Stop treating others as you would like to be treated
- Stop doing annual performance reviews
- Stop trying to treat everyone equally
- Stop thinking of salaries and benefits as an expense
- Stop thinking you have to know the answer.

And what he means is:

- Don't micromanage, and learn to delegate
- Provide a context in which people can manage themselves through guidance rather than direction
- Tell people the results you want, not how to do it
- It's easier to change a job than it is to change a person
- Focus on what the organisation and people are good at
- We're all different so it's a case of treating people as they would like to be treated not as you would like to be treated
- Give regular feedback
- Treat people fairly but not equally because we have different needs and different ways of working
- Think of pay as investment in making your organisation better

- You can't know everything and looking to answers from others will both improve your decision-making and their support of you as a leader.

There's nothing in that list that I disagree with.

Mike Hudson (2009, 344) is another interesting writer with a non-profit perspective. He offers an equally good list of things you shouldn't do:

- Fail to take decisions
- Talk too much in meetings
- Allow team members to talk too much
- Blame the Board
- Fail to hold people to account for their responsibilities
- Always see people's weaknesses rather than their strengths
- Not deliver on tasks you have committed to
- Not delegate effectively
- Criticise team members behind their backs
- Reveal by your attitude, behaviour and non-verbal communication whom you like and whom you dislike.

Finally, here's another X list for interns. It's offered in relation to record companies but I think it's relevant to other creative organisations and employment experiences:

- Fail to respect confidentiality of artists or the company by posting stuff online, being indiscrete, gossiping
- Being disrespectful to artists based on your own opinion
- Being inappropriate with artists, e.g. behaving like a crazed fan
- Behaving inappropriately in the office, e.g. excessive use of phones; allowing dress code to become too casual

- Making no effort to understand the culture and the people of the company
- Bringing unrealistic expectations to the relationship
- "An excess of exuberance with regards to alcohol at a company event" (Saintilan & Schreiber 2018, 19–20).

Most management and leadership education is about learning new things and how to do things better but sometimes the best answer is to stop doing some things. I think these lists are useful because they increase your self-awareness through reflection. I've already confessed to many of the things that I've got wrong along the way. It's worth remembering Grey's (2005) point that management is an ever-failing enterprise. This doesn't mean that you give up before you start. It just means that checking your work is just as important as checking the work of others.

See also: Knowledge, Learning, Management, People

References

Durel, J. *It's Time to Start a "Stop Doing" List*, www.qm2.org/Durel/It_s_Time_to_Start_a_Stop_Doing_List.pdf [accessed 1 March 2015].

Grey, C. 2005 *A Very Short, Fairly Interesting and Reasonably Cheap Book About Studying Organisations*, London: Sage Publications.

Hudson, M. 2009 *Managing Without Profit: Leadership, Management and Governance of Third Sector Organisations in Australia*, Sydney: UNSW Press.

Saintilan, P. & Schreiber, D. 2018 *Managing Organizations in the Creative Economy: Organizational Behaviour for the Cultural Sector*, Abingdon: Routledge.

Note

1 Having found the original source in 2015, the website has since been disabled.

Y

You

Being a good manager is a combination of competencies and character. Both of these are more important than personality. I have worked with and for managers of all sorts of personality types. The flamboyant and the quiet, the noisy and the reflective, the introvert and the extrovert, the direct and the gentle – and their effectiveness or otherwise wasn't mainly driven by their personalities. What mattered, and what made them good to work with and for, was a very different collection of qualities combined with action. Were they trustworthy? Did I feel safe? Did they care about and help me? Were they generous with their time and their praise? And were they any good at doing their job?

Covey (1992), writing about principle-centred leadership, proposes three necessary character traits:

1. Integrity – being honest and honourable
2. Maturity – which Covey describes as "the balance between courage and consideration. If a person can express his (sic) feelings and convictions with courage balanced with consideration for the feelings and convictions of others, he (sic) is mature" (61)
3. Abundance mentality – sharing with others rather than fighting to get your part of a small pie.

Understanding yourself is one of the keys to being a good manager. Hewison and Holden (2011, 56–57) provide a long list of questions you should ask about you, you and others, and the environment in which you want to work in order to see if you are actually prepared to be an arts manager. Thinking back to when I embarked on this career I would have said "yes" to a number of them (Can you keep your temper? Are you honest? Are you ready to work long and often irregular hours?) but my answer to other questions on their list would have been "I don't know yet" (Can you cope with complexity? Can you take the blame? Can you mobilise others? Are you ready to take risks?). The one question that you have to be able to answer "yes" to regardless of the answers to all the others is "Do you like people?"

Although I'm not overly fond of psychological testing, one way of gaining insight into your strengths and weaknesses is doing tests such as Myer Briggs' Dimensions of Leadership Profile or Keirsey Temperament Sorter (Crosby & Bryson 2005). In an emerging leadership program for arts managers, the participants did the Margerison-McCannTeam Performance quiz, shared their feedback and put their learnings into practice for the rest of the course. The result was improved insight into both the individual and the way the group worked. When the CEO of an arts organisation put together a new management team, one of the first things she arranged was for all of them to do a psychological test so that they could learn early and quickly the nature of each other's working styles. Whether it's a psychological test or a training program, a mentor or subscription to a management journal, always be open to new ideas and new information about how to do your job better. If you aren't competent then you won't be a successful manager.

Assuming that you are competent, your staff will want to see and know you as a person. Elsner (2001, 3–4) says "[i]t is not your exquisite technique or management genius that endears you to others. It is how you have been formed by life, by experiences, by connections to others". In an interesting article applying improvisation techniques to management, Parker (2010) says that a key "improv" principle is to "look after yourself first". This means that although "we are usually unable to control the behavioural responses of others, we do have control over our own behaviour" (110). She's making the point that we need to understand ourselves, the motivations that get us going, the emotional traps to avoid and the importance of embodying values.

In deciding how we want to lead, Sinclair (2007, 85) says that a "powerful action is to leave". If you're in an organisation where you can't be an ethical leader, where the organisation culture isn't a safe or positive one, if your manager is incompetent, then leaving and telling the hierarchy why you're leaving might just lead to the change that you haven't been able to make happen by staying in the company.

Having started at "A" with a beautiful quote from John Tusa, it seems appropriate, close to the end of the book, to share another one:

Ultimately, leading an arts organisation is the most human of activities, calling on the most natural of human qualities: a sense of fun; a readiness to apologise and be vulnerable; an ability to say "no"; the capacity to be ruthless but to be fair at the same time. Leadership is about the relationship with those being led. The rest is management speak.

(Tusa 2007a, 24)

The conclusions I offer to my arts management students are slightly less poetic (and in no particular order):

- There isn't a simple answer to any management question
- Focus on learning about yourself and learning about others
- Try empathy – putting yourself into the position of another
- Only make life difficult for someone else if they are making life difficult for the people around them or for the organization
- Continue to learn about management but continue to challenge the theories you are offered from ethical, humanist and political perspectives
- Amanda Sinclair (2007) suggests yoga but it could be anything that improves your physical and emotional health
- Have fun with people, care for others and make sure you have time for your family, your friends and your hobbies (Friedman 2008)
- Say "no" sometimes – turn off the phone, limit the emails
- Delegate and develop others
- Find ways to give back to the industry
- Doubt is fine if it leads to self-reflection but not if it leads to indecision
- Humility is essential because you're dealing with people's lives.

With only one letter to go, I'd like to share the words of another writer whose advice I value. A. C. Grayling is a philosopher but also a playwright. I don't know whether he was thinking about our industry when he wrote the following words but as our role as arts managers is to add value to the artists we work with and the organisations we work for, it feels appropriate:

> Almost everyone wishes to live a life that is satisfying and fulfilling, in which there is achievement and pleasure, and which has the respect of people whose respect is worth having. Such a life is one that adds value – to the experience of the person living it, and to the world that the person occupies. To add value to things involves making good choices. To make good choices requires being informed and reflective. To be both these things one must read, enquire, debate and consider.
>
> (Grayling 2005, Introduction)

References

Crosby, B. C. & Bryson, J. M. 2005 *Leadership for the Common Good* (2nd ed), San Francisco, CA: Jossey-Bass.

Covey, S. R. 1992 *Principle-Centred Leadership*, London: Pocket Books.

Elsner, P. A. 2001 *Authenticity and Leadership: Integrating Our Inner Lives with Our Work*, Iowa State University: Leadership Forum.

Friedman, S. D. 2008 "Be a Better Leader, Have a Richer Life", *Harvard Business Review*, 86(4), 112–118.

Grayling, A. C. 2005 *The Heart of Things*, London: Weidenfeld and Nicholson.

Hewison, R. & Holden, J. 2011 *The Cultural Leadership Handbook*, Farnham: F Gower.

Parker, D. 2010 "The Improvising Leader: Developing Leadership Capacity Through Improvisation", in Kay, S. & Venner, S. (eds) *A Cultural Leader's Handbook*, London: Creative Choices, 106–112.

Sinclair, A. 2007 *Leadership for the Disillusioned*, Sydney: Allen & Unwin.

Tusa, J. 2007a *Engaged with the Arts*, London: I.B. Tauris & Co Ltd.

Z

Z

Z is another letter in the alphabet on which management writers have little to say. The best I could come up with after trawling though endless numbers of textbooks was "zero-based budgeting" and "Zen Buddhism". I addressed the former in the section on *Money* and I'm afraid that I have little to say on the latter. I went searching in my *Dictionary of Proverbs* for final words of advice but the only listings were warnings against zeal. As zeal means great energy or enthusiasm in pursuit of a cause or an objective, that's last thing I want to warn you against. You'll need every bit of energy and enthusiasm you can muster to do your job well.

After the first edition of the A to Z was published, I came across an article by John Tusa (2000) called *The A-to-Z of Running an Arts Centre*. He found another way around the challenge of Z. He chose "zing" and "zip" because you need those qualities to fulfil all the responsibilities of being an arts manager.

Finally, I did find another appropriate Z work in the wonderfully named *Mrs Byrne's Dictionary of Unusual, Obscure and Preposterous Words*. It is "zetetic" which means asking and questioning – a good way, combined with zeal and zing and zip, to become an effective manager.

References

Byrne, J. H. 1974 *Mrs Byrne's Dictionary of Unusual, Obscure and Preposterous Words*, Secaucus, NJ: Citadel Press.
Fergusson, R. & Law, J. 2000 *Dictionary of Proverbs*, London: Penguin Reference.
Tusa, J. 2000 *Art Matters*, London: Methuen.

APPENDIX

Reading

I like to keep adding to my understanding of the world and am always on the lookout for interesting things to read. Sometimes it's blogs or websites but mainly (because I'm just old-fashioned), it's books and journals. Here's my list of some interesting arts management resources:

Books

Arts management books worth reading include William Byrnes 5th edition of *Management and the Arts*, *The Arts Management Handbook* by Brindle and DeVereaux, Hewison and Holden's *The Cultural Leaders Handbook*, Varbanova's *Strategic Management in the Arts* and Walter's *Arts Management: An Entrepreneurial Approach*. There's also a good collection of articles about managing venues in Lamber and Williams' *Performing Arts Center Management* and on managing various aspects of the music industry in *Organising Music* by Beech and Gilmore.

A good collection of stories of arts leadership can be found in two books of international case studies edited by Josephine Caust – *Arts Leadership* and *Arts and Cultural Leadership in Asia*. If you're interested in managing artists, Guy Morrow's book on this subject, examining agility in the creative and cultural industries is worth a read.

Michael Kaiser's writing is always useful – highly practical and informed by years as a brilliantly successful arts manager in the USA and the UK. His work includes *The Cycle, Leading Roles* and *The Art of the Turnaround*.

As well as Kaiser's book on Boards, another good one in particular for Australian and New Zealand readers is David Fishel's *The Book of The Board: Effective Governance for Non-Profit Organisations*.

An up-to-date textbook on Management or Human Resource Management or Organisational Behaviour is also good to have as a reference. For example, a 9th edition of Raymond J. Stone's *Managing Human Resources* was published in 2018 but any good textbook used in a reputable university course is worth reading.

If you want insights into managing people, try Jeremy Adams' *Managing People in Organizations: Contemporary Theory and Practice* (2007). It's based on his reading of 600 research papers from the late 1990s to 2005. I just hope he's got the energy to do an update on the next 10 years' research.

And as this is all about working with creative people, it's worth exploring the books of interviews of artists compiled by John Tusa including *On Creativity* and *The Janus Aspect* as well as the other books he's written about working in the arts.

Sandy Adirondack's book *Just About Managing?* is a practical, insightful book about managing in the non-profit sector. Although it's more than 10 years old, some things never change and its depth of hands on advice is impressive.

There are endless American books on philanthropy and fundraising because it's such an essential part of their funding model for non-profit organisations. A good practical starting point is *Fundraising for Dummies*. I've read the 3rd edition (2010) but I'm sure they will just keep reissuing it. This practical how to do it book is well balanced by reading Fischer's *Ethical Decision Making in Fund Raising*.

There are dozens of books full of practical advice about communication but one that is worth checking out are *Business Communication Today* by Courtland L. Bovee and John V. Thill. On the basis that it's up to its 14th edition in 2020, I assume that it's a textbook used all over the world. For those who are interested in an Australian slant, try Judith Dwyer's *Communication in Business*.

One of the more interesting writers on general leadership is Amanda Sinclair because she looks at new ways of thinking about the role, informed by gender studies and her own experience.

If you want to know more about economics and cultural policy, try the reading the work of David Throsby.

Journals

Although the *Harvard Business Review* is mainly focused on the for-profit sector, they usually have interesting articles on leadership and people management and occasionally have good articles on the not-for-profit sector. They even feature the work of a different visual artist in each edition.

The *International Journal of Arts Management* is a must read for any serious arts manager.

Some of the articles may be too academic for you but you can usually gain insight from the introduction and end of such articles. It's a great way of getting a picture of what's happening across the world.

Every so often there's an edition of the *Asia Pacific Journal of Arts and Cultural Management* which is worth keeping an eye out for.

As you will have noticed from the references, other journals that feature articles on arts and cultural management include the *International Journal of Cultural Policy*, *The Journal of Arts Management, Law, and Society* and *Nonprofit Management and Leadership*.

Websites

There's a great set of references including business and financial strategies and toolkits at www.missionmodelsmoney.org.uk/ and www.ourcommunity.com.au/

In Australia, websites such as Creative Foyer www.creativefoyer.com.au/ and *Arts Hub* www.artshub.com.au/ are good for jobs, news and ideas and the latter also has a UK site: www.artshub.co.uk/about-artshub/.

Douglas McLennan's daily *Arts Journal* www.artsjournal.com/ is worth signing up for as is the *Arts Management Newsletter* www.artsmanagement.net/. *Arts Journal* covers a range of topics and ideas and it's worth signing up for their newsletter: www.artsjournal.com/.

And then there's all the newsletter and websites produced by specific industry associations. The point is: stay in touch.

BIBLIOGRAPHY

A

ABC News 2019 "Dutch Historian Rutger Bregman Goes Viral After Challenging Davos Panel to Talk about Taxing the Wealthy", 31 January, www.abc.net.au/news/2019-01-31/dutch-historian-rutger-bregman-goes-viral-after-davos-tax-speech/10766504 [accessed 10 March 2019].

Abruzzo, J. 2009 "Arts Leaders and Arts Managers", *Arts Management Newsletter*, 94, 10–11.

Abruzzo, J. 2014 "Creating the Company Culture", *Arts Management Newsletter*, 118.

Adair, J. 2005 *The Inspirational Leader: How to Motivate, Encourage and Achieve Success*, London: Kogan Page.

Adams, J. 2007 *Managing People in Organizations: Contemporary Theory and Practice*, Basingstoke: Palgrave Macmillan.

Adirondack, S. 2005 *Just About Managing?* (4th ed), London: London Voluntary Service Council.

Alvesson, M. & Spicer, A. 2016 *The Stupidity Paradox*, London: Profile Books.

Alvesson, M. & Spicer, A. 2016b *Why Smart People Buy into Stupid Ideas: The Stupidity Paradox*, Australian Financial Review, 17 June, www.afr.com/leadership/why-smart-people-buy-into-stupid-ideas-20160613-gpi56s [accessed 16 March 2019].

Amabile, T. M. 1996 *Creativity in Context*, Boulder, CO: Westview Press.

Ambile, T. & Kramer, S. J. 2011 "The Power of Small Wins", *Harvard Business Review*, May https://hbr.org/2011/05/the-power-of-small-wins [accessed 27 February 2019].

Anonymous 2011 "The Problem with Financial Incentives – And What to Do About It', *Knowledge@Wharton*, http://knowledge.wharton.upenn.edu/article/ the-problem-with-financial-incentives-and-what-to-do-about-it/ [accessed on 27 February 2019].

Anonymous 2015 "The Sponsorship Files: Who Funds Our Biggest Arts Institutions", *The Guardian*, www.theguardian.com/culture/2015/mar/02/arts-corporate-sponsorship-tate-british-museum [accessed 16 March 2019].

Archee, R., Gurney, M. & Mohan, T. 2013 *Communicating as Professionals* (3rd ed), Melbourne: Cengage.

Ariely, D. 2013 *What Makes Us Feel Good About Our Work*, TED Talk, www.ted.com/talks/dan_ariely_what_makes_us_feel_good_about_our_work.html [accessed 10 March 2019].

Ariely, D. 2016 *Payoff*, London: TED Books.

Arts Centre Melbourne 2017 *The Role You Play*, Melbourne: ACM.

ArtsHub News 2014 "If the Sydney Biennale Doesn't Need Transfield's Money, Why Should They Be Asking for Ours?" *ArtsHub*, 13 March, www.artshub.com.au/news-article/news/trends-and-analysis/-if-the-sydney-biennale-doesnt-need-transfields-money-why-should-they-be-asking-for-ours--198432 [accessed 16 March 2019].

Assheton, D. 2011 "Coaching at Hitchinson 3", in O'Toole, S., Ferres, N. & Connell, J. (eds) *People Development: An Inside View*, Melbourne: Tilde University Press, 58–64.

Atwood, M. 2016 *Hag-seed*, London: Hogarth.

Australia Council 2015 *Arts Nation: An Overview of Australian Arts*, Sydney: Australia Council.

Australia Council "Strategic Plan Framework: A Guide for Arts Organisations", Sydney: Australia Council, www.australiacouncil.gov.au/workspace/uploads/files/arts-organisations-strategic-p-54c1867bca7bf.pdf [accessed 11 March 2019].

Australia Council, *Artistic Vibrancy*, www. australiacouncil.gov.au/ebook/artistic-vibrancy/publication/contents/pdfweb.pdf [accessed 16 March 2019].

Australian Dairy Industry Council 2014 *Australian Dairy Industry Sustainability Framework Progress Report – December 2014*, Melbourne Dairy Australia.

Autry, J. A. 2001 *The Servant Leader*, New York: Three Rivers Press.

Avery, J., Fournier, S. & Wittenbrake, J. 2014 "Unlock the Mysteries of Your Customer Relationships", *Harvard Business Review*, 92(7/8), 72–81.

B

Bagwell, S., Corry, D. & Rotheroe, A. 2015 "The Future of Finding: Options for Heritage and Cultural Organisations", *Cultural Trends*, 24(1), 28–33.

Baird, L., Post, J. & Mahon, J. 1990 *Management: Functions and Responsibilities*, New York: Harper & Row.

Baker, D., Johnson, M. & Denniss, R. 2014 *Walking the Tightrope: Have Australians Achieved Work/Life Balance?* Canberra: The Australian Institute.

Bakhshi, H., Freeman, A. & Hitchen, G. 2009 *Measuring Intrinsic Value: How to Stop Worrying and Love Economics*, http://culturehive.co.uk/wp-content/uploads/2013/10/Measuring-Intrinsic-Value-Hasan-Bakhshi-Alan-Freeman-Graham-Hitchen-2009_0_0.pdf [accessed 16 March 2019].

Bakke, D. W. 2005 *Joy at Work*, Seattle, WA: PVG.

Baldoni, J. 2010 *Lead Your Boss*, New York: American Management Association.

Balnave, N., Brown J., Maconachie, G. & Stone, R. J. 2009 *Employment Relations in Australia* (2nd ed), Milton QLD: John Wiley & Sons.

Barclays 2009 *Philanthropy: The Evolution of Giving*, https://wealth.barclays.com/content/dam/bwpublic/global/documents/wealth_management/Philanthropy-The-Evolution-Of-Giving.pdf [accessed 10 March 2019].

Barsade, S. & O'Neill, O. A. 2016 "Manage Your Emotional Culture", *Harvard Business Review*, 94(1/2), 58–66.

Barton, D. & Wiseman M. 2015 "Where Boards Fall Short", *Harvard Business Review*, 93(1/2), 98–104.

Bass, B. & Avolio, B. 2000 *The Multifactor Leadership Questionnaire* (2nd ed), Redwood City, CA: Mind Garden.

Bass, B. M. 1970 "When Planning for Others", *Journal of Applied Behavioural Management*, 1(2), 1551–1571.

Baughan-Young, K. 2001 "The Color of Success", *Journal of Property Management*, 66(5), 68–70.

Baumol, W. & Bowen, W. 1966 *Performing Arts, The Economic Dilemma: A Study of Problems Common to Theater, Opera, Music, and Dance*, New York: Twentieth Century Fund.

Baxter, A. 2017a *How Marketing Can Help Influence Philanthropists to Give to your Not-for-profit Cause*, www.andrewbillybaxter.com.au/blog/2017/9/15/how-marketing-can-help-influence-philanthropists-to-give-to-your-not-for-profit-cause [accessed 10 March 2019].

Baxter, A. 2017b "Performance Pressure: Arts Companies Need to Lift Their Game When It Comes to Reaching Out and Growing Their Audiences", www.adma.com.au/resources/performance-pressure-arts-companies-need-to-lift-their-game-when-it-comes-to-reaching-out [accessed 27 February 2019].

Baxter, L. 2010 "From Luxury to Necessity: The Changing Role of Qualitative Research in the Arts", in O'Reilly, D. & Kerrigan, F. (eds) *Marketing the Arts: A Fresh Approach*, London: Routledge, 121–140.

Bazerman, M. H. & Tenbrunsel, A. E. 2011 "Ethical Breakdowns", *Harvard Business Review*, 89(4), 58–65.

Beard, A. 2012a "Dual Leadership and Budgeting in the Performing Arts: A Tale of Two Organizations", in Beard, A. (ed.) *No Money, No Mission – Financial Performance, Leadership Structure and Budgeting in Nonprofit Performing Arts Organisations*, PhD, New York, 9–54.

Beard, A. 2012b "Financial Performance in Arts Organizations – An Empirical Look at Its Relationship to Leadership Structure, in Beard, A. (ed.) *No Money, No Mission – Financial Performance, Leadership Structure and Budgeting in Nonprofit Performing Arts Organisations*, PhD, New York, 55–96.

Beard, A. 2012c "Revenue Structure in Nonprofit Arts Organizations – Do Dual Leadership or Budgeting Matter?" in *No Money, No Mission – Financial Performance, Leadership*

Structure and Budgeting In Nonprofit Performing Arts Organizations, New York, 97–140.

Beard, A. 2014 "Leading with Humor", *Harvard Business Review*, 92(5), 130–131.

Becker, K., Antuar, N. & Everett, C. 2011 "Implementing an Employee Performance Management System in a Nonprofit Organization", *Nonprofit Management & Leadership*, 21(3), 255–271.

Beech, N. & Gilmore, C. (eds) 2015 *Organising Music: Theory, Practice, Performance*, Cambridge: Cambridge University Press.

Beech, N., Broad, S., Cunliffe, A., Duffy, C. & Gilmore, C. 2015 "Developments in Organisation Theory and Organising Music", in Beech, N. & Gilmore, C. (eds) *Organising Music: Theory, Practice, Performance*, Cambridge: Cambridge University Press, 1–24.

Beirne, M. & Knight, S. 2002 "Principles and Consistent Management in the Arts: Lessons from British Theatre", *International Journal of Cultural Policy*, 8(1), 75–89.

Beirne, M. 2012 "Creative Tension? Negotiating the Space Between the Arts and Management", *Journal of Arts & Communities*, 4(3), 149–160.

Belfiore, E. 2015 "'Impact', 'Value' and 'Bad Economics': Making Sense of the Problem of Value in the Arts and Humanities", *Arts & Humanities in Higher Education*, 14(1), 95–110.

Bell, J. 2010 "Financial Leadership in Nonprofit Organizations", in Renz, D. O. (ed.) *The Jossey-Bass Handbook of Nonprofit Leadership and Management* (3rd ed), San Francisco, CA: John Wiley & Sons, 461–481.

Bell, J., Moyers, R. & Wolfred, T. 2006 *Daring to Lead 2006: A National Study of Nonprofit Executive Leadership*, www.compasspoint. org/sites/default/files/documents/194_ daringtolead06final.pdf [accessed 22 February 2019].

Benko, C. & Pelster, B. 2013 "How Women Decide", *Harvard Business Review*, 91(9),78–84.

Benson, J. & Brown, M. 2011 "Generations at Work: Are There Differences and Do They Matter?", *International Journal of Human Resources Management*, 22(9), 1843–1865.

Berryman, J. 2013 "Art and National Interest: The Diplomatic Origins of the 'Blockbuster Exhibition' in Australia", *Journal of Australian Studies*, 37(2), 159–173.

Besana, A., Bagnasco, A. M., Esposito, A. & Calzolari, A. 2018 "It's a Matter of Attention: The Marketing of Theatres in the Age of Social Media", *International Journal of Arts Management*, 20(3), 20–37.

Beugelsdijk, S. & Maseland, R. 2011 *Culture in Economics*, Cambridge: Cambridge University Press.

Bianchi, M. 2008 "Time and Preferences in Cultural Consumption", in Hutter, M. & Throsby, D. (eds), *Beyond Price*, Cambridge: Cambridge University Press, 236–257.

Billing, Y. D. & Alversson, M. 2000 "Questioning the Notion of Feminine Leadership: A Critical Perspective on the Gender Labelling of Leadership", *Gender, Work & Organization*, 7(3), 144–157.

Bilton, C. & Cummings, S. 2015 "Creative Strategy: Notes from a Small Label", in Beech, N. & Gilmore, C. (eds) *Organising Music: Theory, Practice, Performance*, Cambridge: Cambridge University Press, 83–98.

Bilton, C. & Leary, R. 2010 "What Can Managers Do for Creativity? Brokering Creativity in the Creative Industries", *International Journal of Cultural Policy*, 8(1), 49–64.

Bilton, C., Cummings, S. & Wilson, D. 2003 "Strategy as Creativity", in Cummings, S. & Wilson, D. (eds) *Images of Strategy*, Oxford: Blackwell Publishing, 197–227.

Bilton, C. & Leary, R. 2010 "What Can Managers Do for Creativity? Brokering Creativity in the Creative Industries", *International Journal of Cultural Policy*, 8(1) 49–64.

Blair, L. 2017 "Hate Your Open-plan Office? Join the Club", *The Age*, 26 October, 19.

Boehm, M. 2014 "San Diego Opera's Crowdfunding Campaign Has Strong Start", *Los Angeles Times*, 29 April, www.latimes. com/entertainment/arts/culture/la-et-cm-san-diego-opera-emergency-fundraising-campaign-20140429-story.html, [accessed 11 March 2019].

Boerner, S. & Jobst, J. 2011 "Stakeholder Management and Program Planning in German Public Theaters", *Nonprofit Management & Leadership*, 22(1), 67–84.

Boeuf, B., Darveau, J. & Legoux, R. 2014 "Financing Creativity: Crowdfunding as a New Approach for Theatre Projects", *International Journal of Arts Management*, 16(3), 33–48.

Boland, M. 2018 "Powerhouse Museum Uses Public Money to Prop Up Fashion Fundraiser, FOI Reveals", www.abc.net.au/news/ 2018-07-25/powerhouse-museum-uses-public-money-to-prop-up-fashion-party/ 10026264 [accessed 22 February 2019].

Bolman, L. G. & Deal, T. E. 2013 *Reframing Organizations* (5th ed), San Francisco, CA: Jossey-Bass.

Bonet, L., Cubelles, X. & Rosello, J. 1997 "Management Control and Evaluation of Public Cultural Centres", Fitzgibbon, M. & Kelly, A. (eds) *From Maestro to Manager*, Dublin: Oak Tree Press, 85–95.

Bonner, B. L. & Bolnger, A. R. 2014 "Bring Out the Best in Your Team", *Harvard Business Review*, 92(9), 26.

Boorsma, M. & Chiaravalloti, F. 2010 "Arts Marketing Performance: An Artistic-Mission-Led Approach to Evaluation", *The Journal of Arts Management, Law, and Society*, 40(4), 297–312.

Bossidy, L. 2007 "What Your Leader Expects from You – And What You Should Expect in Return", *Harvard Business Review*, 85(4), 58–65.

Boudier-Pailler, D. & Urbain, C. 2015 "How Do the Underprivileged Access Culture?', *International Journal of Arts Manager*, 18(1), 65–77.

Bovee, C. L. & Thill, J, L. 2010 *Business Communication Today* (10th ed), Upper Saddle, NJ: Pearson.

Bowman, W. 2011 *Finance Fundamentals for Non-profits*, Hoboken, NJ: John Wiley & Sons.

Bray, M., Waring, P. & Cooper, R. 2009 *Employment Relations*, Sydney: McGraw Hill.

Breeze, B. & Jollymore, G. 2017 "Understanding Solicitation: Beyond the Binary Variable of Being Asked or Not Asked", *International Journal of Nonprofit and Voluntary Sector Marketing*, 22, e1607, https://doi.org/ 10.1002/nvsm.1607

Brindle, M. & DeVereaux, C. (eds) 2011 *The Arts Management Handbook: New Directions for Students and Practitioner*, Armon, NY: M.E. Sharpe.

Brkić, A. 2019 "Death of the Arts Manager", in DeVereaux, C, (ed.) *Arts and Cultural Management: Sense and Sensibilities in the State of the Field*, New York: Routledge, 75–88.

Brokensha, P. & Tonks, A. 1986 *Culture and Community: Economics and Expectations of the Arts in South Australia*, Sydney: Social Science Press.

Brokensha, P. & Tonks, A. 1994 *Adelaide Festival of Arts 1984: The Economic Impact (interim Report)*, Adelaide: SAIT.

Brokensha, P. 2007 *Getting to Wisdom Slowly*, Adelaide: Peacock Publications.

Brooks, A. W. 2015 "Emotion and the Art of Negotiation", *Harvard Business Review*, 93(12), 57–64.

Brousseau, K. R., Driver, M. J., Hourihan, G. & Larsson, R. 2006 "The Seasoned Executive's Decision Making Style", *Harvard Business Review*, 84(2), 110–121.

Brown, C., Killick, A. & Renaud, K. 2013 "To Reduce E-mail, Start at the Top", *Harvard Business Review*, 91(9), 26.

Brudney, J. L. 2010 "Designing and Managing Volunteer Programs", in Renz, D. O. (ed.) *The Jossey-Bass Handbook of Nonprofit Leadership and Management* (3rd ed), San Francisco, CA: John Wiley & Sons, 753–793.

Bryant, P. & Pozdeev, N. 2011 "'Don't Have Time to Drain the Swap: Too Busy Dealing with Alligators': Defining the Governance Skills Sets that Enhance Volunteer Retention and Recruitment in Small Arts and Cultural Organisations", Antwerp: 11th AIMAC International Conference.

Bryson, A., Cappellari, L. & Lucifora, C. 2004 "Does Union Membership Really Reduce Job Satisfaction?" *British Journal of Industrial Relations*, 42(3), 439–459.

Bunting, M. 2016 *The Mindful Leader*, Milton, QLD: Wiley.

Burnside, J. 2018 "'Why Does Art Matter? Why Should We Support the Arts?", *Daily Review*, 10 May, https://dailyreview.com.au/art-matter-support-arts/74511/ [accessed 22 February 2019].

Button, J. 2012 *Speechless: A Year in My Father's Business*, Melbourne: Melbourne University Press.

Byrne, J. H. 1974 *Mrs Byrne's Dictionary of Unusual, Obscure and Preposterous Words*, Secaucus, NJ: Citadel Press.

Byrnes, W. J. 2015 *Management and the Arts* (5th ed), Burlington, MA: Focal Press.

Byrnes, W. J. 2019 "Foreword", in DeVereaux, C. (ed.) *Arts and Cultural Management: Sense and Sensibility in the State of the Field*, New York: Routledge, ix–xi.

C

Cameron, S. & Lapierre, L. 2007 "Mikhail Piotrovsky and the State Hermitage Museum", *International Journal of Arts Management*, 10(1), 65–77.

Cameron, S. & Lapierre, L. 2013 "Mikhail Piotrovsky and the State Hermitage Museum", in Caust, J. (ed.) *Arts Leadership: Internal Case Studies*, Melbourne: Tilde University Press, 3–18.

Cappelli, P. 2013 "HR for Neophytes", *Harvard Business Review*, 91(10), 25–27.

Carlopio, J., Andrewartha, G. & Armstrong, H. 2005 *Developing Management Skills*, Sydney: Pearson Education.

Carr, M. D. & Mellizo, P. 2013 "The Relative Effect of Voice, Autonomy, and the Wage on Satisfaction with Work", *The International Journal of Human Resource Management*, 24(6), 1186–1201.

Carroll, D. 2018 "What Sponsors Want from the Arts'" *ArtsHub*, 14 May, www.artshub. com.au/news-article/features/grants-and-funding/diana-carroll/what-sponsors-want-from-the-arts-255672 [accessed 16 March 2019].

Casciaro, T., Gino, F. & Kouchaki, M. 2016 "Managing Yourself – Learn to Love Networking", *Harvard Business Review*, 94(5), 104–107.

Caust, J. 2003 "Putting the 'Art' Back into Arts Policy Making: How Arts Policy Has Been 'Captured' by the Economist and the Marketers", *The International Journal of Cultural Policy*, 9(1), 51–63.

Caust, J. 2005 "Does It Matter Who Is in Charge? The Influence of the Business Paradigm on Arts Leadership and Management", *Asia Pacific Journal of Arts and Cultural Management*, 3(1), 153–165.

Caust, J. 2010 "Does the Art End When the Management Begins?", *Asia Pacific Journal of Arts and Cultural Management*, 7(2), 570–584.

Caust, J. 2013 "Thriving or Surviving: Artists as Leaders of Smaller Arts Organizations", in Caust, J. (ed.) *Arts Leadership: Internal Case Studies,* Melbourne: Tilde University Press, 194–209.

Caust, J. (ed.) 2015a *Arts and Cultural Leadership in Asia*, London: Routledge.

Caust, J. 2015b "Different Culture but Similar Roles: Leadership of Major Performing Arts Centers", in Caust, J. (ed.) *Arts and Cultural Leadership in Asia*, London: Routledge, 148–162.

Caust, J. 2018a *Arts Leadership in Contemporary Contexts*, London: Routledge.

Caust, J. 2018b "To Fix Gender Inequity in Arts Organisations We Need More Women in Politics and Chairing Boards", *The Conversation*, 12 June, https://theconversation.com/to-fix-gender-inequity-in-arts-leadership-we-need-more-women-in-politics-and-chairing-boards-97782 [accessed 22 February 2019].

Caust, J. & Glow, H. 2011 "Festivals, Artists and Entrepreneurialism: The Role of The Adelaide Fringe Festival", *International Journal of Event Management Research*, 6(2), 1–14.

Cave, J. 2016 *Digital Marketing vs Traditional Marketing: which one is better?*, Digital Doughnut, 14 July, www.digitaldoughnut.com/articles/2016/july/digital-marketing-vs-traditional-marketing [accessed 27 February 2019].

Chappell, M. & Knell, J. 2012 *Public Value Measurement Framework*, Perth: Government of Western Australia, Department of Culture and the Arts.

Charity Navigator n.d. *Giving Statistics*, www.charitynavigator.org/index.cfm?bay=content.view&cpid=42 [accessed 10 March 2019].

Chew, S. & Hallo, L. 2015 "On Your Toes: Perception of Leadership Influences in Dance Companies in Singapore", in Caust, J. (ed.) *Arts and Cultural Leadership in Asia*, London: Routledge, 129–147.

Chiaravalloti, F. & Piber, M. 2011 "Ethical and Political Implications of Methodological Settings in Arts Management Research: The Case of Performance Evaluation", Antwerp: AIMAC International Conference.

Chie, T. Y. 2015 *The Best Social Media Site to Promote Your Art?* Parkablogs, 19 October, www.parkablogs.com/content/imfa-13-best-social-media-site-promote-your-art [accessed 27 February 2019].

Chin, W.-K. & Yun, S.-W. 2013 "The Predicament of Competition for Cultural Resources among Hong Kong Art Troupes", *LEAP Magazine*, May 23, in Caust, J, (ed,) Arts and Cultural Leadership in Asia, London: Routledge.

Chong, T. 2015 "Deviance and Nation-building", in Caust, J. (ed.) *Arts and Cultural Leadership in Asia*, London: Routledge, 15–25.

Clancy, P. 1997 "Skills and Competencies: The Cultural Manager", in Fitzgibbon, M. & Kelly, A. (eds) *From Maestro to Manager*, Dublin: Oak Tree Press, 341–366.

Clare, R. 2010 "A Cultural Leadership Reader 47 Leadership in a Matrix ... Or Getting Things Done in More Than One Dimension", in Kay, S. & Venner, K. (eds) *A Cultural Leader's Handbook*, London: Creative Choices, 46–49.

Classens, M. 2015 "What's in It for the Volunteers?", *Nonprofit Management & Leadership*, 26(2), 145–156.

Cleveland, H. 2002 *Nobody in Charge: Essays on the Future of Leadership*, Hoboken, NJ: Wiley.

Cloake, M. 1997 "Management, The Arts and Innovation", in Fitzgibbon, M. & Kelly, A. (eds) *From Maestro to Manager*, Dublin: Oak Tree Press, 271–295.

Cloonan, M. 2015 "Managing the Zoeys: Some Reminiscences", in Beech, N. & Gilmore, C. (eds) *Organising Music: Theory, Practice and Performance*, Cambridge: Cambridge University Press, 226–235.

Coffee, S. 2013 "Top Ten Myths about Creativity", *Arts Hub*, 18 August, www.artshub.com.au/news-article/features/trends-and-analysis/top-ten-myths-about-creativity-196291 [accessed 20 February 2019].

Cohen, S. G. & March, J. G. 1974 *Leadership and Ambiguity*, New York: McGraw Hill.

Cohendet, P. & Simon, L. 2014 "Financing Creativity: New Issues and New Approaches", *International Journal of Arts Management*, 16(3), 3–5.

Colbert, F. 2007 *Le Marketing des Arts et de la Culture*, Montreal: Gaetan Morin Editeur.

Colbert, F. 2009 *Beyond Branding: Contemporary Marketing Challenges for Arts Organizations*, Geelong: Kenneth Myer Lecture, Deakin University.

Collins, J. 2005 *Good to Great and the Social Sectors*, Boulder, CO: Jim Collins.

Collins, J. C. & Porras, J. I. 1994 *Built to Last: Successful Habits of Visionary Companies*, New York: HarperBusiness.

Commonwealth of Australia 2017 *Giving Australia 2016*, www.communitybusinesspartnership. gov.au/wp-content/uploads/2017/04/giving_australia_2016_philanthropy_and_philanthropists_report.pdf [accessed 10 March 2019].

Congdon, C., Flynn, D. & Redman, M. 2014 "Balancing 'We' and 'Me'", *Harvard Business Review*, 92(11), 51–57.

Connolly, S. 2015 "Film Funding: Just who will be walking the plank", http://dailyreview. crikey.com.au/film-funding-just-who-will-be-walking-the-plank/11507 [accessed 16 March 2019].

Conte, D. M. & Langley, S. 2007 *Theatre Management*, Hollywood, CA: EntertainmentPro.

Cooke, P. 1997 "The Culture of Management and the Management of Culture", in Fitzgibbon, M. & Kelly, A. (eds) *From Maestro to Manager*, Dublin: Oak Tree Press, 31–40.

Cooperrider, D. L., Whitney, D. & Stavros, J. M. 2005 *Appreciative Inquiry Handbook*, Brunswick OH: Crown Custom Publishing.

Coorey, P. 2011 "I Want to Be Able to Look My Children in the Face", *Sydney Morning Herald*, www.smh.com.au/environment/climate-change/i-want-to-be-able-to-look-my-children-in-the-face-20110530-1fd01. html [accessed on 20 February 2019].

Corrigan, P. 1999 *Shakespeare on Management*, London: Kogan Page.

Coslovich, G. 2011 "If Religious Zeal Inhibits Art We Are All Poorer", *The Age*, 3 October, www.theage.com.au/it-pro/if-religious-zeal-inhibits-art-we-are-all-poorer-20111002-1l3q3.html [accessed 20 February 2019].

Courtney, H., Lovallo, D. & Clarke, C. 2013 "Deciding How to Decide", *Harvard Business Review*, 91(11), 64–70.

Courtney, R. 2002 *Strategic Management for Voluntary Non-profit Organizations*, London: Routledge.

Covey, S. R. 1992 *Principle-Centred Leadership*, London: Pocket Books.

Craumer, M. 2013 "When the Direct Approach Backfires, Try Indirect Influence", in Hill, L. A. & Lineback, K. "Managing Your Boss", in *HBR Guide to Managing Up and Across*, Boston, MA: Harvard Business Review Press, 185–188.

Craumer, M. 2013 "'When the Direct Approach Backfires, Try Indirect Influence", in Hill, L. A. & Lineback, K. "Managing Your Boss", in *HBR Guide to Managing Up and Across*, Boston, MA: Harvard Business Review Press, 185–188.

Craven, P. 2015 "Reacting to the Sting of Critics Casts Light Where One Might Prefer Shadows", *The Weekend Australian*,

10–11 January, 17 www.theaustralian. com.au/arts/opinion/reacting-to-the-sting-of-critics-casts-light-where-one-might-prefer-shadows/story-fn9n9z9n-1227180052396 [accessed 8 February 2015].

Cray, D. & Inglis, L. 2011 "Strategic Decision Making in Arts Organizations", *Journal of Arts Management, Law and Society*, 41(2), 84–102.

Cray, D., Inglis, L. & Freeman, S. 2007 "Managing the Arts: Leadership and Decision Making under Dual Rationalities", *The Journal of Arts Management, Law and Society*, 36(4), 295–313.

Croggon, A. 2013 "The Perfect Storm: Playwright vs. Director", *ABC Arts*, www.abc.net.au/arts/blog/Alison-Croggon/playwright-versus-Director-130731/ [accessed 23 January 2015].

Cropanzano, R. & Wright, T. A. 2001 "When a 'Happy' Worker is Really a 'Productive' Worker: A Review and Further Refinement of the Happy-productive Worker Thesis", *Consulting Psychology Journal: Practice & Research*, 53(3), 182–199.

Crosby, B. C. & Bryson, J. M. 2005 *Leadership for the Common Good* (2nd ed), San Francisco, CA: Jossey-Bass.

Crutchfield, L. R. & Grant, H. M. 2008 *Forces for Good: The Six Practices of High-Impact Nonprofits*, San Francisco, CA: Jossey-Bass.

Cuadrado-García, M. 2017 "Teatro Olympia: A Family-Run Venue Entering a New Century", *International Journal of Arts Management*, 19(3), 71–78.

Cuddy, A. 2013 "Empowering through Body Language – Top Tips on Essential Assertiveness", *TED Talk*, www.youtube.com/watch?v=TdU2I0i2Wh0 [accessed on 22 February 2019].

Culbert, S. 2015 "Performance Reviews: Get Rid of Them", *The Age*, 18 February, 45, www.smh.com.au/comment/performance-reviews-get-rid-of-them-20150217-13gozk.html [accessed 10 March 2019].

Culture Counts n.d. "5 Key Principles", https://culturecounts.cc/about/ [accessed 22 February 2019].

Cummings, S. 2003 "Strategy as Ethos", in Cummings, S. & Wilson, D. (eds) *Images of Strategy*, Oxford: Blackwell Publishing, 41–73.

Cuyler, A. C. 2013 "Affirmative Action and Diversity: Implications for Arts Management", *Journal of Arts Management, Law, and Society*, 43(2), 98–105.

Cyr, C. 2014 "Roger Parent and Realizations Inc. Montreal: A Flair for Creativity", *International Journal of Arts Management*, 16(3), 60–70.

D

D'Aprix, R. 2011 "Challenges of Employee Engagement", in Gillis, T. L. (ed.) *The IABC Handbook of Organizational Communication* (2nd ed), San Francisco, CA: Jossey-Bass, 257–269.

Daft, R. L. 1999 *Leadership Theory and Practice*, Fort Worth, TX: Dryden Press.

Dalglish, P. & Miller, C. 2011 *The Leader in You: Developing Your Leadership Potential*, Melbourne: Tilde University Press.

Dancert, S. & Yeates, C. 2018 "NAB's Culture Could Take 10 Years to Fix, Chairman Says", *The Sydney Morning Herald*, 26 November 2018, www.smh.com.au/business/banking-and-finance/nab-s-culture-could-take-10-years-to-fix-chairman-says-20181126-p50igk.html [accessed 27 February 2019].

Davidson, H. 2018 "Q&A on #MeToo: Actors Use Sexual Energy to Connect, Neil Armfield Says", *The Guardian*, 30 October, www.theguardian.com/australia-news/2018/oct/30/qa-on-metoo-actors-use-sexual-energy-to-connect-neil-armfield-says [accessed 27 February 2019].

Davidson, R. & Poor, N. 2015 "The Barriers Facing Artists' Use of Crowdfunding Platforms: Personality, Emotional Labor, and Going to the Well One Too Many Times", *New Media & Society*, 17(2), 289–307.

Davis, G. 2008 *The Leaders and the Gang: Reflections on Leadership*, Victoria: Leadership Victoria, 5 June.

De Botton, A. 2009 *The Pleasures and Sorrows of Work*, London: Hamish Hamilton.

De Kretser, M. 2012 *Questions of Travel*, Sydney: Allen & Unwin.

De Paoli, D. 2011 "The Role of Leadership in Changing Art Institutions – The Case of the National Museum of Art in Oslo, Norway", Antwerp: 11th AIMAC International Conference.

De Pree, M. 1997 *Leading Without Power*, Holland, MI: Shepherd Foundation.

De Rooij, P. & Bastiaansen, M. 2017 "Understanding and Measuring Consumption Motives in the Performing Arts", *Journal of*

Arts Management, Law and Society, 47(2), 118–135.

De Swaan Arons, M., van den Driest, F. & Weed, K. 2014 "The Ultimate Marketing Machine", *Harvard Business Review*, 92(7/8), 55–63.

Deal, T. E. & Kennedy, A. A. 1982 *Corporate Celebration: Play, Purpose and Profit at Work*, San Francisco, CA: Berrett-Koehler.

Dehler, G. E., Welsh, M. A. & Lewis, M. W. 2004 "Critical Pedagogy in the 'New Paradigm'", in Grey, C. & Antonacopoulou, E. (eds) *Essential Readings in Management Learning*, London: Sage Publications, 167–186.

Deloitte 2014 *Deloitte Media Consumer Survey 2014 Australia Media Usage and Preferences*, www2.deloitte.com/content/dam/Deloitte/au/Documents/technology-media-telecommunications/deloitte-au-tmt-media-consumer-survey-2014-infographic-031014.png [accessed 11 March 2019].

Deming, W. 1982 *Out of Crisis*, Cambridge: Cambridge University Press.

Deshpande, S. 2015 "The Studio Safdar Story", in Caust, J. (ed.) *Arts and Cultural Leadership in Asia*, London: Routledge, 91–101.

DeSteno, D. 2014 "Who Can You Trust?" *Harvard Business Review*, 92(3), 112–115.

Detert, J. R. & Burris, E. R. 2016 "Can Your Employees Really Speak Freely?", *Harvard Business Review*, 94(1/2), 81–87.

DeVereaux, C. 2011 "Arts and Cultural Policy", in Brindle, M. & DeVereaux, C. *The Arts management Handbook*, Armon, NY: M.E. Sharpe, 219–251.

DeVereaux, C. (ed.) 2019a *Arts and Cultural Management: Sense and Sensibility in the State of the Field*, New York: Routledge.

DeVereaux, C. 2019b "Cultural Management as a Field", in DeVereaux, C. (ed.) *Arts and Cultural Management: Sense and Sensibility in the State of the Field*, New York: Routledge, 3–12.

DeVereaux, C. 2019c "Cultural Management and Its Discontents", in DeVereaux, C. (ed.) *Arts and Cultural Management: Sense and Sensibility in the State of the Field*, New York: Routledge, 187–204.

Dickie, L. & Dickie, C. 2011 *Cornerstones of Management* (2nd ed), Melbourne: Tilde University Press.

DiMaggio, P. J. 1981 "The Impact of Public Funding on Organizations in the Arts", *Yale Program on Non-Profit Organizations Working Paper 31*, New Haven, CT: Yale University.

Donaldson, T. & Preston, L. E. 1995 "The Stakeholder Theory of the Corporation: Concepts, Evidence, and Implications", *Academy of Management Review*, 20(1), 65–91.

Donnelly, P. 2017a "Managing Venue Operations for a Newly Opened PAC", in Lambert, P. D. & Williams, R. (eds) *Performing Arts Center Management*, New York: Routledge, 142–162.

Donnelly, P. 2011 "Facilities Management", in Brindle, M. & DeVereaux, C. (eds) *The Arts Management Handbook*, Armon, NY: M.E. Sharpe, 13–37.

Dörfler, D. & Ackermann, F. 2012 "Understanding Intuition: The Case for Two Forms of Intuition", *Management Learning*, 43(5), 545–564.

Doyle, P. 2003 "Strategy as Marketing", in Cummings, S. & Wilson, D. (eds) *Images of Strategy*, Oxford: Blackwell Publishing, 331–335.

Drucker, P. F. 1990 *Managing the Non-profit Organization*, New York: HarperCollins.

Drucker, P. F. 2004 "What Makes an Effective Executive", *Harvard Business Review*, 82(6), 58–63.

Dubini, P. & Monti, A. 2018 "Board Composition and Organizational Performance in the Cultural Sector: The Case of Italian Opera Houses", *International Journal of Arts Management*, 20(2), 56–71.

Dubrin, A. J., Dalglish, C. & Miller, P. 2006 *Leadership* (2nd Asia-Pacific ed), Milton, QLD: John Wiley & Sons.

Ducey, L. 2014 "PM Calls Opera Decision Crazy", *The Age*, 9 October, www.theage.com.au/it-pro/tony-abbott-calls-wa-operas-carmen-ban-crazy-20141009-113mc8.html [accessed 23 February 2015].

Durel, J. n.d. *It's Time to Start a "Stop Doing" List*, www.qm2.org/Durel/It_s_Time_to_Start_a_Stop_Doing_List.pdf [accessed 1 March 2015].

Dwyer, J. 2009 *Communication in Business* (4th ed), Sydney: Pearson.

Dym, B., Egmont, S. & Watkins, L. 2011 *Managing Leadership Transition for Nonprofits*, Upper Saddle River, NJ: Pearson Educational.

E

Eagly, A. H. & Carli, L. A. 2007 "Women and the Labyrinth of Leadership", *Harvard Business Review*, 85(9), 63–71.

Ehrich, L. 2011 "Mentoring", in O'Toole, S., Ferres, N. & Connell, J. (eds), *People Development: An Inside View*, Melbourne: Tilde University Press, 7–16.

Eikhof, Dr & Haunschild, A. 2007 "For Art's Sake! Artistic and Economic Logics in Creative Production", *Journal of Organizational Behaviour*, 28, 523–538.

Ekvall, G. 1996 "Organizational Climate for Creativity and Innovation", *European Journal of Work and Organizational Psychology*, 5, 105–123.

Ellyard, P. 2015 Interview on *The Conversation Hour*, ABC Radio National, 26 February, www.abc.net.au/radio/programitem/pgJE6g2bLG?play=true [accessed 11 March 2019].

Elsner, P. A. 2001 *Authenticity and Leadership: Integrating Our Inner Lives with Our Work*, Iowa State University: Leadership Forum.

Eltham, B. 2013 "Evidence-based Policy: The Minefield of Cultural Measurement", *A Cultural Policy Blog*, 17 August, http://culturalpolicyreform.wordpress.com/category/evidence-based-policy/ [accessed 16 March 2019].

Eltham, B. 2014 "Biennale Boycott Backlash: Vicious Ingratitude or Valid Critique?", *ArtsHub*, 12 March, www.artshub.com.au/news-article/opinions-and-analysis/trends-and-analysis/biennale-boycott-backlash-vicious-ingratitude-or-valid-critique-198405 [accessed 16 March 2019].

Eltham, B. 2018 "Why the Australian Arts Sector Could Be in for a Major Reckoning", *Crikey*, 26 April, www.crikey.com.au/2018/04/26/australian-arts-major-reckoning-governance/ [accessed 28 December 2018].

Eltham, B. 2012 "The State of Australia's Performing Arts Centres, and What it Tells Us about the State of the Australian Arts", *Meanjin*, 71(3), 92–101.

Enoch, W. 2014 *Take Me to Your Leader: The Dilemma of Cultural Leadership*, Platform Paper No. 40, Sydney: Currency Press.

Entertainment Assist 2016 *Working in the Australian Entertainment Industry: Key Findings*, EA Melbourne.

Erickson, A., Shaw, J. B. & Agabe, Z. 2007 "An Empirical Investigation of the Antecedents, Behaviors, and Outcomes of Bad Leadership", *Journal of Leadership Studies*, 1(3), 26–43.

F

Fairwork Ombudsman, www.fairwork.gov.au/employee-entitlements/bullying-and-harassment [accessed 20 February 2019].

Fairwork Ombudsman, *National Employment Standards*, www.fairwork.gov.au/employee-entitlements/flexibility-in-the-workplace/flexible-working-arrangements [accessed 22 February 2019].

Faure, F. 2011 "The Emergent Organisation", in O'Toole, S., Ferres, N. & Connell, J. (eds) *People Development: An Inside View*, Melbourne: Tilde University Press, 272–284.

Fergusson, R. & Law, J. 2000 *Dictionary of Proverbs*, London: Penguin Reference.

Ferrazzi, K. 2014 "Managing Change, One Day at a Time", *Harvard Business Review*, 92(7–8), 23–25.

Ferres, N. 2011 "Leadership and Management Development (LMS)", in O'Toole, S., Ferres, N. & Connell, J. (eds) *People Development: An Inside View*, Melbourne: Tilde University Press, 107–123.

Fine, C. 2017 *Testosterone Rex: Unmaking the Myths of our Gendered Minds*, London: Icon Books.

Fischer, M. 2000 *Ethical Decision Making in Fund Raising*, New York: John Wiley & Sons.

Fishel, D. 2003 *The Book of The Board*, Sydney: Federation Press.

Fisher, R. & Ury, W. 1991 *Getting to Yes* (2nd ed), New York: Penguin.

Fitzgerald, S. (ed.) 2008 *Managing Independent Cultural Centres: A Reference Manual*, Singapore: Asia-Europe Foundation.

Fitzgibbon, C. 2012 "Review of 'The Arts Management Handbook: New Directions for Students and Practitioner', edited by Meg Brindle and Constance DeVereaux", *The Journal of Arts Management, Law, and Society*, 42(2), 96–98.

Fitzgibbon, M. & Isaacs, J. 1997 "Speaking for Themselves Part 1", Fitzgibbon, M. & Kelly, A. (eds) *From Maestro to Manager*, Dublin: Oak Tree Press, 41–51.

Fitzgibbon, M. 2001 *Managing Innovation in the Arts*, Westport, CT: Quorum Books.

Fortier, I. & Castellanos Juarez, M. 2017 "How Hypermodern and Accelerated Society is Challenging the Cultural Sector", *The Journal of Arts Management, Law, and Society*, 47(4), 209–217.

Fox, D. F. 2013 "New Ventures to Support your mission: Financial Diversification in Arts & Cultural Institutions", December, *Arts Insights*, www.artsconsulting.com/pdf_arts_insights/insights_dec_2013.pdf [accessed 23 February 2015].

Freeman, R. E. 1984 *Strategic Management: A Stakeholder Approach*, Boston, MA: Pitman.

Frey, B. S. 2008 "What Values Should Count in the Arts: The Tension between Economic Effects and Cultural Value", in Hutter, M. & Throsby, D. (eds) *Beyond Price*, Cambridge: Cambridge University Press, 261–269.

Friedman, S. D. 2008 "Be a Better Leader, Have a Richer Life", *Harvard Business Review*, 86(4), 112–118.

Fulton, A. 2011 "Smith Threatens to Out Rich Who Don't Help Others", *Sydney Morning Herald*, www.smh.com.au/executive-style/smith-threatens-to-out-rich-who-dont-help-others-20110909-1k1sy.html [accessed 10 March 2019].

G

Gabarro, J. J. & Kotter, J. P. 2005 "Managing Your Boss", *Harvard Business Review*, 83, 92–99.

Galanaki, E. & Papalexandris, M. 2013 "Measuring Workplace Bullying in Organisations", *The International Journal of Human Resource Management*, 24(3), 2107–2130.

Galford, R. & Drapeau, S. A. 2003 "The Enemies of Trust", *Harvard Business Review*, 81(2), 88–95.

Gallo, A. 2013a "Dealing with Your Incompetent Boss", in *HBR Guide to Managing Up and Across*, Boston, MA: Harvard Business Review Press, 55–59.

Gallo, A. 2013b "Stop Being Micromanaged", in *HBR Guide to Managing Up and Across*, Boston, MA: Harvard Business Review Press, 47–59.

Galvin, N. 2017 "Sydney Symphony Orchestra Board's Dramatic U-turn On Same-sex Marriage", *Sydney Morning Herald*, 1 October, www.smh.com.au/entertainment/music/sso-boards-dramatic-uturn-on-samesex-marriage-20171001-gys1it.html [accessed 20 February 2019].

Gardner, J. W. 1989 *On Leadership*, New York: Free Press.

Gardner, W. L., Fischer, D. & Hunt, J. G. 2009 "Emotional Labor and Leadership: A Threat to Authenticity?", *The Leadership Quarterly*, 20, 466–482.

George, B., Sims, P., McLean, A. N. & Mayer, D. 2007 "Discovering Your Authentic Leadership", *Harvard Business Review*, 85(2), 129–138.

George, C. S. & Cole, K. 1992 *Supervision in Action*, Sydney: Prentice Hall.

Gierck, M. 2018 "Take Your Time to Really Hear Others", *The Age*, 6 January, 30.

Gigerenzer, G. 2006 "Follow the Leaders, Breakthrough Ideas for 2006, #13", *Harvard Business Review*, 84(2), 58.

Gilhespy, I. 1999 "Measuring the Performance of Cultural Organizations: A Model", *International Journal of Arts Management*, 2(1), 38–52.

Gill, R. 2017a "Queensland Symphony Staff Churn Prompts Claims of a 'Toxic' Work Culture", *Daily Review*, 15 November, https://dailyreview.com.au/queensland-symphony-staff-churn-prompts-claims-toxic-work-culture/68193/ [accessed 11 March 2019].

Gill, R. 2017b "QSO Chair and Musicians say Everything is Fine", *Daily Review*, 17 November, https://dailyreview.com.au/qso-chair-orchestra-say-everything-fine-brisbane/68279/ [accessed 11 March 2019].

Gilley, J. W., Gilley, A. M., Jackson, S. A. & Lawrence, H. 2015 "Managerial Practices and Organizational Conditions that Encourage Employee Growth and Development", *Performance Improvement Quarterly*, 28(3), 71–93.

Gilley, J. W., Shelton, P. & Gilley, A. 2011 "Development Leadership: A New Perspective of HRD", *Advances in Human Resource Development*, 13(3), 386–405.

Gillfillan, G. & McCann, C. 2018 *Trends in Union Membership in Australia*, Parliament of Australia, Canberra, www.aph.gov.au/About_Parliament/Parliamentary_Departments/Parliamentary_Library/pubs/rp/rp1819/UnionMembership [accessed 11 March 2019].

Gilmore, A. 2011 "Not Just CEOs Tweeting: Digital Content, the Arts and the Cultural Politics of Innovation', Antwerp: 11th AIMAC International Conference.

Ginther, R. 2010 *Making the Case for Change: Challenging Hierarchy in Arts and*

Cultural Organizations, Canada: Athabasca University.

Gleeson-White, J. 2012 *Double Entry*, Sydney: Allen & Unwin.

Globe Foundation 2014 *Globe CEO Study 2014*, https://globeproject.com/study_2014 [accessed 28 February 2019].

Godfrey, C. 2010 "Working with Uncertainty", in Kay, S. & Venner, K. (eds), *A Cultural Leader's Handbook*, London: Creative Choices, 78–85.

Goethals, G. R. & Hoyt, C. L. 2011 "What Makes Leadership Necessary, Possible and Effective: The Psychological Dimensions", in Harvey, M. & Riggio, R. E. (eds) *Leadership Studies – The Dialogue of Disciplines*, Cheltenham: Edgar Elgar Publishing, 101–118.

Goffe, R. & Jones, G. 2013 "Creating the Best Workplace on Earth", *Harvard Business Review*, 91(5), 99–106.

Golding, K. 2011 *Essential Governance Practices for Arts Organisations*, Sydney: Australia Council.

Goldman, B. M. & Kernis, M. H. 2002 "The Role of Authenticity in Healthy Psychological Functioning and Subjective Well-being", *Annals of the American Psychotherapy Association*, 5(6), 18–20.

Goleman, D. 2013 "The Focused Leader", *Harvard Business Review*, 76(6), 51–60.

Golensky, M. 2011 *Strategic Leadership and Management in Nonprofit Organizations*, Chicago, IL: Lyceum Books Inc.

Gosling, J. & Mintzberg, H. 2003 "The Five Minds of a Manager", *Harvard Business Review*, 81(11), 54–63.

Grace, K. S. 2005 *Beyond Fundraising: New Strategies for Nonprofit Innovation and Investment*, Hoboken, NJ: Wiley.

Graeber, D. 2018 "My Bullsh*t Career", *Weekend Australian Magazine*, 12 May, 20–23.

Grant, A. & Singh, J. 2014 "The Problem with Financial Incentives – and What to Do About It", Knowledge@Wharton, http://knowledge.wharton.upenn.edu/article/the-problem-with-financial-incentives-and-what-to-do-about-it/ [accessed 10 March 2019].

Grant, A. H., Gino, F. & Hofmann, D. A. 2010 "The Hidden Advantages of Quiet Bosses", *Harvard Business Review*, 88(12), 28.

Grant, P. 2012 *The Business of Giving: The Theory and Practice of Philanthropy, Grantmaking and Social Investment*, New York: Palgrave Macmillan.

Grayling, A. C. 2005 *The Heart of Things*, London: Weidenfeld and Nicholson.

Grayling, A. C. 2011 *The Good Book*, London: Bloomsbury.

Great Place to Work n.d. *The Dawn of the Great Workplace Era*, www.greatplacetowork.net/storage/documents/Publications_Documents/The_Dawn_of_the_Great_Workplace_Era.pdf [accessed 16 March 2019].

Grehan, H. & Eckersall, P. (eds) 2013 *"We're People Who Do Shows" Back to Back Theatre*, Aberystwyth: Performance Research Books.

Grey, C. 2005 *A Very Short, Fairly Interesting and Reasonably Cheap Book About Studying Organisations*, London: Sage Publications.

Griffin, R. W. 1999 *Management* (6th ed), Boston, MA: Houghton Mifflin Company.

Groves, D. 2014 "Veteran Actor Quits Equity Committee", *if.com.au*, http://if.com.au/2014/06/26/article/Veteran-actor-quits-Equity-committee/TKXBFNUWBE.html [accessed 11 March 2019].

Groysberg, B. & Abrahams, R. 2014 "Manager Your Work, Manager Your Life", *Harvard Business Review*, 92(3), 58–66.

Groysberg, B. & Connolly, K. 2013 "Great Leaders Who Make the Mix Work". *Harvard Business Review*, 91(9), 69–76.

Guillon, O, 2017 "Do Employees in the Cultural Sector Adhere More Strongly to Their Organization's Goals than Employees in Other Sectors", *International Journal of Arts Management*, 19(2), 4–13.

H

Hackley, C. 2015 "Branding and the Music Market", in Beech, N. & Gilmore, C. (eds) *Organising Music: Theory, Practice, Performance*, Cambridge: Cambridge University Press, 127–134.

Hackman J. R. interviewed by Coutu, D. 2009 "Why Teams Don't Work", *Harvard Business Review*, 87(5), 98–105.

Hager, M. A. & Brudney, J. L. 2015 "In Search of Strategy: Universalistic, Contingent and Configurational Adoption of Volunteer Management Practices", *Nonprofit Management & Leadership*, 25(3), 235–254.

Hagoort, G. 2005 *Art Management: Entrepreneurial Style* (5th ed), Delft: Eburon.

Halvorson, G. 2014 "Getting to 'us'", *Harvard Business Review*, 92(9), 38.

Hamlin, R. G. 2004 "In Support of Universalistic Models of Managerial and Leadership Effectiveness: Implications of HRD Research and Practice", *Human Resource Development Quarterly*, 15(2), 189–215.

Hands, K. 2011 *The Impact of Artistic Directors on Australian Performing Arts Organisations*, Antwerp: AIMAC.

Hannan, R. L. 2005 "The Combined Effect of Wages and Firm Profit on Employee Effort", *Accounting Review*, 80(1), 167–188.

Hare, D. 2004 *Acting Up* (2nd ed), London: Faber and Faber.

Harris, M. 1989 "The Governing Body Role: Problems and Perceptions in Implementation", *Non-profit and Voluntary Sector Quarterly*, 18 (3), 317–232.

Haunschild, A. & Eikhof, D. R. 2009 "From HRM to Employment Rules and Lifestyles", *German Journal of Human Resource Research*, 23(2), 107–124.

Hawthorne, M. 2015 "Study Sashes Myth of Roadie Lifestyle", *The Age*, 23 February, 8.

Hayes, D. & Roodhouse, S. 2010 "From Missionary to Market Maker", in O'Reilly, D. & Kerrigan, F. (eds) *Marketing the Arts: A Fresh Approach*, London: Routledge, 40–53.

Haywood, C. 2001 "Wish You Weren't Here", *Financial Management (CIMA)*, July/August, 42–45.

HBR Editor 2015 "Collaboration: Team Building in the Cafeteria", *Harvard Business Review*, 93(12), 24–25.

HBR Staff 2018 "Best Performing CEOs in the World", https://hbr.org/2018/11/the-best-performing-ceos-in-the-world-2018 [accessed 18 January 2019].

Heenan, D. A. & Bennis, D. 1999 *Co-Leaders: The Power of Great Partnerships*, New York: John Wiley & Sons.

Heffron, F. 1989 *Organisation Theory and Public Organisations: The Political Connection*, Englewood Cliffs, NJ: Prentice Hall.

Hein, H. H. 2011 "Stepping into Character", Antwerp: AIMAC International Conference.

Heinze, D. 2013 "Editorial", *Arts Management Newsletter*, October.

Helle Hedegaard Hein 2011 "Stepping into Character", Antwerp: AIMAC.

Hendrix, W. H. 2006 "Foreword", in Sarros, J., Cooper, B. K., Hartican, A. M. & Barker, C. J. (eds) *The Character of Leadership*, Milton, QLD: John Wiley & Sons, ix–x.

Henley, J. 2018 "French Teenagers Swipe Up for Arts on Macron's App", *The Guardian*, 18 August, www.theguardian.com/world/2018/aug/18/french-teenagers-swipe-up-for-arts-electronic-culture-pass-emmanuel-macron [accessed 20 February 2019].

Henrique-Gomes, L. 2018 "'It's Not a Billboard': Anger at Use of Sydney Opera House for Horse Racing Ads", *The Guardian*, 6 October, www.theguardian.com/australia-news/2018/oct/06/its-not-a-billboard-anger-at-use-of-sydney-opera-house-for-horse-racing-ads [accessed 11 March 2019].

Herman, R. D. 2010 "Executive Leadership", in Renz, D. O. (ed.) *The Jossey-Bass Handbook of Nonprofit Leadership and Management* (3rd ed), San Francisco, CA: John Wiley & Sons, 157–177.

Herman, R. D. & Renz, D. O. 2008 "Advancing Nonprofit Organizational Effectiveness Research and Theory: Nine Theses", *Nonprofit Management & Leadership*, 18(4), 399–415.

Hewison, R. & Holden, J. 2011 *The Cultural Leadership Handbook*, Farnham: F Gower.

Hewison, R., Holden, J. & Jones, S. 2013 "Leadership and Transformation at the Royal Shakespeare Company", in Caust, J. (ed.) *Arts Leadership*, Melbourne: Tilde University Press, 144–158.

Hill, L. 2014 "How to Manage for Collective Creativity?", *TED Talk*, www.ted.com/talks/linda_hill_how_to_manage_for_collective_creativity?language=en#t-7224 [accessed 11 March 2019].

Hill, L. A. & Lineback, K. 2011 "Are You a Good Boss or a Great One?", *Harvard Business Review*, 89(1/2), 124–131.

Hill, L. A. & Lineback, K. 2013 "Managing Your Boss", in *HBR Guide to Managing Up and Across*, Boston, MA: Harvard Business Review Press, 3–16.

Hoedemaekers, C. & Ybema, S. 2015 "All of Me: Art, Industry and Identity Struggles", in Beech, N. & Gilmore, C. (eds) *Organising Music: Theory, Practice, Performance*, Cambridge: Cambridge University Press, 172–180.

Hoffmann, E. A. 2015 "Emotions and Emotional Labor at Work-Owned Businesses: Deep Acting, Surface Acting, and Genuine Emotions", *The Sociological Quarterly*, 57, 152–173.

Hofstede, G. 1994 *Uncommon Sense about Organizations: Case Studies and Field Observations*, Thousand Oaks, CA: Sage.

Holden, J. 2008 *Democratic Culture: Opening up the Arts to Everyone*, London: Demos.

Holmquist, J. P. 2013 "Workplace Ethics at the Time Clock: Fudging Time with Respect to Western and Eastern Views", *The International Journal of Human Resource Management*, 24(11), 2221–2236.

Howell, J. M. & Avolio, B. J. 1993 "Transformational Leadership, Transactional Leadership, Locus of Control, and Support for Innovation: Key Predictors of Consolidated-Business-Unit Performance", *Journal of Applied Psychology*, 78, 891–902.

Hsin-tien, L. 2015 "Interlocution and Engagement", in Caust, J. (ed.) *Arts and Cultural Leadership in Asia*, London: Routledge, 48–58.

Hubbard, D. 1992 "The Effective Board", in Drucker P. (ed.) *Managing the Non-profit Organisation*, London: Butterworth Heinemann.

Hudson, M. 2005 *Managing at the Leading Edge*, San Francisco, CA: John Wiley.

Hudson, M. 2009 *Managing Without Profit: Leadership, Management and Governance of Third Sector Organisations in Australia*, Sydney: UNSW Press.

Hudson, M. *Change Management*, http://compasspartnership.co.uk/pdf/CM.pdf [accessed 20 February 2019].

Hughes, L. W. 2005 "Developing Transparent relationships through Humour in the Authentic Leader-follower Relationship", *Authentic Leadership Theory and Practice: Origins, Effects and Development, Monographs in Leadership and Management*, 3, 83–106.

Hughes, P., Luksetich, W. & Rooney, P. 2014 "Crowding-Out and Fundraising Efforts: The Impact of Government Grants on Symphony Orchestras", *Nonprofit Management and Leadership*, 24(4), 445–465.

Hume, M., Mort, G. S., Liesch, P. W. & Winzar, H. 2006 "Understanding Service Experience in Non-profit Performing Arts: Implications for Operations and Service Management", *Journal of Operations Management*, 24, 304–324.

Humphrey, R. H., Pollack, J. M. & Hawver, T. 2008 "Leading with Emotional Labor", *Journal of Managerial Psychology*, 23(2), 151–168.

I

Ibarra, H. & Hunter, M. 2007 "How Leaders Create and Use Networks", *Harvard Business Review*, 85(1), 40–47.

Ibarra, H. 2015 "The Authenticity Paradox", *Harvard Business Review*, 93(1/2), 52–59.

Ignatius, A. 2014 "Leaders for the Long Term", *Harvard Business Review*, 92(11), 48–56.

Ilies, R., Morgeson, F. P. & Nahrgang, J. D. 2005 "Authentic Leadership and Eudaemonic Well-being: Understanding Leader-follower Outcomes", *The Leadership Quarterly*, 16(3), 373–394.

Inglis, L. & Cray, D. 2011 "Leadership in Australian Arts Organisations: A Shared Experience?", *Third Sector Review*, 17(2), 107–130.

Inglis, L., Cray, D. & Freeman, S. 2006 *Leading Arts Organizations: Traditional Styles or Different Realities?*, Department of Management Working Paper, Melbourne: Monash University.

Innes, G. 2014 *Press Club Speech*, 2 July, Canberra, www.abc.net.au/news/2014-07-02/national-press-club-graeme-innes/5567150 [accessed 19 January 2015].

Institute of Community Directors Australia, *Risk Management: Ten Steps to a Safer Organisation*, Our Community Melbourne, www.communitydirectors.com.au/icda/tools/?articleId=1363 [accessed 10 March 2019].

J

Jackson, J. & McIver, R. 2007a *Macroeconomics* (8th ed), Sydney: McGraw Hill.

Jackson, J& McIver, R. 2007b *Microeconomics* (8th ed), Sydney: McGraw Hill.

Jacques, R. 1996 *Manufacturing the Employee*, London: Sage.

Jager, U. P. & Rehli, F. 2012 "Cooperative Power Relations between Nonprofit Board Chairs and Executive Directors", *Nonprofit Management & Leadership*, 23(2), 219–236.

Järvinen, M., Ansio, H. & Houni, P. 2015 "New Variations of Dual Leadership: Insights from Finnish Theatre", *International Journal of Arts Management*, 17(3), 16–27.

Jaskyte, K., Byerly, C. Bryant, A. & Koksarova, J. 2010 "Transforming a Nonprofit Work Environment for Creativity", *Nonprofit Management & Leadership*, 21(1), 77–92.

Jeavons, T. H. 1994 "Ethics in Nonprofit Management: Creating a Culture of

Integrity", in Herman, H. D. (ed.) *The Jossey-Bass Handbook of Nonprofit Leadership and Management*, San Francisco, CA: Jossey-Bass, 184–207.

Johnson, P. & Indvik, J. 2001 "Slings and Arrows of Rudeness: Incivility in the Workplace", *Journal of Management Development*, 20(8), 705–714.

Julie's Bicycle 2013 "Practical Guides: Environmental Policy & Action Plan Guidelines", www.juliesbicycle.com/Handlers/Download.ashx?IDMF=dece678c-682c-4362-80c0-bd8744047213 [accessed 11 March 2019].

Julie's Bicycle 2010 *Long Horizons: An Exploration of Art and Climate Change*, London: British Council.

K

Kaiser, M. M. 2008 *The Art of the Turnaround: Creating and Maintaining Healthy Arts Organizations*, Waltham, MA: Brandeis University Press.

Kaiser, M. M. 2010 *Leading Roles*, Waltham, MA: Brandeis University Press.

Kaiser, M. M. 2013 *The Circle*, Waltham, MA: Brandeis University Press.

Keating, E. K. & Frumkin, P. 2001 *How to Assess Nonprofit Financial Performance*, Washington, DC: Aspen Institute.

Kelly, H. 2012 "How the Hobbit Dispute Was Said to Justify Curbs to the Actors' Union", *The Guardian*, www.theguardian.com/commentisfree/2012/nov/30/hobbit-actor-union-dispute [accessed 11 March 2019].

Kelly, K. 1998 *Effective Fund-Raising Management*, Mahwah, NJ: Lawrence Erlbaum Associates.

Kelly, P. 2014 "The Tragedy of Kevin Rudd Can Be Traced to a Personality Flaw", *Weekend Australian*, 23–24 August, www.theaustralian.com.au/opinion/columnists/the-tragedy-of-kevin-rudd-can-be-traced-to-a-personality-flaw/story-e6frg74x-1227033724468 [accessed 30 January 2015].

Kempa, E. & Pooleb, S. M. 2016 "Arts Audiences: Establishing a Gateway to Audience Development and Engagement", *Journal of Arts Management, Law and Society*, 64(2), 53–62.

Kernis, M. H. 2003 "Toward a Conceptualization of Optimal Self-esteem", *Psychological Inquiry*, 14(1), 1–26.

Kim, S. 2002 "Participative Management and Job Satisfaction: Lessons from Management Leadership", *Public Administration Review*, 62(2), 231–241.

Kirby, J. & Myer, R. 2009 *Richard Pratt: One Out of the Box*, Milton, QLD: John Wiley & Sons.

Kirchberg, V. & Zembylas, T. 2010 "Arts Management: A Sociological Inquiry", *The Journal of Arts Management, Law, and Society*, 40(1), 1–5.

Kirchberg, V. 2003 "Corporate Arts Sponsorship", in Towse, R. (ed.) *A Handbook of Cultural Economics*, Cheltenham: Edward Elgar Publishing.

Kirchberg, V. 2019 "Managing Real Utopias: Artistic and Creative Visions and Implementation", in DeVereaux, C. (ed.) *Arts and Cultural Management: Sense and Sensibility in the State of the Field*, New York: Routledge, 226–246.

Kirchner, T. A., Mottner, S. & Ford, J. B. 2013 "Business Continuity/Disaster Recovery Readiness of Nonprofit Arts Organizations?", Bogota: 12th AIMAC International Conference, 394–403.

Knott, M. 2015 "ABC Maternity Leave Workers Vie for Jobs in 'Hunger Games-style' Redundancy Process", *Sydney Morning Herald*, www.smh.com.au/federal-politics/political-news/abc-maternity-leave-workers-vie-for-jobs-in-hunger-gamesstyle-redundancy-process-20150117-12r808.html [accessed 22 February 2019].

Kolsteeg, J. 2013 "Developing the Practice of Organisation Design", Bogota: Session G3, AIMAC International Conference, 987–993.

Konrad, E. D., Moog, P. & Rentschler, R. (eds) 2018 "Editorial", *International Journal of Arts Management*, 48(2).

Kotler, P. & Scheff, J. 1997 *Standing Room Only*, Boston, MA: Harvard Business School Press.

Kotter, J. P. & Cohen, D. S. 2002 *The Heart of Change: Real Life Stories of How People Change Their Organizations*, Boston, MA: Harvard Business School Press.

Kotter, J. P. 1996 *Leading Change*, Boston, MA: Harvard Business School Press.

Kouzes, J. & Posner, B. 2007 *The Leadership Challenge* (4th ed), Hoboken, NJ: Jossey-Bass.

Krause, D. E. 2015 "Four Types of Leadership and Orchestra Quality", *Nonprofit Management & Leadership*, 25(4), 421–447.

Krug, K. & Weinberg, C. B. 2004 "Mission, Money and Merit: Strategic Decisions Making by Nonprofit Managers", *Nonprofit Management and Leadership*, 14(3), 325–342.

Krznaric, R. www.romankrznaric.com/blog [accessed 26 February 2016].

Krznaric, R. 2013 "Six Habits of Highly Emphatic People", www.dailygood.org/story/518/six-habits-of-highly-empathic-people-roman-krznaric/ [accessed 22 February 2019].

Kuester, I. 2010 "Arts Managers as Liaisons between Finance and Art: A Qualitative Study Inspired by the Theory of Functional Differentiation", *The Journal of Arts Management, Law, and Society*, 40(1), 43–57.

Kumra, S. & Manfredi, S. 2012 *Managing Equality and Diversity*, Oxford: Oxford University Press.

Kurtzberg, T. 2005 "Feeling Creative, Being Creative: An Empirical Study of Diversity and Creativity in Teams", *Creativity Research Journal*, 17(1), 51–65.

L

La Fortune, A., Rousseau, J. G. & Begin, L. 1999 "An Exploration of Management Control in the Arts and Cultural Sector", *International Journal of Arts Management*, 2(1), 64–76.

Ladkin, D. 2010 "Creating an Aesthetic of Inclusivity: A New Solution to the 'Problem' of Women Leaders", in Kay, S. & Venner, K. (eds) *A Cultural Leader's Handbook*, London: Creative Choices, 32–39.

Lally, E. & Miller, S. 2012 *Women in Theatre*, Sydney: Australia Council, http://australiacouncil.gov.au/workspace/uploads/files/research/women-in-theatre-april-2012-54325827577ea.pdf [accessed 20 February 2019].

Landry, P. 2013 "The Succession of Artistic Directors in Cultural Organizations and Organizational identity: A Typological Approach", Session B4, Bogota: 12th, AIMAC International Conference, 213–223.

Lang, C. & Lee, C. H. 2010 "Workplace Humor and Organizational Creativity", *The International Journal of Human Resource Management*, 21(1), 46–60.

Langer, E. 2014 "Mindfulness in the Age of Complexity", *Harvard Business Review*, 92(3), 68–73.

Langley, D. 2010 "Leadership Development: A Critical Question", in Kay, S. & Venner, K. (eds) *A Cultural Leader's Handbook*, London: Creative Choices, 64–70.

Lapierre, L. 2001 "Leadership and Arts Management", *International Journal of Arts Management*, 3(3), 4–12.

Larcker, D. F., Meehan, W. F., Donatiello, N. & Tayan, B. 2015 *Survey on Board of Directors of Nonprofit Organisations*, Stanford, CA: Stanford Graduate School of Business & Rock Center for Corporate Governance.

Lawrence, S. 2003 "Recruitment Agencies Must Be Vigilant", *Australian Financial Review*, 11 April.

Lebow, R. & Spitzer, R. 2002 *Accountability*, San Francisco, CA: Berrett-Koehler Publishing.

Legge, K. 2003 "Strategy as Organizing", in Cummings, S. & Wilson, D. (eds) *Images of Strategy*, Oxford: Blackwell Publishing, 74–104.

Leicester, G. 2007 *Rising to the Occasion*, Fife: International Futures Forum, March.

Leicester, G. 2010 "Real Cultural Leadership: Leading the Culture in a Time of Crisis", in Kay, S. & Venner, K. (eds) *A Cultural Leader's Handbook*, London: Creative Choices, 16–22.

Leigh, A. & Maynard, M. 2003 *Perfect Leader*, London: Random House Business Books.

Lencioni, P. 2000 *The Four Obsessions of an Extraordinary Executive*, San Francisco, CA: Jossey-Bass.

Lencioni, P. 2005 *The Five Dysfunctions of a Team: A Field Guide to Managers, Leaders and Facilitators*, San Francisco, CA: Jossey-Bass.

Leung, C. C. & Tung, K. Y. 2015 "Dual Roles: Collaborative Leadership in a Newly Developed Music Ensemble", in Caust, J. (ed.) *Arts and Cultural Leadership in Asia*, London: Routledge, 105–120.

Lewandowska, K. 2015 "From Sponsorship to Partnership in Arts and Business Relations", *The Journal of Arts Management, Law and Society*, 45, 33–50.

Liao-Troth, M. A. 2001 "Attitude Differences between Paid Workers and Volunteers", *Non-profit Management and Leadership*, 11(4), 423–442.

Libman, S. 2014 "The Dignity of the Job Search", *Arts Management Newsletter*, Issue No. 118, February, 4–7.

Light, P. C. 2004 *Sustaining Nonprofit Performance: The Case for Capacity Building and the Evidence to Support It*, Washington, DC: Brookings Institution.

Lindqvist, K. 2012 "Effects of Public Sector Reforms on the Management of Cultural Organizations in Europe", *International Studies of Management and Organization*, 42(2), 9–28.

Lissy, D. & Beard, A. 2015 "Life's Work: An Interview with Bill T. Jones", *Harvard Business Review*, November, 93(11), 156.

Live Performance Australia 2017 *LPA Ticket Attendance and Revenue Report 2017*, Melbourne: LPA.

Live Performance Australia 2018 *Australian Live Performance Industry Code of Practice: Discrimination, Harassment, Sexual Harassment and Bullying*, http://members.liveperformance.com.au/uploads/files/Combined%20-%20LPA%20Discrimination.H.SH.B%20resources%20-%20Consultation%20Draft%20 23.02.2018-1519365284.pdf [accessed 20 February 2019].

Long, R. J. & Shields, J. L. 2010 "From Pay to Praise? Non-cash Employee Recognition in Canadian and Australian Firms", *International Journal of Human Resource Management*, 21(8), 1145–1172.

Longstaff, S. 2014a *The Twin Foundations of Leadership*, Sydney: St James Ethics Centre, www.ethics.org.au/on-ethics/our-articles/before-2014/the-twin-foundations-of-leadership [accessed 27 February 2019].

Longstaff, S. 2014b Speech at the "Communities in Control Conference", Melbourne, broadcast on Radio National's *Big Ideas*, 28 May.

Lorsch, J. W. & McTague, E. 2016 "Culture is Not the Culprit", *Harvard Business Review*, April, 96–105.

M

MAAS 2014 *Strategic Plan*, Sydney: MAAS.

Mabey C. 2018 "What it Really Takes to Juggle an Arts Organisation with Family Life", *Arts Hub*, 8 November, www.artshub.com.au/education/news-article/career-advice/professional-development/claire-mabey/what-it-really-takes-to-juggle-an-arts-organisation-with-family-life-256772 [accessed 22 February 2019].

Macduff, N., Netting, F. E. & O'Connor, M. K. 2009 "Multiple Ways of Coordinating Volunteers with Differing Styles of Service", *Journal of Community Practice*, 17, 400–423.

Macken, D. 2000 "Desperately Seeking Holiday", *Australian Financial Review*, 2–3 December.

MacNeil, K., Tonks, A. & Reynolds, S. 2012 "Authenticity and the Other", *Journal of Leadership Studies*, 6(3), 6–16.

MacNeill, K. & Tonks, A. 2009 "Co-leadership and Gender in the Performing Arts", *Asia Pacific Journal of Arts and Cultural Management*, 6(1), 291–404.

MacNeill, K. & Tonks, A. 2013 "Leadership in Australian Arts Companies: One Size Does Not Fit All", in Caust, J. (ed.) *Arts Leadership*, Melbourne: Tilde University Press.

MacNeill, K., Tonks, A. & Reynolds, S. 2012 "Authenticity and the Other", *Journal of Leadership Studies*, 6(3), 6–16.

MacNeill, K., Reynolds, S. & Tonks, A. 2013 "A Double Act: Coleadership and the Performing Arts", Bogota: 12th AIMAC International Conference, 1158–1169.

Maddux, R. B. 1989 *Successful Negotiations* (3rd ed), San Francisco, CA: Crisp Publications.

Madlock, P. E. & Dillow, M. E. 2012 "The Consequences of Verbal Aggression in the Workplace: An Application of the Investment Model", *Communication Studies*, 63(5), 583–607.

Maifeld, K. 2012 "Review of 'The Cultural Leadership Handbook: How to Run a Creative Organization' by Robert Hewison and John Holden", *The Journal of Arts Management, Law, and Society*, 42(4), 217–219.

Major, S. & Gould-Lardelli, R. 2011 "Becoming an Arts Manager: A Matter of Choice or Chance?", Antwerp: 11th AIMAC International Conference.

Maloney, S. 2004 *The Brush Off*, Melbourne: Text Publishing.

Mandel, E. S. J. 2014 *Station Eleven*, London: Picador.

Mankins, M., Brahm, C. & and Caimi, G. 2014 "Your Scarcest Resource", *Harvard Business Review*, 92(5), 74–80.

March, J. G. 2006 "Ideas as Art: Interviewed by Diane Coutu", *Harvard Business Review*, 84(10), 83–89.

Martin, R. L. 2013 "The Big Lie of Strategic Planning", *Harvard Business Review*, 91(1/2), 78–84.

Martinez, C., Euzéby, F. & Lallement, J. 2018 "The Importance of the Venue in an Information Search: Online Ticket Purchase in the Performing Arts", *International Journal of Arts Management*, 20(3), 60–74.

Masanauskas, J. 2006 "Ushering in a New Era", *Herald Sun*, www.heraldsun.com.au/news/victoria/ushering-in-a-new-era/story-e6frf7kx-1111112605388 [accessed 27 February 2019].

Mastracci, S. H. & Herring, C. 2010 "Nonprofit Management Practices and Work Processes to Promote Gender Diversity", *Nonprofit Management & Leadership*, 21(2), 155–175.

Mathews, W. K. 2011 "Media Relations", in Gillis, T. L. (ed.) *The IABC Handbook of Organizational Communication* (2nd ed), San Francisco, CA: Jossey-Bass, 301–313.

Mayor of London 2008 *Green Theatre: Taking Action on Climate Change*, London: Greater London Authority.

McCall, K. 2019 "The Reality of Cultural Work", in DeVereaux, C. (ed.) *Arts and Cultural Management: Sense and Sensibility in the State of the Field*, New York: Routledge, 167–184.

McCann, J. M. 2008 "Development: Leadership as Creativity", *Arts Management Newsletter*, No. 82.

McDaniel, N. & Thorn, G. 1993 *Towards A New Arts Order*, New York: Arts Action Research.

McEwan, I. 1999 *Amsterdam*, London: Vintage.

McFarlan, F. W. 1999 "Working on Nonprofit Boards – Don't Assume the Shoe Fits", *Harvard Business Review*, 77(6), 64–80.

McGovern, G. 2014 "Lead from the Heart", *Harvard Business Review*, 92(3), 38.

McIntyre, C. 2008 "Museum Food Service Offers – Experience Design Dimensions", *Journal of Foodservice*, 19(3), 177–188.

McKnight, D. H., Ahmad, S. & Schroeder, R. G. 2001 "When Do Feedback, Incentive Control, and Autonomy Improve Morale? The Importance of Employee-Management Relationship Closeness", *Journal of Managerial Issues*, 13(4), 466–482.

McMillan, E. 2010 *Not-For-Profit Budgeting and Financial Management* (4th ed), Hoboken, NJ: Wiley.

McShane, S. & Travaglione, T. 2003 *Organisational Behaviour on the Pacific Rim*, Sydney: McGraw Hill.

Meade, A. 2018 "Sacked ABC Boss Michelle Guthrie Was Seen as Arrogant by Colleagues, Inquiry Told", 30 November, www.theguardian.com/media/2018/nov/30/michelle-guthrie-was-pressured-to-reprimand-abc-presenter-jon-faine-inquiry-told [accessed 27 February 2019].

Meehan, W. F. & Jonker, K. S. 2017 *Stanford Survey on Leadership and Management in the Nonprofit Sector*, Stanford, CA: Stanford Graduate School of Business.

Mendelssohn, J. 2013a "Déjà vu: Women and Leadership in the Visual Arts", *NAVA Quarterly*, 4–5.

Mendelssohn, J. 2013b "Why Are so Many Arts Organisations Run by Blokes?" *The Conversation*, 10 May, http://theconversation.com/why-are-so-many-arts-organisations-run-by-blokes-13217 [accessed 22 February 2019].

Merton, T. 1971 *Contemplation in a World of Action*, New York: Doubleday.

Meyer, J. W. & Allen, N. J. 1997 *Commitment in the Workplace: Theory, Research and Application*, London: Sage.

Meyrick, J., Phiddian, R. & Barnett, J. 2018 *What Matters? Talking Value in Australian Culture*, Melbourne: Monash University Publishing.

Meyrick, J., Phillips, S. & Tonks, A. 2004 *The Drama Continues*, Melbourne: MTC.

Middleton, M. 1987 "Nonprofit Boards of Directors: Beyond the Governance Function", in Powell, W. W. (ed.) *The Nonprofit Sector: A Research Handbook*, New Haven, CT: Yale University Press.

Miles, S. A. & Watkins, M. D. 2007 "The Leadership Team: Complementary Strengths or Conflicting Agendas", *Harvard Business Review*, 85(4), 90–98.

Milliken, B., Alstein T. & Sun, S. 2018 *Restoring Trust in Financial Services in the Digital Era*, Melbourne: Deloitte Consulting.

Mills, R. 2003 *The Australian*, 4 July, 15.

Minguet, L. 2014 "Creating a Culturally Sensitive Corporation", *Harvard Business Review*, 92(5), 78.

Minister for Women 2018 "Australia's First Gender Equality Bill: Have Your Say", 21 August, www.premier.vic.gov.au/australias-first-gender-equality-bill-have-your-say/ [accessed 20 February 2019].

Mintzberg, H. 1989 *Mintzberg on Management*, New York: The Free Press.

Mintzberg, H. 1994 *The Rise and Fall of Strategic Planning: Reconceiving Roles for Planning, Plans, Planners*, New York: Free Press.

Minzberg, H. 1998 "Covert Leadership", *Harvard Business Review*, November–December, https://hbr.org/1998/11/covert-leadership-notes-on-managing-professionals [accessed 16 March 2019].

Minzberg, H. 2009 "Rebuilding Companies as Communities", *Harvard Business Review*, https://hbr.org/2009/07/rebuilding-companies-as-communities [accessed 20 February 2019].

Mirvis, P. 1992 "The Quality of Employment in the Non-profit Sector: An Update on Employee Attitudes in Nonprofits versus Business and Government", *Nonprofit Management and Leadership*, 3(1), 23–41.

Mitchell, L. & Russell, D. S. 2015 "Organising Music Festivals", in Beech, N. & Gilmore, C. (eds) *Organising Music: Theory, Practice, Performance*, Cambridge: Cambridge University Press, 213–217.

Mitroff, I. 2005 *Why Some Companies Emerge Stronger and Better from a Crisis: 7 Essential Lessons for Surviving Disaster*, Saranac Lake, NY: AMACOM Books.

Montgomery, C. A. 2008 "Putting Leadership Back into Strategy", *Harvard Business Review*, https://hbr.org/2008/01/putting-leadership-back-into-strategy [accessed 31 March 2019].

Morgan, M. & Rentschler, R. 2011 "Mission Fulfilment: The Role of Board Performance", Antwerp: 11th AIMAC International Conference.

Morganti, I. & Nuccio, M. 2011 "Towards an Enhanced Framework for Impact Evaluation of Cultural Events", Antwerp, Belgium: 11th AMAIC International Conference.

Morieux, Y. 2011 "Smart Rules: Six Ways to Get People to Solve Problems Without You", *bcg perspectives*, Boston Consulting Group, www.bcgperspectives.com/content/articles/organization_design_engagement_culture_hbr_smart_rules_six_ways_get_people_solve_problems_without_you/ [accessed 10 March 2019].

Morieux, Y. 2013 "As Work Gets More Complex, 6 Rules to Simplify", *TED Talk*, www.ted.com/talks/yves_morieux_as_work_gets_more_complex_6_rules_to_simplify [accessed 10 March 2019].

Morris, M. 2001 "Genius at Work: A Conversation with Mark Morris", *Harvard Business Review*, 79(9), 63–68.

Morrow, G. 2018 *Artist Management: Agility and the Creative and Cultural Industries*, London: Routledge.

Morrow, G. 2018b "Distributed Agility: Artist Co-management in the Music Attention Economy", *International Journal of Arts Management*, 20(3), 38–48.

Moskow, M. H. 1970 "Trade Unions in the Performing Arts", *Monthly Labor Review*, 93(3), 16–20.

Moss, S., Callanan, J. & Wilson, S. 2012 *The Moonlight Effect*, Melbourne: Tilde University Press.

Moss, S., Callanan, J. & Wilson, S. 2012 *The Moonlight Effect*, Melbourne: Tilde University Press.

Moyers, R. 2011 *Daring to Lead 2011 – The Board Paradox*, Meyer Foundation, http://daringtolead.org/wp-content/uploads/Daring-Brief-3-080511.pdf [accessed 22 February 2019].

Mullen, M. 2012 "Taking Care and Playing it Safe: Tensions in the Management of Funding Relations", *Journal of Arts & Communities*, 4(3), 181–198.

Mutz, J. & Murray, K. 2010 *Fundraising for Dummies* (3rd ed), Hoboken, NJ: Wiley Publishing.

Myers, R. 2014 "The Artistic Director: On the Way to Extinction", 2014 Philip Parsons Memorial Lecture, http://belvoir.com.au/wp-content/uploads/2014/12/2014-Philip-Parsons-Memorial-Lecture-by-Ralph-Myers.pdf [accessed 20 February 2019].

N

Nair, N. & Bhatnagar, D. 2011 "Understanding Workplace Deviant Behaviour in Nonprofit Organizations", *Nonprofit Management and Leadership*, 21(3), 289–309.

Neill, R. 2018 "New Rules of Engagement", *The Weekend Australian*, 8–9 December, 8–9.

Ng, D. & Boehm, M. 2014 "Questions Roil San Diego Opera in Aftermath of its Decision to Close", *Los Angeles Times*, 5 April, http://articles.latimes.com/2014/apr/05/entertainment/la-et-san-diego-opera-20140405 [accessed 11 March 2019].

Nicholass, T. W. & Erakovich, R. 2013 "Authentic Leadership and Implicit Theory: A Normative

Form of Leadership?", *Leadership and Organisational Development Journal*, 24(20), 182–195.

Nielsen, R. & Marrone, J. A. 2018 "Humility: Our Current Understanding of the Construct and its Role in Organizations", *International Journal of Management Reviews*, 20, 805–824.

Nisbett, M. & Walmsley, B. 2013 "The Romanticization of Charismatic Leadership in the Arts", Bogota: AIMAC International Conference, 1145–1157.

Norbury, C. 2010 "Relationships Are at the Heart of Good Cultural Leadership", in Kay, S. & Venner, S. (eds) *A Cultural Leader's Handbook*, London: Creative Choices, 50–57.

Northouse, P. G. 2010 *Leadership* (5th ed), Los Angeles: Sage Publications.

Nugent, H. 1999 *Securing the Future: Major Performing Arts – Final Report*, Canberra: Department of Communications, Information Technology and the Arts.

O

O'Connell, A. 1997 "Strategic Planning and the Arts Organization", in Fitzgibbon, M. & Kelly, A. (eds) *From Maestro to Manager*, Dublin: Oak Tree Press, 69–84.

O'Connor, J. 2014 "What Got Lost between 'Cultural' and 'Creative' Industries", 27 February, http://theconversation.com/what-got-lost-between-cultural-and-creative-industries-23658 [accessed 20 February 2019].

O'Sullivan, P. 1997 "Marketing the Arts: from Paradigm to Plan", Fitzgibbon, M. & Kelly, A. (eds) *From Maestro to Manager*, Dublin: Oak Tree Press, 139–181.

O'Toole, J. Anderson, M., Adam, R., Burton, B. & Ewing, R. (eds) 2014 *Young Audiences, Theatre and the Cultural Conversation*, Netherlands: Springer.

O'Toole, J., Galbraith, J. & Lawler, E. E. 2002 "When Two (or More) Heads Are Better than One", *California Management Review*, 44(4), 65–83.

O'Toole, S., Ferres, N. & Connell, J. (eds) 2011 *People Development: An Inside View*, Melbourne: Tilde University Press.

Obaidalahe, Z., Sarlerno, F. &Colbert, F. 2017 "Subscribers' Overall Evaluation of a Multi-experience Cultural Service, Tolerance for Disappointment, and Sustainable Loyalty", *International Journal of Arts Management*, 20(1), 21–30.

Obama, M. 2018 *Becoming*, New York: Crown Publishing Group.

Onsman, H. 1991 *How to Manage Change in the Workplace*, Sydney: ABC.

Osborne, A. & Rentschler, R. "Conversation, Collaboration and Cooperation", in O'Reilly, D. & Kerrigan, F. (eds) 2010 *Marketing the Arts: A Fresh Approach*, London: Routledge, 54–71.

Ouellett, P. & Lapierre, L. 1997 "Management Boards of Arts Organisations", in Fitzgibbon, M. & Kelly, A. (eds) *From Maestro to Manager*, Dublin: Oak Tree Press, 367–377.

Our Community 2007 *The Complete Community Fundraising Handbook*, Melbourne: ourcommunity.com.au.

Our Community Group n.d. "Managing a Media Crisis", www.ourcommunity.com.au/marketing/marketing_article.jsp?articleId=1520 [accessed 2 September 2019].

Our Community Group n.d. "Our Community Manifesto", www.ourcommunity.com.au/ [accessed 27 February 2019].

P

Pankratz, D. B. 2011 "Evaluation in the Arts", in Brindle, M. & DeVereaux, C. (eds) *The Arts Management Handbook*, Armon, NY: M.E. Sharpe, 319–347.

Paquette, J. 2012 "Mentoring and Change in Cultural Organizations: The Experience of Directors in British National Museums", *Journal of Arts Management, Society and Law*, 42(4), 205–216.

Parker, D. 2010 "The Improvising Leader: Developing Leadership Capacity through Improvisation", in Kay, S. & Venner, S. (eds) *A Cultural Leader's Handbook*, London: Creative Choices, 106–112.

Parker, M. 2012 *Ethics 101 Conversations to Have with Your Kids*, Sydney: Jane Curry Publishing.

Parsons, R. D. & Feigen, M. A. 2014 "The Boardroom's Quiet Revolution", *Harvard Business Review*, 92(3), 99–104.

Pässilä, A. 2012 *Reflexive Model of Research-Based Theatre*, Finland: PhD paper.

Patel, J. 2010 "Doing the Right Thing: The Ethics of Cultural Leadership", in Kay, S. & Venner,

K. (eds) *A Cultural Leader's Handbook*, London: Creative Choices, 72–77.

Patty, A. 2014 "ABC Staff Reject 'Cruel and Inhumane' Approach to Redundancies", *Sydney Morning Herald*, www.smh.com.au/nsw/abc-staff-reject-cruel-and-inhumane-approach-to-redundancies-20141204-11zvtd.html [accessed 22 February 2019].

Patty, A. 2014 "Work-life Balance is Getting Worse for Australians: New Report", *Sydney Morning Herald*, www.smh.com.au/nsw/worklife-balance-is-getting-worse-for-australians-new-report-20141118-11otw6.html [accessed 27 February 2019].

Pekerti, A. A. & Sendjaya, S. 2010 "Exploring Servant Leadership Across Cultures: Comparative Study in Australia and Indonesia", *The International Journal of Human Resource Management*, 21(5), 754–780.

Perlow, L. 2014 "Manage Your Team's Collective Time", *Harvard Business Review*, June, 23–25.

Peter Grant 2012 *The Business of Giving: The Theory and Practice of Philanthropy, Grantmaking and Social Investment*, New York: Palgrave Macmillan.

Peterson, R. A. 1986 "From Impresario to Arts Administrator", in DiMaggio, P. J. (ed.) *Nonprofit Enterprise in the Arts*, New York: Oxford University Press, 161–183.

Pfeffer, J. & Sutton, R. I. 2006 *Hard Facts, Dangerous Half-Truths, and Total Nonsense*, Boston, MA: Harvard Business School Press.

Philip-Harbutt, L. 2009 "Am I An Ethical Arts Worker?" *Asia Pacific Journal of Arts and Cultural Management*, 6(2), 504–511.

Phillips, S. & Tonks, A. 2012 *Play On: Melbourne Theatre Company 2000–2011*, Melbourne: MTC.

Phills, J. A. 2005 *Integrating Mission and Strategy for Nonprofit Organizations*, New York: Oxford University Press.

Pienaar, J. M. 2010 "What Lies Beneath Leadership Ineffectiveness? – A Theoretical Overview", *Proceedings of the European Conference on Management, Leadership & Governance*, 280–286.

Pilbrow, R. 2017 "Magic of Place: An Unrecognized Revolution in Theater Architecture", in Lambert, P. D. & Williams, R. (eds) *Performing Arts Center Management*, New York: Routledge, 84–102.

Pink, D. 2009 *On Motivation*, www.ted.com/talks/dan_pink_on_motivation.html [accessed 27 February 2019].

Pink, D. 2010 *Drive: The Surprising Truth About What Motivates Us*, Edinburgh: Canongate.

Pittard, M. 2013 "Australian Employment Regulation", in Teicher, J., Holland, P. & Gough, R. (eds) *Australian Workplace Relations*, Cambridge: Cambridge University Press, 81–100.

Plas, J. M. & Lewis, S. E. 2001 *Person-Centered Leadership of Nonprofit Organizations*, Thousand Oaks, CA: Sage Publications.

Poisson-de Haro, S. & Montpetit, D. 2012 "Surviving in Times of Turmoil: Adaptation of the Theatre Les Deux Mondes Business Model", *International Journal of Arts Management*, 14(1), 16–31.

Porath, C. 2016 "Managing Yourself: An Antidote to Incivility", *Harvard Business Review*, 94(4), 108–111.

Potts, J. 2013 "You've Got $7 Billion – So How Will You Fund the Arts?", *The Conversation*, 4 November, http://theconversation.com/youve-got-7-billion-so-how-will-you-fund-the-arts-18839 [accessed 16 March 2019].

Preece, S. B. 2015 "Acquiring Start-up Funding for New Arts Organisations", *Nonprofit Management & Leadership*, 25(4), 463–474.

Price, J. 2018 "Guthrie's Morale Boost Fail Was Last Straw for Miserable ABC Staff", 25 September 2018, *Sydney Morning Herald*, www.smh.com.au/national/guthries-morale-boost-fail-was-last-straw-for-miserable-abc-staff-20180924-p505p2.html [accessed 20 February 2019].

Proteau, J. 2018 "Reducing Risky Relationships: Criteria for Forming Positive Museum-corporate Sponsorships", *Museum Management and Curatorship*, 33(3), 235–242.

Protherough, R. & Pick, J. 2002 *Managing Britannia*, Exeter: Brinmill Press.

Pyman, A., Holland, P., Teicher, J. & Cooper, B. 2013 "The Dynamics of Employee Voice in Australia", in Teicher, J., Holland, P. & Gough, R. (eds) *Australian Workplace Relations*, Cambridge: Cambridge University Press, 118–136.

Q

Qiao, L. 2015 "Re-negotiating the Arts in China", in Caust, J. (ed.) *Arts and Cultural Leadership in Asia*, London: Routledge, 26–38.

Quigg, A. M. 2011 *Bullying in the Arts*, Farnham: Gower.

R

Radbourne, J. & Fraser, M. 1996 *Arts Management*, Sydney: Allen and Unwin.

Radbourne, J. & Watkins, K. 2015 *Philanthropy and the Arts*, Melbourne: Melbourne University Press.

Radbourne, J., Johanson, K., Glow, H. & White, T. 2009 "The Audience Experience: Measuring Quality in the Performing Arts", *International Journal of Arts Management*, 11(3), 16–29.

Radbourne, K. 1995 "What Is an Arts Manager?" Brisbane: QUT, 16 March.

Rankin, S. 2014 "Soggy Biscuit", in Schultz, J. (ed.) *Griffith Review 44*, Brisbane: Queensland University of Technology, 12–32.

Rao, H. 2010 "What 17th Century Pirates Can Teach about Job Design", *Harvard Business Review*, 88(10), 44.

Reid, W. & Karambayya, R. 2009 "Impact of Dual Executive Leadership Dynamics in Creative Organizations", *Human Relations*, 62(7), 1073–1112.

Reid, W. 2013 "Dual Executive Leadership in the Arts", in Caust, J. (ed.) *Arts Leadership: Internal Case Studies*, Melbourne: Tilde University Press, 98–111.

Rentschler, R. 1998 "Museum and Performing Arts Marketing: A Climate of Change", *Journal of Arts Management, Law and Society*, 28(1), 83–96.

Rentschler, R. 2002 "Museum and Performing Arts Marketing: The Age of Discovery", *Journal of Arts Management, Law and Society*, 32(1), 7–14.

Rentschler, R. 2015 *Arts Governance: People, Passion Performance*, Abingdon, Oxon: Routledge.

Rentschler, R. & Jogulu, U. 2012 "Are Passion and Ambition Enough to Support the Career of a Female Arts Manager?", in Hausmann, A. & Murzik, L. (eds) *Anthology of Cultural Institutions HRM and Leadership*, Frankfurt: Springer Verlag, 143–155.

Rentschler, R., Jogulu, U. & Richardson, J. 2013 "Occupational Calling as a Platform for Career Advancement in Arts Management: When Passion isn't Enough", Bogota: 12th AIMAC International Conference, 46–54.

Renz, D. O. 2004 "An Overview of Nonprofit Governance", *Philanthropy in America*, www.energycollection.us/Board-Of-Directors/Governance/Overview-Nonprofit-governance.pdf [accessed 15 March 2015].

Reynolds, S., Tonks A. & MacNeill, K. 2017 "Collaborative Leadership in the Arts as a Unique Form of Dual Leadership", *The Journal of Arts Management, Law, and Society*, 47(2), 89–104.

Rhode, D. L. & Packel, A. K. 2009 "Ethics and Nonprofits", *Stanford Social Innovation Review*, 7(3), 29–35.

Rice, M. R., DiMeo, R. A. & Porter, M. P. 2012 *Nonprofit Asset Management: Effective Investment Strategies and Oversight*, Hoboken NJ: Wiley.

Richards, L. 2018 "Part of the Furniture", *Arts Professional*, 8 November, www.artsprofessional.co.uk/magazine/319/case-study/part-furniture?utm_source=Weekly-Good-Reads&utm_medium=email&utm_content=nid-209836&utm_campaign=8th-November-2018 [accessed 9 November 2018].

Ridley, F. F. "Cultural Economics and the Culture of Economics", *Journal of Cultural Economics*, 7(1), 1–18.

Robertson, D. 2016 "Why Should You Care About Art?", *Stuart Challender Talk*, www.ampag.com.au/article/why-should-you-care-about-art [accessed 20 February 2019].

Robin, M. 2013 *Australia Post Employees Who Sent Porn at Work Reinstated by Fair Work Commission with Back Pay*, www.smartcompany.com.au/people/industrial-relations/34744-australia-post-employees-who-sent-porn-at-work-reinstated-by-fair-work-commission-with-back-pay.html# [accessed 22 February 2019].

Roderick, T. 2018 *Does This Job Make My Desk Look Big?*, University of Sydney, https://sydney.edu.au/content/dam/corporate/documents/sydney-policy-lab/all-roles-flex-report.pdf [accessed 18 January 2019].

Rosewall, E. 2014 *Arts Management: Uniting Arts and Audiences in the 21st Century*, New York: Oxford University Press.

Rosh, L. & Offermann, L. 2013 "Be Yourself, But Carefully", *Harvard Business Review*, 91(10), 135–139.

Rosner, B. & Halcrow, A. 2010 *The Boss's Survival Guide* (2nd ed), New York McGraw Hill.

Ross, A. 2003 *No Collar: The Human Workplace and Its Hidden Costs*, New York: Basic Books.

Rothwell, W. J. 2011 "Succession Planning", in O'Toole, S., Ferres, N. & Connell, J. (eds) *People Development: An Inside View*, Melbourne: Tilde University Press, 148–165.

Rowe, W. G. & Dato-on, M. C. (eds) 2013 *Introduction to Nonprofit Management*, Thousand Oaks, CA: Sage.

Rowold, J. & Rohmann, A. 2009 "Transformational and Transactional Leadership Styles Followers' Positive and Negative Emotions, and Performance in German Nonprofit Orchestras", *Nonprofit Management & Leadership*, 20(1), 41–59.

Røyseng, S. 2008 "Arts Management and the Autonomy of Art", *International Journal of Cultural Policy*, 14(1), 37–48.

Rudd, K. 2008 "Kevin Rudd's Sorry Speech", *Sydney Morning Herald*, 13 February, www.smh.com.au/news/national/kevin-rudds-sorry-speech/2008/02/13/1202760379056.html [accessed 27 February 2019].

Ryan, A., Fenton, M. & Sangiori, D. 2010 "A Night at the Theatre", in O'Reilly, D. & Kerrigan, F. (eds) *Marketing the Arts: A Fresh Approach*, London: Routledge, 214–230.

S

Sadler-Smith, E. & Shefy, E. 2004 "The Intuitive Executive: Understanding and Applying 'Gut Feel' in Decision-making", *Academy of Management Executive*, 18(4), 76–91.

Safe Theatres Australia, www.safetheatresaustralia.com [accessed 27 February 2019].

Saffie-Robertson, M. C. & Brutus, S. 2014 "The Impact of Interdependence on Performance Evaluations: The Mediating Role of Discomfort with Performance Appraisal", *The International Journal of Human Resource Management*, 25(3), 459–473.

Saintilan, P. & Schreiber, D. 2018 *Managing Organizations in the Creative Economy: Organizational Behaviour for the Cultural Sector*, Abingdon: Routledge.

Samuelson, M. 2015 "Analysis Group's CEO on Managing with Soft Metrics", *Harvard Business Review*, November, 43–46.

Sarros, J., Cooper, B. K., Hartican, A. M. & Barker, C. J. 2006 *The Character of Leadership*, Milton, QLD: John Wiley & Sons.

Sartain, L. & Finney, M. I. 2003 *HR from the Heart*, New York: AMACOM.

Schien, E. H. 1988 *Organisational Psychology*, New York: Prentice Hall.

Schultz, J. 2014 "The Fourth Pillar", *Griffith Review*, Brisbane, 44, 7–9.

Schumann, D. M. 2011 "The Engagement of Brands", in Gillis, T. L. (ed.) *The IABC Handbook of Organizational Communication* (2nd ed), San Francisco, CA: Jossey-Bass, 393–403.

Sendjaya, S., Pekertie, A., Hartel, C., Hirst, G. & Butarbutar, I. 2016 "Are Authentic Leaders Always Moral? The Role of Machiavellianism in the Relationship Between Authentic Leadership and Morality", *Journal of Business Ethics*, 133(1), 125–139.

Severino, F. 2014 "Cultural Sponsorship and Entrepreneurial Mistrust", in Aiello, L. (ed.) *Handbook of Research on Management of Cultural Products*, Hershey PA: IGI Global, 113–125.

Shane, R. 2013 "Resurgence or Deterioration? The State of Cultural Unions in the 21st Century", *The Journal of Arts Management, Law, and Society*, 43, 139–152.

Shea, M. & Hamilton, R. D.,2015 "Who Determines How Nonprofits Confront Uncertainty?", *Nonprofit Management & Leadership*, 25(4), 383–401.

Sheehan, C., De Cieri, H. & Holland, P. 2013 "The Changing Role of Human Resources Management in the Employment Relationship", in Teicher, J., Holland, P. & Gough, R. (eds) *Australian Workplace Relations*, Cambridge: Cambridge University Press, 103–117.

Shockley-Zalabak, P. & Morreale, S. 2011 "Communication and the High Trust Organization", in Gillis, T. L. (ed.) *The IABC Handbook of Organizational Communication* (2nd ed), San Francisco, CA: Jossey-Bass, 41–53.

Siber, L. 1999 *Career Management for the Creative Person*, New York: Three Rivers Press.

Sigurjónsson, N. 2019 "Silence in Cultural Management", in DeVereaux, C. (ed.) *Arts and Cultural Management: Sense and Sensibility in the State of the Field*, New York: Routledge, 205–225.

Simon, H. A. 1987 "Making Management Decisions: The Role of Intuition and Emotion", *Academy of Management Executive*, February, 57–64.

Simpson Solicitors "Sponsorship", http://simpsons.com.au/wp-content/uploads/chapter-21-sponsorship.pdf [accessed 16 March 2019].

Sinclair, A. 2004 "Journey Around Leadership", *Discourse: Studies in the Cultural Politics of Education*, 25(1), 8–19.

Sinclair, A. 2004 "Teaching Managers about Masculinities: Are You Kidding?", in Grey, C. & Antonacopoulou, E. (eds) *Essential Readings in Management Learning*, London: Sage Publications, 218–236.

Sinclair, A. 2005 *Doing Leadership Differently*, Melbourne: Melbourne University Press.

Sinclair, A. 2007a *Leadership for the Disillusioned*, Sydney: Allen & Unwin.

Sinclair, A. 2007b "Taming the Monkey", *afrboss. com.au*, http://works.bepress.com/cgi/viewcontent.cgi?article=1020&context=amanda_sinclair [accessed 27 February 2019].

Skringar, E. R. & Stevens, T. 2008 *Driving Change and Developing Organisations* (1st ed), Melbourne: Tilde University Press.

Smith, A. & Billett, S. 2005 "Myth and Reality: Employer Sponsored Training in Australia", *International Journal of Training Research*, 3, 16–29.

Snowden, D. J. & Boone, M. E. 2007 "A Leader's Framework for Decision Making", *Harvard Business Review*, 85(11), 68–76.

Sommerton, J. 2010 "The Place of Practical Wisdom in Cultural Leadership Development", in Kay, S. & Venner, K. (eds) *A Cultural Leader's Handbook*, London: Creative Choices, 114–119.

Spears, L. C. (ed.) 1995 *Reflections on Leadership*, New York: John Wiley & Sons.

Spitzmuller, M. & Ilies, R. 2010 "Do They [All] See My True Self? Leader's Relational Authenticity and Followers' Assessment of Transformational Leadership", *European Journal of Work and Organizational Psychology*, 19(3), 304–332.

Stacey, R. 1996 *Complexity and Creativity in Organisations*, San Francisco, CA: Berrett-Koehler.

Stack, L. 2017 "Et Tu, Delta? Shakespeare in the Park Sponsors Withdraw from Trump-Like 'Julius Caesar'", 11 June, www.nytimes.com/2017/06/11/arts/delta-airline-trump-public-theater-julius-caesar.html [accessed 16 March 2019].

Stahl, J. & Tröndle, M. 2019 "Toward a Practical Theory of Managing the Arts", in DeVereaux, C. (ed.) *Arts and Cultural Management: Sense and Sensibility in the State of the Field*, New York: Routledge, 245–266.

Stevens, R. 2014 "White Ears and Whistling Duck", *Griffith Review*, Brisbane, 44, 231–243.

Stewart, M. 2009 *The Management Myth*, New York: W.W. Norton & Co.

Stone, R. J. 2013 *Managing Human Resources* (4th ed), Milton, QLD: John Wiley & Sons.

Stover, C. F. 1984 "A Public Interest in Art – Its Recognition and Stewardship", *Journal of Arts Management and Law*, 14(3), 5–12.

Suchy, S. 1999 "Emotional Intelligence, Passion and Museum Leadership, Museum Management and Curatorship", *Museum Management and Curatorship*, 18(1), 57–71.

Summerton, J. & Hutchins, M. (eds) 2005 *Diverse Voices: Personal Journeys, All Ways Learning*, Brighton: All Ways Learning.

Sumner, J. 1993 *Recollections at Play*, Melbourne: Melbourne University Press.

Sunstein, C. R. & Hastie, R. 2014 "Making Dumb Groups Smarter", *Harvard Business Review*, 92(12), 90–98.

Sutherland, I. & Gosling, J. 2010 "Cultural Leadership: Mobilizing Culture from Affordances to Dwelling", *Journal of Arts Management, Law, and Society*, 40(1), 6–26.

Sutherland, I. & Gosling, J. 2010 "Cultural Leadership: Mobilizing Culture from Affordances to Dwelling", *Journal of Arts Management, Law, and Society*, 40(1), 6–26.

Swanson, C. 2014 "A Balancing Act", *Superfunds*, October, 39–40.

Sweeney, T. 2012 "Creative Talk with ACMI's Director, Tony Sweeney", *Creative Foyer*, www.artnewsportal.com.au/art-news/creative-talk-with-acmi-s-Director-tony-sweeney [accessed 12 December 2019].

Szczepanski, J. 2017 "Understanding Donor Motivations", *Museum Management and Curatorship*, 32(3), 272–280.

Szulanski, G. & Amin, K. 2001 "Learning to Make Strategy: Balancing Discipline and Imagination", *Long Range Planning*, 34(5), 537–556.

T

Taylor, A. & Ting, I. 2016 "What Arts Bosses in Australia Earn, and How Women Get Less", *Sydney Morning Herald*, 10 June, www.smh.com.au/entertainment/art-and-design/what-arts-bosses-in-australia-earn-and-how-women-get-less-20160603-gpahfn.html [accessed 18 January 2018].

Taylor, A. 2010 "Artists, Businesses, and Other Mythological Beasts", *The Artful Manager*, www.artsjournal.com/artfulmanager/main/artists_businesses_and_other_m.php [accessed 20 February 2019].

Taylor, A. 2013a "All Revenue Comes at a Cost", *The Artful Manager*, 22 July, www.artsjournal.com/artfulmanager/main/all-revenue-comes-at-a-cost.php [accessed 27 February 2019].

Taylor, A. 2013b "Managing a Mess", *The Artful Manager*, www.artsjournal.com/artfulmanager/main/managing-a-mess.php [accessed 10 March 2019].

Taylor, A. 2015 "The Theory of Strategy", *The Artful Manager*, 6 February, www.artsjournal.com/artfulmanager/main/the-theory-of-strategy.php [accessed 11 March 2019].

Teicher, J. & Bryan, D. 2006 "Globalisation, Economic Policy and the Labour Market", in Teicher, J., Holland, P. & Gough, R. (eds) *Employee Relations Management* (2nd ed), Sydney: Pearson Education Australia, 11–25.

Teicher, J., Holland, P. & Gough, R. 2006 *Employee Relations Management* (2nd ed), Sydney: Pearson Education Australia.

Teicher, J., Holland, P. & Gough, R. 2013 *Australian Workplace Relations*, Melbourne: Cambridge University Press.

Ten Brummelhuis, L. L., Haar, J. M. & van der Lippe, T. 2010 "Collegiality Under Pressure: The Effects of Family Demands and Flexible Work Arrangements in the Netherlands", *The International Journal of Human Resource Management*, 21(15), 2831–2847.

Tharp, T. 2003 *The Creative Habit. Learnt It and Use It for Life*, New York: Simon & Schuster.

"The Marketing of Theatres in the Age of Social Media", *International Journal of Arts Management*, 20(3), 20–37.

Thelwall, S. 2007 *Capitalising Creativity: Developing Earned Income Streams in Cultural Industries Organisations*, Proboscis Cultural Snapshot 14.

Thomas, M. T. 2008 *Leadership in the Arts: An Inside View*, Bloomington, IN: AuthorHouse.

Thomas, R. 2015 "Resisting Change and Changing Resistance", in Beech, N. & Gilmore, C. (eds) *Organising Music: Theory, Practice, Performance*, Cambridge: Cambridge University Press, 61–71.

Thompson, C. 2016 "Are We Done Crowdfunding?", *Dance Magazine*, January, 80–82.

Throsby, D. 1994 "The Production and Consumption of the Arts: A View of Cultural Economics", *Journal of Economic Literature*, 32, 1–29.

Throsby, D. 1992 "Artists as Workers", in Towse, R. & Khakee, A. (eds) *Cultural Economics*, Berlin: Springer Verlag.

Throsby, D. 2001 *Economics and Culture*, Cambridge: Cambridge University Press.

Throsby, D. 2010 *The Economics of Cultural Policy*, Cambridge: Cambridge University Press.

Tilley, D. 2014 "Moving Sue McCreadie", *Arts Hub*, http://screen.artshub.com.au/news-article/news/television/meaa-moving-sue-mccreadie-244470?utm_source=ArtsHub+Australia&utm_campaign=aa98b581ad-UA-828966-1&utm_medium=email&utm_term=0_2a8ea75e81-aa98b581ad-303971961 [accessed 11 March 2019].

Tonks, A. 2009 "Building a Theatre in the 21st Century", in *Innovation and Transformation*, Kaohsiung, Taiwan: International Symposium on Theater Arts and Cultural Administration.

Townsend, A. M. 2000 "An Exploratory Study of Administrative Workers in the Arts", *Public Personnel Management*, 29(3), 423–433.

Trevino, L. K. & Nelson, K. A. 2011 *Managing Business Ethics* (5th ed), Danvers, MA: John Wiley & Sons.

Tropman, J. E. 1996 *Effective Meetings: Improving Group Decision Making* (2nd ed), San Francisco, CA: Sage Publications.

Tshirhart, M. 1996 *Artful Leadership*, Bloomington, IN: Indiana University Press.

Tucker, P. B. & Parker, L. D. 2013 "Managerial Control and Strategy in Nonprofit Organizations", *Nonprofit Management and Leadership*, 24(1), 87–107.

Turbide, J. 2011 "Poor Governance Sickens the Arts – We Have the Cure", *Kenneth Myer Lecture*, Geelong: Deakin University.

Tusa, J. 2000 *Art Matters*, London: Methuen.

Tusa, J. 2007a *Engaged with the Arts*, London: I.B. Tauris & Co Ltd.

Tusa, J. 2007b "The New ABC of the Arts", *Arts Education Policy Review*, 108(4), 3–6.

Tusa, J. 2011 "Finding a Necessary Language for the Arts", www.theguardian.com/culture-professionals-network/culture-professionals-blog/2011/nov/16/finding-necessary-language-arts [accessed 20 February 2019].

Tusa, J. 2014, *Pain in the Arts*, London: I.B. Tauris.

U

Underhill, E. 2013 "The Challenge to Workplace Health and Safety and the Changing Nature of Work and the Working Environment", in Teicher, J., Holland, P. & Gough, R., *Australian Workplace Relations*, Cambridge: Cambridge University Press, 191–208.

V

Van den Born, A., van Klink, P. & Witteloostuijn, A. 2011 "Subsidizing Performing Arts: between Civilization and Addiction", Antwerp: 11th AIMAC International Conference.

Van den Braber, H. 2011 "Pushy Patrons or Selfless Philanthropists? The Debate on Private Support for the arts in the Netherlands *2001–2010*", Antwerp: 11th AIMAC International Conference.

Van Den Broek, A. 2013 "Arts Participation and the Three Faces of Time: A Reflection on Disentangling the Impact of Life Stage, Period and Socialization on Arts Participation, Exemplified by an Analysis of the US Arts Audience", *Cultural Trends*, 22(1), 46–53.

Van der Wagen, L. 2007 *Human Resource Management for Events*, Oxford: Elsevier.

Van Iddeking, C. H., McFarland, L. A. and Raymark, P. H. 2007 "Antecedents of Impression Management Use and Effectiveness in a Structure Interview", *Journal of Management*, 33(5), 752–773.

Varbanova, L. 2013 *Strategic Management in the Arts*, New York: Routledge.

Vera, D. & Rodriquez Lopez, A 2004 "Strategic Virtues: Humility as a Source of Competitive Advantage", *Organisational Dynamics*, 33(4), 393–408.

Verghis, S. 2014 "Black Ballet Superstar Misty Copeland on Swan Lake and Racial Prejudice", *The Australian*, 9 August, www.theaustralian.com.au/arts/review/black-ballet-superstar-misty-copeland-on-swan-lake-and-racial-prejudice/story-fn9n8gph-1227017793784 [accessed 19 January 2015].

Vernis, A., Iglesias, M., Sanz, B. & Saz-Carranza, A. 2006 *Nonprofit Organizations, Challenges and Collaboration*, New York: Palgrave Macmillan.

Victoria University 2015 *Researching the Rock 'n Roll Lifestyle*, 24 February, www.vu.edu.au/news-events/news/researching-the-rock-n-roll-lifestyle [accessed 27 February 2019].

Volz, J. 2017 *Introduction to Arts Management*, London: Bloomsbury Methuen Drama.

W

WA Inc Royal Commission 2000 www.slp.wa.gov.au/publications/publications.nsf/inquiries+and+commissions?openpage [accessed 22 February 2019].

Waber, B., Magnolfi, J. & Lindsay, G. 2014 "Workplaces That Move People", *Harvard Business Review*, November, 92(11), 69–77.

Wademan, D. 2005 "The Best Advice I Ever Got", in *Harvard Business Review on Managing Yourself*, Boston, MA: Harvard Business School Publishing, 103–127.

Wadman, M. S. & Koping, A. S. 2009 "Aesthetic Relations in the Place of the Lone Hero in Arts Management: Examples from Film Making and Orchestral Performance", *International Journal of Arts Management*, 12(1), 31–43.

Wallis, L. 2011 "Opinion: Cultural Leadership in the Arts", Australia Council, Sydney, http://australiacouncil.gov.au/news/media-centre/speeches/opinion-cultural-leadership-in-the-theatre/ [accessed 20 February 2019].

Walmsley, B. 2013 "Rethinking the Regional Theatre: Organizational Change at West Yorkshire Playhouse", Bogota: AIMAC International Conference, 224–237.

Walmsley, B. 2011 "'A Big Part of My Life': A Qualitative Study of the Impact of Theatre", Antwerp: AIMAC 11th International Conference.

Walmsley, B. 2012 "Whose Value Is It Anyway? A Neo-institutionalist Approach to Articulating and Evaluating Artistic Value", *Journal of Arts and Communities*, 4(3), 199–215.

Walmsley, B. 2013 "Rethinking the Regional Theatre: Organizational Change at West Yorkshire Playhouse", Bogota: 12th AIMAC International Conference, 224–237.

Walmsley, B. 2016 "Deep Hanging Out in the Arts: An Anthropological Approach to Capturing Cultural Value", *International Journal of Cultural Policy*, 24(2), 272–291.

Walter, C. 2015 *Arts Management: An Entrepreneurial Approach*, New York: Routledge.

Walumbwa, F. O., Avolio, B. J., Gardner, W. L., Wernsing, T. S. & Peterson, S. J. 2008 "Authentic Leadership: Development and Validation of a Theory-based Measure", *Journal of Management*, 34(1), 89–126.

Wanchap, G. & Litson, J. 2017 "QSO Chairman Responds to Claims of Low Morale", *Limelight*, 17 November, www.limelightmagazine.com.au/news/qso-chairman-responds-claims-low-morale/ [accessed 27 February 2019].

Watkins, J. M., Mohr B. & Kelly, R. 2011 *Appreciative Inquiry* (2nd ed), San Francisco, CA: Pfeiffer.

Watkins, M. D. 2016 "Leading the Team You Inherit", *Harvard Business Review*, 94(6), 61–67.

Watson, D. 2010 "The Invasion of Management Language", *fora.tv*, www.youtube.com/watch?v=RsVTDz6sunA [accessed 27 February 2019].

Watson, T. 2014 "Women Hit Glass Ceiling in Gallery Jobs", *ArtsHub*, 20 October, http://visual.artshub.com.au/news-article/features/museums/women-hit-glass-ceiling-in-gallery-jobs-246170 [accessed 26 February 2019].

Watts, R. 2013 "What to Do When You're Defunded?" *Arts Hub*, 7 November, www.artshub.com.au/news-article/news-article/feature/all-arts/what-to-do-when-youre-defunded-197230 [accessed 20 February 2019].

Watts, R. 2018 "Three Tips for Emerging Producers", *Arts Hub*, 5 November, www.artshub.com.au/education/news-article/career-advice/professional-development/richard-watts/top-3-tips-for-emerging-producers-256759 [accessed 5 November 2018].

Webb, D. 2017 "Trends in the Development and Operation of Performing Arts Centers", in Lambert, P. D. & Williams, R. (eds) *Performing Arts Center Management*, New York: Routledge, 45–62.

Webb, D. 2017 "Trends in the Development and Operation of Performing Arts Centers", in Lambert, P. D. & Williams, R. (eds) *Performing Arts Center Management*, New York: Routledge, 45–62.

Webb, S. & Dowling, M. 2015 "The Organising and Artistic Demands of Orchestral Performances", in Beech, N. & Gilmore, C. (eds) *Organising Music: Theory, Practice, Performance*, Cambridge: Cambridge University Press, 251–257.

Weinstein, S. 2009 *The Complete Guide to Fundraising Management* (3rd ed), Hoboken, NJ: John Wiley & Sons.

Welch, R. & McCarville, R. E. 2003 "Discovering Conditions for Staff Acceptance of Organizational Change", *Journal of Park and Recreation Administration*, 21(2), 22–43.

Westman, M. & Etzion, D. 2001 "The Impact of Vacation and Job Stress on Burnout and Absenteeism", *Psychology & Health*, 16(5), 595–606.

Westwood, M. 2013 "Curtain Slow to Rise on Multicultural Theatre", *The Australian*, 12 July, www.theaustralian.com.au/arts/stage/curtain-slow-to-rise-on-multicultural-theatre/story-fn9d344c-1226677904294 [accessed 20 February 2019].

White, J. 2017 *Culture Heist: Art versus Money*, Blackheath, NSW: Bandl & Schlesinger.

Wiggins, J., Song, C., Trivedi, D. & Preece S. B. 2017 "Consumer Perceptions of Arts Organizations' Strategies for Responding to Online Reviews", *International Journal of Arts Management*, 20(1), 4–20.

Williams, J. 2010 "Black Leadership and the White Gaze", in Kay, S. & Venner, K. (eds) *A Cultural Leader's Handbook*, London: Creative Choices, 41–45.

Williams, R., Harris, K. & Lambert, P. D. 2017 "Executive Leadership for Performing Arts Centers", in Lambert, P. D. & Williams, R. (eds) *Performing Arts Center Management*, New York: Routledge, 238–259.

Wilson, S. M. & Ferch, S. R. 2005 "Enhancing Resilience in the Workplace through the Practice of Caring Relationships", *Organizational Development Journal*, 23(4), 45–49.

Woiceshyn, J. 2009 "Lessons from 'Good Minds': How CEOs Use Intuition, Analysis and Guiding Principles to Make Strategic Decisions", *Long Range Planning*, 42(3), 298–319.

Wolf, T. 1999 *Managing a Nonprofit Organizations in the Twenty-First Century* (2nd ed), New York: Simon Schuster.

Wolfers, J. 2014 Interviewed on *Sunday Profile*, Radio National, 14 December, http://mpegmedia.abc.net.au/rn/podcast/2014/12/spe_20141214.mp3 [accessed 10 March 2019].

Wolff, S. A. 2017 "The Evolution of the Performing Arts Centre: What Does Success Look Like", in Lambert, P. D. & Williams, R. (eds) *Performing Arts Center Management*, New York: Routledge, 20–44.

Wood, S. J. & de Menezes, L. M. 2010 "Family-friendly Management, Organizational Performance and Social Legitimacy", *The*

International Journal of Human Resource Management, 21(10), 1575–1597.

Woodruff Arts Center 2016 "Woodruff Arts Center and Live Nation Reach New Operating Agreement at Verizon Wireless Amphitheatre", www.woodruffcenter.org/news/new-operating-agreement-at-verizon-wireless-amphitheatre/ [accessed 1 September 2019].

Woronkowicz, J. 2017 "Building Performing Arts Centers", in Lambert, P. D. & Williams, R. (eds) *Performing Arts Center Management,* New York: Routledge, 102–109.

Woronkowicz, J., Joynes, D. C., Frumkin, D., Kolendo, A., Seaman, B., Gertner, R. & Bradburn, N. 2012 *Set in Stone: Building America's New Generation of Arts Facilities, 1994–2008,* Chicago, IL: Cultural Policy Center, University of Chicago, http://culturalpolicy.uchicago.edu/setinstone/ [accessed 20 February 2019].

Worrall, A. 2015 "'Pay as You Feel' Eatery Hit by Lack of Largesse", *The Age,* 9 February, 8.

Z

Zan, L. 2006 *Managerial Rhetoric and Arts Organizations,* Houndmills: Palgrave Macmillan.

Zietlow, J. 2010 "Nonprofit Financial Objectives and Financial Responses to a Tough Economy", *Journal of Corporate Treasury Management,* 3(3), 238–248.

Zietlow, J., Hankin, J. & Seidner, A. G. 2007 *Financial Management for Nonprofit Organizations: Policies and Procedures,* Hoboken, NJ: John Wiley & Sons, Inc.

Zineldin, M. & Hytter, A. 2012 "Leaders' Negative Emotions and Leadership Styles Influencing Subordinates' Well-being", *The International Journal of Human Resource Management,* 23(4), 748–758.